Critique in
German Philosophy

SUNY series, Intersections: Philosophy and Critical Theory

Rodolphe Gasché, editor

Critique in German Philosophy

From Kant to Critical Theory

Edited by

María del Rosario Acosta López
and J. Colin McQuillan

Cover credit: *Wege der Weltweisheit: die Hermanns-Schlacht*, 1978.
Copyright Anselm Kiefer. Photo Credit: Atelier Anselm Kiefer.
Collection Deutsche Bank Frankfurt im Städel Museum Frankfurt.

Published by State University of New York Press, Albany

© 2020 State University of New York

All rights reserved

No part of this book may be used or reproduced in any manner whatsoever without written permission. No part of this book may be stored in a retrieval system or transmitted in any form or by any means including electronic, electrostatic, magnetic tape, mechanical, photocopying, recording, or otherwise without the prior permission in writing of the publisher.

For information, contact State University of New York Press, Albany, NY
www.sunypress.edu

Library of Congress Cataloging-in-Publication Data

Names: Acosta López, María del Rosario, editor. | McQuillan, J. Colin, 1979– editor.
Title: Critique in German philosophy : from Kant to critical theory / María del Rosario Acosta López and J. Colin McQuillan., eds.
Description: Albany : State University of New York Press, 2020. | Series: SUNY series, Intersections: Philosophy and Critical Theory | Includes bibliographical references and index.
Identifiers: LCCN 2020000095 | ISBN 9781438480275 (hardcover : alk. paper) | ISBN 9781438480268 (pbk. : alk. paper) | ISBN 9781438480282 (ebook)
Subjects: LCSH: Philosophy, German.
Classification: LCC B2521 .C75 2020 | DDC 193—dc23
LC record available at https://lccn.loc.gov/2020000095

10 9 8 7 6 5 4 3 2 1

Contents

Acknowledgments — ix

Abbreviations — xi

Introduction — 1
    María del Rosario Acosta López and J. Colin McQuillan

1. The Struggle between Dogmatism and Skepticism in the Prussian Academy: A Precedent for Kantian Critique — 21
    Catalina González

2. Pure Sensibility as a Source of Corruption: Kant's Critique of Metaphysics in the *Inaugural Dissertation* and *Critique of Pure Reason* — 39
    Karin de Boer

3. Critique in Kant's *Critique of Practical Reason*: Why This *Critique* Is Not a Critique of Pure Practical Reason — 61
    Avery Goldman

4. On an Aesthetic Dimension of Critique: The Time of the Beautiful in Schiller's *Aesthetic Letters* — 89
    María del Rosario Acosta López

5. Not Yet a System, Not Yet a Science: Reinhold and Fichte on Kant's Critique — 111
    J. Colin McQuillan

6 Schelling's Philosophical Letters on Doctrine and Critique   133
    G. Anthony Bruno

7 Critique With a Small *C*: Herder's Critical Philosophical
    Practice and Anticritical Polemics   155
    Rachel Zuckert

8 Irony and the Possibility of Romantic Criticism:
    Friedrich Schlegel as Poet-Critic   173
    Karolin Mirzakhan

9 Alexander von Humboldt: A Critic of Nature   185
    Elizabeth Millán Brusslan

10 Critique, Refutation, Appropriation: Strategies of
    Hegel's Dialectic   201
    Angelica Nuzzo

11 Abstraction and Critique in Marx: The Case of Debt   221
    Rocío Zambrana

12 Nietzsche's Project of Reevaluation: What Kind of Critique?   237
    Daniel R. Rodríguez-Navas

13 Kantian Critique, Its Ethical Purification by Hermann Cohen,
    and Its Reflective Transformation by Wilhelm Dilthey   263
    Rudolf A. Makkreel

14 Transcendental Phenomenology as Radical Immanent Critique:
    Subversions and Matrices of Intelligibility   281
    Andreea Smaranda Aldea

15 From the Metaphysics of Law to the Critique of Violence   301
    Peter Fenves

16 Is There Critique in Critical Theory? The Claim of Happiness
    on Theory   317
    Richard A. Lee Jr.

17 Critique as Melancholy Science   335
     Amy Allen

18 Reality and Resistance: Habermas and Haslanger on
     Objectivity, Social Critique, and the Possibility of Change   357
     Federica Gregoratto

19 The Critique of Law and the Law of Critique   377
     Christoph Menke

Works Cited   395

Contributors   415

Index   417

Acknowledgments

Many of the chapters included in this volume were presented at a conference that took place in Chicago at DePaul University in November, 2017. The editors would like to thank everyone who participated in the conference—those who attended and those who presented their papers. We would especially like to thank Luis Guzmán, Thomas Khurana, Ronald Mendoza de Jesús, and Daniel R. Rodríguez-Navas for serving as moderators, as well as Ashley Fleshman, Khafiz Kerimov, Ashleigh Morales, and Gisela Reyes for their assistance throughout the conference.

We would also like to express our gratitude to the *Deutscher Akademischer Austauschdienst* (DAAD), DePaul University Research Council, and St. Mary's University Research Council for awarding us grants that made the conference and this volume possible. The support provided by Michael Thomanek and the DAAD was essential to the success of the conference. The time, effort, and resources devoted to the conference by the chair of the Department of Philosophy at DePaul University, William McNeill, and the department assistant, Mary Amico, were absolutely crucial. So was the administrative support provided by Anndria Flores and Rose Mary Gallegos from St. Mary's University.

Finally, we would like to thank everyone at SUNY Press for supporting the publication of this volume. Andrew Kenyon, Jenn Bennett-Genthner, and Rebecca Colesworthy, our editors, were extremely helpful throughout the publication process. We appreciate their consistent support of the project, as well as their patience. The encouragement and recommendations of the two anonymous reviewers were also very helpful. Greg Convertino provided invaluable assistance with the proofs and index. Last, but certainly not least, we are proud to see this volume published in a series edited by Rodolphe Gasché, whose work has always been an inspiration to us.

Abbreviations

The following abbreviations are used in the notes for citing the following works:

Ak.   Kant, Immanuel. *Kants gesammelte Schriften (Akademie Ausgabe)*. Edited by the Royal Prussian (later German) Academy of Sciences. Berlin: Georg Reimer, later Walter de Gruyter, 1900–.

AF   Schlegel, Friedrich. *Athenaeum* fragments. In *Kritische Friedrich-Schlegel-Ausgabe*. Edited by Ernst Behler, Jean Jacques Anstett, and Hans Eichner. München: F. Schöningh, 1958.

CF   Schlegel, Friedrich. Critical (*Lyceum*) fragments. In *Kritische Friedrich-Schlegel-Ausgabe*. Edited by Ernst Behler, Jean Jacques Anstett, and Hans Eichner. München: F. Schöningh, 1958.

GA   Fichte, Johann Gottlieb. *Gesamtausgabe der Bayerischen Akademie der Wissenschaften*. Edited by Erich Fuchs, Hans Gliwitzky, Reinhard Lauth, and Peter K. Schneider. Stuttgart: Frommann-Holzboog, 1962–2012.

GS   Dilthey, Wilhelm. *Gesammelte Schriften*. Göttingen: Vandenhoeck & Ruprecht, 1913–2005.

HA   Schiller, Friedrich. *Werke in Drei Bänden*. Edited by Gerhard Fricke and Herbert Göpfert. München: Hanser Verlag, 1966.

Hua   Husserl, Edmund. *Husserliana*. Edited by Rudolph Bernet and Ullrich Melle. Dodrecht: Springer, 1950–. Individual works cited by volume number: 1: *Cartesianische Meditationen und Pariser Vorträge*, ed. Stephan Strasser (Den Haag: Martinus Nijhoff, 1950); 3/1: *Ideen zu einer reinen Phänomenologie und phänomenologischen Philosophie I: Allgemeine Einführung in die reine Phänomenologie*, ed. Karl Schuhmann (Den Haag: Martinus Nijhoff, 1976); 4: *Ideen zur einer reinen Phänomenologie und phänomenologischen Philosophie II: Phänomenologische Untersuchungen zur Konstitution*, ed. Marly Biemel (Den Haag: Martinus Nijhoff, 1952); 6: *Die Krisis de Europäischen Wissenschaften und die Transzendentale Phänomenologie*, ed. Walter Biemel (Den Haag: Martinus Nijhoff, 1954); 11: *Analysen zur Passiven Synthesis. Aus Vorlesungs- und Forschungsmanuskripten 1918–1926*, ed. Margot Fleischer (Den Haag: Martinus Nijhoff, 1966); 23: *Phantasie, Bildbewusstsein, Erinnerung 1898–1925*, ed. Eduard Marbach (Den Haag: Martinus Nijhoff, 1980); 29: *Die Krisis der Europäischen Wissenschaften und die Transzendentale Phänomenologie, Ergänzungsband, Texte aus dem Nachlass 1934–1937*, ed. Reinhold N. Smid (Dordrecht: Kluwer, 1993).

IF   Schlegel, Friedrich. *Ideas* fragments. In *Kritische Friedrich-Schlegel-Ausgabe*. Edited by Ernst Behler, Jean Jacques Anstett, and Hans Eichner. München: F. Schöningh, 1958.

KFSA   Schlegel, Friedrich. *Kritische Friedrich-Schlegel-Ausgabe*. Edited by Ernst Behler, Jean Jacques Anstett, and Hans Eichner. München: F. Schöningh, 1958.

NA   Schiller, Friedrich. *Schillers Werke—Nationalausgabe*. Edited by Julius Petersen und Gerhard Fricke. Weimar: Hermann Böhlaus Nachfolger, 1943–.

ND   Adorno, Theodor. *Negative Dialektik*. In *Gesammelte Schriften*, edited by Rolf Tiedemann. Frankfurt am Main: Suhrkamp, 1970–1997.

SW   *One of three references, distinguished by context:*

Dilthey, Wilhelm. *Selected Works*. Edited by Rudolf Makkreel and Frithjof Rodi. Princeton, NJ: Princeton University Press, 1989–.

Fichte, Johann Gottlieb. *Sämmtliche Werke*. Edited by Immanuel Hermann Fichte. Berlin: Walter de Gruyter, 1971.

Schelling, Friedrich Wilhelm Joseph von. *Friedrich Wilhelm Joseph Schellings sämmtliche Werke*. Edited by K.F.A. Schelling. Stuttgart: Cotta, 1856–1861.

TW   Hegel, Georg Wilhelm Friedrich. *Werke in zwanzig Bände*. Edited by Eva Moldenhauer and Karl Markus Michel. Frankfurt am Main: Suhrkamp Verlag, 1970.

Introduction

MARÍA DEL ROSARIO ACOSTA LÓPEZ
AND J. COLIN McQUILLAN

The main goal of this volume is to provide an overview of the conceptual history of critique in modern German philosophy. Such a history would reconstruct the ways in which the concept of "critique" was generated, transmitted, appropriated, and transformed over the course of the eighteenth, nineteenth, and twentieth centuries; how it was applied in different parts of philosophy, such as aesthetics, epistemology, ethics, metaphysics, and political philosophy; and the role it played in the self-understanding of philosophical movements and schools like German Idealism, Romanticism, Marxism, Neo-Kantianism, Phenomenology, and Critical Theory. The chapters included in this volume show that the conceptual history of "critique" in German philosophy is long and varied, starting with a Kantian phase in the late eighteenth century that gives way to German Idealism and Romanticism in the early nineteenth century, followed by a Hegelian phase in the middle of the nineteenth century, which concludes in a late-nineteenth- and early-twentieth-century phase that reformulates and rearticulates central aspects of the two earlier phases. The volume ends with a series of chapters on the legacy of the Frankfurt School and the prospects of critical theory today.

1. Kant and German Idealism

Kant did not introduce the word "critique" (*Kritik*) into German, as some commentators have claimed.[1] The *Deutsches Wörterbuch*, originally published by Jacob and Wilhelm Grimm, shows that its use in German predates the publication of the first *Critique* by more than a century.[2] Nor was Kant the first German philosopher to employ the term. It was already used in the title of *Attempt at a Critical Poetics for the Germans* (*Versuch einer critischen Dichtkunst vor die Deutschen*, 1730) by Johann Christoph Gottsched, who insisted that his poetics was "critical" because it was grounded in philosophical principles.[3] As Catalina González demonstrates in the chapter that opens this volume, "The Struggle between Dogmatism and Skepticism in the Prussian Academy: A Precedent for Kantian Critique," there is also ample precedent in German philosophy for many of the philosophical methods, doctrines, and themes that we associate with Kantian critique.[4] González shows how the members of the Prussian Academy used skeptical arguments to defend religious orthodoxy, blurring the lines between dogmatism and skepticism, and highlighting the need for "mature judgment" about the limits of reason in philosophy and religion. Thus, she concludes, the Prussian Academy's anti-skepticism can be seen as an important precedent for Kant's "critical" philosophy.

In her chapter, "Pure Sensibility as a Source of Corruption: Kant's Critique of Metaphysics in the *Inaugural Dissertation* and *Critique of Pure Reason*," Karin de Boer traces the development of Kant's conception of critique from his inaugural dissertation *On the Form and Principles of the Sensible and the Intelligible World* (1770) to the publication of the *Critique of Pure Reason* (1781/1787). Although she sees the two works as largely continuous, de Boer shows how, in his dissertation, Kant sought to purify metaphysics, understood as a science of purely intellectual cognition, by eliminating any contamination from sensible cognition, which, in his view, led to "fallacies of subreption." Kant continues to exclude sensation from metaphysics in the first *Critique*, but de Boer recounts how he also came to realize that the pure concepts of the understanding depend on sensibility, and, particularly, on time, the form of inner sense, for the schema of their application. This insight allows Kant to identify the sources of metaphysical cognition in pure reason in his critique, while strictly delimiting the extent and boundaries of the science of metaphysics, which Kant planned to survey in subsequent works called *The Metaphysics of Nature* and *The Metaphysics of Morals*. Kant's critique was merely a propaedeutic to the system and science of metaphysics that would be contained in these works.[5]

Instead of moving to complete his system in the years following the publication of the first *Critique*, Kant dramatically expanded the scope of his propaedeutic. In his chapter, "Critique in Kant's *Critique of Practical Reason*: Why This *Critique* Is Not a Critique of Pure Practical Reason," Avery Goldman argues that while Kant's first *Critique* instituted a tribunal to "discipline" pure reason and limit its speculative excesses, his *Groundwork of the Metaphysics of Morals* (1785) and *Critique of Practical Reason* (1788) begin the construction of a "canon" that will justify the extension of pure reason beyond the bounds of possible experience in Kant's moral philosophy. Goldman traces the development of this canon from the Third Antinomy of the Transcendental Dialectic in the first *Critique*, where Kant presents a negative demonstration of the possibility of freedom; to Part III of the *Groundwork*, where Kant argues that a positive conception of freedom is essential for uniting the good will and the moral law; to the account of freedom as a fact of pure practical reason in the second *Critique*; and, finally, to Kant's account of the highest good, which unites an Epicurean conception of happiness with a Stoic notion of moral virtue. Goldman holds that the ideal of the highest good is the culmination of Kant's canon and the completion of his shift from a negative to a positive conception of critique, because it emphasizes the necessity of presupposing, not only freedom, but also the postulates of pure practical reason—the existence of God and the immortality of the soul.

Later, in the *Critique of the Power of Judgment* (1790), Kant turned from the metaphysics of nature and morality to the *a priori* principles of aesthetic and teleological judgment. In her chapter, "On an Aesthetic Dimension of Critique: The Time of the Beautiful in Schiller's *Aesthetic Letters*," María del Rosario Acosta López recounts how Kant's "Critique of the Aesthetic Power of Judgment" inspired Friedrich Schiller. Schiller first became fascinated by the resistance of beauty to conceptualization in Kant's aesthetics. However, in his *Letters on the Aesthetic Education of Humanity* (1793–1795), Schiller related this resistance to a particular form of temporality—"lingering" over the beautiful. Acosta López shows that, for Schiller, lingering over the beautiful opens up a critical dimension of aesthetics, in which the experience of beauty resists the violence that characterizes modernity, as well as an aesthetic dimension of critique, which inaugurates another kind of time, outside the causal order of events, in which it becomes possible to "play" freely, and thus critically, with the historical determinations of the present.

Despite the success of his three *Critiques*, Kant struggled to complete the science of metaphysics and system of pure reason that he promised in the first *Critique*. In his chapter, "From the Metaphysics of Law to the Critique of Violence," Peter Fenves attributes these struggles to a "brain cramp," similar to the one that prevented Kant from completing the transition from his *Metaphysical Foundations of Natural Science* (1786) to "pure physics" in the *Opus postumum* (c. 1796–1801).[6] J. Colin McQuillan's chapter, "Not Yet a System, Not Yet a Science: Reinhold and Fichte on Kant's Critique," explores the response to the incompleteness of Kant's critique in the works of two early post-Kantian idealists: Karl Leonhard Reinhold and Johann Gottlob Fichte. McQuillan explains that Reinhold thought Kant had failed to complete his system because his critique was merely a propaedeutic. As such, it had not provided a general account of the faculty of representation, founded on a first principle. The idea that sciences and systems must be grounded in a single principle is not to be found in Kant's critique, which holds that they could be founded on multiple principles, as long as those principles are *a priori*; yet McQuillan shows that the search for a first principle became a central concern in Reinhold's Elementary Philosophy and Fichte's *Wissenschaftslehre*.

Reinhold maintains that all of the principles of philosophy and science can be derived from the "principle of consciousness," which states that "in consciousness, the subject distinguishes the representation from the subject and object and relates the representation to both."[7] Because it is a first principle, Reinhold denies that the validity of the principle of consciousness can be demonstrated through any other principle. Consciousness must be accepted as a "fact."[8] Recognizing the vulnerability of a system grounded in an indemonstrable "fact," but accepting Reinhold's argument that philosophy, as a science and a system, must be grounded in a first principle, Fichte maintains that the first principle of philosophy and science should instead be considered an "act" and, more specifically, a free act of self-positing that determines the subject (I), the object (not-I), and their relation within consciousness.[9] In his *Wissenschaftslehre*, Fichte insists that this argument remained true to the idealist spirit of Kant's critique, which traces our knowledge of objects back to the spontaneous activity of the human mind.[10]

By grounding his *Wissenschaftslehre* in a free act of self-positing, Fichte had opposed his critical idealism to determinism, which was, as a result of the Pantheism controversy, associated with Spinozist dogmatism in Germany at the end of the eighteenth century.[11] Friedrich Wilhelm Joseph von Schelling stages a confrontation between these two systems in early works like *On the I as a Principle of Philosophy* (1795) and *Philosophical Letters on Dogmatism and Criticism* (1795–1796), arguing, further, that

Kant's critique "is destined to deduce from the essence of reason the very possibility of two exactly opposed systems; it is destined to establish a system of criticism (conceived as complete) or, more precisely, a system of idealism as well as in exact opposition to it, a system of dogmatism or realism."[12] G. Anthony Bruno's chapter, "Schelling's Philosophical Letters on Doctrine and Critique," shows how, for Schelling, critique came to represent "the spirit in which one pursues a system," instead of being just one philosophical system opposed to another. Bruno argues that Schelling's conception of critique identifies philosophical systems with the striving to realize them in practice—to live them. Since he recognizes that many, but not all, philosophical systems are livable, Bruno maintains that Schelling defends a kind of meta-philosophical pluralism in his *Letters* and throughout his career.

2. German Romanticism

Despite the influence of Kant's three *Critiques* and the attempts by the early German idealists to complete Kant's system and discover its first principles, many of Kant's contemporaries remained unconvinced by his critique. One of the most vocal critics was Kant's former student, Johann Gottfried Herder, whose *Ideas for the Philosophy of History of Humanity* (1784–1791) had been the subject of a series of extremely hostile reviews by his former teacher during the 1780s.[13] Venting his frustration, Herder complains, in his "Metacritique of the Critique of Pure Reason" (1799), that Kant had misused the term "critique" by calling his investigation of our capacity for *a priori* cognition a "critique" of pure reason.[14] Rachel Zuckert shows, in her chapter, "Critique With a Small C: Herder's Critical Philosophical Practice and Anticritical Polemics," that critique is, for Herder, more appropriately used to describe judgments about the products of human activity—works of art, technological innovations—than it is to cognitive faculties. Zuckert argues that this objection is not as petty as it might seem. In fact, it is based on a respect for ordinary language and social convention that Herder took Kant to have scorned. According to Zuckert, Herder insisted that critique must always be a part of an "intersubjective conversation concerning publicly accessible objects" that relies on "shared criteria, including a shared language, and common natural capacities," instead of involving itself in scholastic disputes.[15]

Romantic thinkers like Friedrich Schlegel also questioned whether Kant and his followers were really as critical as they claimed to be. In the

Athenaeum Fragments (1798), Schlegel suggests that "the philosophy of the Kantians is probably termed critical *per antiphrasin*; or else it is an *epithet ornans*."[16] The philosophy that prides itself on being "critical" is, in other words, a form of dogmatism that boasts about its depth, profundity, and insight, without taking the time to look critically at itself and understand its limitations. Schlegel makes the same point in his essay "On Incomprehensibility" (1800), which parodies Kant's claim that his age is "the genuine age of criticism" by adding "soon now everything is going to be criticized, except the age itself."[17] Karolin Mirzakhan shows, in her chapter "Irony and the Possibility of Romantic Criticism: Friedrich Schlegel as Poet-Critic," that Schlegel sought to escape this dogmatism through a new form of romantic criticism, which was to be both ironic and poetic. Through irony, Mirzakhan argues, Schlegel hoped to help the reader adopt a more critical stance, which would help them consider contradictory claims simultaneously and, ultimately, "to inhabit different worlds, views, and interpretations."[18] Mirzakhan argues that Schlegel's essay "On Incomprehensibility" is ironic in this sense. Instead of explaining the fragments that had baffled so many readers and fixing their meaning, Schlegel intensifies the irony of his fragments by writing ironically about their irony. This way of writing also exemplifies Schlegel's conception of poetic criticism, which does not merely analyze a work of art, but completes it and fulfills the work by repeating what is most essential to it.

Extending romantic criticism from art to nature, Elizabeth Millán Brusslan shows, in her chapter, "Alexander von Humboldt: A Critic of Nature," how the German naturalist immersed himself in careful empirical studies of the natural world, which allowed him to include a wealth of quantified, empirical data in his descriptions of nature, while still savoring the "free enjoyment of its charms and the awe of its power."[19] Humboldt's writings combine empirical science with aesthetic appreciation in a way that is similar to the early German romantics, who also sought to overcome the boundaries between art, philosophy, and science. The proximity between Humboldt and Romanticism is perhaps most evident in works like *Views of Nature,* in which Humboldt employs a literary form, the *Naturgëmalde,* that is central to his critique of nature. Millán Brusslan points out that, for Humboldt, *Naturgëmalde* is meant to create an "impression of nature" (*Natureindruck*) on the reader, similar to that of a landscape painting. The form also helps to incorporate empirical details into scientific writing in a way that highlights their aesthetic relevance, so that readers gain a greater appreciation of the significance of knowledge about nature, while also developing an appreciation for its aesthetic value. The task of a critique of nature is, for Humboldt, to combine knowledge and enjoyment in a way that will guide the public toward a more serious engagement with and appreciation for nature.

3. Hegel, Marx, and Nietzsche

The Kantian conception of critique that dominated the end of the eighteenth century and the beginning of the nineteenth century also served as a starting point for Georg Wilhelm Friedrich Hegel's dialectical conception of critique. As Angelica Nuzzo shows in her chapter "Critique, Refutation, Appropriation: Strategies of Hegel's Dialectic," it was not only by refuting, but also by critically appropriating Kant's and Spinoza's systems—and, moreover, Kant's and Spinoza's conceptions of philosophy as a system—that Hegel gave shape to his own dialectical systematicity. Nuzzo argues that, for Hegel, dialectical systematicity replaces transcendental critique, but only after it has adopted and understood transcendental critique as an essential moment of the system as a whole. Any act of critical refutation is, thus, an exercise in self-refutation, since it is only by appropriating and transforming philosophy's own history that critique can incorporate the moments of the system and bring them to a completion that is also a new beginning. Contrary to interpretations that see Hegelian dialectics as an appropriation that totalizes without remainder, or as a refutation that replaces the truths of the past with its own, Nuzzo shows that dialectical critique is only truly complete, for Hegel, when it leaves refutation behind and lets go of what it has appropriated, setting it free "in its own right."[20] This is, Nuzzo claims, the standpoint of the absolute or, better yet, the absolute standpoint that philosophy adopts whenever it approaches completion. Thus, philosophy, as critique, begins by taking on the task of comprehending its history, preparing and liberating the present for an "unprecedented way of acting and being" that is, in Nuzzo's words, "not yet there, not even in outline . . . but must be entirely invented, imagined anew."[21]

Understood in this way, Hegel's conception of critique can serve as a model for the conceptual history of critique during the nineteenth century. Consider, for example, Karl Marx's rejection of what he calls "the German ideology"—the systems of Kant, Hegel, and other German philosophers, which abstract from the material conditions under which human individuals live and idealize the forms of their social relationships.[22] Against this ideology, Marx asserts that there is only one true science, history, which concerns itself with "real individuals, their activity, and the material conditions under which they live, both those which they find already existing and those produced by their activity."[23] Keeping Nuzzo's interpretation of Hegel in mind, we can see that Marx not only refutes but also transformatively appropriates Hegelian idealism to orient his philosophical critique and to formulate his historical materialism. For Marx, it is historical determinateness that provides the framework and the content for philosophy, keeping in mind that history, in turn, can itself be dialecticized through critique and set into motion toward the actualization of the possibilities that are already embedded within, but have not yet been explored by, the contradictions at the heart of the present.

Working within this new framework in her chapter, "Abstraction and Critique in Marx: The Case of Debt," Rocío Zambrana shows how Marx's fundamental orientation toward the material conditions of existence gives rise to a multidimensional and intersectional conception of critique, particularly in the critique of capitalism in Marx's mature writings on political economy. Zambrana develops an account of Marx's critique that highlights the multiple ways in which capitalism is not merely an economic system, but also, following Nancy Fraser, "an institutionalized social order."[24] This allows Zambrana to show how Marx's critique of capitalism can elucidate "the structural links between the economy *and* racial and gender oppression, political domination, and ecological degradation."[25] These links become evident, in Zambrana's argument, through Marx's analysis of debt and the corresponding critique of "anti-value," which has recently been rearticulated in the work of David Harvey. Thus, Zambrana shows how Marx's critique of capitalism and his analysis of economies of debt remain essential for an historical and materialist critique of financialized capitalism today—a critique that, by tracking the ways different forms of oppression become entangled with one another, can denounce and dismantle capitalism's gendered, racialized, and ecologically destructive forms of expropriation.

Although he insists that psychology, rather than history, was "the queen of the sciences," Friedrich Nietzsche echoes Marx's critique of the idealist prejudices of German philosophy.[26] Psychology is, for Nietzsche, an investigation of human drives, interests, and motives, particularly as they relate to values, so it is easy to see the "critique of moral values" that he presents in *The Genealogy of Morals* as a psychological critique of the interests and drives that have led, over the course of Western history, to "morality"—a system of values that presents itself as "good in itself."[27] Nietzsche presents his critique of morality in the *Genealogy* as a "re-evaluation of all values" (*Umwerthung aller Werthe*), but, as Daniel R. Rodríguez-Navas points out in his chapter, "Nietzsche's Project of Reevaluation: What Kind of Critique?," it remains unclear what kind of critique this "re-evaluation" is supposed to be. Rodríguez-Navas argues that contemporary interpretations of Nietzsche's critique, particularly those that try to determine whether his *Umwertung* constitutes an "internal" or "external" critique of moral values, remain too close to the form of traditional Western moral rationality and, as a result, Rodríguez-Navas argues, they overlook some of Nietzsche's most important insights into the experience of value. To uncover this experience, Rodríguez-Navas shows that Nietzsche situates his critique within a historical genealogy, which is not identical to his critique, but which helps Nietzsche formulate a "typology of morals." This typology allows Nietzsche's critique to re-evaluate morality's claim to being good in itself and to reveal the structures of rationality and moral justification that lie at the foundations of our (historically determined) experience of value. By genealogically tracing the origin of those structures, Nietzsche is able to render them visible in their contingency, to radically break with traditional conceptions of values, and to open up other forms of rationality that have remained silent or invisible, or even unconceivable, given our already saturated, overdetermined, and to a certain extent, as Rodríguez-Navas insists, incapacitating conceptions of critique.

4. Neo-Kantianism, Phenomenology, and Critical Theory

The end of the nineteenth century and the beginning of the twentieth century saw a return to transcendental critique in both Neo-Kantianism and Phenomenology. Neo-Kantians like Hermann Cohen regarded the *a priori* principles that Kant derived from the faculties of sensibility and the understanding in the first *Critique*—the pure forms of intuition (space and time) and the pure concepts of the understanding (the categories)—as formal conditions of experience, whose universality and necessity were guaranteed by the laws of mathematics and physics.[28] Along with his students Paul Natorp and Ernst Cassirer, the later Cohen sought to formulate an *a priori* logic that would demonstrate the objectivity of both the natural and human sciences (*Naturwissenschaften* and *Geisteswissenschaften*).[29] Taking a different route, Edmund Husserl characterized phenomenology as a form of transcendental idealism in his *Cartesian Meditations* (1931), because it is "nothing more than . . . an explication of my ego as subject of every possible cognition, and, indeed, with respect to every sense of what exists, wherewith the latter might be able to *have* a sense for me."[30] Even Martin Heidegger characterized his project, in his early lectures, as a "phenomenological critique" and, later, identified his own fundamental ontology as a kind of transcendental philosophy in *Being and Time* (1927).[31]

Despite their preoccupation with *a priori* principles, transcendental subjectivity, and, more generally, philosophy "as a rigorous science," Neo-Kantians and phenomenologists did not neglect the social and historical world. Indeed, it was in these contexts that they made some of their most important contributions, as Rudolf Makkreel demonstrates in his chapter "Kantian Critique, Its Ethical Purification by Hermann Cohen, and Its Reflective Transformation by Wilhelm Dilthey." Makkreel begins by distinguishing three kinds of critique in Kant: a constitutive critique that seeks the conditions of the possibility of experience; a regulative critique that orients us toward theoretical and practical ideals; and a reflective critique that is normative, but, instead of orienting us toward ideals, considers our judgments in relation to others and seeks consensus. Makkreel shows that Kant presents a reflective justification for property rights in the *Metaphysics of Morals*, which Cohen replaces with a regulative defense of legal rights, based on the ideal relation between the parties to a contract—mutual consent. Cohen argues that this principle lies at the foundation of "the idea of socialism" and uses it to distinguish states that promote the interests of the dominant classes through might (*Macht*) and those that are justified by the principles of right (*Recht*). In the last section of his chapter, Makkreel presents an alternative formulation of the basis of right, which is found in Wilhelm Dilthey's ethics. Dilthey grounds right in what Makkreel calls "a reflective ethics of cooperation."[32] Dilthey's ethics is reflective because it eschews the legislative model employed by both Kant and Cohen, focusing, instead, on "setting contextually appropriate priorities."[33] Emphasizing both the social nature of these contexts and their basis in human solidarity, Dilthey's ethics of cooperation promotes a kind of "reciprocal fidelity" that acknowledges what we have in common, while respecting our differences.

Likewise, in her chapter "Transcendental Phenomenology as Radical Immanent Critique: Subversions and Matrices of Intelligibility," Andreea Smaranda Aldea argues that transcendental phenomenology provides "powerful tools for critically investigating the historical forces shaping our present reality, doing justice not only to their epistemic weight, but also to their normative weight."[34] Drawing on Husserl's later work, from the 1930s, Aldea points out that the experiential evidence with which the phenomenologist is concerned derives from the lifeworld, which is constituted over time by the sedimentation of theoretical accomplishments and practical commitments. Aldea does not think the origin of this evidence in the lifeworld compromises its legitimacy as evidence for transcendental phenomenology. On the contrary, she maintains, it is by sifting through the different layers of epistemic and normative sedimentation in this evidence that phenomenologists distance themselves from their own sense of "lived possibility"—the conditioned set of possibilities they come to expect from their own historical world. Aldea characterizes the phenomenological analysis of lived possibility, and the limits of what is conceivable, possible, necessary, and impossible in the context of the lifeworld, as a kind of "immanent critique." By undertaking this critique, phenomenologists adopt a "critical" rather than a "normalizing" stance toward lived possibility, exposing the sedimentation of meanings that constitutes the lifeworld without naturalizing or reinforcing them. Through this critique, the phenomenologist gains the ability to distinguish what is historically conceivable from what is transcendentally necessary, advancing the cause of transcendental phenomenology at the same time as they uncover the historicity of experience.

In his chapter, "From the Metaphysics of Law to the Critique of Violence," Peter Fenves goes "back to Kant" in a very different way than we find in either Neo-Kantianism or Phenomenology. Recounting Kant's attempt to ground the doctrine of law in his *Metaphysical Foundations of the Doctrine of Right*, the first part of the *Metaphysics of Morals* (1797), Fenves shows that Kant's difficulties constructing the conceptual foundation of the law derive from his need to reconcile "universal reciprocal coercion with everyone's freedom" without reducing law to either "physical supremacy" or "wild lawless freedom."[35] The inconsistencies in the text of the *Doctrine of Right* represent, for Fenves, Kant's unresolved struggle to unite two things—coercion and freedom—that are mutually exclusive and yet essential to the law. Fenves then turns to Walter Benjamin, an astute reader of Kant's late writings, and shows how he takes up Kant's problem in his early works. Unlike Kant, Fenves argues, Benjamin will admit that the conceptual construction of law "bars the way to justice."[36] However, the solution Benjamin presents in his essay "Towards a Critique of Violence" (*Zur Kritik der Gewalt*, 1920–1921) is itself modeled on Kant's *Critique of Practical Reason*. Just as Kant denies that the second *Critique* is a critique of "pure" practical reason, so too Benjamin will argue that there can be no critique of "pure" *Gewalt*.[37] And as in Kant's conception of pure practical reason, pure *Gewalt* is what Benjamin's critique aims to promote, even though it would be unrecognizable whenever and wherever there would be an instance of such a *Gewalt*. Ultimately, for Benjamin, this would amount to a critique of an unrecognizable and un-possessable form of *Gewalt* that would guarantee the (always unjustifiable, arbitrary) step from law to justice that Kant had failed to complete. Fenves's chapter not only establishes a clear connection between Kant's *Metaphysics of Morals* and Benjamin's critique of violence, it also highlights a novel conception of critique that was being developed by one of the most important thinkers associated with the Frankfurt School, even before Horkheimer published his programmatic essay "Traditional and Critical Theory."

The surprising absence of a definition of "critique" in Horkheimer's essay leads Richard A. Lee Jr. to ask, in his chapter, "Is There Critique in Critical Theory?" While traditional theory not only naturalizes historical and contingent features of social relations, but also covers over this very same operation of naturalization, critical theory, Horkheimer argues, must resist and expose this operation. Thus, in order to understand what makes theory critical, and what prevents it from becoming, in Horkheimer words, "inhuman," Lee argues that one needs to contrast Horkheimer's Marxist conception of critique with Kant's. While Kant's critique sought to constrain the speculative excesses of reason, Horkheimer's critique draws on Marx's attention to the material and social conditions of human existence and, in particular, the way they are presented as "given." Thus, Horkheimer's critique seeks to "rein in the pretension of what is socially given" and its claims to "rationality or even reasonableness."[38] It is this same conception of critique, Lee argues, that inspired Adorno "to hold metaphysics to its promise."[39] Adorno will insist that there can only be critique where there is transcendence, because it is only where one can point out the tension between the factical and the transcendental, and the failure of the factical to live up to its ideal, that one can pose an "otherwise" that differs from what is given. As Lee points out, the difficulty is that such an "otherwise" is already a social fact. As such, metaphysics must be held accountable for the ways in which it has fallen short of its promise, while holding open the possibility of an "otherwise," whose "index" is happiness. Adorno's conception of redemption reminds us that, in Lee's words, "the only form of critique that belongs to critical theory is a Marxist social critique that risks being metaphysical for the sake of a happiness that is the very promise of metaphysics."[40]

Whether the promise of metaphysics can be saved from metaphysics itself is a question that has led Amy Allen to challenge the presuppositions of the early critical theorists in her most recent work, oriented by the question of what kind of responsibility is called for in our reception of this theory today.[41] In her contribution to the volume, "Critique as Melancholy Science," Allen goes back to the question of redemption, this time to highlight the continuity between Adorno's critical theory and Foucault's conception of critique. Against interpretations that take Adorno's naturalism to be incompatible with Foucault's historicism and constructivism, Allen argues that, despite their differences, Adorno and Foucault share a similar conception of critique—one that is attentive to the cracks and fissures of social reality and remains entirely immanent while sustaining a kind of transcendence. Allen will even argue that, given Adorno's singular conception of nature as nothing other than ontology—an ontology that, following Benjamin, needs to understand itself, and nature, as radically historicized, instead of being "naturalized"—Adorno's "critical naturalism" has much in common with Foucault's historical ontology. Thus, in a way that is continuous with Lee's contribution, and by means of a productive comparison with Foucault, Allen shows to what extent Adorno's commitment to metaphysics, understood through the psychoanalytical concept of "melancholy," is not a renunciation but rather an intensification of critical theory, and of a profoundly historical, social and materialist conception of critique.

5. Critical Theory Today

The final chapters in this volume are dedicated to the current state of critical theory in the work of a second and third generation of critical theorists, namely Jürgen Habermas and Christoph Menke. In her chapter, "Reality and Resistance: Habermas and Haslanger on Objectivity, Social Critique, and the Possibility of Change," Federica Gregoratto puts the later works of Habermas in dialogue with Sally Haslanger, a contemporary American philosopher who was trained as an analytic metaphysician, but whose investigations of "social kinds" has led her to formulate her own version of critical theory in recent years. Gregoratto shows that Habermas's and Haslanger's approaches to social critique are complementary in a number of ways.[42] She argues that the pragmatic conceptions of truth and objectivity that Habermas articulates in later works like *Truth and Justification* (1999/2004) can be enriched by Haslanger's analyses, in *Resisting Reality* (2012), of the social construction of categories like race and gender, which show that we do not have to reject realism and objectivity in order to acknowledge their construction. At the same time, Haslanger's analyses can be supplemented by Habermas' account of the intersubjectivity of experience, since it is the violation of intersubjectively shared norms concerning interpersonal communication, social interaction, and dealing with the objective world that motivates critique. To this account, however, Gregoratto argues, we should add Haslanger's conception of "resisting reality," which explains why social critique is so difficult. The social world we inhabit is "congealed, reified, opaque," so it "resists our attempts to conceptually penetrate the structural layers that enable and reproduce injustice and oppression and to practically change even some of them."[43] Despite these difficulties, Gregoratto argues, critical theory has the potential to illuminate the nature of social reality and to challenge the kinds of social injustice that arise from the way the social world has been constructed.

Extending the arguments he began to formulate in his book *Recht und Gewalt* (2012), and has more recently continued in *Kritik der Rechte* (2015), Christoph Menke's chapter, "The Critique of Law and the Law of Critique," reflects on the paradoxical ways in which critique and law are intertwined, focusing, this time, on the consequences of this paradox for critique.[44] If critique is to be fully consistent, Menke argues, it must always engage in a critique of itself, and thus, of its own law. Every critique must therefore be, to a certain extent, "the critique of the legality of critique, and thus, a critique of law."[45] However, critique is also fundamental for law's operation. Indeed, one could say that the operation of law is nothing but the practice of critique, insofar as the law imposes, rationalizes, and systematizes normative distinctions and decisions. So, how can there be critique at all, if every critique is a critique of the law, but critique is, at the same time, constitutive of law's operation? Such is the aporia that leads Menke to ask whether there is, perhaps, a non-legal form of critique that would put an end to this apparently vicious circle. To answer this question, Menke considers what he calls a "romanticizing" and "geneaological" form of critique. Following Adorno back to Marx and Marx back to Schlegel, Menke describes a form of critique that concerns itself with the genesis of forms while attending simultaneously to their presentation. Such a critique would, Menke argues, take both the product and the act of production into consideration, showing the genealogy of the forms of the present, their production of reality as presentation, and the presentation of this reality as ideological—that is, as hiding the fact that it has been produced.

Critique, understood in this sense, is always transformative, because it is "a co-presentation of its own form of presenting."[46] In its operation, Menke argues, critique not only reveals the contingency of the existing order, but also reconceptualizes the normative, legal dimension of critique. This is the case because, in its way of operating, it confronts the legality and non-legality of critique, puts them in relation, and renders a judgment that is no longer legal, or better, a judgment that reveals the other, non-legal, and, hence, Menke adds, violent side of the law. This, Menke insists, is the fundamental and often overlooked or misinterpreted gesture of critical theory. Critique means, in this context, to consider a given form as the presentation of the paradox that lies at its foundation, while also allowing us to understand the reasons why this paradox assumes a specific social and historical form. This form of critique seems to escape the aporia present in more traditional, and, as Menke points out, dogmatic, conceptions of critique. Not because it conceives of an *alegal* form of critique, but because critique can recognize and make evident the fundamental paradox at the heart of all legality, even at the heart of the law of critique. Genealogical critique, Menke concludes, dissolves the dogmatism of normative critique while also explaining its necessity. In doing so, it produces a different, less aporetic, and perhaps less violent form of critique, though one that is no less paradoxical, since it always, by the nature of its legal character, decides in the name of undecidability.

This introduction, as well as this volume as a whole, provides only a brief sketch of the conceptual history of "critique" in modern and contemporary German philosophy. There is much more to say about the figures and works, ideas and arguments that contributed to this history than we have mentioned, and those that we have not mentioned, as will become evident in the chapters that follow. While a complete history remains beyond the scope of a volume like this one, we think the following chapters provide an account of history of the concept of "critique" in German philosophy that is accurate, nuanced, and, above all, critical. At a time where our very notions of critique are being radically challenged and called into question, and rightly so, by non-Western, decolonial, and feminist criticism, as well as new perspectives coming from critical race theory and gender studies, we are hoping that a volume that re-examines the traditional Western—and, in this case, specifically German—history of this concept can help to make visible both the strengths and the limitations of that tradition for contemporary philosophy and our critical accounts of the present.

Notes

1. See Norman Kemp Smith, *A Commentary to Kant's Critique of Pure Reason* (1918; repr., New York: Palgrave, 2003), 1.

2. See the entry on *"Kritik"* in Jacob and Wilhelm Grimm, *Deutsches Wörterbuch* (Leipzig: Hirzel Verlag, 1873), 5:2334. The most recent, online edition of the Grimms' Dictionary is available at http://dwb.uni-trier.de/de/die-digitale-version/online-version/ and the entry on *Kritik* is at http://woerterbuchnetz.de/cgi-bin/WBNetz/genFOplus.tcl?sigle=DWB&lemid=GK14447. See also Claus von Bormann, Giorgio Tonelli, and Helmut Holzhey, "Kritik" in *Historisches Wörterbuch der Philosophie,* ed. Joachim Ritter et al. (Basel: Schwabe Verlag, 1976), 1249.

3. Johann Christoph Gottsched, *Versuch einer critischen Dichtkunst vor die Deutschen* (Leipzig: Bernhard Christoph Breitkopf, 1730).

4. The similarities between Kant's views and those of his German contemporaries are also explored in Corey W. Dyck and Falk Wunderlich, eds., *Kant and his German Contemporaries*, vol. 1, *Logic, Mind, Epistemology, Science, and Ethics* (Cambridge: Cambridge University Press, 2018), and Daniel O. Dahlstrom, ed., *Kant and his German Contemporaries*, vol. 2, *Aesthetics, History, Politics, and Religion* (Cambridge: Cambridge University Press, 2018).

5. Immanuel Kant, *Critique of Pure Reason*, ed. and trans. Paul Guyer and Allen W. Wood (New York: Cambridge University Press, 1998), Axii. All references to Kant's first *Critique,* here and throughout the volume, use the standard A/B pagination of the first (1781, A) and second (1787, B) editions. References to Kant's other works are accompanied by a parenthetical reference, cited as *Ak.*, to the volume and page number of the passage in Immanuel Kant, *Kants gesammelte Schriften (Akademie Ausgabe),* ed. Royal Prussian (later German) Academy of Sciences, et al. (Berlin: Georg Reimer, later Walter de Gruyter, 1900–).

6. See Fenves, "From the Metaphysics of Law to the Critique of Violence." See also Eckart Förster, *Kant's Final Synthesis: An Essay on the Opus postumum* (Cambridge: Harvard Univesrity Press, 2000), and Oliver Thordike, *Kant's Transition Project and Late Philosophy: Connecting the Opus postumum and the Metaphysics of Morals* (London: Bloomsbury, 2018).

7. Karl Leonhard Reinhold, *Beiträge zur Berichtigung bisheriger Mißverständnisse der Philosophen,* ed. Faustino Fabbianelli (Hamburg: Felix Meiner Verlag, 2004), 1:113. See also Martin Bondeli, *Das Anfangsproblem bei Karl Leonhard Reinhold* (Frankfurt am Main: Vittorio Klostermann, 1995), and Elise Frketich, "The Starting Point of Reinhold's *Elementarphilosophie*" (forthcoming).

8. Reinhold, *Beiträge* 1: 98–100.

9. Johann Gottlieb Fichte, *Early Philosophical Writings,* ed. and trans. Daniel Breazeale (Ithaca: Cornell University Press, 1988), 64. This is also discussed in Bruno, "Schelling's Philosophical Letters on Doctrine and Critique."

10. Johann Gottlieb Fichte, *The Science of Knowledge*, ed. and trans. Peter Heath and John Lachs (New York: Cambridge University Press, 1982), 51–52. This is also discussed in Bruno, "Schelling's Philosophical Letters on Doctrine and Critique."

11. On the pantheism controversy, see Frederick Beiser, *The Fate of Reason: German Philosophy from Kant to Fichte* (Cambridge: Harvard University Press, 1987), 44–108.

12. Friedrich Wilhelm Joseph von Schelling, *The Unconditioned in Human Knowledge: Four Early Essays 1794–1796*, trans. Fritz Marti (Lewisburg, PA: Bucknell University Press, 1980), 169.

13. See Immanuel Kant, *Anthropology, History, and Education*, ed. Robert B. Louden and Günther Zöller (Cambridge: Cambridge University Press, 2007), 121–142 (Ak. 8:45–66). See also John H. Zammito, *Kant, Herder, and the Birth of Anthropology* (Chicago: University of Chicago Press, 2002). Jennifer Mensch shows that Kant's campaign against Herder continued into the 1790s in Jennifer Mensch, "Kant and the Skull Collectors: German Anthropology from Blumenbach to Kant," in *Kant and His German Contemporaries*, vol. 1, *Logic, Mind, Epistemology, Science, and Ethics*, ed. Corey W. Dyck and Falk Wunderlich (Cambridge: Cambridge University Press, 2018), 192–210.

14. Johann Gottfried Herder, *Werke in zehn Bänden*, ed. Ulrich Gaier et al. (Deutsche Klassische Verlag, Frankfurt, 1985–2000), 8:318.

15. Zuckert, "Critique with a Small C."

16. Friedrich Schlegel, *Friedrich Schlegel's Lucinde and the Fragments*, ed. and trans. Peter Firchow (Minneapolis: University of Minnesota Press, 1971), 167.

17. Kant, *Critique of Pure Reason*, Axi; Schlegel, *Friedrich Schlegel's Lucinde and the Fragments*, 261.

18. See Mirzakhan "Irony and the Possibility of Romantic Criticism."

19. See Millán, "Alexander von Humboldt."

20. See Nuzzo, "Critique, Refutation, Appropriation."

21. See Nuzzo, "Critique, Refutation, Appropriation."

22. Karl Marx and Friedrich Engels, *The German Ideology*, in Karl Marx and Friedrich Engels, *Collected Works* (Chadwell Heath: Lawrence & Wishart, 1975–2004), 5:31. On the distinction between ideology and science in Marx, see also Louis Althusser, *For Marx*, trans. Ben Brewster (London: Verso, 2005), 13–14.

23. Marx and Engels, *The German Ideology*, 28.

24. Nancy Fraser, "Expropriation and Exploitation in Racialized Capitalism," *Critical Historical Studies* 3, no. 1 (2016), 163. See also Zambrana, "Abstraction and Critique in Marx."

25. Zambrana, "Abstraction and Critique in Marx."

26. Friedrich Nietzsche, *Beyond Good and Evil*, trans. Walter Kaufmann (New York: Vintage, 1989), §23.

27. Friedrich Nietzsche, *The Genealogy of Morals*, trans. Carol Diethe, ed. Keith Ansel Pearson (Cambridge: Cambridge University Press, 1997), 7 (Preface, §6). On Nietzsche's psychology, see Paul Katsafanas, "Nietzsche's Philosophical Psychology" in *The Oxford Handbook on Nietzsche*, ed. John Richardson and Ken Gemes (Oxford: Oxford University Press, 2013), 727–755; John Richardson, "Nietzsche's Psychology" in *Nietzsches Wissenschaftsphilosophie*, ed. H. Heit, G. Abel, and M. Brusotti (Berlin: Walter de Gruyter, 2011), 311–328; and Robert Pippin, *Nietzsche, Psychology, and First Philosophy* (Chicago: University of Chicago Press, 2010), 1–21.

28. Hermann Cohen, *Kants Theorie der Erfahrung* (Berlin: Dümmler, 1871/1885). See also Klaus Christian Kohnke, *The Rise of NeoKantianism: German Philosophy Between Idealism and Positivism*, trans. R.J. Hollingdale (Cambridge: Cambridge University Press, 1991), 178–197; Andrea Pomona, *The Critical Philosophy of Hermann Cohen*, trans. John Denton (Albany: State University of New York Press, 1997), 6–20; and, more recently, Frederick Beiser, *The Genesis of Neo-Kantianism, 1796–1880* (Oxford: Oxford University Press, 2014), 482–491.

29. Hermann Cohen, *System der Philosophie, Erster Teil: Logik der reinen Erkenntnis* (Berlin: Bruno Cassirer, 1920). See also Paul Natorp, *Logik: Grundlegung und logischer Aufbau der Mathematik und mathematischen Naturwissenschaften in Leitsätzen zu akademischen Vorlesungen* (Marburg: Elwert, 1910) and Ernst Cassirer, *The Logic of the Cultural Sciences*, trans. S.G. Lofts (New Haven: Yale University Press, 2000).

30. Edmund Husserl, *Cartesian Meditations: An Introduction to Phenomenology*, trans. Dorion Cairns (The Hague: Matinus Nijhoff, 1960), 86.

31. Martin Heidegger, *Toward the Definition of Philosophy*, trans. Ted Sadler (London: Continuum, 2002), 103–109. See also Martin Heidegger, *Being and Time*, trans. John Macquarrie and Edward Robinson (Oxford: Blackwell, 1962), §4–§8. Theodore Kisiel traces Heidegger's famous *Destruktion* (often translated as "destruction," "destructuring," or "deconstruction") of the history of ontology back to his earlier conception of "phenomenological critique." See Theodore Kisiel, *The Genesis of Heidegger's Being and Time* (Berkeley: University of California Press, 1993), 59–61.

32. Makkreel, "Kantian Critique, Its Ethical Purification by Hermann Cohen, and Its Reflective Transformation by Wilhelm Dilthey."

33. Makkreel, "Kantian Critique, Its Ethical Purification by Hermann Cohen, and Its Reflective Transformation by Wilhelm Dilthey."

34. Aldea, "Transcendental Phenomenology as Radical Immanent Critique."

35. Kant, *Practical Philosophy*, 459 (*Ak.* 6:316). See also Christoph Menke, *Recht und Gewalt* (Berlin: August Verlag, 2011), 7; Christoph Menke, *Law and Violence: Christoph Menke in Dialogue*, trans. Gerrit Jackson (Manchester: Manchester University Press, 2018), 3; and Fenves, "From the Metaphysics of Law to the Critique of Violence."

36. Fenves, "From the Metaphysics of Law to the Critique of Violence."

37. See Goldman, "Critique in Kant's Critique of Practical Reason." See also Fenves, "From the Metaphysics of Law to the Critique of Violence."
38. Lee, "Is There Critique in Critical Theory?"
39. Lee, "Is There Critique in Critical Theory?"
40. Lee, "Is There Critique in Critical Theory?"
41. See Amy Allen, *The End of Progress: Decolonizing the Normative Foundations of Critical Theory* (New York: Columbia University Press, 2016).
42. On Haslanger's conception of critical theory, see her 2015 Spinoza Lecture, published as Sally Haslanger, *Critical Theory and Practice: Spinoza Lectures* (Amsterdam: Koninklijke van Gorcum, 2017).
43. Gregoratto, "Reality and Resistance."
44. Menke, *Recht und Gewalt,* has recently been translated into English in Menke, *Law and Violence: Christoph Menke in Dialogue.* See also Christoph Menke, *Kritik der Rechte* (Frankfurt am Main: Suhrkamp, 2015).
45. Menke, "The Critique of Law and the Law of Critique."
46. Menke, "The Critique of Law and the Law of Critique."

1

The Struggle between Dogmatism and Skepticism in the Prussian Academy

A Precedent for Kantian Critique

CATALINA GONZÁLEZ

1. Introduction

Kant's notion of critique may have been historically preceded and prepared for by one of the quarrels in which dogmatism and skepticism were central themes: namely, the critique of skepticism in the Prussian Royal Academy of Sciences during the eighteenth century. At the center of the dispute was an "anti-skeptical" treatise, Jean-Pierre de Crousaz's *Examen du pyrrhonisme ancien et moderne*. The work was published in French in 1733, later abridged and then translated into German by two important members of the Prussian Academy, Samuel Formey and Albrecht von Haller, respectively. It appeared to the German public in 1751 with the title *Prüfung der Secte, die an allem zweifelt*. Kant himself recommended this text as a good source for modern skepticism in his *Lectures on Logic*: "If one wants closer instruction in the *scepticismus* of modern times, then one can read with great profit the writing that Haller published under the title: *Examination of the sect that doubts everything*."[1]

In this paper, I will examine the introduction to Crousaz's work, first, to gain a general idea of the confrontation between dogmatic and skeptical philosophers with regard to religious issues in the eighteenth century, and second, to identify some of the skeptical topics that Crousaz uses in his defense of religion. Then I will observe how this text may have contributed to a progressive dissolution of the boundaries between skepticism and dogmatism, leading to Kant's critical standpoint. In fact, according to John Christian Laursen, the attitude of the Prussian Academy involved not only the defense of religion from skeptical outlooks but also the assimilation of skeptical strategies and arguments, and in doing so, it promoted the emergence of a philosophical middle ground. He argues:

> There were good reasons for defending some sort of skepticism at the Berlin Academy. For one thing, enlightened philosophes of the Academy were worried as much by the dogmatists of enthusiasm and superstition as they were about the skeptics. They had to defend a middle way to protect their positions and way of doing philosophy.[2]

On the basis of Laursen's suggestion, I argue in this paper that this philosophical middle ground importantly influenced Kant's critical viewpoint. To develop this claim, I will begin by sketching out Laursen's account of the role of the Prussian Academy's anti-skepticism in the popularization of modern skepticism. Then I will outline some of the most important anti-skeptical arguments in Crousaz's *Examen du pyrrhonism ancien et moderne* as well as some rhetorical topics that may have informed Kant's formulation of a "critique" of pure reason, such as the identification of this critique with a "mature" exercise of reason. Finally, I will describe the way in which Crousaz's views, which I consider to be a form of "skeptical anti-skepticism," may have helped in the construction of Kant's critical philosophy.

2. Crousaz and the Prussian Anti-skeptical Academy

In a series of articles published with Richard H. Popkin, Laursen has drawn attention to the influence of the Prussian Anti-skeptical Academy in eighteenth-century German philosophy.[3] Originally founded in 1700 by Leibniz under Elector Frederick III of Brandenburg, the Academy was reformed in 1744 by Frederick the Great. It was predominantly francophone between the '40s and '90s, given that several of its members, some of them

Huguenots in exile, arrived in Germany from France and from Switzerland.[4] Prominent among these members are P. L. Maupertius, Formey, Haller, Mérian, Sulzer, and de Castillon. They engaged in the translation and commentary of skeptical treatises, such as Hume's *Enquiry Concerning Human Understanding* and Cicero's *Academica*.[5] Their purpose, however, was not to spread the skeptical outlook, but rather to attack it, in order to defend Christian faith from the outbreaks of fideism, deism, and atheism that became notorious in the eighteenth century.

According to Laursen, the arguments used by Prussian anti-skeptics have two important features: (1) they are moral and religious arguments, not directed to showing the unsoundness of the skeptical views but only to revealing their harmful practical consequences;[6] and (2) they resort to skeptical topics in order to draw anti-skeptical conclusions.[7] In view of the latter, Laursen argues, the Academy's attitude toward skepticism was rather ambivalent, since, "to the extent that they actually domesticated many a skeptical point into their own canons of argument, they contributed to the process of assimilating skepticism into the modern world view."[8] Thus, the Academy's anti-skeptical efforts proved rather useful in popularizing the writings of the main modern and ancient skeptics, by making their arguments accessible to a more widespread public, and perhaps also by giving them a mystified aura of irreligiousness and immorality.

According to Laursen, one of the most important sources of inspiration for the Academy was Crousaz's extensive treatment of modern Pyrrhonism in his *Examen du pyrrhonisme ancien et moderne*.[9] Formey composed an abridged version of this work with the title *Le triomphe de l'évidence* in 1738, which could not be published immediately for financial reasons.[10] Later, he gave the manuscript to Haller, who translated it into German under the title *Prüfung der Secte die an allem zweifelt*, and this version was published in 1751.[11] To underline the anti-skeptical tone of the work, Laursen quotes Haller's introduction, where the latter argues that "atheistic skeptics will kill their own fathers, skeptical judges will judge according to their own desires, the poor will rob from the rich, the 'philosophical' masses will over-throw princes, and 'philosophical' princes will rule according to their whims."[12] In the same vein, Jacqueline E. de la Harpe indicates that, in his correspondence with Crousaz, Haller shows that he was pleased to translate the abridged form of the treatise, for "in a century where superstition and atheism have such great progress, I am often afraid of seeing in my days the dreadful period when Providence would take away from us the light of reason, to which we already pay so little attention, in order to plunge us back into the darkness of popery, from which we can only escape by falling into irreligion."[13]

In these two testimonies, we can observe how Haller intended his translation to contribute to the defense of Christian orthodoxy and to the refutation of skeptical views that he considered so likely to spread irreligious attitudes.

Now, Crousaz's treatise intends to refute the skepticism of Sextus Empiricus and Bayle, the most important ancient and modern representatives of Pyrrhonism. The first part gives a general account of Pyrrhonism; the second comprises an abridged translation of some sections of Sextus's *Outlines of Pyrrhonism* and *Adversus Matematicos*, with a criticism of his main arguments; and the third part is a refutation of Bayle's skepticism in his *Dictionary*. I will refer to the general introduction of the work, where Crousaz expresses his intentions and explains the causes of the influence of Pyrrhonism in modern times.

At the beginning of his discussion, Crousaz acknowledges that his endeavor may encounter opposition from those who think they do not need such an explanation, for they already know what Phyrrhonism is; or from those that doubt that there could actually be any philosophers that follow such a strange doctrine. Nonetheless, he argues, he will not presuppose what Pyrrhonism means, but rather will begin by explaining it thoroughly, since his objective is not merely to attack some of the skeptic's views but to undermine their whole system, in order to "establish the certainty of our cognitions on their primary foundations."[14]

Having clarified his objective, the author sets the discussion in an imaginary scene. In this scene, he has been transported to a country in the Indies, where he holds a conversation with a curious philosopher, who wants to know about the foundation and development of the sciences in Europe. The author begins his account with ancient Greek philosophy, but moves quickly to modern times, referring to the philosophies of Bacon, Descartes, Malebranche, Locke, and others. His imaginary listener responds that such a diversity of philosophical systems must perplex the learned, who most probably want to "secure the truth." He continues arguing that, given the diversity of doctrines, several disputes must arise, from prejudice, partisanship, or envy, and that to examine every system and distinguish the true from the false in each case would require an excessive amount of time, which would make the situation even more unbearable.[15] He concludes his point by asking, "what maturity of judgment is needed to pronounce oneself on the disputes of such illustrious partisans?"[16]

In the context of this discussion, Crousaz describes the ongoing dispute between dogmatists and skeptics in Europe, claiming that there are, in fact, some who "defend the systems they hold passionately" and others who "think that it is necessary to completely renounce their thinking . . . and they even go so far as to deny to the human being the power of securing any truth, either general or particular."[17]

At this point of the dialogue, the Indian philosopher expresses his astonishment. He claims that he cannot believe there may be philosophers who consider every knowledge uncertain or, if indeed there are, he argues that they could not possibly live and act normally. To this objection, the author answers that the Pyrrhonists are in fact not always hesitant, but they abandon and resume the state of doubt. Then he explains their method, stating that whenever a scientist or a philosopher, for instance, explains the causes of some physical phenomenon, they object to this explanation. If the scientist then states the principles on which the inference rests, the skeptics object to this principle too, and so on. For "their delight in contradicting, embarrassing others and holding paradoxes grows more and more alluring with every objection. . . . But when the dispute ends, they go back to their natural sentiments, and act and think like the rest of humans."[18] This is the famous *apraxia* objection that dogmatists from ancient times used to direct to the skeptics.[19] It is interesting that Crousaz, undoubtedly knowing the force of this objection, chooses rather not to dwell on it, and argues instead that suspension of judgment is not a constant attitude of the Pyrrhonists. The reason lies in his intention to depict the skeptics as having a morally flawed character. Crousaz wants to stress the Phyrrhonists' insincerity, rather than their inability to act.[20] In fact, in the next paragraph the Indian philosopher formulates this very criticism. He says that, being dishonest about their doubts—for they do not hold permanently the state of suspense—no reasonable person could ever trust them. Since they feign insanity, insists the Indian, their views should not find favor with either the learned or the general public. Crousaz agrees with his fellow's criticism and proceeds to elaborate on it—the Pyrrhonists unite laziness with vanity, they let their obstinate passions contradict their ideas, and they delight in opposing against each other the useful, the agreeable, and the rightful.[21]

This moral criticism serves as a preamble to the issue that most interests Crousaz: the skeptics' attitude toward revealed religion. According to Crousaz, the Pyrrhonists are, in fact, a very dangerous sect, insofar as they "overturn all the obstacles that prevent the corruption of the heart and the relaxation of customs."[22] He argues, however, that the Europeans have gradually learned to live with the skeptics and blames the dogmatists for their prevalence. The argument proceeds as follows: The sacred scriptures offer a variety of proofs of the religious truths that are "as forceful as demonstrations."[23] Although reason naturally directs us to understand these truths, revelation has perfected them in a "brilliant and sublime" way, so that human beings can have a more noble access to them.[24] In spite of their clarity, however, we have had the temerity of altering or adorning them in such a way that several different Christian dogmas have appeared, leading their followers to engage in endless disputes with each other. In the history of these disputes, every sect has become more and more dogmatic, so that not only have invectives and anathemas been pronounced, but also much blood has been shed.

To make things even worse, a sect of Phyrronists has arisen who claim that reason is deceitful and its principles uncertain. They hold that those who distrust reason are wise, and argue that religion should be founded on faith, instead of on reason. Because of this, the author claims, they should rather be considered as a group of "mystics." However, their views are so far from being uniform that there is also conflict and perplexity among them, particularly when it comes to defining the source of their divine inspiration.[25]

At the heart of this situation lies a deficiency in religious education.[26] In Europe, Crousaz says, the education of children is entrusted to mediocre instructors, who lack the intellectual curiosity and honesty required for the task. When a child questions the principles of religion, instead of answering her openly, the instructors accuse the young mind of having been influenced by the devil.[27] In this way, the Europeans grow up believing what they do out of custom, example, and authority, not on the grounds of reasoned argument.[28] Hence, it does not surprise anyone when a Pyrrhonist claims that reason has no role in the foundation of religious belief, for this is the realm of faith alone.

The solution, however, is not to silence the Pyrrhonists. They bring about a corruption of customs that should actually be tolerated, along with the undesirable effects of other heretical sects—such as the deists—in order to avoid the even more harmful consequences of their public repression:[29]

> If we punished the deists, we would soon conclude that we ought to punish those who only accept a Providence that only gives rewards and punishment in this life and not in the afterlife; then, we would consider dangerous and worth punishing

the sentiment of those who think that the soul is by nature mortal but immortal by God's direct power; then we would abuse those that believe in their immortality but would not agree in considering it a substance different from the corporeal; afterwards we would persecute those that believe that thinking is not essential to the soul and that we do not always think when we act, and that stupid men do not ever think. And, since everyone believes to have the truth on their side, we would go from disputes to invectives, from invectives to blows, and the zeal for truth would become a pretext for fighting.[30]

The tolerant tone of the passage is, in fact, in agreement with the Enlightenment attitude that the Prussian Academy intended to spread. The author is quite conscious of the risks of religious fanaticism and wants to persuade the Indian philosopher of the importance of avoiding religious persecution and oppression.[31] He is also ready to acknowledge the social circumstances that fostered the emergence of modern Pyrrhonism, particularly the lack of proper religious education and the endless disputes among the different Christian denominations.

In his introduction to the treatise, then, Crousaz acts not merely as a conservative thinker, but also as a representative of the Enlightenment.[32] His attitude toward religious skepticism is rooted in the conviction that religious belief should be grounded in reason, and that such a foundation proves essential for the avoidance of superstition, enthusiasm, and prejudice. Neither does Crousaz claim a blind adherence to traditional theology, but he rather supports a reflexive awareness of the relationship between reason and revelation, so that Christians may reinforce the truths of revelation with reasonable inferences and further their rational and moral goals with the aid of revealed prescriptions.

3. Toward the Critical Attitude: Skeptical Arguments against Skepticism

As Laursen indicates, the arguments used and popularized by the anti-skeptics of the Prussian Academy were in fact skeptical in nature.[33] We can observe this in the previously summarized discussion of the introduction to Crousaz's *Examen du pyrrhonisme*. First, Crousaz employs the very skeptical genre of the *dialogue* to explain his views against the Pyrrhonists.[34]

This strategy allows him to situate the discussion in an imaginary setting, where the characters can freely express their opinions, objections, and doubts. However, in contrast to most skeptical dialogues, the speakers in the *Examen* are not so much refuting each other as supplementing a more-or-less unified perspective with their alternating arguments. In fact, Crousaz and the Indian philosopher tend to agree on the main points of the issue (i.e., the flawed character of the Pyrrhonists, the rational foundation of religion, the harmful consequences of the skeptical views, etc.), differing only slightly on the degree of their negative evaluation. In this sense, we could say that the skeptical form of the dialogue has, in Crousaz's writing, a rather dogmatic and explanatory aim: the objections of the Indian philosopher are taken as opportunities to illuminate complex circumstances and, in this way, to nuance the Indian's evaluation of the situation, but never to challenge his initial point of view.

Second, the very figure of an Indian philosopher, who has a more neutral and unbiased point of view, is also a skeptical topic worth noticing.[35] The function of the Indian philosopher in this dialogue is precisely to show how absurd the skeptical views seem to a sensible spectator, who is not involved in the passionate disputes about religion of eighteenth-century Europe. Yet, as I have mentioned, the Indian's role in this dialogue is not to refute, from his own perspective, the arguments of Crousaz, but rather to invite the author to expand them and to support the latter's criticism of the Pyrrhonists. Thus, the Indian offers an apparently neutral platform, from where Pyrronism can be seen in its "true colors."

Third, when Crousaz rebukes the religious skeptics—the so-called "mystics"—for not having a clear way of detecting a true source of "divine inspiration" from a false one, he is employing one of the most important skeptical strategies, that is, the argument on the invalidity of any internal criterion of truth.[36] If a true representation or judgment cannot be objectively recognized in virtue of an inherent mark, then any representation or judgment is equally uncertain. According to Crousaz, a religion founded on mere faith lacks such an objective character, and thus, every individual may consider her or his own inspiration as divine, which makes a real community of belief impossible. In other words, fideism leads to such a variety of religious views that no agreement on any grounds, theological or moral, is ever attainable and, hence, no unified doctrine can be defended. This refutation of fideism by means of a skeptical topic is, in my opinion, quite subtle. According to Crousaz, skepticism—in the form of fideism—actually leads to a sort of subjective dogmatism that can only be disabused through skeptical argumentation.

Finally, it is worth noticing Crousaz's use of the sorites in the above passage about the need to tolerate the Phyrrhonists. If we were to punish the Pyrrhonist, says Crousaz, we would also have to punish those who hold that divine Providence only rewards and punishes in this life, not in the afterlife; and if so, we would have to persecute those who think the soul is mortal; and, then, we would have to chastise those who consider that thinking is not essential to the soul, etc., until we finish by censuring any belief without distinction.[37] The sorites is also a very common form of skeptical refutation, in spite of its logical limitations.[38] Crousaz must have been quite aware of its argumentative use and its persuasive force.

By way of conclusion, we can see that Crousaz's standpoint is not easy to classify: he was not religiously orthodox, at least in his argumentative style, which incorporated many skeptical strategies. Neither was he a "free-thinker"—a term that in the eighteenth century referred mainly to the deists and fideists—although he did advocate for a free examination of the grounds of religious belief.[39] In my view, scholars like Crousaz and the members of the Prussian Academy contributed to a progressive dissolution of the boundaries between skepticism and dogmatism by employing skeptical arguments with dogmatic goals. In doing so they helped to develop a new critical attitude, one in which the dogmatists learned the habit of examining their own principles, while the skeptics gradually complemented their practice of dialectical refutation with a reserved acceptance of fallible conclusions. I will now refer to this difficult equilibrium, as it is described in Kant's *Critique of Pure Reason*, in order to situate the influence of Crousaz and the Prussian Academy in the origin of Kant's critical philosophy.

4. Kant's *Critique* and the Maturity of Reason

When he describes the standpoint of his "critique" of pure reason, Kant employs the well-known metaphor of the ages of reason:

> The first step in matters of pure reason, which characterizes its childhood is **dogmatic.** The just mentioned second step is **skeptical** and gives evidence of the caution of the power of judgment sharpened by experience. Now, however, a third step is still necessary, which pertains only to the mature and adult

> power of judgment, which has at its basis firm maxims of proven universality, that, namely, which subjects to evaluation not the *facta* of reason but reason itself, as concerns its entire capacity and suitability for pure *a priori* cognitions.[40]

For Kant, only mature reason can exercise the critical effort that is necessary to delineate reason's boundaries. However, to reach this state of maturity, reason must first have gone through the previous phases of infantile dogmatism and youthful skepticism. Therefore, for Kant, dogmatism and skepticism are not necessarily defective or misguided outlooks; instead, they are immature attempts at self-knowledge, the mark of reason's later development. In this way, dogmatism and skepticism should be not avoided or corrected, but rather assimilated in a new critical stance.

Tracing the origins of the term "critique" in eighteenth-century philology, aesthetics and logic, Colin McQuillan has argued, against traditional interpretations, that Kant's critical project was not directed to overcoming dogmatism and skepticism, but rather to examine the principles that lead to them.[41] Indeed, in contemporary Kantian scholarship, the idea that Kant's critical project is directed less to refuting skepticism or dogmatism than to making use of skeptical and dogmatic methods, has become influential.[42] As Rudolf Makkreel argues: "Kant sketches a history of pure reason in which his critical philosophy surpasses both dogmatism and skepticism. But by his own admission, critical philosophy still makes use of dogmatic and skeptical procedures."[43] Thus, although Kant in fact uses very derogatory language to describe both skeptics and dogmatists—calling skeptics a "kind of nomads who abhor all permanent cultivation of the soil" and considering dogmatism as a "worm-eaten" perspective—he still employs the "skeptical method" in the Transcendental Dialectic to tear down the edifice of traditional metaphysics, and he makes use of the "dogmatic method" in the Analytic to lay out the principles of *a priori* knowledge.[44] In this way, his critique incorporates both approaches—the dogmatic method of inferring from principles and the skeptical method of revising principles through thesis and antithesis—in order to ascertain the legitimacy of reason's claims. Once this legitimacy is obtained, reason can be sure of its domain and establish its boundaries: "This is not the censorship but the critique of pure reason, whereby not merely the **limits** but rather the determinate **boundaries** of it—not merely ignorance in one part or another, but ignorance in regard to all possible questions of a certain sort—are not merely suspected but are proved from principles."[45]

As we have seen previously, some of the views that appear in Crousaz's *Examen*, for instance, his claim that much "maturity of judgment" is needed to intercede in the disputes of the different Christian denominations, and his intention of refuting skepticism in order to "establish the certainty of our cognitions on their primary foundations," find a parallel in Kant's conception of a critique of reason.[46]

Still, does this parallel allows us to consider Crousaz as a precursor of the Kantian notion of critique? Is Crousaz's obscure treatise, abridged and translated into German by members of the Prussian Academy, an important precedent for Kant's project? Perhaps. However, even if Kant actually read the German version of the text, and referred directly to it in the *Lectures on Logic*—something that Kant did not do often—in my opinion, we would be hasty to conclude that the notion of critique was retrieved from this work.[47] One main reason for refraining from this conclusion is the fact that Crousaz was in fact not a very original thinker.[48] Thus, we can expect that his references to a "mature exercise of reason" and to the need for a revision of the "certainty of its principles" were rather general formulas that circulated in Enlightenment academic circles. Most probably, Crousaz repeated them as rhetorical devices, intended to make more persuasive his own arguments directed to the refutation of skepticism and the defense of Christian religion.

Yet I still believe that Crousaz's use of skeptical argumentative strategies and topics—such as the structure of the dialogue, the character of the Indian philosopher, the argument about the invalidity of an internal criterion of truth, and the employment of the *sorites*—somehow expresses the historical intellectual state of affairs that preceded the Kantian conception of a critique. As Laursen mentioned, the use of skeptical strategies to refute skepticism is a characteristic shared by most anti-skeptical members of the Prussian Academy, and we can probably extend it to other Enlightenment centers of learning.[49] Thus, what Crousaz's text shows, in my opinion, is the way in which eighteenth-century religious dogmatism appropriated skeptical forms of argumentation or, as I have already claimed, how dogmatism and skepticism intertwined and influenced each other during the Enlightenment, so as to finally give rise to Kant's critical philosophy. If the critique of reason incorporates the methods of both skepticism and dogmatism, then we can say that a good predecessor of this attitude is one in which dogmatism incorporates skeptical strategies. This would be an attitude not yet fully critical, but partially so. And, as I have shown above, this is, in fact, the case for Crousaz's work.

Now, there are many differences between what Crousaz did and what Kant thinks should be done in metaphysics and religion. One of them has to do with the moral and religious attack on skepticism. The use of *ad hominem* arguments that point to the faulty character of the skeptic is clearly not the most suitable form of examination of the rational legitimacy of a claim. Indeed, criticizing skeptical views by merely attributing to them a corrupting influence on customs is far removed from the critical exercise of reason. Thus, the perspective of this sort of moralist—a self-appointed guardian of moral and religious principles—although popular, cannot be considered critical in the Kantian sense of the term. It is instead a dogmatic attitude, as Kant himself describes: "the presumption of getting on solely with pure cognition from (philosophical) concepts according to principles, which reason has been using for a long time, without first inquiring in what way and by what right it has obtained them."[50] Another important point of divergence concerns the rational foundation of religion. Even though neither Crousaz nor Kant thinks religion ought to be entirely grounded on irrational faith, Kant's critical position precisely shows that at the basis of religion there cannot be found "truths" that are "as forceful as demonstrations," as Crousaz holds.[51] Kant's exhibition of the dialectical illusions that lie at the foundations of the proofs of the existence of God, in the Ideal of Pure Reason of the *Critique of Pure Reason*, traces in a very clear way the limits of reason in theological endeavors. Thus, nothing could be further removed from Kant's idea of a critique than Crousaz's optimistic rationalism regarding the "truths" of religion.[52]

In conclusion, inasmuch as Crousaz uses skeptical arguments to further his dogmatic goals, it cannot be said that his outlook is yet a critical one. But his approach does prefigure in many ways the critical exercise of reason. Perhaps it could be said that his defense of religion is an interesting mixture of infantile dogmatic impulses with youthful rebelliousness—the sort of immature impetus that is necessary, but not sufficient, to make a decisive step toward mature judgment.

5. Conclusion

In this paper, I have attempted to articulate one possible example of the Enlightenment intellectual attitude that may have decisively preceded Kant's conception of a critique of reason. In my view, the Prussian Academy contributed not only, as Laursen claims, to the popularization of skepticism, but also to the dissolution of the limits between skepticism and dogmatism—a dissolution that was necessary to give rise to the critical examination of human reason. Even though Crousaz's *Examen* is still a dogmatic defense of religion, his work is worthy of philosophical interest insofar as it makes use of skeptical strategies and topics to refute skepticism. In my view, when the traditional topics of skepticism become a weapon in the hands of dogmatism, the method of doubt has become a species of second nature, which can begin to be applied not only to the adversary but also to oneself. In the Kantian critical attitude, we can see this happening: both sorts of methods, skeptical and dogmatic, are used to examine the claims of reason itself. Thus, skepticism and dogmatism merge in order to provide a new ground to resolve endlessly unproductive and practically harmful disputes, in religion as well as in other domains of human inquiry.

As for Crousaz's *Examen*, I agree with Laursen and Matytsin in that it cannot be readily classified as a work of orthodox apologetics.[53] Rather, it expresses the effort of a conservative form of Enlightenment, which promoted a more reflective and tolerant religious attitude, an attitude that may have influenced the subsequent secularizing impetus of the second half of the eighteenth century.[54] Far from rejecting it as irrelevant, I think historians of philosophy (and not only of modern skepticism) should examine more closely its development and impact.

Notes

1. Immanuel Kant, *Lectures on Logic*, ed. and trans. J. Michael Young (Cambridge: Cambridge University Press, 1992), 172–173 (*Ak.* 24:218). All references to Kant's first *Critique* use the standard A/B pagination of the first (1781, A) and second (1787, B) editions. References to Kant's other works are accompanied by a parenthetical reference, cited as *Ak.*, to the volume and page number of the passage in *Kants gesammelte Schriften (Akademie Ausgabe)*, ed. Royal Prussian (later German) Academy of Sciences, et al. (Berlin: Georg Reimer, later Walter de Gruyter, 1900–).

2. John Christian Laursen, "Swiss Anti-skeptics in Berlin," in *Schweizer im Berlin des 18. Jahrhunderts*, ed. M. Fontius and H. Holzhey (Berlin: Akademie Verlag, 1996), 265.

3. See John Christian Laursen, "Swiss Anti-skeptics in Berlin," 261–282; and "Cicero in the Prussian Academy," 117–126; John Christian Laursen, Richard H. Popkin, and Peter Briscoe, "Hume in the Prussian Academy: Jean Bernard Mérian's 'On the Phenomenalism of David Hume,'" *Hume Studies* 23, no. 1 (1997): 153–162.

4. Laursen et al., "Hume in the Prussian Academy," 156.

5. Cicero's *Academica* was translated to French and commented upon by J. de Castillon in 1779. Hume's first *Enquiry* was translated to French by Mérian in 1758, with an introduction and notes by J.H.S. Formey. G. Sulzer wrote the introduction and notes to the German translation (translator unknown) in 1755.

6. For a different assessment of Crousaz's and other anti-skeptics' arguments, see Anton Matytsin, "The Protestant Critics of Bayle at the Dawn of the Enlightenment," in *Scepticism in the Eighteenth Century: Enlightment, Lumières, Aufkärung*, eds. Sébastian Charles and Plínio J. Smith (Dordrecht: Springer, 2013). According to Matytsin, Crousaz and Boullier "sought to articulate rational counter-claims that combined various epistemological systems of their period and, in their views, made convincing cases, against the onslaught of Pyrrhonian doubt" (64). I agree with his appraisal of some of Crousaz's arguments.

7. Laursen, "Cicero in the Prussian Academy," 263.

8. Laursen et al., "Hume in the Prussian Academy," 155. See also Laursen, "Swiss Anti-skeptics in Berlin," 261–282.

9. Laursen et al., "Hume in the Prussian Academy," 154.

10. According to de la Harpe, "In order to spread the good doctrine contained in the work of Crousaz, Samuel Formey, from a family of refugees, holder of the chair of Eloquence in Berlin and member of the Academy of Sciences of this city, composed an abridged version, of which, in 1738, he submitted some passages to the author, who declared himself satisfied and ready to give his approval to the print. But difficulties, first, from the part of a librarian in Strasbourg, and then from De Hondt at The Hague—who opposed the printing of the abridged version for financial reasons—prevented the publication." See Jacqueline E. de la Harpe, *Jean-Pierre de Crousaz et le conflit des idées au siècle des lumières* (Berkeley: University of California Press, 1955), 226.

11. "In 1941, Formey informed his correspondent that the manuscript was at Göttingen in the hands of professor Albert de Haller, who intended to make a translation into German." See de la Harpe, *Jean-Pierre de Crousaz*, 226.

12. Cited by Laursen et al., "Hume in the Prussian Academy," 155.

13. See de la Harpe, *Jean-Pierre de Crousaz*, 227.

14. Jean-Pierre de Crousaz, *Examen du pyrrhonisme ancien et moderne* (Den Haag: Pierre de Hondt, 1733), 1.

15. Crousaz, *Examen du pyrrhonisme*, 2.

16. Crousaz, *Examen du pyrrhonisme*, 2.

17. Crousaz, *Examen du pyrrhonisme*, 2.

18. Crousaz, *Examen du pyrrhonisme*, 3.

19. About the *apraxia* objection, see Myles Burnyeat, "Can the Sceptic Live his Scepticism?" in *The Original Sceptics: A Controversy*, ed. Myles Burnyeat and Michael Frede (Indianapolis: Hackett Publishing Company, 1997); K.M. Vogt, "Scepticism and Action," in *The Cambridge Companion to Ancient Scepticism*,

ed. Richard Bett (Cambridge: Cambridge University Press, 2010); Harald Thorsrud, "Sextus Empiricus on Skeptical Piety," in *New essays on Ancient Pyrrhonism*, ed. Diego E. Machuca (Leiden: Brill, 2011); Suzanne Obdrzalek, "From Skepticism to Paralysis: The Apraxia Argument in Cicero's Academica," *Ancient Philosophy* 32, no. 2 (2012); Alfonso Correa Motta, "¿Es posible vivir el escepticismo?" in *Convertir la vida en arte: una introducción a la filosofía como forma de vida*, ed. A. Lozano and G. Meléndez (Bogotá: Universidad Nacional de Colombia, 2016).

20. For a similar interpretation of Crousaz's charge of insincerity to the skeptic, see Matytsin, "The Protestant Critics of Bayle," 70–72.

21. Crousaz, *Examen du pyrrhonisme*, 4.

22. Ibid.

23. Ibid.

24. Ibid., 5.

25. Ibid., 6.

26. One of the most important matters of reflection for Crousaz is education. In 1718, he published anonymously the *Nouvelle maximes sur l'éducation des enfants*; and in 1722 the *Traité de l'éducation des enfants*. See de la Harpe, *Jean-Pierre de Crousaz*, 213–220.

27. Crousaz, *Examen du pyrrhonisme*, 7.

28. This is also a topic in Montaigne. In his essay "Apologie de Raimond de Sebonde" he says we are Christians for the same reasons we are Perigourdins or Germans ("Nous somes Chrétiens à même tritre que nous sommes ou Périgordins ou Alemans"). See Michel de Montaigne, "Apologie de Raimond de Sebonde" in *Les Essais* (Paris: Librarie Générale Française, 2001), 700.

29. In the same polemic vein, Crousaz had already written a refutation of the deist work of Anthony Collins, *Discourse on Free-Thinking*, in 1718. In his refutation, he accused Collins of Pyrrhonism (cf. de la Harpe, *Jean-Pierre de Crousaz*, 221).

30. Crousaz, *Examen du pyrrhonisme*, 8.

31. See Matytsin, "The Protestant Critics of Bayle," 64–66.

32. See de la Harpe, *Jean-Pierre de Crousaz*, 236.

33. Laursen et al., "Hume in the Prussian Academy," 155.

34. Indeed, the "dialogue" has been one of the favorite genres of the skeptical tradition. Many skeptical philosophers found their inspiration in Plato's Socratic dialogues and considered this the best philosophical form to express the dialectical movement of thesis and antithesis, that is, the so-called skeptical equipollence or *isostenia*. Instances of this use of the dialogical form range from Cicero's philosophical treatises such as *Academica* and *De Natura Deorum* to Hume's famous *Dialogues concerning Natural Religion*.

35. It also appears in Montaigne's "Des Cannibales." See Montaigne, *Les Essais*, 312–333.The difference in customs is also Sextus' tenth trope in the *Outlines*. See Sextus Empiricus, *Outlines of Scepticism*, ed. Julia Annas and Jonathan Barnes (Cambridge: Cambridge University Press, 2000), xiv, 145.

36. This argument is developed fundamentally by the Platonic Academy as a refutation of the Stoic criterion of truth (i.e., the "kataleptic impression"). According to the Academy, if it is not possible to distinguish a kataleptic impression from a non-kataleptic one, no internal criterion of truth exists, and everything ought to be uncertain (even the affirmation that "everything is uncertain"). See Cicero, *On Academic Skepticism*, trans. C. Brittain (Indianapolis-Cambridge: Hackett Publishing Company, 2006), 48 (*Luc.* 83).

37. Crousaz, *Examen du pyrrhonisme*, 8.

38. See Cicero, *On Academic Skepticism*, 30 (*Luc.* 49).

39. See de la Harpe, *Jean-Pierre de Crousaz*, 236.

40. Immanuel Kant, *Critique of Pure Reason*, trans. Paul Guyer and Allen W. Wood (New York: Cambridge University Press, 1998), A761/B789.The formulation in the *Dreams of a Spirit-Seer* is very curious, and indicates that even in the pre-critical period Kant had already in mind the outline of the ages of reason: "For that about which one knows a great deal early on his life as a child—of that, one can be sure, one will certainly know nothing later on life when one has reached maturity. And the man of thoroughness will in the end at best be the sophist of his youthful delusions" (*Ak.* 2:320).

41. J. Colin McQuillan, *Immanuel Kant: The Very Idea of a Critique of Reason* (Evanston, IL: Northwestern University Press, 2016), 68–69.

42. See Manfred Kuehn "The Reception of Hume in Germany," in *The Reception of David Hume in Europe*, ed. Peter Jones (London: Bloomsbury, 2005); Giorgio Tonelli, "Kant and the Ancient Sceptics," in *Scepticism in the Enlightenment*, ed. Richard H. Popkin, Ezequiel de Olaso, and Giorgio Tonelli (Dordrecht: Kluwer, 1997); Rudolf A. Makkreel, "Kant's Responses to Skepticism," in *The Skeptical Tradition around 1800: Skepticism in Philosophy, Science, and Society*, ed. Johan van der Zande and Richard H. Popkin (Dordrecht: Kluwer, 1998); Michael N. Forster, *Kant and Skepticism* (Princeton, NJ: Princeton University Press, 2008); Paul Guyer, "Kant on Common Sense and Scepticism," *Kantian Review* 7, no. 1 (2003); Catalina Gonzalez, "Pyrrhonism vs. Academic Skepticism in Kant's *Critique of Pure Reason*," *Philosophy Today* 55, Supplement (2011).

43. Makkreel, "Kant's Responses to Skepticism," 101.

44. Kant, *Critique of Pure Reason*, Aix–x.For definitions of the skeptical and dogmatic method, see Kant, *Critique of Pure Reason*, Bxxxv–xxxvi, A424/B452, A486/B514, A507/B535. See also Kant, *Lectures on Logic*, 163, 164–165, 332–333, 478–479, 585 (*Ak.* 9:84; 24:206, 208, 744–745, 885).

45. Kant, *Critique of Pure Reason*, A761/B789.

46. Crousaz, *Examen du pyrrhonisme*, 1–2.

47. Kant, *Lectures on Logic*, 172–173 (*Ak.* 24:218).

48. See de la Harpe, *Jean-Pierre de Crousaz*, 245–264.

49. Laursen et al., "Hume in the Prussian Academy," 155.

50. Kant, *Critique of Pure Reason*, Bxxxv.

51. Crousaz, *Examen du pyrrhonisme*, 4.

52. Kant, *Critique of Pure Reason*, A567–647/B595–670. According to de la Harpe, Crousaz's optimism has two features—on the one hand, God has given us a reason that allows us to direct our life in accordance with his precepts; and on the other, God has ordained the world in a rational way, so that we can know its natural laws and replicate them in our social systems. This is why "Crousaz rose with such vigor against the Pyrrhonists, libertines and immoralists: their doubts and disorders placed a discording note in this beautiful universe." See de la Harpe, *Jean-Pierre de Crousaz*, 257.

53. See Matytsin, "The Protestant Critics of Bayle," 66.

54. For a characterization of conservative Enlightenment, see Laursen, "Cicero in the Prussian Academy," 117–126.

2

Pure Sensibility as a Source of Corruption

Kant's Critique of Metaphysics in the *Inaugural Dissertation* and *Critique of Pure Reason*

KARIN DE BOER

1. Introduction

A hallmark of Enlightenment thought, Kant's critical philosophy has inspired widely diverging modes of philosophical critique throughout the nineteenth and twentieth centuries.[1] Given the abstruse reflections on the conditions of possibility of cognition carried out in the *Critique of Pure Reason*, however, the significance of Kant's notion of critique is not easy to grasp. As a result, our understanding of the relationship between Kant and post-Kantian modes of critical philosophy lacks precision as well. Do we know for sure that Kant is as modern as we take him to be?

In this chapter, I answer this question in the negative. Accordingly, I hold that Kant's famous presentation of the *Critique of Pure Reason* as a Copernican revolution is misleading.[2] Commentators have embraced the image of a revolution because it suggests that Kant's mature philosophy is modern and highly relevant to questions we have concerning the ultimate grounds of physics and empirical knowledge. Contextualizing Kant's notion of critique, I argue that the *Critique of Pure Reason* targets eighteenth-century German metaphysics in order to determine which of its elements need to be abolished and which of its elements need to be preserved. I maintain, in other words, that what Kant means by critique is very different from a wholesale rejection of metaphysics.

More specifically, this chapter challenges the alleged break between the dogmatic and critical phases of Kant's thought by highlighting the critical impetus of Kant's 1770 *Inaugural Dissertation*. According to the prevailing view, the *Dissertation* is pre-critical in that it considers the human mind to be capable of purely intellectual cognition of things in themselves.[3] I aim to show, by contrast, that Kant in this short treatise establishes the distinction between sensibility and thought for the sake of a thoroughgoing critique of his dogmatic predecessors and, on the other hand, that the *Critique of Pure Reason* both retains and radicalizes this critique. In this way, I hope to show that the critique of metaphysics for which Kant is famous rests on two criteria, namely, intellectual purity and objectivity, neither of which entails the impossibility of the scientific metaphysical system he envisioned.[4]

After outlining the mode of critique developed in the *Inaugural Dissertation* in section 2, I turn in section 3 to Kant's presentation of the task carried out in the *Critique of Pure Reason*. Section 4 zooms in on a number of passages from this work to show that Kant's mature critique of metaphysics rests on these two complementary layers of critique.

2. Kant's Notion of Critique in *Dreams of a Spirit-Seer* and the *Inaugural Dissertation*

While Kant's engagement with metaphysics betrays a critical impetus from at least 1755 onward, one of his first reflections on the act of critique can be found in *Dreams of a Spirit-Seer*. Published in 1766, *Dreams* is a complex text in which Kant elaborates his critique of Wolffian metaphysics by attacking Swedenborg's speculations about unembodied spirits, a strategy to which he refers at one point as a "tiresome detour."[5] In the final chapter, Kant presents this act as a mode of philosophy intended to determine the boundaries of human reason: "But if this enquiry turns into a philosophy that passes judgment on its own procedure and achieves knowledge not only of objects, but also of their relation to the human understanding, its boundaries [*Grenze*] will contract and its boundary-stones [*Marksteine*] will be placed in such a way that the enquiry can never again stray from its proper realm [*eigenthümlicher Bezirk*]."[6] It is clear that Kant assigns these boundary-stones the task of keeping out speculations about things such as the soul that are completely disconnected from the "data" given in sensation.[7] This is not to say, however, that Kant in this work renounces metaphysics as such. *Dreams* first and foremost targets judgments "such as those concerning the way in which my soul moves my body, or the way in which it is now or may in the future be related to beings of the same kind."[8] What Kant seeks to preserve, conversely, consists in metaphysics qua "companion of wisdom," that is, qua discipline devoted to questions such as "spiritual nature, freedom and predestination, the future state" on behalf of the moral destination of humankind.[9] But how can this useful element of metaphysics be purged from the vain speculations that have so far occupied its terrain? A clear-cut answer to this question had to wait until the publication of the *Inaugural Dissertation*.

Although Kant in the *Inaugural Dissertation* does not explicitly refer to the act of critique, he clearly takes the treatise to contain a critique of metaphysics. As Kant sees it, the main problem of metaphysics so far is its incapacity to limit itself to a purely intellectual consideration of things such as the soul or the world. Judging, for example, that the soul occupies a space or causes the body to move is unwarranted not because these judgments treat of the soul, but because the concepts involved in its determination *partly stem from sensibility*.[10] In order to purify metaphysics from the sensible elements by which it is infected, Kant calls for a preparatory investigation that radically distinguishes between sensible and intellectual cognition: "The philosophy that contains the first principles of the use of the pure intellect is metaphysics. But the science that is propaedeutic to it teaches the distinction between sensible and intellectual cognition; it is of this science that I am offering a specimen in my present dissertation."[11] The task of this propaedeutic is to critically examine, among other things, "a considerable part" of the method employed in metaphysics so far, a method that Kant claims rests on "the contagion of intellectual cognition by sensible cognition."[12]

One of the principles targeted in the *Dissertation* is Crusius's principle according to which "whatever is, is somewhere and somewhen."[13] Its use in metaphysics is "subreptic," Kant claims, because a predicate such as "somewhere" concerns the content of our sensible representations and cannot be attributed to things as such and, hence, to the soul or God.[14] If the meaning of a predicate presupposes sensibility, in other words, it may not be predicated and stated objectively of an intellectual concept; it may be predicated only as the condition without which the sensible cognition of the given concept cannot occur.[15]

Unlike *Dreams*, the *Dissertation* diagnoses the problems that result from the subreptive use of sensible predicates primarily by means of examples taken from general cosmology. However, Kant writes that these problems are not limited to this discipline, but "have disastrously permeated the whole of metaphysics."[16] In this sense, the discussion of general cosmology in the *Dissertation* should be regarded as a case study rather than a treatise on the world insofar as it can be grasped by the intellect.[17]

But how does Kant think metaphysics can be cured of its infection with sensibility? With regard to general cosmology, he argues in the first section of the text that a concept such as "composition" can acquire two different meanings: it can be used either as a purely intellectual concept or as a concept that refers to the mental act of adding one element to the next, an act that can be repeated *ad infinitum*. In the latter case, the meaning of the concept relies on time and is, for that reason, not suitable to be used with regard to the world considered as the object of general cosmology. He writes:

> It is one thing, given the parts, to conceive the composition of the whole by using an abstract concept of the intellect, and another thing to carry out this general concept by means of the sensible faculty of cognition . . . that is to say, to represent it concretely in a determinate intuition. The former is done by means of the concept of composition in general . . . and thus by means of universal ideas of the intellect. The latter case rests upon the conditions of time, insofar as it is possible, by the successive addition of part to part, to arrive genetically, that is to say, by SYNTHESIS, at the concept of a compound; this case falls under the laws of intuition.[18]

Metaphysics goes wrong, according to Kant, if it attempts to make judgments about the world qua object of the intellect by using a concept of composition that relies on the temporal act of synthesis, in other words, if it uses a "thick" notion of composition.

This example makes it clear that, for Kant, establishing the distinction between sensible and intellectual cognition is a necessary step within the propaedeutic discipline rather than an end in itself. This distinction has to be drawn in order to show that the allegedly intellectual cognitions of which metaphysics consists tend to be contaminated by sensible principles. By identifying this contamination, the propaedeutic should be able to establish metaphysics as a purely intellectual discipline. Thus, the upshot of Kant's propaedeutic reflection on the method to be employed in metaphysics is simple: "The whole method employed by metaphysics . . . amounts to this essential prescription: great care must be taken that the principles native to sensible cognition do not transgress their limits and affect intellectual cognitions."[19] In a letter to Lambert written shortly after the *Dissertation*, Kant summarizes the gist of the *Dissertation* in similar terms:

> The large role that the most universal laws of sensibility play in metaphysics, in which only concepts and principles of pure reason are at issue, is unwarranted. It seems that metaphysics must be preceded by a quite special, though purely negative science . . . in which *the validity and limitations of the principles of sensibility is determined*, so that the latter cannot confuse [*verwirren*] the judgments about objects of pure reason, as has heretofore almost always happened. For space and time, and the axioms for considering all things under these conditions, are, with respect to empirical knowledge and all objects of sense, very real and actually contain the conditions of all appearances and empirical judgments. But extremely mistaken positions emerge if we apply the basic concepts of sensibility to something . . . thought through a universal or a pure concept of the understanding as a thing or substance as such, and so on.[20]

Thus, Kant intended the purely negative, propaedeutic science that he envisioned and partly carried out in the *Dissertation* to purge metaphysics from principles the meaning of which presupposed space or time, in other words, to limit the use of such principles to the realm of appearances.[21] He accordingly held that the rational core of metaphysics could be salvaged by reducing its domain to, first, a systematic treatment of purely intellectual concepts and, second, judgments about the world as such, the soul, and God by means of such concepts. Even though the *Dissertation* takes issue with the role of sensible principles rather than the intellect, I consider Kant's 1770 reflection on the predicament of metaphysics a mode of critique proper. As we will see, moreover, this early guise of critique is not completely superseded by the one that dominates the *Critique of Pure Reason*.

3. The Notion of Critique in the *Critique of Pure Reason*

Clearly, the idea of a propaedeutic required to turn metaphysics into a science that we find in *Dreams* and the *Dissertation* results in the *Critique of Pure Reason*. Contrary to the earlier works, however, the *Critique* rejects the purely intellectual cognitions of objects that metaphysics purported to possess. For this reason, one might expect Kant to give an account of the aim to be achieved in the *Critique of Pure Reason* that deviates considerably from his account in *Dreams* and the *Dissertation*. In order to determine the exact difference, this section compares this early understanding of critique to some of Kant's well-known remarks on the topic in the two versions of the Preface and Introduction of the *Critique of Pure Reason*.[22] On my reading, only one of the four main elements that can be distinguished is actually new.

> a. *Critique as investigation into the possibility and boundaries of metaphysics.* In the Preface of the 1781 edition, Kant defines a critique of pure reason as "the critique of the faculty of reason as such, in respect of all the cognitions after which it might strive independently of all experience, and hence [as] the decision about the possibility or impossibility of a metaphysics as such (*überhaupt*), and the determination of its sources, as well as its extent and boundaries."[23] Clearly, Kant considers reason—taken in a broad sense—to produce the *a priori* cognitions of objects at stake in metaphysics. In accordance with the *Dissertation*, he suggests that a critique of metaphysics must examine these cognitions in view of their possible sources, that is, sensibility and thought, in order to determine the limits within which metaphysics is warranted.

> b. *Critique as propaedeutic to the system of pure reason.* As was mentioned above, Kant retains the idea put forward in the *Dissertation* that a critique of pure reason, qua propaedeutic investigation, must precede metaphysics proper. In the *Critique of Pure Reason*, he repeatedly refers to the metaphysics he intended to elaborate on the basis of this critique as a "system of pure reason."[24] As he puts it, critique, qua "science of the mere estimation of pure reason, of its sources and boundaries," must be regarded as "the propaedeutic to the system of pure reason" and provide "the

touchstone of the worth or worthlessness of all cognitions *a priori*."[25] This characterization is completely in line with his earlier remarks on the topic.

c. *The utility of critique.* Between 1770 and 1781, Kant did not change his mind on the usefulness of a critique of pure reason either. In the 1781 Introduction of the *Critique* he emphasizes that such a critique is useful only in a negative sense: "Such a propaedeutic would . . . have to be called . . . merely a critique of pure reason, and its utility would really be only negative. It would not be suited for the amplification of our reason, but only for its purification [*Läuterung*] and for keeping it free of errors, by which a great deal is already won."[26] The idea that metaphysics must be purified is clearly in line with the *Dissertation*. In the 1787 edition of the *Critique*, Kant specifies his position by explaining that critique plays this negative role only with regard to the speculations that used to be developed within the *theoretical* part of metaphysics. The utility of critique, he writes, "becomes positive when we realize that the principles with which speculative reason ventures beyond its boundaries do not in fact result in extending our use of reason, but rather . . . inevitably result in narrowing this use, namely, insofar as these principles threaten to extend the boundaries of sensibility, to which they really belong, beyond everything, and so to shut out [*verdrängen*] the use of pure (practical) reason."[27] Insofar as metaphysics draws on principles that "in fact reach only to objects of possible experience," it undermines the possibility "to assume God, freedom and immortality for the sake of the necessary practical use of . . . reason."[28] This is the case, Kant writes, because these principles transform that which cannot become an object of experience into an appearance.[29] As was seen above, Kant already in *Dreams* took his attack on metaphysical speculations to serve the purpose of practical philosophy.

While the passages just cited are well known, Kant's specific point about the principles he mentions in this context might easily be overlooked. Given his claim that they "really belong" to sensibility, the principles Kant has in mind must include the kind put forward by Crusius: since the principle according to which "whatever is, is somewhere and somewhen" does not distinguish between appearances and things insofar as they can be thought, it threatens to put the soul and God on a par with the spatio-temporal things governed by the laws of nature. This would threaten the possibility to conceive of human beings as free and of the world as a sphere within which this freedom can be realized.[30] But Kant's critique also applies, I hold, to the use of pure concepts such as substance and causality in Wolffian proofs of the immortality of the soul or the existence of God. Notwithstanding their purity, the use of such concepts relies on sensibility and accordingly ought to be limited to possible objects of experience alone. As I see it, Kant's explanation in the 1787 Preface of what is wrong with the principles used in metaphysics only makes sense if read in conjunction with the *Dissertation*. This early strand inconspicuously resurfaces in the 1787 Preface and, as we will see, in other sections of the *Critique of Pure Reason* as well.

d. *Critique qua rejection of purely intellectual cognition of objects*. Shortly after 1770, Kant must have realized that the mode of critique put forward in the *Dissertation* was not sufficiently radical.[31] In the *Critique of Pure Reason*, Kant is no longer satisfied with turning metaphysics into a purely intellectual discipline. Complementing the 1770 strand of critique, the strand carried out in the Transcendental Analytic seeks to demonstrate that predicating purely intellectual concepts of purely intellectual quasi-objects is a matter of thought rather than cognition proper. Kant considers the "analytical part" of the work to prove "that space and time are only forms of sensible intuition, and . . . further that we have no concepts of the understanding and hence no elements for the cognition of things except insofar as an intuition can be given corresponding to these concepts, consequently *that we can have cognition of no object as a thing in itself*, but only insofar as it is an object of sensible intuition, i.e. as an appearance."[32] While Kant's new criticism may seem to amount to empiricism, he distinguishes his position from the latter in two respects. First, he holds that the cognitions we can obtain of objects of experience includes *a priori* cognitions, that is, *a priori* judgments concerned with the determinations that *anything* must possess in order to count as an object of experience. Hence the pivotal role he assigns to the question concerning the possibility of synthetic *a priori* judgments.[33] Second, Kant holds that conceiving of things in themselves such as the soul, the world as such, and God by purely intellectual means is possible, and even necessary, on the condition that we do not purport to obtain *cognitions of objects* in this way. Kant's new critique of pure reason entails, that is, "the limitation of all even possible speculative cognition of reason to mere objects of experience. Yet . . . even if we cannot cognize these same objects as things in themselves, we at least must be able to think them as things in themselves."[34] Thus, the *Critique of Pure Reason* seeks to determine not only the limits within which the *a priori* use of *sensible* principles is warranted, but also the limits within which pure *reason*, taken in the broad sense of intellect, can obtain cognition proper.[35] In both cases, this limit is defined by the realm of possible objects of experience: a pure concept such as causality constitutes an *a priori* determination of any such objects, but cannot be used to determine alleged objects of pure reason such as the soul, the world as such, or God. As far as the theoretical part of metaphysics is concerned, any effort on the part of pure reason to determine non-sensible objects is a matter of thought rather than cognition proper.

In order to reject the assumption of metaphysics that cognition of objects can be achieved by means of the intellect alone, the *Critique* seeks to identify the conditions required to constitute something as an object of cognition at all. As I see it, this task is carried out in particular in the chapters of the Transcendental Analytic devoted to the transcendental deduction of the pure concepts of the understanding and the account of the schematism of the pure understanding.[36] For present purposes, it suffices to note that the *Critique* seeks to demonstrate that any synthetic *a priori* judgment must rely on time qua pure intuition in order to count as cognition of an object. Such judgments, in short, must be based on pure concepts the meaning of which presupposes sensibility, that is to say, on thick concepts.[37] It follows from this new "touchstone" that synthetic *a priori* cognitions are warranted if they pertain to appearances, but not if they pertain to purely intellectual concepts such as the world, the soul, and God.

Given the result of this new mode of critique, no one needs to doubt, Kant tells the reader, whether

> pure concepts of the understanding . . . as conditions of a possible experience . . . relate a priori solely to appearances, or whether, as conditions of the possibility of things as such, they can be extended to objects in themselves. . . . For we have seen there that . . . pure concepts a priori, in addition to the function of the understanding in the category, must also contain *a priori formal conditions of sensibility* (namely of the inner sense) that contain the general condition under which alone the category can be applied to any object.[38]

Kant's mature critique of metaphysics dominates the *Critique of Pure Reason* as a whole. Yet I hold that this new strand obscures the strand it has in common with the *Dissertation*. In the next section I will try to unearth this older layer within the *Critique of Pure Reason* and, on that basis, try to clarify their relationship.

4. The Purification and Self-Limitation of Metaphysics in the *Critique of Pure Reason*

As we have seen, in the *Critique of Pure Reason* Kant does not abandon his earlier view that metaphysics must be purified from all heterogeneous elements. As he writes in the Architectonic, human reason has so far not elaborated a metaphysics "in a manner sufficiently purified of everything foreign to it," that is, of the impact of empirical principles.[39] To achieve a purely intellectual mode of metaphysics, or a system of pure reason, the capacity to think something by means of pure concepts—the pure understanding—must be completely isolated from sensibility: "The pure understanding separates itself completely not only from everything empirical, but even from all sensibility. It is therefore a unity that subsists on its own, which is sufficient by itself, and which is not to be supplemented by any external additions. Hence the sum total of its cognitions will constitute a system that is to be grasped and determined under one idea."⁴⁰ This passage suggests that Kant's 1781 critique of metaphysics no less than its precursor hinges on the distinction between sensibility and thought established in the *Dissertation*.

The analysis of space and time as forms of intuition put forward in 1770 is repeated in the Transcendental Aesthetic. But Kant now makes use of this analysis for two complementary purposes: on the one hand, he aims to show that concepts and principles tainted by sensibility *must be expelled* from metaphysics because sensibility does not give us access to things insofar as they can be conceived by the intellect, that is, to things as they are in themselves. This strand of his critique is the one developed in the *Dissertation*. On the other hand, Kant aims to show that pure sensibility—in particular, time—is *required* to produce synthetic *a priori* cognitions of any object whatsoever. Given the complementary requirement that metaphysics be purely intellectual, this second strand entails, as the Transcendental Dialectic seeks to demonstrate in detail, that metaphysical cognition of quasi-objects such as the soul, the world as such, and God is impossible. In order to clarify how Kant in the *Critique of Pure Reason* conceives of the relationship between the early and mature strand of his critique of metaphysics, I will refer to them as [1] and [2] respectively.

As I see it, Kant must have developed the more radical version of his critique on the basis of his 1770 insight that pure concepts such as "composition" can function *either* as purely intellectual determinations of a purely intellectual object *or* as rules that allow the mind to carry out the synthesis of successive representations, rules that presuppose time qua form of intuition. Only in the latter case, I take the first *Critique* to argue, can pure concepts be used to achieve *a priori* cognitions of objects.

While passages that bring together both strands are rare, they can be found in both the Transcendental Analytic and the Transcendental Dialectic. In the chapter concerned with the distinction between *phaenomena* and *noumena*, Kant stresses that the pure understanding can and must stake out a realm of things that can only be thought, that is, of *noumena* in the negative sense of the term.⁴¹ By dint of the latter, the pure understanding is said to "set limits" to sensibility, which I take to mean that it prevents principles that depend on sensible determinations from encroaching upon metaphysics qua purely intellectual discipline.⁴² This is strand [1] of Kant's critique of metaphysics. As was mentioned above, it can be traced back to the *Dissertation* and is required to safeguard freedom and morality. This strand concerns not the alleged *objectivity* of synthetic *a priori* judgments, but their alleged *purity*. According to this strand, metaphysics can develop into a science if it establishes itself as a purely intellectual discipline concerned with determining purely intellectual concepts by means of other purely intellectual concepts.

Yet Kant moves beyond his position in the *Dissertation* by arguing, in the same passage, that in order for categories to *relate to objects at all*, "more than merely the unity of thinking must be given, namely a possible intuition to which they can be applied."[43] This is strand [2] of his critique of metaphysics. It is developed most explicitly in the Schematism chapter and, as was mentioned above, takes the upper hand in the *Critique of Pure Reason* as a whole. Kant takes himself to demonstrate in this work that cognition proper, or cognition of an object, requires that a sensible manifold be unified according to *a priori* rules the application of which involves time, in other words, "thick" versions of pure concepts such as causality and substance. On this account, synthetic *a priori* cognitions of objects are warranted insofar as they concern possible objects of experience, but not insofar as they concern particular quasi-objects such as the world, the soul, and God: a pure concept such as "composition," to recall the example from the *Dissertation*, is empty if used, as is done in metaphysics, to determine the world as it is in itself.

Bringing the two strands together, Kant writes that the pure understanding must not only restrict the realm of sensibility, but "also immediately [set] boundaries for itself, not cognizing these things through categories, hence merely thinking them under the name of an unknown something."[44] Thus, unlike the *Dissertation*, the *Critique of Pure Reason* maintains that metaphysics cannot solve the problems that afflict it unless it not only *purges* its domain from sensibility, but also accepts that cognition proper *requires* sensibility and, hence, that cognition proper of quasi-objects such as the soul, the world as such, and God is impossible.

In order to clarify this point, Kant's discussion of the first antinomy in the Transcendental Dialectic can serve as example.[45] Clearly, the synthetic *a priori* judgment "the world must have a beginning in time" is based on the spurious principle according to which all things are spatio-temporal. Without mentioning Crusius by name, Kant writes, "The cause of this illusion is that our reason . . . contains basic rules and maxims for its use that look entirely like objective principles, such that *the subjective necessity of a certain connection of our concepts on behalf of the understanding* is taken for an objective necessity, that is, a necessity that concerns the determination of things in themselves."⁴⁶ Once again, this passage echoes the *Dissertation*. As was discussed above, Kant already in this work argued that principles that involve sensibility merely concern the way in which the human mind unifies its sensible representations. Accordingly, he claims that Crusius's principle holds true of appearances alone and cannot be extended to things insofar as they can be conceived by the intellect. Even though Kant in the passage just quoted does not refer to sensibility, I hold that, for him, principles the meaning of which presupposes a form of intuition are nothing but ways in which the understanding unifies given representations and consequently cannot be used to determine the world considered as *noumenon*.

However, neither in 1770 nor in 1781 is Kant's critique of metaphysics limited to Crusius's principle. The more interesting cases are those where judgments that purport to be purely intellectual depend on concepts infected with sensibility in a less conspicuous way. As I see it, Kant does not object to a purely intellectual conception of the world qua sum total of things in themselves: "The synthesis of the conditioned with its condition is a synthesis of the mere understanding, which represents things as they are."⁴⁷ In this case, there is no "succession" involved and, accordingly, no erroneous infusion of the intellectual with the sensible.⁴⁸ I take Kant to hold that the pure understanding can err in two ways. First, it can err by positing an idea of reason—the world as such—as a potential object of cognition, whereas it is nothing but a *noumenon* in the negative sense of the term.⁴⁹ Second, it can err by determining this alleged object by means of pure concepts that purport to be purely intellectual, but are actually applicable to appearances alone.

For example, by asking whether the world as such is infinite or finite as regards its composition or divisibility, the pure understanding implicitly relies on pure concepts the meaning of which presupposes time qua form of intuition, namely, the act of adding one unit to the next:

> The synthesis of the conditioned with its condition . . . carries with it no limitation through time and no concept of succession. The empirical synthesis, on the contrary, . . . is necessarily given successively and is given only in time, one after another; consequently here I could not presuppose the absolute totality of synthesis and the series represented by it, as I could in the previous case, because . . . here [the members of the series] are possible only through the successive regress, which is given only insofar as one actually carries it out.⁵⁰

For this reason, it cannot be said that the world as such is either infinite or finite, and the same, Kant notes, holds for the other antinomies.[51] Such antinomies arise if the distinction between *noumena* and *phaenomena* is ignored and the former are determined by means of concepts the use of which is warranted with regard to the latter alone.

Metaphysics gets caught in transcendental illusion, that is, if the pure understanding determines a purely intellectual quasi-object by means of pure concepts infected by pure sensibility, in other words, by means of "thick" concepts that are nothing but rules for the unification of sensible representations. Kant summarizes this insight by noting that "transcendental subreption" occurs if "we take the empirical principle of our concepts of the possibility of things as appearances to be a transcendental principle of the possibility of things in general."[52] Although I cannot elaborate on this point, I believe that Kant's critique of rational psychology and rational cosmology in the Transcendental Dialectic is likewise informed by the view that metaphysics tends to draw on pure concepts the actual meaning of which is not purely intellectual, that is, on a subreptic use of such concepts.[53] Thus, while the pure understanding treats the soul as a purely intellectual object, it seeks to determine the latter by means of a concept of substance that presupposes permanence and, hence, time.[54]

In sum, I take the Transcendental Dialectic—and the *Critique of Pure Reason* as such—to argue that synthetic *a priori* cognition of objects *must* rely on schematized concepts, and so on time [strand 2], but that metaphysics *cannot* rely on such concepts if it is to establish itself as a purely intellectual discipline [strand 1]. Seen in this way, the critical distinction between "thin" and "thick" versions of pure concepts elaborated in the *Dissertation* sheds light on Kant's mature account of transcendental illusion and the critique of metaphysics at stake in the *Critique of Pure Reason*.

Since, as I have argued, the mature version of Kant's critique is more radical than the one developed in the *Dissertation*, one might infer that Kant by 1781 had become very skeptical about the prospects of a truly scientific metaphysics. I do not think that this conclusion is warranted. Quite the contrary: his mature critique merely targets the assumption that the activities carried out by the intellect ought to result in the cognition of *particular objects*. Yet metaphysics, as regards its theoretical part, need not aspire to the latter. According to Kant, in order for a doctrine to be called a science, it merely has to be "a system, that is, a whole of cognition ordered according to principles."[55] Given this definition, nothing prevents a mode of cognition concerned "not so much with objects as with our a priori concepts of objects as such" to develop into a "system of such concepts,"[56] that is, into the purely intellectual system of pure reason for which the *Critique of Pure Reason* was supposed to pave the way.[57]

We know from the Architectonic that Kant intended to include a rational cosmology in this metaphysical system.[58] Arrived at this point, we can briefly reconsider the *Dissertation* and ask how different Kant's projected rational cosmology would have been from the cosmology sketched in the *Dissertation*. Take, for example, the passage from the beginning of the *Dissertation*, discussed above, insofar as it deals with a purely intellectual conception of the world:

> When a substantial compound has been given, we arrive without difficulty at the idea of things which are simple by taking away generally the concept of composition, which derives from the intellect. . . . To conceive for oneself the composition of the whole, using an abstract concept of the intellect . . . is done by means of the concept of composition in general, insofar as a number of things are contained under it . . . and thus by means of ideas of the intellect which are universal.[59]

Can this account of the world be rejected on the basis of the twofold touchstone established in the *Critique of Pure Reason*? There is no reason to assume that Kant at the time of the *Dissertation* conceived of judgments that assign purely intellectual concepts to things insofar as they can be thought as cognitions of objects in a strict sense. Such concepts, he wrote already in 1770, are "empty of all intuition" and consequently afford us only "symbolic cognition."[60] Considered in this way, even the apparently dogmatic strand of the *Dissertation* turns out to be immune to Kant's mature critique of pure reason.

5. Conclusion

I have argued that, from 1770 onward, Kant's critique of metaphysics rests on the view that the two different meanings pure concepts can acquire limit their warranted use to either the purely intellectual determination of *noumena* or the production of objects of experience. This guiding thread has allowed me to argue, first, that the purification of metaphysics at stake in the *Dissertation* makes it a truly critical work and, second, that this purification remains one of the aims of the critique of metaphysics carried out in the *Critique of Pure Reason*.

Unlike commentaries that regard the *Dissertation* as an inexplicable regression into dogmatism, my reading has no difficulties of making sense of Kant's famous note that the year of 1769 brought him "great light."[61] Moreover, in this note and elsewhere, Kant suggests that this breakthrough ensued from a critical examination of antinomies and the "illusion" to which they testified. This is in agreement with my claim that Kant's 1781 account of the antinomies is motivated by the same concern—intellectual purity—as the *Dissertation*.[62]

The reading I have proposed is also supported by another famous passage, namely, Kant's 1772 question to Herz as to the ground of the relation between the "intellectual representations" stemming from the "inner activity" of the understanding and the object.[63] This remark arguably announces Kant's extensive investigation, in the Transcendental Analytic, into the conditions that allow the human mind to obtain *a priori* cognition of objects at all. While this investigation denotes an important difference between the *Dissertation* and the *Critique of Pure Reason*, I hope to have shown that its result affects neither the critical thrust of the former nor the ambition of the latter to turn metaphysics into a purely intellectual system of reason.[64]

Notes

1. On this, see Karin de Boer and Ruth Sonderegger, *Conceptions of Critique in Modern and Contemporary Philosophy* (Basingstoke: Palgrave Macmillan, 2012).

2. Immanuel Kant, *Critique of Pure Reason*, ed. and trans. Paul Guyer and Allen W. Wood (New York: Cambridge University Press, 1998), Bxxii. All references to the *Critique of Pure Reason* are to the A and B pagination of the first and second editions. I use the following translations for other works by Kant: Immanuel Kant, *Theoretical Philosophy, 1755–1770*, ed. and trans. David Walford and Ralf Meerbote (Cambridge: Cambridge University Press, 1992); Immanuel Kant, *Correspondence*, ed. and trans. Arnulf Zweig (Cambridge: Cambridge University Press, 1999); Immanuel Kant, *Theoretical Philosophy after 1781*, ed. Henry Allison and Peter Heath (Cambridge: Cambridge University Press, 2002). I have sometimes added emphasis and minor modifications to the translations in the quotations. Each quotation from a translation is accompanied by the volume and page of the passage in Immanuel Kant, *Kants gesammelte Schriften (Akademie Ausgabe)*, ed. the Royal Prussian (later German) Academy of Sciences, et al. (Berlin: Georg

Reimer, later Walter de Gruyter, 1900–).

3. According to De Vleeschauer, for example, Kant in 1770 "adopts a standpoint . . . opposed to the critical standpoint which is to come." Ertl asserts that Kant interrupted his dogmatic slumber in 1768–69 "only temporarily" because of "the utterly un-Kantian view that the human understanding has access to the world of *noumena*" put forward in the *Dissertation*. See Hermann-Jean de Vleeschauer, *The Development of Kantian Thought*, trans. A.R.C. Duncan (Edinburgh: Thomas Nelson and Sons, 1962), 56. See also Wolfgang Ertl, "Hume's Antinomy and Kant's Critical Turn," *British Journal for the History of Philosophy* 10, no. 4 (2002), 635. Beiser takes the more nuanced view that whereas Kant in both *Dreams* and the *Inaugural Dissertation* targets "speculations about an unknown spiritual world," he in the latter text seeks to establish an ontology that anticipates the *Critique of Pure Reason*. However, he disregards Kant's focus in the *Dissertation* on general cosmology rather than ontology. See Frederick Beiser, "Kant's Intellectual Development: 1746–1781," in *The Cambridge Companion to Kant*, ed. Paul Guyer (Cambridge: Cambridge University Press, 1992), 49–50. My own approach converges with that of Moledo, who likewise considers Kant's effort to establish metaphysics as a purely intellectual discipline to testify to the critical impetus of the text. See Fernando Moledo, "Die neue Auffassung der Metaphysik als reine Philosophie in der Inauguraldissertation und ihre propädeutische Bedeutung im Rahmen der Entwicklungsgeschichte der Kritik der reinen Vernunft," *Kant-Studien* 107, no. 3 (2016).

4. The current chapter draws on earlier work on the Schematism chapter of the *Critique of Pure Reason* and Kant's notion of sensible concepts in the *Inaugural Dissertation*. See Karin de Boer, "Categories versus Schemata: Kant's Two-Aspect Theory of Pure Concepts and his Critique of Wolffian Metaphysics," *Journal of the History of Philosophy* 54, no. 3 (2016), and Karin de Boer, "Kant's Account of Sensible Concepts in the *Inaugural Dissertation* and the *Critique of Pure Reason*," in *Akten des XII. Internationalen Kant-Kongresses*, ed. Violetta Waibel and Margit Ruffing (Berlin: Walter de Gruyter, 2018). It differs from both by discussing the continuity between the two works in more detail and by putting the notion of critique center stage. See Karin de Boer, *Kant's Reform of Metaphysics: The Critique of Pure Reason Reconsidered* (Cambridge: Cambridge University Press, 2020), for a more in-depth elaboration of the reading put forward in the present chapter.

5. Kant, *Theoretical Philosophy, 1755–1770* (*Dreams of a Spirit-Seer*), 354 (*Ak.* 2:367).

6. Ibid., 356 (*Ak.* 2:369–370).

7. Ibid., 354 (*Ak.* 2:368).

8. Ibid., 357 (*Ak.* 2:371).

9. Ibid., 356 (*Ak.* 2:369).

10. On the debate among Kant's predecessors as to whether the soul occupies space, Heßbrüggen-Walter points out that Crusius defended a strong version of what he calls "localism." See Stefan Heßbrüggen-Walter, "Putting Our Soul in

Place," *Kant Yearbook* 6 (2014), 25. For present purposes, I limit my account to the ontological principle that supports Crusius's account of the soul.

11. Kant, *Theoretical Philosophy, 1755–1770* (*Inaugural Dissertation*), 387 (*Ak.* 2:395).

12. I will translate "sensitivus" as "sensible" rather than "sensitive" because the German equivalent "sinnlich" is normally translated as "sensible." Since the *Dissertation* does not yet clearly distinguish between the understanding and reason, I will translate "intellectualis" as "intellectual" throughout: what Kant calls intellectual concepts includes what he will come to call ideas of reason.

13. Kant, *Theoretical Philosophy, 1755–1770* (*Inaugural Dissertation*), 408–409, see also 399–400 (*Ak.* 2:413–414, see also 406). Kant does not mention Crusius by name, and the formulation of the principle is his. See Christian August Crusius, *Entwurf der nothwendigen Vernunft-Wahrheiten, wiefern sie den Zufälligen entgegen gesetzet werden* (Leipzig: Gleditsch, 1745), §46. Crusius here states that the expression "a substance exists" means "that it is immediately present in a determinate somewhere, or space, and at a determinate time." While Grier briefly discusses Kant's endorsement of Crusius's criticism of the principle of sufficient reason in the 1760s, her account of the *Inaugural Dissertation* disregards Kant's criticism of Crusius's principle of the spatio-temporality of everything that exists. See Michelle Grier, *Kant's Doctrine of Transcendental Illusion* (Cambridge: Cambridge University Press, 2001).

14. Kant, *Theoretical Philosophy, 1755–1770* (*Inaugural Dissertation*), 408 (*Ak.* 2:412).

15. Ibid.

16. Ibid.

17. Kant briefly discusses problems in natural theology in Kant, *Theoretical Philosophy, 1755–1770* (*Inaugural Dissertation*), 409–411 (*Ak.* 2:414–415). For an interpretation of the *Dissertation* that centers on Kant's effort to establish a general cosmology that does not conceive of substances as spatio-temporal, see Andree Hahmann, "Die Reaktion der spekulativen Weltweisheit: Kant und die Kritik an den einfachen Substanzen." *Kant-Studien* 100, no. 4 (2009).

18. Kant, *Theoretical Philosophy, 1755–1770* (*Inaugural Dissertation*), 377–378 (*Ak.* 2:387).

19. Ibid., 407 (*Ak.* 2:411).

20. Kant, *Correspondence* (*Kant to Lambert, September 2, 1770*), 108–109, translation modified, emphasis added (*Ak.* 10:98). Kant here seems to use "reason" and "understanding" indiscriminately.

21. On this point, I disagree with Beiser, who considers Kant's treatment of concepts such as divisibility in the *Inaugural Dissertation* to stem from his attempt to solve disputes between metaphysics and mathematics. See Beiser, "Kant's Intellectual Development: 1746–1781," 51.

22. I will limit my account to these introductory sections. For a more extensive treatment see J. Colin McQuillan, *Immanuel Kant: The Very Idea of a Critique of Pure Reason* (Evanston, IL: Northwestern University Press, 2016).

23. Kant, *Critique of Pure Reason*, Axii; see also Axxi, A10, Bxxii–xxiii.

24. Ibid., Axxi, A83/B109, A841/B869.

25. Ibid., A11–12/B25–26; see also B27. See also Kant, *Theoretical Philosophy after 1781* (*Prolegomena*), 131, 165, 169 (*Ak.* 4:340, 378, 383).

26. Kant, *Critique of Pure Reason*, A11.

27. Ibid., Bxxiv–xxv.

28. Ibid., Bxxx.

29. Ibid., Bxxx.

30. Ibid., Bxxvii–xxviii.

31. Already in 1771, Kant mentioned to Herz a manuscript he was working on with the title *The Limits of Sensibility and Reason*, suggesting that reason not only exclude sensible principles from its proper realm, but also put limits on its purely intellectual activities. See Kant, *Correspondence* (*Kant to Herz, June 7, 1771*), 126–127 (10:122–123). On the plan for this project, see McQuillan, *Immanuel Kant*, 51–54, who, however, sees no real break between this project and the *Dissertation* and does not consider it to anticipate the *Critique of Pure Reason*.

32. Kant, *Critique of Pure Reason*, Bxxv–xxvi (emphasis added).

33. Ibid., A10, B19.

34. Ibid., Bxxvi.

35. Grier ignores the corrupting effect Kant attributes to pure sensibility in this context. Whereas she holds that Kant regarded *any* use of the categories beyond the realm of experience as "erroneous," I argue that he only opposes the use of their "thick" versions. Seen from this perspective, Kant's projected metaphysics salvages not only the regulative use of the ideas of reason, as Grier and most commentators maintain, but also the sum-total of their purely intellectual determinations. See Grier, *Kant's Doctrine of Transcendental Illusion*, 109–110, 263–301.

36. In what follows, I disregard, among others, the role of the metaphysical deduction and Kant's distinction between the pure understanding and pure reason.

37. I take this to be the result of the Schematism chapter. See, for instance, Kant, *Critique of Pure Reason*, A145–146/B185 and my discussion in Karin de Boer, "Categories versus Schemata," 441–468.

38. Kant, *Critique of Pure Reason*, A139–140/B178–179 (emphasis added). Similarly, Kant writes that "merely intelligible objects," or "those things that are thought through pure categories, without any schema of sensibility," are impossible because "the condition of the objective use of all our concepts of understanding is merely the manner of our sensible intuition, through which objects are given to us, and, if we abstract from the latter, then the former have no relation at all to any object whatsoever." See Kant, *Critique of Pure Reason*, A286/B342; see also A147/B186–187.

39. Kant, *Critique of Pure Reason*, A842/B870. Kant notes in the *Dissertation* that "empirical concepts do not, in virtue of being raised to greater universality, become intellectual in the real sense," but "always remain sensible" (2:394); see Kant, *Critique of Pure Reason*, A843/B871 for a similar claim.

40. Ibid., A65/B89–90.

41. Ibid., B309.

42. Ibid., A256/B311.

43. Ibid., A256/B311.

44. Ibid., A256/B312.

45. A discussion of Kant's intricate account of transcendental illusion in the Transcendental Dialectic falls outside the scope of this chapter.

46. Kant, *Critique of Pure Reason*, A297/B353 (emphasis added).

47. Ibid., A498/B526.

48. Ibid., A500/B528. This point is stressed in an unpublished paper on the antinomies by Miguel Herszenbaun.

49. Transcendent ideas, Kant notes, "have a merely intelligible object, which one is of course allowed to admit as a transcendental object." Yet it is not justified, in his view, to conceive of such an object "as a thing determinable by its distinguishing and inner predicates." See Kant, *Critique of Pure Reason*, A566/B594. Thus, Kant suggests that pure reason, in its attempt to conceive of something as a totality, unwarrantedly entangles itself with the pure understanding's attempt to determine objects, an attempt that, in its turn, relies on the use of pure concepts the meaning of which presupposes sensibility. This is to say that I agree with Grier's point that the understanding's effect on reason causes the fallacies, but not with her assumption that sensibility is irrelevant in this regard. See Grier, *Kant's Doctrine of Transcendental Illusion*, 110–111.

50. Kant, *Critique of Pure Reason*, A500–501/B528–529; see also A528/B556.

51. Ibid., A505/B533.

52. Ibid., A582–583/B660–661.

53. Ibid., A509/B537.

54. Kant argues that we can conceive of ourselves as subject, but cannot determine ourselves as substances, because the concept of substance that we thus bring into play "is always related to intuitions, which in me cannot be other than sensible, and hence must lie wholly outside the field of the understanding and its thinking, which is all that is really under discussion here if it is said that the I in thinking is simple." See Kant, *Critique of Pure Reason*, B408; see also A401. In this case, our use of the category is "empirical," that is, valid with regard to appearances alone. If the category in *this "thick" sense* is used with regard to the I or the soul qua *noumenon*, I take Kant to argue, then it is used surreptitiously. The term "transcendental subreption" is also used in relation to rational theology. See Kant, *Critique of Pure Reason*, A402, A619/B647.

55. Kant, *Theoretical Philosophy after 1781* (*Metaphysical Foundations of Natural Science*), 183 (*Ak.* 4:467).

56. Kant, *Critique of Pure Reason*, A11–12; see also A57/B81.

57. Thus, I submit that for a body of cognitions to be a science, these cognitions need not be cognitions of objects. Given his references to his propaedeutic as a mode of knowledge (Axv, Axx) or self-knowledge (Axi), I hold that Kant thought of his projected system of pure reason as a purely intellectual mode of cognition as well. See Kant, *Critique of Pure Reason*, Axi, Axv, Axx.

58. Kant, *Critique of Pure Reason*, A846/B874.

59. Kant, *Theoretical Philosophy, 1755–1770* (*Inaugural Dissertation*), 378 (*Ak.* 2:387).

60. Ibid., 387 (*Ak.* 2:396).

61. Kant, Reflexion 5037, dated 1776–1778 (*Ak.* 18:69).

62. See Kant, *Theoretical Philosophy after 1781* (*Prolegomena*), 129 (*Ak.* 4:338), and Kant, *Correspondence* (*Kant to Garve, September 21, 1798*), 552 (*Ak.* 12:258–259). These reports need not be at odds with Kant's claim in the *Prolegomena* that it was Hume who aroused him from his dogmatic slumber. See Kant, *Theoretical Philosophy after 1781* (*Prolegomena*), 57 (*Ak.* 4:260). I discuss Kant's engagement with Hume in Karin de Boer, "Kant's Response to Hume's Critique of Pure Reason," *Archiv für Geschichte der Philosophie* (2019).

63. Kant, *Correspondence* (*Kant to Herz, February 21, 1772*), 133 (*Ak.* 10:130).

64. I am grateful to G. Anthony Bruno, Miguel Herszenbaun, J. Colin McQuillan, Angelica Nuzzo, Rachel Zuckert, and members of the Leuven Research Group in Classical German Philosophy for their comments and suggestions on earlier versions of this paper.

3

Critique in Kant's *Critique of Practical Reason*

Why This *Critique* Is Not a Critique of Pure Practical Reason

AVERY GOLDMAN

Kant begins his second *Critique*, the *Critique of Practical Reason* (1788), by explaining why the book is not called the *Critique of Pure Practical Reason*. While the latter title would have paralleled the title of his first *Critique*, the *Critique of Pure Reason* (1781/1787), he explains that practical reason does not need its pure, which is to say non-empirical, pursuits limited.[1] Critique in the realm of pure (speculative) reason plays the role of a tribunal—a "court of justice"—limiting the metaphysical tendencies of the faculty of reason, which otherwise lead to unending controversies.[2] Kant deems such a "negative" sense of critique a "discipline" that limits the pursuit of metaphysics to the narrowly construed realm of experience.[3] It is this "negative" sense of critique that Kant famously proclaims in the Preface to the *Critique of Pure Reason*: "our age is the genuine age of criticism, to which everything must submit."[4] However, on the first page of his *Critique of Practical Reason*, Kant explains that the critique of practical reason requires no such tribunal. This is not to say that just six years after the publication of the *Critique of Pure Reason* Kant had joined forces with anti-Enlightenment voices, renounced the "age of criticism," and embraced a morality of custom. Rather, he offers here an addendum to the tribunal he institutes in the name of critique in the *Critique of Pure Reason*.

In his first *Critique* Kant rejects the possibility of knowledge of the ideas of reason. Reason has been limited, but Kant still hints at the positive role played by setting such a boundary. Disciplining reason both protects the realm of empirical cognition from metaphysical speculation and determines the possibility of metaphysics after it has been delimited by critique.[5] Kant explains late in the first *Critique* that his critique "is not the censorship but the critique of pure reason, whereby not merely limits [*Schranken*] but rather the determinate boundaries [*Grenzen*] of it . . . are not merely suspected but are proved from principles."[6] In the *Prolegomena* Kant explains that limits "are mere negations that affect a magnitude insofar as it does not possess absolute completeness," but boundaries refer beyond what is negated, and so "presuppose a space that is found outside a certain fixed location."[7] Kant is referring to such a determinate "space" of metaphysics in the preface to the first edition, when he explains that critique will not deny our metaphysical tendency but will determine its "extent and boundaries."[8]

In the first *Critique* Kant describes such a positive sense of critique, an investigation of the *a priori* principles of pure reason, as a "canon," and locates it in reason's "practical use."[9] Kant's third Antinomy raises just such a possibility for reason. In pitting mechanism against freedom, its solution offers both a "discipline" that excludes the possibility of a mechanical explanation of the world in its entirety and a "canon," raising the possibility that pure reason could exist in the noumenal sphere as a causality that does not contradict the mechanistic causality of phenomenal nature. *Both* senses of critique are thus initiated in the *Critique of Pure Reason*.[10]

The *Critique of Practical Reason* begins at precisely this point, investigating the transcendental idea of freedom, and attempting to show that such a possibility can be said to exist. In relation to practical reason, critique is thus neither a "tribunal" nor a "discipline" that sets limits to reason's use, but a "canon" searching for pure reason within the boundaries that the critique of speculative reason has determined.[11] Kant goes on to say that once pure reason is shown to exist in the practical sphere, it will not need to be disciplined, for, as practical rather than speculative, it has already had its speculative pretensions denied.[12]

Such a development of the Kantian conception of critique in the second *Critique* offers a new way to investigate the transcendental idea of freedom raised by Kant in the first *Critique*. This paper will investigate not only the broadening of the Kantian conception of critique from "discipline" to "canon," but also the transformation in the conception of practical reason that it affords. For it comes as some surprise that, when one finally reaches the Dialectic of the *Critique of Practical Reason*, one finds Kant's search for pure practical reason returning to the Epicurean happiness that he would seem to have rejected in favor of his Stoic morality. Kant explains that while moral virtue has been shown to be "the supreme good [*das oberste Gut*]" of human life, it is not "the highest good [*das höchste Gut*], in the sense of the complete good, for that would require happiness as well."[13] Kant calls the combination of morality and happiness, the virtue of the Stoic and the pleasure of the Epicurean, the "highest good," but it is hardly clear how these two pursuits can avoid contradicting each other.[14] By addressing Kant's antinomy of pure practical reason, this paper will be able to solve this apparent contradiction without denying humanity's "supreme good," the transcendental freedom first broached by Kant in the third Antinomy. What will become apparent is that critique for Kant is not only a "discipline" that guards against error, but a "canon" that works to extend the reach of pure reason. This extension, initiated by the pursuit of transcendental freedom, will lead Kant to defend the pursuit of (Epicurean) happiness alongside the pursuit of (Stoic) moral responsibility.

1. The Moral Law

Kant famously addresses the question of free will in his third Antinomy, in the Transcendental Dialectic of the *Critique of Pure Reason*. By this point in the book Kant has defended a mechanistic account of nature by narrowing the defense of causality to the world as it appears to us, that of phenomena. The Transcendental Analytic addresses the conditions of the possibility of such appearances within the spatio-temporal limits set by the Transcendental Aesthetic and deduces mechanistic causality as one of the twelve *a priori* concepts of the understanding.

The Transcendental Dialectic takes up the investigation at this point. While the categories have been deduced from the limited field of spatial appearances designated by the Transcendental Aesthetic, the categories of relation, substance, causality, and community, are not in themselves limited to appearances.[15] Kant's Transcendental Dialectic follows these three categories as they direct us, beyond appearances, to the unconditioned, to the ideas toward which the syllogisms point. The first concept of relation, that of substance, points toward the thinking subject and so relates to psychology; the second, causality, points toward the unity of all appearances and so to cosmology; and the third concept, community, points toward the unity of all thought and so to theology.[16] These extensions of the categories are, Kant explains, "necessary . . . as they are grounded in the nature of human reason, even if these transcendental concepts lack a suitable use *in concreto*."[17] The extension of our concepts is, thus, shown by Kant to follow "from the nature of our reason" even if no object can be determined for them.[18] In the second edition of the first *Critique*, Kant adds a footnote that goes even further, naming the "transcendental concepts" toward which reason, in each of the three cases, proceeds: the first of these inquiries, psychology, is connected to the metaphysical idea of immortality; the second, cosmology, is connected to the idea of freedom; and the third, theology, is tied to the idea of God.[19]

What is particularly noteworthy, in the context of this chapter, is the second of these ideas, freedom. Mechanistic causality is said to have as its "proper end" the idea of freedom.[20] While we are accustomed to Kant's complex solution to the distinction between phenomenal mechanism and noumenal freedom, it is worth pointing out just how odd it would have been to have read such a connection of mechanism and freedom for the first time. The completion of the series of mechanistic causes, which is to say determinism, would seem to exclude all possibility of human freedom; and yet, Kant claims that freedom, human freedom and not God's, is the idea to which mechanism points. Leibniz's defense of freedom makes use of the impossibility of completing just such a series. For Leibniz, while God is all knowing, human reason includes both necessary truths and contingent ones, both of which follow the principle of sufficient reason, and yet contingent truths, in evading analysis, permit human freedom.[21] So, for Leibniz, human freedom is neither opposed to the rational nor located at its completion; rather, freedom can be said to take place within the region of such "contingent futurities"—rational truths that cannot yet be explained.[22] Kant, on the other hand, raises freedom as the idea toward which the entire series of conditions proceeds. It is not an unexplained cause but something distinct from the chain of causes, and yet it is still related to the series of causes in some as of yet unexplained manner. In the introductory discussions of the Transcendental Dialectic, Kant says nothing about how the idea of causality is to be thought to relate to that of freedom. Kant addresses this question in the Antinomy of Pure Reason chapter of the Transcendental Dialectic.

In the introductory material to the Antinomies, Kant explains that "reason demands an absolute totality on the side of conditions."[23] Such a demand leads Kant into the third Antinomy. If reason directs us to complete the series of appearances, then how can freedom be anything apart from this causal chain? Kant's third Antinomy begins from the perspective developed in the Transcendental Analytic. Causality, as an *a priori* concept of understanding, is a condition of the possibility of experience. This is made most explicit in the second Analogy of Experience.[24] The *a priori* concept of substance has already been shown in the first Analogy of Experience to explain how what appears successively can be understood to be a persisting object.[25] In the second Analogy Kant asks how the subsisting substance can be conceived. If substance is distinguished by the persistence of what is successive, Kant now asks how what is not only successive, but is, in fact, altered in such succession, can be said to persist. The answer that Kant offers is that all alterations that relate to the persisting substance "occur in accordance with the law of the connection of cause and effect."[26] Without such a law we would not be able to explain how substance both subsists (first Analogy) and alters (second Analogy).[27] While the Transcendental Deduction has argued for the dependence of experience on the *a priori* concepts of the understanding, Kant, in the Analogies, explains that when conceived as the rules governing spatial appearances, such *a priori* concepts of relation produce the "principles [*Grundsätze*]," or empirical rules, of experience.[28] All "alteration" of substances can be said to follow the law of causality such that "all change (succession) of appearances" can be said to be merely the transformation of what subsists.

The third Antinomy begins from this point. The question for Kant is whether such an account of the dependence of all alteration of substance on the *a priori* concept of causality rules out the possibility of a conception of freedom distinct from the chain of nature. This is to ask: Can Kant offer a more robust account of freedom than that of Leibniz's ever diminishing region of "contingent futurities"? Kant's thesis attempts to prove that distinct from causal nature a causality by means of freedom must also be embraced. To do so, Kant begins with the opposite assumption, "assume that there is no other causality than that in accordance with laws of nature," proceeding, as he will in the antithesis as well, by means of the *reductio ad impossibilem* (proof by contradiction).[29] If there is only natural causality, then everything that happens presupposes a prior state, and such prior states themselves presuppose prior states.[30] Kant explains that such a conception of nature, as that which is defended in the second Analogy, claims that "nothing happens without a cause sufficiently determined *a priori*." And yet, at any given time analysis of the complete series of causes is impossible; there is no "first beginning" only a relative or "subordinate [*subaltern*]" beginning.[31] But here the law of causality contradicts itself, as it says both that everything that happens has a cause that can be explained, and that, in fact, at any given time we have no such explanatory reach. And so, by means of a proof by contradiction, we can say that our assumption was mistaken. To claim that there is only natural causality leads to a contradiction, and thus we have proven that there must be a causality apart from nature, in which something can be said to happen spontaneously and not only as following from prior acts.

The antithesis attempts to prove the opposite, that everything that happens in the realm of appearances is governed by the laws of nature, so there is no freedom, only causal necessity. Kant again proceeds by assuming the opposite: assume that freedom as a type of causality could be proven to exist alongside natural necessity. If this were the case, Kant explains, then this causality would be an absolute beginning, the start of a series with nothing that precedes it. But natural causality explains that every action presupposes "a state of the not yet acting cause," of a cause that is itself the effect of another cause.[32] This is precisely what causal freedom denies, so the assumption that there exists a causal freedom apart from natural necessity, with which the antithesis began, is proven false. The antithesis has shown that freedom, as a further type of causality, cannot exist alongside natural causality. Thus, in the third Antinomy, the thesis has proven that freedom exists, and the antithesis has proven the opposite, that freedom cannot exist.

Where does this leave us? The mathematical antinomies offer only contradiction, as they remain within the realm of appearances, arguing over whether the world has a beginning in space and time (first Antinomy) and whether composite substances are made up of simple parts (second Antinomy). The dynamical antinomies, however, "insofar as they are suited to the ideas of reason," can be "**mediated** to the satisfaction of both parties."[33] While the mathematical antinomies make opposing claims within the phenomenal realm, the dynamical antinomies do not. While one claim remains within the sensible, that of nature's causality, the other, freedom, points beyond the series of conditions and so addresses the intelligible realm.[34] Kant explains that "in this way reason can be given satisfaction and the understanding can be posited prior to appearances without confounding the series of appearances, which is always conditioned, and without any violation of principles of understanding."[35] Freedom would violate the "principle of understanding" by proclaiming the possibility of a cause that was not itself a temporal event, if it claimed that such a beginning anew was a phenomenal event. Kantian freedom raises the possibility of "beginning a state **from itself**," not in the phenomenal realm but in the noumenal realm.[36] Kant describes such causality by means of freedom as the "**transcendental** idea of **freedom**" and explains that the "practical concept of freedom" is "grounded upon it."[37] And yet, the "idea" of freedom is raised merely "problematically, as not impossible to think."[38] Kant does not explain in the first *Critique* how a positive account of practical freedom, a "canon," can be attained, claiming that "how such a faculty is possible is not so necessary to answer"—at least, we must add, in this work.[39]

Kant first addresses the question of how one pursues the goal of practical freedom that is raised by the idea of transcendental freedom in his *Groundwork of the Metaphysics of Morals* (1785). There Kant introduces the conception of a good will, as the only thing "in the world, or indeed even beyond it, that could be considered good without limitation."[40] Such a will, Kant explains, is not defined by anything that it could attain for us.[41] It is good, Kant explains, insofar as it can be conceived to "stand under objective laws (of the good)" and so as distinguishing itself from the mechanical laws of nature.[42] Kant explains that while we are unable to deduce such moral laws, we can test the maxims of our actions to see whether they could in any way conform to such an objective, moral law. The categorical imperative affords such a test, elucidating how we can test the maxims of our actions, deeming the will worthy of the goal of practical freedom. Kant explains that such an imperative, which commands the will not for this or that hypothetical goal, but universally, offers a "practical **law**."[43] Such a law commands you to "act only according to the maxim through which you can at the same time will that it become a universal law."[44] Without any positive content for the moral law, the categorical imperative tests the maxims to distinguish whether they could be universal laws of nature and whether, in willing them, you are also willing them universally. By willing them universally, you are subjecting yourself to the universal law. Kant goes on to describe a will that pursues the universality of the law itself as autonomous—as a law unto itself.[45] In this way Kant distinguishes rational beings who possess a causality distinct from the natural necessity that is the sole cause of non-rational beings.[46] Such autonomous, rational beings are, Kant explains, free.[47]

Kant makes clear that further inquiry is needed to explain the idea of reason toward which this kind of freedom points.[48] In the third and final section of the *Groundwork*, Kant explains that the concept of freedom that has been elucidated so far is a negative one. The third Antinomy has raised the possibility of free action, undetermined by material causality, and the first two sections of the *Groundwork* have explained the way that we can test the maxims of our actions in order to rid the will of mechanistic causes. Freedom is, in this way, defined negatively: we can strive toward practical freedom directed by such a test of our maxims, ensuring that the maxims of our actions, at a minimum, conform to the categorical imperative. Transcendental freedom is thus conceived in terms of critique as a tribunal, a discipline, determining that our actions *could be* guided by a causality distinct from that of mechanism. What this causality entails, what sort of claim concerning pure reason follows from this conception of freedom, remains unclear, but Kant suggests that the relation of the good will and the universal law it pursues is a "synthetic proposition."[49] The question, according to Kant, concerns how they are joined together—how can the will conceive of itself as choosing in a manner that is consistent with the law? The answer to this question promises a positive and not merely a negative account of the connection between the good will and the moral law.

2. The Highest Good

In the third section of the *Groundwork*, Kant explains that, in addition to the negative conception of freedom offered by the categorical imperative, there is also a positive one expressed in the principle of morality—a canon to compliment the discipline.[50] To claim not just that one's actions are undetermined by natural necessity, but that universal maxims deem one's will absolutely good, is to go beyond a mere negative definition of morality, since no mere analysis of the idea of the good will distinguishes the ideal state of its maxims. Kant describes such a positive or synthetic claim as requiring some third cognition in a manner similar to the role that "the sensible world" plays in distinguishing empirical causes. The sensible world, the world of empirical objects, must be given in order to synthetically connect empirical causes with their effects, and so subsume experience under the category of causality.[51] Freedom, understood positively, as a canon and not merely a discipline, points toward a "third" thing that allows for our synthetic confidence that the maxims of the good will are universalizable. Kant goes on to say in the third section of the *Groundwork* that this "third" thing must be *a priori*.[52] But what such positive freedom might be, what pure practical reason offers transcendental freedom as such a "third cognition," Kant does not develop in this elusive section.

It is perhaps a surprise to see Kant, in the third section of the *Groundwork*, pointing beyond the transcendental idea of freedom to an idea of reason from which such freedom can be deduced. Kantian morality has typically been conceived in terms of the negative test of the categorical imperative, so any reference to a positive statement of the idea of morality would seem to claim more than what Kant's critique of metaphysics permits. Kant, however, offers an account of how ideas of metaphysics can be retained without leading us into endless controversies in the first *Critique*. Kant is most explicit about this in relation to the cosmological idea—the idea of the world in its entirety. Kant's solution of the third Antinomy is to view mechanistic causality as only an explanatory principle of phenomena, the world of mere appearances, permitting one to conceive of an alternate form of causality in the noumenal realm of things in themselves. While the solution to the third Antinomy rejects the possibility of the complete determination of the world, it maintains such an idea as a regulative principle that directs "an **indeterminately continued regress** (*in indefinitum*)."[53]

In the Appendix to the Transcendental Dialectic of the first *Critique* Kant describes this use of metaphysical ideas as the "hypothetical use of reason."[54] In relation to the cosmological idea, it is to view the world "**as if** it began absolutely," even though such absolute beginning is indeterminable.[55] Thus, the disciplining of reason undertaken in the Transcendental Dialectic still allows us to make use of the ideas of reason in ways that avoid error. Freedom, however, as raised in the solution to the third Antinomy, offers no such direction. Transcendental freedom does not even afford the conceptual determinacy that is found in the ideas of reason, which are derived from *a priori* concepts that go beyond the limits of possible experience and, as such, lack empirical determinacy.[56] Freedom is merely negatively defined as that which evades mechanistic causality, so it would seem that such freedom does not even constitute a regulative principle. This is the picture of Kantian morality derived from the first two sections of the *Groundwork*, but Kant's introduction of the question of pure reason in the third section raises the possibility that pure practical reason might have more to offer the pursuit of morality.

Unfortunately, Kant goes on in section three of the *Groundwork* to say that in this work he cannot explain the idea of pure reason from which freedom must be deduced. However, just three years later, Kant addresses the same issue in the opening pages of the *Critique of Practical Reason*.

There Kant takes up the discussion of transcendental freedom precisely at this point, attempting to show not only how one can strive for such a practical goal, but also how such a conception of transcendental freedom can be said to exist within the context of the critique of metaphysics offered in the Transcendental Dialectic of the first *Critique*. In the opening pages of the second *Critique*, Kant promises to undertake this investigation of the conception of pure reason to which transcendental freedom can be said to refer.[57] And he does so in the Dialectic of Pure Practical Reason, where he explains that practical reason, like speculative reason, seeks the unconditioned for the conditioned. In the case of speculative reason, this dialectic leads to the attempt to extend the determination of causal conditions to their completion in the third Antinomy. In practical reason, the dialectic seeks the "totality of the object of pure practical reason."[58] In other words, it pursues the unconditioned totality of which the moral law is a part. Kant calls this unconditioned goal "the highest good [*das höchste Gut*]."

An investigation of the highest good, as the practical idea of pure reason, seems strange. The moral law might have been assumed to be just such a good and the categorical imperative allows us to pursue it. In the *Critique of Practical Reason*, however, Kant goes further, claiming that our consciousness of this moral law is "a fact of reason [*ein Faktum der Vernunft*]" and, indeed, "the sole fact of pure reason."[59] What sort of "fact" this is, however, remains elusive.[60] Kant says that the "fact of pure reason of which we are *a priori* conscious . . . is apodictically certain," but he also explains "that no example or exact observance of it can be found in experience," so that the "objective reality of the moral law cannot be proved by any deduction."[61] And yet, Kant concludes, such a fact "is nevertheless firmly established of itself."[62] The moral law establishes itself as an undeniable fact of which we are conscious but its "objective reality" cannot be deduced. Kant explains that the fact of the moral law is neither drawn from the sensible world, nor determined by the theoretical use of reason.[63] And yet, Kant explains, such a fact "points to a pure world of the understanding and, indeed, even determines it positively and lets us cognize something of it, namely a law."[64] The fact of reason is not an idea of reason, an unattainable object of metaphysical speculation, but, as a consciousness of the moral law, it is an intimation of the noumenal sphere.[65] If the third Antinomy shows us that a causality apart from natural necessity is at least possible, and the categorical imperative explains how it can be pursued, then the "moral feeling" of "respect" describes our motivation, the fact of reason that offers its foundation in our human nature, and "even determines it positively."[66] Is this then the completed "canon," the positive account of pure reason that Kant, in the first *Critique*, had suggested was located in the practical sphere?[67] If so then it would seem that there would be no reason for Kant to continue the search for this positive sense of critique into the Dialectic, pursuing pure practical reason as he does, toward the "highest good."[68]

Kant explains, while the moral law is given to us as a "fact of reason," and is thus the "sole determining ground of the will," it is merely "formal," offering the form of law according to which practical freedom can be determined.[69] Kant describes the "fact in which pure reason in us proves itself actually practical" as "autonomy," as the "consciousness of freedom of the will."[70] The will is conscious of itself as both "subject to laws of causality" and "determinable in an intelligible order of things."[71] And it is such a consciousness, promoted by the moral feeling of "respect," that directs the will to elucidate the categorical imperative, the test for the universality of its maxims. But such universality remains formal; it is the law of a possible universal, an affirmation that our actions do not offend the moral law that could be developed from this fact of reason. But what, the Dialectic asks, can be said beyond the formality of this moral order, what is the idea of practical reason toward which the "fact of reason" is directed?

Kant cautions us that "the highest good" that the Dialectic pursues should not supplant the moral law and its "fact of reason" as the "determining ground" of the good will.[72] We should not let ourselves be tempted to think that we can attain knowledge of this "highest good," for not only would that lead our practical reason into the metaphysical illusions of speculative reason, but it would also risk corrupting the will. Kant explains that, "if one assumes any object under the name of a good as a determining ground of the will prior to the moral law," even the highest good, "and then derives from it the supreme practical principle, this would always produce heteronomy and supplant the moral principle."[73] If the highest good is what directs us to pursue the moral law, then even the highest good would interfere with our autonomy, replacing it with heteronomy. And so the Dialectic of the second *Critique* investigates the highest good, not in order to replace the fact of reason as it directs us to the moral law, but as an attempt to augment it, to ask about that toward which the "fact of reason" points. In this sense the "fact of reason" initiates the positive account of critique, reason's canon, which is aided by the categorical imperative. And the idea of the "highest good" promises to augment this positive account of pure practical reason that had been distinguished only negatively in the third Antinomy.

What, then, is the "highest good"? Kant explains that there is some ambiguity in the term "highest," as it could refer either to that which is itself highest, in this case "the supreme [*supremum*] good," the moral law; or it could refer to the "complete [*consummatum*] good," which includes "happiness [*Glückseligkeit*]" as well as "the supreme good" of the moral law.[74] It is the latter conception of a "complete" good that Kant intends by the "highest" good. The highest good is not just being worthy of happiness, but actually attaining it, with virtue produced by the moral law as its "supreme" condition.[75] Kant describes the completeness of the highest good as "the ideal of the highest good" and the *summum bonum*, which consists in "morality coupled with happiness to the highest degree."[76] The categorical imperative allows us to test our maxims, determine that we are not motivated by any expected result, and so pursue the moral law, the "supreme" good. This is the negative sense of critique, a court of justice whose goal is not to determine whether we have achieved the moral law, in fact claiming nothing about the law itself, but only to mark out the territory within which morality can be conceived. What has now been added to the negative sense of critique is the beginning of the positive critique promised by Kant in section 3 of the *Groundwork* and the first page of the *Critique of Practical Reason*. The negative test of the categorical imperative itself presupposes the idea of the highest good for the human being, the unity of morality and happiness that offers itself as an elusive goal.

In relation to practical reason, critique is thus not a "discipline," a tribunal that sets limits to reason's use. Instead, it is a "canon" searching for pure practical reason without overstepping the boundaries that the investigation of speculative reason has determined. But what exactly does this "canon" entail for practical reason? In the Canon of Pure Reason chapter of the Transcendental Doctrine of Method that closes the first *Critique* Kant explains that the interests of reason, both speculative and practical, relate to three questions:

1. "What can I know?"
2. "What should I do?"
3. "What may I hope?"[77]

The first is the topic of the *Critique of Pure Reason*, the second that of the *Critique of Practical Reason*, and the third, Kant explains, relates to "happiness," understood as "the satisfaction of all of our inclinations."[78] Happiness, Kant explains, offers only pragmatic rules of prudence, mere hypothetical imperatives, but no role for reason. In its pursuit of the law of morality, reason, in the form of the categorical imperative, determines only "the worthiness to be happy."[79] In his *Groundwork of the Metaphysics of Morals* (1785) Kant makes this point in a striking fashion, explaining that reason is so ill suited for the pursuit of happiness that if happiness were its goal, misology would be its fate.[80]

And yet, in the Dialectic of the *Critique of Practical Reason*, written just seven years after the first edition of the first *Critique*, and three years after the *Groundwork*, Kant reintroduces the question of happiness into the search for pure practical reason. The highest good of a human being is said to include not only the formal freedom offered by such self-governance but also material happiness. Kant is able to defend a Stoic conception of practical freedom only by introducing a conception of pure reason that raises the possibility of Epicurean happiness. And while the second *Critique* will be shown to have merely introduced the postulates of pure reason to which we are committed in our pursuit of the highest good, it raises important questions about the possible coexistence of virtue and happiness in Kant's moral philosophy. If reason authorizes the pursuit of not only virtue but also happiness, then has Kant changed his view and affirmed that happiness is rationally determinable?

3. The Antinomy of Practical Reason

Kant addresses such questions in the Antinomy of Practical Reason. The issue, he explains, concerns how virtue and happiness, the two constitutive parts of the positive sense of critique, are connected in the highest good.[81] Kant says they are either analytically connected, which would mean they are identical, so that virtue is happiness, and happiness virtue; or else they are connected synthetically, as cause and effect, one producing the other.[82] Kant explains that the two great Ancient traditions accepted the analytic nature of this relationship—Stoics claimed that to be conscious of one's virtue is happiness, while Epicureans claimed that to be conscious of the means to attain one's happiness is virtue.[83] And yet, Kant explains, neither school quite accepted the equivalence of virtue and happiness, with the

Stoics claiming that virtue is the complete good and happiness is merely an effect of the awareness of one's virtue; and the Epicureans claiming that happiness is the complete good and virtue merely the means of achieving it. Kant has argued that the difference between virtue and happiness is more pronounced, that they are neither identical nor coextensive, that the virtuous person might not be happy, and that the happy person is often not virtuous.[84] The question for Kant is then how happiness and virtue can be said to constitute the highest good, not empirically as an *a posteriori* combination, but *a priori*, affording that to which transcendental freedom points merely negatively.[85]

Kant offers two possibilities for the highest good, the two sides of the antinomy of practical reason. Kant explains that the thesis, that the desire for happiness is "the motive [*die Bewegursache*] to maxims of virtue," has been proven false in the Analytic of the *Critique of Practical Reason*.[86] The antithesis, that virtue is "the efficient cause [*die wirkende Ursache*] of happiness," also appears false, since the effects of virtuous actions are not determined by the moral disposition of the will but by the mechanical laws of nature. What then can be said of the highest good to which freedom is ultimately directed? Kant explains that this antinomy appears unsolvable, as neither side of the antinomy appears able to determine the highest good. However, Kant explains, the highest good can be conceived as attainable when, in a manner reminiscent of the third Antinomy, the phenomenal/noumenal distinction is invoked. The thesis, the Epicurean idea that happiness leads to virtue, is absolutely false; yet the antithesis, the Stoic idea that virtue leads to happiness, is not absolutely false. If one distinguishes the noumenal from the phenomenal realms, then virtue in the noumenal realm need not exclude the possibility of happiness in the phenomenal realm. Virtue could lead to happiness. Kantian moral autonomy (Stoic virtue) can be conceived as necessarily connected to happiness (Epicurean pleasure) by means of the idea of "an intelligible author of nature."[87]

Kant already hinted at such a defense of the pursuit of happiness in the Analytic of the second *Critique*, and so prior to the elucidation of the antinomy of practical reason. In the concluding "Critical Elucidation" Kant explains that "this distinction of the principle of happiness from that of morality" is not "an opposition between them."[88] The pursuit of pure practical reason does not mean that one must renounce happiness, "only that *as soon as duty is in question* one should renounce claims to happiness."[89] In this we already have a first version of the solution to the antinomy of practical reason. Happiness can be thought to be consistent with morality as long as its pursuit does not take precedence over the negative test of the moral law. As Kant had earlier stated, while "the law of morality commands," in the pursuit of happiness "the maxim of self-love (prudence) merely advises."[90]

Kant does not here offer any explanation of how one is to pursue both morality and happiness, only that they can be conceived as consistent when conceived in relation to the idea of a noumenal God. In this one might be tempted to claim a similarity with the solution to the third Antinomy in the first *Critique*. There Kant raises the possibility of human freedom as a causality that escapes mechanistic necessity, without developing an account of how such a noumenal causality could be attained. Kant leaves such an undertaking to the *Groundwork* and the second *Critique*. Here too Kant initiates a further project, that of investigating the way that the pursuit of happiness can be thought to be consistent with morality, a task that is begun in the final sections of the *Critique of the Power of Judgment* (1790) and continued in Kant's political writings. I will address such a development of the possibility of the highest good raised in the Antinomy of Practical Reason in what follows, but it is first important to explain how this solution differs from that of the third Antinomy. In the third Antinomy, the possibility of freedom limits claims about mechanical causality. Freedom is possible when we refrain from claiming knowledge of the world in its entirety. Metaphysics is limited, disciplined, while the formulation of a further, positive canon of pure reason is begun. The second *Critique* contributes to the development of this canon, but the task of its critique is to establish pure reason's rightful claims, not to discipline its groundless pretensions. While the antinomy of practical reason does not lead to an investigation of how morality and happiness can be achieved in this life, it does explain the metaphysical presuppositions of their possible combination. Kant follows the solution to the antinomy of practical reason with an investigation into what must be claimed on behalf of pure reason such that the highest good can be determined in this way. The task of the book, elucidating pure practical reason, culminates in the Postulates.

Kant explains that the "will determinable by the moral law" has its "necessary object" in the highest good, encompassing both morality and happiness.[91] Kant's task in the sections of the Postulates is to explain what pure practical reason must presuppose in order to claim that the highest good, as such a "necessary object," is at least in principle achievable. Kant explains that by a postulate he means "a theoretical proposition" that cannot be demonstrated but that nevertheless follows from a practical law.[92] He begins with the moral law. What must we presuppose in order to claim the possibility of the will's conformity with the moral law? The complete conformity of the will with the moral law would be "holiness [*Heiligkeit*]," a perfection, Kant explains, unattainable by human beings.[93] Only progress toward such a goal is possible for human beings, but if we are to think of this progress as infinite, and so not merely as progress to an achievable, merely human end (which would then replace the goal of complete conformity with the moral law), then we must presuppose the endless existence of rational beings, and so postulate the immortality of the soul.

Kant then moves on to the question of happiness. He asks what must be presupposed such that we can conceive of the correspondence of happiness and morality, and so of the highest good. The answer Kant offers is that since the moral law in no way promises happiness, the highest good requires the presupposition of the possibility of their correspondence. Kant explains that what is required is "the existence of a cause of all nature, distinct from nature," a cause that could permit nature, and the mechanistic happiness achieved therein, to correspond to the moral law.[94] To presuppose such a cause apart from nature that permits the highest good is to postulate the existence of God.

Interestingly, in summing up the discussion of the postulates, Kant refers to three postulates of pure reason, including freedom alongside the soul's immortality and God's existence.[95] Kant explains that by freedom he does not mean the mere negative conception that is raised in the third Antinomy of the first *Critique*. There mechanistic analysis of nature is limited by the possibility of transcendental freedom. Freedom, conceived as a postulate, is "considered positively (as the causality of a being insofar as it belongs to the intelligible world)."[96] While the third Antinomy raises the possibility of such freedom, the second *Critique* designates such "independence from the sensible world" as a postulate that must be presupposed in order to pursue the highest good.[97]

The moral law leads Kant to uncover the highest good of the will that the moral law commands. And what has now been added is that such a highest good presupposes the postulates, the soul, freedom, and God, offering the long-awaited account of pure practical reason. The ideas of reason that theoretical reason cannot cognize, and that offer only regulative principles after their speculative pretentions have been disciplined, offer practical reason "(transcendent) thoughts [(*transzendente*) *Gedanken*] in which there is nothing impossible."[98] And such "thoughts" are already presupposed in the command of the moral law. Such thoughts are not cognitions. The limit on cognition introduced in the first *Critique* has not been transgressed. The ideas of reason that theoretical reason cannot determine have had their "objective reality [*objektive Realität*]" distinguished by practical reason.[99] While we still cannot "show how their concept refers to an object," the highest good of the human will (morality and happiness) requires the ideas of reason to be "postulated [*postuliert*]."[100]

4. The Complete Good

This reintroduction of the ideas of reason in the Dialectic of the Critique of Practical Reason neither introduces a reified goal that conflicts with Kantian freedom nor merely returns us to the solution to the third Antinomy;[101] rather, Kant is able to explain the postulates of pure practical reason in relation to the highest good in a manner that raises the possibility of the consistency of the pursuit of both freedom and happiness. Kant's solution to the antinomy of practical reason—that morality, and the categorical imperative that permits its pursuit, need not conflict with happiness—not only generates the practical postulates of immortality and God, elucidating pure practical reason, but also raises the possibility of such contentment within the context of a life lived in pursuit of freedom. Yet Kant does not develop such an analysis in the second *Critique*, as the highest good merely introduces the postulates to which we are committed by our moral inquiries and so demonstrates pure reason in the practical sphere. Kant has clearly distinguished freedom, that is, Stoic moral virtue, from the pursuit of Epicurean happiness, which is not our supreme good but remains a constitutive element of our highest good. If happiness is both distinct from the moral law and at least potentially consistent with it, then the question for Kant is how we can pursue it, how such a constitutive good can be conceived as an end for us.

It is in the third *Critique* that Kant investigates such ends. While the first *Critique* deems God, the theological idea, to be unknowable, Kant already announced in the appendix to the Transcendental Dialectic that such an idea can still be used regulatively, directing inquiry into the "absolute unity" of the mechanistic laws of possible experience.[102] Kant calls this the "hypothetical use of reason."[103] The third *Critique* further develops this claim, introducing the reflecting power of judgment in order to explain how reason pursues its ends hypothetically when guided by the theological idea as a regulative principle. Such a regulative principle directs the reflecting power of judgment to pursue unity when none can be mechanistically determined, and so promises that nature is governed by rules, the "purposiveness" of nature for our reflecting judgment.

In the closing sections of the third *Critique*, after having earlier prioritized the internal purposiveness of living organisms, Kant returns to the external purposiveness of natural systems. Teleological, reflecting judgment permits us to search for systematic unity in the varied causal laws that determine nature. And it is here that Kant broaches the question of teleological judgments concerning humanity's place in nature and returns to the question of happiness. He explains that if we investigate plants and ask why they exist, we are lead on the path of teleological inquiry to the herbivores that eat them.[104] If we at some point ask "for what is the natural kingdom good," then we cannot determine "a final end" of nature, an end or purpose apart from its phenomenal appearance; however, by judging nature's purposes reflectively we are offering ourselves as the perspective from which such systematic unity is to be judged.[105] We who judge are "the ultimate end" of the nature we judge, not because we posit that nature exists in a particular way apart from our judging, but because without such an assumption, without such a regulative principle, we would not be able to judge nature as a system and we would be limited to elucidating discrete mechanistic laws.[106] While we are not nature's "final" end, we cannot help but posit ourselves as the "ultimate" end of our judgments. Kant explains that we judge such an end or purpose in terms of both the "happiness [*Glückseligkeit*]" and the "culture [*Kultur*]" of the human being.[107] Both happiness and culture are teleological judgments of the external purposiveness of nature. So the theological idea functions not only as a postulate of the highest good, offering the possibility of the moral life as happy in the second *Critique*, but also as a regulative principle that directs the pursuit of the systematicity offered by the theological idea in the third *Critique*, which includes both happiness and culture.

Kant makes one final suggestive distinction in §83 of the *Critique of the Power of Judgment*. While both "happiness" and "culture" offer the human being as the end of nature, it is culture that offers "the ultimate end [*den letzten Zweck*]" of our reflecting judgment of nature.[108] Kant explains that while neither happiness nor culture offers an end apart from the mechanistic laws of phenomenal nature, culture prepares us for morality, which departs from phenomenal nature, and so offers itself as our ultimate end and as a preparation for the final, moral end that we are.[109] Kant describes such an ultimate end as "the culture of training (discipline) [*die Kultur der Zucht* (*Disziplin*)]," the pursuit of "the liberation of the will from the despotism of desires."[110] In this way such a culture of discipline offers itself as the ultimate end of nature insofar as it prepares us to pursue our freedom, and treats us as a final end with a causality distinct from that of nature. Kant then goes on to explain that when nature offers itself too abundantly, there is less incentive to develop such an end, which explains why "inequality among people," and competition among them for limited resources, is needed to promote the culture of discipline. If there is no competition with others, and if our needs are so generously met by nature's beneficence, then we will not be encouraged to investigate our freedom from such mechanistic desires.[111] With competition and need we are both threatened from without by others and internally dissatisfied with our situation, and this "splendid misery" leads to the development of a culture of discipline that reaches its high point, Kant explains, in a cosmopolitan organization of states.[112]

The question of how culture can be said to benefit human beings as rational ends is the teleological project of Kant's historical-political writings, but what is already clear is that the idea of God that is deemed in the second *Critique* a postulate of pure practical reason is in the third *Critique* the regulative principle of teleological judgment that directs the pursuit, not only of human happiness, but also of the political system that disciplines us, prepares us for our moral lives, and stands as our ultimate, if not final, end.[113]

The *Critique of Practical Reason* announces on its first page that it is not a critique of pure practical reason, not a discipline to rein in speculation. In the sphere of practical reason, critique can be understood as a canon, a positive attempt to justify pure practical reason. The antinomy in which pure practical reason comes to the fore in relation to the highest good, the *summum bonum*, is the culmination of this canon, for it explains that the moral law must presuppose not only the possibility of human freedom, but also the postulates of the immortality of the soul and the existence of God, if it is to claim to represent not merely "the supreme good [*das oberste* Gut]" but also "the highest good [*das höchste Gut*]," in the sense of "the complete good [*das vollendete Gute*]" of a human being.[114]

Notes

1. Immanuel Kant, *Critique of Pure Reason*, ed. and trans. Paul Guyer and Allen W. Wood (New York: Cambridge University Press, 1998), A395. All references to Kant's first *Critique* use the standard A/B pagination of the first (1781, A) and

second (1787, B) editions. References to Kant's other works are accompanied by a parenthetical reference, cited as *Ak.*, to the volume and page number of the passage in Immanuel Kant, *Kants gesammelte Schriften (Akademie Ausgabe)*, ed. Royal Prussian (later German) Academy of Sciences, et al. (Berlin: Georg Reimer, later Walter de Gruyter, 1900–). Comparing the *Critique of Pure Reason* and the *Critique of Practical Reason*, Kant refers to the first *Critique* as the "speculative *Critique*" and even refers to the "Critique of Pure Speculative Reason." See Immanuel Kant, *Practical Philosophy*, ed. and trans. Mary Gregor (Cambridge: Cambridge University Press, 1996), 141, 149 (*Ak.* 5:6, 16). Why the first is not so titled—*Critique of Pure Speculative Reason* or *Pure Theoretical Reason*—particularly with Kant's emphasis in that work on the primacy of the practical, is not clear. It could be that Kant saw no need for an adjective in the title of his first *Critique* because he had not yet conceived of the need for a second, a critique of reason as practical rather than as speculative. Kant had clearly come to understand such a need by the time of his 1785 *Groundwork of the Metaphysics of Morals*, explaining that what was required was both a critique of pure speculative reason and a critique of pure practical reason, neither reference in the form of the respective books' actual titles. See Kant, *Practical Philosophy*, 47 (*Ak.* 4:391). Another possibility is that the first *Critique* needs no adjective limiting the conception of reason because it is addressing reason generally, laying the foundation even for the practical. Karl Ameriks makes such a claim. He explains: "For surely, the main overall aim of that philosophy [initiated in the first *Critique*] is to scrutinize—and in part attack and in part vindicate—the pure contentions of 'reason' in the broadest sense." See Karl Ameriks, "Reality, Reason, and Religion in the Development of Kant's Ethics," in *Kant's Moral Metaphysics: God, Freedom, and Immortality*, ed. James Krueger and Benjamin J. Bruxvoort Lipscomb (Berlin: Walter de Gruyter, 2010), 25.

2. Kant, *Critique of Pure Reason*, A751/B779.
3. Ibid., A709/B737.
4. Ibid., Axi.
5. Ibid., Axii. For a thorough discussion of the various descriptions of critique offered in the Prefaces and Introductions of the two editions of the *Critique of Pure Reason* see J. Colin McQuillan, *Immanuel Kant: The Very Idea of a Critique of Pure Reason* (Evanston, IL: Northwestern University Press, 2016), 63–88.
6. Kant, *Critique of Pure Reason*, A761/B789.
7. Immanuel Kant, *Theoretical Philosophy after 1781*, ed. Henry Allison and Peter Heath (Cambridge: Cambridge University Press, 2002), 142 (*Ak.* 4:352).
8. Kant, *Critique of Pure Reason*, Axii.
9. Kant, *Critique of Pure Reason*, A795–796/B823–824. Kant distinguishes such a "canon," which makes use of *a priori* principles "for the assessment of empirical use," from an organon, which would "dare to synthetically judge . . . about objects in general with the pure understanding alone." In the Introduction to the first *Critique* Kant hints suggestively that such an organon, "a system of

pure reason," might be attainable, although he explains that "it is still an open question whether such an amplification of our knowledge is possible at all." The Transcendental Doctrine of Method that closes the book makes it appear that this is no longer a possibility. What is possible is not only the transcendental analytic as a "canon" for the pure understanding, but also a "canon" for pure reason in its "practical use." See Kant, *Critique of Pure Reason*, A11/B25, A63/B88, A131/B170, A795/B823, A797/B825. Kant would appear to be following Epicurus in his opposition to an Aristotelian "organon" as he refers in the *Jäsche Logic* to "the universal art of reason" as *"canonica Epicuri."* See Immanuel Kant, *Lectures on Logic*, ed. and trans. J. Michael Young (Cambridge: Cambridge University Press, 1992), 529 (*Ak.* 9:13). Epicurus's lost work *On the Criterion, or Canon* is mentioned in Diogenes Laërtius, *Lives of Eminent Philosophers*, trans. R.D. Hicks (Cambridge: Harvard University Press, 1925), 2:556–557.

10. For a discussion of the historical background of the term "critique" see Giorgio Tonelli, "Critique and Related Terms Prior to Kant: A Historical Survey," *Kant-Studien* 69 (1978), 119–148, and McQuillan, *Immanuel Kant*, 3–20.

11. Critique as both discipline and canon is propaedeutic to metaphysics proper, which in relation to practical reason entails a "metaphysics of morals," and in 1797 a book of that name, which Kant explains refers to "the principles [*Prinzipien*] which determine action and omission *a priori* and make them necessary." See Kant, *Critique of Pure Reason*, A841–A842/B869–870. Interestingly, Kant does not refer to such post-critical metaphysics as an "organon."

12. Kant, *Practical Philosophy*, 139, 148–149 (*Ak.* 5:3, 16). In the first *Critique* Kant describes the practical accomplishments thus: "there it thus has a possession the legitimacy of which need not be proved, and the proof of which it could not in fact give." See Kant, *Critique of Pure Reason*, A776/B804.

13. Kant, *Practical Philosophy*, 228–229 (*Ak.* 5:110–111).

14. Ibid., 229 (*Ak.* 5:111).

15. Kant, *Critique of Pure Reason*, A323/B379.

16. Ibid., B391/A334.

17. Ibid., A323/B380.

18. Kant explains that while no "objective deduction" can be offered a "subjective derivation [*Ableitung*]" is possible. See Kant, *Critique of Pure Reason*, A336/B393. Here I follow Benno Erdmann in reading *Ableitung* (derivation) rather than *Anleitung* (introduction). See Kant, *Ak.* 4:590.

19. Kant, *Critique of Pure Reason*, B395.

20. Ibid., B395n.

21. Leibniz explains that both necessary and contingent truths of reason can be said to be *a priori*. See Gottfried Wilhelm Leibniz, "Primary Truths," in *Philosophical Essays*, trans. Roger Ariew and Daniel Garber (Indianapolis: Hackett Publishing, 1989), 31; *Opuscules et fragments inédits de Leibniz*, ed. Louis Couturat (Paris: Presses Universitaires de France, 1903; repr., Hildesheim: Georg Olms, 1961), 519.

22. Gottfried Wilhelm Leibniz, *Theodicy: Essays on the Goodness of God, the Freedom of Man, and the Origin of Evil*, ed. Austin Farrer, trans. E.M. Huggard (La Salle, IL: Open Court, 1985), 82–83 (§14). See also Gottfried Wilhelm Leibniz, *Die Philosophischen Schriften von Gottfried Wilhelm Leibniz*, ed. C.I. Gerhardt (Hildesheim: Georg Olms, 1961), 6:414.

23. Kant, *Critique of Pure Reason*, A409/B436.

24. Ibid., A189–211/B232–256.

25. Ibid., A182–189/B224–232.

26. Ibid., B232.

27. After arguing that the *a priori* concept of causality deems all occurrences determined by what preceeds them, Kant explains that this means that "the principle of sufficient reason is the ground of possible experience [*der Satz vom zureichenden Grunde*]." Kant, *Critique of Pure Reason*, A201/B246. The principle of sufficient reason has been defended by Kant within the phenomenal realm of experience.

28. "*Grundsätze*" is the term used by Kant to refer to the empirical rules that follow from the *a priori* concepts of the understanding. They are, Kant explains, not quite *Prinzipien*, not quite principles that permit cognition merely through concepts, as they require sensible content for cognition. Kant explains that they can be called "principles comparatively [*komperative Prinzipien*]." See Kant, *Critique of Pure Reason*, A301/B357. Reason, Kant explains, is the faculty of *Prinzipien*, the faculty that pursues purely conceptual cognition, while understanding offers only *Grundsätze*. See Kant, *Critique of Pure Reason*, A299–301/B356–358.

29. Kant, *Critique of Pure Reason*, A444/B472.

30. Ibid.

31. Ibid., A446/B474.

32. Ibid., A445/B473.

33. Ibid., A530/B558, A529/B557. In what follows I will explain the third Antinomy, with its opposition of mechanism and freedom, but one could make a similar argument for the fourth Antinomy, in which claims for and against a necessary being are contrasted. See Kant, *Critique of Pure Reason*, A452–460/B480–488. The latter Antinomy prefigures the analysis of the theological idea in the Ideal of Pure Reason.

34. Ibid., A530/B558.

35. Ibid., A531/B560.

36. Ibid., A533/B561.

37. Ibid.; see also A448/B476.

38. Kant, *Practical Philosophy*, 139 (*Ak.* 5:3).

39. Kant, *Critique of Pure Reason*, A448/B476. In the remark on the thesis of the third Antinomy, in his defense of freedom as an alternative causality, Kant writes, "if (for example) I am now entirely free, and get up from my chair without the necessarily determining influences of natural causes, then on this occurrence, along with its natural consequences to infinity, there begins an absolutely new series, even though as far as time is concerned this occurrence is only the contin-

uation of a previous series." See Kant, *Critique of Pure Reason*, A450/B478. How we might know that we are in this way "entirely free," Kant does not here explain.

40. Kant, *Practical Philosophy*, 49 (*Ak.* 4:393).

41. "Power, riches, even health and that complete well-being and satisfaction with one's condition called happiness [*Glückseligkeit*] produce boldness and often arrogance as well unless a good will is present." See Kant, *Practical Philosophy*, 49 (*Ak.* 4:393).

42. Kant, *Practical Philosophy*, 67 (*Ak.* 4:414).

43. Ibid., 72 (*Ak.* 4:420).

44. Ibid., 73 (*Ak.* 4:421).

45. Ibid., 83, 89 (*Ak.* 4:433, 440).

46. Ibid., 94 (*Ak.* 4:446).

47. Ibid.

48. Ibid., 95 (*Ak.* 4:447).

49. Ibid.

50. Ibid.

51. Ibid.

52. Ibid.

53. Kant, *Critique of Pure Reason*, A518/B546. See also A509/B537.

54. Ibid., A647/B675.

55. Ibid., A685/B713.

56. Ibid., A320/B377.

57. Kant, *Practical Philosophy*, 139 (*Ak.* 5:3).

58. Ibid., 227 (*Ak.* 5:108).

59. Ibid., 165 (*Ak.* 5:31).

60. Many commentators reject the fact of reason as a dogmatic claim illicitly introduced by Kant. Guyer describes the fact of reason as a "mystery" in Paul Guyer, *Kant on Freedom, Law, and Happiness* (Cambridge: Cambridge University Press, 2000), 138. Wood calls the fact of reason "moralistic bluster" in Allen W. Wood, *Kantian Ethics* (Cambridge: Cambridge University Press, 2008), 135.

61. Kant, *Practical Philosophy*, 177–178 (*Ak.* 5:4).

62. Ibid., 178 (*Ak.* 5:47). Patrick Cain explains that the "fact of reason" can be understood as an "analogue of sensible intuition within the account of theoretical cognition." See Patrick Cain, "Practical Cognition, Intuition, and the Fact of Reason," in *Kant's Moral Metaphysics: God, Freedom, and Immortality*, ed. James Krueger and Benjamin J. Bruxvoort Lipscomb (Berlin/New York: de Gruyter, 2010), 220. Lewis White Beck makes a similar point in Beck, *A Commentary on Kant's Critique of Practical Reason* (Chicago: University of Chicago Press, 1960), 273n.

63. Kant, *Practical Philosophy*, 174 (*Ak.* 5:43).

64. Ibid.

65. In §29 of the third *Critique*, while describing the dynamically sublime, Kant explains that the sublime requires the cultural development of "moral ideas,"

but it does not find its source in "convention." Rather, "it has its foundation in human nature . . . in the predisposition to the feeling for (practical) ideas, i.e., to that which is moral." See Immanuel Kant, *Critique of the Power of Judgment*, trans. Paul Guyer and Eric Matthews (Cambridge: Cambridge University Press, 2000), 149 (*Ak.* 5:265). Could such a "foundation in human nature" refer to the fact of reason?

66. Kant, *Practical Philosophy*, 174 (*Ak.* 5:43). Kant writes, "For, the moral law proves its reality, so as even to satisfy the *Critique* of speculative reason, by adding a positive determination (*positive Bestimmung*) to a causality thought only negatively." See Kant, *Practical Philosophy*, 178 (*Ak.* 5:48).

67. Kant, *Critique of Pure Reason*, A795–796/B823–824.

68. What follows is a response to a question raised by Angelica Nuzzo at the conference on which the essays in this volume are based.

69. Kant, *Practical Philosophy*, 164 (*Ak.* 5:31). By "formal" Kant explains that the moral law "requires only that the form of a maxim be universally lawgiving." See Kant, *Practical Philosophy*, 227, *Ak.* 5:109).

70. Ibid., 173 (*Ak.* 5:42).

71. Ibid.

72. Ibid., 227–228 (*Ak.* 5:109).

73. Ibid., 228 (*Ak.* 5:109).

74. Kant uses the word *Glückseligkeit* rather than *Glück*. In avoiding *Glück*, which can refer to both happiness and luck, Kant is de-emphasizing the role of what is uncontrollable, of fate and fortune, in human happiness. The term *Glückseligkeit*, with the addition of the noun *Seligkeit*, blessedness, differentiates such happiness from that born of luck, by connecting it with worthiness, and so distinguishing it as the state of one who is deserving of a blessing. *Glückseligkeit* is the German term used to translate Aristotle's *eudaimonia*, the happiness that is born of virtue. See Aristotle, *Nicomachean Ethics*, in *The Complete Works of Aristotle: The Revised Oxford Translation*, ed. Jonathan Barnes (Princeton: Princeton University Press, 1984), 2:1097a15–1098b7. Christian Helmreich is right to point out, in his entry on *Glück/Glückseligkeit* in the *Dictionary of Untranslatables*, that Kant shows some ambivalence toward this Aristotelian tradition. Not only does Kant continue to use the adjective *glücklich* rather than *glückselig*, even as he uses the noun *Glückseligkeit* rather than *Glück*, but he also complicates the distinction by describing *Glückseligkeit* as inaccessible to our reason. However, I think Helmreich goes too far in claiming that Kant "destroys the efforts made in Germany to differentiate" happiness from fortune, as what Kant will be seen to offer in the antinomy of practical reason is a way for reason to pursue the not fully cognizable goal of *Glückseligkeit*. See Barbara Cassin, ed., *Dictionary of Untranslatables: A Philosophical Lexicon* (Princeton: Princeton University Press, 2014), 400–401. See also Kant, *Critique of Pure Reason*, A806/B834, and Kant, *Practical Philosophy*, 159 (*Ak.* 5:25).

75. Kant, *Critique of Pure Reason*, A806/B834, and Kant, *Practical Philosophy*, 228–229 (*Ak.* 5:110–111).

76. Kant, *Critique of Pure Reason*, A810/B839. See also Kant, *Lectures on Ethics*, trans. Peter Heath and J.B. Schneewind (Cambridge: Cambridge University Press, 1997), 440 (*Ak.* 27:717).

77. In the *Logic* Kant appends a fourth question—"what is man?"—to these three. See Kant, *Lectures on Logic*, 538 (*Ak.* 9:25). He connects this final question to anthropology, and then claims that the other three questions relate to it. For a discussion of the conception of anthropology here initiated, see Avery Goldman, *Kant and the Subject of Critique* (Bloomington: Indiana University Press, 2012), 175–178. See also Martin Heidegger, *Kant and the Problem of Metaphysics*, 5th ed., enlarged, trans. Richard Taft (Bloomington: Indiana University Press, 1997), 152 (217).

78. Kant, *Critique of Pure Reason*, A806/B834.

79. Ibid., A806/B834, and Kant, *Practical Philosophy*, 49 (*Ak.* 4:393). Kant uses the adjective *glücklich* and the noun *Glückseligkeit* in both texts. See also Kant's *Lectures on Ethics*, where he explains, "we find in the world that virtue does not always make for happiness [*Glückseligkeit*]. Virtue has to do solely with the worth of our person, and not with our condition." See Kant, *Lectures on Ethics*, 241 (*Ak.* 29:623).

80. Kant, *Practical Philosophy*, 51 (*Ak.* 4:395–396).

81. Ibid., 231 (*Ak.* 5:113).

82. Ibid., 231 (*Ak.* 5:113–114).

83. Ibid., 229 (*Ak.* 5:111).

84. Kant, *Lectures on Ethics*, 241 (*Ak.* 29:623). In the *Groundwork* Kant explains, "power, riches, honor, even health and that complete well-being and satisfaction with one's condition called happiness [*Glückseligkeit*] produce boldness and thereby often arrogance as well unless a good will is present." He continues by explaining that "even if by a special disfavor of fortune . . . this will should wholly lack the capacity to carry out its purpose . . . then like a jewel it would still shine by itself . . . as something that has its full worth in itself." See Kant, *Practical Philosophy*, 49 (*Ak.* 4:393).

85. Lewis White Beck denies the importance of the highest good, that of the moral law and happiness, "for any practical consequences it might have." Beck claims that such a concept has only architectonic importance for the system as a whole. He writes, "But we must not allow ourselves to be deceived, as I believe Kant was, into thinking its possibility is directly necessary to morality." See Beck, *A Commentary on Kant's Critique of Practical Reason*, 245. John Silber defends Kant's account of the highest good, arguing that Kant attempts to integrate virtue and happiness in the highest good in order to overcome the divide between our sensible and intellectual natures. He writes, "his obligation must be presented in terms of action in the *sensible world* and not merely in terms of the form of

action itself, as mere autonomy or virtue." See John Silber, "The Importance of the Highest Good in Kant's Ethics," *Ethics* 73, No. 3 (1963), 193. And yet, Kant has offered the Typic of Pure Practical Judgment and the discussion of "respect" in order to explain how the divide between the intellectual and the sensible can be bridged. See Kant, *Practical Philosophy*, 194–206 (*Ak.* 5:67–82). This has already been accomplished in the Analytic by the time the Dialectic and the discussion of the highest good have been reached. What will be argued here is that such an idea of the highest good has a systematic role to play in relating practical and theoretical philosophy, one that is not merely for architectonic purposes, but leads to the development of Kant's political philosophy.

86. Kant, *Practical Philosophy*, 231 (*Ak.* 5:113).
87. Ibid., 232, 235–236 (*Ak.* 5:114–115, 119).
88. Ibid., 214 (*Ak.* 5:93). Kant explains that the principle of happiness is the "direct opposite" of the principle of morality. See Kant, *Practical Philosophy*, 168 (*Ak.* 5:35).
89. Kant, *Practical Philosophy*, 214, emphasis added (*Ak.* 5:93).
90. Ibid., 169 (*Ak.* 5:36); see also 160 (*Ak.* 5:26).
91. Ibid., 238 (*Ak.* 5:122).
92. Ibid.
93. Ibid.
94. Ibid., 240 (*Ak.* 5:125).
95. Ibid., 246 (*Ak.* 5:132).
96. Ibid.
97. Marcus Willaschek argues that the argument for freedom as a postulate can be found in the account of the fact of reason. See Marcus Willaschek, "Freedom as a Postulate," in *Kant on Persons and Agency*, ed. Eric Watkins (Cambridge: Cambridge University Press, 2018), 113–116.
98. Kant, *Practical Philosophy*, 248 (*Ak.* 5:135).
99. Ibid.
100. Ibid., 248 (*Ak.* 5:134).
101. See Alenka Zupančič, *Ethics of the Real, Kant, Lacan* (New York: Verso, 2000), 164. See also Gabriela Basterra, *The Subject of Freedom: Kant, Levinas* (New York: Fordham University Press, 2015), 108.
102. Kant, *Critique of Pure Reason*, A672/B700.
103. Ibid., A647/B675.
104. Kant, *Critique of the Power of Judgment*, 294 (*Ak.* 5:426).
105. Ibid., 294 (*Ak.* 5:426). See also Kant, *Critique of Pure Reason*, A647/B675.
106. Kant, *Critique of the Power of Judgment*, 297 (*Ak.* 5:429).
107. Ibid., 297 (*Ak.* 5:430).
108. Ibid., 297–299 (*Ak.* 5:430–432).
109. Ibid., 298–299 (*Ak.* 5:431).
110. Ibid., 299 (*Ak.* 5:432).

111. While Kant does not here offer an example of such hindrances caused by natural abundance, he argues in a similar fashion in the *Groundwork*, and elsewhere, when he uses "the South Sea Islanders" as the example of those whose "comfortable circumstances," which is to say the ease of life when nature offers itself with such abundance, leads them to neglect their "natural gifts." See Kant, *Practical Philosophy*, 74–75 (Ak. 4:423). And while such an example raises the question of eighteenth-century European prejudices and Kant's racism, one need not look to a people for such an example. For is this not what is meant by spoiling a child, when too much is given such that there is no incentive for the child to develop her talents?

112. Kant, *Practical Philosophy*, 168 (Ak. 5:35). See also Kant, *Critique of the Power of Judgment*, 299 (Ak. 5:432).

113. See "Perpetual Peace" and *Metaphysics of Morals* in Kant, *Practical Philosophy*, 311–351, 353–604 (Ak. 6:203–492; 8:341–386).

114. Kant, *Practical Philosophy*, 228–229 (Ak. 5:110–111).

4

On an Aesthetic Dimension of Critique

The Time of the Beautiful in Schiller's *Aesthetic Letters*

MARÍA DEL ROSARIO ACOSTA LÓPEZ

"To thinking belongs movement as well as the arrest of thoughts. Where thinking comes to a standstill in a constellation saturated with tensions—there the dialectical image appears. It is the caesura in the movement of thought. Its position is naturally not an arbitrary one. It is to be found, in a word, where the tension between dialectical opposites is greatest."

—Walter Benjamin, *The Arcades Project*[1]

1. From a Critique of Aesthetics to Aesthetics as Critique

The National Schiller Museum in Marbach holds Schiller's two annotated copies of Kant's *Critique of Judgment*. A mere glance at the markings and notes that Schiller wrote the first time he read Kant's third *Critique* show how, for Schiller, what was most fundamental about this work—and what was already, at the time, fundamental for his own aesthetics—were the passages where the connection between ethics and aesthetics is either evident or can be traced.[2] This connection, however, is not only to be found in those places where Kant would most evidently admit it. For Schiller, the singular experience of the beautiful, analyzed by Kant as reflective aesthetic judgment, is not only relevant to ethics in the experience of the sublime, as a mere indication of a moral character, or as a symbol of the good.[3] Already at the core of the transcendental analysis of the judgment of taste, in the specific response of the cognitive faculties to the resistance of the "beautiful object" to be subsumed by the concepts of the understanding, Schiller recognizes the "free play" of the understanding and imagination as an ethically relevant concept. As one can see in many of the essays he wrote in response to, and, in his mind, as a continuation of Kant's critical project, Schiller finds in Kant's aesthetics something more than a mere transcendental critique—and, as I would like to argue here, also something more than a mere transcendental conception *of* critique.

As Dieter Henrich suggests, to understand Schiller's reading of Kant, one needs to understand that, for Schiller, "beauty had to be something more fundamental than the mere modification of a cognitive activity which makes no difference to human beings."[4] It is starting with this very same modification, however, that beauty for Schiller can be understood, as Henrich writes, as something more "fundamental" for philosophical critique. Rather than reading Kant's analysis of the judgment of taste in the Analytic of the Beautiful of the *Critique of the Power of Judgment* as a specific activity of thought, related to, even if not entirely delimited by, our cognitive mental capacities, Schiller understands Kant's conception of aesthetic pleasure as the opening of an entirely different dimension of experience. By making possible another relation within ourselves, and, as a consequence, another relation to others and to the world, beauty becomes for Schiller the opening of another perspective that can eventually be turned into an attitude, a disposition, a way of being and thinking that Schiller will call "aesthetic." The singularity of the aesthetic provides for Schiller, in itself, a standpoint for critique.[5]

Such a standpoint is not, as it would have been for Kant, a transcendental perspective on the conditions of the possibility of experience, and, therefore, on the delimitations of the territory that will provide justification for our judgments. This is, as we know, Kant's project of a critique of aesthetics, or, even more precisely, Kant's analysis of aesthetic judgments as an essential part of his critical project. Schiller's philosophical project, however, is not transcendental but rather historical-political. By this I mean that Schiller is not preoccupied with studying the conditions of the possibility for every possible experience. He is, rather, interested in understanding what he sees as a modern, and thus historically determined, mode of experience—alienated, subjected to forms of violence that come from a misinterpretation of both sensibility and reason as coercive forces—and in uncovering and questioning the conceptual categories that give shape to it. Critique in Schiller—and the standpoint provided for it by the experience of the beautiful—is thus a philosophical-historical activity, one that is not only preoccupied with addressing the historical conditions of the present, but even more so, the very conceptions of history and of experience that are a-critically assumed and structurally operative (and the latter even more so because of the former) in his present.

Thus, the "aesthetic," in Schiller, is not just one way of being among others. If Schiller read Kant's third *Critique* as an ethical and political work, this is because the aesthetic dimension is, for Schiller, already *the* critical dimension par excellence. And critique, here, becomes something else, different from the Kantian project, and closer to what we today understand by this term, as a material, historical critique, made possible by a standpoint that allows us to imagine an otherwise, by diagnosing the contradictions lying at the core of the present.[6] Schiller, I want to argue, is an important moment in the history of this change. More specifically, it is his reading of Kant's aesthetics, and his particular understanding—and misunderstanding, as some have also argued—of the nature of Kant's critical philosophy, that allows for the change from transcendental to historical-political critique to take shape in his work.[7]

In order to show how Schiller's work brings about this change, one must follow the double gesture performed in its conceptual development. On the one hand, it is important to understand the move from Kant's critique of aesthetics to Schiller's idea of aesthetics as critique. On the other hand, it is also necessary to explore the ways in which this turn requires Schiller to develop a different conception of philosophical critique, a redefinition of its task that draws on aesthetics as a critical standpoint. My purpose is therefore twofold. I want to understand how in Schiller aesthetics becomes, on the one hand, a *critical dimension*. I also want to understand how this leads in turn, in Schiller's work, to an *aesthetic dimension for critique*.

Such a project requires a careful analysis of Schiller's essays on aesthetics after his reading of Kant, one that I cannot develop thoroughly here. This paper is therefore the second part of a more extensive argument that I have started elsewhere and that will also have to be continued elsewhere. In a first part of this project, I consider Schiller's first attempt at a systematic reading of Kant in his 1793 letters to Körner, published as *Kallias or Concerning Beauty*.[8] In these letters, one can see how Schiller is already concerned with understanding how the critical dimension of aesthetics—and, furthermore, aesthetics as critique—is made possible by Kant's emphasis on beauty's resistance (*Widerstand*) to conceptual determination.[9] Such a resistance—that, in the case of Schiller, belongs also to the "beautiful" object and not only to the exclusively subjective realm of aesthetic pleasure—brings to light a mode of relation (of judgment, of experience) that not only resists categorization, but also, and simultaneously, exhibits the violence involved in categorization.[10] By making it visible and opening a form of relation that suspends the violence of this operation, both the judgment and experience of the beautiful, on the one hand, and the existence of the beautiful object, on the other, call for another mode of being that is, in fact, opened up and made possible by this resistance.[11]

Thus, Schiller's attention to the connection between beauty and resistance, in Kant's analysis of the judgment of taste, leads to a conception of resistance as a force or a power (*Kraft*) in beauty that defies, without opposing, the forms of violence (*Gewalt*) otherwise imposed on imagination by the understanding, or, in Schiller's terms, imposed on sensibility by an abstract use of reason, imposed on matter by (a simplistic understanding of) form.[12] This, in turn, allows for a shift in *Kallias* from the idea of a resistance *in* beauty, to the idea of beauty *as* resistance. Resistance, I argue, becomes the inaugurating gesture for a new mode or kind of philosophical critique made possible by aesthetics—one that Schiller extends to, or better, never conceives apart from, historical-political critique.[13]

In this second part of the project, I want to explore the way Schiller developed his initial reading of Kant's Critique of the Aesthetic Power of Judgment in his *Aesthetic Letters*. I am most intrigued, here, by the way that resistance, as Schiller interprets it in *Kallias*, following Kant, as a suspension or permanent delaying of all determination, is related in the *Aesthetic Letters* to a particular experience of temporality—both a suspension of temporality and the temporality of suspension—that Schiller associates with Kant's description of the experience of the beautiful as a "lingering" (*weilen*).[14] Thus, Schiller develops in the *Aesthetic Letters* what was in *Kallias* just one aspect of beauty as resistance, namely, the potentiality of aesthetic experience to suspend or interrupt violence (the violence of categorization). This time, however, Schiller adds the historical perspective to the analysis. Beauty not only serves as a model for resistance, the suspension or interruption of an operation of the cognitive faculties; it is also the point of departure for an interruption of the violence entailed in the modern—and alienating—reduction of experience to productivity and of thought to knowledge, displaying therefore the potentiality of the aesthetic dimension (inaugurated and opened up by, but not reduced to, beauty) to render inoperative the forms of violence that, according to Schiller, saturate his historical present. This gives way, as I will show, to a conception of critique as interruption or suspension of the logics and structures at work in the present, and as an opening, within time, of another time, another set of historical possibilities that are contained within the present, through what Schiller describes as the "real and active determinability" inaugurated by the experience and the *time* of the beautiful.[15] Hence, suspension and interruption become, in Schiller's (second) response to Kant's aesthetics, the fundamental gestures of aesthetic critique—or, better still, fundamental gestures of a dimension of critique opened up and configured by aesthetics.

My argument is structured in two parts, following what I consider to be the two forms of suspension at play in Schiller's own argument. In section 2, I want to pay attention to Schiller's transformation in the *Aesthetic Letters* of what he had understood in *Kallias* as resistance—the suspension of conceptualization that takes place in Kant's analysis of the judgment of taste and the very specific relation between the faculties that results from this suspension. For Schiller, this inaugurates a new possibility of temporality, and with it, a new philosophical standpoint to relate to time and history. This will allow me to move, in the third and final section, from the particular experience of time inaugurated by the beautiful to the suspension or opening *within* time made possible by beauty—an experience of a *caesura* or interruption saturated with possibilities for conceiving the present otherwise. Thus, I will move, following Schiller, from the suspension of time made possible by beauty to the time of suspension inaugurated by the beautiful; from the description of the kind of experience made possible by the suspension of determination to suspension as the time and the temporality of the beautiful, a time simultaneously subtracted from and full of time, as Schiller will describe it, which makes of beauty a radical opening in the present of the present's possibilities of interruption.

2. A Standstill at the Greatest Tension: Aesthetics as a Critical Dimension

The fact that Schiller understands aesthetics—and, precisely, Kantian aesthetics—as inaugurating a new dimension for thought, and, with it, introducing a new standpoint for critique, is made visible in the presentation of his project in the first part of the *Aesthetic Letters*. Given the historical and political turmoil of the present times (the *Letters* were written between 1793 and 1795, in the midst of the events unchained by the French Revolution), Schiller writes, an investigation on aesthetics and the question of the beautiful may seem superfluous. However, he insists, "I hope to convince you that the subject I have chosen is far less alien to the needs of our age than to its taste. More than this: if we are ever to solve the problem of politics in practice *we must take the path of aesthetics* [*durch das ästhetische den Weg nehmen muss*], because it is only through beauty that we make our way to freedom."[16] Schiller appeals to the urgency and the necessity of another path, different from an empirical, historical-political perspective, in order to take up the double task he lays out for the *Aesthetic Letters*.

On the one hand, Schiller wants to present a *diagnosis* of his time—a critical assessment of the causes of the forms of violence that, as symptoms of a more structural illness, seem to pervade the modern human condition (including, but not limited to, the political sphere). The language of illness and diagnosis is not arbitrary, since Schiller was trained as a physician and always understood the task of philosophical critique as one closely connected to medical diagnosis, treatment, and remedy, or even (in a slightly less optimistic tone in his later essays) as a form of inoculation.[17]

On the other hand, the aesthetic path seems to make possible a standpoint that, in addition to making these forms of violence visible, together with their structural causes, will also provide a way out of the corrupted way of thinking—tainted by these very same structures—pervasive in modernity. Schiller speaks here of a *vicious circle*, and of the aesthetic dimension or pathway as the only standpoint capable of escaping the forms of power dominating the present. He writes: "But this is not perhaps to argue in a circle? . . . how under the influence of a barbarous constitution is character ever to become ennobled? To this end we should presumably have to seek out some instrument not provided by the state, and to open up living springs that, whatever the political corruption, would remain clear and pure."[18] The aesthetic—and especially art as the first step toward the opening of an aesthetic dimension in the present—allows for a perspective that not only escapes the logics of the present, but also, as we will see, interrupts its reductive and overdetermining logics. Already from its very way of being, from its own presentation (*Darstellung*) and resistance to conceptualization, and therefore to any appropriation by the logics of production, the experience of beauty challenges the ways of being to which historical forces seem to condemn everything that exists and is produced under their scope.[19]

This critical dimension of the aesthetic is provided, Schiller continues, by what he describes as a "pure rational concept of beauty,"[20] which is Schiller's own translation of a transcendental perspective, that is, the task Kant has undertaken in his Critique of Aesthetic Judgment. Since experience, in its current historical circumstances, does not show itself as the "best judgment seat before which an issue as this can be decided," there is the need to appeal to a "concept of beauty derived from a source other than experience" or "deduced from the sheer potentialities of our sensuous-rational nature."[21] "True," Schiller continues, "this *transcendental way* will lead us out of the familiar circle of human existence . . . but . . . he who never ventures beyond actuality [*Wirklichkeit*] will never win the prize of truth."[22] It is clear from these quotations, as from many others in the *Aesthetic Letters*, that Schiller is reading Kant's analysis of the beautiful as an *alternative* perspective to historically overdetermined modes of existence—and not only, as Kant intends, as another mode of relation between the faculties of cognition that explains and justifies the use of another analysis and deduction of our judgments of taste. "Transcendental" here means for Schiller therefore not so much the conditions of possibility for every possible experience, as is the case in Kant, but rather, as Schiller puts it, the conditions of possibility for our historical (and thus modern) human condition. "Beauty," Schiller writes, "has to be shown to be a necessary condition of human being."[23] In beauty, in the kind of experience that it represents when analyzed from a Kantian transcendental perspective, Schiller finds a *critical standpoint* that, as a suspension of the *modes of existence* pervasive within the present, can allow for a critical interruption of its determinations.

This particular interpretation of the transcendental as an analysis of the conditions of the possibility of our human condition is one of the reasons why Schiller reads Kant's description of the free play of the faculties in the *Critique of Judgment* not only as an analysis of the specific kind of pleasure proper to the beautiful, and thus as an explanation of the conditions of the possibility for our judgments of taste (that is, for both the singular pleasure that grounds them and the universal demand for assent with which they are associated in Kant). The play between the faculties that allows in Kant for a reciprocal action between understanding and imagination, where the one is unable to determine the other given the unconceptualizable nature of the experience of beauty, and, therefore, where both "freely" perform their activities and mutually enliven their powers, also represents for Schiller an alternative to the two one-sided relations between the faculties—and beyond the faculties, between our "natural drives," that is, our sensuous and rational "natures"—that Schiller sees as a consequence of the present historical circumstances.[24]

It is history, according to Schiller, that has led both reason and sensibility to develop independently of each other as empty and arbitrary versions of what they could and should be when considered together, as different but complementary drives of human nature. He writes: "It was culture [*Kultur*] itself that inflicted this wound upon modern humanity [*Menschheit*] . . . the intuitive and the speculative understanding now withdrew in hostility to take up positions in their respective fields, whose frontiers they now began to guard with jealous mistrust; and with this confining activity to a particular sphere we have given ourselves a master within, who not infrequently ends up suppressing the rest of our potentialities.[25]" This is the reason why, Schiller continues, "with us [moderns], one might almost be tempted to assert, the various faculties appear as separate in practice as they are distinguished by the psychologist in theory."[26] Kant's analytical description of the separation of the faculties in his critical philosophy (Schiller is thinking here, particularly, of Kant's notion of freedom as a rational suppression of our sensuous impulses) is therefore not only transcendental, but rather coincides, in the case of modernity, with a diagnosis of the present and the forms of domination and violence that are, for Schiller, entailed by the abstract separation of our natural human drives. Either the barbaric domination of (a one-sided notion of) reason over and against the forces of imagination and sensibility, or the reaction of sensibility to this arbitrary domination in a violent regression to the natural state: these are the two modes of relation between the human drives that describe for Schiller a typology of violence, perpetuated by, and installed at the core of, modernity—the two ways in which "humanity can be at odds with itself."[27] "In other words," Schiller continues, they are "the two extremes of human depravity, and both united in a single epoch!"[28]

The relation between the faculties or drives is very different in the case of the beautiful, where the particular resistance to being conceptualized suspends the forceful determination that the understanding exercises over imagination, giving way to a very different kind of relationship. In the experience of the beautiful, Schiller writes, "the activity of the one [drive] both gives rise to, and sets limits to, the activity of the other . . . [in such a way that] each in itself achieves its highest manifestation precisely by reason of the other being active."[29] Kant's free play of the faculties thus introduces an alternative to what Schiller sees as the one-sided determinations and forms of domination that are characteristic of modernity.[30] Continuing his previous investigations in *Kallias*, he describes beauty as the exhibition of another idea of humanity, and consequently, as the opening of another realm of existence. Both in its presentation, and in the experience it makes possible, beauty opens another dimension, another perspective from which we can judge, and act, in the world. The aesthetic, Schiller insists, is both a condition and a disposition, a character and a perspective for judgment.[31]

Simply through its *presentation* (*Darstellung*), beauty suspends the violence of both rationality and sensibility taken in isolation, in abstraction from one another, and thus, in an empty misinterpretation of their powers.[32] The presentation of the beautiful, we know from *Kallias*, not only displays this possibility (makes it possible by way of its appearance) but also communicates it as an invitation and an exhortation to actualize it. As Schiller writes in *Kallias*: "That is why the realm of taste is the realm of freedom—every object of natural beauty outside me is a happy citizen who calls to me: be free like me."[33] The experience of beauty is for Schiller not only, as in Kant, a momentary suspension of our usual way of relating to the world, one that, as much as it enables for an enlivening of the faculties and even, as Kant puts it, provides a particular "feeling of ourselves," is not really meant to fundamentally change our relation toward the world.[34] For Schiller, to experience beauty means also to be somehow already summoned into an aesthetic disposition, to be called toward a transformation of the relationship we hold toward ourselves—a call that, as with Kant's experience of beauty, we do not simply choose whether or not to respond to; rather, it catches us by surprise in the harmonious free play of our faculties.

Such an experience, for Schiller, does not remain exclusively in the realm of pleasure. It is much more powerful and has a real effect on our determinations. Schiller writes: "Should there be cases in which he were to have this twofold experience simultaneously, in which he were . . . at one and the same time to feel himself matter and come to know himself as mind, that he would in such cases have a complete intuition of his human nature . . . they would awaken in him a *new drive* that, precisely because these two drives cooperate within it, would be opposed to each one of them considered separately."[35] Beauty is, itself, a *force* and a drive, not merely the reconciliation of the opposition between the rational and sensible, formal and material drives, but the drive that allows the other drives to balance one another in the tension and the difficult, fragile, suspension that is made possible by their opposition. This is what Schiller calls in the *Letters* the "play drive," following Kant's description of the free "play" of the faculties in the judgment of taste.

It is in this way, Schiller writes, that in beauty the sensible and rational drives "overcome their respective forms of violence [*ihre bestimmende Gewalt gegenseitig aufheben*] and bring about a negation by means of an opposition. . . . The scales of the balance stand level when they are empty; but they also stand level when they contain equal weights."[36] It is not by opposing violence that beauty achieves the interruption of its vicious circle, but rather by exhibiting and eliciting in us another kind of relation between the faculties. And it does so, not by eliminating the tension between them (which would mean merely a reconciliation between the drives), but rather by bringing the faculties to a standstill at the highest point of their opposition (*Wechselwirkung*), deactivating thereby the violence (*Gewalt*) implicated in the one-sidedness of their exercise. Schiller writes:

> Exclusive domination by either of his two basic drives is for him [man] a state of constraint and violence, and freedom [made possible by beauty] lies only in the cooperation of both his natures. The man one-sidedly dominated by feeling . . . will be released and set free by means of form; the man one-sidedly dominated by law . . . will be released and set free by means of matter. In order to be adequate to this twofold task, beauty will therefore reveal herself under two different guises. First, as tranquil form, she will assuage the violence of life, and pave the way that leads from sensation to thought. Secondly, as living image, she will arm abstract form with sensuous power, lead concept back to intuition, and law back to feeling.[37]

The aesthetic state, for Schiller, is thus conceived as a state, a relation, and a way of being outside violence. By suspending the logics that make violence possible in the first place, it renders these forms of violence inoperative, allowing for another kind of relationship between faculties that would otherwise seek unilateral domination.[38]

The *form of critique* offered by beauty, and thus by the aesthetic dimension and perspective that it allows and elicits, is on the one hand a diagnosis of Schiller's time—it makes visible the one-sidedness of the two main forms of violence that dominate the age. On the other hand, it is also a force or a drive that suspends these forms of violence. Beauty as critique (or as a critical standpoint) interrupts the vicious circle of violence. Rather than positing itself in a relation of opposition to violence (engaging thereby in a dialectical relation to it that would only end up reinstituting its causal power), the aesthetic offers an alternative that renders violence, and its structural causes, inoperative. Instead of criticizing merely the effects of violence, aesthetics as a critical dimension dismantles the very structures on which violence is grounded. As we are about to see, this is made possible, above all, by displacing the *temporal framework* required for its operation. I will devote the last section of this paper to explaining what this means for Schiller and what this means for his conception of aesthetics, or, better, given the specific character of aesthetic experience, for what I see in Schiller's work as the development of an *aesthetic dimension of critique*.

3. The Time of the Beautiful: An Aesthetic Dimension of Critique

The analysis of the pleasure of the beautiful in Kant's *Critique of the Power of Judgment* is tied to a very particular form of causality. Only under the framework of causality, Kant argues, can the beautiful be understood as pleasure, even though this pleasure cannot be the immediate result of the experience of the object, in which case the pleasure of the beautiful would be no different from the agreeable, nor can the judgment merely precede pleasure, in which case the latter would not constitute the (universally communicable) ground for the judgment of taste.[39] Thus, Kant writes, the solution to "whether in the judgment of taste the feeling of pleasure precedes the judging [*Beurteilung*] of the object, or the latter precedes the former," constitutes "the *key* to the critique of taste."[40] The question of the *succession* of the pleasure by the judging or the judging by the pleasure—even though we come to learn throughout the analysis that we need to consider them also simultaneously, or even better as one and the same—is one that Schiller will consider very carefully, in light of what we have seen so far, namely, the kind of suspension that the free play of the faculties represents in the judgment of taste, and of its consequences for the "temporal framework" that constitutes and is constituted by the experience of the beautiful.

Already in *Kallias* Schiller starts to consider the aesthetic as an "outlook," a standpoint, whose framework, following Kant, must disrupt temporal logics of means and ends. Schiller writes: "We never want to see coercion [*Zwang*], even if it is reason itself which exercises it; we want even nature's freedom to be respected because "we regard every being in aesthetic judgement as an end in itself" and "it disgusts (outrages) us, for whom freedom is the highest thing, that something should be sacrificed for something else, and used as a means."[41] Beauty, indeed, disrupts the temporality of succession, namely, the temporality required for any logics of means and ends which, for Schiller, as representative of an instrumental form of reason, constitutes the framework that makes the operation of violence possible—or at least, as Schiller analyzes it in the context of *Kallias*, that makes possible the "sacrificial" and coercive domination of the imagination by the understanding and of reason over and against the "freedom" of nature.[42] The aesthetic, indeed, not only understood as an experience, but even more so as a criterion of judgment, demands that we disrupt the very temporality required by instrumentality, or, at least, that we consider experience under a framework different from the temporal succession required by the logics of means to ends.

Schiller is here following Kant, for whom the analysis of the singularity of the pleasure of beauty in the *Critique of the Power of Judgment* forces him to introduce the paradoxical formula of "purposiveness without a purpose"—a "causality in itself," Kant explains, that is only occupied with "maintaining the state of the representation of the mind and the occupation of the cognitive powers without a further aim."[43] It is this very particular causality, without any further aim, that leads Kant to characterize the experience of the beautiful as a form of suspension. Kant writes, "we linger [*weilen*] over the consideration of the beautiful because this consideration strengthens and reproduces itself."[44] Whether this means that the beautiful brings with it and inaugurates its own kind of temporality is not entirely clear in Kant's text.[45] What is clear, however, is that the experience of the beautiful needs to suspend the normal temporal framework that is presupposed in any other form of experience. The pleasure of the beautiful, if it is causal at all, is a form of causality that cannot be understood with reference to its effect, even though it must still be comprehended as purposive, as end in itself—or, one could even imagine, if "lingering" describes the structure of the experience, as a means without an end.

This is, in any case, the way Schiller interprets Kant on this point. He writes: "While every other state into which we can enter, refers us back to a preceding one and requires for its termination a subsequent one; the aesthetic alone is a whole in itself, since it comprises within itself all the conditions of both its origin and its continuance. Here alone do we feel *ripped out of time [aus der Zeit gerissen]*."[46] It is not only that the experience of the beautiful suspends the order of temporality, ripping us out of time and dismantling the frameworks through which violence operates. Precisely in its capacity for suspension, the beautiful seems to introduce and to sustain an interruptive mode of experience, one that is itself experienced precisely *as* suspension—the suspension of time, being out of time, but also, in a way, as the "lingering" also suggests, being "over" time. This capacity for suspension, for placing ourselves outside of time—without losing sight, however, of the purposiveness of this lingering—is what Schiller, since the beginning of the *Letters*, associates with art's capacity to offer a standpoint for critique. He writes, "The artist is indeed the child of his age; but woe to him if he is at the same time its ward or, worse still, its minion! . . . His theme he will, indeed, take from the present; but his form he will borrow from a nobler time, nay, from beyond time altogether [*jenseits aller Zeit*]."[47]

Beauty as the standpoint for critique does not find its sources in a better time, another time in history, perhaps, that may serve as its inspiration. Instead, it is in an experience "outside" of time that allows for the artist to "return, as a stranger, to its own century; not, however, to gladden it by his appearance, but rather, terrible as Agamemnon's son, to cleanse and to purify it."[48] Beauty, therefore, is not from another time. It makes possible and inaugurates, in its capacity for suspension, an outside of time while also, simoultenously, remaining within time; namely, a critical standpoint that finds its source (*Quelle*) in a form of experience that Schiller characterizes as "whole in itself," neither active nor passive, neither past nor present, but whole in its potentiality, its capacity for "preparing the shape of things to come."[49]

This mode of potentiality offered by beauty does not come exactly, as is also the case in Kant's judgments of taste, from a *lack of determination* or actualization. The verb *weilen* in German suggests both a lingering and a tarrying as much as a delay and a deferral.[50] In Kant, this means that the moment of conceptual determination in the case of the judgment of taste is somehow indefinitely postponed. What is obtained through the deferral of determination is not merely indetermination but rather *determinability*. Here I follow Rodolphe Gasché's interpretation of this moment in Kant's *Critique of the Power of Judgment*. Gasché writes, "To judge an undetermined empirical thing as beautiful, is merely to state that it can be intuited (in its appearing) as having the phenomenal form of something *determinable* in principle; that is, something with *open determinability*."[51] This is not the language used by Kant, but it is precisely the language that Schiller uses, when reading Kant, to describe the standpoint opened up by beauty—the aesthetic dimension of critique—that comes to be through the suspension of every determination, *while* preserving them all. "This condition of *real and active determinability*," Schiller continues, "is the aesthetic."[52]

Real determinability is not, Schiller clarifies, "complete absence of determination."[53] Instead, it is the combination of "such sheer absence of determination, and an equally unlimited determinability, with the greatest possible content."[54] This is made possible, Schiller explains, by the play drive, which is to say by the balancing out of the sensuous and the formal drives, which produces in turn a new drive, one capable of sustaining, *at the same time*, the combination and the canceling out of the forces involved in each one of the drives. Schiller writes, "the problem is therefore at one and the same time to destroy and to maintain the determination of the condition—and this is possible in one way only: by confronting it with another determination."[55] This is, as we have seen above, what the experience of the beautiful makes possible, by creating a new drive, the play drive, which is not the result of the negation of the other two drives, the sensuous and the formal, but rather of the balanced relation between them. As Schiller continues: "our psyche passes then from sensation to thought via a middle disposition in which sense and reason are both active *at the same time* . . . this middle disposition . . . preeminently deserves to be called . . . aesthetic."[56]

The aesthetic, as a perspective and dimension for thought, "does not reside in the exclusion of certain realities," Schiller insists, "but in the absolute inclusion of all."[57] It is a standpoint that can contemplate and linger over the present without having to operate through the usual distinction between possibility and actuality, since through beauty, thanks to the suspension of the temporal order that we experience in the free encounter and reciprocal action (*Wechselwirkung*) between our sensible and rational drives, we enter into the realm of real (existing) potentiality. Schiller writes, "In the pleasure we take in knowledge we distinguish without difficulty the transition from passivity to activity and are clearly aware that the first is over when the latter begins. In the delight we take in beauty, by contrast, no such succession of activity and passivity can be discerned."[58] Precisely in its capacity for suspension, the beautiful inaugurates in turn an interruptive experience of temporality, one that is itself experienced precisely *as* suspension. Thus, the suspension of temporality in the beautiful—and of the usual distinctions between cause and effect, activity and passivity—opens up another experience of temporality, a temporality of *another kind*. Not a temporality *in* another time, however, but one opened up in the midst of the present. "That drive," Schiller writes, "in which both the others [drives] work in concert (permit me for the time being to call it the *play drive*), would be directed therefore towards overcoming [suspending while preserving] time within time [*die Zeit in der Zeit aufgehoben*]."[59]

This capacity for suspension not only guarantees the critical dimension of the aesthetic. It is also, Schiller realizes, the temporality *of* the beautiful, and thus, the temporality of a mode of potentiality that the beautiful inaugurates for critique. The time of the beautiful *is* the time of critique, the time of interruption and suspension, that renders all the historical determinations inoperative but determinable; that opens, in the midst of time, and within time, an *inoperative–interruptive mode of experience*. Beauty gives time enough time to introduce a pause in the heart of the present, to produce a standstill where the forms of violence that are operative in the present are not only made visible but brought to a halt, in order to conceive, to imagine and to give shape, even if only as an image, to things to come.[60] This image, however, is not just one image among others. It results from the encounter of all the forces inhabiting the present; it is saturated with their tension. And it does not generate just one possibility among many; on the contrary, it changes the realm of the possible, giving shape to something radically different in kind in the realm of experience, something other than time, another time, that historical time cannot suppress even if it can also not hold onto.

I find the ambiguity of the phrase "the time of the beautiful" intriguing, since it seems to contain precisely an ambiguity involved in the multiple interpretations of Schiller's aesthetical-political project. On the one hand, the *Aesthetic Letters* could be interpreted as a call to step into *another time*. The time of the beautiful in this case would correspond to the usual interpretation of Schiller, which attributes to him a teleological philosophy of history, whose end and goal would indeed be the "beautiful State" understood both as a character (a disposition, a state of mind) and a political project (the overcoming of the natural state as well as the abstract and merely formally understood moral state, along with the kinds of violence that each reproduces, given their structural roles in the implementation of the Enlightenment project). On the other hand, following the interpretation I have proposed, "the time of the beautiful" could refer to the experience of a different kind of temporality, inaugurated and made possible by the experience of the beautiful—a radical opening and interruption within the present of "another time"—that disrupts the logics—the conceptual and temporal frameworks—that make violence possible in the first place. This "time of an otherwise" is, for Schiller, the time of a potentiality that the beautiful makes possible and inaugurates for critique. Thus, the time of the beautiful is, from this perspective, here and now. It is the time opened up by the critical dimension of aesthetics, and makes possible, thereby, an aesthetic dimension for critique.

Notes

1. Walter Benjamin, *The Arcades Project*, ed. Rolf Tiedemann, trans. Howard Eiland and Kevin Mclaughlin (Cambridge, MA: Harvard University Press, 1999), 475 (Convolute N, N10a, 3). The first version of this paper was delivered as a lecture in a special panel on Aesthetics at the 2017 Pacific APA, in Seattle, at the invitation of Daniela Vallega-Neu. I am thankful for the questions and comments during the Q&A, and particularly to J. Colin McQuillan for his patient reading of different versions of this text.

2. This material has been compiled in Jens Kulenkampff, ed., *Materialen zu Kants 'Kritik der Urteilskraft'* (Frankfurt am Main: Suhrkamp, 1974), 126–144. Also, for a thorough analysis of how Schiller's own perspective on aesthetics did not change but was simply reinforced by his reading of Kant's third critique, see Laura Anna Macor's work on Schiller, particularly *Der morastige Zirkel der menschlichen Bestimmung: Friedrich Schillers Weg von der Aufklärung zu Kant* (Würzburg: Königshausen & Neumann, 2010).

3. See Immanuel Kant, *Critique of the Power of Judgment*, ed. and trans. Paul Guyer and Eric Matthews (Cambridge: Cambridge University Press, 2000), §23–29, §42, §59. Subsequent quotations from Kant's third *Critique* are accompanied by a reference (indicated with *Ak.*) to the relevant volume and page number in Immanuel Kant, *Kants gesammelte Schriften (Akademie Ausgabe)*, ed. the Royal Prussian (later German) Academy of Sciences (Berlin: Georg Reimer, later Walter de Gruyter, 1900–).

4. Dieter Henrich, "Beauty and Freedom: Schiller's Struggle with Kant's Aesthetics," in *Essays in Kant's Aesthetics*, ed. Ted Cohen and Paul Guyer (Chicago: University of Chicago Press, 1982), 244.

5. Schiller already speaks of beauty and the aesthetic as a certain "view" (*Ansicht*) in his *Kallias* letters. See Friedrich Schiller, "*Kallias* or Concerning Beauty: Letters to Gottfried Körner," in *Classic and Romantic German Aesthetics*, ed. J.M. Bernstein, trans. Stefan Bird-Pollan (Cambridge: Cambridge University

Press, 2003), 154; Friedrich Schiller, "Kallias oder über die Schönheit," in *Werke in Drei Bänden* (cited hereafter as *HA*), ed. Gerhard Fricke and Herbert Göpfert (Munich: Hanser Verlag, 1966), 2: 357. In the *Aesthetic Letters*, Schiller speaks of the "anthropological view [*Schätzung*]," and of the aesthetic character as criteria for judgement [*Beurtheilung*]. See Friedrich Schiller, "Letters on the Aesthetic Education of Man," in *Essays*, ed. Walter Hindereder and Daniel Dahlstrom (New York: Continuum, 2001), Letter 4, 93, and Letter 20, 146, respectively; Friedrich Schiller, "Über die ästhetische Erziehung des Menschen in einer Reihe von Briefen," in *Schillers Werke—Nationalausgabe* (cited hereafter as *NA*), ed. Julius Petersen und Gerhard Fricke (Weimar: Hermann Böhlaus Nachfolger, 1963), 20:316 and 376. However, he will refer explicitly to the aesthetic as a "perspective" (*Gesichtspunkt*) and "standpoint" (*Standpunct*) only later, in his text "Concerning the Sublime." See Friedrich Schiller, "Concerning the Sublime," in *Essays*, 81; and Friedrich Schiller, "Über das Erhabene," *NA* 21:49–50. I will not be able to devote space in this paper to the analysis of this later essay. For a detailed analysis, see María del Rosario Acosta López, *La tragedia como conjuro: el problema de lo sublime en Friedrich Schiller* (Bogotá: Universidad Nacional de Colombia, 2008), 321ff.

6. Hence the quote that serves as an epigraph to this chapter, the connection to which I will not be able to develop, but which I would at least like to suggest here; namely, a connection (closer than is usually recognized) between Schiller's conception of critique, as opened up by the aesthetic realm, and the kind of philosophical critique we usually trace back to the tradition of critical theory. That is, a conception of critique as historical materialism, or, as is very clearly the case in Benjamin's work, a critique of historical and political forms of violence. The very idea that inspired this volume, as J. Colin McQuillan and I suggest in the introduction, is to remind us of those connections that are usually forgotten in the process of compartmentalizing the history of philosophy and the different traditions of philosophical critique.

7. The question of Schiller's misappropriation and/or misunderstanding of Kant is characteristic of Schiller's philosophical secondary literature, particularly in the twentieth century. For a detailed recount of this see Frederick Beiser, *Schiller as Philosopher: A Re-Examination* (New York: Oxford University Press, 2005), 1–12. See also Beiser's "Un lamento," in *Friedrich Schiller: Estética y Libertad*, ed. María del Rosario Acosta López (Bogotá: Universidad Nacional, 2008). Rather than denying these misappropriations, in my own work on Schiller I have been interested in making them productive, showing how Schiller's idiosyncratic reading of Kant is only one side of a very rich and consistent philosophical project, already on the way by the time Schiller read Kant, and for which Kant's aesthetics and practical philosophy were a fundamental source of inspiration, even if not always taken rigorously and to "the letter." I have developed different productive sides of this misappropriation elsewhere; among others, see María del Rosario Acosta López, "¿Una superación estética del deber? La crítica de Schiller a Kant," *Episteme N.S.* 28, no. 2 (2008),

3–24; María del Rosario Acosta López, "Making Other People's Feelings our Own: From the Aesthetic to the Political in Schiller's *Aesthetic Letters*," in *Who Is This Schiller Now?*, ed. Jeffery High, Nicholas Martin, and N. Oellers (London: Camden House, 2011), 187–203; and María del Rosario Acosta López, "The Resistance of Beauty: On Schiller's *Kallias Briefe* in Response to Kant's Aesthetics," *Epoche* 21, no. 1 (2016), 235–249.

    8. Schiller, *Kallias*, 145–84; Schiller, *HA* 2: 352–81.

    9. Schiller, *Kallias*, 145–84; Schiller, *HA* 2: 353.

    10. The German word for "violence" is *Gewalt*, which Schiller uses in *Kallias* as opposed to "force" or "power" (*Kraft*) to denote an unjustified, unilateral, and pernicious use of one's drives, faculties, or potentialities. However, one also needs to be careful about the different connotations, not always self-evident, of the German word *Gewalt*. The English translations of Schiller's texts are a clear sign of the difficulties of translating this notion as consistent with its context. I will make a point of indicating the presence of the word in Schiller's quotes, and of changing the translation when I consider it necessary to maintain some consistency with the German. For a thorough discussion of this word and its connotations, see Peter Fenves's contribution in this volume.

    11. See Acosta López, "The Resistance of Beauty," 235–249. By emphasizing on resistance as an essential moment of beauty, Schiller is already blurring the distintinctions between beauty and the sublime. In this paper I am mostly concerned with Schiller's conception of the beautiful in his reading of Kant's Analytic of the Beautiful. However, when Schiller speaks of aesthetic experience, particularly in the *Aesthetic Letters*, one needs to think of the beautiful and the sublime as two different points of the same spectrum of experiences that Schiller is considering under this concept. Thus, even though the sublime will not make an appearance in my paper—and it rarely makes an appearance in the *Aesthetic Letters*—it is in the background of Schiller's analysis of the aesthetic. The third part of this project will have to deal with the specificity of the question of the sublime and how it contributes, in its own way, to Schiller's development of a new concept of critique. See for now Acosta, *La tragedia como conjuro*, and Acosta, "Making Other People's Feelings Our Own."

    12. See Schiller, *Kallias*, 164–165; Schiller, *HA* 2: 367–368.

    13. And, as I argue elsewhere, also never conceived apart from a philosophical critique of historical-political violence. See María del Rosario Acosta López, "The Violence of Reason: Schiller and Hegel on the French Revolution," in *Aesthetic Reason and Imaginative Freedom: Friedrich Schiller and Philosophy*, ed. María del Rosario Acosta López and Jeffrey Powell (Albany: State University of New York Press, 2018), 59–82.

    14. Kant, *Critique of the Power of Judgment*, 107 (*Ak*. 5: 222).

    15. Schiller, "Aesthetic Letters," Letter 20, 145; Schiller, *NA* 20:375.

    16. Schiller, "Aesthetic Letters," Letter 2, 90 (translation modified); Schiller, *NA* 20:312.

17. See for instance Friedrich Schiller, "Concerning the Sublime," 83; Schiller, *NA* 21:51. For an analysis of this metaphor in connection to the question of the role of aesthetics as critique in Schiller, see Acosta López, *La tragedia como conjuro*, 321ff. Also, this is the reason why, as we are about to see in the pages below, Schiller moves from the language of faculties to the language of drives, and thus from the Kantian transcendental analysis of the relation between imagination and understanding to the more general "anthropological" reflection, as Schiller calls it, on the relation between the sensuous and the rational drives, or the sensuous drive (*sinnliche Trieb*) and the formal drive (*Formtrieb*). This is just one of those instances of "misappropriation" of Kant's argument that are productive for understanding Schiller's own take on the potentialities lying in the "aesthetic" standpoint.

18. "Aesthetic Letters," Letter 9, 107–108; Schiller, *NA* 20:332.

19. Schiller is, of course, aware that even art can be appropriated and made into an instrument of the State. But art, when it remains free and autonomous, can also be and remains always the site where another possibility is to be "exhibited" (*darstellt*) to us. By means of this exhibition, art and beauty become the first step toward the development of a critical disposition toward the logics of one's historical present. This is guaranteed not through its contents, but rather through the kind of experience, and the kind of pleasure, it elicits. As we are about to see, this is all tied to Schiller's reading of Kant's free play of the faculties.

20. Schiller, "Aesthetic Letters," Letter 10, 114; Schiller, *NA* 20:340.

21. Schiller, "Aesthetic Letters," Letter 10, 114–115; Schiller, *NA* 20:340.

22. Schiller, "Aesthetic Letters," Letter 10, 115; Schiller, *NA* 20:341.

23. Schiller, "Aesthetic Letters," Letter 10, 115; Schiller, *NA* 20:340.

24. Kant speaks here of the "animation of both faculties," of "an activity that is indeterminate but yet . . . in unison" between them, and of the "facilitated play of both powers of the mind (imagination and understanding), enlivened through mutual agreement." See Kant, *Critique of the Power of Judgment*, 104 (Ak. 5:219).

25. Schiller, "Aesthetic Letters," Letter 6, 99 (translation modified); Schiller, *NA* 20:322–323.

26. Schiller, "Aesthetic Letters," Letter 6, 98; Schiller, *NA* 20:322.

27. Schiller, "Aesthetic Letters," Letter 4, 95 (translation modified); Schiller, *NA* 20:318. The entire passage reads: "But man can be at odds with himself in two ways: either as savage, when feeling predominates over principle; or as barbarian, when principle destroys feeling. The savage despises civilization and acknowledges nature as his sovereign mistress. The barbarian derides and dishonors nature, but, more contemptible than the savage, as often as not continues to be the slave of his slave."

28. Schiller, "Aesthetic Letters," Letter 5, 96; Schiller, *NA* 20:319.

29. Schiller, "Aesthetic Letters," Letter 14, 125; Schiller, *NA* 20:352.

30. Not only Kant, but also Fichte, are here in the background of what Schiller describes in the *Letters* as the *Wechselwirkung* between the two drives: "Once you postulate a primary, and therefore necessary, antagonism between these

two drives, there is of course, no other means of maintaining unity in the human being than by unconditionally subordinating the sensuous drive to the rational. From this, however, only uniformity can result, never harmony, and man goes on forever being divided. Subordination there must, of course, be; but it must be reciprocal. . . . Both principles are, therefore, at once subordinated to each other and coordinated with each other, that is to say, they stand in reciprocal relation [*Wechselwirkung*] to one another: without form no matter, and without matter no form. (This concept of reciprocal action, and its fundamental importance, is admirably set forth in Fichte's Fundaments of the Theory of Knowledge, Leipzg, 1794.)" See Schiller, "Aesthetic Letters," Letter 113, 121; Schiller, *NA* 20:348. The role of this reciprocal relation or effect (*Wirkung*), as conceptualized by Fichte, and its connection to Schiller's reformulation not only of a way of being, but also of a way of thinking and doing, even writing, philosophy, can be traced back to their dispute regarding Fichte's denial of publication by Schiller in *Die Hören*. See María del Rosario Acosta López, "On the Poetical Nature of Philosophical Writing: A Controversy about Style between Schiller and Fichte" in *Philosophers and their Poets: The Poetic Turn in German Philosophy Since Kant*, ed. Charles Barnbach and Theodore George (Albany: State University of New York Press, 2019), 21–46.

31. See Schiller, "Aesthetic Letters," Letter 20, 146; Schiller, *NA* 20:376.

32. Moreover, as I have shown elsewhere concerning Schiller's analysis of the beautiful in *Kallias*, this mode of relation displayed and exhibited by beauty introduces for Schiller the possibility of another *conception of freedom*, another mode of relation between the sensible and the rational, whereby lawfulness remains operative but is no longer experienced as a constraint. This is connected to Schiller's interpretation and extension of Kant's conception of purposiveness without a purpose in the Analytic of the Beautiful. Schiller refers to this as "aesthetic freedom" and even speaks about an overcoming of duty through the aesthetic. See Schiller, "Aesthetic Letters," Letter 19, 143 ("the opposition of two drives gives rise to freedom"); Schiller, *NA* 20:373; and also his long footnote at the end of the twentieth letter, Schiller, "Aesthetic Letters," Letter 20, 146; Schiller, *NA* 20:376. See Acosta López, "The Resistance of Beauty," 241ff.

33. Schiller, *Kallias*, 173 (translation modified); Schiller, *HA* 2:375.

34. Kant speaks of the "subject feeling itself" in the experience of the beautiful. See Kant, *Critique of the Power of Judgement*, 89 (*Ak.* 5:204).

35. Schiller, "Aesthetic Letters," Letter 14, 126; Schiller, *NA* 20:353.

36. Schiller, "Aesthetic Letters," Letter 20, 145 (translation modified); Schiller, *NA* 20:375.

37. Schiller, "Aesthetic Letters," Letter 17, 136; Schiller, *NA* 20:365.

38. This is also the case, for Schiller, with the conception of the political that an aesthetic perspective allows to undertake. Schiller is very clear about this in his comparison between the "forms of production" involved in artisanal and artistic operations, and the very particular form of relation between form and

matter, and even more importantly, between means and ends, that is required by the political. He writes: "When the artisan lays hands upon the formless mass in order to shape it to his ends, he has no scruple in doing it violence [*Gewalt*]; for the natural material he is working merits no respect for itself, and the concern is not with the whole for the sake of the parts, but with the parts for the sake of the whole. When the artist lays hands upon the same mass, he has just as little scruple in doing it violence [*Gewalt*]; but he avoids showing it. For the material he is handling he has not a whit more respect than has the artisan; but the eye that would seek to protect the freedom of the material he will endeavor to deceive by a show of yielding to this latter. With the pedagogic or the political artist things are very different indeed. For him human being is at once the material on which he works and the goal toward which he strives. In this case the end turns back upon itself and becomes identical with the medium; and it is only inasmuch as the whole serves the parts that the parts are in any way bound to submit to the whole. The statesman-artist must approach his material with a quite different kind of respect from that which the maker of beauty feigns toward his. The consideration he must accord to its uniqueness and individuality is not merely subjective, and aimed at creating an illusion for the senses, but objective and directed to its innermost being." See Schiller, "Aesthetic Letters," Letter 4, 94; Schiller, *NA* 20:317–318.

39. Kant, *Critique of the Power of Judgement*, 102 (*Ak*. 5:217).

40. Kant, *Critique of the Power of Judgement*, 102 (emphasis added, *Ak*. 5:217).

41. Schiller, *Kallias*, 159; Schiller, *HA* 2:362.

42. I am aware that all these are a number of unexplained steps in the argument. Schiller goes from one to the next in his *Kallias* letters, but each one of these needs justification. I have offered a careful reading of Schiller's different moves—and particularly, in what is relevant in this specific passage, of his move from the resistance of the beautiful object to an understanding of this resistance as the appearance of freedom in nature, in *Kallias*—in Acosta López, "The Resistance of Beauty," 235–249.

43. Kant, *Critique of the Power of Judgement*, 107 (*Ak*. 5:222).

44. Ibid.

45. I owe the idea of such a temporality, coming out of the *Critique of Judgment* and Kant's analysis of the "time of the beautiful," to Khafiz Kerimov, one of my students at DePaul, who does a superb job interpreting Kant's *Critique of Judgment* in the light of the question of time. See "The Time of the Beautiful in Kant's *Critique of Judgment*," *Epoche* 24, no. 1 (2019).

46. Schiller, "Aesthetic Letters," Letter 22, 149 (translation modified); Schiller, *NA* 20:379.

47. Schiller, "Aesthetic Letters," Letter 9, 108; Schiller, *NA* 20:333.

48. Ibid.

49. Schiller, "Aesthetic Letters," Letter 9, 109; Schiller, *NA* 20:334.

50. See also Kerimov, "The time of the beautiful."

51. Rodolphe Gasché, *The Idea of Form: Rethinking Kant's Aesthetics* (Stanford, CA: Stanford University Press, 2003), 35 (emphasis added).

52. Schiller, "Aesthetic Letters," Letter 20, 145; Schiller, *NA* 20:375.

53. Ibid.

54. Ibid.

55. Ibid.

56. Ibid.

57. Schiller, "Aesthetic Letters," Letter 18, 139; Schiller, *NA* 20:367.

58. Schiller, "Aesthetic Letters," Letter 25, 164; Schiller, *NA* 20:396.

59. Schiller, "Aesthetic Letters," Letter 14, 126 (translation modified); Schiller, *NA* 20:353.

60. This introduction of time within time, the need to give (historical) time some more time to go where it needs to go, is related to Schiller's criticisms of the French Revolution and what he describes as the "unpreparedness" of the times to actualize the demands of a still too abstract ideal of reason. Schiller writes, "If, then, reason does away with the natural state (as she of necessity must if she would put her own in its place), she jeopardizes the physical man who actually exists for the sake of a moral man who is as yet hypothetical; risks this very existence of society for a merely hypothetical idea of society. She takes from humankind something they actually possess, and without which they possess nothing, and refers them instead to something that they could and should possess. . . . Before they have had time to cleave unto the law with the full force of their moral will, she [reason] would have drawn from under their feet the ladder of nature." See Schiller, "Aesthetic Letters," Letter 3, 91; Schiller, *NA* 20:314. The aesthetic as a middle term starts to take shape in Schiller's *Letters* precisely as the possibility of introducing a passage that allows for time to catch up with itself. The aesthetic state rips time open, therefore, to make more time for what otherwise can only manifest itself as violence. The idea of a middle term is substituted progressively in Schiller's argument throughout the *Letters* by the idea of a new drive, a new state, the "aesthetic," which is no longer conceived exclusively as a means, but precisely, as we have seen, as the interruption of any logic that defines history in terms of means and ends. See also Acosta López, "The Violence of Reason," 71ff.

5

Not Yet a System, Not Yet a Science

Reinhold and Fichte on Kant's Critique

J. COLIN McQUILLAN

I am just as sincerely convinced that nothing following Kant's spirit of genius, could contribute more to philosophy than Reinhold's systematic spirit.

—Fichte, *Concerning the Concept of the Wissenschaftslehre* (1794)[1]

Through the work of Kant, and still more through that of Fichte, the idea of a science, and particularly of philosophy as a science, has been established.

—Hegel, "The Essence of Philosophical Criticism" (1802)[2]

1. Introduction

Although he promises that his *Critique of Pure Reason* (1781/1787) will finally set metaphysics on the "secure path of science," Immanuel Kant warns his readers, in the Introduction, that they will not find in its pages a complete system of the science of metaphysics.[3] Kant explains that his critique undertakes "the mere estimation of pure reason, of its sources and boundaries, as the propaedeutic to the system of pure reason."[4] Critique is, as such, a "special science" that will clear the way and lay the foundation for the system of pure reason and the science of metaphysics that Kant hoped to present under the titles *The Metaphysics of Nature* and *The Metaphysics of Morals*.[5]

Despite his reputation as a systematic philosopher, Kant never completed the system he promised. He claims, in a 1785 letter to Christian Gottfried Schütz, that his *Metaphysical Foundations of Natural Science* (1786) is an application of the principles contained in *The Metaphysics of Nature*, even though Kant had not yet published the work in which he was supposed to demonstrate these principles.[6] The fragments contained in the *Opus postumum* (written 1796–1801, published 1936–1938) are meant to bridge the gap between the principles Kant articulated in the *Metaphysical Foundations* and physics, understood as "a system of the special laws of nature," so they are no substitute for the general principles that were supposed to be contained in *The Metaphysics of Nature*. Kant eventually published a work with the title *The Metaphysics of Morals* (1797), but it is hard to see it as the completion of his system of the science of metaphysics. It contains a variety of principles that are not discussed in *The Groundwork of the Metaphysics of Morals* (1785) or the *Critique of Practical Reason* (1788), but Kant admits in the Preface that the work contains only the "metaphysical first principles" of right and virtue.[7] It excludes the numerous principles that would govern the application of these "first principles" to particular cases, even though these principles are essential for the construction of "a system of pure reason" according to the first *Critique*.[8] Consequently, it is hard to avoid the conclusion that Kant failed to make metaphysics a science, according to his own definition, even if he did manage to set metaphysics on the right path and lay a foundation on which other philosophers could build.

In this chapter, I would like to focus on two post-Kantian philosophers who saw Kant's failure to complete the system he had promised as one of the greatest weaknesses of his critique, but also as an opportunity to achieve something that Kant had not. Karl Leonhard Reinhold was one of Kant's earliest and most vigorous defenders, but, in time, he came to regard Kant's critique as merely the first step toward a complete system and science of philosophy. In his *Elementarphilosophie*, Reinhold sought to go beyond Kant's critique and formulate a single first principle from which every other principle, in every other part of philosophy and, indeed, in every other science, could be derived. Johann Gottlieb Fichte concurred with Reinhold's criticisms of Kant and took over his attempt to ground philosophy in a single principle in his *Wissenschaftslehre*, though Fichte had notably different ideas about the kind of principle with which philosophy and science must begin. By examining Reinhold's and Fichte's objections to Kant's critique in greater detail, I hope to shed new light on Kant's critique and illuminate the way the concepts of "critique," "system," and "science" were understood by post-Kantian philosophers.

2. Kant's Critique of Pure Reason

Before we turn our attention to Reinhold and Fichte, it will be helpful to consider the passage in which Kant distinguishes his critique from a complete system of pure reason.[9] This passage is found in the Introduction to the Critique of Pure Reason, where it is preceded by three other definitions of critique in the Preface to the first (A, 1781) and second (B, 1787) editions. There, Kant says his critique is a court of justice, a critique of faculty of reason, and an attempt to transform the method of metaphysics. As a court of justice, the critique of pure reason dismisses reason's groundless pretensions and asserts its rightful claims about metaphysics—a subject Kant considers too important to abandon to indifference.[10] As a critique of the faculty of reason, Kant's critique determines what we can know *a priori*, which establishes the possibility of metaphysics.[11] And, as an attempt to transform the method of metaphysics, Kant's critique insists that human reason can and should measure its own capacity for *a priori* cognition, instead of seeking the conditions of our knowledge in external objects.[12] This leads, finally, to the account of the critique of pure reason in the Introduction, where Kant describes his critique as "a special science" that has as its object "the mere estimation of pure reason, of its sources and boundaries," and which serves as "the propaedeutic to the system of pure reason."[13]

In the Introduction, Kant calls his critique "a special science" to distinguish it from the complete system of pure reason. He says that such a system would have to be based on the "exhaustive application" of the "organon of pure reason," which he defines as "a sum total of those principles in accordance with which all pure *a priori* cognitions can be acquired and actually brought about."[14] But he admits that an organon "requires a lot" that cannot be accomplished while "it is still an open question whether such an amplification of our cognition is possible at all and in what cases it would be possible."[15] To answer this question, and lay the foundation for the system he hoped to construct, Kant holds that a critique must first determine whether and how much we can know *a priori*. He had already suggested as much when he defined his critique as a critique of the faculty of reason and indicated that this critique was necessary to determine the possibility of metaphysics in the Preface to the first (A) edition; yet the passage from the Introduction differs from the definition in the Preface, because it goes beyond the assertion of reason's rightful claims, the demonstration of our capacity for *a priori* cognition, and the transformation of the method of metaphysics. Kant's critique is also a special science that serves as "the propaedeutic to the system of pure reason" and "a preparation, if possible, for an organon, and, if this cannot be accomplished, then at least for a canon, in accordance with which the complete system of the philosophy of pure reason, whether it is to consist in the amplification or mere limitation of its cognition, can in any case at least someday be exhibited both analytically and synthetically."[16] The construction of this system is the ultimate goal of the critique of pure reason.

Kant indicates, in the passage from the Introduction, that the object of the "special science" that he presents in the first *Critique* is "pure reason" (*reine Vernunft*). Kant says cognition is "pure" (*rein*) when "no experience or sensation at all is mixed in, and that is thus fully *a priori*."[17] "Reason" (*Vernunft*) is defined in the Introduction as "the faculty that provides the principles of cognition *a priori*."[18] This definition is broad enough to include principles derived from the faculties of sensibility, the understanding, and reason, since the pure forms of sensible intuition (space and time), the pure concepts of the understanding (the categories), and the concepts of pure reason (the transcendental ideas) are all sources of *a priori* cognition.[19] The pure forms of sensible intuition and the pure concepts of the understanding are constitutive principles, because they are the universal and necessary conditions of the possibility of our knowledge and experience of objects.[20] The ideas of reason serve as regulative principles, guiding reason in its search for systematic order and unity in nature, even though their objects—God, freedom, and the immortality of the soul—cannot be given in experience.[21] None of the principles that Kant derives from the faculties of sensibility, the understanding, and reason are derived from experience or sensation, not even the pure forms of sensible intuition, so they can all be included in the system of "pure reason" as it is defined in the Introduction.

The same passage in the Introduction explains the relationship between Kant's critique, the system of pure reason, and transcendental philosophy. Kant uses the term "transcendental" to refer to cognition that is concerned "not so much with objects but rather with our *a priori* concepts of objects in general," so he defines transcendental philosophy as "a system of such concepts."[22] A few paragraphs later, he expands on this definition and says transcendental philosophy constitutes "a philosophy of pure, merely speculative reason," though it excludes "the concepts of pleasure and displeasure, of desires and inclinations, of choice."[23] Curiously, Kant thinks these practical concepts are related to feelings, "which belong among empirical sources of cognition," and, therefore, lack the purity that defines transcendental philosophy.[24] Even if transcendental philosophy is only concerned with the part of pure reason that is "merely speculative," which Kant seems to be using as a synonym for "theoretical" in this context, it is still included in the system of pure reason that he proposes earlier in the Introduction, since transcendental concepts are *a priori* cognitions. What is more, Kant says that the critique that is to lay the foundation for this system can be understood as a "transcendental critique," since it "does not aim at the amplification of the cognitions themselves, but only at their correction, and is to supply the touchstone of the worth or worthlessness of all cognitions *a priori*."[25] Transcendental critique must be distinguished from the "completed system of the philosophy of pure reason," but Kant insists that such a system is possible, because its object "is not the nature of things, which is inexhaustible, but the understanding, which judges about the nature of things, and this in turn only in regard to its *a priori* cognition."[26] Because we do not need to search for this cognition externally, in nature, but only in our own understanding, he concludes that it "cannot remain hidden from us."[27] He is also convinced that the quantity of this cognition is "small enough to be completely recorded, its worth or worthlessness assessed, and subjected to a correct appraisal," so he does not think the scope of the search for the *a priori* concepts that constitute transcendental philosophy and the *a priori* cognitions that belong to the system of pure reason will pose any impediment to completion of these systems.[28]

In the Introduction, Kant says transcendental philosophy is "only an idea, for which the critique of pure reason is to outline the entire plan **architectonically**, i.e., from principles, with a full guarantee for the completeness and certainty of all the components that comprise this edifice."[29] This statement is meant to emphasize, again, the propaedeutic nature of Kant's critique and the incompleteness of the system of pure reason. However, we get a glimpse of what Kant expected the completed edifice of the system of pure reason to look like in the chapter on The Architectonic of Pure Reason at the end of the first *Critique*. There Kant proposes to complete the task of his critique by "merely outlining the **architectonic** of all cognition from **pure reason**."[30] He begins by drawing distinctions between rational and empirical cognition, and then divides rational cognition into cognition from concepts and cognition from the construction of concepts, which allows him to distinguish philosophy from mathematics. Philosophy is a system of rational cognition from concepts, though it admits a distinction between a propaedeutic, which "investigates the faculty of reason in regard to all pure *a priori cognition*," and the system of pure reason itself, which contains the entirety of "philosophical cognition from pure reason in systematic interconnection." Kant identifies the former (propaedeutic) with critique and the latter (system) with metaphysics. Metaphysics may be further divided into "the metaphysics of the **speculative** and the **practical** use of pure reason and is therefore either **metaphysics of nature** or **metaphysics of morals**." Kant says the former "contains all rational principles from mere concepts (hence with the exclusion of mathematics) for the **theoretical** cognition of things; the latter, the principles which determine **action and omission** *a priori* and make them necessary."[31] This appears to contradict Kant's remarks about practical philosophy in the Introduction, since it suggests that practical concepts may be pure, rather than empirical, and, thus, may be included in a system of pure reason. But he clarifies, later in the Architectonic, that transcendental philosophy is a part of metaphysics in a "narrower sense," insofar as it "considers only the understanding and reason itself in a system of all concepts and principles that are related to objects in general, without assuming objects that **would be given** (*Ontologia*)." As such, it is only a part of the science of metaphysics, which extends beyond transcendental philosophy to include all of the principles of *a priori* cognition, whether they are derived from the faculties of sensibility, the understanding, or reason, and whether they are theoretical or practical. This conception of the science of metaphysics is identical, in both form and content, to the system of pure reason that Kant discussed in the Introduction.

In the years following the publication of the *Critique of Pure Reason*, Kant pursued a number of different projects. He published a revised second (B) edition of the first *Critique* in 1787, which was soon followed by a second *Critique* (*Critique of Practical Reason*, 1788) and a third *Critique* (*Critique of the Power of Judgment*, 1790). He also published numerous works on natural science, moral philosophy, religion, politics, and history, many of which were popular, several of which were controversial, and some of which were censored. He even began publishing textbooks based on lecture courses he had delivered on anthropology (*Anthropology from a Pragmatic Point of View*, 1798), logic (*Immanuel Kant's Logic*, 1800), physical geography (*Immanuel Kant's Physical Geography*, 1802), and pedagogy (*On Pedagogy*, 1803). Yet he never published the *Metaphysics of Nature* he promised in the first *Critique*, despite the fact that he had published the *Metaphysical Foundations of Natural Science* in 1786 and had begun working on the transition between the metaphysical foundations and the science of physics in 1796. Nor does the *Metaphysics of Morals* that he published 1797 present an exhaustive account of all the *a priori* principles of practical philosophy, as one would expect from a work with that title. The incompleteness of the system Kant had described in his Introduction and outlined in the Architectonic chapter was painfully obvious to post-Kantian philosophers like Reinhold and Fichte, despite their initial enthusiasm for Kant's critique.

3. Reinhold's Elementary Philosophy

Reinhold gained his reputation as a defender of Kant's philosophy through his *Letters on the Kantian Philosophy* (1786–1787, 1790, 1792), which first appeared in *Der Teutsche Merkur* in 1786–1787. In his *Letters*, Reinhold presents Kant's critique as the solution to two problems. Following Kant, Reinhold sees philosophy at the end of the eighteenth century as a "battleground of endless controversies," in which philosophers have embroiled themselves in pointless disputes, failed to answer the questions that matter the most, and, as a result, diminished the authority of reason. The pantheism controversy, which set the defenders of rational philosophy against the proponents of religious faith, was merely a local manifestation of a more global crisis of faith in reason.[32] Reinhold believed that both could be resolved through Kant's critique. By demonstrating the possibility of metaphysics, the impossibility of an apodictic proof of God's existence, and the practical necessity of faith in morality and religion, Reinhold thought Kant's critique had shown both sides of the pantheism controversy, the dogmatic rationalists as well as the religious skeptics, that philosophy could do justice to competing claims and resolve its "endless controversies."[33] In the process, Reinhold thought Kant had determined which questions philosophers could answer and which questions they could not, placing the authority of reason on a firm foundation for the first time.

The popular success of Reinhold's *Letters* won him Kant's support and a position as *Professor Extraordinarius* at the University of Jena, where he began lecturing on Kant's philosophy in 1787. In his essay "On What Has

Been Happening with the Kantian Philosophy" (1789), Reinhold shifts his focus from the salutary effects of Kant's critique for morality and religion to its theoretical achievements. He presents Kant's critique as a response to the decline of the Leibnizian-Wolffian philosophy and the rise of four new systems: Spinozist dogmatism; supernaturalism, inspired by Pascal; dogmatic skepticism, inspired by Hume; and a popular philosophy that remains indifferent to abstruse metaphysical questions.[34] Reinhold thinks Kant's first *Critique* refutes all these new systems by presenting a "complete and perfectly satisfying theory of the human cognitive faculty, the only possible source of universally accepted principles and the system of all systems founded on the nature of the human mind."[35] Reinhold contends that materialism and spiritualism are both refuted by Kant's critique, because both depend on claims about the nature of things in themselves. Nor can skepticism, in either its dogmatic or popular forms, be defended in the face of the "universally valid" principles of Kant's critique, which proves that metaphysics is possible. Yet that does not mean Kant's philosophy had or would achieve universal acceptance. Reinhold compares Kant's critique to the Protestant Reformation, which threatened everything that was supposed to be certain; Newtonian physics, whose mathematical sophistication perplexed its supporters as well as its critics; and the rise of Cartesian and Leibnizian-Wolffian philosophy, both of which were "initially rejected as unconditionally as they were subsequently adopted and advanced."[36] Given these historical precedents, Reinhold does not think we should be surprised that Kant's critique has not been "universally accepted."[37]

Despite his praise for Kant's critique, there is one point that Reinhold thinks Kant has overlooked. At the end of "On What Has Been Happening," Reinhold accuses Kant of presenting a theory of the human cognitive faculty that relies on a "merely presupposed" concept of representation (*Vorstellung*), even though Kant appeals to that concept "on every page" of the first *Critique*.[38] This realization led Reinhold to write works like his *Essay on a New Theory of the Human Faculty of Representation* (1789), *Contributions to the Correction of Previous Misunderstandings of the Philosophers* (1790/1794), and *On the Foundation of Philosophical Knowledge* (1791). Together, these works are often called Reinhold's "Elementary Philosophy" (*Elementarphilosophie*).[39] Each one is meant to define and defend the conception of representation that is missing from Kant's critique, relying solely on "consciousness as it functions in all people according to basic laws."[40] After arguing, in his *Essay on a New Theory*, that "it is absolutely impossible to reach agreement about the universally valid concept of the cognitive faculty while there is different thinking about the nature of the faculty of representation," Reinhold goes on to describe the nature of this faculty and the conception of representation that is associated with it.[41] The faculty of representation is, for Reinhold, the set of inner conditions that are necessary for representation.[42] In the end, he identifies the faculty of representation with consciousness, though he distinguishes consciousness from both the object that is represented in consciousness and the representing subject that possesses this consciousness.[43] The object that is represented constitutes the content of a representation, while the faculties of the representing subject determine the way that content will be represented—as sensation, thought, intuition, concept, or idea. Still, the subject and object of representation are both distinguished from one another and related to each another in our consciousness of a representation, so Reinhold concludes that consciousness itself is the ultimate condition of representation.

Reinhold repeatedly insists, in his *Essay on a New Theory* and in later works, that consciousness cannot be defined and is impossible to explain.[44] It is simply a *fact* that we are conscious and that the subject and object of our consciousness are related in representation.[45] Instead of trying to define or explain this fact through other terms, Reinhold argues, we should regard the terms that are employed in philosophical discourse and the logic of its arguments as conscious representations. As such, Reinhold thinks philosophical terms and arguments can be explained by the principle of consciousness, which states that "in consciousness, the subject distinguishes the representation from the subject and object and relates the representation to both."[46] In his *Contributions*, Reinhold calls this principle "the fundamental doctrine" and "first principle" of his Elementary Philosophy, because it explains the content and form of all our representations and cannot be explained by anything prior to our consciousness of a representation. Even the term "representation" and the claim "the principle of consciousness is the first principle of philosophy" must be understood as conscious representations, consisting of a subject and a object that are both distinguished and related by the subject in our consciousness of each representation. Consciousness is, thus, immediate and original.[47] It is the source and condition of all representations, of all cognitions, as well as the cognitive faculty that was the subject of Kant's critique. Since his Elementary Philosophy demonstrates a principle that is more fundamental than any of the principles Kant demonstrates in the first *Critique,* and upon which Kant's critique can be shown to depend,

Reinhold thinks the principle of consciousness justifies his claim to have presented a truly "elementary" philosophy—a philosophy so basic and so necessary for any other science that it can be identified with philosophy in itself and as such, what Reinhold will call "philosophy without surnames" in *On the Foundation*.[48]

Reinhold's *Contributions* and *On the Foundation* make the case for the principle of consciousness as the first principle of all philosophy and all science. Reinhold maintains, in these works, that Kant's critique is neither systematic nor scientific, because it is not grounded on a first principle like the principle of consciousness. Kant's distinction between critique and system comes to represent, for Reinhold, the partiality and uncertainty of his philosophy. For example, he argues in *On the Foundation* that, however successful Kant was in "demonstrating that the foundation of philosophical knowledge lies in the *possibility of experience*" in the first *Critique*, he still cannot deny that "his newly uncovered foundation fails to ground the *whole* of philosophical knowledge; on the contrary, it can only ground *one part* of it."[49] Reinhold explains that "the only part of philosophical knowledge that Kant grounded is that philosophical science properly called metaphysics," which is "the *science of objects proper*, that is to say, of objects that are distinguished in consciousness from all mere representations or the properties of representations."[50] Kant's critique demonstrates that "any metaphysics not meant to be the science of objects of possible experience is untenable, unfounded, and contradictory," but it remains merely a propaedeutic to the system and science of metaphysics, because it does not contain the "first principle . . . to which metaphysics owes its systematic unity and its rank as philosophical science."[51] Reinhold thinks he has provided this first principle, the principle of consciousness, in his Elementary Philosophy. Consequently, he takes himself to have completed what Kant's critique began, and to have finally discovered "the ultimate and proper foundation of philosophy" as a system and a science.[52]

The beginning of the second (1794) volume of the *Contributions* suggests that "the only possible system of scientific philosophy without surnames" is still "to come" (*künftige*) and can only be constructed "bit by bit" (*nach und nach*). Reinhold could be said to have made some progress toward the completion of his system through the discussions of the foundations of morality, religion, and taste in the second volume of his *Contributions*; however, he does not derive any of these foundations from the principle of consciousness, so their relation to the Elementary Philosophy as a whole remains unclear. His subsequent vacillations between Fichtean idealism (1798), the realism of C. G. Bardili (1800), and the philosophy of language in his later works (1806) further suggest that Reinhold's Elementary Philosophy suffered the same fate as Kant's critique—a propaedeutic to an unfinished system.

4. Fichte's *Wissenschaftslehre*

Like Reinhold, Fichte first became known to the German public as a Kantian. In 1792, he anonymously published his *Attempt at a Critique of All Revelation*, in which he tries to demonstrate the possibility of revelation from *a priori* principles and establish the criteria necessary for distinguishing true revelations from false ones.[53] The work was thought by many to be Kant's own, until Kant publicly identified Fichte as the author in a letter he published in the *Allegemeine Literatur Zeitung*.[54] On the strength of this publication, and the apparent endorsement of Kant's statement concerning its authorship, Fichte was appointed to the position Reinhold had vacated at the University of Jena when he moved to Kiel in 1793. Before he took up his new position, however, Fichte spent several months in Zurich studying Reinhold's Elementary Philosophy. Fichte's notes from this period are contained in his *Personal Meditations on Elementary Philosophy/Practical Philosophy* (1793/1794), which show a great deal of sympathy for Reinhold's philosophy, but also reveal his concerns about the principle of consciousness. At several points in the *Personal Meditations*, Fichte notes that the principle of consciousness seems to presuppose the concept of the "I." He also points out that the concepts of the self, consciousness, and representation depend on one another and constitute a circle, instead of being derived from a single foundational principle.[55]

Fichte's ambivalence about Reinhold became public in a review of Gottlob Ernst Schulze's *Aenesidemus, Or Concerning the Foundations of Professor Reinhold's Elementary Philosophy, Together with a Defense of Skepticism Against the Pretensions of the Critique of Reason* (1792). Schulze had raised a number of objections to Reinhold's principle of consciousness, noting, first, that it is "not an absolutely first principle," since it is a proposition and, as such, its validity is established by logic and, at the most basic level, by the principle of non-contradiction; second, that the principle of consciousness is "not a proposition completely determined through itself," because it is determined by the distinctions and relations between the subjects and objects of our representations; and, finally, that the principle of consciousness does not "express a fact" that is beyond definition or explanation.[56] Fichte responds to each of these objections in his review. He argues that Reinhold is right to think that the principle of non-contradiction is founded on the principle of consciousness, since the formal validity of logic must be established through an examination of the relation between the subject and object of a representation in consciousness.[57] Fichte also defends Reinhold against the charge that the principle of consciousness is not self-determining on the grounds that distinctions and relations must be understood through the concepts of identity and difference, which are grounded in our consciousness of a representation. It is only within this consciousness, and not outside it, that the distinctions and relations between the subject and object of a representation can be determined.[58] However, Fichte will concede that Schulze is right when he says that the principle of consciousness cannot be regarded as a "fact" of consciousness. Fichte says he is "convinced that the principle of consciousness is a theorem which is based on another first principle, from which, however, the principle of consciousness can be strictly derived, *a priori*, and independently of all experience."[59] "Such a principle does not have to express a fact," he continues, "it can also express an act."[60] The rest of his review suggests that the first principle to which he refers is an act of intellectual intuition through which the subject an object of empirical representation are "originally posited" in our consciousness by an "absolute subject."[61] Although this act differs in important ways from Reinhold's principle of consciousness, Fichte thinks it performs the same function as Reinhold's principle. As the ultimate condition of the possibility of representation, it can be regarded as the first principle of all of philosophy as a system and a science.

Fichte published *Concerning the Concept of the Wissenschaftslehre* (1794) as an introduction to the system that would be based on his new first principle. In the Preface, he pays tribute to Kant's "spirit of genius" as well as Reinhold's "systematic spirit" before introducing his own system, which goes by the name *Wissenschaftslehre*. This title could be translated literally as "Doctrine of Science," but Fichte often says it could simply be called "science" (*die Wissenschaft*) or "the science of science in general" (*die Wissenschaft von einer Wissenschaft überhaupt*).[62] Instead of trying to survey the whole of his "science of science" in *Concerning the Concept*, Fichte presents the work as a "critique" similar to Kant's *Critique of Pure Reason*. According to Fichte, critique is "not metaphysics, but lies beyond metaphysics. It is related to metaphysics in exactly the same way that metaphysics is related to the ordinary point of view, and metaphysics is itself explained by critique."[63] This is actually a novel conception of critique, because it implies that a critique is not merely a propaedeutic to a system, but rather that it has an explanatory function. Instead of formulating and presenting the basic principles from which subsequent principles can be derived, Fichte thinks his "critique" of the *Wissenschaftslehre* "describes the relation of the *Wissenschaftslehre* to ordinary knowledge and to those sciences which are possible from the standpoint of ordinary knowledge, and it describes this in terms of the content of knowledge."[64] To this end, Fichte focuses on the form and content of scientific knowledge; the need for an absolutely certain first principle; how such a principle can be demonstrated; and how the principles of every other science can be derived from an absolutely first principle. He does not develop his account of the act that posits a representation in consciousness and distinguishes the subject (I) and object (not-I) of that representation. Nor does Fichte defend his reference to intellectual intuition in the *Review of Aenesidemus* from the objections Kant, Reinhold, and their followers might have raised against the appeal to a faculty whose existence Kant had denied in the *Critique of Pure Reason*.[65] Those arguments are reserved for a later presentation of the *Wissenschaftslehre*, because Fichte thinks they are part of the *Wissenschaftslehre* and would, as such, be out of place in a critique that explains what it means for the *Wissenschaftslehre* to be a "science of science."

It could be argued that Fichte never finished his *Wissenschaftslehre*, just as Kant never finished the system of pure reason he promised in the first *Critique*. Unlike Kant, however, Fichte attempted, on a number of different occasions, to present the whole of his "science of science." His first attempt, published as *Foundations of the Entire Wissenschaftslehre* (1794–1795), contains extensive discussions of the "first, absolutely unconditioned principle" of the *Wissenschaftslehre* along with the foundational principles of theoretical and practical philosophy. It is in this work that Fichte defends the claims he first advanced in the *Review of Aenesidemus*, arguing, for example, that the act of self-positing by the absolute I constitutes the "absolutely unconditioned first principle" of the *Wissenschaftslehre*, because all human knowledge depends on the existence of consciousness (I am) and its identity (I am I) to determine the form and content of the relationship between the subject (I) and object (not-I) of our representations. Unless we recognize this act of self-positing as the ultimate condition of all knowledge, Fichte thinks we are doomed to a kind of dogmatism that denies our freedom and turns the subject into an object—a conclusion that

Fichte believes even the most consistent dogmatist, like Spinoza, could not actually accept.[66] Similarly, he argues that this first principle must be given through intellectual intuition, because any thought or action can be shown, upon reflection, to depend on an immediate awareness of oneself, not only as the subject that represents an object, but as the consciousness that unites subject and object within itself, through its own activity—a position that Fichte identifies with idealism, the counterpoint to Spinozist dogmatism.[67] It is on the basis of these arguments that Fichte proceeds to discuss the principles of theoretical philosophy, which explain the reciprocal determination of subject (I) and object (not-I) in any act of representation; and practical philosophy, which concern the activity of the subject (I) to determine the object (not-I) in accordance with its own ends.[68]

Instead of proceeding to a more articulated division of the kinds and parts of theoretical and practical philosophy, Fichte's next contribution to the *Wissenschaftslehre* presented the same material according to a new method. He hoped this would make his work more comprehensible to those who remained unconvinced by the *Foundations*, but he apparently failed to achieve this lofty goal. Fichte abandoned his *Attempt at a New Presentation of the Wissenschaftslehre* (1797) after publishing two introductions and a first chapter. Subsequent presentations of the *Wissenschaftslehre* suffered the same fate. Even if Fichte was convinced that his deductions were "universally valid," they never attained the "universal acceptance" he thought they deserved, so, instead of moving on and completing his system, he returned to the same material again and again in a futile attempt to make his readers understand.

5. Critique, System, Science

Kant responded to the charges, leveled by Reinhold and Fichte, that he had failed to complete the system he had promised in his "Declaration Concerning Fichte's *Wissenschaftslehre*" (1799). Kant's *Declaration*, published in the same journal in which he had identified Fichte as the author of the *Attempt at a Critique of All Revelation*, denounces the *Wissenschaftslehre* as a "totally indefensible system" and maintains that the "pure theory of science (*reine Wissenschaftslehre*) is nothing more than logic, which is purely formal and cannot lead to any material knowledge of objects, and is, therefore, completely inadequate to the task of constructing a system and science of metaphysics.[69] Kant also declares the charge that "I have intended to publish only a *propaedeutic* to transcendental philosophy and not the actual system of this philosophy" to be "incomprehensible," since "I have praised the completed whole of pure philosophy in the *Critique of Pure Reason* as the best indication of its truth."[70] It remains unclear whether Kant now wants his readers to think the first *Critique* contains the completed system of pure reason or whether his affirmation of the possibility of completing such a system in the first *Critique* is to be treated as evidence of his commitment to going beyond a mere propaedeutic. The former would contradict a number of statements he made in the first *Critique*, where Kant explicitly said that his critique was only a propaedeutic to the system of pure reason and the science of metaphysics, but it was defended by several of Kant's followers.[71] The latter would highlight his failure to complete the *Metaphysics of Nature* and the gap that separates the *Metaphysics of Morals* he had published in 1797 and the one he had promised in the Architectonic chapter of the first *Critique*. Neither of these interpretations would have satisfied his critics, nor did they stop the German idealists from pursuing new and even more radical conceptions of system and science than Reinhold and Fichte.

Kant's praise for "the completed whole of pure philosophy" would not have satisfied Reinhold, because, no matter how much Reinhold admired Kant, and no matter how much he had already departed from the original plan for his Elementary Philosophy by the time Kant published his *Declaration*, the point of Reinhold's criticism is that a propaedeutic is not enough. Kant had failed to complete the system of pure reason his critique had not only praised but promised. Even if Kant had made more progress toward the completion of *The Metaphysics of Nature* and *The Metaphysics of Morals* than he actually did, Reinhold's criticism still would have argued that Kant's critique had not laid their foundation properly.

Kant's system was supposed to be grounded in a small set of *a priori* principles, which he took to be satisfactory, as long as their universality and necessity could be demonstrated and other *a priori* principles of theoretical and practical philosophy could be derived from them. Reinhold's conception of a system was more radically foundationalist than Kant's. Reinhold thinks a system should be—indeed, has to be—derived from a single, first principle—a principle that not only precedes every other principle in the system, but determines them, without having been determined by them. This poses numerous challenges for the construction and defense of the Elementary Philosophy, since Reinhold insists that its first principle have to precede and determine the validity of basic logical principles such as the principle of non-contradiction. Yet he still insists, at least during the late 1780s and early 1790s, that the principle of consciousness could meet this challenge and ground a system in a way that Kant's critique could not. That is why, in a chapter on the relationship between his theory of the faculty of representation and Kant's critique in the first volume of the *Contributions* (1790), Reinhold argues that the principle of consciousness is prior to Kant's accounts of sensibility, concepts, and ideas in the first *Critique*.[72] It is also the reason why Reinhold thinks his Elementary Philosophy remains faithful to the spirit of Kant's critique. By providing Kant's critique, and, indeed, all of philosophy with a foundation, the Elementary Philosophy is taking an important step toward the completion of the system of "pure philosophy" that Kant had outlined in the *Critique of Pure Reason*.

It is likely that Fichte would have echoed these sentiments, though he would have had additional reasons to object to Kant's *Declaration*. Fichte follows Reinhold in maintaining that even the most basic logical principles, like the principle of non-contradiction, have to be derived from a more basic philosophical principle, so he would reject Kant's claim that the "pure theory of science" (*reine Wissenschaftslehre*) is "nothing more than logic." He would also reject Kant's claim that the *Wissenschaftslehre* is "purely formal" and "cannot lead to any material knowledge of objects." Fichte insists, in *Concerning the Concept*, that "a science is supposed to be something unified and whole," so he denies that the *Wissenschaftslehre* is "purely formal."[73] Indeed, he maintains that the *Wissenschaftslehre* grounds both the formal and material dimensions of science, its method as well as its content, since both are necessary for scientific knowledge. Fichte also contends that the *Wissenschaftslehre* provides the foundational principles necessary for knowledge of objects and discusses these principles at length in the second part of the *Foundations*, which is devoted to theoretical philosophy.

However, Fichte also thinks it is necessary for the *Wissenschaftslehre* to go beyond these principles to explain "the possibility of any first principles whatsoever—to show how, to what extent, under what conditions, and perhaps to what degree anything at all can be certain, as well as what the phrase '*to be certain*' means."[74] It is this explanation that makes the *Wissenschaftslehre* critical, since Fichte thinks a critique concerns "the possibility, the real meaning, and the rules governing such a science" as philosophy or metaphysics.[75] Thus it could be argued that, in addition to failing to complete the system of pure reason that he announced in the first *Critique*, Kant also failed to make metaphysics a science because he misunderstood the conditions under which a part of philosophy like metaphysics could become a science. For Fichte, the ultimate foundation of scientific knowledge is not the pure forms of intuition or the pure concepts of the understanding, but a free act of the absolute I that posits both the I and the not-I, their differences as well as their relations. Even if Fichte's account of this act is inspired by Kant and remains "in the spirit" of Kant's critique, it also implies that Kant's critique remains incomplete both as a theory of science and as a system.

Notes

1. Johann Gottlieb Fichte, *Early Philosophical Writings*, ed. and trans. Daniel Breazeale (Ithaca, NY: Cornell University Press, 1988), 96.

2. George di Giovanni and H.S. Harris, *Between Kant and Hegel: Texts in the Development of Post-Kantian Idealism*, revised edition (Indianapolis, IN: Hackett, 2000), 278.

3. Immanuel Kant, *Critique of Pure Reason*, ed. and trans. Paul Guyer and Allen W. Wood (New York: Cambridge University Press, 1998), Bxv. All references to Kant's first *Critique* use the standard A/B pagination of the first (1781, A) and second (1787, B) editions. References to Kant's other works cite the volume in which the work is included in Immanuel Kant, *The Cambridge Edition of the Works of Immanuel Kant in Translation*, ed. Paul Guyer and Allen W. Wood (Cambridge: Cambridge University Press, 1992–2016). They are accompanied by a parenthetical reference to the volume and page number (indicated with *Ak.*) of the passage in Immanuel Kant, *Kant's gesammelte Schriften (Akademie Ausgabe)*, ed. Royal Prussian (later German) Academy of Sciences (Berlin: Georg Reimer, later Walter de Gruyter, 1900–).

4. Kant, *Critique of Pure Reason*, A12/B25.

5. Kant, *Critique of Pure Reason*, A10/B24, A841/B869.

6. Immanuel Kant, *Correspondence*, ed. and trans. Arnulf Zweig (Cambridge: Cambridge University Press, 1999), 229 (*Ak.* 10:406).

7. Immanuel Kant, *Practical Philosophy*, ed. and trans. Mary Gregor (New York: Cambridge University Press, 1996), 365 (*Ak.* 6:205–206).

8. Kant, *Critique of Pure Reason*, A11/B24–25.

9. I focus in this section on Kant's system as a system of pure reason, because this is the first description of his system in the first *Critique*. An alternative account of Kant's system as a system of the unity of nature and freedom is to be found in other works. See Paul Guyer, *Kant's System of Nature and Freedom* (Oxford: Oxford University Press, 2005), esp. 277–313. In the end, I think Kant considered the system of pure reason and the system of nature and freedom to be the same, but the difference between the two accounts should be noted.

10. Kant, *Critique of Pure Reason*, Axi. See also J. Colin McQuillan, *Immanuel Kant: The Very Idea of a Critique of Pure Reason* (Evanston, IL: Northwestern University Press, 2016), 65–70.

11. Kant, *Critique of Pure Reason*, Axii. See also McQuillan, *Immanuel Kant*, 70–77.

12. Kant, *Critique of Pure Reason*, Bxxii. See also McQuillan, *Immanuel Kant*, 78–86.

13. Kant, *Critique of Pure Reason*, A10–A12/B23–B25. See also McQuillan, *Immanuel Kant*, 86–88.

14. Kant, *Critique of Pure Reason*, A11/B24.

15. Ibid., A11/B25.

16. Ibid., A12/B26.

17. Ibid., A10/B24.

18. Ibid.

19. There is a long tradition in the scholarly literature of distinguishing between broader and narrower conceptions of reason in Kant's critique. The definition of pure reason that Kant presents in the Introduction would be, perhaps, the broadest conception of reason he employs, since it could include cognition from the faculties of sensibility and the understanding as well as reason. The definition of reason in the Transcendental Dialectic, where Kant calls reason "the faculty of the unity of the rules of the understanding under principles," presents a much narrower and more specific conception of reason than we find in the Introduction, insofar as it does not include all *a priori* cognition. See Kant, *Critique of Pure Reason*, A10/B24, A302/B359. See also Hans Vaihinger, *Commentar zu Kants Kritik der reinen Vernunft* (Stuttgart: Spemann Verlag, 1881), 1:116–118.

20. Kant, *Critique of Pure Reason*, A178–179/B221.

21. Ibid., A327/B383–384.

22. Ibid., A11/B25.

23. Ibid., A14/B28.

24. Ibid., A15/B29. This is notably at odds with what Kant says about practical concepts elsewhere in his moral philosophy. See, for example, the *Groundwork of the Metaphysics of Morals*, where Kant distinguishes between practical concepts that occur "only *a posteriori* or *a priori* as well," indicating that there are non-empirical practical concepts. See also the *Critique of Practical Reason*, where Kant warns against the "empiricism of practical reason, which places the practical concepts of good and evil merely in experiential consequences (so-called happiness)." Kant, *Practical Philosophy*, 46, 197 (*Ak.* 4:391 and *Ak.* 5:70).

25. Kant, *Critique of Pure Reason*, A12/B26.

26. Ibid., A13/B26.

27. Ibid.

28. Ibid.

29. Ibid., A13/B27.

30. Ibid., A835/864.

31. Ibid., A841/B869.

32. On the relationship between Reinhold's *Letters* and the Pantheism controversy, see Frederick Beiser, *The Fate of Reason: German Philosophy from Kant to Fichte* (Cambridge: Harvard University Press, 1987), 332–336.

33. Kant, *Critique of Pure Reason*, Aviii.

34. Karl Leonhard Reinhold, *Essay on a New Theory of the Human Capacity for Representation*, trans. Tim Mehigan and Barry Empson (Berlin: Walter de Gruyter, 2011), 7. Karl Ameriks has suggested that the title of Reinhold's preface to the *Essay on a New Theory* ("On What Has Been Happening with the Kantian Philosophy") as well as his tendency to frame philosophical problems in relation to historical developments in the *Letters*, *Essay on a New Theory*, and (perhaps most notably) the *Contributions*, are indicative of "a constant and explicit attempt to confront the chaotic character of philosophy as a historical enterprise" that Ameriks takes to be novel. See Karl Ameriks, *Kant and the Historical Turn: Philosophy as Critical Interpretation* (New York: Oxford University Press, 2006), 194. Hegel sharply criticized Reinhold for this tendency in his *Differenzschrift*, where he calls Reinhold's philosophy "a bit of contemporary flotsam in time's stream." See Georg Wilhelm Friedrich Hegel, *The Difference between Fichte's and Schelling's System of Philosophy*, ed. and trans. H. S. Harris and Walter Cerf (Albany: State University of New York Press, 1977), 82.

35. Reinhold, *Essay on a New Theory*, 7–8 (translation modified).

36. Ibid., 10–16.

37. Ibid., 11.

38. Ibid., 25–26. Reinhold elaborates on this point at much greater length in Karl Leonhard Reinhold, *Beiträge zur Berichtigung bisheriger Mißverständnisse der Philosophen*, ed. Faustino Fabbianelli (Hamburg: Felix Meiner Verlag, 2004), 1:179–228.

39. There is some disagreement in the scholarly literature about whether Reinhold's *Essay on a New Theory* and the second (1794) volume of his *Contributions* belong to the Elementary Philosophy. Commentators rightly note that Reinhold does not mention or propose an Elementary Philosophy in *Essay on a New Theory*, though its content is clearly continuous with the first (1790) volume of the *Contributions* and *On the Foundation*. Some also maintain that the changes Reinhold introduces in the second volume of the *Contributions* are substantial enough to constitute a "new" Elementary Philosophy. See the introductions by Faustino Fabbianelli in Reinhold, *Beiträge (I)*, xvi–xxv and *Beiträge (II)*, xi–xxiii. See also Elise Frketich, "Reinhold's Elementarphilosophie: A Scholastic of Critical Philosophical System?" *Kant Yearbook* 8 (2016): 17–18. The most detailed and comprehensive account of the development of Reinhold's Elementary Philosophy remains Martin Bondeli, *Das Anfangsproblem bei Karl Leonhard Reinhold* (Frankfurt am Main: Vittorio Klostermann, 1995).

40. Reinhold, *Essay on a New Theory*, 26.
41. Ibid., 86 (translation modified).
42. Ibid., 89.
43. Ibid., 92.
44. Ibid., 105. See also di Giovanni and Harris, *Between Kant and Hegel*, 71–72 (80–82).
45. Reinhold, *Beiträge (I)*, 98–100. See also Di Giovanni and Harris, *Between Kant and Hegel*, 70 (77–78).
46. Ibid., 113.
47. Ibid.
48. Di Giovanni and Harris, *Between Kant and Hegel*, 93.
49. Ibid., 64.
50. Ibid.
51. Ibid., 66.
52. Ibid., 67–68.
53. Johann Gottlieb Fichte, *Attempt at a Critique of All Revelation*, trans. Garrett Green, ed. Allen Wood (Cambridge: Cambridge University Press, 2010), 131–134.
54. Kant, *Ak.* 12: 359–360. Kant published "Über den Verfasser" in the *Allgemeine Literatur Zeitung* in response to a review published in the journal that attributed the work to him. Kant states that "the author of *Attempt at a Critique of All Revelation* is someone who visited Königsberg for a short time last year, a native of Lusatia, who is now tutor to the Count of Krockow, in Krockow in West Prussia, standing candidate in Theology, Mr. Fichte, as one can see from this year's Easter catalog from Mr. Hartung of Königsberg, his publisher. Moreover, neither in writing nor verbally do I have anything to do with this work by the skillful man, as [indicated by] the notice in the *Allgemeine Literatur Zeitung*."
55. Johann Gottlieb Fichte, *Gesamtausgabe der Bayerischen Akademie der Wissenschaften* (hereafter cited as *GA*), ed. Erich Fuchs, Hans Gliwitzky, Reinhard Lauth, and Peter K. Schneider (Stuttgart: Frommann-Holzboog, 1962–2012), 2.3:26.
56. Fichte, *Early Philosophical Writings*, 61–62.
57. Ibid.
58. Ibid., 62.
59. Ibid., 64.
60. Ibid.
61. Ibid.
62. Ibid., 106.
63. Ibid., 97.
64. Ibid., 98. Günter Zöller helpfully calls this conception of critique a "metacritique" in Günter Zöller, "From Critique to Metacritique: Fichte's Transformation of Kant's Transcendental Idealism," in *The Reception of Kant's Critical Philosophy*, ed. Sally Sedgwich (New York: Cambridge University Press, 2000), 129–146.

65. Some discussion of the (three!) first principles of the *Wissenschaftslehre* is included in Part III: Hypothetical Division of the *Wissenschaftslehre* in *Concerning the Concept*, but this amounts to only the end of a paragraph indicating that the theoretical and practical parts of the *Wissenschaftslehre* depend on them. See Fichte, *Early Philosophical Writings*, 135 (1:66).

66. Johann Gottlieb Fichte, *The Science of Knowledge*, ed. and trans. Peter Heath and John Lachs (New York: Cambridge University Press, 1982), 81–82.

67. On the difference between dogmatism and idealism, see Fichte, *The Science of Knowledge*, 8–28. On Fichte's appeals to intellectual intuition, see Dieter Henrich, "Fichte's Original Insight," trans. David Lachterman, *Contemporary German Philosophy* 1 (1982), 15–52. See also Daniel Breazeale, *Thinking through the Wissenschaftslehre: Themes from Fichte's Early Philosophy* (New York: Oxford University Press, 2014), 197–229.

68. Fichte, *The Science of Knowledge*, 122–123.

69. Kant, *Correspondence*, 559 (*Ak.* 12:370). Although he also found Reinhold's Elementary Philosophy to be "weighed down with obscure abstractions" and warned his correspondents about his "hypercritical friends Fichte and Reinhold," Kant refrained from criticizing Reinhold in print and even discouraged Beck from writing a work critical of Reinhold, because he had done so much to promote Kant's critique through his *Letters on the Kantian Philosophy*. See Kant, *Correspondence*, 392, 394, 528 (*Ak.* 11:291, 304; 12:207).

70. Kant, *Correspondence*, 559–560 (*Ak.* 12:371, translation modified).

71. The view that the *Critique of Pure Reason* constituted a system was defended by Johann Schultz and Jacob Sigismund Beck. See McQuillan, *Immanuel Kant*, 119.

72. Reinhold, *Beiträge (I)*, 181–228, esp. 209–228.

73. Fichte, *Early Philosophical Writings*, 102.

74. Ibid., 108.

75. Ibid., 97.

6

Schelling's Philosophical Letters on Doctrine and Critique

G. ANTHONY BRUNO

My whole tendency and I believe the tendency of all men who ever tried to write or talk Ethics or Religion was to run against the boundaries of language. This running against the walls of our cage is perfectly, absolutely hopeless. Ethics so far as it springs from the desire to say something about the ultimate meaning of life, the absolute good, the absolute valuable, can be no science. What it says does not add to our knowledge in any sense. But it is a document of a tendency in the human mind which I personally cannot help respecting deeply and I would not for my life ridicule it.

—Wittgenstein, "A Lecture on Ethics"[1]

I can only say: I don't belittle this human tendency; I take my hat off to it. And here it is essential that this is not a sociological description but that I speak *for myself*.

—Wittgenstein, in Waismann, "Notes on Talks with Wittgenstein"[2]

1. Introduction

In 1795 and 1796, Schelling published an essay in two parts in *Philosophical Journal of a Society of German Scholars*, co-edited by Fichte and

Niethammer. While they appeared under the familiar title *Philosophical Letters on Dogmatism and Criticism* (*Philosophische Briefe über Dogmatismus und Kriticismus*), the first part was originally entitled *Philosophical Letters on Dogmaticism and Criticism* (*Philosophische Briefe über Dogmaticismus und Kriticismus*). Without informing Schelling, Niethammer replaced "Dogmaticism" with "Dogmatism," assuming the author had intended a term more common among philosophers and germane to readers of Kant.[3] Additionally, the text's English translation mistranslates "Dogmaticismus" as "dogmatism" at two key junctures.[4] These historical matters obscure what is, in fact, an important philosophical matter, namely, Schelling's appropriation of Kant's distinction between critique and doctrine in the former's attack on dogmaticism.

The *Letters* repurpose Kant's distinction in response to the surging interest in philosophical systematicity in Germany in the 1780s and 1790s. They argue that a system is constituted by "perpetual striving," an activity whose goal is "the object of an endless task."[5] According to Schelling, critique furnishes the method of striving for any system, including dogmatism—by which he means Spinozism. Critique secures this method by investigating the subject's essence, namely, the freedom by which she lives the system of her choice. Critique accordingly favors no system, not even criticism—by which Schelling means Fichteanism. By contrast, dogmaticism flouts critique by asserting the actual attainment of doctrinal or systematic knowledge. Dogmaticism mistakes a system for "an object of *knowledge*" rather than "an object of *freedom*," indulging a delusion to which Schelling thinks critics and dogmatists—Fichteans and Spinozists—are equally susceptible.[6]

Removing publication and translation errors surrounding the *Letters* reveals that whereas "dogmatism" and "criticism" refer to the systems of Spinoza and Fichte involved in the pantheism controversy of the late eighteenth century, "dogmaticism" invokes one of Kant's chief methodological distinctions. As we will see, Schelling relies on the distinction between critique and doctrine in asserting that the *Critique of Pure Reason* provides the "universal methodology" by which alone Spinozism and Fichteanism may be authentic systems for living.[7]

In section 2, I articulate Kant's distinction between critique and doctrine. In section 3, I explicate Fichte's claim for the identity of critique and doctrine, which rests on his idea of intellectual intuition. In sections 4 and 5, I account for Schelling's rejection of Fichte's identity claim by reconstructing the *Letters*' two-step argument that critique concerns the spirit in which one pursues a system and that this pursuit is inconsistent with intellectual intuition. According to this argument, a system is nothing beyond our activity of striving to realize it practically—nothing beyond its livability—and insofar as intellectual intuition feigns this activity's completion—its achievement of a doctrine—it is dogmaticist and thus unlivable. We will see that this argument expresses the *Letters*' metaphilosophical pluralism, a commitment to the valid multiplicity of systems, which Schelling defends often throughout his career.

2. Kant's Distinction

In the Preface to the first *Critique*, Kant provides a definition of a critique of reason that is meant to orient the reader through the text as a whole. He says that our power of judgment demands of reason "the most difficult of all its tasks, namely, that of self-knowledge, and to institute a court of justice, by which reason may secure its rightful claims while dismissing all its groundless pretensions, and this not by mere decrees but according to its own eternal and unchangeable laws; and this court is none other than the critique of pure reason itself."[8] Self-knowledge is described in this definition as the absence of delusion regarding the claims to which reason is entitled. Self-knowledge is furthermore portrayed as emerging from a trial in which reason's claims are pressed for their entitlement. So defined, a critique of reason may appear to consist strictly in providing a transcendental deduction in response to the question *quid juris* regarding reason's right to the categories, a right which grounds the possibility of judgments that are universal and necessary yet ampliative. This appearance would agree with the idea that the first *Critique* must solve what, in the Introduction, Kant calls the "real problem of pure reason," namely, the possibility of synthetic *a priori* judgments.[9]

However, Kant clarifies his definition in the next sentence: "by this I do not understand a critique of books and systems, but a critique of the faculty of reason in general, in respect of all the cognitions after which reason might strive independently of all experience, and hence the decision about the possibility or impossibility of a metaphysics in general, and the determination of its sources, as well as its extent and boundaries, all, however, from principles."[10] According to this clarification, critique includes, yet exceeds, the "real problem of pure reason," for while it must solve this problem by determining the "sources" of reason's *a priori* cognitions, it must also determine the "boundaries" of such cognitions. As Kant says in the Discipline of Pure Reason, "philosophy consists precisely in knowing its bounds."[11] Thus, the sort of self-knowledge attained through critique is knowledge of oneself within one's proper cognitive limitations.

Kant's full definition of a critique of reason helps to clarify his later assertion that "without critique" nothing can "bring [us] to self-knowledge."[12] It also serves to contextualize his distinction between critique and doctrine.

In the Preface and Introduction, Kant assigns critique a methodological function. He says that critique aims "to transform the accepted procedure of metaphysics," calling it a "method" that "catalogues the entire outline of the science of metaphysics, both in respect of its boundaries and in respect of its entire internal structure."[13] This method assesses "the worth or worthlessness of all cognitions *a priori*," which has the "negative" utility of correcting the use of pure reason. Critique thus differs from doctrine, which, beyond a mere corrective, purports to amplify cognitions of pure reason through an organon. Whereas cataloging the *a priori* principles of reason's correct use yields a "canon," an "organon of pure reason would be a sum total of those principles in accordance with which all pure *a priori* cognitions can be acquired and actually brought about. The exhaustive application of such an organon would create a system of pure reason." By asserting the "exhaustive application" of *a priori* principles in an organon, a doctrine lays claim to metaphysics as a science. Critique, by contrast, is simply "the propaedeutic to the system of pure reason."[14]

Doctrine expresses what Kant calls the "prejudice" that speculative reason can make progress in metaphysics without critique, a prejudice he labels "dogmatism."[15] Dogmatism is a state of self-delusion in which reason's habit of "groundless pretensions" "leads to groundless assertions" and "thus to skepticism."[16] Hence, it impairs philosophy's "aim of revealing the deceptions of a reason that misjudges its own boundaries and of bringing the self-conceit of speculation back to modest but thorough self-knowledge by means of a sufficient illumination of our concepts."[17] Without self-knowledge secured through critique, reason's maturation stalls at the "childhood" of dogmatism.[18]

Kant connects the foregoing concepts in the Analytic of Principles: "although, for the expansion of the role of the understanding in the field of pure cognitions *a priori*, hence as a doctrine, philosophy seems entirely unnecessary or rather ill-suited, since after all its previous attempts little or no territory has been won, yet as critique . . . philosophy with all of its perspicacity and art of scrutiny is called up (even though its utility is then only negative)."[19] The endless controversies and inevitable skepticism to which dogmatism leads show that philosophy, which consists in "knowing its bounds," is best suited for self-knowledge rather than self-delusion—for critique instead of doctrine.

3. Fichte's Identity Claim

Although Fichte claims to inherit the spirit of Kant's philosophy, he predicates his *Wissenschaftslehre* on *identifying* critique and doctrine, not differentiating them. It is crucial to grasp Fichte's argument for this identity claim if we are to comprehend Schelling's defense of Kant's distinction in the *Letters*. First, in 1794 Schelling publishes and sends Fichte *On the Possibility of a Form of Philosophy in General*, which is indebted to Fichte's *On the Concept of the Wissenschaftslehre* published that year. Fichte then sends Schelling fascicles of *Foundations of the Entire Wissenschaftslehre*, inspiring Schelling in 1795 to write *Of the I as Principle of Philosophy*. Thus, by the time Schelling writes the *Letters*, he is steeped in Fichte's work. Second, the *Letters* attack the idea of intellectual intuition and the idea that critique secures more than the method for philosophy. Since both of these ideas support Fichte's argument for the identity of critique and doctrine, their development in his early Jena texts bears considerably on our understanding of Schelling's rejection of the identity claim.

We can see in a prefatory way that the *Wissenschaftslehre* is critical, insofar as it defines our "first demand" as the turn toward the first-person standpoint, yet doctrinal, insofar as it sets as our first "task" the grounding of a systematic account of experience on a first principle.[20] On the one hand, it is by a critical turn inward that we determine the conditions of experience. Our first demand is thus, not only the Kantian requirement of securing reason's right to its claims, but the equally Kantian requirement of regarding reason as self-determining in the deduction of this right, as subject and object of critique. As Fichte says in *On the Concept*, his science "is not something that exists independently of us and without our help. On the contrary, it is something which can only be produced by the freedom of our mind."[21] On the other hand, critique is not merely the propaedeutic to a system. Fichte transforms critique into a system grounded on a first principle, namely, the absolute freedom of reason or "the I."[22] Enshrining freedom as a first principle is necessary to refute dogmatism, the system that nihilistically rules out human freedom. Fichte describes dogmatism in the *Foundations* as "appealing to the supposedly higher concept of the *thing*" or "the not-I." Positing such a principle is *"transcendent*, since it goes on beyond the I. So far as dogmatism can be consistent, Spinozism is its most logical outcome."[23] Dogmatism is refutable only if philosophy's first principle can be known to be the I and the *Wissenschaftslehre* thereby proven to be the one true doctrine.

Positing a first principle depends, as Fichte says in the 1797/98 *Attempt at a New Presentation of the Wissenschaftslehre*, on the kind of person one is.[24] This may tempt us to ascribe to him the view that one may legitimately endorse dogmatism and genuinely live as a Spinozist. Yet we find that, for Fichte, one is either a willful or a failed idealist. In the *Foundations*, he says that there is "no explaining how any thinker should ever have been able to go beyond the I . . . if we did not encounter a practical datum which completely accounts for this phenomenon. It was a practical datum . . . which drove the dogmatist on beyond the I . . . namely, the feeling of a necessary subordination and unity of the entire not-I under the practical laws of the I."[25] A dogmatist cannot explain how to transcend the first-person standpoint of the I, for her philosophy expresses a "practical datum" that conflicts with her nihilistic view, namely, her feeling of freedom, of "a necessary subordination" of the world to her "practical laws." Her very act of positing the not-I as first principle betrays this datum insofar as she seeks to reconcile the world with her practical perspective. As Fichte says in the *New Presentation*, something in a dogmatist's "inner self" agrees with her idealist opponent.[26] Thus, although one cannot be forced to accept idealism, as this acceptance "depends on freedom,"[27] and while one can at most be "summoned"[28] to embrace one's freedom, the dogmatist undermines her system through the performative contradiction of positing a principle that rules out this practical datum. Fichte concludes that the "only type of philosophy that remains possible is idealism," from which it follows that a person must either rise to "the level of idealism" and act in good faith or else fail to do so and live in bad faith.[29]

Embracing freedom is a cognitive act that Fichte calls "intellectual intuition." This term does not appear in the *Foundations*. Fichte introduces it in his 1794 review of Schulze's 1792 *Aenesidemus* and develops it, after Schelling's *Letters*, in the 1796–99 *Wissenschaftslehre Nova Methodo* lectures and in the *New Presentation*. However, we can see that the concept behind the term is at work in the *Foundations* if we consider Fichte's description of philosophy's first principle in the *Aenesidemus* review.

As Paul Franks has shown, Schulze's attack on Reinhold in *Aenesidemus* elicits Fichte's qualified concession.[30] Fichte agrees that Reinhold's principle—that every act of consciousness is mediated by representation—cannot be a first principle. But he denies that this is because, as Schulze holds, the mind must be immediately conscious of objects as transcendentally real. Rather, Fichte argues that acts of consciousness mediated by representation form a regress unless the mind has immediate awareness of a single unconditioned ground. Reinhold's principle cannot express this ground, for it asserts that consciousness is always mediated by representation, which means that grasping this principle is itself mediated by representation. But representation, Fichte says, is *"empirically* given" and so conditioned: Reinhold's principle is thereby homogeneous with what it conditions, which forms a regress.[31] Thus, it cannot express an unconditioned ground.

Fichte's review locates philosophy's first principle in "an *Act*" of the I, which the *Foundations* will describe as "that *Act* which does not and cannot appear among the empirical states of our consciousness, but rather lies at the basis of all consciousness and alone makes it possible."[32] In the review, he says that the I is "posited" and "realized through intellectual intuition, through the *I am*, and indeed, through the *I simply am, because I am*."[33] This prefigures his formulation in the *Foundations* that "the I *exists* because it *posits itself*, and *posits itself* because *it exists*."[34] Finally, Fichte's claim against Schulze that "[o]ur knowledge can extend no further" than intellectual intuition of the I is echoed in the *Foundations'* claim that the I's self-positing is the principle of "all human knowledge."[35] Thus, while the term recedes briefly in the early Jena period, the concept of intellectual intuition plays a crucial role in the *Foundations*.

For a detailed account of intellectual intuition, however, we must look to the *Nova Methodo*. As we saw, proving that idealism is the one true doctrine depends on positing a principle that expresses an unconditioned ground. To this end, Fichte summons us to think the I and to observe that, whatever we represent, the I is active in this. Grasping the concept of the I as essentially active allows us then to observe that, in thinking this very concept, "the thinking subject and the object one is thinking of, the thinker and the thought, are here one and the same."[36] We overcome both subjective and objective conditions in thinking the I, for, in doing so, subject and object are inseparable. As Fichte says in the *Foundations*, the I is both "the active, and what the activity brings about."[37] Cognizing the I as "a subject-object" thus secures an unconditioned ground. Fichte calls this cognition "intellectual intuition." It apprehends the I's "self-positing," the freedom whereby it pervades all representation.[38] This apprehension is intellectual, since it does not depend on passive sensation, yet intuitive, since it is not mediated by either subjective or objective conditions.[39]

In an 1801 reply to Kant's 1799 public repudiation of the *Wissenschaftslehre*,[40] Fichte clarifies that his use of "intellectual intuition" is meant to signify apprehension, not of an object, but of reason's own activity. It is, he says, "*cognition of reason itself by means of reason itself.*" Although this recalls Kant's view of critique as a kind of self-knowledge, and while Fichte attributes this idea's "discovery" to Kant, he adds that Kant "failed to carry it through to completion," namely, by converting critique into a "system" or doctrine.[41] How does intellectual intuition facilitate this conversion?

In his review, Fichte chides Schulze for demanding a thing-in-itself outside the I's activity: "[the I] is the circle within which every finite understanding, that is, every understanding that we can conceive, is necessarily confined. Anyone who wants to escape from this circle does not understand himself and does not know what he wants. . . . Within this circle, on the other hand, [critique] furnishes us with the greatest coherence in all of our knowledge."[42] The idea of the thing-in-itself is "a piece of whimsy, a pipe dream, [and] a non-thought" insofar as it feigns a faculty "different from ours."[43] This agrees with Kant's view that critique corrects the self-delusion by which one craves an alien perspective: "complaints . . . that we do not understand through pure reason what the things that appear to us might be in themselves . . . are entirely improper and irrational; for they would have us be able to cognize things, thus intuit them, even without senses, consequently they would have it that we have a faculty of cognition entirely distinct from the human not merely in degree but even in intuition and kind, and thus that we ought to be not humans but beings that we cannot even say are possible, let alone how they are constituted."[44] Despite their idealist accord, however, Fichte rejects Kant's insistence on thinking the thing-in-itself. In such thinking, "*one always thinks of oneself, as an intellect striving to know the thing.*"[45] The idea of the thing-in-itself is "nothing but another way of looking at the I"[46] and is otherwise "a pure invention which possesses no reality whatsoever."[47] Critique rightly confines us to the circle of the I's activity, but it errs in retaining the idea of the thing-in-itself. But what exactly is Kant's error, given that he denies this idea any actuality and regulatively rehabilitates it for theoretical reason's systematic ends?

According to Fichte, the idea of the thing-in-itself is the remnant of a needless deception. In the Transcendental Dialectic, Kant describes transcendental illusion as the "natural and unavoidable" confusion of the "subjective necessity of a connection of our concepts" with "objective necessity in the determination of things in themselves."[48] It is the illusion that we know, not appearances, but "things in general in a systematic doctrine."[49] Fichte denies that we can diagnose an illusion without thereby removing it: "[Kant refers to] *a deception that continually recurs, despite the fact that one knows that it is a deception. . . .* To know that one is deceived and yet to remain deceived: this is not a state of conviction and harmony with oneself; instead it is a state of serious inner conflict."[50] Transcendental illusion is a deception that can be "completely extirpated," for we ourselves have "invented" the thing-in-itself,[51] and must be extirpated, on pain of a divided standpoint in which, as Kant himself admits, we "irremediably" chase "false hopes," "even after we have exposed the mirage."[52] Once we see that appearances compose "our commonly shared truth," the "false philosophy" of the thing-in-itself "will fall away—like scales from our eyes—never to recur again."[53] The *Wissenschaftslehre* presents critique freed from this idea, having refuted the system grounded on the thing-in-itself, that is, on the dogmatist's not-I. As we saw, it does so by means of intellectual intuition. This, then, is how intellectual intuition converts critique into a doctrine: in cognizing the I as the absolute ground of experience, it decisively vindicates a system that is no longer threatened either by Spinozistic dogmatism or by transcendental illusion.

4. Schelling's First Premise

Freedom is the practical datum expressed by positing any first principle, a datum that apparently refutes Spinozism. This insight inspires Fichte to defend our intellectual intuition of the I as the ground of the sole possible system, from which he infers the identity of critique and doctrine. In the *Letters*, Schelling argues that critique strictly concerns our endless striving for doctrine and that intellectual intuition is only the pretense of achieving this goal. We will see that this two-step argument supports his rejection of Fichte's identity claim.

In the Fifth Letter, Schelling declares,

> Nothing, it seems to me, proves more strikingly how little of the *spirit* of the *Critique of Pure Reason* the majority have grasped than the almost universal belief that the *Critique of Pure Reason* belongs to one system alone, since it precisely must be the

> peculiarity of a critique of reason *that* it can favour *no* system exclusively, but rather must either truly establish, or at least prepare, a canon for *all*. Of course, the universal methodology belongs to a canon for *all* systems as a necessary part; but nothing worse can befall such a work than if one takes the method that it sets up for *all* systems as the system itself. . . . [T]he *Critique of Pure Reason* is not destined to establish any one *system* exclusively. . . . Rather, as far as I understand it, it is destined precisely to deduce from the essence of reason the possibility of two directly opposed systems and to establish a system of criticism (conceived in its completion) or, better said, of idealism as well as, directly opposing it, a system of dogmatism or of realism. . . . The *Critique of Pure Reason* alone is or contains the actual doctrine of science [*Wissenschaftslehre*] because it is valid for all *science*.[54]

This passage wrests from Fichte both the claim to critique and the title of *Wissenschaftslehre*, ascribing them to the "canon" and "method" whereby criticism and dogmatism can with equal validity be pursued. I will examine in turn the premises that lead to this conclusion.

To advance the premise that critique concerns our striving for doctrine, Schelling reassesses the practical datum that Fichte discerns in the dogmatist. Rather than dismiss her feeling of freedom as self-refuting, Schelling situates it within a "consistent dogmatistic ethics."[55] In the Fifth Letter, he asks, "why did Spinoza present his philosophy in a system *of ethics*? Certainly he did not do so in vain. Of him, one can really say: 'he lived in his system.' But surely he also thought of it as more than a theoretical castle in the sky, in which a spirit like his could hardly have found the calm and the '*heaven in understanding*' in which he so visibly lived and moved."[56] Spinoza's is an ethics in that it offers a way of living in accord with nature by rendering nature fully intelligible. Systematic knowledge of nature is the "highest good" for Spinoza because the mind is active to the extent that it understands: the more it knows, the more it acts from virtue.[57] Instead of the nihilism that appalls Fichte, Schelling sees in dogmatism the desire common to all systems: to live in systematic knowledge of the world.[58] As he says in the Seventh Letter, dogmatism, "like any other ethics," aims to solve "the problem of the existence of the world."[59] Schelling thus reserves for Spinoza a capacity that Fichte unqualifiedly denies to him, namely, action. This is why he ascribes "*vol-*

untary annihilation" to dogmatism, for although Spinoza concludes that we are not free, he is moved by an active *"love* of the infinite" to live out his doctrine.[60] By drawing attention to the "practical intention" that drives Spinoza's ethics, Schelling underscores what the practical datum of dogmatism shares with that of criticism.[61]

Stressing Spinoza's practical starting point may appear to ignore his necessitarian conclusions. However, dogmatism can no more definitively prove its conclusions than can criticism, for this requires intellectual intuition, which, as Schelling's second premise will show, is unlivable.

Returning to the first premise, if we grant that dogmatism and criticism both start from a desire for systematic knowledge, why should we regard critique as investigating this practical datum, rather than the bounds of our cognitive faculty? Schelling claims that adducing the "weakness" of this faculty affords merely a privative conception of our essence, on the basis of which we cannot fully lay claim to the laws of experience. By contrast, adducing what he calls "the freedom of minds" affords a positive conception of our essence.[62] Schelling develops this conception by considering what makes the dispute between criticism and dogmatism possible in the first place.

In the Third Letter, Schelling argues that no real dispute occurs between systems "except in a field they had in common." Their shared field of dispute is not the absolute, in which "the strife of different systems would never have arisen."[63] It rather originates in an *"original* opposition in the human mind."[64] Schelling describes this opposition in terms of "the last great question (to be or not to be?)."[65] What is the precise meaning of this question and how does it account for systems' shared field of dispute?

Experience raises the question of how we amplify our cognition or how we *"come to judge synthetically."* Schelling claims that systems disagree, "not about the question whether there are any synthetic judgments, but about a decidedly higher question concerning the principle of that unity which is expressed in the synthetic judgment."[66] Experience raises the question of the unconditioned "principle" that unifies synthetic judgment. It thereby draws criticism and dogmatism into the "domain of *practical* philosophy," which *"demands* the *act* through which [the unconditioned] *ought* to be realized."[67] We have seen why experience ultimately raises a *"practical"* problem. Recall that systems confront "the problem of the existence of the world," which, at root, is the problem of how one should decide to live. We can therefore see why systems' shared field of dispute arises from an opposition "in the human mind," in the subject who faces a momentous decision. Experience confronts us with the question of whether to live by one system rather than another—of whether "to be or not to be" in accord with that system.[68]

This, then, is why Schelling construes critique as investigating "the freedom of minds" rather than the bounds of our cognitive faculty.[69] Striving for systematic knowledge in response to the world's existence is a positive feature of our essence. As Schelling says in the Sixth Letter, "Which of the two [systems] we choose depends on the freedom of spirit which we have ourselves acquired. We must *be* what we call ourselves theoretically. And nothing can convince us of being that, except our very *striving* to be just that. This striving realizes our knowledge of ourselves, and thus this knowledge becomes the pure product of our freedom. We ourselves must have worked our way up to the point from which we want to start: one cannot *reason oneself up to that point*, nor can others."[70] Critically construed, freedom is the decision to *"be,"* to practically strive to realize the unconditioned according to one or another system.

Notice that deciding to be an idealist or a realist is not the conclusion to an argument. Endorsing a system "depends on the freedom of spirit" by which one responds to the problem of how to live.[71] For this very reason, Schelling infers that either of dogmatism and criticism "is just as possible as the other, and both will coexist as long as finite beings do not all stand on the same level of freedom."[72] As a matter of freedom, these systems are equally possible: however much Schelling prefers idealism, dogmatism remains a practical possibility. Crucially, these systems would remain equally possible even if all subjects came to occupy either a realist or an idealist level of freedom, for their opposition is *"original"* to the human mind. Thus, whereas Fichte restricts systematicity to the "level of idealism," Schelling recognizes distinct—and valid—modes of freedom.

Schelling thus arrives at his first premise. Since the mode of striving is what differentiates an idealist from a realist, critique must delve into the *"peculiar* spirit"[73] in which one strives to live out the realization of the unconditioned. Criticism differs from dogmatism, "not in the ultimate *goal* which both of them set up, but in the *approach* to it, in the *realization* of it. . . . And philosophy inquires into the ultimate *goal* of our human vocation only in order to be able to answer the much more urgent question as to our vocation itself."[74] This explains Schelling's declaration above that the first *Critique* must "deduce from the essence of reason the very possibility of two exactly opposed systems." Reason's essence consists, not in cognition, but in the decisive spirit by which one strives to *"be."* As he says in the Sixth Letter, "if we want to establish a system and, therefore, principles, we cannot do it except by an *anticipation* of the practical decision. We should not establish those principles unless our freedom had already decided about them; at the beginning of our knowledge they are nothing but proleptic assertions or . . . *original insuperable prejudices.*"[75] We will now see that, insofar as knowledge begins with the prejudice of deciding to realize a system, it is incompatible with intellectual intuition.

5. Schelling's Second Premise

A philosophical system is a response to the ethical problem of the existence of the world, the practical problem of how to be in the world. A system is accordingly nothing beyond our living it. By investigating our essence as agents in search of systematic knowledge, critique shows that "every *system* bears the stamp of individuality on its face because none can be completed otherwise than *practically* (i.e., subjectively). The more closely a philosophy approaches a system, the greater share *freedom* and *individuality* have in it and the less claim it has to universal validity."[76]

Now, if a system is subjectively valid, it would be illusory to regard it as an unrivaled doctrine. Consequently, Fichte's identity claim would be false, inasmuch as it rests on intellectual intuition of the first principle of a universally valid doctrine. This is precisely Schelling's second premise.

As Kant defines it, dogmatism is driven to uncritical metaphysical claims by the "fanaticism" or "delusion" that we are capable of intellectual intuition.[77] In the Fifth Letter, Schelling says that when the first *Critique* renounces dogmatism, it in fact speaks "against dogmaticism."[78] Schelling's earlier defense of the practical datum of dogmatism explains his choice of a different term here to denote what Kant calls "dogmatism." In doing so, he no more spares Spinoza than attacks Fichte (if not by name), for an essential mark of dogmaticism is its claim to intellectual intuition. Why is such a claim fanatical?

Schelling argues in the Eighth Letter that consciousness depends on "resistance." Without objects resisting my activity and without my ability to resist their force, "there is infinite expansion. But the intensity of our consciousness is in inverse ratio to the extension of our being."[79] Consciousness would vanish were the subject to annihilate the object's difference from it. As we saw, intellectual intuition aims to extend beyond the division between subject and object in order to secure an unconditioned ground. If this extension stands inversely to consciousness, however, then we cannot sustain such an intuition: "We awaken from intellectual intuition as from a state of death. We awaken through *reflection*, i.e., through a forced return to ourselves. But no return is thinkable without resistance, no reflection without an *object*. We designate as alive an activity directed at objects *alone* and as dead an activity losing itself in itself. Man ought to be neither lifeless nor merely living. His activity is necessarily intent upon objects, but with equal necessity it returns into itself. The *latter* distinguishes him from the merely living (animal) being, the *former* from the lifeless."[80] Schelling likens intellectual intuition to death because it effaces the resistance on which mere life depends in order to survive in its environment and on which rational life depends in order to reflect on its possibilities.[81] Insofar as reflectively mediated sensation constitutes rational life, it makes intellectual intuition unlivable: "as long as intuition is intent upon objects, i.e., as long as it is sensible intuition, there is no danger of losing oneself. The I, on finding resistance, is *obliged* to take a stand against it, i.e., to return into self. However, where sensible intuition ceases, where everything objective vanishes, there is nothing but infinite expansion without a return into self. Should I maintain intellectual intuition I would cease to live; I would go 'from time into eternity.'" I resist what I intuit, grasping it *as* an object. With no such resistance, Schelling says, "I would cease to be *I*."[82]

Intellectual intuition seeks a point at which the subject is "annihilated." This, Schelling says, is the "delusion" of a "fanatic," for one must think of oneself *as* a subject in order to think of oneself as annihilated.[83] The fanatic mistakes intellectual intuition for what Schelling calls "self-intuition." By this, he means our capacity to withdraw from the "experience of objects" to an "experience produced by ourselves," which "alone can breathe life" into a system. Self-intuition is our response to experience, which, as we saw, raises the problem of the world's existence and how to live in it. To solve it, we withdraw from experience to an intuition that is "in the strictest sense our own experience," namely, our freedom to decide by which system to live.[84] Self-intuition is thus no knowledge of an unconditioned. Indeed, no proposition is "more *groundless*" than one that "asserts an absolute in human knowledge. Just because it affirms that which is absolute, no further ground can be given for the proposition. As soon as we enter the realm of proofs, we enter the realm of that which is conditioned and, vice versa, entering the realm of that which is conditioned, we enter the realm of philosophical problems."[85] The realm of "problems" or "proofs" is experience, a realm that leads us to dispute about its ultimate condition. Claiming to resolve this dispute through intellectual intuition is fanatical because any response to the question of experience presupposes experience: "to answer this question we first must have left the realm of experience; but if we had left that realm the very question would cease."[86] The question instead leads us to "*create* a new realm" where "*knowledge* ceases," where we are faced with "*giving* reality" to our first principles in such a way that "they themselves merge into life and existence."[87]

By ruling out intellectual intuition, Schelling refutes Fichte's claim to doctrine. As he says, "criticism would deteriorate into fanaticism if it should represent this ultimate goal as attainable," a reproach it can be spared "as little as can dogmatism."[88] We must instead strive under the guidance of critique, which establishes "neither an absolute principle nor a definite and complete system," but only "the canon for all principles and systems."[89] It is "vain" and "blind dogmaticism" to regard doctrine as achievable through "the mere choice of principles"—vain because principles are "*insuperable prejudices*," blind because restricting us to one principle "coerce[s] our freedom."[90] As we saw, positing a principle is an intuition of the freedom of spirit with which I meet the problem of experience and exemplify my life as a response to it.[91] My vocation is not to achieve systematic knowledge in the form of a doctrine. It is to demand of myself the endless realization of my system of choice—*to be what I call myself*. As Schelling says, "even dogmatism, by its *practical* intention, is distinguished from blind dogmaticism, which uses the absolute as a constitutive principle for our *knowledge*, while dogmatism uses it merely as a constitutive principle for our vocation."[92] Criticism and dogmatism differ, not in their "vocation," but in the spirit of their "approach," which, according to Schelling's first premise, is critique's proper topic. To assert one's arrival at a doctrine—to assert the cessation of one's approach—is to deny one's essence as free. It is to evade oneself, misunderstanding oneself beyond one's bounds.[93] It is, moreover, to deny others' essence as free: "for a spirit who has made itself free and who owes *its* philosophy only to itself, nothing must be more unbearable than the despotism of narrow minds who cannot tolerate another system beside their own."[94] I can, like Fichte, summon you to embrace your freedom, but not, on pain of dogmaticism, to adhere to my principle as sacrosanct. I can even exemplify my life as a response to the problem of existence, but I cannot decide for all how to live.[95]

Schelling's two-step rejection of Fichte's claim for the identity of critique and doctrine shows that philosophy starts, not with a conclusive cognition, but with a decision whose form can be neither determined in advance nor vindicated against alternatives. To borrow a concept that Schelling develops in the 1809 *Philosophical Investigations into the Essence of Human Freedom*, such a beginning is *unprethinkable*.[96] My first principle is thinkable, but only as that which thought cannot anticipate, on which thought cannot enforce any prior rule. While my principle opens a way of life, it is, for that life, a foregone commitment lying outside legitimate, internal questions. On Schelling's reading, critique awakens us to the spirit of striving that is expressed by a first principle, and alerts us to the dogmaticist temptation to misconstrue as livable the resolution of this striving in a doctrine. By retrieving the idea of dogmaticism, we thus better understand Schelling's *Letters*, while registering the impact of a core Kantian distinction on the development of German idealism.

Notes

1. Ludwig Wittgenstein, "A Lecture on Ethics," *Philosophical Review* 74, no. 1 (1965), 11–12.

2. Friedrich Waismann, "Notes on Talks with Wittgenstein," *Philosophical Review* 74, no. 1 (1965), 16.

3. See Annemarie Pieper, "Editorischer Bericht zu Schellings Briefe über Dogmatismus und Kritizismus," in Friedrich Wilhelm Joseph von Schelling, *Schelling: Historisch-Kritische Ausgabe* (Stuttgart: Frommann-Holzboog, 1982).

4. See Friedrich Wilhelm Joseph von Schelling, *The Unconditioned in Human Knowledge: Four Early Essays 1794–1796*, trans. F. Marti (Lewisburg: Bucknell University Press, 1980), 172, 176. I modify this translation in some citations from this text.

5. Friedrich Wilhelm Joseph von Schelling, *Friedrich Wilhelm Joseph Schellings sämmtliche Werke* (cited hereafter as *SW*), ed. K.F.A. Schelling (Stuttgart: Cotta, 1856–1861), 1/1:315, 331.

6. Schelling, *SW* 1/1:331.

7. Schelling, *SW* 1/1:301.

8. Immanuel Kant, *Critique of Pure Reason*, ed. and trans. Paul Guyer and Allen W. Wood (New York: Cambridge University Press, 1998), Axi–xii. All references to Kant's first *Critique* use the standard A/B pagination of the first (1781, A) and second (1787, B) editions.

9. Ibid., B19.

10. Ibid., Axii.

11. Ibid., A727/B755.

12. Ibid., A763/B791.

13. Ibid., Bxxii–xxiii.

14. Ibid., A11–12/B25–26.

15. Ibid., *Critique of Pure Reason*, Bxxx. Dogmatism differs from what Kant calls reason's dogmatic procedure: "Criticism is not opposed to the dogmatic procedure of reason in its pure cognition as science (for science must always be dogmatic, i.e., it must prove its conclusions strictly *a priori* from secure principles); rather, it is opposed only to dogmatism, i.e., to the presumption of getting on solely with pure cognition from (philosophical) concepts according to principles, which reason has been using for a long time without first inquiring in what way and by what right it has obtained them. Dogmatism is therefore the dogmatic procedure of pure reason, without an antecedent critique of its own capacity." Kant, *Critique of Pure Reason*, Bxxxv. A dogmatic procedure is one in which reason proceeds from *a priori* principles. This becomes dogmatism if reason does not deduce its right to such principles as part of a "careful examination of its condition" (Kant, *Critique of Pure Reason*, A757/B785). This is to proceed pre-judicially, that is, without a prior judgment of right.

16. Kant, *Critique of Pure Reason*, B22–23.

17. Ibid., A735/B763.

18. Ibid., A761/B789.

19. Ibid., A135/B174. As Kant states in the Preface, however, "a critique that limits the speculative use of reason is, to be sure, to that extent negative, but because it simultaneously removes an obstacle that limits or even threatens to wipe out the practical use of reason, this critique is also in fact of positive and very important utility, as soon as we have convinced ourselves that there is an absolutely necessary practical use of pure reason (the moral use), in which reason unavoidably extends itself beyond the boundaries of sensibility, without needing any assistance from speculative reason, but in which it must also be made secure against any counteraction from the latter, in order not to fall into contradiction with itself." Kant, *Critique of Pure Reason*, Bxxiv.

20. Johann Gottlieb Fichte, *Sämmtliche Werke* (cited hereafter as *SW*), ed. Immanuel Hermann Fichte (Berlin: Walter de Gruyter, 1971), 1:422–426.

21. Fichte, *SW* 1:46.

22. See: "What then is the overall gist of the *Wissenschaftslehre*, summarized in a few words? It is this: Reason is absolutely self-sufficient; it exists only for itself." Fichte, *SW* 1:474.

23. Fichte, *SW* 1:120–121.

24. Ibid., 1:434.

25. Ibid., 1:121.

26. Ibid., 1:434.

27. Ibid., 1:499.

28. Ibid., 1:462.

29. Ibid., 1:438, 434.

30. See Paul Franks, *All or Nothing: Systematicity, Transcendental Arguments, and Skepticism in German Idealism* (Cambridge, MA: Harvard University Press, 2005), 219–236.
31. Fichte, *SW* 1:8.
32. Ibid., 1:8, 91.
33. Ibid., 1:10, 16.
34. Ibid., 1:134.
35. Ibid., 1:16, 91.
36. Johann Gottlieb Fichte, *Gesamtausgabe der Bayerischen Akademie der Wissenschaften* (cited hereafter as *GA*), ed. Erich Fuchs, Hans Gliwitzky, Reinhard Lauth, and Peter K. Schneider (Stuttgart: Frommann-Holzboog, 1962–2012), 4/2:29.
37. Fichte, *SW* 1:96.
38. Fichte, *GA* 4/2:31, 40.
39. If vindicating idealism is necessary to refute the view that human action is a mode of a dead mechanism, intellectual intuition would be apt. As Fichte says in the *New Presentation*, it is in virtue of my immediate awareness of the I's freedom that, in any action, "I know that *I* do this." It is in this sense that intellectual intuition "contains within itself the source of life, and apart from it there is nothing but death." Fichte, *SW* 1:463.
40. See Immanuel Kant, "Open Letter on Fichte's *Wissenschaftslehre*," in *Philosophical Correspondence 1759–99*, ed. and trans. Arnulf Zweig (Chicago, IL: University of Chicago Press, 1967), 253–254.
41. Fichte, *GA* 1/7:159. Cf.: "The intellectual intuition of which the *Wissenschaftslehre* speaks is not directed towards any sort of being whatsoever; instead, it is directed at an acting—and this is something that Kant does not even mention (except, perhaps, under the name 'pure apperception'). . . . I have just as much right to use this term to designate this type of consciousness as Kant has to use it to designate something else, something that is actually nothing at all." Fichte, *SW* 1:472. And cf.: "Less rational than Kant's denial of the possibility of intellectual intuition is the behaviour of those who have continued to reject intellectual intuition even after it has been deduced in their presence (e.g., the author of the review [namely, Erhard], published in 1796 in the *Allgemeine Literatur-Zeitung*, of Schelling's *On the I*). People of this sort will never become conscious of their own freedom of thinking." Fichte, *GA* 4/2:32.
42. Fichte, *SW* 1:11, 15. Cf. Kant: "Our reason is not like an indeterminably extended plane, the limits of which one can cognize only in general, but must rather be compared with a sphere, the radius of which can be found out from the curvature of an arc on its surface (from the nature of synthetic *a priori* propositions), from which its content and its boundary can also be ascertained with certainty. Outside this sphere (field of experience) nothing is an object for it; indeed even questions about such supposed objects concern only subjective principles of a thoroughgoing determination of the relations that can obtain among the concepts of understanding inside of this sphere." Kant, *Critique of Pure Reason*, A762/B790.

43. Fichte, *SW* 1:16, 17. Cf. Fichte's claim that the idea of the in itself is "the uttermost perversion of reason, and a concept perfectly absurd." Fichte, *SW* 1:472.

44. Kant, *Critique of Pure Reason*, A277–278/B333–334. Cf. Stanley Cavell, *Must We Mean What We Say?* (Cambridge: Cambridge University Press, 1967), 96: "philosophy concerns those necessities we cannot, being human, fail to know. Except that nothing is more human than to deny them."

45. Fichte, *SW* 1:19.

46. Fichte, *GA* 4/2:42.

47. Fichte, *SW* 1:428.

48. Kant, *Critique of Pure Reason*, A297/B354.

49. See Kant, *Critique of Pure Reason*, A247/B303.

50. Fichte, *SW* 1:513–514.

51. Fichte, *SW* 1:514.

52. Kant, *Critique of Pure Reason*, A298/B354–355.

53. Fichte, *SW* 1:514.

54. Schelling, *SW* 1/1:301–304.

55. Ibid., 1/1:299.

56. Ibid., 1/1:305. Contrast Fichte: "*Spinoza* could not have been convinced by his own philosophy. He could only have *thought* of it; he could not have *believed* it. For this is a philosophy that directly contradicts those convictions that Spinoza must necessarily have adopted in his everyday life, by virtue of which he had to consider himself to be free and self-sufficient." Fichte, *SW* 1:513.

57. Baruch Spinoza, *The Ethics*, trans. S. Shirley (Indianapolis, IN: Hackett, 1992), 4p28.

58. See also: "The ideas to which our speculation has risen cease to be objects of an idle occupation that tires our spirit all too soon; they become the law of our *life*, and as they themselves merge into life and existence—and become objects of *experience*—they free us forever from the tedious business of ascertaining their reality by way of speculation *a priori*." Schelling, *SW* 1/1:341.

59. Ibid., 1/1:313.

60. Ibid., 1/1:284, 316, first italics added. See also: "A *system* of knowledge is either a stunt or intellectual game (you know that nothing could be more repugnant to the serious spirit of Spinoza)—or it must *obtain* reality . . . not by *knowledge*, but by *action*. . . . You say: 'I can understand how Spinoza could keep out of sight the contradiction involved in his ethical principle. However, granting that, how was it possible for the serene spirit of Spinoza to bear that destructive and annihilating principle itself? For his is a serenity which illumines with its mild light his whole life and all his writings.' I cannot reply except by saying: 'Read his writings in just *this* respect, and you will find the answer to your question yourself.'" Schelling, *SW* 1/1:305, 317.

61. Schelling, *SW* 1/1:333. See also: "[dogmatism] is practically *refutable* if one realizes *in oneself* an absolutely opposing system. But it is irrefutable for him who is able to realize it *practically*, who can bear the thought of working at his

own annihilation, of abolishing every free causality in himself, and of being the modification of an object in whose infinitude he will sooner or later find his own (moral) ruin." Schelling, *SW* 1/1:339.

62. Ibid., 1/1:290–92.

63. Ibid., 1/1:293. See also: "if we had never left its sphere we should all agree about the absolute, and if we had never stepped out from it, we should have no other field for dispute. . . . [I]n the absolute . . . [idealism and realism] must cease as opposite systems." Schelling, *SW* 1/1:294, 330.

64. Ibid., 1/1:294.

65. Ibid., 1/1:339.

66. Ibid., 1/1:294–295.

67. Ibid., 1/1:299.

68. Schelling's pluralism repudiates Fichte's claim that idealism is the only possible system and the sole measure of personality. They agree that philosophy requires systematicity, not simply through a critical turn to the first-person standpoint, but through an *authentic* turn to the essential freedom of that standpoint. However, Fichte denies any common discourse for idealists and realists: "Each denies everything included within the opposite system. They do not have a single point in common on the basis of which they might be able to achieve mutual understanding and be united with one another. Even when they appear to be in agreement concerning the words of some proposition, they understand these same words to mean two different things." See Fichte, *SW* 1:429. A defense of idealism, for Fichte, is conclusive yet potentially alienating, whereas for Schelling it is inconclusive yet genuinely discursive.

69. This may suggest that Schelling's notion of critique surpasses Kant's, which concerns an analysis of our faculties of cognition. Goldman argues that Kant's analysis is in fact guided by the regulative idea of the self. This idea can be seen as orienting thought, in the first place, toward a consideration of our faculties. See Avery Goldman, "What is Orientation in Critique?" in *Recht und Frieden in der Philosophie Kants: Akten des X. Internationalen Kant-Kongresses*, ed. Valerio Rohden et al (Berlin: Walter de Gruyter, 2008), 252. Goldman argues, furthermore, that Kant provides a deduction of this idea in order to establish the conditions of the possibility of critical inquiry generally and the division between the empirical and transcendental use of concepts in particular. See Avery Goldman, "Critique and the Mind: Towards a Defense of Kant's Transcendental Method," *Kant-Studien* 98, no. 4 (2007), 408–414. Connecting Kant's idea of the self and what Schelling regards as the freedom of minds may accordingly reveal more common ground concerning their concepts of critique.

70. Schelling, *SW* 1/1:308.

71. "The highest dignity of philosophy is precisely that it expects everything of human *freedom*." Schelling, *SW* 1/1:306.

72. Ibid., 1/1:307. See also: "Nothing more disgusts the philosophical mind than when it hears that henceforth all philosophy shall lie captive in the fetters of a single system." Schelling, *SW* 1/1:306.

73. Ibid., 1/1:304.

74. Ibid., 1/1:332. Dogmatism and criticism "can only differ in the spirit of the action." Schelling, *SW* 1/1:334.

75. Ibid., 1/1:312–313.

76. Ibid., 1/1: 304. Contrast Schelling's claim in the 1804 *System of the Whole of Philosophy and the Philosophy of Nature in Particular* that in "*reason* all subjectivity ceases" and that "it is not *me* who recognizes this identity, but it recognizes itself, and I am merely its organ." Not coincidentally, this text describes reason's self-recognition as "an *intellectual intuition*." Schelling, *SW* 1/6:142–143, 153.

77. See Kant, *Ak.* 5: 275; 8: 398, 405; *Critique of Pure Reason*, Axiii, Bxxxiv.

78. Schelling, *SW* 1/1:302.

79. Ibid., 1/1:324. Cf.: "There is no consciousness without something that is at the same time excluded and contracted. That which is conscious excludes that of which it is conscious as not itself. Yet it must again attract it precisely as that of which it is conscious as itself, only in a different form." Schelling, *SW* 1/8:262.

80. Ibid., 1/1:325.

81. Cf.: "Without opposition [there is] no life. Indeed, such [opposition] inheres in man and in all existence." Schelling, *SW* 1/7:435.

82. Ibid., 1/1:325.

83. Ibid., 1/1:319–320. For an account of the relation between intellectual intuition and death in Schelling's *Letters*, see G. Anthony Bruno, "'As From a State of Death': Schelling's Idealism as Mortalism," *Comparative and Continental Philosophy* 8, no. 3 (2016).

84. Schelling, *SW* 1/1:318–319.

85. Ibid., 1/1:308–309. A realm of problems is qualitatively unlike the absolute, in which "all is intelligible" (Schelling, *SW* 1/1:308).

86. Ibid., 1/1:310–311.

87. Ibid., *SW* 1/1:310–311, 341. Cf. Nagel: "What sustains us, in belief as in action, is not reason or justification, but something more basic than these—for we go on in the same way even after we are convinced that the reasons have given out. If we tried to rely entirely on reason, and pressed it hard, our lives and beliefs would collapse—a form of madness that may actually occur if the inertial force of taking the world and life for granted is somehow lost. If we lose our grip on that, reason will not give it back to us." Thomas Nagel, "The Absurd," *The Journal of Philosophy* 68, no. 20 (1971), 724.

88. Schelling, *SW* 1/1:327–328, 335.

89. Ibid., 1/1:304–305.

90. Ibid., 1/1:312. See also: *"Philosophy*, an admirable word! If this author has a vote, he casts it for the retention of this old word. For, as far as he sees, our whole knowledge will always remain *philosophy*, i.e., always merely progressing knowledge, whose higher or lower degrees we owe only to our *love* for wisdom, i.e., to our freedom. —Least of all would he wish to displace this word through a philosophy that has for the first time undertaken to save the freedom in philosophizing from the presumptions of dogmaticism, through a philosophy that presupposes the self-achieved freedom of the spirit and that therefore will be eternally incomprehensible for every slave of system." Schelling, *SW* 1/1:307n.

91. See Schelling: "as soon as we are in the contest, those very principles as set up in the beginning are no longer valid in and by themselves; now only is it to be decided, practically and by our freedom, whether they are valid or not." Schelling, *SW* 1/1:312.

92. Ibid., 1/1:333. See also Kant: "The mistake that most obviously leads to [creating a field of objects beyond appearances], and can certainly be excused though not justified, lies in this: that the use of the understanding, contrary to its vocation, is made transcendental, and the objects, i.e., possible intuitions, are made to conform themselves to concepts, but concepts are not made to conform themselves to possible intuitions (on which alone rests their objective validity)." Kant, *Critique of Pure Reason*, A289/B345.

93. Cf. Cavell: "Nothing is more human than the wish to deny one's humanity. . . . A fitting title for the history of philosophy would be: Philosophy and the Rejection of the Human." Stanley Cavell, *The Claim of Reason: Wittgenstein, Skepticism, Morality and Tragedy* (Oxford: Oxford University Press, 1999), 109, 207.

94. Schelling, *SW* 1/1:306. Cf.: "Nothing could more enrage a youthful and fiery sensibility, burning for the truth, than the intention of a teacher to prepare his audience for some one special or particular system, wishing in this way to emasculate them by underhandedly removing the freedom of inquiry" (Schelling, *SW* 2/3:16).

95. See Cavell: "To say 'Follow me and you will be saved,' you must be sure you are of God. But to say 'Follow in yourself what I follow in mine and you will be saved,' you merely have to be sure you are following yourself." Stanley Cavell, "An Emerson Mood," in *Emerson's Transcendental Etudes* (Stanford, CA: Stanford University Press, 2003), 32. We can hear Fichte in the first instruction and Schelling in the second.

96. For an account of the *Freedom* essay's development of the *Letters'* view of the act that grounds philosophy, see G. Anthony Bruno, "Freedom and Pluralism in Schelling's Critique of Fichte's Jena *Wissenschaftslehre*," *Idealistic Studies* 43, no. 1/2 (2014).

7

Critique with a Small *C*

Herder's Critical Philosophical Practice
and Anticritical Polemics

RACHEL ZUCKERT

1. Introduction

As a student in Königsberg, Johann Gottfried Herder was deeply influenced by his teacher, Immanuel Kant, and incorporated into his own philosophical position much from Kant's philosophy of that precritical period.[1] In his late career, he wrote widely quoted, admiring descriptions of Kant as an urbane, insightful teacher.[2] But in his late career Herder also engaged in lengthy, bitter anti-Kantian polemics in two works, *Metacritique* (1799) and *Calligone* (1800). One may attribute the bitterness of these polemics in part to Herder's dismay at Kant's negative reviews of his own work[3]— but he also is dismayed at the transformation in his admired teacher's philosophical approach. He emphatically rejects the project of Kantian Critique as such.

In a less technical sense, however, Herder is also a thoroughly critical thinker: many of his works are formulated as responses—reactive, corrective, critical—to other writers' views. Indeed, as Herder notes, the very title of the work on which I shall focus here, his polemic against Kant's *Critique of Pure Reason—Metacritique*—itself testifies that his view of philosophical critique is twofold. He is against "critical philosophy," the name he consistently gives to Kant's mature philosophy, and to which I refer as Critique (with a capital *C*). But precisely in that attack, Herder takes himself to be engaging in, and indeed writing in favor of, some other form of critique (lowercase *c*); one might call this "criticism" or even critical thinking.[4] In this chapter I attempt to delineate this two-sided position: to discern some central points in Herder's case against Kantian Critique, and to reconstruct the positive Herderian conception of philosophical critique. That is, I aim to spell out more explicitly than Herder himself does: what can it mean to critique critique, critically to attack criticism?

To focus this question, in turn, I use as a guiding thread a striking and puzzling passage from the beginning of the *Metacritique*: "*Critique of Pure Reason*: the title is alienating. One does not criticize a natural human capacity; one rather investigates, determines, limits it, shows its use and misuse. One criticizes arts, sciences, considered as products of human beings."[5] This passage provocatively sums up the difficulty in understanding Herder's view. For Herder here endorses critique not just in some general or commonsense form—thinking critically, or "testing" claims as he puts it on the following page—but even, apparently, Kant's own Critical project.[6] For he appears to agree with Kant that one ought to establish the correct use and limits of human cognitive capacities. He disagrees only in claiming that this project should not be conceived as critique. So my question about Herder's position may be formulated more precisely: why is Kant wrong to call his project a "critique"? What is critique—"testing" claims—such that it is not appropriately directed toward natural human capacities, but rather toward human "products," as its objects?

In answer to these questions, I shall propose that Herderian critique, as practiced in *Metacritique* and elsewhere, is intersubjective conversation concerning publicly accessible objects (understood broadly, to include texts and doctrines), mobilizing more or less oppositional individual positions to judge the success or failure of such objects, by appeal to shared criteria, including a shared language, and common natural capacities. Those capacities—as appealed to *by* critique, and as not themselves publicly accessible—are thus not appropriate objects of critique. I shall develop this view by discussing the various elements of Herder's position as articulated in my guiding passage (quoted above), beginning with his accusation that Kant misuses the word, "critique."

2. "The Title is Alienating"

I have stated the aim of this paper narrowly: to spell out some points of Herder's criticism of Kant. This qualification is necessary because Herder is an unrelenting critic of Kant, on points large and small, organizational, methodological, and substantive; no single paper could treat even all major points of dispute. To name two important examples that will just be touched upon here, Herder objects not only to Kantian Critique, but also vehemently and repeatedly both to Kant's idealism and to his commitment to *a priori* knowledge and corresponding philosophical methodology. The unrelenting character of Herder's criticism, his apparent unwillingness to let any (to him) objectionable Kantian doctrine or phrase pass without contrary comment, in part explains the negative reception and scholarly neglect of the *Metacritique* (as well as the similar *Calligone*).[7] It is not only difficult to discern what Herder's own position (or even central objection) might be, amid the flurry of objections, but the work also acquires thereby a bitter flavor, off-putting to most of its likely readers (i.e., those who find Kant's critical philosophy of interest). Thus here I use my guiding passage—and the theme of critique—to select *some* lines of criticism for more concentrated attention.

Herder's remark that Kant's title is "alienating" (*befremdet*) exemplifies one of his most frequent and seemingly nit-pickiest forms of criticism: his repeated complaints that Kantian vocabulary is overly technical or arbitrary, distant from common usage.[8] So might one read my guiding passage as well: Kant *misuses the term* "critique" in describing his project of determining the limits of our cognitive capacities (even though the project itself is fine).

Students and other first-time (or non-Kantian) readers of Kantian texts might sympathize with such criticisms, as well as with Herder's tone of scornful frustration in offering them. And Herder is often right, as here, concerning critique (at least to my ear). In Herder's and Kant's time, "*Kritik*" was probably most often used to characterize art criticism, that is, judgment of a human product (an artwork) in order to establish and perhaps communicate its success or failure—not investigation of human faculties.[9] In the wake of Kant, we now of course use the term more widely. Still, I suspect that one rarely considers its subject matter to be cognitive faculties or natural capacities: "critique of hearing" or "critique of the understanding" have a strange ring to them. "Critique of reason" does not—but only, I suggest, because it recalls Kant's work, just as the book titles that modify this phrase (*Critique of Postcolonial Reason*, *Critique of Cynical Reason*, *Critique of Black Reason*) clearly allude to Kant's title and promise some relation (critical or otherwise) to Kant's thought.[10]

Ultimately, though, this kind of Herderian criticism seems petty. Why does it matter what one calls it, if the project is well conceived, if one explains what one means by one's terms? Herder even explicitly acknowledges, at least sometimes, that Kant does explain what he means.[11]

Though one cannot on my view defend all such linguistic objections made by Herder (nor their frequency), they are not entirely petty, but reflect more substantive points. First, Herder takes it that such misleading use of language contributes to a problem he identifies in the effect or reception of Kantian Critical philosophy. Namely, he alleges that Kant's Critique in fact brought about not critical thinking but dogmatism, in a form to which Kant himself objected: Kantians take up the very arrogant, self-promoting dogmatism of a philosophical school that Kant negatively portrayed in the Preface to the second edition of the *Critique of Pure Reason*. They claim to know other and better than everyone else, particularly the common folk; they purport to be somehow impervious to the "discipline" they exert against others' use of reason.[12]

Kantian technical vocabulary is instrumental to this problematic social formation, Herder suggests: the language is used to separate the inner circle from those outside, to mark those who do not use or even understand it as "alien," or indeed to "alienate" them, to exclude them from discussion, to disallow criticism or objections, as resting solely on misunderstandings.[13] Indeed, Herder argues, the alienness of Kant's technical terms also encourages disciples to become *mere* disciples, i.e., to parrot the terms, to manipulate them within that "language game" without themselves actually being clear about (or remembering and truly internalizing) what the terms mean.[14]

Second, Herder argues, more strongly, not only that Kant's disciples use Kantian terms without understanding them, but that those alienating, abstract terms simply have no meaning, are "empty" and "say nothing."[15] For, on Herder's empiricist view, terms that refer to purportedly **pure** *a priori* representations in fact refer to nothing, since we have no such representations.[16] And it is obviously problematic to use empty words as if they mean something, as the classical empiricists had insisted against traditional (rationalist, scholastic) metaphysics.

This objection seems, however, dismissive, too quick to rule out meanings that other people recognize and employ. (One might be tempted to employ it rather against the classical empiricists and Herder: if their semantic theories cannot account for such meanings, this does not show that there are no such meanings, but rather that the theories are faulty.) One may understand this line of thought in a somewhat more complex way, however: Herder acknowledges (at least sometimes) that Kant's terms have meaning, but provides alternative (anti-Kantian) accounts of the contents and origins of such meaning or, perhaps, error theories about how one could come to think the Kantian terms have (coherent) meaning.[17] According to this line of thought, the Kantian terms do have a sort of cobbled-together meaning or a meaning transferred from one register to another, from the "normal" meaning in everyday use to a more exotic, abstract, and specialized philosophical use. So, for example, might one read Herder's claims that "intuition" (*Anschauung*) is a term ordinarily used to describe visual experience, and secondarily to describe insight that one has through the understanding of self-evident truths (one can tell that they are true "just by looking"). Kant then repurposes this term, exploiting some aspects of its meaning (e.g., its connection to sensibility), combining it with other terms and everyday meanings with which we are also familiar, such as the idea that objects "affect" us sensibly.[18] Similarly, though Herder does not argue so explicitly, on a Herderian view one could say that Kant repurposes the language of "*Kritik*," ordinarily used to characterize the evaluation of artworks, to refer to the investigation of natural capacities.

But, Herder objects: precisely because one is using familiar words in unfamiliar or newly defined ways, one is encouraged to think that one knows what one means, when in fact one does not. Or, perhaps: one knows that one is dealing with a term used technically, with specially designed meaning, but does not always hold fast to that knowledge, nor really examine that specially designed meaning, slipping back into one's more common understanding of the term and correlative confidence in its coherence and meaningfulness. Because meanings of such technically used terms are recombined or transferred from one register to another, moreover, they are in greater danger of being incoherent—jumbled—while one's own resources (one's sense of ordinary meanings and usage) for detecting such incoherence are weakened.[19] Such unknowing ignorance is particularly problematic in philosophy, which—in Herder's as in Kant's view—is concerned with promoting one's ability to think for oneself, and bringing about human self-knowledge, including knowledge of our own limits. This last is of course, specifically, the project that Herder thinks is misnamed "critique," to which project and accusation I now turn more directly.

3. "One Does Not Criticize a Natural Capacity"

Given the preceding reflections, one might think Herder opposes all novel definitions or word usages, all transformations in meaning, proposing instead that one adhere to and be guided by common sense or tradition, that one eschew revolutionary or oppositional criticism such as that practiced by Kant. So Herder's (and Kant's) friend, Johann Georg Hamann, argued against Kant in his own brief *Metacritique*.[20] So Herder himself perhaps suggests in his exhortation to the youth to leave Kantian discipleship aside, with which he opens the *Metacritique*. Rather than repeating the words of one's teacher, Herder writes, "you [should] learn for yourself, for your own future vocation, for the world. . . . [I]t is a world that you did not create, nor should you, nor can you, create it. Learn to know it, become useful to it."[21]

This interpretation of Herder's position is on the right track, I think, but as stated it is too broad: someone who clearly delights in formulating nasty neologisms—word-ghosts, word-clamors, word-fog, foggy word-spirit, fog arts, word-foam[22]—to describe his opponent's work would seem hard pressed to rule out linguistic innovation altogether (at least consistently). I suggest, then, that one should formulate Herder's position more precisely, taking direction from my guiding passage: Kant's (own, particular) neologisms are problematic because they express, perhaps instantiate, a confusion of the natural and given with the artifactual. For in objecting to Kant's language and indeed in his own marked neological formulations, Herder conveys not just that Kant is hard to understand (though he does insist upon that point), but also that Kant's language is itself manufactured: it is an artificial linguistic construct, building its concepts out of previously given materials (those of natural language). Yet the Kantian approach does not acknowledge its reliance upon, nor its artifactual (artificial) transformation of, those prior natural-linguistic materials.

This unacknowledged manufactured-ness of Kantian technical language in turn symbolizes for Herder Kant's mistaken (Critical) approach to discussing the cognitive faculties. Herder explains this reasoning in the following passage, commenting on the Introduction to the *Critique of Pure Reason*. One should not ask how human understanding and reason are possible, he writes, "as if these were to be established [*setzen*] or made [*fabrizieren*] in the first place; rather, since they are already *established* and *given*, since they are indeed the noblest gifts that we can know and use, the question is rather: 'What are understanding and reason? How do they come to their concepts? What right do we have to think of some of them as universal and necessary?'"[23] Herder here objects that in the *Critique* Kant treats the cognitive faculties as if they were to be made or established (posited or placed—*gesetzt*), whereas they are in fact "given," even noble "gifts."

In Herder's language of "noble gifts," we may hear a theistically inspired accusation of ingratitude: we are furnished with gifts (from God), and it is arrogant to question or criticize them. Herder indeed does accuse Kant of ingratitude or (better) arrogance, perhaps especially in discussing Kant's idealism, which he takes to be insufficiently cognizant of human dependence—on others, on external, existing objects that affect the senses and thereby give rise to cognition, and so forth. In Herder's view, Kantian idealism therefore amounts to a false assertion, or immoral demand, that the world goes according to one's own thought and will, a denial that we are, like everything else, dependent and subordinate parts of nature.[24]

But this accusation can also be articulated in non-theistic (and less moralized) terms, as an objection that Kant fails to recognize the character and constraints of human making (including the "making" of cognitive claims). So Herder suggests in discussing Kant's distinction between sensible matter and spatiotemporal form of appearance[25]: "Matter means materials for building [*Bauzeug*]; form is the construction of the building. When the senses [the source of materials in the case of the purported manufacture of experience] furnish it with materials [*Bauzeug*], the builder-soul cannot give them any form it likes or build with a material that would please it, but is not given to it."[26] Here again Herder uses the language of the "given": when we construct things, we use previously given materials and provide them with a new form, rearrange them and their parts. (As Herder takes it that Kant does in constructing his own technical language, as discussed above.) Herder in effect argues that human making is therefore constrained by the given materials in at least two ways: it is dependent on materials being given at all, and it is constrained by the specific character of the materials. Not every form can be given to every material—skyscrapers cannot be made out of cotton wool.

We can see here one reason why natural capacities—as *given*, not as to be made—are not appropriate subject matters for critique, in Herder's view: we do not have other options.[27] They are one part of the "given" from or out of or using which we will "make" something further. We cannot, in other words, get "outside" the use of these capacities in our doing, making, thinking, outside enough to choose other "materials" (we don't have those) or to give them an entirely other "form." What we most basically are is not subject to our wills: "Like everything else around us," Herder writes, "the human being is itself a *given*; he did not establish [*setzte*] himself there, but *finds* himself."[28]

In the case of understanding and reason, moreover, they are our "noblest" gifts, Herder claims. They are, he insists against Kant, *themselves* the way in which we figure out if something has gone well or badly, if it achieves its purposes, and so forth. Thus, they too provide constraints on what may be made: *criteria* according to which something (especially a cognitive claim) may be praised or criticized. So then, Herder asks: by what criteria, except reason's own, could one judge reason? Herder's objection to Kant here may be reconstructed in the form of a dilemma. In embarking on a critique of reason, *either* one does not use reason, in which case one is rejecting criteria—engaging not in rational critique, but in arbitrary accusation. *Or*, if one *is* using reason, the project is self-undermining or self-refuting: as Herder puts it, reason would then have to be both "party and judge," "law and witness."[29]

As noted above, Herder grants, in my guiding passage, that natural capacities may be used properly or misused (as, he must think, Kant is misusing reason and perhaps also imagination[30]), and that one ought to investigate them to find those limits. In denying the title "critique" to this project, however, Herder means to distinguish between two sorts of projects: two sorts of subject matters of inquiry, and correspondingly different ways of engaging in it. On one hand, there are products, claims, doctrines, objects made for purposes, subject to our wills, that may be evaluated according to external criteria, or for reasons. These may be judged globally (or in large part) in "yes/no" or success/failure terms, and, if failures, may be discarded. On the other hand, there are natural capacities, the character of which is not under our control, and which cannot be abandoned (on pain of stopping one's cognitive life, anyway). They furnish the criteria for the first sort of project—critique proper—while they themselves are not evaluated thus from "outside" as it were. Rather, Herder writes, "true, noble powers have the rules of their use in themselves" (8:311). They are, then, to be explored, investigated, tried out perhaps, but not judged. Again, Herder finds Kant's treatment of reason especially problematic in this regard: it is incoherent, he alleges, to think that that our most ultimately determinative cognitive faculty could itself be aimed in the wrong direction, could of its very nature produce errors, its use itself more or less constituting a misuse.[31] Alternatively put: how could such a faculty, which purportedly by its very nature generates illusions and error, correct itself?[32] All we have—at best what we have—is the smooth, self-ruling, (ideally) self-correcting use of our natural faculties.

4. "One Criticizes Arts and Sciences as Products of Human Beings"

Herder thus alleges that critique of natural faculties is a wrong-headed project. In discussing this point, we have also started to articulate what philosophical critique is and should be on his view: reasoned, "yes/no," success/failure judgment of human products, that is, of items that are (not given but rather) subject to our will and dependent on us. These items may be understood as new arrangements of the given and they are subject to judgment in accord with given criteria: to consideration whether such forms are well fitted to the materials from which they are made, and to judgment in light of the internal rules of the cognitive faculties. Such critique is of course itself a use of natural cognitive capacities and rules, and is understood to be situated within and responsive to a given array of potential materials for formation, both natural (e.g., the operations of the senses and the information they glean) and cultural (e.g., the meanings of words in ordinary usage).

Herder's conception of philosophical critique is, then, *local*: focused on particular and conditioned products of human artifice, and judging them according to criteria external to them, provided by the constraints exerted by the materials (and faculties) used, or, more broadly put, by the context in which the work was produced and the critic criticizes.[33] Because the focal objects of critique, that is, human products, are made for purposes or according to intentions, they also may be judged as successful or unsuccessful in light of those purposes and intentions. That is: here "critique" means pretty much what we usually tend to think it is. And Herder would of course embrace such a return to familiar meaning and common practice.[34] It is "critique" with a small *c*.

Herder's own philosophical practice instantiates such critique, moreover. To return to (and correct) my first formulation of my central question in this essay, Herder does not in fact criticize criticism, or critique critique. If anything, the contrary, since he is arguing that one may not judge (critique) the operation of cognitive capacities (such as our capacity to criticize). Rather, he judges a particular human product, namely Kant's book, the *Critique of Pure Reason*, and the doctrine presented in it. Here we may see a direct contrast to Kant's proclamation in the Introduction to the *Critique of Pure Reason* that one can here expect "even less . . . a critique of the books and systems of pure reason, but rather that of the pure faculty of reason itself."[35]

Herder emphasizes indeed that his object of critique, this book (or its doctrine), *is* a specific, human product. He brings out its "materiality" as it were—the words of which it is made—and calls the reader's attention to the author's hand in choosing and forming those materials. He adduces common experiences—of occupying a place, for example—and anthropological-historical facts—for example, concerning human historical interpretation and representation of time (as, e.g., cycling through the seasons or phases of the moon)—to give a sense of a shared, larger (historical, experiential) context, in which this product is made, in light of which it may be judged.[36] And Herder criticizes this product on the grounds that it mishandles its given materials (e.g., in constructing new, misleading terms) and violates criteria given by the internal rules of the faculties, e.g., in claiming to go beyond what one cannot go beyond, the use of one's cognitive faculties, which are used in making the claim itself.[37] And of course Herder objects that Kant's theory does not provide what it intended, namely self-knowledge—but rather just word-fog.

Even if he does not merely endorse adherence to common sense or tradition, then, Herder's conception of critique does prove somewhat conservative. This (relative) conservatism reflects in turn a real difference between his view and Kant's or, perhaps better, between Herder's view and what he takes to be Kant's "true message," as revealed (again) in his reception, for example by Fichte. Insofar as one engages in (or claims to be engaging in) critique—sitting in external judgment—of natural human capacities, one is also thereby suggesting that one may create oneself or remake oneself radically, that such human constitution is up to and dependent on our wills.[38] And this Herder rejects as both impossible in fact and arrogant in intention.

Even if one grants these Herderian points, his conception of critique may raise some questions: if we are always to criticize in light of common understandings as they are expressed (embalmed?) in the shared linguistic meanings of everyday language, how can we come to recognize errors in that common thinking, unclarity in that everyday language? Must we just accept the status quo, as furnishing un-criticizable constraints and "materials" (context)? It may seem, too, that Herder glosses over the difficulty of discerning the "internal rules" of use, and so ruling out corresponding misuse, of the natural faculties: how are we to "investigate" or "observe" the faculties, in order to discern such rules? We may grant to Herder that we cannot get outside or beyond them, but does he indicate at all how we are to find their proper, best directions?

Herder does mention (if not fully articulate or explore) a panoply of strategies—more conservative, less revolutionary ones—to try to investigate our shared meanings, and the proper use of our cognitive faculties. He mentions biographies and doctors' reports as sources of information about how human powers operate, what they are, and endorses the empirical scientific study of psychology to understand ourselves and abilities better.[39] He endorses and engages in etymological and other linguistic analysis to determine and specify the meanings of words. (And thereby also concepts, for Herder holds, famously, that thought and language are intimately connected: "What is it *to think*? *To speak inwardly*," he writes.)[40] Correspondingly, he takes it that the central tasks of philosophy include conceptual analysis, and (for him, closely related) historical investigation of human language use, meanings, experiences, and practices.[41] He proposes that the different cognitive powers may correct one another, as we correct visual illusions through touch, for example.[42] There are, in sum, many ways to investigate human cognitive faculties and clarify natural-linguistic meanings.[43]

We have not yet accounted, however, for the centrality of critique—precisely in its localized form—to Herder's philosophy. So far, as I have presented it, his position appears to be negative or hypothetical: *if* one wishes to engage in critique, this—and not the bad, Kantian version—is what it should be. But critique is more important for Herder: it is not an optional, hypothetical philosophical enterprise, but rather central to philosophy, as is manifested less in stated doctrine than in his philosophical practice itself. For, as mentioned above, Herder's own philosophy proceeds in large part *through* critique (indeed, often polemic), to a degree unequaled, I think, by any other philosopher, even those of similarly cantankerous temperaments, such as Schopenhauer. Though Herder does not state this view explicitly (to my knowledge), I think that this critical practice is for him crucial to the philosophical project of self-knowledge, precisely for reasons expressed in the questions raised above. If we cannot stand outside of—if we cannot critique according to external criteria—our practices, contexts, inherited meanings, operations of our faculties, how can we discover the "internal rules" of the faculties, or correct their misuse? The answer to this question for Herder is, I think, philosophy as conversation, the interchange of positions, arguments, and so forth, from many individual, localized subjects' points of view. Such conversational practice in philosophy includes, I think, Herder's much-heralded practice of *Einfühlung*, "feeling one's way" into others' perspectives. Sympathetic interpretation allows one not only to broaden one's understanding of what human beings can do, believe, or value—and so also of the uses of natural faculties—but also to take up another perspective, and thus potentially to correct one's own blind spots or errors.[44] But it also, and prominently, includes more direct critique—testing, challenging—of others' views.[45]

Let me spell out a bit the character of such conversation, and so both fill out my characterization of Herderian critique, as well as suggest how it can contribute to the project of clarifying linguistic meaning or investigating the (proper) use of the faculties (even if it does not consist in "testing" the faculties, as we have seen). Artificers (notably here, authors) obviously use their faculties to produce their works, whether artworks or philosophical doctrines (and so forth). They thus manifest and make more determinate what those faculties are like, what they can do. A strong version of this claim is the core of the position Charles Taylor has termed Herder's expressivism: internal states or frames of mind only come to be known, indeed gain determinacy at all, through external manifestation.[46] This view indeed furnishes a further reason, not much thematized in the *Metacritique*, why on Herder's view natural capacities as such cannot be critiqued: they have too many uses, are too indeterminate in themselves, to be as such objects of critique. By contrast, works produced by and expressing natural capacities *do* furnish determinate (fixed, specific) "objects"—claims, formulations, doctrines—to which one can attend, concretely, in detail, so as to test them, evaluate their success or failure, and so forth.

Authors (or other artificers) not only render the operation of natural capacities manifest and determinate, and so scrutable, in producing their works, but also thereby put that scrutable expression into a public realm, making it available to others' examination. And this examination, if it proceeds in accord with Herder's conception of critical practice (as discussed above), will appeal to common standards, to criteria shared between author and critic, between critic and "common people."[47] By so appealing, it can clarify what those rules (e.g., our criteria of rationality) actually are, to what we do or could appeal. The language of "clarify" and "appeal" (not "critique") is important here, to reflect the way in which Herderian critics take themselves to judge: they take themselves to accord with or to be subject to already-given criteria. But Herder acknowledges that these criteria may need to be discovered, investigated, made more consciously explicit or precise.[48]

The critical—oppositional, even polemical—aspect of criticism is important here as well, if, again, in a more local way.[49] The public realm, the context for and audience to which expressions are addressed, obviously comprises many other people, operating within a complex historical, experiential, linguistic context, who all—as limited, particular beings—occupy different "places" within that common context, with different experiential reference points or senses of what is important.[50] Herder adheres in fact to a form of Leibnizean monadology, reinterpreted in a realist and naturalist vein: because of their physical, cultural, and historical positions in the world, in the complex nexus of causes, individual human beings will of necessity have different conceptions of the world, reflecting their own particular, distinctive viewpoints upon it, the particular causes that have made them who they are.[51] This difference, if harnessed to the ends of critique (careful, specific, local testing, in light of appealed-to common norms), can bring to light uses of cognitive faculties that are in fact misuses or call attention to presumed common norms that are not such. Opposition means *looking for* errors and presumptions of agreement where there is none, bringing up different evidence that is more salient from one's own distinct viewpoint than it is from the author's, and so forth. Critical friction among viewpoints can foment, bring to one's attention, and also then rub away (as it were) distortions, prejudices, mistakes in the use of the cognitive faculties or in thoughts about their rules.[52]

Herderian critique is, then, localized not just with respect to its objects, but also and importantly in its subjects: the bite and opposition of critique, necessary for its role in the philosophical task of self-knowledge, is based in the locality and so the diversity of those engaged in it. With this point, we have completed my proposed picture of Herderian critique, as practiced in *Metacritique* and elsewhere: it is intersubjective conversation concerning publicly accessible "objects," specifically human products, which appeals to shared criteria, including a shared language and common natural capacities, and is practiced by particular, located, diverse individuals. This is why—to return to the discussion in section 2—we must strive to share a language, to employ terms meaningful to all. Only so can we converse.

Notes

1. Herder studied, in part with Kant, at the University of Königsberg in 1762–64. On Herder's education by and relation to Kant, see Rudolf Haym, *Herder* (Berlin: Aufbau, 1954), 1:44ff. and 2:663–768. Unless otherwise indicated, citations

of Herder are to the title of the work, followed by the volume and page number of the passage in Johann Gottfried Herder, *Werke in zehn Bänden*, ed. Ulrich Gaier et al. (Deutsche Klassische Verlag, Frankfurt, 1985–2000). I refer most to volume 8, ed. Hans Dietrich Irmscher, published in 1998. Where available, English translations are subsequently cited; otherwise, translations are my own.

2. See, for example, Herder, *Letters for the Advancement of Humanity*, 7:424–425, 794ff. Herder even praises Kant similarly in the *Calligone* (where he subjects the *Critique of Judgment* to blistering criticism), at 8:651ff.

3. See Immanuel Kant, "Review of J.G. Herder's *Ideas for the philosophy of the history of humanity*," trans. Allen W. Wood, in Kant, *Anthropology, History, and Education*, ed. Robert Louden and Günther Zöller (Cambridge: Cambridge University Press, 2007), 124–142. These reviews can also be found in Immanuel Kant, *Kants gesammelte Schriften (Akademie Ausgabe)*, ed. the Royal Prussian (later German) Academy of Sciences (Berlin: Georg Reimer, later Walter de Gruyter, 1900–), 8:45–66, and reproduced in Herder, *Werke*, 8:1089–1115.

4. Herder, *Metacritique*, 8:319.

5. Ibid., 8:318.

6. Ibid., 8:319.

7. Scholars have tended to focus on Herder's earlier works, perhaps because they were historically most influential, perhaps because they fit better historiographical conceptions of Herder's place in the Western philosophical tradition, e.g., as anti- or counter-Enlightenment, a now somewhat disputed characterization popularized by Isaiah Berlin in *Vico and Herder*, reissued in Berlin, *Three Critics of the Enlightenment: Vico, Hamann, Herder* (Princeton, NJ: Princeton University Press, 2000). I would argue that this focus is also prompted by the more positive, productive character of the earlier works by comparison to the later anti-Kant polemics: though many early works are also written as critical commentary on other works, they do not have this unrelenting, negative character.

8. See, e.g., Herder, *Metacritique* 8:346–347 on Kant's use of "Anschauung" and "Erscheinung" and so forth as arbitrary and alien to ordinary language use. On Herder's criticism of Kant's account of sensibility (of which this passage is part), see Angelica Nuzzo, "Sensibility in Kant and Herder's *Metakritik*," in *Herders 'Metakritik': Analysen und Interpretationen*, ed. Marion Heinz (Stuttgart: Fromann-Holzboog, 2013), 17–42.

9. In the Grimms' dictionary, *"Kritik"* is identified as originally Greek but borrowed from the French "critique." The first use listed, denominated "proper" (*eigentlich*), is "the art of judging or evaluating in matters of the arts and sciences," while Kant's usage (*Vernunftkritik*) is briefly listed among the "broadened" (*erweiterte*) usages at the very end of the entry. See Jacob and Wilhelm Grimm, *Deutsches Wörterbuch* (Leipzig: Hirzel Verlag, 1873), 5:2334. (For the current online edition, see http://dwb.uni-trier.de/de/die-digitale-version/online-version/; the Kritik

entry is at: http://woerterbuchnetz.de/cgi-bin/WBNetz/genFOplus.tcl?sigle=DWB&lemid=GK14447.) "Kritik" is similarly defined in Johann Christoph Adelung, *Grammatisch-kritisch Wörterbuch der hochdeutschen Mundart* (Leipzig: Breitkopf, 1793), though with greater emphasis on the art of interpreting ancient authors, in addition to that of judging artworks according to rules.

10. See Gayatri Chakravorty Spivak, *Critique of Postcolonial Reason: Toward a History of the Vanishing Present* (Cambridge, MA: Harvard University Press, 1999); Peter Sloterdijk, *Critique of Cynical Reason*, trans. Michael Eldred (Minneapolis: University of Minnesota Press, 1988); Achille Mbembe, *Critique of Black Reason*, trans. Laurent Dubois (Durham, NC: Duke University Press, 2017).

11. E.g., in the passage just cited—Herder, *Metacritique*, 346–347—Herder seems to understand perfectly well Kant's explanations of what he (Kant) means by the terms in question.

12. Herder, *Metacritique*, 8:308, 310, 312; compare to Immanuel Kant, *Critique of Pure Reason*, ed. and trans. Paul Guyer and Allen W. Wood (Cambridge: Cambridge University Press, 1998), Bxxxiii.

13. Herder, *Metacritique*, 8:312.

14. Ibid., 8:306. Of course, if one is to judge a work by its reception, Herder's *Metacritique* will not come out well either: it was strongly attacked already in 1800, more or less immediately after its publication (see Irmscher's editorial notes to the *Metacritique*, at Herder, *Werke*, 8:1063–1064) and has not been taken seriously as an engagement with Kant's Critical philosophy. It did not produce disciples, however.

15. Ibid., 8:363, 395.

16. Apart from Herder's sarcasm about "pure a priori" representations that arise "without any objects" on nearly every page of the *Metacritique* (see, e.g., Herder, *Metacritique*, 8:380), he provides an empiricist account of the origins of human concepts at Herder, *Metacritique*, 8:384ff., explicitly opposed to the Kantian claim that there are *a priori* concepts.

17. So I would distinguish, as Herder himself does not quite, between his accusations (Herder, *Metacritique*, 8:363) that Kantian terms are "contentless" on one hand, and "ill-formed" and "contradictory" on the other (where they do have cobbled-together, if ultimately unsatisfactory, content).

18. One might so interpret the discussion cited above from Herder, *Metacritique*, 8:345–346.

19. Herder raises such concerns also concerning the use of Latin in philosophy by moderns, who (because it is not their native language) are less able to detect meaningless or incoherent terminology; see *Metacritique*, 8:568.

20. This essay was written in 1783–84, but remained unpublished in Hamann's lifetime. Herder read it in manuscript well before he composed his own *Metacritique*. See Irmscher's editorial notes, Herder, *Werke*, 8: 1064–1065; the essay itself is reproduced in Herder, *Werke*, 8: 1115–1123, and may be found

in English translation in *What is Enlightenment? Eighteenth-Century Answers and Twentieth-Century Questions*, ed. James Schmidt (Berkeley and Los Angeles: University of California Press, 1996), 154–167.

21. Herder, *Metacritique*, 8:306.

22. Ibid., 8:306, 311–313.

23. Ibid., 8:343 (emphasis altered). So stated, this criticism is unfair, since Kant in fact writes that he is *not* going to ask "how is the faculty of thinking itself possible?" but only whether its knowledge *a priori* is possible (Kant, *Critique of Pure Reason*, Axvii). Herder may not have been familiar with this passage from the first edition, as he cites the second (B) edition of the *Critique*. Perhaps one could respond on his behalf also that Kant nonetheless emphasizes in section 7 of the Introduction (present in both editions) that he is criticizing not particular claims or systems, but rather the faculty of reason itself, its *"mode of cognition of objects* insofar as it is to be possible a priori" (Kant, *Critique of Pure Reason*, A11/B25, emphasis added).

24. Herder, *Metacritique*, 8:466; see also Herder, *Metacritique*, 8:371–375, 390. Herder takes even the Kantian *question* how thought might attain to objects to betray an unjustifiedly exceptionalist mode of thinking: our natural powers (here of sensation and thought) are just like all other organic powers, our minds simply part of nature (Herder, *Metacritique*, 8:388–389).

25. At Kant, *Critique of Pure Reason*, A20/B34.

26. Herder, *Metacritique*, 8:347.

27. See, e.g., Herder, *Metacritique*, 8:324–325, where Herder so objects, in a way intertwined with his empiricist objections to Kant: one cannot think beyond or apart from oneself (one has no other options), and one's self is constituted empirically, by one's inner and outer experiences.

28. Herder, *Metacritique*, 8:452.

29. Herder, *Metacritique*, 8:319. Kant is of course well aware of this self-referential—and self-limiting—character of the Critique of pure reason (and indeed of reason itself on his view). Here one might think that the German Idealists (who in their own way concur with this Herderian criticism of Kant) are more acute critics, in seeing that in order to resist this Kantian conception of reason, one must attend rather less dismissively than (unfortunately) does Herder to Kant's account of reason's self-transcendence and thus self-diagnosis (of its own errors and limits) in the Transcendental Dialectic of the *Critique of Pure Reason*.

30. At Herder, *Metacritique*, 8:370, 449, Herder suggests that Kant's views are products of fantasy (imagination) rather than reason proper; it is hard to know whether this would be, strictly speaking, a *misuse* of imagination.

31. Kant portrays reason as "eine Betrügerin ohne Kanon, ohne End und Zweck," as the "Endlosen Betrug selbst" (Herder, *Metacritique*, 8:311).

32. Herder, *Metacritique*, 8:498, 562.

33. See Herder, *Metacritique*, 8:326 for endorsement of localized critique (with respect also to the subjects exercising critique, see below).

34. I owe this observation to Mark Alznauer.

35. See Kant, *Critique of Pure Reason*, A13/B27. Colin McQuillan drew my attention to this passage.

36. Herder, *Metacritique*, 8:357ff.

37. E.g., Herder, *Metacritique*, 8:342.

38. See, e.g., Herder, *Metacritique*, 8:342–343. See also Manfred Baum, "Herder über Kants 'vefehlte Kritik der reinen Vernunft,'" in *Herders 'Metakritik'. Analysen und Interpretationen*, ed. Marion Heinz (Stuttgart: Fromann-Holzboog, 2013), 195–208, 221–222, and Irmscher's editorial notes in Herder, *Werke* 8:1065.

39. Herder, *On the Cognition and Sensation of the Human Soul*, 4:340–345 and in Herder, *Philosophical Writings*, ed. and trans. Michael Forster (Cambridge: Cambridge University Press, 2002), 197–200; Herder, "How Philosophy can become more useful and universal for the Benefit of the People," 1:111–114, and in Herder, *Philosophical Writings*, 9–11.

40. Herder, *Metacritique*, 8:389. Herder famously argues for the co-dependence of thought and language in his *Treatise on the Origin of Language*. This doctrine of course strongly motivates Herder's criticisms of Kant's language, in addition to the considerations adduced above.

41. For an endorsement of this Herderian philosophical practice, represented throughout his texts, see *Metacritique*, 8:342–343. One might argue, following Christoph Menke, that for Herder critique simply is such genealogical investigation; he certainly employs it to debunk claims concerning (e.g.) the *a priori* origin or meaning of concepts. Yet such practice can also, I suggest, simply clarify, render more vivid and meaningful, terms and practices by connecting them to the lived experience and deep human needs from which they arose; it need not, that is, have a critical (undermining, testing) function. Menke also emphasizes that Herder takes such genealogical investigation to find the conditions that precede or underlie the subject and her capacities, thus suggesting that she/her capacities are not given on Herder's view in that way that I have been emphasizing concerning the *Metacritique*, but rather are constructed over the course of individual or social history. I remain unsure how to reconcile these two aspects of Herder's views. See Christoph Menke, *Force: A Fundamental Concept of Aesthetic Anthropology*, trans. Gerrit Jackson (New York: Fordham University Press, 2013), 33–35, 41, 47.

42. Herder, *Metacritique*, 8:456.

43. On Herder's philosophical methodology (in comparison to Kant's), see Liisa Steinby, "Zur 'Wissenschaftlichkeit' von Herders Methode," *Herder Jahrbuch/ Yearbook* 13 (2016), 103–128.

44. This aspect of Herder's philosophical practice is celebrated by Isaiah Berlin (in *Three Critics*), and more recently in Kristin Gjesdal, *Herder's Hermeneutics: History, Poetry, Enlightenment* (Cambridge: Cambridge University Press, 2017).

45. See Herder, *Fourth Critical Grove*, 2:258, and Herder, *Selected Writings on Aesthetics*, trans. Gregory Moore (Princeton, NJ: Princeton University Press, 2006), 183. Here Herder insists upon the need for reasoned, interpersonal discussion

instead of trusting the unanalyzable dispensation of immediate feelings. He is at the same time *performing* such conversation, in the form of critique (even mockery) of the formulations and position of his opponent, Friedrich Just Riedel.

46. See Herder, *Metacritique*, 8:452; Charles Taylor, *Sources of the Self* (Cambridge, MA: Harvard University Press, 1989), esp. 374; Charles Taylor, *Hegel* (Cambridge: Cambridge University Press, 1975), 14–16.

47. Herder sometimes suggests that criticism, like artistic creation, requires genius (e.g., Herder, *Letters for Advancement*, 7:569). Nonetheless, he does not consider critics to be outside, beyond, above ordinary language or shared social contexts; for example, he claims about his own *Metacritique* that many others could make similar criticisms (Herder, *Metacritique*, 8:313).

48. At Herder, *Metacritique*, 8:318–319, where Herder denies that reason can be both judge and witness (quoted above), he nonetheless also emphasizes that judges must clarify the laws according to which they judge, as well as make the judgments themselves as clear as possible.

49. Astonishingly, given his own practice, Herder rejects the "polemical use" of reason (Herder, *Metacritique*, 8:578–579), not on the grounds that polemic can be misleading, too extreme (as one might worry), but on the grounds that, once errors have been removed, reason will not engage in fighting. This suggests that Herder sees his own texts as somehow preliminary, clearing the way for philosophy proper, as of course Kant also does.

50. At Herder, *Metacritique*, 8:350–352, Herder analyzes space as an image generated by the imagination, on the basis of being aware of limited beings (in the first instance oneself) as occupying particular places. I am expanding this account in a way I think friendly to Herder's approach.

51. Herder's inheritance (and reinterpretation) of Leibnizean doctrines has been discussed by, among others, Nigel DeSouza. See Nigel DeSouza, "The Metaphysical and Epistemological Foundations of Herder's Philosophical Anthropology" in *Herder: Philosophy and Anthropology*, ed. Anik Waldow and Nigel DeSouza (Oxford: Oxford University Press, 2017), 52–71, though with a more idealist slant than I would endorse (see Herder, *Metacritique*, 8:465: all idealism fails).

52. Frederick Beiser argues that Herder uses his historicist approach as a way to critique his own time. See Frederick Beiser, *Enlightenment, Revolution, and Romanticism: The Genesis of Modern German Political Thought 1790–1800* (Cambridge, MA: Harvard University Press, 1992), esp. 202–206. I take this proposal in turn to be an (historical) expansion of the practice of critique I am sketching, namely the productive critical oppositions that can arise when different subjects are at different places but are also appealing to (or take themselves to have to appeal to) common standards. (I therefore take it that Herder's historicism cannot be a form of relativism, since then it would lose its critical import.)

8

Irony and the Possibility of Romantic Criticism
Friedrich Schlegel as Poet-Critic

KAROLIN MIRZAKHAN

1. Introduction

Friedrich Schlegel's anti-foundationalist, romantic philosophy was a critical response to the philosophers of his time, particularly Kant and Fichte. In order to understand both his critique of the tradition and the role of critique within Schlegel's own philosophy, I will examine the central role of irony in his fragmentary writings. I will first argue that Schlegel's use of irony, which he defines as the "form of paradox," fosters a critical stance in his reader. Second, I will argue that Schlegel's response to his own critics can itself be regarded as an ideal moment of critique wherein the poet and critic are one and the same individual.

Throughout this chapter, I will be operating with a distinction between three definitions of critique as it pertains to philosophy and to art works. The first is what Schlegel calls ordinary critique. This type of critique is analytical—it determines what the thing is and places it within a context. The second form is critique in the Kantian sense, which is concerned with determining the boundaries of reason and dismissing reason's groundless pretensions in order to assert its rightful claims to metaphysics.[1] Schlegel is critical of this second form of critique, because it does not question itself and does not consider the limits of critique itself. He articulates this problem in *Athenaeum* fragment 56 and in his essay "On Incomprehensibility."[2] In the fragment he writes, "Since nowadays philosophy criticizes everything that comes in front of its nose, a criticism of philosophy would be nothing more than justifiable retaliation."[3] Schlegel echoes this claim when he writes in "On Incomprehensibility" that we now live in the "Critical Age" in which everything is criticized except the age itself; that is, criticism as the limitation of the faculties is not itself reined in.[4] Finally, the third sense of critique is romantic criticism, which is the form I will be developing out of Schlegel's fragments and his own response to critics who merely evaluated his work. Romantic critique is concerned neither with limitation as the evaluation of the work nor with drawing boundaries (of the understanding or of reason), but rather with the completion of the work through its reception.

2. Irony and the Critical Stance

The early German romantic movement, or *Frühromantik*, lasted from 1794 to 1808 in Jena and Berlin. Friedrich Schlegel's philosophical writings during this period are comprised primarily of his fragments published in the *Athenaeum*. Schlegel founded the *Athenaeum* journal with his brother, August Wilhelm, and though only three issues were published between 1798 and 1800, it was a major vehicle for the philosophy of the early German romantics. In addition to the Schlegel brothers, other contributors included Novalis and Schleiermacher. Schlegel also published a short essay in the last issue of the *Athenaeum* entitled "On Incomprehensibility," which was a response to the unfavorable reception of his fragments, many of which were deemed incomprehensible by his critics. I will return to this short essay where Schlegel declares that the misunderstanding of the fragments was due to their irony in the second half of the chapter, after I first provide an account of how irony cultivates the stance necessary for romantic critique.

Irony, which Schlegel defines in Critical fragment 48 as the "form of paradox," is capable of holding two, often opposing, positions simultaneously without conflating or reducing either.[5] Irony has several crucial functions in Schlegel's fragments. First, it allows Schlegel to enter into a conversation with his reader. In a conversation, each participant posits a view and is often presented with an opposing view by her interlocutor. A conversation is a back-and-forth movement between two or more participants. Schlegel is not able to be physically present with his reader, and therefore he uses irony as a technique that activates this characteristic movement of the conversation. Through irony's capacity for holding multiple views simultaneously, it thrusts the reader out of dichotomous thinking and forces her to consider two contradictory claims simultaneously. This oscillating movement between two claims is performed by the irony of the fragments and mirrors the movement of a conversation. Through irony's capacity for holding multiple claims without conflating them and thus also for holding a space for the possibility of (further) meanings, the irony of the fragments accomplishes its second role of bringing its reader "nearer" to the Absolute. The Absolute, defined as the whole or the unconditioned, must "contain" not only that which is, but also the empty space that allows for the possibility of that which is yet to be. Finally, and of primary interest in this chapter, Schlegel employs irony in his fragments in order to train his reader to have an agile mind, one capable of holding contradicting views. The fragments are multiple and it is through repeated encounters with ironic texts that the reader develops an agility of mind, and therefore also a capacity for "understanding" irony. This agility of mind can also be connected to the role of art. Fred Rush astutely points out in "Irony and Romantic Subjectivity" that art allows the viewer to inhabit many different viewpoints, and ironic art does this even more so. It is precisely irony that allows for the agility of mind to inhabit different worlds, views, and interpretations.[6] This shuttling back and forth does not only happen between multiple works of art, but it can also happen within the same work, as is the case, for example, in the Wallace Stevens poem "Thirteen Ways of Looking at a Blackbird." The poem is composed of fragments; each of the thirteen stanzas stands on its own, and, at the same time, refers to the same object: the blackbird. The shift in meaning from one stanza to the next cultivates an agility of mind in the reader, who is quickly and repeatedly transported to new viewpoints.

The agility of mind cultivated by irony creates the possibility for critique that is not merely an evaluative judgment, but rather a critical stance of its reader. This critical stance names the capacity for shuttling between multiple interpretations or views. The critic is the one who can shuttle between the work and its reception, or between multiple interpretations of the same work. This capacity, cultivated by irony, allows the work of art to open up beyond its self-imposed limits. Describing the cultivated work (and the same could be said of the cultivated individual), Schlegel writes in *Athenaeum* fragment 297, "[a] work is cultivated when it is everywhere sharply delimited, but within those limits limitless and inexhaustible; when it is completely faithful to itself, entirely homogenous, and nonetheless exalted above itself."[7] Schlegel challenges his reader to consider the work of art as self-contained and autonomous, while being simultaneously open beyond itself. One significant way in which it is open beyond itself is through its reception by an audience, i.e., through critique that interprets its meaning. This ironic description of the work as simultaneously self-contained and reaching beyond itself describes the work's relationship to criticism, or its criticizability; at the same time, as an ironic fragment, it cultivates the agility of mind required for romantic critique.

In "Criticism Underway: Walter Benjamin's Romantic Concept of Criticism," Samuel Weber argues that romantic criticism is not primarily an evaluation of the work but rather its fulfillment or *Vollendung* ("completion" or "consummation").[8] Following Benjamin's dissertation *The Concept of Art Criticism in German Romanticism*, Weber claims that works of art are autonomous and have an intrinsically coherent structure. At the same time, by virtue of their structure, they are "criticizable." Criticism refers here to the "culmination and continuation" of the structure immanent to the work of art.[9] Critique that completes the work is distinguished by Schlegel from ordinary critique, which merely analyzes the work. In "On Goethe's Meister," Schlegel distinguishes poetic criticism from critique that "[acts] as a mere inscription, and merely [says] what the thing is, and where it stands and should stand in the world."[10] In "Friedrich Schlegel's Literary Criticism," Victor Lange clarifies the role of the poet-critic who "must do more" than the ordinary critic.[11] Lange writes, "[the poetic-critic] must, in a sense, repeat the original performance, re-imagine the original imagery, and then extend and re-form the poem."[12] Lange claims that what distinguishes the romantic from the ordinary critic is respect; the romantic critic does not dissect the poem into its elements, which are dead outside of their relationship to the whole and to their "total poetic purpose."[13] This re-performance is best accomplished, Lange argues, by the one who is both critic and poet at once.[14] Schlegel articulates this point when he writes in Critical fragment 117, "Poetry can only be criticized by way of poetry. A critical judgment of an artistic production has no civil rights in the realm of art if it isn't itself a work of art, either in its substance, as a representation of a necessary impression in the state of becoming, or in the beauty of its form and open tone, like that of the old Roman satires."[15] In order to elaborate this view that poetry can only be criticized by way of poetry, I will closely examine Schlegel's short essay "On Incomprehensibility" in the following section. I will argue that an instance in which critique functions as the work's completion or fulfillment can be found in Schlegel's response to his critics who did not understand his fragments. This essay is an exemplary moment in which the romantic author and critic are one and the same individual and in which Schlegel's response to his critics enhances the meaning of the fragments without destroying their deliberately ironic form. Schlegel does not merely clarify the meaning of the fragments, rendering them comprehensible and destroying their irony in the process. Rather, this text is a romantic critique; it is a self-aware ironic treatise on irony that gives life and fuller meaning to the fragments without betraying the very force that led to their misunderstanding in the first place. In this essay, Schlegel is at once the romantic poet and critic.

3. Romantic Criticism and the Limits of Comprehension

Because the charge of incomprehensibility had been repeatedly directed against the *Athenaeum*, Schlegel begins his response "right at where the shoe actually hurts" with the "notorious fragment" in which he wrote, "The French Revolution, Fichte's philosophy, and Goethe's *Meister* are the greatest tendencies [*Tendenzen*] of the age."[16] Schlegel claims, at least initially, that he wrote this fragment with almost no irony at all, and defends the importance of the Revolution, *Wilhelm Meister*, and Fichte's philosophy for the German spirit. He quickly changes gears, however, and states that perhaps the misunderstanding lies with the multiple meanings of the word "tendency," and thus the misunderstanding of the fragment does indeed lie with its irony. That is, by "tendency" Schlegel could have meant a temporary venture that has not yet been brought into completion; or, he could have meant tendency as a partial venture in which the author relies upon the work of others. He illustrates this latter meaning of the term by stating that perhaps he is now placing himself on Fichte's shoulders, who had in turn placed himself on Reinhold's, who had placed himself on Kant's shoulders, and so on.[17] The possible double meanings of the term are also opposite senses of incompleteness; tendency marks a work as incomplete either because it is unfinished or because it is dependent on something else for its beginning, instead of being autonomous. This structure of incompleteness, or beginning in the middle of things, is also the structure of this essay on incomprehensibility. The essay does not begin with a first principle or foundation; it starts where we find ourselves in

Schlegel's present, i.e., the negative reception of his fragments. Nor does it work toward a conclusion by providing a definitive interpretation or final word on the meaning of the fragments.[18]

After providing a couple of meanings for the term "tendency" as a potential site the for the source of misunderstanding (although he is skeptical that his readers actually caught onto this), Schlegel declares "[a] great part of the incomprehensibility of the *Athenaeum* is unquestionably due to the *irony* that to a greater or lesser extent is to be found everywhere in it."[19] After proclaiming that irony is indeed the source for the misunderstanding of the fragments, Schlegel immediately defines irony by quoting his own Critical fragments 38 and 108, where he defines irony as the "form of paradox" and where he defines Socratic irony, respectively. The irony of the fragments is thus, given the definitions to which he refers, their capacity to posit multiple, often contradictory, meanings at once, and their capacity, like Socratic irony, to be simultaneously "playful and serious," to be at once "the freest of all licenses" and "absolutely necessary."[20]

Schlegel does not stop there; he does not merely state that the fragments are ironic and that their irony is the source of the misunderstanding. He re-performs the structure of their irony in a categorization of irony, and thus performs a romantic critique of the fragments. Schlegel models his system of irony on the French poet Boufflers's categories of hearts: "*Grands, petits, minces, gros, médiocres, énormes.*"[21] This gesture to construct a system of irony is itself ironic insofar as irony is that very force which, by positing multiple meanings simultaneously, undercuts our efforts at creating a completed system. The first and most rudimentary type of irony, "coarse irony," is found in the nature of things. As Elaine Miller has pointed out, crystals, which the romantics were fond of, have splitting and unity as a part of their organic structure.[22] Crystals are an example of irony, as the coincidence of opposites, in the nature of things. This type of irony is also found in the forces of love and strife in the pre-Socratic philosopher Empedocles, as well as in the forces of yin and yang as darkness and light in ancient Chinese contexts. Thus, coarse irony courses through the very nature of things as their paradoxical structure, and is a "basis," which is not singular, for the other forms of irony. The next two types of irony are "fine" and "extra fine." The latter consists in insulting someone without their being aware. This type is tied to the traditional meaning of irony as saying one thing but meaning another. Ernst Behler has pointed out that this type of irony is found in the liars and charlatans of Aristophanic comedies.[23] In dramatic irony, the author becomes a new person in the fourth act—a transformation that is signaled by a sudden shift in the storyline. Dramatic irony is similar to the idea of a parabasis or anacoluthon, which are, as Paul de Man argues in "The Concept of Irony," marked by a shift or interruption in the narrative structure.[24] Double irony, as the name suggests, entails two meanings, which are located in different places in the theater—one for gallery and one for boxes.[25]

And, finally, at the peak, or perhaps in the depths, of this system is the "irony of irony." Schlegel lists examples of the irony of irony:

> if one speaks of irony without using it, as I have just done; if one speaks of irony ironically without in process being aware of having fallen into a more noticeable irony; if one can't disentangle oneself from irony anymore, as seems to be happening in this essay on incomprehensibility; if irony turns into a mannerism, and becomes, as it were, ironical about the author; if one has promised to be ironical for some useless book without first having checked one's supply and then having to produce it against one's will, like an actor full of aches and pains; and if irony runs wild and can't be controlled any longer.[26]

In this list of examples of the "irony of irony," Schlegel is simultaneously instructing his audience about irony and performing many of the types as he lists them. In the categories prior to the "irony of irony," Schlegel was unironically providing definitions of irony, and thus committing the irony of irony. Now, as he continues, he cannot disentangle himself from irony. The reader gets a sense, as this list goes on, that irony is indeed running wild and that this essay, which began by stating that the fragment in question was meant in earnest, can no longer escape irony. This taxonomy is itself ironic. Schlegel does not betray the irony of the fragments by unironically parsing their meanings, but rather performs irony while narrating it to his audience. This is perhaps why he thinks this essay will produce people who know how to read. A new class of readers will exist in the future who will not find the fragments indigestible, because they will have been trained to read them.

This short essay, which begins by stating that the fragment in question regarding the three tendencies of the age was indeed written almost entirely without irony, ends with Schlegel's proclamation that the fragments were indeed written in the "heat of irony" and that to parse their meanings would do "violence" to that irony.[27] Moreover, as I have argued earlier, irony is not an incidental stylistic technique employed by Schlegel, but rather the very method by which he achieves the romantic aim of bringing the reader "nearer" to the Absolute. It is irony that is the source of the misunderstanding of the fragments by Schlegel's readers, but it is also irony that is the means by which he enters into a conversation with them through a dynamic movement oscillating between two poles, which brings his readers closer to the Absolute. Because irony does not directly communicate what it means, it cannot rely on a system of complete agreement between speaker and listener, and thus there is always the possibility of misunderstanding, and with that misunderstanding the failure of the fragments to accomplish the romantic aim of the realization of the Absolute.

As a romantic critic, Schlegel does not commit violence against the fragments by parsing their meanings, by analyzing them, or by limiting their irony. He does not attempt to make their meaning comprehensible to the reader, but rather he allows for their fulfillment by pointing to the limits of comprehensibility itself. Rather than destroying the ironic fragments by making them un-ironic in order to explain their meanings, he elaborates, in the following passage, the crucial role of irony, which shows us the limits of human knowing. Schlegel asks his readers,

> But is incomprehensibility really something so unmitigatedly contemptible and evil? Methinks the salvation of families and nations rests upon it. If I am not wholly deceived, then states and systems, the most artificial products of man, are often so artificial that one simply can't admire the wisdom of their creator enough. Only an incredibly minute quantity of it suffices: as long as its truth and purity remain inviolate and no blasphemous rationality dares approach its sacred confines. Yes, even man's most precious possession, his own inner happiness, depends in the last analysis, as anybody can easily verify, on some such point of strength that must be left in the dark, but that nonetheless shores up and supports the whole burden and would crumble the moment one subjected it to rational analysis. Verily, it would fare badly with you if, as you demand, the whole world were ever to become wholly comprehensible in earnest. And isn't this entire unending world constructed by the understanding out of incomprehensibility or chaos?[28]

In this passage, Schlegel claims that the most precious thing we possess, our "own inner happiness," depends on "something" that must be left in the dark, without being subjected to "blasphemous rationality" (*frevelnder Verstand*). The terms translated here as "rationality" or "rational analysis" are better translated from the German "*Verstand*" as the English "understanding." For Schlegel, the understanding names a watered-down way of looking at the world, which cuts it apart in order to know it. If to understand means to dissect, the understanding can never reach the Absolute as the whole. It will only ever know it in part or, better yet, *in relation to* the structures of human knowledge. If we were to subject everything to the understanding, we would destroy that which we seek to know. Schlegel is warning his readers of the disastrous consequences of trying to make the whole world comprehensible (*verständlich*). Human structures are constructed, according to Schlegel, by the understanding out of "incomprehensibility or chaos."[29] This means that there is a limit to human knowing and rational scrutiny. There is "something" that must be allowed to remain in the dark, but which supports the entire structure. Schlegel is not only warning his readers of the dangerous consequences of their need to criticize everything (except, as he says, the "Critical Age" itself), but also pointing to the limits of human knowing. Schlegel is gesturing toward what exceeds the comprehensible but makes comprehensibility itself possible, i.e., the incomprehensibility or chaos out of which the possibility of comprehensibility arises.

Schlegel is not performing critique in the Kantian sense of defining the limits of the understanding or of reason, because the means by which limitation is revealed is irony. Irony points out the limits of our claims to sovereignty, by demonstrating that words have a "secret brotherhood" and often outwit those who use them.[30] By showing us that we cannot have complete mastery over language, irony humbles the knower and points out the limits of her sovereignty. And by exposing our own limitations, irony produces an agile mind capable of sensing, but not knowing, that which lies outside the realm of the human. Schlegel describes this agility in terms of versatility in *Ideas* fragment 55, where he writes, "Versatility [*Vielseitigkeit*] consists not just in a comprehensive system but also in a feeling [*Sinn*] for the chaos outside the system, like man's feeling [*Sinn*] for something beyond man."[31] *Vielseitigkeit*, or many-sidedness, does not aim merely at a more comprehensive system, i.e., one that contains more as an aggregation. Rather, versatility names a multifaceted approach, which has a feeling for that which lies outside our human attempts at knowing. True versatility feels its own limits.

4. Conclusion

Schlegel's essay "On Incomprehensibility" does not perform critique by circumscribing irony's role and is thus not critique in the Kantian sense outlined earlier. Nor is it an example of what Schlegel calls ordinary criticism, i.e., a form of critique that merely places the work in its proper context and says what it is; it is not a defense of his earlier claims that provides the reader with historical and social context. It is a romantic critique that re-performs the work, and through which the work culminates. As a romantic critique, Schlegel's essay does not betray the irony of his fragments in order to parse out their meanings and make them easier to digest by their audience. The fragments remain, as Ricarda Huch puts it, "hard-shelled nuts," which require the energetic effort of their reader, whom they simultaneously train to read.[32] This essay does not betray the irony of the fragments, because it is itself ironic. For example, in its exposition of irony, it produces an ironic classification system, which is both illuminating and frustrating for the reader who wants to know what irony "is" and "where" exactly it is located. It re-performs the irony of the fragments, but in a way that opens up their meaning, that exposes more about the work of irony, i.e., that irony points us toward the limits of human knowing without allowing for complete mastery, because it shows us that words have a "secret brotherhood." Without directly stating, it reveals that it would be absurd to write an essay about irony that attempted to have full mastery, and moreover that doing so would truly betray the irony of the *Athenaeum* fragments.[33] Like Socratic irony, the essay as a whole is simultaneously serious and playful; it contains both moments of clarification and further obfuscation of the meaning of the fragments. In this essay, Schlegel is poet-critic; he is at once the author of the ironic and witty fragments and the author of their critique in a romantic sense. He re-performs the irony of the original work, the *Athenaeum* fragments, in a way that opens these "hard-shelled nuts" without cracking them, i.e., without destroying their peculiar ironic form.[34] This essay is the *Vollendung* or completion of the fragments, in which their irony is both preserved and illuminated for the reader.

Notes

1. A fuller account of this second form can be form in J. Colin McQuillan's contribution to this volume, "Not Yet a System, Not Yet a Science: Reinhold and Fichte on Kant's Critique."

2. References to the fragments are cited according to their number and abbreviated as follows: AF = *Athenaeum* fragments, CF = Critical [*Lyceum*] fragments, IF = *Ideas* fragments. References in the original German are from Friedrich Schlegel, *Kritische Friedrich-Schlegel-Ausgabe* (cited hereafter as *KFSA*), ed. Ernst Behler, Jean Jacques Anstett, and Hans Eichner (Munich: F. Schöningh, 1958). Translations are from Friedrich Schlegel, *Friedrich Schlegel's Lucinde and the Fragments*, ed. and trans. Peter Firchow (Minneapolis: University of Minnesota Press, 1971).

3. Schlegel, *Lucinde and the Fragments*, 168; CF 56.

4. Schlegel, "On Incomprehensibility," in *Classic and Romantic German Aesthetics*, ed. J. M. Bernstein (Cambridge: Cambridge University Press, 2003), 299.

5. "Ironie ist die Form die Paradoxen. Paradox ist alles, was zugleich gut und groß ist." See Schlegel, *KFSA* 2:153; CF 48.

6. Fred Rush, "Irony and Romantic Subjectivity" in *Philosophical Romanticism*, ed. Nikolas Kompridis (New York: Routledge, 2006), 182–183.

7. Schlegel, *Lucinde and the Fragments*, 204; *KFSA* 2:215; AF 297.

8. Samuel Weber, "Criticism Underway: Walter Benjamin's Romantic Concept of Criticism," in *Romantic Revolutions: Criticism and Theory*, ed. Kenneth R. Johnston et al. (Bloomington: Indiana University Press, 1990), 302–319.

9. Ibid., 309.

10. Friedrich Schlegel, "On Goethe's Meister," in *Classic and Romantic German Aesthetics*, ed. J. M. Bernstein (Cambridge: Cambridge University Press, 2003), 281.

11. Victor Lange, "Friedrich Schlegel's Literary Criticism," *Comparative Literature* 7, no. 4 (1955), 289–305.

12. Schlegel, "On Goethe's Meister," 298.

13. Ibid.

14. Ibid., 297.

15. Schlegel, *Lucinde and the Fragments*, 204; CF 117.

16. Schlegel, "On Incomprehensibility," 300.

17. Ibid., 301.

18. Schlegel, *Lucinde and the Fragments*, 171; *KFSA* 2:178; AF 84. "Subjective betrachetet, fängt die Philosophie doch immer in der Mitte an, wie das epische Gedicht."

19. Schlegel, "On Incomprehensibility," 302.

20. Schlegel, *Friedrich Schlegel's Lucinde and the Fragments*, 155–156; *KFSA* 2:160; CF 108.

21. Schlegel, "On Incomprehensibility," 303.

22. See Elaine Miller, "Romanticism and Continental Thought," in *The Palgrave Handbook of German Romantic Philosophy*, ed. Elizabeth Millán Brusslan (New York: Palgrave, forthcoming).

23. Ernst Behler, *Irony and the Discourse of Modernity* (Seattle: University of Washington Press, 1990), 78.

24. Paul de Man, *Aesthetic Ideology*, ed. Andrzej Warminski (Minneapolis: University of Minnesota Press, 1996), 178.

25. Schlegel, "On Incomprehensibility," 303–304.

26. Ibid., 304.

27. Ibid., 305.

28. Ibid.; see also Schlegel, *KFSA* 2:370.

29. Schlegel, "On Incomprehensibility," 305.

30. Schlegel, "On Incomprehensibility," 298; *KFSA* 2:364.

31. Schlegel, *Friedrich Schlegel's Lucinde and the Fragments*, 246; *KFSA* 2:262; IF 55.

32. Dennis McCort, "Jena Romanticism and Zen," *Discourse* 27, no. 1 (2005), 104.

33. Schlegel's contemporary and friend Novalis makes a similar claim in his 'Monologue' when he writes that language is concerned only with itself, and that when one attempts "to talk about something definite, the whims of language make him say the most ridiculous false stuff." It is only when, on the contrary, we speak merely for the sake of speaking that "the most splendid, original truths" are uttered. Novalis, 'Monologue,' in *Classic and Romantic German Aesthetics*, ed. J.M. Bernstein (Cambridge: Cambridge University Press, 2003), 214–215.

34. McCort, "Jena Romanticism and Zen," 104.

9

Alexander von Humboldt

A Critic of Nature

ELIZABETH MILLÁN BRUSSLAN[1]

1. Introduction

As Ronald Hepburn points out in his seminal essay, "The Trivial and Serious in Aesthetic Appreciation of Nature," art includes "a continuing practice of criticism and philosophical study," from which we develop criteria for appreciating art.[2] "In the case of nature," Hepburn points out, "we have far less guidance."[3] Yet, as Hepburn emphasizes, "it must matter, [in nature] too, to distinguish trivial from serious encounters."[4] In my view, Alexander von Humboldt (1769–1859), engaged as he was in the sort of presentation of nature that balanced the empirical data of the phenomena of nature with an appreciation of the aesthetic elements of those phenomena, served as a critic of nature, teaching his readers to distinguish the trivial from the serious in nature. Humboldt's work as a critic of nature enabled him to open his readers to a serious engagement with nature, especially the landscape of Latin America, which became the main focus of his work after his voyage to the "equinoctial region of the earth," as Spanish America was known at the time (1799–1804).

The *Naturgemälde*, a canvas or *tableau* of nature, was part of Humboldt's lifelong attempt to achieve a *Gesamteindruck* of nature. In his ambition to present a *Gesamteindruck* of nature, Humboldt did not become entangled in the "metaphysically extravagant" claims to which accounts of natural beauty guided by a concept of unity all too often succumb, and which often lead a thinker to abandon the empirical details that Humboldt found indispensable to any presentation of nature.[5] Humboldt claims that nature is the "realm of freedom" whose living breath should not be suffocated by its presenter, and for some philosophical minimalists such a claim is indeed metaphysically extravagant. Yet such a flight to the realm of ideas, part of what might be understood as giving wings to plodding science, is always tempered in Humboldt's work, by an emphasis on the empirical detail of the phenomena of nature. Humboldt's commitment to preserving the "living breath of nature" engaged him in a nuanced balancing act. In his presentation of nature, Humboldt attempted to balance the empirical mastery of nature, i.e., a quantified, scientific presentation, with those aspects of nature that could not be mastered, the free enjoyment of its charms and the awe of its power, i.e., an aesthetic presentation of nature. He believed that without empirical knowledge of nature, our aesthetic appreciation of it would be impoverished in significant ways. Yet, to transform nature, "the realm of freedom," into merely a set of quantifiable data points would strip it of its poetry and of its life force, and hence would be equally problematic. In his canvases of nature, we find systematic depictions of nature, that is to say, charts and graphs with empirical information on the quantifiable aspects of nature. Humboldt's *Naturgemälde* resist the reductionist tendency that would kill the living breath of nature that Humboldt sought to preserve. In what follows, I shall argue that the *Naturgemälde* Humboldt created with his writings on nature are best understood as literary acts of preservation—acts of preservation that presented the empirical side of natural phenomena, while maintaining space for the freedom of nature. Humboldt was *not* offering a metaphysical account of nature; rather, he was offering a presentation of nature that would be as faithful as possible to his experience of nature's beauty and its wonder. In short (though this is not a short story, and I can only tell a fraction of the larger story here), Humboldt took on the task of a critique of nature. Humboldt's task as a critic of nature was influenced by the constellation of ideas that took shape with the early German Romantics, especially their focus on the merging of borders between poetry, science, and philosophy. This move to merge borders is part of a philosophical project aimed at overturning hierarchies. Humboldt's role as a critic of nature is connected to the early German Romantics' embrace of the aesthetic, and their sustained call to open philosophy to science and to poetry. Of particular interest to the story of Humboldt as a critic of nature is the influence of early German Romantic thought on Critical Theory, in particular on the work of Walter Benjamin and Theodor Adorno. Margarete Kohlenbach situates the work of Adorno within the context of ideas developed by the early German Romantics: "Adorno's last work, *Ästhetische Theorie* (written 1961–69; *Aesthetic Theory*) was . . . less a philosophical work about aesthetics than a philosophical meditation that itself was aesthetic and thus represented a twentieth-century adoption of the postulate of the unity of philosophy and *Poesie* that Friedrich Schlegel . . . had first formulated at the time of historical Romanticism."[6] Kohlenbach develops a most productive line of connection between early German Romanticism and Critical Theory, one that takes seriously the role of the aesthetic in the early German Romantic movement. Adorno is one of the few philosophers who addressed Humboldt's presentation of nature in his work. That he addresses Humboldt in a work on aesthetics is particularly relevant, for it reveals that Adorno did indeed understand that Humboldt, who was a scientist, was engaged with an ambitious aesthetic project. To understand just how radical and philosophically relevant Humboldt's presentation of nature was, we need to place it into historical context. Humboldt's role as a critic of nature is part of a larger history of the dialogue between the early German Romantics and their more contemporary heirs (Adorno and Benjamin). In Humboldt's writing on nature, the realm of nature's beauty and delight brings us to the realm of aesthetic experience and of freedom—a freedom that is not exhausted by human agency or human willing.[7] Humboldt could become the critic of nature he became in part because of the efforts of the early German Romantics to make philosophy itself more critical.

Friedrich Schlegel, a leading thinker of early German Romanticism, called for philosophy to be critical in a way that it had not been even for Kant, the great critical philosopher himself. As I have already noted, a central goal of the early German Romantics' project was to bring philosophy into closer company with other disciplines, including poetry and history—strange bedfellows in the wake of Kant's *Critique of Pure Reason*, a work that celebrated philosophy's relation to the ahistorical sciences. In Schlegel's *Letter on the Novel*, which is one of his most detailed statements on the meaning of the term "romantic," he claims that, "romantic poetry rests entirely on historical grounds."[8] As we learn in *Athenaeum* fragment 116, "romantic poetry is a progressive universal poetry"—a poetic ideal that is progressive because it is always in a state of becoming, never reaching completion. Historical grounds bring romantic poetry into conversation with the tradition of which it is a part. And like poetry, philosophy is also in need of history for orientation. Schlegel never tired of emphasizing this point, and he even scolded Kant, the great critical philosopher himself, for his neglect of history, insisting that no critique can succeed without a history of philosophy. In several fragments, Schlegel claims that a critique of philosophy cannot succeed without a history of philosophy, that an age that calls itself a critical age must not leave the age itself uncriticized; in short, that Kant's critical project did not go far enough.[9] Schlegel frequently criticizes other philosophers for the one-sidedness (*Einseitigkeit*) of their approach, an *Einseitigkeit* reflected in their literary form, where there is only the voice of one author, of one position, and not enough attention to the historical context of the ideas presented. Schlegel's use of fragments, dialogues, and even the form of the novel, was his way of escaping what he understood to be the *Einseitigkeit* born of a view that philosophy could begin with first principle and achieve certainty. For Schlegel, a critical philosophy would be a blend of science and art, and his literary form reflected the innovative approach and content of his romantic, critical philosophy.

In the new literary form developed by Humboldt, the literary canvases of nature or *Naturgemälde*, we also find a reflection of some of his theoretical commitments. Committed as he was to a presentation of nature that would not kill its living breath, Humboldt was searching for a literary tool that would present nature as both an empirical realm to be mastered and a realm of beauty and delight that was beyond mastery. Humboldt wanted to avoid the vicious empiricism (*rohe Empirie*) that he found so troubling in other accounts of nature. Empiricism is vicious, he argued, only when it is deployed as the *only* way to understand nature, a way to dominate the forces of nature and tell just one side of the story of nature's meaning. We must step out of mastery to understand the full story of nature's meaning, and Humboldt's aesthetic turn is just such a move away from mastery.

Humboldt's aesthetic courage in attempting to present to his European reading public scenes of nature that were utterly unfamiliar to them was bold and, if his enduringly warm reception in the countries of Latin America is any indication, successful at wearing away at some of the troubling anti-American stereotypes that circulated widely in the late eighteenth century and well into the 1800s. Humboldt not only enacts *Naturgemälde* through his writings, especially in his *Ansichten der Natur*, which is where we find the clearest example of the *Naturgemälde* as a literary form, but he also speaks about *Naturgemälde* throughout his writings on nature.[10] The best place to examine Humboldt's reflections on the *Naturgemälde* is in the pages of his final work, *Kosmos/Cosmos* (written between 1843 and 1844, but published in1845), which became the first scientific best seller of the nineteenth century.[11] While Humboldt created his portraits of nature in *Ansichten der Natur/Views of Nature*, I will focus on what he had to say in *Kosmos/Cosmos about* how he viewed the role of the *Naturgemälde*, as I think that will take us to the heart of his critical enterprise.

2. The Task of the Critic: Concretizing Natural Beauty

Humboldt's expressed goal in *Cosmos* is to "grasp nature as one great whole, moved and animated by internal forces."[12] In the preface to *Cosmos*, Humboldt explicitly asks what literary form could possibly do justice to this task. He writes, "The very abundance of the materials which the ordering spirit should master, necessarily impart no inconsiderable difficulties in the choice of the form under which such a work must be presented, if it would aspire to the honor of being regarded as a literary composition."[13] Humboldt acknowledges that a full mastery of the abundant materials of nature will not be accomplished, but an effort toward mastery will be attempted. The ordering spirit to which Humboldt refers will be complemented by an appreciating spirit, so that in his *Naturgemälde*, order and control will join freedom and appreciation in the presentation of nature. Humboldt goes on to emphasize that descriptions of nature "ought not to be stripped of the breath of life" and so must avoid the "mere enumeration of a series of general results" and the "elaborate accumulation of the individual data of observation."[14] The mere accumulation of individual data points to quantify nature would indeed be wearying to the reader and would not do justice to the majesty of nature. To illustrate his point of what the description of nature ought to achieve, Humboldt refers to his earlier publication, *Views of Nature*. This collection of seven essays on nature was, along with *Cosmos*, one of the few he wrote in German, and it was close to his literary heart. In *Cosmos*, Humboldt claims that the success of *Views of Nature* gave him hope that he could indeed present nature to the public without weighing down the presentation with a collection of isolated empirical facts that would undermine the view of nature as a living whole:

> This work [*Ansichten der Natur*] treats, under general points of view, of separate branches of physical geography (such as the forms of vegetation, grassy plains, and deserts). The effect produced by this small volume has doubtlessly been more powerfully manifested in the influence it has exercised on the sensitive minds of the young, whose imaginative faculties are so strongly manifested, than by means of anything which it could itself impart. In the work on the *Cosmos* on which I am now engaged, I have endeavored to show, as in that entitled *Ansichten der Natur*, that a certain degree of scientific completeness in the treatment of individual facts does not necessarily entail colorlessness in its presentation.[15]

Humboldt's humility is overstated, for his *Ansichten* accomplished much more than what he describes above; its effect on the sensitive minds of the young readers was due not merely to the imaginative faculties of the young readers, but also, undoubtedly, to the literary achievement accomplished by Humboldt in the pages of his text. Humboldt's achievement notwithstanding, it is important to keep in mind that Humboldt's view of the importance of his work takes into account the *effects* of his work on his readers; he wanted to cause a change in his readers, to lead them to a greater appreciation for nature. Long before our present age of interdisciplinarity, Humboldt was well aware that certain concepts could best be approached by a perspective that drew from a variety of disciplines and methods, rather than just one. Humboldt wanted to free science from the narrow boundaries of the specialist and make it something that would be intelligible to all thoughtful people; he wanted to achieve a lively, colorful portrait of nature for his readers. In *Cosmos*, Humboldt cites Goethe's criticism of the dubious German talent for making science inaccessible to the public. He writes, "There is perhaps some truth in the accusation advanced against many German scientific works, that they lessen the value of general views by an accumulation of detail, and do not sufficiently distinguish between those great results which form, as it were, the beacon lights of science, and the long series of means by which they have been attained. This method of treating scientific subjects has led the most illustrious of our poets to exclaim with impatience, 'The Germans have the art of making science inaccessible.'"[16] Humboldt helped to correct this dubious German "talent." His writings on nature were intended not only to uncover truths about the physical world, but also to reach as many readers as possible and, even more importantly, to cultivate within his readers a "genuine love of the study of nature."[17] Humboldt's work as a critic of nature involved presenting the story of nature to his readers in a compelling way that paid tribute to both the empirical and aesthetic dimensions of nature.

In the preface to *Cosmos*, Humboldt charts the vision of nature that will guide his work, a vision intimately connected to the method of presentation that would best serve his reading public. The *Naturgemälde* are central to Humboldt's task of presenting nature, so it is not surprising that, in the introduction to *Cosmos*, we are given several clear accounts of what precisely the *Naturgemälde* are. We are told that they are "ordered according to guiding ideas, not just to pleasantly occupy the spirit. Their sequence can also indicate the grades of the impressions of nature [*Natureindrücke*], which we have followed, ranging from the gradually increasing intensity from the empty, plantless plains to the inexhaustible fertility of the torrid zone."[18] As we immediately see, the *Naturgemälde* are associated with feelings of pleasure, they are meant not only to occupy our spirit in a pleasant way, but they are also intended to present the empirical details of nature, the grades of diversity from the barren to the lush landscapes of the reaches of the earth. Already in the preface to *Cosmos*, Humboldt explicitly states that his presentation of nature will be twofold. He writes, "The first portion of [*Cosmos*] contains introductory considerations regarding the diversity in the degrees of enjoyment to be derived from nature and the knowledge of the laws by which the universe is governed, it also considers the limitations and the scientific mode of treating a physical description of the universe, and gives a general picture of nature which contains a view of all the phenomena comprised in the cosmos."[19] Like a landscape artist, Humboldt presents nature as a canvas that will illustrate the beauty of nature, an illustration, Humboldt believes, that cannot be achieved without due attention to the empirical details of nature, details that are presented via the methods of the natural sciences. An accurate presentation of nature is a goal of both the natural scientist and the landscape artist, and Humboldt sees common ground in both circles of thinkers: "in scientific circles as in the carefree circles of landscape poetry and painting, the presentation of nature gains in clarity and objective liveliness when the individual elements are decisively grasped and delimited."[20]

The common ground between science and art to which Humboldt refers and which he was devoted to cultivating remains a fertile area of analysis for contemporary philosophers. In contemporary discussions of the aesthetic appreciation of nature, we are often taken back to the problem

Humboldt brought into sharp focus so many years ago, namely, the role of empirical knowledge in our aesthetic appreciation of nature. Unfortunately, contemporary philosophers tend to neglect Humboldt's valuable contributions to this issue. For example, Malcolm Budd opens his work, *The Aesthetic Appreciation of Nature*, with a detailed discussion of what kind of understanding of nature a correct and full aesthetic of nature requires: this is precisely the sort of problem with which Humboldt grappled. Some attention to Humboldt's contributions to the problem of the role of knowledge in our aesthetic appreciation of nature would enrich the discussion we continue to have. In the context of discussing our aesthetic appreciation of nature, Budd writes:

> Do we need the knowledge of the natural scientist—the naturalist, the geologist, the biologist, and the ecologist. Does experiencing something with 'scientific' understanding of it deepen or enhance the aesthetic appreciation of it? Does it matter aesthetically whether you correctly experience something as being a certain type of natural phenomenon or of natural kind K? Does it matter whether you mis-experience something as being of a natural kind? Does it matter whether you are not mistaken about but ignorant of the natural kind you are appreciating? . . . People have thicker or thinner conceptions of the nature of the phenomena which they see or otherwise perceive under concepts of those phenomena: children have exceptionally thin conceptions, adults have conceptions of greater and varying thickness. The thicker the conception, the greater the material available to transform the subject's aesthetic experience of nature. . . . If you have the right kind of understanding of nature, you can recruit to your perceptual experience of nature relevant thoughts, emotions, and images unavailable to those who lack that understanding.[21]

These lines take us back to Hepburn's insight, namely, that the task of the critic in helping us to distinguish the trivial from the serious is no less important to our encounters with nature than it is to our encounters with art. Budd's reference to the "right kind of understanding of nature" and his emphasis on the recruitment of "relevant thoughts, emotions, and images" to enrich the aesthetic experience of nature also put him in close company with Humboldt's project of cultivating the common ground between art and science. Humboldt would not put the problem in the terms used by Budd, but Budd's clarity is helpful in highlighting the sorts of issues with which Humboldt grapples and which he addressed, albeit more implicitly than Budd does, in his work. Humboldt's presentation of nature helped "thicken" his readers' conception of the phenomena of nature without ossifying its elements. He believed that knowledge of nature augmented our aesthetic appreciation of it, in part, because knowledge of nature, especially of the history of the phenomena of nature, helped the viewer make connections between the individual phenomena in order to get at the whole or cosmos idea that he thought would help bring the idea of nature as the realm of freedom into sharper focus.

Humboldt's work has affinities not only with contemporary work on the aesthetic appreciation of nature, but also with the philosophical commitments of the early German Romantics, in particular, with their work as critics. In several of his *Athenaeum* fragments, Schlegel presents his view of poetry and the central role it plays in philosophy. The most famous of all fragments is arguably *Athenaeum* fragment 116, where Schlegel claims that "romantic poetry is a progressive, universal poetry. Its aim isn't merely to reunite all the separate species of poetry and put poetry in touch with philosophy and rhetoric. It tries to and should mix and fuse poetry and prose, inspiration and criticism, the poetry of art and the poetry of nature."[22] With Schlegel's notion of "romantic poetry," we are most decidedly *not* dealing with a fixed genre category. Schlegel pushes for a fusion of poetry and philosophy: just as all poetry should be romantic, for Schlegel, philosophy and poetry should be made one. Schlegel's notion of poetry and of irony is guided by his view that both poetry and irony are practices that help us appreciate our relation to the Absolute.[23]

Fred Rush has recently pointed out that, "just as poetry and philosophy are optimally interchangeable, criticism is supposed to be poetic."[24] Schlegel writes in Critical fragment 115 that "the whole history of modern poetry is a running commentary on the following brief philosophical text: all art [*Kunst*] should become science [*Wissenschaft*] and all science art; poetry [*Poesie*] and philosophy should be made one."[25] And in *Ideas* fragment 108, we find that the claim that "whatever can be done while poetry and philosophy are separated has been done and accomplished. So the time has come to unite the two."[26] In this cluster of claims, we find the threads for the development of a romantic hermeneutics of nature, one that would culminate in the "poetry of nature" announced by Schlegel in *Athenaeum* fragment 116. Schlegel is pushing for a broader conception of

Wissenschaft, and certainly, if nature is understood, as Humboldt insisted, as the "realm of freedom," a science of nature would almost have to be poetic, and would certainly not be laughable.[27] Indeed, such a romantic science of nature would be critical.

Humboldt, committed as he was to a presentation of nature that would not kill its living breath, was after a way to present nature as *both* an empirical realm to be mastered and a realm of beauty and delight that is beyond mastery. As I have mentioned, Humboldt wanted to avoid the vicious empiricism (*rohe Empirie*) that he found so troubling in other accounts of nature. He emphasized in his work that empiricism is vicious only when it is deployed as the *only* way to understand nature, a way to dominate the forces of nature and tell just one side of the story of nature's meaning. Let us now consider Humboldt's take on a crucial dimension of our aesthetic appreciation of nature: pleasure. Balancing our empirical knowledge of nature with our pleasure in nature's beauty was one of Humboldt's aims and part of his legacy as a critic of nature, a legacy that connects his work with Adorno's.

Writing in 1969, Adorno, in his characteristically trenchant way, lamented the fading of natural beauty from the stage of philosophy: "Natural beauty, which was still the occasion of the most penetrating insights of the *Critique of Judgment*, is now scarcely a topic of theory. The reason for this is not that natural beauty was dialectically transcended, both negated and maintained on a higher plane as Hegel's theory propounded, but rather, that it was repressed. The concept of natural beauty rubs on a wound and little is needed to prompt one to associate this wound with the violence that the artwork—a pure artifact—inflicts on nature."[28] Adorno goes on to tell us that Humboldt occupies a position between Kant and Hegel, "in that he holds fast to natural beauty yet in contrast to Kantian formalism endeavors to concretize it."[29] The delicate balancing act that Humboldt performs in his *Naturgemälde* attempts to blend our experience of nature's beauty with a detailed account of its objective properties. Let us now turn to some examples of how Humboldt presents natural beauty and how he concretizes it.

3. The Aesthetic Appreciation of Nature through Thick and Thin

In *Cosmos*, Humboldt maintains that the pleasure we take in nature is the result of having arrived at or at least approximated a presentation of nature as a totality.³⁰ In order to understand nature in its totality, and so to deepen our delight in nature, we need a method that enables us to capture not only the empirical facts of the objects of nature, but also the individual elements of nature in a coherent way leading to a sense of nature's whole. For Humboldt, the task of connecting the individual elements of nature into some harmonious whole was of high importance, for the meaning and value of nature could not be appreciated if the elements of nature remained a group of disconnected individual items. In Humboldt's work we find a focus on the "general connection" (*allgemeiner Zusammenhang*) present in the phenomena of nature and his desire to grasp nature in its unity. The chain of connection that will lead us to the whole of nature is built of both knowledge of nature and appreciation for the phenomena of nature. Consider the following claim from *Cosmos*: "In considering the study of physical phenomena, not merely in its bearings on the material wants of life, but in its general influence on the intellectual advancement of mankind; we find its noblest and most important result to be a knowledge of the chain of connection, by which all natural forces are linked together, and made mutually dependent upon each other; and it is the perception of these relations that exalts our views and ennobles our enjoyments."³¹ Humboldt delineates two types of pleasure: (1) sensual or physical pleasure and (2) intellectual pleasure. He describes sensual pleasure in the following way: "One [sensual pleasure] arouses the open, childlike sense of humans, the entrance to free action and the dark feeling of unison, which dominate in the eternal change of nature's silent drive."³² So, on the one hand, the pleasure we have in nature is something primitive, an intuitive feeling, something sensual. This sort of pleasure is available, to speak with Budd, to those with even the thinnest conceptions of nature, young children finding pleasure in spring's first bright red tulip, for example. But there is also the intellectual pleasure we take in the contemplation of nature, which "comes from the comprehension of the order of the world and of collaboration of the physical forces within the world."³³ This sort of pleasure, again invoking the lines cited above from Budd's account, is a pleasure born of a thicker conception of nature, found in the experience of the mountaineer who not only enjoys the thrill of the view from atop the Chimborazo, but who is also aware of the precise altitude of her vista point and is well aware of the mountain's composition and history—facts that connect the vista to a history of the mountain and the mountain's place within the history of the earth, creating a connection between an individual experience of nature and nature as a whole (that is, the web of forces and phenomena comprising our experience of nature). Like Budd, Humboldt stresses the "right kind of understanding of nature," as he puts it: "if we would correctly comprehend nature, we must not entirely or absolutely separate the consideration of the present state of things from that of the successive phases through which they have passed. We cannot form a just conception of their nature without looking back on the mode of their formation. It is not organic matter alone that is continually undergoing change and being dissolved to form new combinations. The globe itself reveals at every phase of its existence the mystery of its former conditions."[34] The sort of recruitment of relevant thoughts, emotions, and images referenced by Budd finds company in Humboldt's emphasis on creating a context that provides a fuller understanding of the phenomena of nature and its appreciation. For Humboldt, the description of nature is "intimately tied with its history."[35] The critic of nature is the figure poised to place the empirical details of nature into a context that enables a deeper story of its meaning to emerge. I will end with some comments on how that takes place in Humboldt's work.

4. Assimilation and the Task of the Critic

Mere accumulation of historical facts about nature or of empirical facts about natural phenomena is not enough to bring us to an aesthetic appreciation of nature. We must assimilate our knowledge of nature (be that knowledge of nature's history or of its empirical data) into our aesthetic experience of nature. As Jerome Stolnitz points out, "[m]erely to acquire knowledge is not enough and may even be detrimental to aesthetic appreciation."[36] Knowledge about something must be assimilated into our aesthetic experience of that thing; otherwise, it remains aesthetically irrelevant. Knowledge of a given object, be that object a painting by Picasso or a flower in a field, is, to speak with Stolnitz, aesthetically irrelevant if that knowledge remains external to our aesthetic experience of the object. In his presentation of nature, Humboldt attempts to make knowledge of nature aesthetically relevant to our experience of nature. Intellectual recognition and aesthetic enjoyment of the phenomena of nature are assimilated in Humboldt's *Naturgemälde*. Knowledge of nature plays a role in creating connections between phenomena, and when that knowledge of nature is assimilated into our aesthetic experience of nature, the level of appreciation deepens, and the project of approximating the whole of nature is further developed.

Enjoyment of nature and knowledge of it are two distinct experiences. Humboldt's *Naturgemälde* blend enjoyment and knowledge of nature so that our knowledge of nature can deepen our aesthetic appreciation of it. His *Naturgemälde* serve to guide the reader in her appreciation of nature, much the same way a good critic of art can guide the viewer of a work to a deeper appreciation of a painting's value. Humboldt, engaged as he was in the sort of presentation of nature that balanced the empirical data of the phenomena of nature with an appreciation of the beauty of those phenomena, served as a critic of nature, teaching his readers to distinguish the trivial from the serious in nature. This work as a critic of nature enabled him to open his readers to a deep appreciation for and a serious engagement with nature.

Notes

1. With thanks to María Acosta and Colin McQuillan for comments that helped me develop several points with more detail.
2. Ronald Hepburn, "Trivial and Serious in Aesthetic Appreciation of Nature," in *Landscape, Natural beauty, and the Arts*, ed. Salim Kemal and Ivan Gaskell (Cambridge: Cambridge University Press, 1993), 65.
3. Ibid.
4. Ibid.
5. I take this way of describing the pitfalls of those seeking "unity" accounts of nature from Hepburn's watershed (as far as renewed attention to the aesthetic dimensions of nature go) article, R.W. Hepburn, "Contemporary Aesthetics and the Neglect of Natural Beauty" in *British Analytical Philosophy*, ed. Bernard Williams and Alan Montefiore (New York: The Humanities Press, 1966), 285–310, here 299.
6. Margarete Kohlenbach, "Transformations of German Romanticism 1830–2000," in *The Cambridge Companion to German Romanticism*, ed. Nicholas Saul (Cambridge: Cambridge University Press, 2009), 273.
7. Martin Seel develops one of the most original lines of work connecting Humboldt to critical theory. See his *Eine Ästhetik der Natur* (Frankfurt am Main: Suhrkamp, 1996). His *Aesthetics of Appearing*, trans. John Farrell (Stanford: Stanford University Press, 2005) is also a valuable source for exploring the nuances and aesthetic implications of Adorno's thought.
8. All references to Schlegel's work are to Friedrich Schlegel, *Kritische Friedrich-Schlegel-Ausgabe* (cited hereafter as *KFSA*), ed. Ernst Behler, Jean Jacques Anstett, and Hans Eichner (Munich: F. Schöningh, 1958), 2:334. Some of Schlegel's fragments have been translated by Peter Firchow, in Friedrich Schlegel, *Friedrich Schlegel's Lucinde and the Fragments*, ed. and trans. Peter Firchow (Minneapolis:

University of Minnesota Press, 1971). When I have used Firchow's translation, the reference is to this edition, cited hereafter as Firchow.

9. See for example, Schlegel, *KFSA* 2:165, no. 1; *KFSA* 2:364; *KFSA* 12:286; *KFSA* 18:21, no. 35; *KFSA* 18:21, no. 36; *KFSA* 19:346, no. 296.

10. *Ansichten der Natur* was first published in 1807, with new editions published in 1826 (which included the essays,"Versuch über den Bau und die Wirkungsart der Vulkane in den verschiedenen Erdstrichen" and "Die Lebenskraft oder der rhodische Genius") and in 1849. See Alexander von Humboldt, *Ansichten der Natur*, ed. Hanno Beck (Darmstadt: Wissenschaftliche Buchgesellschaft, 1987). This has been translated as Alexander von Humboldt, *Views of Nature or Contemplations on the Sublime Phenomena of Creation,* trans. E.C. Otté and Henry G. Bohn (London: Henry G. Bohn, 1850). A more recent translation is Alexander von Humboldt, *Views of Nature,* ed. Stephen T. Jackson and Laura Dassow Walls, trans. Mark W. Person (Chicago IL: University of Chicago Press, 2014). References to *Views of Nature* are to the Otté translation. All references to *Ansichten* are to the Beck edition.

11. Gisela Brude-Firnau, "Alexander von Humboldt's Sociopolitical Intentions: Science and Poetics" in *Traditions of Experiment from the Enlightenment to the Present: Essays in Honor of Peter Demetz*, ed. Nancy Kaiser and David Wellbery (Ann Arbor: University of Michigan Press, 1992), 45–61.

12. Alexander von Humboldt, *Cosmos: A Sketch of the Physical Description of the Universe*, trans. E.C. Otté (Baltimore, MD: Johns Hopkins University Press, 1997), 24. All English-language references are to this edition, hereafter *Cosmos*. I have often, for the sake of greater precision, modified the translation (indicated by "translation modified") or simply translated the passage anew when I have found the Otté translation wanting (indicated as "my translation"). The German references to *Kosmos* are to Alexander von Humboldt, *Kosmos: Entwurf einer physischen Weltbeschreibung*, 5 vols. (Stuttgart/Tübingen: J.G. Cotta, 1845–1862). See also Humboldt, *Cosmos*, 7, translation modified. "[D]ie Natur als ein durch innere Kräfte bewegtes und belebtes Ganzes aufzufassen" (Humboldt, *Kosmos*, vi).

13. Humboldt, *Cosmos*, 8–9, translation modified. "Bei der reichen Fülle des Materials, welches der ordende Geist beherrschen soll, ist die Form eines solchen Werkes, wenn es sich irgend eines literischen Vorzugs erfreuen soll, von großer Schwierigkeit" (Humboldt, *Kosmos*, viii).

14. Humboldt, *Cosmos*, 9; Humboldt, *Kosmos*, viii.

15. Humboldt, *Cosmos*, 9, translation modified. "Diese Schrift behandelte einzelne Teile des Erdlebens (Pflanzengestaltung, Grasfluren und Wüsten) unter generellen Beziehungen. Sie hat mehr durch das gewirkt, was sie in empfänglichen, mit Phantasie begabten jungen Gemüthern erweckt hat, als durch das, was sie geben konnte. In dem *Kosmos*, an welchem ich jetzt arbeite, wie in der *Ansichten der Natur* habe ich zu zeigen gesucht, daß eine gewisse Gründlichkeit in der Behandlung der einzelnen Thatsachen nicht unbedingt Farbenlosigkeit in der Darstellung erheischt" (Humboldt, *Kosmos*, ix).

16. Humboldt, *Cosmos*, 47. "Man hat vielleicht mit einigem Rechte wissenschaftlichen Werken unserer Literatur vorgeworfen, das Allgemeine nicht genugsam von dem Einzelnen, die Übersicht des bereits Ergründeten nicht von der Herzählung der Mittel zu trennen, durch welche die Resultate erlangt worden sind. Dieser Vorwurf hat sogar den grössten Dichter unserer Zeit [Goethe] zu dem humoristischen Ausruf verleitet: die Deutschen besitzen die Gabe, die Wissenschaften unzugänglich zu machen" (Humboldt, *Kosmos*, 29).

17. Humboldt, *Cosmos*, 12; Humboldt, *Kosmos*, xv.

18. Humboldt, *Cosmos*, 27–28, translation modified. "Naturgemälde, nach leitenden Ideen aneinander gereiht, sind nicht allein dazu bestimmt, unseren Geist angenehm zu beschäftigen, ihre Reihenfolge kann auch die Graduation der Natureindrücke bezeichnen, deren allmähli gesteigerten Intensität wir aus der einförmigen Leere pflanzenloser Ebenen bis zu der üppigen Blütenfülle der heissen Zone gefolgt sind" (Humboldt, *Kosmos*, 10).

19. Humboldt, *Cosmos*, 10, translation modified. "Der erste Band meines Werkes enhält: Einleitende Betrachtungen über die Verschiedenartigkeit des Naturgenusses und die Ergründing der Weltgesetze; Begrenzung und wissenschaftliche Behandlung der physischen Weltbeschreibung; ein allgemeines Naturgemälde als Übersicht der Erscheinungen im Kosmos" (Humboldt, *Kosmos*, xii).

20. Humboldt, *Cosmos*, 34, translation modified. "Aber in dem wissenschaftlichen Kreis wie in den heiteren Kreisen der Landschaftsdichtung und Landschaftsmalerei, gewinnt die Darstellung um so mehr an Klarheit und objektiver Lebendigkeit als das enzelne bestimmt aufgefaßt und begrenzt ist" (Humboldt, *Kosmos*, 12–13).

21. Malcolm Budd, *The Aesthetic Appreciation of Nature* (Oxford: Oxford University Press, 2002), 20.

22. Schlegel, *KFSA* 2:182; Firchow, 31.

23. For more on Schlegel's view that poetry and irony are practices that help us appreciate our relation to the Absolute, see Fred Rush, *Irony and Idealism: Rereading Schlegel, Hegel, and Kierkegaard* (Oxford: Oxford University Press, 2017).

24. Rush, *Irony and Idealism*, 73.

25. Schlegel, *KFSA* 2:161; Firchow, 14.

26. Schlegel, *KFSA* 2:267; Firchow, 104.

27. While Schlegel pushes for the unity of philosophy, poetry, and science, he also claims that "taken strictly the idea of a scientific poetry is just as laughable as that of a poetic science" (Critical fragment 61, Schlegel, *KFSA* 2:154). Cited by Rush, *Irony and Idealism*, 73n106.

28. Theodor W. Adorno, *Aesthetic Theory*, trans. Robert Hullot-Kentor (Minneapolis: University of Minnesota Press, 1997), 62.

29. For a more detailed discussion of the connections between Humboldt's presentation of nature and the aesthetic views of Adorno, see Elizabeth Millán Brusslan, "Protecting Natural Beauty from Humanism's Violence: The Healing Effects of Alexander von Humboldt's *Naturgemälde*," in *Post-humanism in the Age of Humanism. Late 18th- and Early 19th-Century Cognitive, Materialist,*

and Idealist Contentions, ed., Edgar Landgraf, Gabriel Trop, and Leif Weatherby (Bloomsbury, 2019): 183–200.

30. Eberhard Knobloch has analyzed the relation between pleasure and the portraits of nature in *Cosmos*. See Eberhard Knobloch, "Naturgenuss und Weltgemälde—Gedanken zu Humboldt Kosmos," *Internationale Zeitschrift für Humboldt-Studien* 5, no. 9 (2004), 34–48.

31. Humboldt, *Cosmos*, 23. "Wer die Resultate der Naturfoschung nicht in ihrem Verhältnis zu einzelnen Stufen der Bildung oder zu den individuellen Bedürfnissen des geselligen Lebens, sondern in ihrer großen Beziehung auf die gesamte Menschheit betrachtet, dem bietet sich als die erfreulichste Frucht dieser Forschung der Gewinn dar, durch Einsicht in den Zusammenhang der Erscheinungen den Genuss der Natur vermehrt und veredelt zu sehen" (Humboldt, *Kosmos*, 4).

32. Humboldt, *Cosmos*, 24, translation modified. "Den einen erregt in dem offenen kindlichen Sinn des Menschen der Eintritt in die freie Natur und das dunkle Gefühl des Einklangs, welcher in dem ewigen Wechsel ihres stillen Treibens herrscht" (Humboldt, *Kosmos*, 5).

33. "Entspringt aus der Einsicht in die Ordnung des Weltalls und in das Zusammenwirken der physischen Kräfte" (Humboldt, *Kosmos*, 5).

34. Humboldt, *Cosmos*, 72.

35. Ibid.

36. Jerome Stolnitz, *Aesthetics and Art Criticism. A Critical Introduction* (Boston, MA: Houghton Mifflin, 1960), 58.

10

Critique, Refutation, Appropriation

Strategies of Hegel's Dialectic

ANGELICA NUZZO

In presenting the project of a dialectic-speculative logic in contrast both to traditional logic and to Kant's transcendental logic—i.e., the positions he generally subsumes under the designation of *Verstandeslogik*—Hegel curiously insists on the fact that this foundational part of his system is ultimately not such a novelty after all. In downplaying the originality of his logic, Hegel highlights, rather, the apparent continuity with the tradition, a continuity confirmed by the persistence of a seemingly unalterable logical content. This is, after all, what Kant had claimed with regard to the scientific status of formal logic in the 1787 Preface to the *Critique of Pure Reason* looking back to Aristotle, a claim that Hegel now duly repeats. Because of its formality, logic seems to be a concluded and perfected science since its very inception—and to never "have had to go backwards a single step," as Kant puts it.[1] Kant, however, had also insisted on the unprecedented character of a logic that instead of being "generally" formal, i.e., instead of concerning the mere form of thinking as such (*Denken*), addresses the particular form of our knowledge (*Erkennen*) of objects in their truth, thereby reclaiming an objective content and a crucial epistemological validity.[2] Thereby the distinctive transcendental character of Kant's logic is indicated. To this logic belongs a fundamentally critical function with regard to reason's speculative knowledge and its objects. Next to the Analytic, the Dialectic as "transcendental dialectic" becomes part of the critique of (pure) reason.

While insisting on the presence of the contents of traditional logic in his "science of logic," Hegel also sides with Kant's content-based transcendental logic and its critical function with regard to metaphysics. The new logic is characterized as *dialectic-speculative* (in contrast to formal or transcendental or even phenomenological) not by its content but by the "method" which shapes that content in the form of a "science of logic." In fact, the content, Hegel announces, is the same "received material," the same well-known "thought forms" inherited from the tradition and critically explored by Kant—notably, among them, the traditional ontological determinations featured in the Logic of Being and Essence, and the forms of concepts, judgments, and syllogisms featured in the Logic of the Concept. Such content, however, given the way it is generally handled in the logical presentation, displays the appearance of "dead bones of a skeleton thrown together in a disorderly heap."[3] The logical "thought forms" (*Denkformen*), Hegel maintains, are the supporting skeleton of an organism now inexorably dead and quickly decaying. They are nothing more than dead bones scattered haphazardly, unmoved, and without life. According to this image, the task of the new logic and, more precisely, of the new "method" is to restore the living function of that inert skeleton, to coherently organize those bones in the self-supporting structure of a living organism, i.e., of a self-moving systematic whole. As the "soul" is the principle of life, Hegel claims in Aristotle's aftermath, the task is to animate those dead bones with soul; and furthermore, as the soul is the principle of movement, at stake is the task of presenting the life of the logical organism in the dynamic process that first institutes it precisely as a living whole. Now the dialectic-speculative method is the "soul" or "living pulse"[4] that alone can bring back to life the dead spoils of the tradition. The paradox is that the living organism thereby obtained turns out to be an entirely new creature.

A significant *critical* objective is outlined in Hegel's program. Indeed, only the act of thoroughly re-thinking the tradition can lead to radical innovation. If at stake is the "truth" of the logical forms, as Kant had already maintained by asking Pilate's question—"What is truth?"—such truth is inseparable from the actual, realized life of the organism that instantiates it or brings it about.[5] Truth is the dynamic movement in which the life and action of pure thinking discursively unfolds. If the organism is dead and unmoved, this is, *ipso facto*, the proof of the failure of the method employed. Now, as Hegel's logic takes up the critical task of Kant's transcendental logic, it does so as system whereby it is presented as the true "system of pure reason."[6] System, then, is critique—or: for Hegel, dialectical systematicity replaces transcendental critique. That is to say, critique is carried out by the methodological act that organizes the content in the form of a system, thereby reinstituting the life of the organism (truth is, famously, "the whole" and is alive only as such whole).[7] The system concerns the articulation of truth as its discursive process-like actualization. Herein truth and freedom ultimately converge. The speculative concept—*Begriff*—is the structure that articulates this convergence. Indeed, it is at the beginning of the Logic of the Concept that Hegel raises Pilate's question, "What is truth?" echoing Kant with regard to the systematic place in which the logic is expected to raise the question of truth.[8]

While the confrontation with Kant's transcendental logic plays a crucial role in Hegel's presentation of his "science of logic," a well-known slogan from the preface to the *Phenomenology of Spirit* sets the logic (which takes its departure from "absolute knowing" as the result of the phenomenological development) in a critical confrontation with Spinoza. Famously, "everything hangs on apprehending and expressing the truth not merely as substance but also equally as subject."[9] At stake, again, is "truth." But truth cannot be apprehended and expressed as "subject"—or rather, "also equally" as subject in addition to substance—unless the form of the system is achieved. For, ultimately, truth is the full actuality of that discursive system. In the *Phenomenology* as well, Hegel appeals to the image of the dead body to be reanimated in order to make the same point he will make in the *Science of Logic*. The critical target is the contemporary (Schellingian) view of truth as the Absolute, the intuitive first and last that defies development and discursive systematicity. Now, despite their distance from Schelling's Absolute, traditional formal logic and Kant's transcendental logic (i.e., the undialectical *Verstandeslogik*) share the same view of truth as fixed and unchangeable because set apart from falsity and error. Hegel formulates the task—at once logical and historical—as that of "bringing fluidity to fixed thoughts" or, alternatively, as that of "realizing and spiritualizing the universal by overcoming fixed . . . thoughts."[10] Significantly, the fulfillment of this task is identical with the transformation of "pure thoughts" into the speculative concept.

In sum, the problem of the dynamic, living articulation of truth at the center of Hegel's logic, the problem to which "method" and "system" respond, implies a confrontation with—and a critique of—the preceding logical tradition but also Kant and Spinoza. More specifically, Kant and Spinoza are crucial for understanding the dialectic-speculative nature of Hegel's logical *Begriff*. Now, there is a customary way of accounting for Hegel's relation to both his predecessors (and even, more generally, to the entire history of philosophy) that construes it as a powerful (for better or worse) operation of *appropriation* of their views animated, in different degrees, by a *critical* stance. Dialectical *Aufhebung* may be taken, indeed, in this sense, namely, as an appropriative movement of overcoming. On this interpretative view, however, appropriation and critique stand in a problematic and generally unexplored relation. It certainly does not seem *necessary* to appropriate that which is critiqued and thereby overcome—it seems neither necessary *per se* nor necessary for critique to be performed. (If anything, one may suggest the opposite, namely, that only that which survives critique may be appropriated.) What, then, is the relationship that connects Hegelian critique to dialectical appropriation and *Aufhebung*? Ultimately, and more generally, to address this question is to confront the predicament that places philosophical thinking between the past of its historical tradition and the openness of its future.

In this paper, I argue that the dialectical *method* of Hegel's logic—that is, the way thinking's forms are given life and its discursive process immanently and systematically organized—is, first, appropriation: an appropriation that transforms, *transformative appropriation* (an appropriation that transforms, perhaps, to the point of rendering what is appropriated utterly other [than itself], hence uncomfortably unrecognizable). Second, Hegelian dialectic is *refutation* (*Widerlegung*). The ways dialectic transforms what it appropriates is by refuting what it appropriates (or what it has made its own), hence by an act of self-refutation. Herein Hegel's dialectic shares a crucial, although not often underscored, feature with Socrates' *elenchos* and Plato's elenctic dialectic in contrast to Aristotle's: namely, its ethical and indeed educational core validity. Refutation is connected to thinking's freedom. It is significant that while the transformative appropriation of traditional logical and metaphysical contents may seem practiced throughout the logic, *Widerlegung* is appealed to explicitly and thematically only at the crucial juncture in which Spinoza and Kant are confronted: in the transition from the Objective to the Subjective Logic (or from Being and Essence to the Concept). And it is furthermore significant that such critical confrontation is considered *logically necessary* in order for the problem of truth to be addressed in its full scope as the problem of freedom. It is precisely at this juncture that Hegel repeats Pilate's question, "What is truth?"[11] Refutation is the process of truth's actualization as freedom. It is not, however, the highest act of freedom itself—it is not the highest act of the logical subject in which Spinoza's substance is finally transformed and by which it is fully refuted. The final act of freedom is the gesture of "letting go" and "letting be"—the *frei Entlassen* that is ostensibly the very opposite of that initial appropriation, the act of relinquishing whatever has been appropriated thereby letting it be free from the subject, free for itself or in its own right, free for new possibilities. Thus, the subject established by the dialectical process is free not as possessor or proprietor of truth but in the very act of letting truth be beyond the subject itself. Appropriation is not a final goal, and is not what freedom in its fullness consists in. Its function is rather to be always revoked as a substantial appropriation—"to be let go of." This is the highest act of freedom.

In sum, my suggestion is that Hegel's dialectical critique as method for instituting truth and freedom is the articulation of three interconnected moments or actions: first, transformative appropriation; second, refutation as self-refutation; and the final act of letting go. In what follows, I will discuss these moments by looking at three crucial passages of the *Science of Logic*: the Absolute in which the Logic of Essence appropriates Spinoza's substance; the *Widerlegung* of Spinozism as the "genesis" of the *Begriff* and the beginning of freedom; and the act of *frei Entlassen* by which the "absolute idea" brings the logic as a whole to the end, leading logical thinking beyond itself to its radical other.

1. Transformative Appropriation

Let's begin by going back to the quoted passage from the *Phenomenology*. At stake is the task of "bringing fluidity to fixed thoughts," of "realizing and spiritualizing the universal by overcoming fixed . . . thoughts."[12] Hegel suggests that thinking is set in motion when the "the pure consciousness of itself makes abstraction from itself,"[13] i.e., when pure thinking yields to the negative power of its own activity, and consents on becoming a "moment" of a more comprehensive process. Once this change of perspective has taken effect, it becomes clear that truth belongs to the larger overall process (indeed, to the "whole");[14] that each partial moment owes its truth to the whole of which is part; and that each partial moment, taken in isolation (and because of it), is simply false. Becoming fluid and lifelike requires a humbling gesture, namely, the recognition that the whole is not yet available and that the whole is not what thinking itself in its inception is (thinking is instead only a "moment"). The requirement that the pure consciousness of itself make abstraction from itself implies not that thinking must be "eliminated or left aside" but that it abandons "the fixity" of its self-conferred autarchic position. If the *Phenomenology* aims at instituting truth as the subject beyond mere (Spinozistic) substance, the subjectivity Hegel is after is not the unmoved "I think" of transcendental philosophy. For, on Hegel's view, reason's "critique" notwithstanding, Kant's subject still belongs to the autarchic order of an unmoved and still absolutistic truth.

The standpoint of science results from a development in which consciousness achieves truth only by mediating its initial immediacy, thereby activating the negative power of the self and losing its fixity and guaranteed uniqueness. To recognize that knowledge in its immediate position is not yet true means to recognize that a fundamental "difference"[15] still separates consciousness from its content. This lack of identity or adequacy between consciousness and object—this lack of truth, as it were—determines the "fluid," process-like character of thinking on its path to science. Difference (hence the lack of adequacy which is untruth) is the "negative" that immanently moves the phenomenological process. Thereby Hegel draws to the center what traditional logic and the activity of *Verstand* strenuously labor to keep out. The negative is by definition a "lack" (*Mangel*), is the falsity that general logic, being necessarily concerned with truth (and *only* with truth), must block out of thinking. On Hegel's view, by contrast, the negative is the "soul" and the moving principle of the process *toward truth*, and this process only is the movement *of truth*.[16] To claim that a "difference" (*Unterschied*) separates consciousness from its object is to claim that the imbalance of an *Ungleichheit*—a lack of (self-) identity—affects substance in its relation to itself. In order to eliminate such difference the recognition is required that what appears as an external "action" that substance only suffers is truly *its own* action. Only at this point is substance *proved* subject, i.e., when suffered external action is turned into one's own free act of self-determination.[17] Herein truth and freedom converge.

In the *Phenomenology*, truth is achieved when the substantial content has become "immediate property of the I," when truth's actuality has finally become "property of consciousness."[18] Truth becomes truth by an act of appropriation, thereby becoming itself *Eigentum*—property as that which is proper (*eigen*) to its possessor, allegedly identical with it (thereby erasing the *Ungleichheit* still affecting consciousness on its way toward truth). Such *"selbstisch"* possession—substance beginning to acquire the form of the "self" (*selbst*)—is "the concept."[19] However, truth is a "property" that stands under a twofold limiting condition. First, possession is more properly the phenomenological process of appropriation or of becoming intellectually worthy (or, minimally, capable) of possessing truth: it is not the passive inheritance of an already given—initial, original, and allegedly absolute—truth but the act by which the subject progressively and indeed laboriously acquires the position of truth. Kant's property-right model of deduction yields to the notion of the subject's laboring for the appropriation of the truth by which the subject itself is first constituted. Hegel replaces the transcendental *quid juris* with a phenomenological *quid facti*. Or, to put it differently, the story Hegel tells regards the subject's efforts, not her proprietor status as such. Second, the final truth of the *Phenomenology* that consciousness, having reached "absolute knowing," is said to finally "possess" (or which is said to be consciousness's *Eigentum*), is a precarious possession immediately revoked by the utter indeterminacy of the beginning of the Logic in which the phenomenological subject and its truth entirely vanish. As the *Phenomenology* reaches truth and the self seems to eventually "possess" it, what we really have is the beginning of the Logic, i.e., the point of radical immediacy and indeterminateness from which the constitution of purely logical truth begins. In this point there is no subject entitled to possess truth, just as there is no ready-made truth to be possessed. In an important reversal, the form of the concept has rather taken possession of the self.[20] In the Logic, the concept has to "let go" of the (phenomenological) subject, as it were—and this constitutes the specifically *logical* movement of speculative truth, the process that only in the end reaches the logical form of free subjectivity.

While the Logic is the "science of truth in the figure of truth,"[21] the *Phenomenology* is the process in which truth appears in the complete series of its partial figures. Accordingly, truth is herein present along with its negative form, and is itself rather the (totality of the) false. For this reason, Hegel needs to debunk the commonsense representations of falsity, which, like the claims of *Verstandeslogik*, are the major obstacle to gaining "access to truth." Underlying these views is the assumption that truth and falsity are fixed, thoroughly separated, and unmoved determinations (of things or thoughts). Under this condition, however, the question arises: why do we need a "science of the false" or Phenomenology; why can't we start immediately with truth—which is accordingly assumed as a given, unquestioned "absolute"? The understanding's assumption is that truth is separate from the false and immediately graspable as such—no need to labor on finding it, no need to dwell on falsity. In the framework of the logic of the understanding, which separates truth and falsity, the access to speculative truth is inexorably blocked. It follows that such position must be *refuted* if the *Phenomenology* is to lead on to the logic as the science of "truth in the figure of truth": "True and false belong among those determinate notions which are held to be motionless and wholly separate essences, one here and one there, each standing fixed and isolated from the other, with which it has nothing in common. Against this view it must be maintained that truth is not a minted coin that can be given and pocketed ready-made."[22] Herein Hegel explicitly makes Lessing's refutation of the numismatics of truth in *Nathan der Weise* (the truth-coin analogy) his own by turning it against the *Verstandeslogik*.[23] He rejects the common notion that truth and falsity are "determinate thoughts" given once and for all—ready-made and ready at hand for their indifferent exchange, like "minted coin." Such a notion leads to the essentialist view that sets them as "independent essences" separate from each other, and consequently denies any possible "*Gemeinschaft*" or common ground between them.[24] Moreover, Hegel rejects the view of truth and falsity that by positing them as utterly "motionless" deprives them of dynamic development and the possibility of change. The conception of truth as the whole offers the programmatic backdrop for his argument: truth is not given and isolated but is a result, positioned along with the false within the totality of a system progressively and indeed historically developed in the structure of the whole.[25] However, at this juncture, Hegel does not appeal directly to it but endorses Lessing's position to state his disagreement with the numismatics of truth. Echoing Nathan's claim, Hegel simply states, "it must be contended that truth is not minted coin." The fixation in the thing-coin, the unmoved essentialization of value that is consigned to the illusory process of abstract quantitative exchange, the appeal to the minting authority for ultimate validity, the radical separation of truth and falsity—these are the target for both Hegel and Lessing. Thus, in the *Phenomenology*, Lessing's "refutation" of the numismatics of truth becomes the starting point of Hegel's speculative and developmental idea of truth.

It follows that if truth is to become "property" of the self through a process of appropriation, such possession does not fall within the economic realm of monetary activity and exchange. Truth is not minted coin. Moreover, as suggested above, such refutation indirectly implies another critical objective. Truth is not an absolute and is not the Absolute—first and foremost because truth is the result and endpoint of a discursive process, not an intuitive beginning. As the dimension of pure logical thinking obtains from "absolute knowing," the proprietor subject of the *Phenomenology* disappears and truth must be reconstituted by a dialectical process that is now moved by its own "method" or "soul," independently of a substrate, a thinking subject, a phenomenological consciousness or an external reflection. Appropriation becomes a process without proprietor subject.

In the conclusive step of the Logic of Essence, the Absolute—Spinoza's absolute—is dialectically appropriated, as it is made into a necessary step in the conclusive development of essence. The Absolute is not a beginning (as for Schelling) but both a transition point (from Being through Essence to the Concept) and, most importantly, a failed attempt at making the end (i.e., of reaching the Absolute). In fact, the Absolute that substance maintains to be is not the highest or absolute truth—hence not the end—but only the necessary condition for the transition to the concept. As such, however, the dialectically appropriated Absolute is transformed into a contradiction, i.e., into an absolute that being not-absolutely-absolute is *ipso facto* overcome the moment it is posited. Thereby the transition to the sphere of the Concept is achieved.

Hegel claims that "the concept of Spinozistic substance *corresponds* to the concept of the absolute."[26] Spinoza's substance is the monistic whole: "*one* substance, *one* indivisible totality." Hegel underlines that "there is no determinateness that is not contained and dissolved into it." Precisely to this extent, substance is posited as the same totality that essence is, and more precisely, as the absolute with which essence attempts to conclude its movement by positing the highest, absolute truth. This is essence's appropriation of Spinozistic substance. There is no determinateness that is not *contained* in the absolute as its *Grund*. But there is also no determinateness that is not *dissolved* in the absolute as its *Abgrund*. Indeed, Hegel recognizes as a valuable insight of Spinozism that "anything that to the natural way of representing and to the determining understanding appears as self-subsistent is entirely reduced in this necessary concept to a mere *positedness* [*Gesetzsein*]." Hegel famously expresses the "absolute principle" of Spinoza's substance in the proposition "determinateness is negation," a proposition he considers a "true and simple insight" but also a limited one, for it remains at the view of "negation as determinateness or quality" and does not advance to negation as self-negation. Ultimately this means that the individual does not recover from—or does not survive—the negation or annihilation within the absolute; that it does not subsist *as individual* within it. The further limit of Spinoza's position consists in the fact that the "manifold act of determining" lies in "an external thinking." Thinking is "not as determining and informing, *nor as a movement of return that begins from itself.*"[27] In other words, the end, in the case of the absolute (the end that the absolute allegedly makes or represents), is not a turning back to a new beginning. Thinking radically ends in the absolute substance but does not make a return back into itself, hence does not make a new beginning out of itself. Such is, instead, the nature of subjectivity. Despite its definition as *causa sui*, the absolute is not itself a creative power truly determining itself—it is the end but not a new beginning. It is the repetitive power that reproduces itself in a self-identical position, with no otherness and no difference[28]—Nature repeating itself but truly unable to imagine an utterly different order; thinking identical with extension but unable to differentiate itself from it. However, the capacity of making a new beginning *out of itself* and *after the end* is, for Hegel, the necessary condition for anything claiming to be truly "absolute": absolute knowing, absolute idea, absolute spirit. Indeed, the end entails the creative act that requires the production of difference as difference, of otherness as otherness. This is the character of freedom. But it is also the limit of Spinoza's position. The absolute is not "absolutely absolute,"[29] is not the true end. Thinking stalls in the absolute and is indeed "petrified" in the end, unable to turn back to itself and to gain the "concept of an other by which it would have to be formed" anew, as different from itself.[30] Thinking is annihilated in the abyss but does not survive negation.

2. Refutation

Hegel presents the Concept as a double result. It is, first, the result of the entire development of Being and Essence, which contain the "genetic exposition of the concept."[31] But it also results, more directly, from the immediately preceding movement of substance.[32] Significantly, Hegel translates this latter relation in terms of truth. The "concept is the *truth of* substance," and since the modality of substance is "necessity," he concludes that "freedom is the *truth of* necessity and the mode of relation [*Verhältnisweise*] of the concept."[33] Hegel frames the problem of conceptual truth in terms of the immanent process that produces a logical "successor" from the internal dialectic of a determinate logical form. Truth is "truth of" as that genitive's successor; it is that which succeeds or follows an accomplished and concluded movement. If truth is a process (the process in the flux of which dialectical thinking has been transformed), the end of the process is not absolute; truth follows the end. That which is succeeded or overcome (*aufgehoben*), in turn, viewed from the newly gained "height" (and only then) may be seen as false. The false emerges only once truth is established: truth *completes* the false. Accordingly, the concept as the "truth of substance" is the "completion of substance [*Vollendung der Substanz*]" and, as such, it is "a higher structure [*ein Höheres*]," namely, subject.[34] In the concept we attain the transition from substance to subject announced in the preface to the *Phenomenology*. The speculative form of truth expressed in the syntactic form "truth of" is the structure according to which an advancement is made and an ascending oriented movement with a higher and a lower level is established. Moreover, since that which is overcome in the structure of truth specifies or determines this very truth as the "truth *of*," that which precedes and is overcome (i.e., the false) is still present within truth. Clearly, this structure fundamentally alters the linear and static opposition of truth and falsity defended by the logic of the understanding. Speculative truth does not leave anything behind; it is cumulative and inclusive; it is concrete in that it uses the false as the means to acquire determinateness and specification and ultimately completion (*Vollendung*). Thereby Hegel points to the process that leads the concept on to its full realization in the "absolute idea" as the true and final end of the entire logical movement.

While the structure of truth just described brings to mind the general mode of dialectical *Aufhebung* at work throughout the Logic,[35] in order to introduce the form of the *Begriff* at the beginning of the Logic of the Concept Hegel appeals to the different, more specific idea of "refutation"—*Widerlegung*. If the "concept is the *truth of* substance" and its "completion," dialectical refutation is the act that institutes speculative truth by completing what it refutes as it refutes it. Now, on Hegel's view, the philosophical system that paradigmatically "remains stuck [*stehenbleibt*] in the standpoint of substance" is Spinoza's.[36] Significantly, Spinoza is called in at this juncture not because he generically represents the standpoint of substance (the point Hegel makes in the exposition of the Absolute in the sphere of Essence) but because he has taken it as the final, highest, and completed end, has stopped there (he "remains stuck" in it, as it were), and hence has not seen the necessity of "completing" the thought of substance into its truth, namely, the concept. The falsity or shortcoming (*Mangel*) that is involved in Spinoza's position consists in taking substance as the *static*, *final*, and *absolute* truth that as such does not itself need to be completed in a higher truth. In so doing, Spinoza is unable to discover the *speculative truth* of substance, namely, its successor, the *Begriff*.[37] Thus, what Hegel needs to perform at the beginning of the Logic of the Concept is the step that leads from the notion of substance of the Logic of Essence on to the "truth of substance." Now this step takes the form of a "*Widerlegung des Spinozismus*."[38] At stake in such refutation, Hegel warns, is not the opposition between a "true" and a "false" philosophical system with the aim of declaring which one of the two *possesses* the final truth.[39] For, the position of substance belongs, after all, to speculative logic itself as a necessary moment, and is essential to the concept because it constitutes its immanent "genesis" or "genetic exposition."[40] Substance belongs to the concept if the concept is to be declared the "truth of" substance and its *Vollendung*. Reciprocally, truth "arises out" of the position of substance and belongs to it: it is the truth *of* its very standpoint.[41] The completion of substance is its very refutation. Dialectical refutation is completion.

Hegel indicates two conditions for a refutation leading to speculative truth, or for a "true and truthful refutation" to take place: "*wahrhafte Widerlegung*" says Hegel in the *Science of Logic*, echoing Aristotle, or "*gründliche Widerlegung*" as he posits in the *Phenomenology*.[42] First, no polemic *Entgegensetzung* should be tolerated, for head-on opposition blocks the access to truth by making the movement of truth impossible, and rather describes the stalemate resulting from the understanding's separation of truth and falsity. True refutation implies instead inclusion and inclusive confrontation of different positions; it implies the recognition that such positions do in fact share something common or a common ground (the *Gemeinschaftes* mentioned in the passage of the preface to the *Phenomenology* mentioned above),[43] i.e., at least, the quest for truth. Second, refutation should not "come from the outside," namely, from premises and assumptions that lie outside of the system to be refuted, but shall be the immanent, internal process of thinking through the premises of the system itself. Refutation necessarily comes from inside a certain position.[44] In this regard, refutation does presuppose the movement of appropriation as the act of making what one refutes one's own. Thereby Hegel renders the complementary and reciprocal tenet that completes a fundamental principle of Socratic refutation shared by Aristotle's dialectical *peirastike*, namely, the fact that the dialectician must interrogate her interlocutors starting from what they truly believe, not from what they take from the outside or from common and not necessarily shared opinions.[45] While what is at stake in Socrates's *elenchos* is the demand that the interlocutor say what he believes, once the interlocutor's view is appropriated by the refuter, the demand becomes that refutation be truly self-refutation—a conclusion ultimately confirmed in Plato's view as well.

Now, under these two conditions (namely, the exclusion of merely antagonistic opposition and the requirement of immanence), Hegel rejects the opposition to Spinoza's philosophy on the basis, for example, that he does not take the claims of freedom and self-conscious subjectivity into account. For such pretended refutation "comes from the outside," from a different and higher standpoint, and does not really engage the position it criticizes. Taking already for granted the self-proclaimed "truth" of its own standpoint, namely, the already established claim of free subjectivity, it does not recognize the merits of Spinoza's own idea of thinking and its connection with the notion of self-consciousness.[46] In other words, on Hegel's notion of "true" *Widerlegung*, the claim that Spinoza's philosophy lacks the concept of freedom and self-consciousness not only is *not* a refutation but entirely misses the point of his position and remains utterly external to it. Ultimately, this is a refutation that, not having made the other's position its own (i.e., lacking the effort of appropriation), is unable to recognize the root of its own genesis and lacks the critical courage required by a self-refutation. Thus, Hegel claims that against the merely "*äußerliche[s] Widerlegen*" that only yields unilateral results but no higher truth, the "*wahrhafte Widerlegung* must give in to the force of the adversary and place itself in the circle of his power."[47] The point of the immanent and true refutation of Spinozism is to show the necessary *transition* from Spinoza's idea of thinking as attribute of substance to the higher, inclusive truth displayed by the subjectivity of the concept. Significantly, such transition *begins* with Spinoza. The concept results precisely from the process of *thinking through* substance, of "completing" it, as it were, or of thinking it to the end. It follows that the "only possible refutation of Spinozism can consist solely in this, that first its standpoint is recognized as essential and necessary, and second, this standpoint is lifted to the higher one *from itself*."[48]

There is, indeed, an "ethics of refutation" sketched out in this important argument. Freedom arises only on the condition of recognizing the adversary as necessary and constitutive to one's own truth, or on the condition of building truth as inclusive and respectful of difference. Appropriation is not the exercise of an act of power whereby the other is erased and the self is erected as the sole possessor of truth. There is no refutation, let alone "true refutation," going on in this case. This is an important warning when we recall that the concept's universality is constituted by an act of *Übergreifen* (*Begreifen* is also *Über-greifen*). Appropriation is instead the necessary condition of a true refutation insofar as it imposes to take the other's position as seriously as one's own. Refutation is always self-refutation. "Reaching over" the other is not so much the act of power that erases the other's presence as the act that exposes the shortcomings of the self and shows its necessary implication in every act of refutation.

Thus, Hegel's conclusion is that "the *exposition* of substance" in its leading on to the concept is the "true refutation of Spinozism." Thereby "*wahrhafte Widerlegung*" indicates both the properly *speculative* way of conducting a refutation and the refutation that yields a higher, inclusive truth against the blocked, unilateral oppositions of the understanding and against its absolutistic and static view of truth. At this point, conceptual truth achieved by appropriating and refuting Spinoza discloses the "realm of freedom."[49] And yet, "true refutation" is only the *beginning* of the concept's freedom, not yet freedom's full-fledged actualization. For this we have to attain the level of the idea—the "absolute" idea, which, being conclusively "absolute method," brings us back full circle to the problem stated at the beginning.

3. Freedom as "*Frei Entlassen*"

Once the transition to the concept is accomplished, the question "What is truth?" is proposed yet again,[50] this time in relation to the notion of "deduction" put forth by Kant's transcendental logic. Kant's deduction is now criticized (or indeed "refuted") and replaced with the idea of the concept's own process of "realization."[51] Hegel's point is that reality can by no means be placed "outside of the concept"[52]—which is by contrast the premise of Kant's transcendental deduction—since the concept is in itself real. The dimension of freedom implied by the concept's truth consists precisely in staging the process of realization culminating in the structure of the "idea." This task emerges already in the first step of the Logic of the Concept in which Hegel presents the *Begriff* in the "moment" of universality[53] as the "concrete universal." Herein it becomes clear for the first time in what sense the concept is the completion and truth of substance. The concept in its universality is pure identity with itself. It is not, however, abstract identity but identity full of determination. The concept is not only itself concrete but in its immanence within the concrete the concept is the animating "soul of the concrete." In this relationship, the concept shows its identity with and adequacy to itself.[54] To be sure, the concept is a fundamental relation or, better, a way of establishing relations to the other. Ultimately the concept is constituted by such relations. The relationality of the concept, however, is not displayed in the merely external way proper of the *Reflexionsbestimmungen* of essence; it is instead the free action of the concept itself. Hegel expresses all this by saying that the concept is the true "essence" and the true "substance of its determinations," so that what for substance was contingent is now the very mediation of the concept with itself, its "immanent reflection" and the act of its free self-determination.[55] This is indeed the concept's *"Vollendung"* of substance."

And yet, it is only at the end of the logic that the "absolute idea" is able to attain the overarching form of truth or truth in its full logical completion (*"alle Wahrheit"*), and to perform the highest form of free action. Properly, it is only such a free action that can be called "absolute," thereby sanctioning the end of the logical process. Such an action *is* the end: it is neither a beginning allegedly pronounced absolute (Schelling's) nor the *Grund-Abgrund* of an Absolute posited as the end of all things but itself incapable of making a new beginning (Spinoza's), truly only a transition point. It is only the free action of the "absolute idea" that can put an end to the logic as a whole. Such action is free in the sense of being capable of generating an utterly new beginning. Freedom is creation. This act entails the most radical critical stance, which is, at the same time, the consummation—that is, the fulfillment and completion—of both the moment of dialectical appropriation and the movement of true refutation. The last moment of dialectical critique is the act of letting go—*frei Entlassen*—which revokes the appropriative act (and all possessions thereby claimed) while leaving refutation behind.

Hegel presents the end of the logic or its highest, indeed "absolute" truth in apparently simple terms. "As the idea posits itself . . . as the absolute *unity* of the pure concept and its reality and thus gathers itself in the immediacy of being, it is in this form as the totality—nature."[56] The idea gathers or collects itself, and in so doing it re-collects the overall development that has made it what it truly is, namely, the "absolute unity" of concept and reality (which is truth). Then there is a pause in this re-collecting act. And the pause produces a sort of identification, or perhaps only a suggestion, a hint toward the new creative act, which is no longer an act of logical thinking. It is, rather, the *Zeigen*—the act of pointing to and imagining a new beginning.[57] It is the different, indeed logically unprecedented act of intuiting, an "intuition"[58] that discloses a new horizon for thinking, knowing, acting, being, namely, "nature."[59] What follows to the end of the book is Hegel's explanation of this final act.

The action with which the idea makes the end is "neither a having-become [*Gewordensein*] nor a transition [*Übergang*]" in the strict sense. It is, instead, an "absolute liberation"—"*absolute Befreiung*." Since this final liberation is not the positing of a determination that is still immediate or not yet permeated by the concept (as is the case at each step within the logical process), "in this freedom there is no transition that takes place." This freedom is therefore *complete*: "in it" there is no passing over into something other, no refutation is needed to further complete it. The end in its absoluteness is not a transition but the liberating gesture that hints to another story altogether, to another, unprecedented way of acting and being—a way that is not yet there, not even in outline (i.e., indeterminately or immediately), but must be entirely invented, imagined anew. As the idea in a final act of freedom "determines itself" to simple being, this "remains completely transparent to it" and is "the concept that in its determination remains with itself [*der . . . bei sich selbst bleibende Begriff*]."[60] Indeed, "to-remain-with-oneself" is no transition and no becoming; it is, rather, another expression of the highest freedom caught in its concluding act—to-be-with-oneself-in-otherness. However, Hegel suggests that if there is a "transitioning" in this action, it should be taken "in the sense that the idea *freely lets go of itself* [*sich selbst frei entlässt*], absolutely certain of itself and *internally at rest*."[61] The idea's "absolute liberation" is the act whereby the idea frees itself from itself: having fulfilled its (logical) task, it absolves and unbounds itself from it, and is now both retrospectively *free from* it and prospectively *free for* a new life, a new destination, and a new task. Indeed, this can be seen as the accomplishment of the highest critical act. In its freedom, the idea lets itself go or lets go of itself as it has been as *logical* idea, and lets itself go as something utterly other—nature. As the poet puts it: "the power of relinquishing / what one would keep that is freedom."[62] Finally, the "letting go" and "letting be" that describes the ending action of the idea's absolute freedom is "*Entschluss*."[63] This is the act that by ending makes a thoroughly new beginning. Properly, the movement beyond the end begins with both the idea's *Entschluss* and its *Befreiung*—decision and liberation disclose Nature and Spirit beyond the idea's logical end.

And here, conclusively, is the full critical force of the dialectical argument deployed throughout the Logic in what I have indicated as the three moments of appropriation, refutation, and the liberating act of letting go. Discursive or rational truth is no (substantive) Absolute (there for someone to be possessed over and above others). It is, instead, the culminating free act of (logical) subjectivity. No Absolute is a beginning (against Schelling) (and no beginning is absolute); but no Absolute is the end if such an end is unable to creatively generate an utterly new process (against Spinoza). Hence, also: no end is the Absolute. Ultimately, the highest truth is the absolute liberation of a free decision to let go in its realized truth whatever has been appropriated and refuted. Now, if the story of such progressive appropriation and refutation is the "system" of logic achieved at the end of this discipline, the final liberating act in seemingly revoking such a story is the beginning of the development of the different story of nature and spirit.

Notes

1. Immanuel Kant, *Critique of Pure Reason*, ed. and trans. Paul Guyer and Allen W. Wood (New York: Cambridge University Press, 1998), Bviii. All references to Kant's first *Critique* use the standard A/B pagination of the first (1781, A) and second (1787, B) editions.

2. For an extensive development of this topic, see Angelica Nuzzo, "General Logic, Transcendental Logic, Dialectic-Speculative Logic," in *System und Logik bei Hegel—200 Jahren nach der Wissenschaft der Logik*, ed. L. Fonnesu, L. Ziglioli (Hildesheim, Olms, 2016), 63–80.

3. Georg Wilhelm Friedrich Hegel, *Werke in zwanzig Bände* (cited hereafter as *TW*), ed. Eva Moldenhauer and Karl Markus Michel (Frankfurt am Main: Suhrkamp Verlag, 1970), 5:19.

4. Hegel, *TW* 6:551, 5:27.

5. Kant, *Critique of Pure Reason*, A58/B82.

6. Hegel, *TW* 5:44, 61.

7. See Hegel, *TW* 3:24.

8. Hegel, *TW* 6:244; Hegel cites Klopstock, *Der Messiah*, 7. Gesang V. I have examined this reference extensively in "'. . . As if Truth were a Coin!' Lessing and Hegel's Developmental Theory of Truth," in *Hegel-Studien* 44 (2009), 131–155.

9. Hegel, *TW* 3:22.

10. Ibid., 3:37.

11. Ibid., 6:244.

12. Ibid., *TW* 3:37: respectively, "*die festen Gedanken in Flüßigkeit zu bringen*" and "*durch das Aufheben der festen, bestimmten Gedanken das Allgemeine zu verwirklichen und zu begeistern.*"

13. Ibid., 3:37.

14. Ibid., 3:24.
15. Ibid., 3:39: *"Ungleichheit"* and *"Unterschied."*
16. Ibid.: it is its "soul" (*"Seele"*) or "the moving principle" (*"das Bewegende"*).
17. Ibid., 3:39: "Was ausser ihr [der Substanz] vorzugehen, eine Tätigkeit gegen sie zu sein scheint, ist ihr eigenes Tun, und sie zeigt sich wesentlich Subjekt zu sein."
18. Ibid.: *"Eigentum des Bewusstseins,"* *"Eigentum des Ichs."*
19. Ibid.
20. Ibid., 5:25: of the logical determinations of thought we cannot properly say that they "are at our service," we cannot say "that it is we who have them in our possession [*Besitz*]" since it is those determinations "who have us in their possession."
21. Ibid., 3:39–40: *"Wissenschaft des Wahren, das in Gestalt des Wahren ist."*
22. Ibid., 3:40. "Das Wahre und Falsche gehört zu den bestimmten Gedanken, die bewegungslos für eigene Wesen gelten, deren eines drüben, das andre hüben ohne Gemeinschaft mit dem andern isoliert und fest steht. Dagegen muß behauptet werden, dass die Wahrheit nicht eine ausgeprägte Münze ist, die fertig gegeben und so eingestrichen werden kann."
23. For a close examination of Hegel's reference to Lessing's *Nathan*, see Nuzzo, "As if Truth were a Coin," 131–155.
24. This point needs some explanation from Hegel's part: what can the *Gemeinschaft* of truth and falsity indicate? In what sense is there a community between the two—not the spatial separation of "here" and "there" but somehow the unifying basis of a common, shared space?
25. See the programmatic passages in Hegel, *TW* 3:24, 28.
26. Hegel *TW* 6:195 (emphasis added).
27. Ibid. (emphasis added).
28. Ibid., 6:196.
29. Ibid., 6:190.
30. Ibid., 6:196.
31. Ibid., 6:245.
32. Ibid., 6:245f.
33. Ibid., 6:246 (emphasis added).
34. See Hegel, *TW* 6:249.
35. See Hegel's explicit considerations in Hegel, *TW* 5:113f.
36. Hegel, *TW* 6:249.
37. Ibid.
38. Ibid., 6:250.
39. Ibid., 6:249.
40. Ibid., 6:246 and 245 respectively.
41. Ibid., 6:249: *"geht von selbst* der wahre Standpunkt *desselben* . . . hervor" (emphasis added).

42. Ibid., 3:27; see Aristotle, *Sophistical Refutations*, trans. E.S. Forster and D. J. Furley (Cambridge: Harvard University Press, 1978), 9: "refutations may be true as false: for whenever it is possible to demonstrate something, it is also possible to refute the man who maintains the contradictory of the truth."

43. Hegel, *TW* 3:40.

44. Ibid., 6:250; these conditions perfectly correspond to what Hegel claims with regard to a *Widerlegung* that is *"gründlich"* in Hegel, *TW* 3:27.

45. Plato, *Protagoras*, in *Complete Works*, ed. John M. Cooper and D.S. Hutchinson (Indiana: Hackett Publishing, 1997), 332b; Aristotle, *Sophistical Refutations*, 2, 165b4–7; Terence Irwin, "Say What You Believe," *Apeiron: A Journal for Ancient Philosophy and Science* 26, no. 3/4 (1993), 1–16; Louis-André Dorion, "Aristote et l'elenchos Socratique," *Les Études philosophiques* 4 (2011), 569.

46. Hegel, *TW* 6: 250.

47. Ibid.

48. Ibid., 6:250: *"aus sich selbst"*—and the passage goes on "Das Substantialitätsverhältnis, ganz nur *an und für sich selbst* betrachtet, führt sich zu seiner Gegenteil, den *Begriff*, über."

49. Ibid., 6:251.

50. Ibid., 6:266.

51. Ibid., 6:264–266.

52. Ibid., 6:266.

53. Ibid., 6:273.

54. Ibid., 6:276.

55. Ibid., 6:276f.

56. Ibid., 6:573.

57. Ibid., 6:572.

58. Ibid., 8:393 (§244).

59. Ibid., 6:572.

60. Ibid., 6:573.

61. Ibid. (emphasis added).

62. Marianne Moore, "His Shield," in *New Collected Poems*, ed. Heather Cass White (New York: Farrar, Straus and Giroux, 2017), 179.

63. Hegel, *TW* 6:573.

11

Abstraction and Critique in Marx

The Case of Debt

ROCÍO ZAMBRANA

The work of our time [is] to clarify to itself . . . the meaning of its own struggle and its own desires.

—Karl Marx, "For a Ruthless Criticism of Everything Existing"[1]

1. Introduction

"It is largely through debt," Nancy Fraser writes, "that capital now cannibalizes labor, disciplines states, transfers wealth from periphery to core, and sucks value from society and nature. As debt flows through states, regions, communities, households, and firms, the regime is reconfiguring capitalism's constitutive divisions between economy, polity, society, and nature."[2] Although a substantive treatment of debt is not found in her work, Fraser underscores debt as central to a critique of contemporary financialized capitalism and its political contradictions. In recent essays, she turns to Marx's *Capital* to develop such a critique.[3] One of the most significant innovations of *Capital*, Fraser maintains, is an exposition of the dynamics of "*exploitation-cum-expropriation*."[4] *Capital* accounts not only for the structure of exploitation but also for the ongoing expropriation required by a crisis-prone system. Attention to exploitation-cum-expropriation, she suggests, is necessary for clarifying the political contradictions in core and periphery with respect to ecology ("nature"), political economy ("social reproduction"), and politics ("imperialism"). It also clarifies Marx's notion of a critique of capital. It elucidates the fact that Marx combines economic, political, and normative analysis in an effort to address the multidimensionality of capital accumulation and its crises. Exploitation-cum-expropriation, then, allows us to develop Marx's own treatment of debt in ways that speak to today's financialized capitalism.

In what follows, I assess the critique of capitalism at work in Marx's mature writings on political economy, taking Fraser's reading of *Capital* as a point of departure. Specifically, I examine Fraser's claim that her reading of *Capital* moves away from understanding the text as a critique of commodification, paradigmatically articulated in Lukács' conception of reification but reiterated in readings of Marx within and beyond the Frankfurt School. Marx does not view capitalism as a "reified form of ethical life," one "characterized by commodification and monetization," Fraser argues.[5] Exploitation-cum-expropriation establishes capitalism's dependence on a "plurality" of "non-commodified" social "zones" that "embody normative and ontological grammars of their own."[6] Capitalism is not an encroaching economic system, then, but an "institutionalized social order" that *separates* and *entwines* society, polity and nature from and with the economy. A critique of capitalism thus tracks the institutional separation and entwinement within and across commodified and non-commodified zones. It thereby elucidates the structural links between the economy *and* racial and gender oppression, political domination, and ecological degradation. It also illuminates political contradictions within what Fraser calls "boundary struggles," which draw from the distinct normative perspectives of non-commodified zones when resisting capital's rearticulation within a crisis.[7]

I am sympathetic to the view that, given the significance of expropriation, Marx's critique of capitalism exceeds a critique of commodification. However, I want to step back and examine the role of abstraction in Marx's writings on political economy. I do so in order to re-center Marx's economic analysis, though I am not suggesting a return to a one-dimensional, functionalist view of Marx's critique of capital. Rather, I aim to highlight the significance of Marx's exposition of self-expanding value for an understanding of the multidimensionality of his critique of capital. I thus consider how the dialectic of value and "anti-value," as David Harvey has recently put it, affects how we understand the dynamics of exploitation-cum-expropriation.[8] The economy of debt central to financialized capitalism, he maintains, should be examined as a phenomenon in which anti-value becomes a "fundamental driving force" within the circuits of capital. I argue that the account of anti-value elucidates the relation between the two distinct organizing logics of exploitation and expropriation: equalization and hierarchy, respectively. The exposition of self-expanding value thereby helps account for exploitation-cum-expropriation *as* a matter of racial and gender oppression, political domination, and ecological degradation within debt economies. It also helps assess boundary struggles, specifying anti-capitalist struggles that dismantle rather than reinforce racial and gender oppression, political domination, and ecological degradation.

The chapter is composed of two sections and a concluding remark. First, I recount Fraser's reading of Marx, engaging key moments in Marx's writings on political economy. Focusing on two essays, "Marx's Hidden Abode" and "Expropriation and Exploitation in Racialized Capitalism," I assess her claim that we must "shift our gaze" away from political economy to capital's "non-economic" conditions. I examine her exposition of the multidimensionality of Marx's critique of capital and her notion of boundary struggles here as well. Second, I provide an account of Marx's view of capital as self-expanding value drawing from Harvey's work on the dialectic of value and anti-value in *Capital* and other relevant writings. I also examine Harvey's view of the mode of critique at work in these texts and its elucidation of fields of anti-capitalist struggles. I suggest that the critique of anti-value is crucial for a critique of debt economies in their multidimensionality. I close by suggesting that a critique of capital requires recentering Marx's exposition of self-expanding value, thereby affirming Marx's view of critique as self-clarification of the struggles and desires of one's own time.

2. Exploitation-cum-Expropriation

In *Capital*, Fraser argues, Marx offers a two-tiered account.[9] Marx "looked behind the sphere of exchange into the 'hidden abode' of production in order to discover capitalism's secrets," she writes.[10] Marx's move from the "economic foreground" to its "background conditions," that is, from the dynamics of an economic system to its social, historical, and political conditions, makes possible a "critical perspective." Such critical perspective, however, requires linking exploitation and expropriation even more clearly than Marx did. It requires taking a closer look behind the hidden abode of capital (production) to conditions that are "even more hidden" (dispossession).

It is instructive to begin by recalling Marx's conceptions of exploitation and expropriation. Marx's exposition of exploitation moves from the sphere of exchange to the hidden abode of production by considering the commodity. In contrast, his exposition of expropriation accounts for the dispossession that made possible the originary accumulation of capital by considering "so-called" primitive accumulation. I'll argue that exploitation and expropriation represent two distinct social processes that follow heterogeneous logics: reduction through equalization and the institution or intensification of a hierarchy. Distilling the *logic* of each, I'll suggest, is crucial for understanding the structural imbrication of capital and racial and gender oppression, political domination, and ecological degradation.

Marx opens *Capital* with an analysis of the commodity, highlighting the abstraction at work in the move from use-value to exchange-value.[11] Use-value pertains to the properties of a thing that satisfies a human need, and to the fact that the thing takes on these properties as the product of human labor. Exchange-value, in contrast, transcends the sensuousness of the thing in the attempt to establish an identical magnitude among incommensurable things to be exchanged in a market. Such reduction requires a third thing, a common measure—labor time.[12] In the section on the fetishism of the commodity central to Lukács's reading, Marx makes the claim that the commodity form structures social relations. In the commodity, Marx argues, "it is a definite social relation between men, that assumes, in their eyes, the fantastic form of a relation between things."[13] For Lukács, a critique of capital accounts for a social totality rearticulated by the commodity form.[14] Fraser argues that Marx's point is that the fetishism of the commodity points to its material origin, namely, the labor that produces commodities. The abstraction that exchange-value represents is key not because it colonizes society as a whole, but because labor time is the key to the extraction of surplus value distinctive of exploitation. To be sure, the political relation sustaining this economic relation, the distinction between property owner and propertyless worker, exhibits not equalization but the type of hierarchy that we will see in a moment. The critique of commodification, however, explains this hierarchy through the logic of exchange.

Consider how the logic of commodification works in the case of credit and debt. As early as his *Comments on James Mill* (1844) and, for example, in the chapter on money in the *Grundrisse* (1857–61), Marx treats credit in light of this logic. In both texts, Marx speaks of money as a form of alienation.[15] The essence of money, however, is not that "property is alienated in it."[16] Rather, as he puts it in the *Comments*, the "*mediating activity* . . . the *human*, social act by which man's products mutually complement one another, is *estranged* from man and becomes the attribute of money."[17] Social relations are not mediated by an abstraction, money; they are turned into an abstraction. In credit, however, it seems as if the alienation is "abolished."[18] Because it bears on trust, credit seems to reestablish human bonds.[19] This is merely an "appearance," however. "*Credit*," Marx writes, "*is* the *economic* judgment on the *morality* of a man. In credit, the *man* himself, instead of metal or paper, has become the *mediator* of exchange, not however as a man, but as the *mode of existence of capital* and interest."[20] In credit, the reduction of social bonds is intensified. Credit turns individuals themselves into a medium of exchange by preying on trust. It utilizes trust as a medium of exchange.[21] Although Marx is keen on pointing out that it becomes an opportunity to drive the "antithesis between capitalist and worker" even deeper, the point here is that credit is the epitome of capital's articulation of social bonds in light of the logic of exchange.

Marx's exposition of commodification, according to Fraser, draws from the account of self-expanding value, which I discuss in detail below. To read Marx along this thread alone is to reduce his view of capitalism as a social order to an economic system. Yet Marx consistently moves to an account of confiscatory processes that point to "non-economic" conditions of capital. While exploitation is a matter of the dynamic of the extraction of value through labor time, expropriation is a matter of the history of "enclosure, slavery, robbery, murder" that accounts for the originary accumulation of capital. The so-called primitive accumulation of capital concerns the history of the creation of the worker through a process of "becoming free."[22] Workers are free "*from*, unencumbered by, any means of production of their own" and free "*to* become free seller[s] of labor power, who carr[y] [their] commodity wherever [they] find[] a market." Marx acknowledges that this process is not only traceable to the enclosure of the English commons, but also to the "discovery of gold and silver in America, the extirpation, enslavement and entombment in mines of the aboriginal population, the beginning of the conquest and looting of the East Indies, the turning of Africa into a warren for the commercial hunting of black-skins."[23] Rather than the logic of equalization distinctive of exchange, the confiscatory processes that Marx describes institute or intensify hierarchies.

Consider Richard Dienst's argument that Marx's treatment of debt in the *Grundrisse* and in *Capital* refers the ongoing nature of these confiscatory processes.[24] In the *Grundrisse*, Marx suggests that the worker "owes an obligation to capital for the fact that he is alive at all."[25] Debt is the result of the creation of "free" subjects released from feudal obligations and slavery. Dienst draws from this moment to suggest that, in *Capital*, indebtedness is also a matter of the ever-present threat of impoverishment and misery. An example of the legacy of primitive accumulation is thus Marx's notion of a reserve army of labor. It articulates the necessity—to an "increasing extent"—of a laboring population that is "superfluous."[26] Such population addresses the "changing needs of the self-expansion of capital" through the creation of a "mass of human material always ready for exploitation."[27] An army of laborers ready for exploitation consolidates exploitation. The creation of a relative surplus population is the "pivot" on which the law of supply and demand of labor works. It is thus a central "tool of control over labor" and the "domination of capital."[28] Furthermore, the creation of an unproductive sector submits workers and non-workers to a logic of debt. The worker's dispensability is a condition to which all workers are subjected, but it is expressed more precisely in "floating," "latent," and "stagnant" reserves of unproductive, inactive workers.[29] These "unproductive bodies" can only be "fed by submitting to the law of debt."[30]

For Fraser, the significance of expropriation leads to a description of Marx's view of capitalism as an "institutionalized social order." Capitalism depends on non-economic zones—"social, ecological, political"—that embody normative and ontological grammars of their own.[31] Capitalism should thus be theorized as the institutional *separation* of economic production from social reproduction, economy from polity, nature from "human" activity. But it must be understood in terms of the forms of entwinement between commodified and non-commodified zones as well. I add that such separation and entwinement combines the logic of equalization and the logic of hierarchy, though not always mobilizing the latter as a condition for the former. The separation of production and social reproduction, for example, "grounds specifically capitalist forms of male domination, even as it also enables capitalist exploitation of labor power and, through that, its officially sanctioned mode of accumulation." Similarly, the division between nature, seen as raw material for appropriation, and the economy, conceived as a sphere of value produced by and for humans, grounds "practices of extraction and production that have decisive impacts on ecosystems and the earth's atmosphere."[32]

Fraser concludes that the separation and entwinement between and across zones establish the "structural imbrication" of capital expansion and gender and racial oppression, political domination, and ecological degradation.[33] But they do so precisely because we have decentered Marx's analysis of value and its conception of capitalism as self-expanding value, which cannot account for the logic of hierarchy distinctive of expropriation. While I am sympathetic to the view that capitalism depends on "non-commodified" forms of conceiving nature, pursuing social reproduction, and articulating public power, I disagree that such structural imbrication is only established by giving up Marx's exposition of self-expanding value. The latter articulates and/or disarticulates the relation between commodification and its non-commodified conditions.

Consider Fraser's own account of racialized capitalism in her debate with Michael Dawson. Here, Fraser clarifies exploitation-cum-expropriation in terms of "racialized dependent labor."[34] Subjection of those whom capital expropriates within and across core and periphery along racial lines is a condition for the freedom of those whom it exploits. Political representation tracks such distinction-relation as well in the figures of the exploitable citizen-worker and the dependent expropriable subject.[35] Most relevant for our purposes, however, is her exposition of "confiscation-cum-conscription-into-accumulation."[36] Expropriation "works by confiscating capacities and resources and conscripting them into capital's circuits of self-expansion."[37] It is not merely dispossession or outright theft. Rather, it is the conscription of what has been confiscated, from capacities to natural resources, into modes of extracting value, by becoming "exploited proletarians" or a superfluous laboring population.[38]

This dynamic is crucial to the constitution of racialized forms of exploitation today, continuing the legacy of capitalism's "early history" in conquest and enslavement. Yet confiscation-cum-conscription is also "structural," given the aim of "limitless expansion and private accumulation" that moves capitalism. The need to acquire labor and means of production "below cost," Fraser thus argues, establishes the imbrication of capital and racial domination. Within financialized capitalism, Fraser notes, debt becomes a central means of capital expansion in the core and periphery through dispossession and land grabs or consumer debt (housing and education) respectively. Debt becomes a mechanism of confiscation-cum-conscription, driving, one might say, the circuits of capital. We find a new figure in this context, however: the "expropriable-and-exploitable citizen-worker formally free but acutely vulnerable." This is the inverse of the dynamic of confiscation-cum-conscription where the expropiable subject faces the fate of the exploitable worker. Here, the citizen-worker faces the fate of the expropriable subject.

Recall that Fraser maintains that a critique of capital tracks the forms of separation and entwinement that articulate specific shapes of capitalism and that inform boundary struggles. "Precisely *where* and *how* capitalist societies draw the line" not only varies historically. It carves out sites of contestation that draw from distinct normatvities of non-commodified zones, such as "ideals of care, mutual responsibility and solidarity, however hierarchical and parochial these may be." Tracking the work of debt requires elucidating confiscation-cum-conscription along racial lines within and across core and periphery. Fraser does not elaborate the work of critique in this context. I argue that confiscation-cum-conscription requires a different conception of critique than one based on claims about distinct normativities. Despite the ubiquity of precarity, a critique of debt should track the *difference* that racialized subjects face as exploited or expropriated within and across core and periphery. Boundary struggles, accordingly, are not a matter of distinct normative perspectives within non-commodified zones. Rather, they are a matter of articulating anti-capitalist strategies that dismantle rather than exacerbate racial oppression. It is thus a matter of tracking the histories of the entanglement of these two forms of oppression in their material and "logical" registers.

Notice that, despite her efforts to decenter Marx's economic analysis, self-expanding value plays a crucial role in Fraser's account. Indeed, self-expanding value correlates to exploitation-cum-expropriation.[39] It plays an organizing role in the multiple dimensions of exploitation-cum-expropriation through confiscation-cum-conscription. I have argued that the view of critique thus needs to shift, indeed come closer to Marx's. Rather than an emphasis on competing normativities, critique is a mode of clarification that assesses anti-capitalist struggles in their imbrication with racial and gender oppression and ecological degradation. I want to turn to Harvey's *Marx, Capital, and the Madness of Economic Reason* and develop this aspect of Fraser's account. Harvey defends Marx's view of capital as value in motion and elaborates a view of debt economies as the expression of the growing significance of "anti-value." Harvey re-centers Marx's economic analysis without reverting to a functionalist totalizing critique of capital, thereby clarifying the status of Marx's own multidimensional critique.

3. Value, Anti-Value

In *Capital*, Marx describes capital as "value in motion." Recall that the overall circulation process of capital, that is, the circulation of value that *is* capital, is composed of valorization, realization, distribution, and the renovation of money as capital. Valorization is a matter of the extraction of surplus value in production. Realization is a matter of the transformation of value back into the money form through the exchange of commodities in a market. Distribution is a matter of disbursement of value and surplus value among various claimants. Finally, there is a return to valorization through capturing some of the money in circulation in order to convert it into money capital.[40] When Marx speaks of "circuits of capital," he is referring to these "moments" within the process of circulation.

Consider Marx's famous description of the circuits of capital in volume 1 of *Capital*. He begins by recalling us to the fact that "the circulation of commodities is the starting point of capital."[41] He moves on, however, to "abstract from the material substance of the circulation of commodities," from the exchange of the use-values to consider the "economic forms produced by this process of circulation." Money, the "final product of the circulation of commodities," is the "first form in which capital appears." The difference between money and money as capital, he adds, is their form of circulation. Accordingly, the "simplest form" of circulation of commodities is the transformation of commodities into money and the change of money back again into commodities—C-M-C.[42] Here we are selling in order to buy. Alongside this form, however, Marx argues, "we find another specifically different form: M-C-M." Here we have the transformation of money into commodities and the change of commodities back again into money. Here we are buying in order to sell. Money is not spent but rather advanced. For Marx, the latter is crucial. Money is here "transformed into, becomes capital, and is already potentially capital." The circuits of capital follow the extraction of value for the expansion value. Capital is nothing but value in motion.

We can begin to see why, in volume 3 of *Capital*, Marx writes that "the relations of capital assume their most externalized and most fetish-like form in interest-bearing capital. We have here M-M , money creating more money, self-expanding value, without the process that effectuates these two extremes."[43] M-M' abstracts from the material process of production that it in fact organizes. To return to the discussion in volume 1 once more, C-M-C cycles through by ending up in consumption. The "satisfaction of wants," hence use-value, is "its end and aim." In contrast, M-C-M begins and ends with money, hence its "leading motive" and goal is mere exchange-value. This might seemingly buttress Fraser's claim that self-expanding value is a matter of commodification. As we saw in the discussion of credit in the *Comments on Mill* and in the *Grundrisse*, credit is the intensification of the logic of equalization distinctive of exchange. However, attention to the dynamics of "anti-value," as Harvey puts it, allows us to see that inscribed in the self-expansion of value is the combination of equalization and hierarchy central to Fraser's analysis of exploitation-cum-expropriation through confiscation-cum-conscription. As we will see, Harvey argues that "the formation and circulation of interest-bearing capital is in effect the circulation of anti-value," which inscribes the logic of dispossession within the process of commodification.

In the *Grundrisse*, Marx stresses that "the circulation of capital *realizes value*, while living labor *creates value*."[44] The relation between creation and realization is key for Harvey's exposition of devaluation and elaboration of the notion of anti-value. Capital is nothing but value in motion. Devaluation is a loss or slowdown in the movement of capital within its circuits. Marx writes, "As long as (capital) remains in the production process it is not capable of circulating; and it is virtually devalued. As long as it remains in circulation it is not capable of producing. . . . As long as it cannot be brought to market it is fixated as product. As long as it has to remain on the market it is fixated as commodity. As long as it cannot be exchanged for conditions of production, it is fixated as money."[45] The notion of anti-value arises from blocks that occur within the process of circulation, but it is more than such blocks, Harvey argues. It can itself become the source of movement driving the circuits of capital. Harvey reconstructs the notion of anti-value from Marx's gloss on the negation of value internal to the processes of valorization and realization. "While capital is reproduced as value and use value in the production process," Marx for example writes, "it is at the same time posited as not-value, as something which first has to be realized as value by means of exchange."[46] Marx is here straightforwardly Hegelian. He conceives of value as necessarily in motion given its relation to its opposite.[47] For Harvey, Marx's Hegelianism is deeply relevant, since it establishes that the "prospect and reality of anti-value" "are always there."

Marx focuses on valorization, that is, production. Harvey builds on Marx, arguing that debt economies exhibit the dialectic of value and anti-value yet within realization, that is, within the moment of exchange where value is transformed back into the money form. This is heightened in the moment of capture of money within circulation, transforming it into money capital. Harvey argues that this is crucial for understanding the role of debt as a form of anti-value that drives the process of circulation in debt economies, hence exceeding an account of anti-value as the generator of crises through blocks in the moment of valorization (production). But here we see that the role of anti-value and the phenomenon of devaluation are not merely a matter of realization. We see that it bears on the relation between valorization and realization, production and exchange. It is this relation, however, that in being driven by debt integrates expropriation as a social process *and* as an ordering logic. In other words, this account of self-expanding value makes sense of Fraser's notion of confiscation-cum-conscription.

The dialectic of value and anti-value establishes that capitalists are "locked in a perpetual battle not only to produce values but to combat their potential negation," Harvey writes.[48] Anti-value must be overcome, in other words. It must be "redeemed." It can only do so by circling back to the production process, since that is the site of valorization, of the creation of value. It thus becomes key to defining and securing capital's future.[49] Harvey argues that "the money lent out—the debt incurred—becomes a form of anti-value that circulates within the credit system as interest-bearing capital."[50] Credit is crucial to the circulation of capital, as Marx argues in *Capital*, since it "resuscitates hoarded and, therefore, dead money capital and puts it back into motion."[51] Debt, accordingly, is a claim on future value production. Piled up debt that cannot be redeemed is the source of crises, since the future of value production is in peril. But when seen from the perspective of realization and its role in the transformation of captured money into money capital, it is the source of opportunity.[52] As anti-value, then, debt intensifies the relation not only between exchange and production, but between production and dispossession. And it consolidates that relation economically *and* politically. It organizes production (and, in fact, consumption), but it also organizes expropriation through public and private debt peonage and the disciplining of borrowers into being productive laborers.[53] The crucial point is that, as anti-value, debt organizes the distinct logics of commodification and dispossession to aid the circulation of value.

The dialectic of value and anti-value elucidates the economic relations at work in exploitation-cum-expropriation, then. It does so by specifying the organizing logics at work in confiscation-cum-conscription. It thereby also clarifies the structural correlation between the logic of capital, racial/gender oppression, and ecological degradation. It makes it possible to track the intersection of equalization and hierarchy across economic and, for example, racial lines. It is not a view of capital as composed of distinct social zones, some of which are commodified and some of which are not, that can explain the relation between exploitation and expropriation, confiscation-cum-conscription. It is the multiple logics at work in the economic system separating and entwining any such zones that explain capital's dependence on non-commodified forms of being, knowing, and relating. Attention to this dialectic, then, allows us to see capital as *racializing* and *gendering* what Fraser deems as "non-commodified." This brings into focus the critical aspect of Marx's exposition of capital and thus Marx's own conception of critique in his economic writings.

Harvey argues that the dialectic of value and anti-value elucidates "an active field of anti-capitalist struggle" and helps assess ongoing anti-capitalist struggles. In volume 3 of *Capital*, Marx argues that the credit system has a "dual character." "It develops the motives of capitalist production into the purest and most colossal system of gambling and swindling, and restricts even more the already small number of the exploiters of social wealth."[54] It also "constitutes the form of transition towards a new mode of production."[55] Dienst, Randy Martin, and Max Haiven, among others, build on this suggestion by recovering Marx's notion of "fictitious capital." Martin and Haiven, for instance, argue for a subversion of the modes of subjectivation distinctive of financialization.[56] Harvey takes a different route. "Anti-value," he writes, "signals the potential for breakdown in the continuity of capital circulation. It prefigures how capital's crisis tendencies can take different forms."[57] In so doing, I add, it clarifies the terrain of anti-capitalist struggles as a *fraught* terrain, one composed of distinct logics of oppression.

Anti-capitalist struggles seek "the conscious negation of the capitalist law of value in individual and collective lives," according to Harvey. They attempt to subvert or interrupt valorization (production) *or* realization (exchange, but also consumption)—for example, the wages for housework movement or forms of ethical consumerism. Anti-value sheds light on the contradictions of these movements, which inadvertently incorporate forms of activity within value creation and realization. A politics of anti-value, in contrast, draws from Marx's insight that, for example, "a devaluation of credit money . . . would destroy all existing relationships," clarifying, for instance, the role of bank bailouts in the rearticulation of capital within a crisis. Debt repayment or forgiveness, accordingly, can be seen as a site of rearticulation *or* interruption of the movement of capital in its multiple dimensions. Debt repayment *and* the refusal to pay can harnesses the driving force of anti-value to reinforce *or* dismantle distinct forms of domination (racial, gender) at work in debt economies. Rather than a matter of distinct normativities made available by non-commodified zones, critique here is a matter of elucidation of the organizing role of value in separating or entwining multiple forms of oppression *and* their resistance.

5. Concluding Remarks

In the Coda to his book, Harvey writes, "What Marx in *Capital* as well as in his other political-economic writings does is to suggest a way to cut through all the confusions of the daily workings of a capitalist mode of production and get to its essence—its inner laws of motion—through the formulation of abstractions woven into some simple (and in the end not-so-simple) theory of endless capital accumulation."[58] For Harvey, this is the core of Marx's conception of critique. These theoretical abstractions illuminate the "surface of daily life," indeed the "struggles for survival" faced under capitalism. They also help articulate anti-capitalist struggles. This is the type of analysis and the conception of critique that critical theories such as Fraser's outright reject. Rather than a theoretical abstraction, Marx's conception of critique is distinctively concrete, rooted in material conditions, drawing from historical realty.

In a counterintuitive move, I have argued that a multidimensional critique of capital benefits from centering Marx's exposition of self-expanding value, especially given the significance of debt today. I have done so in the spirit of Marx's 1843 definition of critical philosophy as the self-clarification of the meaning of the struggles and desires of one's own time. The critical concepts that Marx develops elucidate not only the root of the struggles for survival under capitalism, but also the contradictions that arise in our practices of critique and resistance. Such clarification allows a "cross-redressing," to speak with Fraser yet thinking of her earlier work.[59] Anti-capitalist struggles are pragmatic and flexible, using measures that address one form of domination to dismantle another. Most importantly, cross-redressing is an awareness of the fact that dismantling one form of domination might intensify the other. In debt economies, Marx's critique of *political economy* should guide such awareness.[60]

Notes

1. Karl Marx, "For a Ruthless Criticism of Everything Existing," in *The Marx-Engels Reader*, ed. Robert C. Tucker (New York: WW Norton, 1978), 15. For an extended discussion of variations of critique in Marx (and Hegel), see Rocío Zambrana, "Critique in Hegel and Marx," in *From Marx to Hegel and Back to the Future*, ed. Victoria Fareld and Hannes Kuch (New York: Bloomsbury Press, 2020).

2. Nancy Fraser, "Legitimation Crisis: On the Political Contradictions of Financialized Capitalism," *Critical Historical Studies* 2, no. 2 (2015), 175–176.

3. In addition to "Legitimation Crisis," see Nancy Fraser, "Behind Marx's Hidden Abode," *New Left Review* 86 (2014), and Nancy Fraser, "Expropriation and Exploitation in Racialized Capitalism," *Critical Historical Studies* 3, no. 1 (2016).

4. See Fraser, "Expropriation and Exploitation," 163–178.

5. Fraser, "Behind Marx's Hidden Abode," 66.

6. Ibid.

7. Ibid., 68ff.

8. David Harvey, *Marx, Capital, and the Madness of Economic Reason* (Oxford: Oxford University Press, 2018), esp. chap. 4.

9. There are four "defining features" of capital discussed in *Capital*, according to Fraser: (1) private property in the means of production, (2) free labor market, (3) self-expanding value, (4) the role of markets in allocating the major inputs to commodity production and in the investment of society's surplus. These four features must be understood in light of the two-tiered account of exploitation and expropriation. See Fraser, "Behind Marx's Hidden Abode," 57ff.

10. Fraser, "Behind Marx's Hidden Abode," 57.

11. See Karl Marx, *Capital: A Critique of Political Economy*, trans. Ben Fowkes (London: Penguin, 1976), 125ff.

12. See Marx, *Capital*, esp. 128ff.

13. Ibid., 165.

14. See György Lukács, "Reification and Consciousness of the Proletariat," in *History and Class Consciousness: Studies in Marxist Dialectics*, trans. Rodney Livingston (London: Merlin Press, 1971).

15. Karl Marx, "Comments on James Mill," in Karl Marx and Friedrich Engels, *Collected Works* (Chadwell Heath: Lawrence & Wishart, 1975–2004), 3:213.

16. Ibid., 3:212.

17. Ibid.

18. Ibid., 3:214.

19. Ibid.
20. Ibid., 3:215.
21. Ibid.
22. Marx, *Capital*, 1:874, emphasis mine.
23. Ibid., 1:915.
24. Richard Dienst, *The Bonds of Debt* (London: Verso, 2011), chap. 6, esp. 150.
25. Quoted in Dienst, *The Bonds of Debt*, 149.
26. Marx, *Capital*, 1:782.
27. Ibid., 1:784.
28. See Marx, *Capital*, 1:792. See John Bellamy Foster and Fred Magdoff, "Disposable Workers: Today's Reserve Army of Labor," *Monthly Review* 55, no. 11 (2004).
29. Marx, *Capital*, 1:794ff.
30. Dienst, *The Bonds of Debt*, 150.
31. Fraser, "Marx's Hidden Abode," 66.
32. Ibid.
33. Ibid., 68.
34. Fraser, "Expropriation and Exploitation," 166.
35. Ibid., 171.
36. Ibid., 167.
37. Ibid., 166.
38. Ibid.
39. Ibid., 167.
40. Harvey, *Marx, Capital, and the Madness of Economic Reason*, 20.
41. Marx, *Capital*, 1:247.
42. Marx, *Capital*, 1:198, 206, 210ff.
43. Karl Marx, *Capital*, vol. 3, *A Critique of Political Economy*, trans. David Fernbach (London: Penguin, 1981), 515.
44. Karl Marx, *Grundrisse*, trans. Martin Nicolaus (London: Penguin, 1993), 543.
45. Ibid., 621.
46. Ibid., 403.
47. See Marx, *Grundrisse*, 415ff.
48. Harvey, *Marx, Capital, and the Madness of Economic Reason*, 75.
49. See Harvey, *Marx, Capital, and the Madness of Economic Reason*, 78.
50. Ibid., 79.
51. Ibid.
52. "Crises typically leave in their wake a mass of devalued assets that can be picked up at fire-sale prices by those who have the cash (or privileged connections) to pay for them" (Harvey, *Marx, Capital, and the Madness of Economic Reason*, 86).
53. Harvey, *Marx, Capital, and the Madness of Economic* Reason, 82.
54. Marx, *Capital*, vol. 3, 572.

55. Ibid., 572. Marx also writes that "it is this dual character that gives the principal spokesmen for credit . . . their nicely mixed character of swindler and prophet" (573).

56. See Randy Martin, "What Difference Do Derivatives Make? From the Technical to the Political Conjuncture," *Culture Unbound* 6 (2014); Randy Martin, "A Precarious Dance: A Derivative Sociality," *TDR: The Drama Review* 56, no. 4 (2012); and Max Haiven, *Cultures of Financialization: Fictitious Capital in Popular Culture and Everyday Life* (New York: Palgrave, 2014).

57. Harvey, *Marx, Capital, and the Madness of Economic Reason*, 93.

58. Ibid., 209.

59. Nancy Fraser and Axel Honneth, *Redistribution or Recognition? A Political-Philosophical Exchange*, trans. Joel Golb, James Ingram, and Christiane Wilke (London: Verso, 2003), 83ff. See also Rocío Zambrana, "Paradoxes of Neoliberalism and the Tasks of Critical Theory," *Critical Horizons* 14, no. 1 (2013), 93–119.

60. It gives us resources for thinking the movement of value as, for example, a form of racialization. See, for example, Paula Chakravartty and Denise Ferreira da Silva, "Accumulation, Dispossession, and Debt: The Racial Logic of Global Capitalism—An Introduction," *American Quarterly* 64, no. 3 (2012), 361–385. This is a key argument in my forthcoming book *Colonial Debts: The Case of Puerto Rico* (Durham, NC: Duke University Press, 2021).

12

Nietzsche's Project of Reevaluation
What Kind of Critique?

DANIEL R. RODRÍGUEZ-NAVAS

1. Introduction

Are good things good because we take them to be good, or do we take them to be good because they are good? According to one of our myths, we came to realize, in one of our foundational moments, that if it is the good we're talking about, the real one, the one that we in fact mean to be talking about when we're talking about *the* good, then the answer is, it ought to be, the latter: we take the good to be good because it is good; the goodness of *the* good is independent from us taking it to be so. Indeed, this conception of the good is so deeply engrained in our way of life, this myth so foundational, that even the suggestion that there might be an alternative, as in the question "Is the good good because we take it to be good?" is liable to strike us as nonsensical.[1]

One version of this myth is found in Plato's *Euthyphro*, where *the good* is discussed under the guise of the divine or the pious. In one of the central moments of the dialogue, Socrates asks Euthyphro whether "the pious is loved by the gods because it is pious, or [whether] it is pious because it is loved by the gods."[2] In its context, the question can seem to be intended to work as a challenge to Euthyphro's attempt to characterize the pious in terms of its being loved by the gods; it can seem to work as a rhetorical question designed to call to mind that the goodness of the pious does not reside in its being loved by the gods, but that on the contrary, the gods too must have reason to love it: they must love it because it is in itself good. Yet this move, which may seem innocuous, is in fact, to speak somewhat grandiosely (and quite anachronistically), one of the "founding moments" of "Western" moral rationality. Saying that what makes the pious good—in the way pious things are good—is not that the gods love it but that it is good in itself, and that if the gods love it is because it is good in itself, and thus only insofar as they are in the business of loving what is in itself love-worthy, effectively amounts to displacing moral authority from the powerful authority that *wills* it to be good to the *rational exercise* of that authority's will. And once we follow Plato's Socrates in thus displacing moral authority from the will of a certain type of individual, endowed with a certain authoritative status, to the rational exercise of its will—once, that is, we sever moral authority from the "authoritative status" of certain individuals and anchor it instead in their ability to let themselves be guided by reason (by moral truth, by goodness)—we are within the space of the form of moral rationality that has dominated "Western" *philosophical* moral discourse since Plato's days.

Moreover, as I suggested, this way of thinking is so deeply engrained in us, and shapes our moral experience to such an extent, that it informs even our ability to conceive possible alternatives. Thus we are prone to think that holding that the good is good because we take it to be so must ultimately amount to holding that there is no good at all. We're led to think, that is, that those who hold that the good is attitude-dependent must be confused in one of two ways: because by thinking of the good as attitude-dependent they effectively (if inadvertently) commit to the view that there is no good, while insisting on their entitlement to treat certain things as good; or because, like the radical nihilist, they explicitly hold that there is no good, while inadvertently treating things as good (as the nihilist who screams "That isn't fair!" in the parking lot scene in *The Big Lebowski*).[3] And so our traditional way of thinking about the good makes it seem as if there is no coherent alternative to it, as if the denial that the good is good in itself invariably could and would have to be traced back to some confusion.

Much of Nietzsche's work, including most of his most widely commented works, is dedicated to a radical critique of traditional morality and to what he would eventually come to refer to as an "Umwerthung aller

Werthe"—what we usually think of, in English, as the reevaluation of all values.[4] And one of the central elements of his approach to morality is the rejection of the idea of the good in itself, of the valuable in itself. Instead, Nietzsche indexes goodness to perspectives, to ways of life and, ultimately, to the will to power of the valuing individual. This all is of course almost too obvious to be worth mentioning. But I mention it nonetheless because it being so, we should expect to find in Nietzsche's work an alternative to what I just described as traditional Western moral rationality, an alternative to a conception of morality and its relationship to rationality that is anchored in the idea that the good is good in itself. And yet, contemporary interpretive trends present a Nietzsche that seems to me to remain too close to the *form* of morality that was in fact the primary target of his critical work. My overarching goal in this paper is to bring into view just this: how the traditional way of thinking—according to which values are valuable in themselves—is, in spite of appearances, still at work in a range of approaches to Nietzsche, and how it renders such approaches blind to some of Nietzsche's most insightful contributions to our understanding of *our experience of value*. Naturally, beyond simply showing that this traditional way of thinking continues to inform Nietzsche scholarship, I shall also endeavor to show why this is exegetically problematic, and to suggest that it is philosophically incapacitating.

It has become commonplace to think of genealogy as a form of critique. It has become common to use the phrase "genealogical critique" to describe Nietzsche's method, and to identify the critical dimension of genealogy with the project of *Umwertung*. "Genealogy," "critique," and re-evaluation" are thus often treated as more or less equivalent terms for referring to Nietzsche's project and method. The tendency is understandable. Nietzsche himself can often seem to suggest that genealogy is part of a critical method. Thus he writes in a passage that has become a *locus classicus* for discussions of this question, "We need a *critique* of moral values, *the value of these values must first be called into question*—and for that there is needed a knowledge of the conditions and circumstances in which they grew, under which they evolved and changed."[5]

Yet in spite of passages like this, and of the uncontroversially close connection that he draws between genealogy on the one hand, and critique and *Umwertung* on the other, it seems to me doubtful that genealogy should be regarded as a proper part of *Umwertung*. Even in this passage, what Nietzsche writes is that the critique of moral values, the calling into question of the value of moral values, *requires genealogical knowledge*; not that such knowledge, or that the production of such knowledge, amounts in itself to a critique of moral values. Similarly, in his account of the *Genealogy* in *Ecce Homo*, he describes the three essays that make up the body of the book as "three decisive preliminary studies by a psychologist for the revaluation of all values."[6] Since Nietzsche himself describes genealogical work as *preliminary* for *Umwertung*, we should exercise caution, and speak, at most, of the *critical vocation* of the genealogical method, not of genealogical critique, of genealogy as *Umwertung*, etc. And note that the point is not innocuous, and the motivation for it is more than a matter of principled fastidiousness. Whether we identify genealogy with critique will have important consequences on our conceptions of Nietzschean methodology and of what we take *Umwertung* to be. And it will have important consequences on our attitude toward the worry that Nietzsche might be guilty of the genetic fallacy.[7] For if genealogy is "history, properly done" and if it is also critique, then the latter worry, the worry that Nietzsche is guilty of the genetic fallacy, is indeed at the very least highly plausible. Nietzsche would be relying on facts about the origin of values in order to appraise them.[8]

Yet even leaving aside, for the time being, and for the sake of simplicity, whether or not genealogy is, properly speaking, part of Nietzsche's project of a critique of morality, and whether the latter can in turn be identified with the Nietzschean project of *Umwertung*; account taken, second, that of these three driving concepts (genealogy, critique, *Umwertung*) the latter is the most distinctively Nietzschean, it should be clear that how we understand *Umwertung* will affect our understanding of the critical vocation of Nietzschean genealogy, of how the genealogical method is meant to function. It is thus our overall understanding of Nietzsche's project of a critique of morality that is at stake in our understanding of *Umwertung*.

With this in view, I can formulate my overarching goal in this paper somewhat more precisely. My goal is to argue that a widespread way of understanding Nietzschean *Umwertung* (and the closely related ideas of critique and genealogy) is still under the grip of a traditional conception of values, and that it renders us blind to another, more Nietzschean and deeper form of *Umwertung*, to the functioning of the genealogical method, and to some of Nietzsche's deepest insights about values.[9]

My strategy will be to focus on an emerging "debate" within Anglo-American Nietzsche scholarship. In the next part of the paper, I will present and analyze, in some detail, this emerging debate, which turns on whether Nietzsche's critique of morality is to be understood as a form of *internal* or *external* critique.[10] I will argue that a central problem with that debate is that it is based on a common assumption about the critical dimension of Nietzsche's work, and in particular of his idea of *Umwertung*—namely, that *Umwertung* consists of an evaluation of values *based on an evaluative standpoint that serves as its ground*. This assumption, as we shall see, is closely related to the traditional conception of values discussed above, the very conception of values that is the primary target of Nietzsche's critique. In the third part of the paper, I will sketch an alternative conception of Nietzschean *Umwertung*, one that brings clearly into view the distinctiveness of Nietzschean style of critique, how it relates to genealogy and, most importantly, how it supposes a more radical break with traditional conceptions of values than is often acknowledged.

2. Internalist and Externalist Interpretations of Nietzsche's Critique of Morality

The last decade has seen the emergence of an interpretive trend regarding Nietzsche's genealogical method. Some interpreters, notably Aaron Ridley, David Owen, and Allison Merrick, have identified a "dominant [exegetical] strategy" according to which "Nietzsche's genealogical descriptions stimulate a transcendent critique of our moral values by appealing to some external benchmark."[11] Their central argument against such *externalist* interpretations, originally formulated by Ridley, is that they would render the genealogical method vulnerable to what they refer to as the *authority problem*. Ridley presents the way of reading Nietzsche that leads to the authority problem as follows:

> The re-evaluation of values, it is said, can only be undertaken from an evaluative standpoint; in order to be authoritative, that standpoint must be somehow immune to re-evaluation (or at any rate to devaluation); Nietzsche, however, gives us no reason to think that his own evaluative standpoint is immune to re-evaluation in the relevant way; therefore, the only thing

that Nietzsche's re-evaluation can tell us about the value of our existing values is how they look from the perspective of his own preferred values, values whose superiority he merely asserts, rather than defends or demonstrates.[12]

Schematically, the source of the authority problem, on Ridley's reconstruction, lies in the following line of reasoning (the labels are mine):

1. *The Grounding Requirement* (Background Assumption): Reevaluation "can only be undertaken from an evaluative standpoint."[13]

2. *The Immunity Constraint* (Premise): A reevaluation has authority only if the standpoint from which it is "undertaken" is "immune to reevaluation."

3. *Nietzschean Vulnerability* (Premise): Nietzsche "gives us no reason to think that his own evaluative standpoint is immune to re-evaluation in the relevant way."

4. *The Authority Problem* (Conclusion): "Nietzsche's evaluative standpoint, and the re-evaluation that he undertakes from it, need have no authority for us" ("if we're comfortable with our existing values, and with our existing evaluations of them").[14]

The argument that, in Ridley's view, leads to the authority problem is based on the second and third items on the list, along with another component of Nietzsche's conception of values. On this way of understanding Nietzsche, reevaluation involves an *evaluating standpoint*—the standpoint from which reevaluation is undertaken—and an *evaluated* standpoint—the standpoint that is the target of reevaluation. Therefore, if, as the Immunity Constraint suggests, the authority of a reevaluation requires that the reevaluating standpoint itself be immune to reevaluation, then unless Nietzsche's reevaluating standpoint is taken to be immune to reevaluation, his reevaluations could have no authority. Moreover, since Nietzsche himself rejected the idea that there are unconditional values (the only kind of values that would be, from any standpoint, invulnerable to reevaluation), from Nietzsche's own perspective, his reevaluations could only have authority over those who subscribe to the evalua*ting* standpoint.[15] Hence the authority problem: "the only thing that Nietzsche's re-evaluation can tell us about the value of our existing values is how they look from the perspective of his own preferred values, values whose superiority he merely asserts, rather than defends or demonstrates."[16] The strategy of Ridley, Owen, and Merrick for avoiding the authority problem is to suggest that genealogy and reevaluation are meant to work as internal critiques, that the evalua*ting* standpoint on which they are grounded coincides with the evaluat*ed* standpoint that is their target.

The conception of Nietzschean *Umwertung* at work in this way of reading Nietzsche, which confers the Grounding Requirement its apparent necessity, is, in my view, rather un-Nietzschean. In order to bring this (i.e. the un-Nietzschean character of this conception of *Umwertung*) into view, I will argue that the latter leads to a number of exegetical impasses regarding Nietzsche's intended audience and regarding the originality and scope of his project of *Umwertung*. Then, in the next section, I will offer an alternative account of how *Umwertung* is meant to work and a brief discussion of what this way of understanding *Umwertung* reveals about Nietzsche's conception of values and of moral rationality.

2.1. Nietzsche's Target Audience

One of the main points of contention between internalists and externalists is the intended audience of Nietzsche's *Umwertungen*. But some of the exegetical problems with the conception of *Umwertung* at work in both interpretations come into view precisely if we consider its implications for the question of Nietzsche's target audience. Internalists and externalists both subscribe to what we may think of as a *restricted audience claim*, according to which Nietzsche's texts are addressed primarily to a certain type of reader. Internalists think that the problem of authority arises precisely when a critique is grounded on a standpoint that isn't shared by those who subscribe to the *criticized* standpoint. Accordingly, in their view, if Nietzsche's reevaluations can be authoritative, it is because the *evaluating* standpoint that grounds his critiques, the *evaluated* standpoint that they target, and the standpoint of his intended audience all coincide, and all differ from Nietzsche's own all-things-considered standpoint.

Externalists, by contrast, take Nietzsche's reevaluations to be grounded in his own standpoint, a standpoint that is external to the target of his critiques. So they think the intended audience of Nietzsche's critical reevaluations are those who already share his standpoint. In their view, the evaluating standpoint that grounds the critique, the standpoint of its intended audience, and Nietzsche's own all-things-considered standpoint coincide, but they differ from, and are external to, the evaluat*ed* standpoint that is criticized. Based on passages like the following, Ridley, Owen, and Merrick all present Brian Leiter as an externalist reader. In *Nietzsche on Morality*, Leiter writes: "recall what Nietzsche's goal is in undertaking a "revaluation of all values": he wants to alert *"higher" types* to the fact that MPS [morality in the pejorative sense] is not, in fact, conducive to their flourishing. Thus, he needs to "wake up" *his appropriate readers*—those whose "ears are related" to his—to the dangers of MPS, a task made all the more difficult by MPS's pretension to be "morality itself." Given, then, that Nietzsche's target is a certain sort of misunderstanding *on the part of higher men*."[17] Now, on a first approximation, the idea of writing for an audience who already shares one's own standpoint, of addressing a critical work to someone who already accepts its results, could seem counterintuitive.[18] Perhaps for this reason, internalists find the idea by default implausible, and think that if externalists endorse it, it is only because they must do so in order to avoid the authority problem. As Merrick writes: "To evade the problem of authority one must argue that Nietzsche limits his audience to those for whom his arguments are compelling, those who already share his descriptive and evaluative sensibilities, those, in other words, who already accept Nietzsche's authority on the matter."[19] In fact, Ridley and Owen go as far as to describe the externalist version of the restricted audience claim as a "somewhat desperate tactic" for avoiding the authority problem.[20]

Yet Nietzsche's numerous remarks about who his books are meant for and how they are to be read is at odds with this off-handed dismissal of the externalist version of the restricted audience claim. Consider, for instance, the second section of the "Preface" to the *Genealogy*, where Nietzsche directly addresses his readers in order to highlight his indifference toward their reception of his claims: "And this is the only thing proper for a philosopher. . . . our thoughts, values, every 'yes,' 'no,' 'if' and 'but' grow from us with the same inevitability as fruits are born on the tree. . . . Do *you* like the taste of our fruit?—But of what concern is that to the trees? And of what concern is that to *us* philosophers?"[21] The closing rhetorical question underscores Nietzsche's indifference to his readers' approval. And while there is, undoubtedly, some interpretive leeway as to what exactly he seeks to accomplish by highlighting this purported indifference, the fact that he does highlight it lends enough plausibility to the externalists' conception of his intended target audience, enough at least to rule out its dismissal as a "somewhat desperate" tactic.

At the same time, it would be hasty to conclude the correctness of the externalist stance, according to which Nietzsche's target audience are *only* those who already share his evaluative standpoint. After all, in the passage, Nietzsche is directly *addressing* readers whose reaction toward the *Genealogy* is, manifestly, still an open question, readers who *may or may not disapprove* of those views and attitudes.[22] So contrary to what externalists suggest, Nietzsche is *not only* writing for those who already share his evaluative standpoint. He also writes for readers who do not share that standpoint; he addresses them, taunts them and works on them from the very beginning of the book.

That Nietzsche simultaneously addresses both types of audience suggests that neither internalist nor externalist interpretations of his critical strategy are correct. However, Ridley's characterization of Nietzsche's position, endorsed by Owen and Merrick, suggests that the distinction between externalist and internalist readings exhausts the interpretive possibilities. For as we saw, the Grounding Requirement, according to which *Umwertungen* "must be undertaken from an evaluative standpoint," is part of a view according to which *Umwertung* necessarily involves an evaluat*ing*, critical standpoint, and an evaluat*ed*, critically examin*ed* standpoint, and the values that are part of the evaluat*ing* standpoint are deployed as standards for assessing those within the reevaluat*ed* standpoint. But if this is right, then one of two things must hold: either the values of the evaluat*ing* standpoint coincide with those of the evaluat*ed* standpoint, and the critique is *internal*, or the two sets of values are disjoint, in which case the critique is *external*.[23]

But perhaps this isn't right. Perhaps rather than attempt to identify Nietzsche's target audience on the basis of the evaluative standpoint on which his critique is grounded, we ought to call into question the Grounding Requirement itself, the idea that his critiques are *grounded* on an evaluative standpoint. As we've just seen, it is this requirement that forces upon us the choice between internalist and externalist interpretations. If, by contrast, Nietzschean *Umwertung* is not grounded on an evaluative standpoint, if it does not consist in the deployment of a set of values as standards for reevaluating a reevaluat*ed* standpoint, then it might be reasonably expected to have the potential to work on readers regardless of their prior axiological commitments.[24]

But how could *Umwertung* not be grounded on an evaluative standpoint? To begin to see this, consider more closely Nietzsche's rhetorical strategy when explicitly addressing various types of readers in single breath.

In his discussion of the title of *Human, All Too Human* (subtitled *A Book for Free Spirits*) in *Ecce Homo*, he writes:

> *Human, All Too Human* is the monument to a crisis. It calls itself a book for *free* spirits: almost every sentence is the manifestation of a victory—I used it to liberate myself from things that *did not belong* to my nature. Idealism is one of them: the title says 'where *you* see ideal things, *I* see—human, oh, only all too human!' . . . I know people *better* . . . The term 'free spirit' does not want to be understood in any other way: a spirit that *has become free*, that has taken hold of itself again.[25]

Through the title alone, Nietzsche sets up an opposition between two standpoints: the standpoint of someone who remains under the spell of idealism (who remains human, all too human), and the standpoint of someone who has liberated herself from that spell (the free spirit). He also attributes these standpoints to two different versions of himself, and, as it turns out, to three possible types of readers. There is the Nietzsche who was under the spell of idealism, who used the book to liberate himself from it. And there is the Nietzsche who occupies the liberated standpoint, the one who wrote the title, who addresses his readers through the title, and who, through a "choral" use of the first person pronoun that brings together in unison the voices of the writer of *Human, All Too Human* and of its commentator in *Ecce Homo*, also addresses his readers in that commentary of the title. As for the types of readers, there is the type to whom the title only *refers*: unliberated, all-too-human readers that still see the world through ideals; and the type to whom, as the subtitle tells us, the book is addressed: the free spirits. But note that in writing that he liberated himself from things that *did not belong to his nature*, Nietzsche also introduces a distinction, within unliberated readers, between those in whose nature it is to remain unfree, and those whose nature is compatible with liberation.

It thus seems that Nietzsche knows well what we are sometimes prone to forget: that reading involves entertaining views and perspectives different from our own while placing the latter on hold (rather than immediately deploying them as standards for mechanically endorsing or dismissing what we read). In deploying this *typology* of potential types of readers through the title and subtitle, and eventually the commentary, of *Human, All Too Human*, he effectively offers his potential readers, regardless of their background, three alternative standpoints for consideration, as if he were saying "it is up to you, identify yourself with the unfree spirit in whose nature it is to remain unfree (and do what you will with this book—of what concern is that for me?); identify yourself with the unfree spirit in whose nature it is *not* to remain unfree—and with the free spirits—and use this book, as I did, to liberate yourself from that which does not belong to your nature; identify yourself with the free spirits, and enjoy this celebration of your crisis and self-overcoming."

So while Nietzsche does, as internalists suggest, explicitly address readers who occupy a different evaluative standpoint than his own, a reader who may disagree with him, who may still be under the grip of *ideals*, who remains all too human, it is not at all obvious that he does it, *or that he would need to do it*, by occupying or pretending to occupy their standpoint. His strategy is rather to *bring into view different standpoints and ethical attitudes*, to *display* and (arguably) even exaggerate the difference between his standpoint and attitude and that of his readers, to taunt them by showing their own in a different light and by showing disdain for the kind of reader who would remain committed to their preconceptions.[26]

But does this not reveal the correctness of the Grounding Assumption, and the corresponding picture of critique that goes in hand with it, according to which a critique of values amounts to the reevaluation of some evalua*ted* values on the basis of some evalua*ting* values? After all, the internalist may point out that Nietzsche's strategy in the title of *Human, All Too Human* and its commentary in *Ecce Homo* could only be effective insofar as there is substantive overlap between his standpoint and that of his readers. Indeed, only readers who, *like Nietzsche*, are committed to freedom as a core value are likely to be moved by his disdain of constitutively unfree spirits, to side with him, and to continue to treat the book as though it might have been written for them, at least potentially free spirits.

The last observation, while true, is tangential to the correctness of the Grounding Assumption and the corresponding picture of critique. There is, after all, a difference between, on the one hand, occupying a standpoint and being motivated by it, and even displaying it and emphasizing it in order to elicit a certain reaction from an audience, and on the other hand, *grounding* a critique on that standpoint by relying on it as a standard for evaluating the target of the critique. It is of course uncontroversial that Nietzsche did not think it possible to occupy an axiologically neutral or disinterested standpoint; his projects are always explicitly undertaken, his texts written, from his particular, non-neutral, axiologically committed perspective, an aspect of his work that he often highlights. But this does not imply, as internalists contend, and externalists seem to grant, that his critique of morality or his *Umwertung* is *grounded* on that standpoint—not, at any rate, in any way that would be analogous to how the conclusions of sound arguments are grounded on their premises, and which would require his target audience to share that standpoint, much in the same way that recognizing the soundness of an argument requires recognizing the truth of its premises. At the risk of sounding repetitive, for the point is important: just as it is possible for someone to deploy an argument whose premises they do not subscribe to, and just as it is possible for someone to entertain and learn something from an argument the premises of which they do not endorse, so it is possible for someone writing from an axiologically committed standpoint to deploy critiques that are not grounded on that standpoint, and for readers to consider critiques that are based on standpoints different than their own and to learn something in the process. What the title and remarks in *Human, All Too Human* show is that it is part of Nietzsche's overall *rhetorical* strategy to *exhibit* his standpoint. The reason Nietzsche's *Umwertungen* are not vulnerable to the authority problem is not that, based on the very evaluative standpoint that they criticize, they function as internal critiques. It is rather that, not being grounded on any particular evaluative standpoint, they give no room for the question of the authority to gain any traction. And indeed, would it not be surprising if for Nietzsche, if from a Nietzschean perspective, the attitude that one is to have toward values were a matter of authority, of rational authority?

But what, then, is Nietzsche's strategy? How are his texts meant to work on his target audience? What is, as we like to say "in philosophy," his argument? This will be the topic of the next section. There are, however, a few other problems with internalist and externalist approaches, and a few related aspects of Nietzsche's idea of *Umwertung*, that I'd like to bring into view before sketching my positive account of Nietzsche's method. For the time being, allow me to settle, first, for noting that in his commentary of the title of *Human, All Too Human*, Nietzsche displays a *typology* of potential readers without spelling out what the reader is to do and how she is to react in the face of this typology; and second, for venturing the suggestion that perhaps this has something to do with the fact that even if Nietzsche is quite aware that bringing this typology into view can have the effect of alerting his readers to the possibility of occupying those various standpoints, it would be quite out of character and confused for him to attempt to derive, from that typology, claims about how his reader is to (must, ought to, should, on pains of irrationality) read his text, or about what reader-type his reader is to (must, ought to, should . . .) identify with.

As for the question of Nietzsche's intended audience, it should be clear that, contrary to what internalists and externalists seem to assume, Nietzsche does not restrict his target audience either to readers who share his evaluative standpoint or to readers who do not. While he certainly says that his books are for those who share his standpoint, he also says that such readers have yet to come into being. And he says this to his actual readers, whom he often characterizes as people who, beyond simply not sharing his standpoint, are not even in a position to understand it.

2.2. The Novelty of *Umwertung*

Another exegetical problem with the conception of *Umwertung* at issue is that it renders Nietzsche's insistence on the historically unprecedented character of his idea of *Umwertung* rather obscure. In the Preface to the *Will to Power* Nietzsche tells us that the book is "the history of the next two centuries," that its author is "a spirit of daring and experiment that has already lost itself once in the labyrinth of the future," a "soothsayer-bird spirit who *looks back* when relating what will come"; and that the title "that this gospel of the future wants to bear" is "The Will to Power: Attempt at a Re-evaluation of All Values" (*Umwerthung aller Werthe*).[27] Nietzsche, that is, goes well out of his way to emphasize the originality of *Umwertung*, so novel indeed that its possibility is only beginning to be explored, and lies ahead even of this soothsayer-bird who must look back at the very moment of relating the future that lies ahead of us. By contrast, the form of revaluation described above, characterized by the Grounding Requirement, and consisting in the assessment of values on the basis of the values that make up an evaluative standpoint, is anything but innovative. For it essentially amounts to reflexively occupying an evaluative standpoint. This, accordingly, is a second problem with the Grounding Requirement: it goes hand in hand with a picture of *Umwertung* that renders Nietzsche's insistence on the novelty of the idea enigmatic.

2.3. The Scope of *Umwertung*

We saw that in *Ecce Homo* Nietzsche describes the essays that make up the *Genealogy* as "three decisive preliminary studies by a psychologist for the revaluation of all values."[28] In discussing that claim, I emphasized that

Nietzsche describes his genealogical essays as preliminary to *Umwertung*. But it is worth noting that he characterizes the latter as bearing upon *all* values. The same is true of the passage from *The Will to Power* we just considered, where he writes about the revaluation of *all* values, not of a particular value, or a particular set of values. In fact, most of Nietzsche's uses of the word *Umwerthung* are within the phrases *"Umwerthung aller Werthe"* and *"Umwerthung der Werthe überhaupt"* ("re-evaluation of all values" and "re-evaluation of values in general").[29] Since at least in these predominant contexts, the target of *Umwertung* is not a particular value or set of values, the conception of reevaluation sketched above, according to which it consists in the assessment of a particular evalua*ted* standpoint on the basis of an evalua*ting* standpoint, does not seem to capture his conception of *Umwertung*. For how could the assessment of particular values on the basis of other values lead to a reevaluation of all values?

2.4. The Novelty and the Scope of the Problems Combined

It might be tempting to think that the answer to this last question is that the slow, piecemeal critique of values might, in the long run, at least approximate the goal of a reevaluation of *all* values. However, the conception of *Umwertung* that then begins to emerge leads to an exacerbated version of the novelty problem, and makes it hard to account for Nietzsche's claim to the effect that genealogy is needed as a preliminary for *Umwertung*.

To see this, suppose that the Grounding Requirement is correct, that reevaluation requires deploying some values as evaluative standards, and consider the values that function as such for some particular reevaluative project, and the reevalua*ting* values at work in it. In order for that reevaluation to be the reevaluation of *all* values, the reevalua*ting* values must themselves be then reevaluated. But since, *ex hypothesi*, they must be reevaluated by reference to themselves, they can at best be said to be reevaluated in a vacuous sense. The reevaluation would, at best, serve to identify and resolve inconsistencies within the overall evalua*ting* standpoint. So in this view, undertaking the reevaluation of all values turns out to be the same as occupying an evaluative standpoint with a modicum of reflexivity. It becomes hard to see whether there is any *substantive* sense in which one may speak of the reevaluation of *all* values (rather than of the reevaluation of all values that aren't one's own on the basis of one's own). It also becomes hard to see what distinguishes reevaluation from the simple fact of having an evaluative standpoint, why Nietzsche took it to be historically unprecedented, or why he took the idea of reevaluation to require genealogical knowledge at all.

But what is the alternative? What else might *Umwertung* consist in? Nietzsche's *Umwertung* functions at the level not of particular values, but, as Nietzsche himself frequently writes, of values *überhaupt* (in general). In other words—and this is crucial—*Umwertung* is primarily the reevaluation of our *conception* of values, of what they are and, most importantly, of the relationship in which we stand to them. This reevaluation corresponds, *grosso modo*, to a shift between the positions mentioned in the *Euthyphro*. It corresponds, that is, to a shift away from a traditional conception of values according to which values are valuable in themselves, and hence according to which a commitment to "the right" values can and ought to be—and in the best cases is—rationally grounded (following a traditional, foundationalist conception of practical rationality), towards a novel, Nietzschean conception of values according to which values are expressions of a way of life, and each person's commitment to values is the commitment to *their* particular way of life. In the next section, I'll offer a more detailed sketch (but a sketch nonetheless) of this conception of *Umwertung*, and how it relates to the project of genealogy and to Nietzsche's methodology more broadly.

3. Genealogy and *Umwertung*

We should admit to ourselves with all due severity exactly *what* will be necessary for a long time to come and *what* is provisionally correct, namely: collecting material, formulating concepts, and putting into order the tremendous realm of tender value feelings and value distinctions that live, grow, reproduce and are destroyed,—and, perhaps, attempting to illustrate the recurring and more frequent shapes of this living crystallization,—all of which would be a preparation for a *typology* of morals. . . . that supposedly modest little *descriptive* project, left in rot and ruin, even though the subtlest hands and senses could hardly be subtle enough for it. Precisely because moral philosophers had only a crude knowledge of moral *facta*, selected

> and arbitrarily abbreviated at random—for instance, as the morality of their surroundings, their class, their church, their *Zeitgeist*, their climate and region,—precisely because they were poorly informed (and not particularly eager to learn more) about peoples, ages, and histories, they completely missed out on the genuine problems that only emerge from a comparison of many *different* moralities.[30]

The passage is from the first section of "On the Natural History of Morals," the central part of *Beyond Good and Evil*. Nietzsche suggests that the problems of morality, what should be the topic of a science of morality, first appear through the comparison of various forms of morality. Hence the need for a typology of morality, for a descriptive, natural history of morality that offers a typology of moralities.

Throughout the section, Nietzsche contrasts this idea of a typology of morals (and the preliminary, information gathering and organizing work that it requires) with what "all philosophers" hitherto have sought to accomplish "under the guise of a science of morals: to ground morality." Ultimately, Nietzsche suggests, because philosophers took this to be the primary goal of a science of morals, they neglected the typology of morals, thereby depriving themselves of the means to identify the proper (*Eigentliche*) problems of morality:

> they completely missed out on the genuine problems that only emerge from a comparison of many *different* moralities. As strange as it may sound, the problem of morality has itself been *missing* from every "science of morals" so far: there was no suspicion that anything was really a problem. Viewed properly, the "grounding of morals" (as philosophers have called it, as they demanded it of themselves) was only an erudite form of good *faith* in the dominant morality, a new way of *expressing* it; as such, it was itself already situated within the terms of a certain morality. In the last analysis, it even constitutes a type of denial that these morals *can* be regarded as a problem.[31]

Or we might say: by taking for granted that they subscribed to their morality because it was good in itself, and not because it was theirs, philosophers thought that the main task of a science of morals was to show that this was indeed morality in itself. They thereby rendered themselves blind to the possibility that they subscribed to it merely because it was theirs. What Nietzsche exposes here is a certain form of parochialism that consists in taking what is familiar, what is the local norm, to be normative for similar phenomena in all contexts; a parochialism that consists, that is, in reifying local ways of acting and interacting with others, and in regarding them as norms that ought to regulate how people in general, human being as such, ought to act; in mistaking local customs for universally valid norms that determine how people ought to act and interact by virtue of the fact that they are human.

There are two important aspects of the traditional moral philosophers' starting assumption: on the metaphysical register, the idea that moral values are valuable in themselves; on the practical register, the corresponding, closely related view that the source of moral commitments, their ground, is recognition of "the" moral values, the ones that are (thought to be) good in themselves. Thus it is not only the idea that moral values are valuable in themselves that is at work in traditional morality, but a whole approach to moral psychology, moral epistemology and moral philosophy that come with it.

But what are "the problems of morality" that Nietzsche alludes to? And how is the idea of a typology of moralities supposed to bring these problems into view? Nietzsche himself does not offer a simple answer to the first question, and so it seems to me that to offer one would be to offer an overdetermined interpretation of the text. But one thing is certain: he is not concerned, at all, by the possibility that denying that values are valuable in themselves would deprive us of the conceptual means to render values, and to render our commitment to our values, intelligible. That is the primary worry of the traditional philosopher who hastens to ground morality before coming to understand the problems of morality. And it is the worry of the nihilists, a worry for the time of nihilism, a time to which, as Nietzsche writes in the Preface to the *Will to Power*, the *Umwertung* of all values is a response.

Thus we can at least safely say that the problems of a science of morals are the host of problems that first come into view once we give up that traditional assumption, once we call into question the rationality of morality, not by denying that morality is rational, but by calling into question the idea that the type of rationality that must necessarily underlie our moral lives is, as it has traditionally been taken to be, structurally analogous to the type of rationality operative in rational belief formation and revision, and according to which our attitudes toward values must ultimately be motivated by, and traceable to, attitude-independent reasons. "The problem of morality" is acknowledging that there is much more decision making, much more of willing, and much less of grounds involved in moral commitment than the tradition has taken there to be.

As for the second question, a typology of moralities and a natural history of morality might contribute to that reconceptualization of moral values by bringing into view the fact that our own particular morality is but one among many possible forms of morality, that different peoples, in different lands, in different periods, have subscribed to different moralities; that moral reasoning and moral-ground-giving are, as Nietzsche suggests in that opening section of "On the Natural History of Morals," only forms of *faith* at work in each particular morality, new ways of *expressing* it, of consolidating it, and that as such, they are themselves always already situated within the bounds of that particular moral standpoint that they purport to ground.

Umwertung, accordingly, works not at the level of particular values. If the idea of *Umwertung* is the idea of an *Umwertung* of all values, if it applies to values *überhaupt* (in general), it is because it operates at the level of *the concept of* morality itself, of what moral values are, of what moral commitment is. What the typology of moralities is meant to bring into view is that there is a host of questions to be raised about these concepts, questions which, through the assumption that the valuable is valuable in itself, the Western philosophical tradition has rendered intractable. *Umwertung* itself, reevaluation, is the outcome of that process of questioning and problematizing morality. It is not merely a reappraisal of existing values on the basis of existing values, and its result is less a new view about which values are highest and which lowest than a new conception of values.

This idea of a typology and its effects, which we find in *Beyond Good and Evil*, are forerunners of the idea of genealogy. If in a typology we see variation of forms of morality, their relationship to the cultural and natural milieus within which they emerge, and (perhaps, as Nietzsche says) recurrent patterns, in a genealogy we see the historical processes of coming into being and disappearing of such forms of morality, what we may describe as the dialectical emergence and development of different moralities and their corresponding moral types.[32] Genealogy is meant to bring into view, perhaps even to emphasize, that the source of moral commitment *tends* to lie not in a disinterested acknowledgment of the truth about "the valuable in itself," but in an effort to preserve and persevere in one's way of life.

And it matters, of course, that this is only a tendency, and that once we come to see that moral commitment tends to be the commitment to a familiar way of life because it is familiar, we can also resist that tendency by calling into question our parochial commitments.

Typology and genealogy are both descriptive historical enterprises: typology produces the record of the different forms of morality that have existed, genealogy the record of the processes whereby they have come into being, undergone transformations, disappeared. Neither amounts to an *Umwertung* of values, but both of them bring into view the possibility and necessity of the task by revealing the need to call into question the conception of moral life and of values operative in traditional philosophy—they bring into view "the problem of morality."

It is true that in writing his histories of morality and of philosophical discourse about morality, Nietzsche never ceases to foreground his own allegiances and commitments. But his argumentative strategy does not consist in offering arguments against traditional morality which would be *grounded* on the values to which he subscribes or on those he criticizes. This would be anathema to the very idea that there is something confused and blinding about the traditional project of grounding morality. His strategy consists rather in displaying a range of moral values and systems of values, and showing that, in each case, the commitment to the relevant set of values can invariably be traced back to something other than what is presented as its grounds and which invariably serves the function of perpetuating the way of life to which those values is bound. And note: the crucial point here is not only that *Umwertung* consists in a revision of what one takes to be one's reasons for valuing the particular values that one values—a view arguably shared by Ridley—but also that this revision is a revision of one's concept of what value is, and that it is brought about through the description of the variety of moral types (in typology) and of their genesis (in genealogy), rather than through the deployment of a range of values as standards of assessment for the reevaluation of one's own.[33]

But how could typology and genealogy, and more generally, how could the history of morality bring someone to call into question traditional morality? Would this not amount to an instance of the genetic fallacy? The question itself should be rejected. Nietzsche's works are not intended to be conclusive, in the sense that they are not intended to *command assent on pains of irrationality*. They couldn't be, since on his view, there is ultimately no rational grounding for morality, no set of claims that would show that being rational *requires* committing to a particular morality.[34]

Typologies and genealogies bring into view that systems of values, and the justificatory discourses surrounding them, tend to be such as to promote and perpetuate the particular ways of life of those who subscribe to them; they bring into view that within any given community, there are strong, generally unacknowledged, practical incentives to treat as good, and as good in itself, what is generally taken to be good within those communities. One may react to such descriptive observations in a number of ways. Schematically:

1. Disputing their accuracy.

2. Accepting their accuracy but maintaining that while in other communities people are committed to values simply because they are the dominant ones within their community and mistakenly treat them as valuable in themselves, one's own case is the exception, as one just happens to be part of the one community built around the values that are actually valuable in themselves. There are, moreover, two versions of this stance: some may claim to be committed to the values of their community only because they are the "right ones"; others may acknowledge that they are committed to them because they take them to be the right ones, while also acknowledging that the fact that they are the dominant values of their community has played an important role in their being committed to them.

3. One may also come to think that one's commitment to one's own values, and the various procedures for vindicating the legitimacy of that commitment and the treatment of those values as valuable in themselves, are largely accidental; they largely result from the fact that one is a member of one's own community, and committed to the way of life that is dominant in that community.

To come to think of values in this last way is, effectively, to begin to operate an *Umwertung aller Werte*. But one of the key points here is that Nietzsche's goal as a writer is not to compel all his readers to adopt one such reaction. Typology or genealogy do not impose, conclusively, this change of attitude. They are preliminary studies that provide the source material for a novel conception of values, a form of moral rationality that offers an alternative to the tradition, and according to which our values are valuable because and insofar as we take them to be valuable.

Once we see this, the oddity of the idea that Nietzschean *Umwertung* could be vulnerable to a *problem of authority* can begin to come into view. The goal of *Umwertung* is precisely to shift away from a conception of values according to which commitment to values is a matter of authority, and thus, according to which the commitment to values must (or even could) be grounded on the authority of rational argument. On Nietzsche's view, commitment to values is *ultimately* groundless; it is the expression of a force, nothing over and above *the individual's commitment* to a way of life, a commitment that can be freely made or passively acquired. Accordingly, the idea of a critique of morality that has the form of a battery of arguments intended to show, *conclusively*, that the reader *should* or *ought* to adopt a difference stance toward their own axiological commitments, and thus, the idea of a critique of morality whose success would depend on its having the authority to command assent over all those whose moral standpoint it targets by virtue of its being grounded on the appropriate evaluative standpoint, is strongly anti-Nietzschean.[35] As Nietzsche himself puts it in his commentary to *Beyond Good and Evil* in *Ecce Homo*, "From this moment forward all my writings are fish hooks: perhaps I know how to fish as well as anyone?—If nothing was caught, I am not to blame. *There were no fish.*"[36]

4. Concluding Remarks

One of the key components of the traditional picture of morality is the idea that values are valuable in themselves. It is widely acknowledged—certainly by sophisticated interpreters—that Nietzsche rejected this idea. So how could one hold that the traditional conception of values is still at work in much of contemporary Nietzsche interpretation? There is a number of ways in which one could reject the notion of the valuable in itself while remaining hostage to the traditional view. To go back to the *Euthyphro*, one might, for instance, opt for the alternative offered by Socrates taken literally: the reason that values are valuable is because the gods, or some other recognized higher authority, value them. But one might also adopt what could seem—somewhat naively, in my view—the only alternative: that the value of values is always instrumental.[37] Common to these two "alternatives" is the idea that the individual's commitment to values is—that is, that it ought to be—rational, in the sense that it must be rationally motivated, hence, *grounded* on reasons: further ends to whose pursuit one is committed, the dictum of what one recognizes as an authority in matters of value, the fact of their being intrinsically valuable. The idea that values are valuable for attitude-independent reasons, and that the commitment to values can and must, accordingly, be grounded on such reasons, is but a notational variant of the traditional idea that values are valuable in themselves.

It is in this respect that I see the traditional conception of morality at work in much contemporary Nietzsche scholarship. It can be seen at work, as I have attempted to show, in conceptions of *Umwertung* according to which the latter is a form of critique consisting in the reappraisal of a set of evalua*ted* values *on the basis of* an evaluative standpoint, and in the very worry about authority that motivates the adoption of such conceptions of *Umwertung*. For the latter are based on the following assumptions: that Nietzsche's aim, as a writer, is to command assent from his target audience; that his strategy is to offer conclusive reasons that must be recognized as such by that audience on pains of irrationality; that such reasons must in fact consist in the audience's pre-existent commitments to a range of values; and that on these values, accordingly, the reevaluation must itself be grounded. But these assumptions jointly betray a conception of values according to which the commitment of values must ultimately be grounded on reason, and according to which the recognition of such reasons ought to be enough to persuade anyone to endorse the relevant values.

To reject such a picture, on the other hand, is not to commit to an irrationalism, both implausible and impracticable, according to which our axiological lives lacks rational structure altogether. It is simply to acknowledge what we have, for a while already, come to accept about epistemic rationality: that being rational does not consist in being able to trace back all our beliefs and values to an unshakable foundation from which they're derivable, but to be able to revise any of them, at any given moment, and to revise them in accordance to the appropriate procedures. Of course, part of Nietzsche's project consists precisely in enquiring into the idea of appropriateness that remains in matters of value, if such a remainder there be. And of course, it is well beyond my present aims to even begin to address that question. My aim has been merely to point out that what is at issue in Nietzschean *Umwertung* is the urgency of this very question: what notion of appropriateness applicable to our commitment to values are we left with once we abandon not only the idea that values are valuable in themselves, but also the more general, and more deeply engrained assumption that the commitment of values must be grounded in the authority of reason?

Notes

1. The alternative at issue here, the one that is likely to strike us as nonsensical, is not one according to which there is no "real" good but merely a collective treating-things-as-though-they-were-good; it is rather one according to which there is such a thing as the good, but what makes it good is that we take it to be so.

2. Plato, *Euthyphro*, in *Complete Works*, trans. G.M.A. Grube, ed. John M. Cooper and D.S. Hutchinson (Indiana: Hackett Publishing, 1997), 10c (with minor modifications).

3. Ethan Coen and Joel Coen, *The Big Lebowski* (Universal City: Universal Studios Home Entertainment, 1998), DVD.

4. The German *Umwertung* is usually translated as "reevaluation" or "revaluation." I suspect that this choice of translation has lent plausibility to a somewhat inaccurate understanding of the notion within Anglophone scholarship. So I shall use the (contemporary) German *Umwertung* in what follows, except when citing discussions that use "reevaluation," and when citing Nietzsche, where I shall rely on his spelling (consistent with conventions of his time) and write "Umwerthung" and "Werthe."

5. Friedrich Nietzsche, *The Genealogy of Morals*, trans. Carol Diethe, ed. Keith Ansel Pearson (Cambridge: Cambridge University Press, 1997), Preface, §6.

6. Friedrich Nietzsche, *Ecce Homo*, in *Basic Writings*, ed. and trans. Walter Kaufmann (New York: Random House, 1992), 769.

7. The genetic fallacy, a subspecies of the naturalistic fallacy, consists in deriving normative claims about something from descriptive claims about its origins (where normative claims can be evaluative claims about the value of something, or prescriptive claims about what the appropriate standpoint toward that thing is). E.g., Edmund was born out of wedlock, therefore he is morally deficient (evaluative claim), and must be treated as such (prescriptive claim).

8. Alexander Nehamas, *Nietzsche: Life as Literature* (Cambridge, MA: Harvard University Press, 1985), 246n1; and Raymond Geuss, "Nietzsche and Genealogy," in *Morality, Culture and History: Essays on German Philosophy* (Cambridge: Cambridge University Press, 1999), 22–23.

9. To suggest this is not, however, to impute to the authors I'll be discussing the view Nietzsche was committed to the idea that values are valuable in themselves. The issue is rather that although they deny this, they operate with, and ascribe to Nietzsche, a concept of "value" that remains too close to the traditional one.

10. A critique of a standpoint S is *external* if and only if it is grounded in (i.e., if the acceptance of its validity requires) the adoption of a standpoint S' that is manifestly excluded by S; otherwise it is *internal*. I shall henceforth use the label "*externalist*" to refer to interpretations according to which Nietzsche's critique of morality was *grounded* in an *evaluative standpoint* external to the moral standpoint it targets, and "*internalist*" to refer to those according to which it is *grounded* on an *evaluative standpoint* internal to its target. In so doing, I am following Ridley et al. in using the pair of labels to refer to views that build on the assumption that Nietzschean critiques are *grounded in evaluative standpoints*, even though this is an assumption that I shall be calling into question.

11. Aaron Ridley, "Nietzsche and the Re-evaluation of Values," in *Nietzsche's On the Genealogy of Morals: Critical Essays*, ed. Christa Davis Acampora (Lanham, MD: Rowman & Littlefield, 2006), 77–92; David Owen, *Nietzsche's Genealogy of Morality* (Stocksfield, UK: Acumen Publishing, 2007), ch. 8; Alison Merrick, "On Genealogy and Transcendent Critique," *Journal of Nietzsche Studies* 47, no. 2 (2016), 228. Although Merrick writes of *immanent* and *transcendent* critiques rather than of *internal* and *external* critiques, her use of the first pair of terms corresponds to my use of the second one.

12. Ridley, "Nietzsche and the Re-evaluation of Values," 78. Note that the passage in question is not written in Ridley's own voice, but is rather a description of the line of reasoning that, on his view, leads to the authority problem. His own solution to the problem, however, is not based on a wholesale rejection of that line of reasoning. He only takes issue with the assumption that the authority of reevaluation must be based on an evaluative standpoint that is *immune* to reevaluation, replacing it by the weaker and more plausible constraint that it be based on a standpoint that is compatible with the one that is the target of reevaluation. Account taken of this emendation, the passage accurately captures Ridley's own conception of how reevaluation is meant to function.

13. Ridley's formulation of the Grounding Requirement, while sufficiently precise for his purposes, is somewhat imprecise for ours. He writes that *"re-evaluation can only be* 'undertaken' *from an evaluative standpoint,"* while the idea is in fact that reevaluation must be *grounded on*, rather than merely undertaken from, an evaluative standpoint. To see the difference, and its importance, note that the view that all standpoints are evaluative (in the sense that part of what it is to have a standpoint is to be committed to a range of evaluative standards) makes it vacuously true that all critiques are undertaken from an evaluative standpoint, and is consistent with the view that it is possible to criticize an evaluative standpoint without grounding the critique on an evaluative standpoint by, say, criticizing the conception of values that undergirds it.

14. All citations are from Ridley, "Nietzsche and the Re-evaluation of Values," 78.

15. As I noted in the introduction, part of my goal is to show that the traditional conception of values, as valuable in themselves, is still operative in the reception of Nietzsche's work. But crucially, the suggestion is not that some contemporary interpreters explicitly (and rather implausibly) attribute Nietzsche a conception of values as valuable in themselves. Ridley's insistence on the importance of the Nietzsche's rejection of unconditional values (i.e., values that are valuable in themselves) as one of the potential sources of the authority problem indicates that if the traditional conception of values is operative in his reading of Nietzsche, it is in a much subtler way than through its overt endorsement.

16. Ridley, "Nietzsche and the Re-evaluation of Values," 78.

17. Brian Leiter, *Nietzsche on Morality* (New York: Routledge, 2002), 125 (emphasis added).

18. This *could* seem counterintuitive *on a first approximation*. But the idea that one writes not to persuade those who disagree with one's standpoint, but to articulate why it might be better to agree, for those who already agree, or who at least are on the fence about agreeing, is of course anything except counterintuitive.

19. Merrick, "On Genealogy and Transcendent Critique," 231.

20. Ridley, "Nietzsche and the Re-evaluation of Values," 133.

21. Nietzsche, *Genealogy*, Preface, §2.

22. In the passage, Nietzsche uses the second person plural to address his target audience: "Ob sie e u c h schmecken, diese unsre Früchte?" Nietzsche, *Genealogy*, Preface, §2.

23. See note 10 above.

24. Here, the distinction between what *motivates someone* to put forth a critique and what *grounds* a critique is essential. The present point is not that we should entertain the view that Nietzsche's critique is not motivated by his own values, or that his critiques are undertaken from a standpoint that is axiologically neutral. The point is only that *deploying* the critique need not require either endorsing or rejecting those aspects of the evaluat*ed* standpoint that it targets.

25. Nietzsche, *Ecce Homo*, 739. Note that in section 2 of the foreword to *The Genealogy*, Nietzsche traces the latter's project back to *Human, All Too Human*.

26. In this regard, it seems to me to be right to emphasize, as Ridley, Janaway, and Owen have, the rhetorical importance of Nietzsche's attention to and work on his readers' affects, so long as one does not take the idea to be that Nietzsche's strategy seeks to persuade his audience primarily by engaging their affective capacities instead of his rational capacities, a dichotomy rejected by Nietzsche (a point emphasized by Owen). See Christopher Janaway, *Beyond Selflessness* (Oxford: Oxford University Press, 2007), esp. chap. 12; Aaron Ridley, *Nietzsche's Conscience: Six Character Studies from the Genealogy* (Ithaca, NY: Cornell University Press, 1998); and David Owen, "Nietzsche's Genealogy Revisited," *Journal of Nietzsche Studies*, no. 35–36 (2008), 147.

27. Friedrich Nietzsche, *The Will to Power*, trans. Walter. Kaufman and R.J. Hollingdale (New York: Vintage Books, 1968), 3.

28. Nietzsche, *Ecce Homo*, 769.

29. This is not to deny that there are contexts in which Nietzsche uses *Umwertung* to refer to the reevaluation, conceived of as a reversal, of particular sets of values by particular groups of people (e.g., Nietzsche, *Genealogy*, I, §7–§8); but only to indicate the need to distinguish between that restricted sense of *Umwertung* primarily in the earlier occurrences of the term in Nietzsche's writings, and the deeper and more comprehensive one that he embarked upon later on.

30. Friedrich Nietzsche, *Beyond Good and Evil*, trans. Walter Kaufmann (New York: Vintage, 1989), 287 (emphasis added).

31. Nietzsche, *Beyond Good and Evil*, 287.

32. Nietzsche's terminology suggests that he is thinking of moral systems, and their corresponding moral types, as analogous to biological species; typology would correspond to taxonomy, genealogy to evolutionary theory.

33. See Ridley, "Nietzsche and the Re-evaluation of Values," 81.

34. That there is no rational foundation of morality in the sense at issue here does not entail that being moral is irrational, but only that it is not a requirement for being rational.

35. To insist, the view that I have been defending is not that any of the contemporary interpreters of Nietzsche that I have been discussing make the sophomoric mistake of taking him to subscribe to the idea of values that are valuable in themselves (see notes 9 and 20). The issue is rather that while denying this in letter, their conception of Nietzschean *Umwertung*, according to which it must be "grounded on" or "draw upon" an evaluative standpoint, and of how Nietzsche's texts are meant to work, which might render them vulnerable to an authority problem, betrays the persistence of this traditional conception of values. Ridley, for instance, while arguing that Nietzsche rejected the idea of unconditional values, relies on the idea of intrinsic values, according to which an individual's attitudes toward particular values must be grounded on reasons.

36. Nietzsche, *Ecce Homo*, 766.

37. While I cannot elaborate on the point here, this is a picture explicitly rejected by Nietzsche in his attack on the British genealogies in the opening sections of the first essay of the *Genealogy*.

13

Kantian Critique, Its Ethical Purification by Hermann Cohen, and Its Reflective Transformation by Wilhelm Dilthey

RUDOLF A. MAKKREEL

1. Introduction

It is possible to derive three kinds of critique from Kant's philosophy, and I will distinguish them as having either constitutive, regulative, or reflective functions. My main aim is to explore the potential of reflective critique and to argue for its relevance when assessing ethical decisions for their social ramifications. To accomplish this, it will be instructive to examine two nineteenth-century responses to Kant's moral philosophy—first that of the orthodox Neo-Kantian Hermann Cohen and then that of the less orthodox or quasi-Kantian Wilhelm Dilthey.

2. The Three Kinds of Critique in Kant

The first kind of Kantian critique is *constitutive and foundational* and provides the basic meaning categories that make it possible to cognize reality. These constitutive concepts of experience define the main project of Kant's *Critique of Pure Reason*, namely, to ground our cognition of the natural world in lawful terms. Wilhelm Dilthey conceived his project of a *Critique of Historical Reason* as an analogous attempt to define some of the constitutive conditions for the cognition of history made possible by the human sciences.[1] But instead of searching for the overarching laws of history, Dilthey saw it as his task to articulate the immanent purposiveness of the evolving sociocultural systems that serve to structure the process of history. This methodical transformation will lead Dilthey in the direction of what I consider to be a reflective critique.

The second or *regulative* kind of Kantian critique is speculative in that it is *ideal-directed*. We see the move in that direction in the Transcendental Dialectic of the *Critique of Pure Reason*, where Kant introduces regulative ideas in an attempt to systematize or comprehend the totality of what we know. But since these ideas of reason go beyond the constitutive concepts of the understanding, they cannot be tested by experience and can readily produce conflicting conclusions or antinomies. In order to cope with the dialectical antinomies that it engenders, regulative critique must be self-limiting.

We can find an even closer relation between constitutive and regulative critique in Kant's *Groundwork of the Metaphysics of Morals*, where the final formulation of the categorical imperative introduces an ideal kingdom of ends.[2] And for us to be held morally responsible for our actions, Kant postulates freedom as "the *ratio essendi* of the moral law"[3] in the *Critique of Practical Reason*. The postulate that we are noumenally free is supplemented by the less essential postulates of immortality and God as conditions, not for the moral law, but for the possibility of attaining the highest good.

In Kant's first two *Critiques*, then, the constitutive makes objective necessity intelligible and the regulative satisfies the higher needs of reason. The regulative needs of reason are spelled out by Kant as follows: "A need of pure reason in its speculative use leads only to hypotheses, that of pure practical reason, however to postulates . . . based on the duty to promote the highest good."[4] Regulative postulates are clearly normative and ideal directed.

The third kind of critique in Kant that I want to focus on was not as fully worked out by him. It is a *reflective and judgment-based critique*, but it can encompass more than the aesthetic and teleological judging discussed in the third *Critique*. A reflective judgment (*reflektirendes Urteil*) is evaluative (*beurteilend*)[5] by relating what we feel to what we think and do. A reflective attitude requires us to appraise the various situations we find ourselves in and confront in life. Like regulative critique, a reflective critical approach is normative, but because it is situational it must consider what we think and do in relation to others. This is already implicit in making a judgment of taste, for as Kant recognizes, my response to something beautiful must take the response of others into account. An aesthetic reflective judgment can only be valid if I have imaginatively engaged with other human beings before finalizing my judgment. More broadly considered, reflective judgment aims to nudge individual attitudes and views toward an intersubjective consensus.[6]

To extend this kind of reflective critique to what we think and decide to do, I will also bring in certain themes introduced in Kant's late *Metaphysics of Morals*. Accordingly, I will argue that the right to acquire property is reflectively justified by Kant relative to the needs of others based on a conditional permissive law rather than an unconditional moral law. Then I will consider how the Neo-Kantian Hermann Cohen attempts to improve on such a reflective defense of legal rights by seeking a more pure ethical justification for them.

Finally, I will turn to Dilthey's *System of Ethics* as the framework for further testing my thesis that a reflective critique should consider what we do, whether through action, work, or the investment of resources, in terms of its impact on others. This kind of reflective critique situates each of us in a shared human world and is orientational. It alone can make the transition from the traditional *Philosophie nach dem Schulbegriff* that Kant aimed to replace with *a Philosophie nach dem Weltbegriff*. Reflective critique moves from conceiving things from the *anywhere* of academic debate to judging them from *somewhere* within this world.

To sum up this initial delineation of the three kinds of critique, we can say that whereas constitutive critique can justify what we know and do within transcendental self-prescribed bounds, regulative critique is speculative by projecting ideals that reason allows us to believe in and hope for. Reflective critique can deepen human understanding by taking into account both self-imposed normative bounds (*Grenzen*) and external contextual limits (*Schranken*) imposed by the world. Reflective critique is essential for coming to terms with a world that is finite.

3. Kant on Rightful Ownership in a World of Limited Resources

Concerning rightful ownership, Kant writes that "nothing external is originally mine, but it can indeed be *acquired* originally, that is, without being derived from what is another's."[7] The problem is how to justify using something as one's own without depriving others of what they need. How can my freedom to possess property coexist with the freedom of others on this earth, which is not equally habitable and offers finite resources? Kant distinguishes three moments in the process of legitimating the acquisition (*Erwerbung*) of property. The first moment is that of simply apprehending (*Apprehension*) "an object that belongs to no one" so that it does not directly "conflict with another's freedom."[8] Apprehending property, whether it be land or a useful thing, is a *unilateral* act that is only permissible if no one else is making a similar claim here and now. But this could merely mean that from where I happen to be, I cannot see any counterclaim and feel that my claim is justified.

The second moment of claiming ownership involves designating (*bezeichnen*) this property "territorially" as mine by an "act of choice [*Willkür*] to exclude everyone else from it."[9] I intend to extend my ownership even if others may come upon it later and make a counterclaim. Designative possession can be seen as a *bilateral* declaration addressed to anyone who might subsequently be in a position to take or occupy it. This second comparative moment points to the realization that proper ownership is not merely a case of possessing *or inhabiting something* (*Inhabung*), but of being entitled to *have* it (*Habens*) and hold on to it over time.[10] To designate something as mine is to also make a normative counterclaim against another subject. At this stage I may feel justified in claiming ownership of a plot of land because I have begun cultivating it and invested resources to improve its productivity.

True entitlement or critical justification requires a third reflective moment of "appropriation [*Zueignung*] as an act of a universal legislative will [*Willens*]."[11] Only if my choice to acquire something can be normatively justified as compatible with the general will of the community will it be fully legitimate. This appropriative moment involves an *omnilateral* claim and amounts to what Kant calls an act of noumenal possession. To have an object legitimately as a *"possessio noumenon"*[12] is to have individual ownership publicly endorsed as compatible with the freedom of all. But this public legitimation presupposes a civil "domain" established by a constitution and its positive laws. The right of private ownership derives from a collective ownership of the earth, or as Kant puts it, "possession of an external object can originally be only a possession in common."[13]

The last phase of appropriating an object is to make it an "intelligible thing in itself [*Ding an sich selbst*]" on the basis of a civil constitution.[14] A phenomenal object is said to become "noumenal" if its availability for the free use of a subject is authorized by a constitution as being compatible with the freedom of all other subjects in the civil condition. The object's intelligibility is derived from an omnilateral insight into its proper placement in the civil world of nation-states. I consider Kant's approach here as being reflective by appropriately contextualizing the individual right to property.

4. Cohen on Property Rights and Contractual Justice

Hermann Cohen was the head of the Marburg school of Neo-Kantianism and the teacher of the better-known Ernst Cassirer. For us he is of interest because he set out to improve on Kant's conception of legal rights by orienting it not to the earth that we inhabit, but to a legislative world-order. Whereas Kant's legal approach to property rights was distributive and comparative, Cohen's approach will be collectivist. Both in his *Kants Begründung der Ethik* (*Kant's Grounding of Ethics*) of 1877 and in his *Ethik des reinen Willens* (*Ethics of the Pure Will*) of 1904, Cohen aims to give a legislative reconstruction of Kant's views on human rights and justice. He argues that the philosophy of right must offer the same kind of *a priori* grounding for the human sciences (*Geisteswissenschaften*)[15] that mathematics offers the natural sciences.[16] Moreover, Cohen claims that if Kant had anticipated the need to legitimate the human sciences that arose in the nineteenth century, he would have expanded his critique of practical reason into a "critique of *pure* practical reason."[17] And it is within a "pure ethics" that Cohen sets out to place the philosophy of right.

At its core, the philosophy of right or legal theory is conceived by Cohen as an *a priori* ethics applied reciprocally so that free wills can act lawfully out of mutual respect. On this basis, the ideal of lawful behavior can be preserved for all the sciences: in the natural sciences we discover the laws that are at work in nature; in the human sciences we establish laws in the normative sense. Cohen is not content with a mere external legality based on the positive laws of nation-states. Legitimacy and justice must be rooted in the same idea of self-legislation that defines moral actions.

What this points to is a critique of Kant's "postulate" of "a permissive law"[18] that we discussed earlier, which allows someone to unilaterally apprehend something momentarily in the absence of a counterclaim. There can be no universal law that allows that. Kant's second bilateral moment of declaring something as mine would have to be even more troubling for

Cohen, for it excludes and preempts others who come later from making a counterclaim. It violates the respect for others that he sees as central to ethics. According to Cohen, we must conceive of the ethical as already involving "a community of purposes,"[19] to guarantee that there is a reciprocity of justice at the core of all human action. Whereas Kant derived the goal of the rightful appropriation of things from an *a priori* communal ownership which is then codified by the civil constitution of the state, Cohen makes the concept of a legal contract that Kant applied to our relation to other persons applicable to our relation to things as well. For Kant each of us has an original right to acquire property, but not an original right to acquire "another's choice, in the sense of my capacity to determine it by my own choice to a certain deed."[20] For that, Kant demands that I enter into a contractual relation with that person through a negotiation consisting of an offer and a reciprocal assent. When concluded, the contractual relation amounts to both a promise and its acceptance. Kant writes that "by a contract I acquire another's promise . . . to *perform* something for me; it is not a *right to a thing*,"[21] but against another person to let me have the thing. And all this is based on the premise that "the legislative demand [*Gesetzgebung*] that promises agreed to [in a contract] must be kept, lies not in ethics but in *Ius*."[22] Thereby Kant establishes a division between the internal obligation of moral laws and the external constraint (*Zwang*) of juridical laws. It is this division that Cohen wants to overcome with a more inclusive ethics. In *Kants Begründung*, he attempts to do so by exposing the fact that the legal constraint of contractual consent has become applicable not only to individual claims against others, but also to institutionally endorsed claims on things that others have labored to produce. Because Cohen considers our ethical actions to be inseparable from the labor relations needed to sustain life within a network of economic exchange, we can no longer appeal to any kind of original acquisition of property. The inequities in property relations that have developed in capitalism require an ethical response.

By expanding the contractual relation into a bilateral ethical agreement between individuals that respect each other, Cohen offers an interesting attempt to update Kantian critique to cope with the challenge of Marx. Like Marx, Cohen no longer looks to nation-states that codify the historical needs of people (*Völker*) to legitimate property rights. But unlike Marx, who appeals to human solidarity, Cohen appeals to an ethical concept of juridical law (*Recht*) as the solution. Thus he adds that only by means of a process of "separating out [*Absonderung*]" the way the "bourgeois state" has been shaped by the "cultural" demands of life, "can we come to understand constraint [*Zwang*] as the special characteristic of justice [*Rechts*]"[23] and recognize its ethical basis. Although Cohen recognizes the need for reflective reciprocity through a *contractual* relation, it is made *contractive* by abstracting from the overall situational context of human decision making.

This purifying tendency is even more evident in Cohen's *Ethik des reinen Willens,* where the project to bring ethics and justice together requires an ideal just state. He prepares for this by declaring that the Kantian demand that each person be treated as an end-in-itself is the basis for "the idea of socialism."[24] In the important chapter on justice (*Gerechtigkeit*), Cohen rightly notes the isolating effects of property relations and how they have been aggravated by the way capitalism has separated workers from the earnings of their products.[25] But his solution relies on a "faith in a new world"[26] in which the earnings of work will no longer be measured in terms of property.[27] Thereby he transforms critique from a constitutive activity into a regulative project. Cohen now distinguishes between actual "empirical states" as *Machtstaaten* that represent "the interests of the dominant classes"[28] and an ideal *Rechtstaat*. When this just state is attained it will become clear that "without justice all ethical virtue is worthless."[29] Only in such an ideal state "will property become harmless to the individual."[30] By incorporating the ideal of justice into ethics itself, Cohen aims to attenuate the very concern with individual rights and property. Ownership will only count as an "indispensable moment" for "consumable things."[31] More lasting resources should belong to "cooperative societies [*Genossenschaften*]."[32] These collective associations are meant to emancipate us from imprecise conceptions of community and prepare the ground for a new kind of "juristic person" who will feel at home in the ideal state.

5. Bringing Ethics Down to Earth and Into a Multicultural World

Cohen's ethical reconstruction of Kant's metaphysics of morals is incisive insofar as it shows that Kant's approach is not always consistent: some claims are constitutive and legislative and others more situational. But the drawback of Cohen's more consistent regulative approach is a kind of utopianism that despite its acknowledgment of basic socioeconomic relations ultimately falls back into an academic stance that abstracts from political and cultural conditions. The reciprocity of a contractual relation whereby one can reflectively take the needs of others and their circumstances into account is submerged into a collectivist perspective. Let us see whether a more consistent application of what I have called "reflective critique" can enrich our understanding of the Kantian moral worldview. Can it draw out what is "authentic" rather than "doctrinal" in thinking about human existence, and can it articulate what it means to philosophize in accordance with the actual world (*nach dem Weltbegriff*)?[33]

One of the virtues of a reflective critique is that it can more directly address the multiple empirical conditions of human interaction and interchange. Cohen moves away from this by focusing on juridical law as universally applicable to socioeconomic conditions everywhere. But the reflective judgment that Kant develops in the *Critique of Judgment* can be used to mediate between a plurality of more localized social and cultural systems and the larger territory of the human world of coexistence. Not enough attention has been given to the way in which judgments are contextualized in the Introduction of Kant's third *Critique*. In the first *Critique*, he already moved beyond the abstract logical definition of judgment as the representation of a relation of two concepts. The traditional representational or mental account of judgment is replaced by a schematic epistemic account that directs "given cognitions to the objective unity of apperception."[34] This means that judgments relate concepts by directing them at objects. In the third *Critique,* Kant expands on this object-directed understanding of judgment by relating concepts, not only to objects, but also to their relevant contexts. Four such judgmental contexts are distinguished,[35] the first being a "field" (*Feld*), which can be considered as the sphere of possibility. An object in the field of thought may or may not be actual. Only actual objects are part of what Kant calls a "territory" (*Boden*). I interpret this as the context of human experience and social interchange. The third kind of context of judgment is a "domain" (*Gebiet*), which is the sphere of lawful necessity carved out by each of the scientific disciplines of the academy. Finally, a judgment can be oriented to the "habitat" (*Aufenthalt*) where we happen to be—it can thus be considered as the context of contingency that each of us constantly contends with. These four modal contexts are not inscribed in the world as separate parts of it but can serve us in sorting out the different kinds of judgmental discourse that can be applied to the world. I see it as the task of reflective judgment, and hermeneutics more generally, to navigate among these spheres that frame the meaning of our lives and which philosophers must take into account if they are to think from a worldly perspective.[36] To not distinguish among the different modes of discourse that characterize these various contexts as they intersect in real life is to be subject to the kinds of confusions that Kant calls "amphibolies."

Whereas Kant's reflective justification of property rights proceeded from the level of our earthly habitat to that of the territory of human counterclaims to finally the domain of civil law, Cohen's legislative approach was almost exclusively focused on the domain of ethical law. Let us now turn to Dilthey's *System of Ethics* to see whether we can find something closer to what I consider to be a reflective critique.

6. Dilthey's Formative Social Ethics and the Reflective Commitment to What Is Right

Like Cohen, Dilthey took note of Marx's critique of economic conditions and his analysis of class conflicts.[37] But as a philosophical historian who is as much interested in cultural life as in economic matters, Dilthey focuses more on the problem of attaining human solidarity. He situates the problem of solidarity in the more concrete Hegelian context of objective spirit. However, Dilthey no longer conceives of objective spirit as a universal determining force that serves to prolong into the present the social, political, and legal institutions that have governed individuals in the past. Instead, Dilthey reinterprets objective spirit as a more local medium of commonalities that individuals are born into and assimilate in their own way. Objective spirit is a way to understand how certain shared aspects of our present life are informed by a common ethnic past. This provides the framework for his *System of Ethics* and for the possibility of what I would call a reflective ethics of cooperation. Dilthey's project is to wean ethics away from the *legislative* model of Kant and from the even more *constructive* elaborations of Hegel and Cohen. Instead, he proposes a *formative* (*bildende*) ethics that shows how our capacities are supported by the heritage of the past and must be further cultivated from within. Whereas a legislative ethics commands us from on high and is still academic in Kant's sense, a formative ethics is worldly in that it works from the ground up and at least partly replaces the constraint of law with that of self-control. Because this self-control must be achieved in a shared context, Dilthey's approach to ethics is social from the start and open enough to analyze empirical evidence for feelings of group solidarity as well as to prescribe certain universal ethical norms.

Dilthey's *System of Ethics* is a posthumously published version of a lecture course he gave in 1890.[38] His formative ethical approach leads him to take our anthropological dispositions into account. Dilthey takes the idea of group solidarity seriously and defines it as a fellow-feeling (*Mitgefühl*) or bondedness with others that goes deeper than the sympathy (*Sympathie*) of the British moralists. Sympathy is a feeling "transferred from one living being to another."[39] It affects us from without and cannot really motivate us in any fundamental way. Dilthey has similar reservations about the "pity" that tragedy is said to arouse and the "compassion" for all living beings that Schopenhauer locates at the root of morality. Sympathy, pity, and compassion are modes of "suffering with" (*Mitleid*) that Dilthey regards as a mere "conjoint movement or being stirred" (*Mitbewegung*)[40] from without. Kant had of course criticized sympathy for being too provincial and passive and ultimately replaced it with an active moral feeling of participation (*thätige Theilnehmung*) in such late writings as *The Metaphysics of Morals* of 1797.[41] Dilthey is less critical of sympathy, but still considers it a superficial psychological response just as he considered pity a mere prelude to the true "tragic sentiment" that generates a more positive sense of "kinship."[42] Solidarity is more important than sympathy, according to Dilthey, because it is a fellow-feeling that stems from within—an inner sense of belonging to the group we grow up with in the familiar locality that Kant referred to as our habitat. Dilthey regards solidarity as an instinctive basis for engaging with others. But because it is instinctive, solidarity cannot become an ethical incentive if it is not transformed into the will to do well (*wohl-wollen*) that characterizes benevolence. It is thus our task to cultivate a local sense of group solidarity into the incentive of benevolence (*Wohlwollen*), which is potentially more encompassing in scope.

Benevolence expands the instinctive bond (*Band*) that is felt in solidarity into a volitional commitment (*Bindung*) to others that extends to the wider territory of humans in general. It is at this point that Dilthey begins to speak of obligations and duties that bind us mutually. Solidarity and benevolence provide the background for the recognition of a reciprocity of obligation. This becomes more evident in the next section on social ethics, where Dilthey delineates what he considers the three subjective volitional incentives that drive the development of ethical life. The first incentive of the will is the striving for personal excellence along the lines of the formative kind of ethics we saw him espouse. The second volitional incentive centers again on benevolence as a social virtue. The third incentive is described as "the consciousness of the commitment that inheres in the duty to do what is right or just."⁴³ At the heart of this sense of commitment is the respect for others as ends in themselves. The respect for others that was reflexive or implicit in instinctive solidarity and explicitly felt in benevolence is now recognized to be at the core of the reflective commitment to do what is right even for those who have little in common with us.

In the final lectures, Dilthey moves from the territorial level of subjective volitional incentives to the level of objective domain-like ethical principles. He does so by drawing on an early essay from 1864 in which he affirmed that moral oughts are unconditional, as Kant had claimed, and that accordingly they may be considered as *synthetic a priori practical judgments*. This may seem strange, not only because Dilthey expressed his reservations about *synthetic a priori theoretical judgments* throughout his life, but also because the just-discussed incentives of will were rooted in empirical instinctive and felt relations such as solidarity. But now Dilthey makes it clear that the ethical commitments we make as adults have a prescriptive and normative quality that is not empirically derivable. The three social incentives that we spoke of earlier are now reformulated as *synthetic a priori ethical principles* and in doing so are given a new ranking. And it is in this reformulation that Dilthey's ethics becomes reflectively critical. Here he appeals to the self-reflection (*Selbstbesinnung*) that became central to his philosophy in all spheres. What is morally *a priori* is not a pre-given of life, which would make it a prejudice, but a product of human self-reflection.

Reflective critique in social ethics, as I am explicating it and expanding on it, is basically about setting contextually appropriate priorities. Thus we see that for Dilthey our "sense of what is right or just" (*Rechtschaffenheit*)⁴⁴ should be given priority over the feeling of benevolence because it represents our deepest commitment. Dilthey refers to character when he describes this social sense of what is right, and although he does not mention Kant here, it is interesting to note that it was at the level of character that Kant invoked this same term *Rechtschaffenheit* for the private virtue of uprightness.⁴⁵ For Kant, too, the responsibility that comes with the recognition of what is right is an achievement that requires active character formation.⁴⁶

Dilthey's first ethical principle demands from each of us an unconditional commitment to do what is right or just based on respect for all human beings as ends in themselves. Dilthey sees no need to derive this respect for self and others from Kantian respect for the moral law. Qua moral principle, the commitment to what is right or just is called a *synthetic principle of unity* because it is rooted in a reciprocal fidelity.

The second ethical principle builds on this sense of fidelity and expects us to cultivate the feeling of benevolence. Benevolence "does not place us into that rigid chain of mutual obligation of the will's sense of what is right, but rather in a free reciprocal relation of human sentiments that, without a feeling of compulsion, pervades the whole moral world."[47] The principle of benevolence transforms the respect for the rights of others into a felt identification with their fate. It adds a more free and open-ended *synthetic principle of multiplicity* that actively embraces both what unites and what differentiates human beings. Although benevolence was also a Kantian virtue, Dilthey's affirmation of it seems to be more in the spirit of Lessing, who encouraged a tolerance of difference.

It is not until he formulates his third ethical principle that Dilthey invokes the universal validity of law. It moves beyond both the universal commitment of equity and what he calls the "unsurveyable" universality of benevolence to finally project a universal ideal of perfection. But this is not the overarching universality of a homogeneous consensus valid for all time. Just as Dilthey thought that laws of historical development would only be valid within specified spheres like economics, he maintains that the project of articulating a perfect morality that is universally valid will produce limited cultural forms over time. He writes, "The urge toward perfection, like benevolence, and fidelity to reciprocal justice, involves a creative synthesis of our moral organization; however, its conception and clarification in consciousness is obtained in combination with the theoretical content of the human spirit. Thus, there are as many different ways to understand the nature and basis of this urge for perfection and value as there are cultural stages."[48] This universal ideal of perfection will produce a *synthetic plurality* of articulated ethical purposes over time.

It is interesting to compare and contrast this progression in Dilthey with the way Kant summarizes his three formulations of the categorical imperative leading up to his ideal of lawgiving as making a communal kingdom of ends possible. Kant sees a progression that moves from the "*unity* [*Einheit*] of form" inherent in our respect for the moral law, to the *multiplicity* (*Vielheit*) of human beings that need to be respected as ends in themselves, to a final "*allness* [*Allheit*] or totality" of a kingdom of ends.[49] Dilthey's reflective critical ethics also moves from a principle of unity to one of multiplicity, but it resists Kant's ideal of an overall consensus, for it cannot properly accommodate the "*plurality*" (*Mehrheit*)"[50] of human situations. At first it may seem that plurality is just another word for multiplicity. I think, however, that multiplicity refers to external differences, whereas plurality points to a reflectively articulated differentiation.

The allness of Kant's kingdom of ends and his ideal of the omnilateral legitimation of human property rights cannot adequately accommodate the distinctive needs and ends of individual human agents. Nor can it do justice to the cultural differences that have developed over time and are still with us. Whereas for Kant the ethical challenge was to take the limited incentive to do good based on sympathy for those who are like us and to transform it into the more active participatory feeling of being part of an overarching kingdom of ends, for Dilthey the challenge would be to replace the feeling of solidarity with one's group with a willingness to engage with members of other groups and cultures without necessarily consolidating them. To the extent that the goal of universal validity is also a search for completeness, it cannot always achieve absolute totality, and will at times have to settle for a plurality of contextually appropriate completions.

7. Conclusion

A reflective ethical critique concerned with the overall impact of human actions must be open to replacing unilateral and bilateral decisions with pluralistic as well as omnilateral solutions. There are, to be sure, basic human rights to life, sustenance, and equity where omnilateral legitimacy can be demanded. But there are also issues about access to resources and to opportunities where simple equity cannot be attained. Then local conditions need to be factored in and compared in order to approximate as fair a mode of distribution as possible. This is where the idea of a reflective equilibrium becomes relevant. Different situations and their cultural conditions may require distinctive paths toward an acceptable equilibrium. Also relevant here is the Rawlsian claim that social laws and institutions will only be accepted as just if they are regarded as being fair by means of public agreement.[51] Such agreement will be context-driven and assumes that as much attention must be given to avoiding unintended, but possible, negative consequences of ethical courses of action as to the original moral intent.

It is important to realize that a reflective critique, being judgment-based and orientational, can also provide the proper framework for the other two kinds of critique. The determinant claims of constitutive and regulative critique tend to be confined by the limited domains of academic scientific disciplines. As I have argued before, Kant's third *Critique* does more than attempt to mediate between the two lawful domains of theoretical and practical reason.[52] These domains were already framed by the infinite field of pure thought and abstract regulative ideas. What the *Critique of Judgment* adds is a more concrete context for the domains of theoretical and practical reason, namely, the worldly territory in which communicative discourse and social interaction can take place. This experiential territory can orient judgment as it grapples with the ways in which more limited contexts such as habitats of existence and the disciplinary systems of the natural and human sciences intersect in human life. At this stage, reflective judgment can be seen to go over into reflective specification.[53] An example of this is the way in which the homogeneous nature of the first *Critique* is specified in the Critique of Teleological Judgment into an inorganic nature where mere mechanistic explanations suffice and an organic nature in which individual organisms manifest an immanent purposiveness that allows us to make reflective sense of their overall functioning, without denying that each of their parts considered separately is mechanically determined. The sociocultural systems that Dilthey delineates in history provide a similar functional reflective understanding of history. But whereas the idea of natural or organic purposiveness is merely regulative and speculative, the purposiveness of sociocultural systems is constituted by human agency. Since the purposive intentions of human participants in these systems can clash and distort each other, sometimes even to the point of canceling each other out, Dilthey ended up specifying sociocultural systems as productive systems (*Wirkungs-zusammenhänge*) rather than as purposive systems (*Zweck-zusammenhänge*).[54] The productive sociocultural systems in which we participate are thus only partly intelligible from within, and as they become increasingly institutionalized their original purposes gradually alter or disappear and need to make room for new historical formations.

In conclusion, I would like to go back to Dilthey's claim that the ideal of perfection leads not to a Kantian omnilateral consensus but to a plurality of competing moral and cultural systems. It is worth remembering that Kant himself appealed to reflective judgment to assess what is beautiful precisely because it does not manifest perfection. Beauty cannot be conceptually defined as the perfection of something. Yet it manifests an orderly representation that produces a pleasure that enhances our feeling of life and allows the various "powers of the mind to reciprocally promote each other" as they hold onto that representation.[55] This creates a state of mind in which we can reflectively engage with each other even without having reached a determinate consensus. What reflective critique must strive for is to extend this attitude to social ethics as different cultural systems evolve over time and potentially clash.

A reflective critique is ultimately, as I see it, a communicative or hermeneutical project that must set priorities among the relevant contexts that come into play in human interaction. A judgment-based reflective critique may orient itself by regulative ideals without being determinantly directed by them. But it should not let the regulative ideal of overall perfection become the enemy of situational goods that can be contextually validated from the ground up.

Notes

1. Dilthey defined the human sciences (*Geisteswissenchaften*) as a complex of humanities and social sciences whose aim is to understand the historical world. He proposed methods for the interpretation of human life, social interactions, and the meaning of cultural achievements, which can be applied when causal explanations are not available or limited. Dilthey thought that at least some human sciences could formulate developmental laws as in linguistics, aesthetics, and economics, but he was skeptical about attempts by Hegel and Comte to come up with valid laws of history at large. See Wilhelm Dilthey, *Selected Works* (cited hereafter as *SW*), ed. Rudolf Makkreel and Frithjof Rodi (Princeton: Princeton University Press, 1989–), esp. vol. 1, *Introduction to the Human Sciences* (1989), and vol. 3, *The Formation of the Historical World in the Human Sciences* (2002).

2. Immanuel Kant, *Practical Philosophy*, ed. and trans. Mary Gregor (Cambridge: Cambridge University Press, 1996), 40–41 (*Ak.* 4:432–433). Citations from Kant are accompanied by a reference to the volume and page number of the passage in Immanuel Kant, *Kants gesammelte Schriften (Akademie Ausgabe)*, ed. the Royal Prussian (later German) Academy of Sciences, et al. (Berlin: Georg Reimer, later Walter de Gruyter, 1900–), cited as *Ak.*

3. Kant, *Practical Philosophy* (*Critique of Practical Reason*), 140n (*Ak.* 5:5).

4. Ibid., 254 (*Ak.* 5:142).

5. See Immanuel Kant, "First Introduction," *Critique of the Power of Judgment*, trans. Paul Guyer and Eric Matthews (Cambridge: Cambridge University Press, 2000), 15 (*Ak.* 20:211). Guyer translates *reflektirendes Urteil* not as "reflective judgment" but as "reflecting judgment," but this makes it possible to confuse it with the simple comparative reflection (*Reflexion*) that even animals are capable of according to Kant.

6. An extended argument for this point is given in Rudolf Makkreel, *Orientation and Judgment in Hermeneutics* (Chicago: University of Chicago Press, 2015), ch. 5.

7. Kant, *Practical Philosophy*, 411 (Ak. 6:258).

8. Ibid.

9. Ibid.

10. See Kant, *Practical Philosophy*, 407 (Ak. 6:253).

11. Ibid., 411 (Ak. 6: 259).

12. Ibid.

13. See Kant, *Practical Philosophy*, 137 (Ak. 6:371).

14. Ibid., 411 (Ak. 6:258).

15. It is interesting that Cohen uses this Diltheyan term, because most subsequent Neo-Kantians replaced it with the term "cultural sciences" (*Kulturwissenschaften*). On the differences between the human and cultural sciences see Rudolf Makkreel, "Wilhelm Dilthey and the Neo-Kantians: On the Conceptual Distinctions between *Geisteswissenchaften* and *Kulturwissenschaften*," in *Neo-Kantianism in Contemporary Philosophy*, ed. Rudolf Makkreel and Sebastian Luft (Bloomington: Indiana University Press, 2010), 253–271.

16. See Hermann Cohen, *Ethik des reinen Willens* (Berlin: Bruno Cassirer, 1907), 66.

17. Cohen, *Ethik des reinen Willens*, 228.

18. Kant, *Practical Philosophy*, 421 (Ak. 6:271).

19. Hermann Cohen, *Kants Begründung der Ethik: Nebst ihren Anwendungen auf Recht, Religion und Geschichte*, 2nd ed. (Berlin: Bruno Cassirer, 1910), 413.

20. Kant, *Practical Philosophy*, 421 (Ak. 6:271).

21. Ibid., 424 (Ak. 6:274).

22. Ibid., 384 (Ak. 6:220).

23. Cohen, *Kants Begründung der Ethik*, 413.

24. Cohen, *Ethik des reinen Willens*, 321.

25. Ibid., 610.

26. Ibid., 616.

27. Ibid., 612–613, 616.

28. Ibid., 615.

29. Ibid., 616.

30. Ibid., 614.

31. Ibid.

32. Ibid., 613.

33. For further discussion of what Kant calls "authentic interpretation" and how it relates to what I consider a reflective, worldly critique, see Makkreel, *Orientation and Judgment in Hermeneutics*, 134–172.

34. Immanuel Kant, *Critique of Pure Reason*, ed. and trans. Paul Guyer and Allen W. Wood (New York: Cambridge University Press, 1998), B141. All references

to Kant's first *Critique* use the standard A/B pagination of the first (1781, A) and second (1787, B) editions.

35. See Kant, *Critique of the Power of Judgment*, 61–63 (*Ak.* 5:174–176).

36. I expand on these and other contexts in Makkreel, *Orientation and Judgment in Hermeneutics*, 59–80.

37. Marx lived from 1818 to 1883, Dilthey from 1833 to 1911, Cohen from 1842 to 1918.

38. This text is the opening work in Dilthey, *Ethical and World-View Philosophy*, *Selected Works* (*SW*), vol. 6, ed. Rudolf Makkreel and Frithjof Rodi (Princeton: Princeton University Press, 2019), 31–139.

39. Dilthey, *SW* 6:89.

40. Dilthey, *SW* 6:89, 96.

41. See Rudolf Makkreel, "Relating aesthetic and sociable feelings to moral and participatory feelings: reassessing Kant on sympathy and honor," in *Kant's Observations and Remarks; A Critical Guide*, ed. Susan Meld and Richard Velkley (Cambridge: Cambridge University Press, 2012), 101–115.

42. Dilthey, *SW* 6:102.

43. Dilthey, *SW* 6:128.

44. Dilthey, *Ibid.*

45. Cohen's chapter on *Gerechtigkeit* or justice does not refer to how humans internalize it as an attitude of *Rechtschaffenheit*.

46. Immanuel Kant, *Lectures on Anthropology*, ed. Allen W. Wood and Robert B. Louden, trans. Robert R. Clewis, Robert B. Louden, G. Felicitas Munzel, and Allen W. Wood (Cambridge: Cambridge University Press, 2012), 178 (*Ak.* 25:632).

47. Dilthey, *SW* 6:135.

48. Dilthey, *SW* 6:136.

49. See Kant, *Practical Philosophy*, 44 (*Ak.* 4:436).

50. Dilthey, *SW* 6:134.

51. See John Rawls, *A Theory of Justice* (Cambridge, MA: Harvard University Press, 1971), 133.

52. See Rudolf Makkreel, *Imagination and Interpretation in Kant: The Hermeneutic Import of the Critique of Judgment* (Chicago, IL: University of Chicago Press, 1990), 2–3.

53. For more detail on this see Makkreel, *Orientation and Judgment in Hermeneutics*, 161–164.

54. Dilthey, *SW* 3:174–184.

55. See Kant, *Critique of the Power of Judgment*, 33 (*Ak.* 20:230–231).

14

Transcendental Phenomenology as Radical Immanent Critique

Subversions and Matrices of Intelligibility

ANDREEA SMARANDA ALDEA

1. Introduction

Claims of neutrality, eidetic insight, and ahistoricity have squarely placed transcendental phenomenology in the camp of philosophical approaches unwilling and/or unable to engage in social critique. Take, for instance, the skepticism surrounding Husserlian methods as resources for feminist inquiry. Concerns here range from phenomenology's inability to do critical justice to the normalized and the contingent, or to the normatively complex dynamic between knowledge and power, or further still, to the radically other/different/novel/strange.[1] While some have sought to defend the import of Husserlian resources for feminist philosophy, the view remains marginal at best.[2] I argue, on the contrary, that Husserlian phenomenology grants us powerful tools for critically investigating the historical forces shaping our present reality, doing justice not only to their epistemic weight, but also to their normative weight.[3]

The distinctively critical dimension of Husserlian phenomenology lies in its ability to *work through* the modally productive tension between its eidetic and historical interests. This tension, seemingly crippling, opens a modal platform of analysis—one dealing in questions regarding conceivability, possibility, necessity, and impossibility—capable of shedding diagnostic as well as prescriptive light both on the experiences under investigation and on phenomenology's own methods of inquiry.[4] In what follows, I will examine this method of "modal-intentional analysis" and explicate its diagnostic (*possibility-mapping*) and prescriptive (*possibility-opening*) abilities. My goal will be to show that what makes phenomenology an *immanent, radical, subversive critique of the present*—a valuable resource to all forms of social critique, including feminist inquiry—is its unique historical-eidetic and teleological approach.

2. Matters of Distance

In his work during the 1930s, Husserl stressed the important issue of the traditionality of theoretical thought, including philosophy, and proposed a critical stance and method able to expose the principles, long-forgotten decisions, and commitments—the very grounds for our "validity foundings" (*Geltungsfundierungen*)—that systemically orient our knowledge acquisition. He referred to this mode of inquiry as "teleological-historical reflection," hermeneutical and ever-at-work: what the "autonomous thinker" must engage in.[5] Through the reductions, we bracket the general thesis of the world, we focus on how we experience (as opposed to the reality of the objects themselves), we zero in on the meaning-constitutive processes qualitatively distinguishing whatever noetic-noematic correlation is under investigation (say imagination and its objects), and we seek to identify the necessary structures all instances of the correlation share in common (if they are to count as such); as a result, we attain a *methodological distance afforded by a shift in attitude*, whereby nothing is lost, but rather all is renewed from a different perspective. The focus of teleological-historical reflection lies elsewhere. The critical distance it grants stems from a different kind of inquiring effort.

While this historical method appears *prima facie* at odds with Husserl's established methods, such as eidetic variation, in what follows, I will argue that only through these disparate methods' collaboration can phenomenology succeed as radical transcendental critique—one able to tackle our orientation toward intelligibility, toward coherent articulations of meanings and possibilities in everyday experience as well as in our theoretical endeavors. This orientation is, according to Husserl, a potent normative force that structures all our epistemic efforts.⁶ It is precisely this orientation, along with the sedimentation of epistemic accomplishments and of normative commitments, that phenomenology as critique must engage if it is to be an "autonomous" philosophical endeavor. This historical inquiry—what Husserl refers to as "teleological-historical reflection"—begins, as it must, in *medias res*. It is, for Husserl, a critique of present systems of knowledge— namely, those pertaining to whatever noetic-noematic correlation is under investigation.⁷ The method seeks to strike through the "crust of historical facts" in order to shed light on the flow (*Gedankenbewegung*) of these systems or matrices of intelligibility, on how they are articulated, on how they have come to hold the epistemic and normative sway that they do.⁸

Such a critical effort, is, needless to say, a hermeneutical, self-transformative task: what comes to light—diagnostically and prescriptively—about *our situation* does not leave the philosopher unchanged.

> In a constant critique, which always regards the total historical complex as a personal one, we are attempting to ultimately discern the historical task which we can acknowledge as the only one which is personally our own. *This we seek to discern not from the outside, from facts, as if the temporal becoming in which we ourselves have evolved were merely an external causal series. Rather, we seek to discern it from the inside.* Only in this way can we, who not only have a spiritual heritage but have become what we are thoroughly and exclusively in a historical-spiritual manner, have a task which truly our own.⁹

Like all theoretical endeavors, phenomenology, too, begins with and through our experience of the *lifeworld*—the intersubjectively communalized correlate of all of our meaning-constituting efforts. The lifeworld itself, as Husserl shows in the *Origin of Geometry*, is permeated by theoretical accomplishments that have seeped back (streamed-in), sedimented. In short, the experiential evidence that phenomenology as transcendental critique works with is layered, historically volatile, touched by many epistemic and normative commitments. The fact that as phenomenologists, we must work to analyze and explicate the intricate, historical, sociocultural layers of this present evidence—what our experience of the lifeworld grants us—does not undermine the legitimacy of this evidence. In other words, shedding light on, contesting, and subverting the normalized layers of this evidence is a critical distancing that gradually secures and guards itself as it unfolds; thus, like the theoretical distance of the phenomenological reductions (understood as shift in attitude, not loss or exclusion!), the critical distance teleological-historical reflection secures remains very much within the purview of going "back to the things themselves!" However, unlike theoretical distance *as shift in attitude*, critical distance remains at risk, precarious, given the epistemically and normatively sedimented layers of the evidence it works with and given the very tranditionality of the phenomenological methods themselves, such that the investigation as a whole, in its eidetic-historical complex, if in methodological good faith, cannot but unfold *as immanent critique.*

> This manner of clarifying history by inquiring back into the primal establishment of the goals which bind together the chain of future generations, insofar as these goals live on in sedimented forms yet can be reawakened again and again and, in their new vitality, be criticized; this manner of inquiring back into the ways in which surviving goals repeatedly bring with them ever new attempts to reach new goals whose unsatisfactory character again and again necessitates their clarification, their improvement, their more or less radical reshaping—this, I say, is nothing other than the philosopher's genuine self-reflection on what they are *truly seeking*, on what is in them as a will coming *from* the will and *as* the will of their spiritual forefathers.[10]

By way of introduction into this examination of the radical and critical dimension of phenomenology, let us begin with *the conceivable*, which constitutes a rich and little explored dimension of phenomenological evidence. Its import for our purposes lies in its relationship, on the one hand, to sedimented norms and concepts and, on the other, to possibility and impossibility.

3. Conceivability, Inconceivability, Difference as Conflict

Our everyday lived possibilities—the possibilities we negotiate for ourselves, the possibilities we share with others—are conditioned, both in their kind and in their systemic articulation (i.e., how they relate to each other), by what we deem conceivable. The conceivable, as Husserl has shown in his synthetic-genetic work on meaning-constitution, is for the most part the correlate of passive, embodied, perceptual, and perceptual-based experiences; these experiences shape what we deem conceivable (*denkbar*) by constantly molding, in an ever-sedimenting, receding manner, the concepts and norms that help us map our *lifeworld*, render it intelligible, make choices, and orient ourselves toward goals. What we deem conceivable depends on these concepts and norms, which play existentially and ethically heavy roles, not just epistemic ones.[11]

While our everyday experiences are primarily interested in individual objects, the habituated and historically sedimenting manners in which experiences relate to each other—what Husserl refers to as associational and memorial modifications and syntheses of likeness—generate a well-delineated projective understanding of ourselves and of our lifeworld.[12] They do so by constituting concepts, understood as empirical generalities, which organize entire systems of possibilities pertaining to the individual objects falling under the category the concept (or type, in the case of passively constituted generalities) seeks to capture.[13] In short, we expect real possibilities in specific ways given our epistemic and normative backgrounds. These possibilities, "lived" insofar as they are intimately intertwined with our daily lives and projects, are conceivable in the manner that they are given these very backgrounds. What we deem meaningful and intelligible, what we deem valuable and worthy of pursuit, is thus necessarily part of our system of conceivable possibilities.

By generating and (re)affirming certain concepts and norms, we are continuously, in for the most part covert ways, delineating and articulating stylistically coherent systems of lived possibilities: veritable, self-reinforcing general styles exhibiting their own lively teleology (*lebendige Fortarbeit*), which keeps us under the spell of our situation.[14] Our styles, both in their epistemic and in their normative aspects, help us navigate the matrices of intelligibility, possibility, and value we share with others. Therein lies, according to Husserl, their seductive character.[15] Since they orient us in well-delineated manners toward certain possibilities, they have more than epistemic expectational import. They inform our expectations, but they also guide us when carving courses of knowledge and action for ourselves.[16]

Both Husserl and Merleau-Ponty provided nuanced analyses of this structure of everyday, positional intentionality. They further deepened its modal facets and reach through their analyses of our "I can" understood as a structural moment of all experiences. In its most basic form, my "I can" pertains to embodied experiences: how I inhabit a lived space, how I negotiate the kinaesthetic possibilities it affords me, how I just "know" what is possible for me.[17] Beyond this basic level, however, my "I can"—and, importantly, its inverse my "I cannot"—refers to that which I deem, passively or actively, covertly or overtly, inconceivable for me in any experience, given any endeavor or project, in any register.[18] Challenging and shedding light on what I deem conceivable and inconceivable is no easy feat, precisely because it must involve a rearticulation of my possibilities and of the possibilities I share with others.

The stylistic orientation types, concepts, and norms provide is driven by a distinctive teleology—a harmonizing, resolution-seeking, totalizing kind of teleology.[19] We see this, as Husserl shows in his synthetic-genetic analyses of the 1920s, especially in our everyday, *personalistic* attitude, which, given its orientation toward epistemic and normative harmony, stubbornly seeks to reinscribe the unfamiliar into the familiar.[20] There is no active decision to do so, since, according to Husserl, such a motivation is a structural feature of our experiences. And while this harmonizing feature pertains primarily to the everyday, non-theoretical attitude, it also marks theoretical endeavors, which are no strangers to similar harmonizing forces. In what follows, I will refer to this feature of meaning and possibility-constitution, irrespective of whether theoretically/methodologically or non-theoretically driven, as the "normalizing stance" and argue that while pervasive, *this stance and its orientation are not impossible to resist*. That in fact, if phenomenology is to be a radical critique, it must expose both the normalizing tendencies of the meaning-constituting process under investigation and the normalizing forces at work in its own critical work. As such, phenomenological analysis must be at once diagnostic and subversive with respect to its subject matter as well as self-reflective with respect to its own methods of investigation and theoretical goals. To accomplish this, I contend, phenomenology *must work through the tension between its eidetic interest* in the universal structures of meaning-constitution—i.e., its motivation toward grasping the necessary features of the *a priori* of correlation under investigation—*and its historical interest* in the epistemic and normative sedimentations and layers pertaining to the meaning-constituting process, along with its corresponding field of conceivable possibilities, together functioning as its inquiring starting point. Phenomenology's historical interest guides its eidetic interest toward the complex articulations/matrices of intelligibility and possibility the meaning-constituting process in question sustains in stylistically homogenous ways. *In short: seeking the transcendentally necessary involves working through the historically conceivable*. The possibility of working through this tension lies in assuming a stance that resists normalization; phenomenology must work with a sense of difference—of the otherwise—that does not amount to experiencing epistemic and normative conflicts in need of swift resolution.

In the normalizing stance, the most pervasive form that conflict takes is our experience of what Husserl refers to as "problematic possibilities."[21] We experience something unexpected. And we deem the unexpected—that which is out of the ordinary (*ausgezeichneit*)—as problematic: something to be dealt with and resolved. This could either be something that defies the immediate modal scope of our expectations (e.g., I teach in a manner I have successfully and repeatedly employed before, but in today's class my pedagogical method fails me). It could also be something that radically departs even from the extended scope or horizon of our respective experiences' conceivable possibilities (e.g., my students read Butler and learn that biological sex, not just gender, could be considered a discursive/social construct without metaphysical grounding in "factual reality"). Our responses to these immediate or extended modal departures, which defy or fall outside of the scope of our conceivability, involve processes that seek to make sense of the interruption in our expectational flow: we experience doubt, uncertainty, vacillation, engagement of alternatives—all processes of doxic and epistemic unease, all processes meant to terminate in some form of satisfactory resolution that would reinstate the stability of the familiar.[22] Depending on our commitment to how things "ought to be" in the given circumstances, our experience of difference may exhibit higher or lower levels of normative and ethical conflict, not just epistemic conflict.

These processes of modality modification, which seek the reinstatement of epistemic and normative stability, play the all-important role of maintaining a unity of sense/unity of articulation with respect to our lives and our lifeworld (what I refer to as a "matrix of intelligibility").[23] They enrich our holistic understanding; they aid us in adapting and responding to our environment. As such, they necessarily exhibit some degree of modal elasticity. However, they also fuel a high degree of resistance to novelty, to that which is out of the ordinary—a resistance that marks the normalizing stance in non-theoretical and theoretical endeavors alike. These processes are behind our stubborn, at times unshakable sense of "I cannot," especially when our normative and ethical commitments are strong, especially when the difference we experience pushes the limits of the scope of what we conceive as possible, valuable, meaningful. In such cases, we struggle to fold that which is "out of the ordinary" back into our totalizing unity of sense. We experience that which is different as defying and resisting the very harmonizing forces fueling our normalizing stance. These forces are nothing other than the types, concepts, norms, and styles we constitute in sedimented, habituated ways. While in the normalizing stance, resisting these forces is all but impossible; however, this is not the only stance we are able to adopt—and this holds, once more, both in our everyday, non-theoretical life and in our theoretical endeavors. In both of these spheres, we can assume what I refer to as the imagining-critical stance.

4. The Imagining Stance: From Substantial to Modal Concepts and Norms

Unlike the normalizing stance, the imagining stance not only relates to its systems of possibilities in a qualitatively different manner; its possibilities are also of a qualitatively different kind than expected and problematic possibilities.[24] Husserl recognized this about the imagination and sought to analyze it through the lenses of distinctive forms of ontic and doxic freedom and neutrality. According to his analyses, imaginative possibilities are "pure" and "open," entirely free of the epistemic and normative bonds of our perceptual-everyday attitude.[25] They are arbitrary, unmotivated, lacking teleological orientation.[26] I argue elsewhere that while Husserl was right to focus on freedom and neutrality as key features of imagining consciousness, his overemphasis of the purity, arbitrariness, and lack of teleological orientation of imagining possibilities sought to grasp the structures of the imagination primarily negatively, by comparing them to those of perception; the result: he generated what I would refer to as a "minimal" descriptive account of a kind of consciousness whose intentional scope is not only wider than what this binary framework can afford, but also qualitatively different and therefore not fully lending itself to this negative comparative framework.[27]

Furthermore, if we follow Husserl's late-1930s synthetic-genetic and historical-critical methods of phenomenological analysis, we see that what marks the imagination cannot be purity understood as "freedom from" our previous epistemic and normative commitments. Such a purity would require not only an ambiguity and anonymity-defying self-transparency, which, as Merleau-Ponty later shows, is not possible for us; it would also require a neat and well-delineated separation between different dimensions of consciousness, different attitudes, difference stances.[28] This, too, is not feasible, since our experiential attitudes—attitudes such as the personalistic, the practical, the everyday—are porous, permeable, ever-morphing in light of epistemic and normative accomplishments pertaining to other attitudes, such as the naturalistic-scientific one. In the *Crisis*, Husserl referred to this process as "streaming-in" (*einströmen*).[29] Thus, the radical-critical potential of the imagination does not lie in its epistemic and normative purity and arbitrariness, in its minimally defined, negative freedom; it lies, among other things, in its stance toward novelty and difference—in how it articulates and re-articulates systems of possibilities.

Husserl was right to claim that the imagination does not exhibit the motivation and teleology pertaining to perceptual and perceptual-founded forms of consciousness—namely, the orientation toward harmony, stability, and unity of sense. He was wrong, however, to hold that the imagination was therefore without motivation and without teleology.[30] The imagination exhibits a distinctive kind of teleological orientation, irrespective of its domain of interest and correlate system of possibilities (e.g., the possibilities pertaining to engaging an alternative pedagogical method). Its *orientation* is toward exploration and experimentation, rather than epistemic and normative stability. Indeed, as Husserl shows, the imagination is not necessarily interested in harmony, finality, and the resolving of epistemic conflicts; but it is interested in the productive creativity stemming from tension, from holding something in suspense, from experiencing something differently, even radically so.[31] In the normalizing stance, difference is a site of epistemic and normative conflict, a conflict to be swiftly resolved through an ossified "I can/I cannot" distinction; the imagining stance engages difference not just "with more epistemic and normative tolerance," but also with an eye for opening new possibilities, which may very well depart from what the respective expectational and conceivable horizons dictate. As such, the imaginative stance can—and often does—involve epistemic and normative *discomfort* or *tension* (not to be confused with conflict in the sense above). But it relates to this discomfort, even passively (i.e., not solely in its active/willed guise), in a manner the normalizing stance never could: it grasps, whether implicitly or explicitly, this discomfort's critical and transformative potential.[32]

This is not to say that the imagination is immune to normalization. But even when normalizing habits seep into our imagining endeavors, the suspicion that things "could be otherwise" colors our epistemic and normative commitments. In other words, the imagination is not "all too easily seduced" by the safety-promising lures of naturalization. Its correlate systems of conceivable possibilities are not necessarily metaphysically loaded.

Nor are they arbitrary and fluid—veritable "free plays" as Husserl would have it.[33] The concepts and norms passively and/or actively organizing these systems of imagined possibilities are not motivated toward stability; they are not structurally bound to resist radical difference. As such, they harbor a critical potential we could tap into and develop. In short: the imagining dimension is not necessarily critical, but it does lend itself to such a stance, even a radical one.

Thus, a necessary condition for the possibility of a critical phenomenological stance is uncovering not only *what kinds* of concepts, styles, norms we rely on, but also *how* we relate to them. Building on a distinction Merleau-Ponty makes in his *Phenomenology of Perception,* I would like to propose that in what I refer to as the "normalizing stance," we view the types and concepts we rely on (e.g., identity, race, gender, sexuality) as substantial.[34] They are meant to capture the essential predicates and relations that all individuals falling under the class in question must exhibit. On this conceptual model, difference—that which falls outside of the scope the concepts/types in question cover—is a violation of essential determinations. To use the language of conceivability and possibility here: for the most part, in the normalizing stance, difference is an inconceivable possibility that points to a metaphysical impossibility. Thus, through a commitment to the substantiality of concepts, the normalizing stance is also naturalizing.

However, a careful phenomenological investigation of how concepts, styles, and norms shape our normalizing meaning-constituting processes reveals them as *modal* rather than substantial. To reiterate: while in the naïve normalizing stance, we deem them substantial, phenomenological investigation reveals these concepts and norms as modal. Following this insight, difference is not a violation of (supposed) metaphysically necessary determinations, but a contingent stylistic variation that could be otherwise. This revealed plasticity of apparently inviolable concepts, styles, and norms, however, also sheds light on the possibility of experiencing difference in terms other than conflict. Phenomenology, drawing on our ability to engage a critical imagining stance, through its diagnostic-descriptive work could thus also sustain a "breaking with a style."[35] This not only opens otherwise inconceivable articulations of meanings and possibilities; it also grants us resources to relate to these meanings and possibilities in ways better equipped to resist the lure of the normalizing and naturalizing forces, which, if Husserl is right, are bound to infiltrate non-theoretical and theoretical endeavors alike. To see how phenomenology sheds light on the modality rather than substantiality of norms and concepts, let us return to its work as variation through the tension between its eidetic and historical interests, especially given the reliance of this work on the imagining stance.

5. Working through the Tension: Transcendental Impossibility and Normalized Inconceivability

The eidetic interest of phenomenology focuses on transcendental necessity: the structures of experience and meaning-constitution that could not be otherwise for us. So, while the historical instantiation or expression of this transcendental necessity is contingent (Husserl's *historical a priori*), many features of human experience and reality constitution are not historically volatile. Take for example the kinaesthetic sense of "I can" expressed through our body schema. This structure of experience is transcendentally necessary and, as such, it is, for Husserl, an essence. However, unlike logical or metaphysical necessity, transcendental necessity refers to what could not be otherwise for us as embodied, meaning-constituting beings oriented toward epistemic, normative, and modal articulations (i.e., articulations of possibilities). Other structures of experience exhibit transcendental necessity in a historical manner—for instance the deep structures of co-constitution binding the body, gender, and epidermal-racial schemas. Exposing the intricate ways in which these schemas affect each other sheds light on fissures where "the otherwise" might emerge; that these schemas are co-constitutive is transcendentally necessary. Whether or not their necessity is ahistorical, i.e., not subject to historical transformation, is something phenomenology can investigate.

In my view, phenomenology is uniquely positioned to ask such questions and investigate the historical volatility of certain structures of meaning and reality constitution precisely in virtue of its commitment to a robust understanding of transcendental necessity. If we are to do justice to our experience of the otherwise, of the unexpected, of the foreign, of the radically contingent—what a diligent critique from within the very matrices it investigates requires—, then we must look to the complex relationship between different kinds of possibilities (normalized, imagining, theoretical, transcendental-ideal) and different kinds of necessity (transcendental ahistorical, transcendental historical, logical, historical-normalized). Unlike a study of experience focusing entirely on the contingent (what most contemporary feminist projects drawing on poststructuralist resources focus on), phenomenology can accomplish this. It is my contention that the distinctive value of phenomenology understood as radical transcendental critique from within lies precisely in this modalities-mapping/modalities-opening work—a work that, if it is to succeed, must unfold through the critically productive tension between two guiding limits: transcendental necessity, on the one hand, and, on the other, normalized inconceivability. The former refers to what is structurally binding in meaning-constituting processes; it is neither metaphysical, nor epistemic, nor logical. The latter parades as metaphysical impossibility (one with hefty epistemic and normative implications), referring either to how the process under investigation constitutes its correlate *or* both to how the process under investigation constitutes its object and how empirical/scientific investigations study the process itself.

It is important to note that as far as transcendental necessity is concerned, its opposite is transcendental impossibility (i.e., what necessarily violates the structures of meaning-constitution); this may or may not overlap with transcendental inconceivability (i.e., what we, as phenomenologists, cannot conceive regarding the structures of meaning-constitution). Uncovering the differences and/or overlap between transcendental impossibility and transcendental inconceivability requires extensive self-reflective work on the part of the phenomenologist (as they engage in their investigations). This necessary work constitutes yet another core dimension of phenomenology as immanent critique, one that complements its diagnostic and prescriptive analyses of the historically and teleologically sedimented layers of evidence.

So how does the process of transcendental, historically informed eidetic variation work? The first point I should stress is that on this understanding of the process, while the invariant remains its eidetic focal point, the process is also motivated by the historical interest in shedding light on normalized conceivable and inconceivable possibilities that parade as necessary—as that which could not be otherwise, in whatever matrix/articulation under investigation. By generating and engaging imagining rather than normalized possibilities, the process accomplishes several things:

1. It overrides the need to deem the different/the otherwise through the lens of conflict to be swiftly resolved, resorbed back into the fold of the familiar/expected, thus making room for heterogeneity and a stance that resists normalization; this stance can very well spill from the phenomenological

attitude into other theoretical endeavors as well as the everyday attitude.

2. It pushes the limits of normalized conceivability by challenging the supposedly inevitable "I cannot" pertaining to meaning-constituting process under investigation—in other words, it reveals the contingency of normalized inconceivability.

3. As it maps the meaning and possibility articulations that span the gap between transcendental necessity and normalized inconceivability, it not only attempts to zero in on the necessary structures of meaning-constitution, but also enriches our understanding of the intentional range the process under investigation can sustain.

In other words, the eidetic orientation of phenomenology does not entail the closure and ossification of the modal horizon pertaining to the experience under investigation. The focus on transcendental necessity, on modally mapping how various experiences constitute distinct kinds of possibilities in the manner that they do, does not (pre)determine which possibilities pertain to these experiences. What phenomenology maps here, through this oft-dreaded eidetic variation, are not exhaustive fields of possibilities. What it maps are the modes of possibility-constitution pertaining to experiences (visual perception, for example) and the sedimented manners in which these, for the most part covertly, unfold. The focus on transcendental necessity smokes out, so to speak, vast arrays of normalized contingencies. The reason why this process does not fall prey to a *petitio principii* fallacy lies in its ever-guarded tension between transcendental impossibility and transcendental inconceivability—a self-reflective tension that drives the inquiring process itself. The eidetic goal of the mapping process remains in question. Yet without this eidetic orientation toward transcendental necessity, the standard of impossibility—what most normalized inconceivabilities claim yet fail to meet—would be neither binding nor high.

These accomplishments are at once diagnostically powerful, subversive, and capable of opening and rearticulating the matrices of meanings and possibilities. They have the ability to undermine otherwise ossified epistemic and normative commitments pertaining to the styles of meaning-constitution of the process under investigation. They constitute a productive/creative breaking with the established style of the respective process of meaning, value, reality constitution. To go back to the intricate co-constituting dynamic among the body/gender/epidermal-racial schemas, using this method of variation in our study of visual meaning-constitution, we can expose ways in which what otherwise presents itself as metaphysically impossible—beyond the reach of our lived possibilities—is actually merely inconceivable in the normalized sense, hence surpassable and replaceable.

Varying through the tension between the eidetic and historical interests maps fields of conceivable possibilities in this diagnostic manner, yet in doing so, it also suggests ways of transforming these fields of possibilities, whether they pertain to our lifeworld or to the world of our theoretical investigations. Thus, the diagnostic dimension of phenomenology as immanent critique also lends itself to robust prescriptive endeavors.

Working through the tension of its eidetic and historical interests as discussed above (i.e., maintaining the tension in the mapping process) safeguards phenomenology from binding itself to predelineated, predetermined fields of possibilities, driven by similarity rather than difference. This is a danger that feminist philosophers have deemed pervasive in phenomenological transcendental-eidetic work.[36] And for this reason, they have been deeply suspicious of Husserlian phenomenological tools. However, given the above explication of the eidetic process, worries about the essentializing tendencies of the process of variation or worries about the inability of the process to engage unexpected, free possibilities emerge as unfounded. If we develop Husserl's *Crisis* insight regarding the need for both the eidetic and the historical dimensions of transcendental phenomenology, if we understand the tension between these two dimensions not as entailing their mutual exclusion but as being critically productive, then we recognize not only phenomenology's ability to speak to pressing, everyday issues of sociocultural injustice, but also its ability to generate new possibilities and venues for surpassing the apparently unavoidable circumstances of our situation, including our theoretical, traditional situation as phenomenologists. And while the possibilities it generates and proposes do not violate the standards of ahistorical transcendental necessity—standards such as the structure of the body schema pertaining to kinaesthetic experiences, for example—neither are they predetermined in a manner that forecloses our openness to the unexpected; they do not even preclude challenging the ahistorical status of some transcendental necessary structures. Transcendental necessity, while intentionally binding, need not entail ahistoricity. Thus, given its reliance on the critical imagining stance, phenomenology has a very different relation to novelty and the unexpected than any normalized non-theoretical or theoretical process. And given its self-reflective character, very much informed by its recognition of its own traditionality as a philosophical method of investigation, the risk of normalization is something it is willing and able to assume and negotiate for itself.

5. Conclusion

Through the collaboration of the methods of reductions, transcendental-eidetic variation, and teleological-historical reflection, phenomenology is able to assume the role of a critique of present systems of knowledge in order to expose the conditions for the possibility of these systems' flow, their *Gedankenbewegung*, their influence on our current situation, which it, like all theoretical endeavors, must draw on.[37] Phenomenology can engage this present situation; in fact, it must.[38] To be successful, it must treat its own situation "genealogically," involving a generational chain of thinkers committed to more or less the same principles and norms.[39] As such, this inquiry occurs through the critical philosopher's "knowing life" as it challenges the very grounds for its own validities and accomplishments.[40] Critical "inquiring back" into traditional commitments is self-reflective in this manner, leaving us "without a ground yet not groundless."[41] It demands that our investigations unfold in virtue of their risks and precarious evidence.

It is tempting, if inclined to endorse the critical value of transcendental phenomenology, to deem its efforts mostly—if not solely—oriented toward the epistemic dimension of experience. By acknowledging, however, its primarily modal framework, we cannot but recognize its normative import also. Its close examinations of conceivability/inconceivability interplays would not succeed but for their focus on the intricate relations between knowledge and power. We would deem sedimentations understood as normalizing and naturalizing processes as "solely epistemic" only in the most minimal and artificial of senses. That phenomenology is not reductionistic in this way is hopefully abundantly clear by now. Nevertheless, much remains to be said about the normative, sociocultural, ethical, and political import of transcendental phenomenological diagnostic and prescriptive work. For now, suffice to say, given the propaedeutic purposes of this essay, that phenomenology as radical transcendental critique must occur from a position of historical privilege: our own living present in all of its depth and unfolding.[42] This is no easy feat, especially given that the impact of a tradition's primal establishments (*Urstiftungen*) becomes more "obviously" mirrored, through its sedimenting re-establishments (*Nachstiftungen*).[43]

This obviousness of both grounds and goals makes them all the more obscure, illusory even, to use Husserl's words, given their epistemic and normative weight: yet it is precisely this lure as "necessary" we can and must question, we can and must resist as we do the work of phenomenology.[44] It is in this vein that we engage questions surrounding the historical versus ahistorical status of certain transcendentally necessary structures of meaning constitution. The resources and commitments we, as theoreticians working within a methodologically robust tradition of inquiry, rely on in our work inform not only how we modally map the field of possibilities spanning transcendental necessity and normalized inconceivability; they also inform our willingness and ability to critically examine our stance toward and the relation between transcendental impossibility and transcendental inconceivability; this latter modal pair regards the transcendental method itself, while the former focuses primarily on the modal range of the experience under investigation. The dynamic between the two pairs likewise does not leave us unchanged. Thus, what matters here for our critical purposes, is not solely the transformative potential of phenomenology as far as its object of investigation is concerned—for example, the co-constitutive relations among the racial/gender/sexual schemas. What matters is also its self-transformative potential, which further deepens its ability to function as radical, subversive critique from within.

Husserl saw the import of "self-variation" in the context of his transcendental-eidetic method.[45] In our phenomenological endeavors, the most radical form of critical stance we could assume necessarily involves "self-variation"—that is, "imagining myself as if I were otherwise," to use Husserl's words.[46] In this active orientation toward self-transformation, what comes to light is not solely what we, as theoreticians, have come to deem conceivable, knowable, worthy of pursuit, but also the guiding concepts and norms we rely on in the manner that we do. The grounds fueling our projects and endeavors become the focus of our inquiring exercise. At the heart of this call to self-transformation lies the lesson of the imagining-critical stance, the lesson of opening to experiencing difference, of risking the comforts of our I cannot/normalized inconceivability in a manner other than conflict, for whom instability, ambiguities, tensions, incomprehensibilities, the unexpected—what phenomenology is bound to delve into according to Husserl—do not pose threats and dangers to our projects, but creatively enhance them instead.[47]

Notes

1. See, for instance, Joan W. Scott, "The Evidence of Experience," *Critical Inquiry* 17, no. 4 (1991); François Dastur, "Phenomenology of the Event: Waiting and Surprise," *Hypatia*, 15, no. 4 (2000); Alia Al-Saji, "Creating Possibility: The Time of the Quebec Student Movement," *Theory & Event* 15, no. 3, Supplement (2012); Johanna Oksala, *Feminist Experiences: Foucauldian and Phenomenological Investigations* (Evanston, IL: Northwestern University Press, 2016).

2. See Linda Fisher, "Feminist Phenomenology," in *Feminist Phenomenology*, ed. Linda Fisher and Lester Embree (Dordrecht: Kluwer, 2000); Linda Fisher, "Phenomenology and Feminism: Perspectives on their Relation," in *Feminist Phenomenology*, ed. Linda Fisher and Lester Embree (Dordrecht: Kluwer, 2000); and Alia Al-Saji, "Bodies and Sensings: On the Uses of Husserlian Phenomenology for Feminist Theory," *Continental Philosophy Review* 43, no. 1 (2010). Most feminist approaches open to drawing on phenomenological resources for the most part turn to Merleau-Ponty; the reason for this remains, largely, the perceived danger of essentialism stemming from Husserl's transcendental-eidetic approach. I argue in Andreea Smaranda Aldea and Julia Jansen, "Imagination in Phenomenology: Variations and Modalities," *Husserl Studies* (forthcoming), that this perceived danger, while indeed non-negligible were it the case, stems from a misunderstanding of the eidetic character and import of transcendental-phenomenological investigations.

3. I would like to thank Amy Allen, Alia Al-Saji, and David Carr for feedback on earlier versions of this paper. References to Husserl's works include the volume and page number of the relevant passage in Edmund Husserl, *Husserliana* (cited hereafter as *Hua*), ed. Rudolph Bernet and Ullrich Melle (Dodrecht: Springer, 1950–). Special thanks also to Colin McQuillan and María Acosta for organizing the conference around this topic and for their editorial work.

4. See Andreea Smaranda Aldea, "Making Sense of Husserl's Notion of Teleology—Normativity, Reason, Progress and Phenomenology as 'Critique from Within,'" *Hegel Bulletin* 38, no. 1 (2017).

5. Edmund Husserl, *Die Krisis de Europäischen Wissenschaften und die Transzendentale Phänomenologie* (cited hereafter as *Hua* 6), ed. Walter Biemel (Den Haag: Martinus Nijhoff, 1954), 191. Translated as Edmund Husserl, *The Crisis of European Sciences and Transcendental Phenomenology*, trans. David Carr (Evanston, IL: Northwestern University Press, 1970). See also Husserl, *Hua* 6:xiv, 72–73, 372–373.

6. Husserl, *Hua* 6:115.
7. Husserl, *Hua* 6:58.
8. Husserl, *Hua* 6:60.
9. See also Husserl, *Hua* 6:72 (emphasis added).
10. Husserl, *Hua* 6:72–73; Husserl, *Crisis*, 71 (emphasis original, translation modified).
11. Edmund Husserl, *Analysen zur Passiven Synthesis: Aus Vorlesungs- und Forschungsmanuskripten 1918–1926* (cited hereafter as *Hua* 11), ed. Margot Fleischer (Den Haag: Martinus Nijhoff, 1966), 40–51. Translated as Edmund Husserl, *Analyses Concerning Passive and Active Synthesis: Lectures on Transcendental Logic*, trans. Anthony J. Steinbock (Dordrecht: Kluwer, 2001). See also Edmund Husserl, *Experience and Judgment*, trans. James S. Churchill and Karl Ameriks (Evanston, IL: Northwestern University Press, 1973), §8–§9.
12. Husserl, *Hua* 11:§26–§27, §36–§40; Husserl, *Experience and Judgment*, 385, 395–396.
13. Husserl, *Experience and Judgment*, §80, §87d.
14. Husserl, *Hua* 6:28–29, 59, 71ff., 103–104, 366. See also Andreea Smaranda Aldea, "Phenomenology as Critique: Teleological-Historical Reflection and Husserl's Transcendental Eidetics," *Husserl Studies* 32 (2016); and Aldea, "Making Sense of Husserl's Notion of Teleology," 104–128.
15. Husserl, *Hua* 6:372.
16. Edmund Husserl, *Phantasie, Bildbewusstsein, Erinnerung 1898–1925* (herafter cited as *Hua* 23), ed. Eduard Marbach (Den Haag: Martinus Nijhoff, 1980), 548. Translated as Edmund Husserl, *Phantasy, Image Consciousness, and Memory (1898–1925)*, trans. John B. Brough (Dordrecht: Springer, 2005). See also Husserl, *Hua* 6:22–23.
17. Edmund Husserl, *Ideen zur einer reinen Phänomenologie und phänomenologischen Philosophie II: Phänomenologische Untersuchungen zur Konstitution* (cited as *Hua* 4), ed. Marly Biemel (Den Haag: Martinus Nijhoff, 1952), 139–142. Translated as Edmund Husserl, *Ideas Pertaining to a Pure Phenomenology and to a Phenomenological Philosophy (Second Book)*, trans. Richard Rojcewicz and André Schuwer (Dordrecht: Kluwer, 1989). See also Maurice Merleau-Ponty, *Phenomenology of Perception*, trans. Donald E. Landes (New York: Routledge, 2012), 169ff.
18. See Alia Al-Saji, "A Phenomenology of Hesitation: Interrupting Racializing Habits of Seeing," in *Living Alterities*, ed. Emily S. Lee (Albany: State University of New York Press, 2014).
19. See Aldea, "Making Sense of Husserl's Notion of Teleology," 104–128.
20. Husserl, *Hua* 4:§34; Husserl, *Hua* 11:§20.
21. Husserl, *Hua* 11:§§5–13; Husserl, *Experience and Judgment*, §79.
22. Husserl, *Hua* 11:83–84; Husserl, *Experience and Judgment*, §67.
23. See Edmund Husserl, *Ideen zu einer reinen Phänomenologie und phänomenologischen Philosophie I: Allgemeine Einführung in die reine Phänomenologie*

(cited hereafter as *Hua* 3/1), ed. Karl Schuhmann (Den Haag: Martinus Nijhoff, 1976), §105. See also Husserl, *Hua* 11:30. This orientation toward homogeneity and harmony also marks the scientific/naturalistic attitude, not just the everyday/personalistic stance.

24. See Aldea, "Phenomenology as Critique," 21–46.

25. Husserl, *Hua* 23:553. See also Husserl, *Hua* 23, nos. 1, 8, 15, 18–20.

26. Husserl, *Hua* 23:535, 561–562. See also Husserl, *Hua* 3/1:§4.

27. Aldea, "Phenomenology as Critique," 21–46. See also Aldea and Jansen, "Imagination in Phenomenology: Variations and Modalities."

28. Merleau-Ponty, *Phenomenology of Perfection*, 403–411.

29. Husserl, *Hua* 6:112–115.

30. Husserl, *Hua* 23, no. 1, also appendix 1.

31. Husserl, *Hua* 23:533–534, 581–582, 589.

32. In his extensive work on the imagination, in his 1904/05 lectures and onward, Husserl emphatically stresses the self-consciousness of the imagination (*Phantasie*). When imagining, even when immersed in the world of irreality, we do not lose the consciousness of difference between reality and irreality (if we were to lose this sense of difference, the experience in question would be/become a hallucination). See Husserl, *Hua* 23, no. 1. I would add in the context of this discussion of critical imagination that the imagination exhibits a consciousness of difference—however vague—between the normalized/the familiar and the otherwise/unfamiliar.

33. See Aldea, "Phenomenology as Critique," 21–46.

34. Merleau-Ponty, *Phenomenology of Perception*, 377–378. See also Sara Heinämaa, *Toward a Phenomenology of Sexual Difference* (London: Rowman & Littlefield, 2003), 41ff.

35. Husserl, *Hua* 6:71ff.

36. See Al-Saji, "Creating Possibility," 10–18, and Oksala, *Feminist Experiences*.

37. Husserl, *Hua* 6:58, 60, 72.

38. Husserl, *Hua* 6:73.

39. Husserl, *Hua* 6:73.

40. Husserl, *Hua* 6:101.

41. Husserl, *Hua* 6:103. See also Edmund Husserl, *Die Krisis der Europäischen Wissenschaften und die Transzendentale Phänomenologie, Ergänzungsband, Texte aus dem Nachlass 1934–1937* (hereafter cited as *Hua* 29), ed. Reinhold N. Smid (Dordrecht: Kluwer, 1993), 373–375.

42. For a rich discussion of what our experience of history entails, especially in its relation to memory and communalization, see David Carr, *Experience and History* (New York: Oxford University Press, 2014). Carr argues convincingly that historicity is a feature of transcendental consciousness itself (Carr, *Experience and History*, 162 *et passim*). For more on the relation between historical reflection and memory, see also Husserl, *Hua* 29, no. 30.

43. Husserl, *Hua* 6:72–73.
44. Husserl, *Hua* 6:50.
45. Edmund Husserl, *Cartesianische Meditationen und Pariser Vorträge* (hereafter cited as *Hua* 1), ed. Stephan Strasser (Den Haag: Martinus Nijhoff, 1950), 105–106.
46. Husserl, *Hua* 1:105–106.
47. Husserl, *Hua* 6:185.

15

From the Metaphysics of Law to the Critique of Violence

PETER FENVES

At the center of a small treatise published under the title *Recht und Gewalt* ("Law and Violence"), Christoph Menke poses and immediately answers a question concerning the possibility of identifying a way of implementing the law that would not amount to an affirmation of its unquestionable supremacy: "How far do we have to go back into the conceptual construction of law to access the possibility of the other mode of its implementation [*Vollzugsweise*]? The answer can only be: to the beginning of law [*der Anfang des Rechts*]."[1] This brief colloquy stands at the crux of Menke's inquiry on the relation between law or right (*Recht*) and force or violence (*Gewalt*), insofar as an alternative mode of implementing law points toward a "liberation from the violent domination of law over the extra- or non-legal."[2] While taking its point of departure from this crucial passage in Menke's inquiry, where reflection on "the beginning of law" is the source of a new conception of the relation between law and violence, this essay moves in a different direction. According to Menke, the beginning can be found in "the insight of (Greek) tragedy."[3] Beyond the fact that the term "Greek tragedy" covers far more than the two plays under discussion in *Law and Violence*, including a vast number of lost works, none of them, it seems to me, can be described as "the beginning of law in its *conceptual construction*"—not even the *Oresteia*, despite its staging of the inception of the

Council of the Areopagus. It is perhaps more productive to begin where *Law and Violence* itself begins: with the inception of Kant's construction of law—more exactly, with the opening paragraphs of Kant's 1797 treatise, *Metaphysische Anfangsgründe der Rechtslehre*, which should probably be translated as *Metaphysical Beginning-Principles of the Doctrine of Right* but, for the sake of simplicity, I will henceforth call the *Doctrine of Law*.

This is, of course, one of the three doctrinal treatises Kant produced as counterparts to the first two of his *Critiques*. Nothing will be said here about the last of these treatises, *Metaphysische Anfangsgründe der Tugendlehre* (Metaphysical Beginning-Principles of the Doctrine of Virtue), which accompanies the *Doctrine of Law* as a relatively unproblematic complement; but a few words are warranted about the deeply problematic treatise Kant published some ten years earlier, *Metaphysische Anfangsgründe der Naturwissenschaft* (Metaphysical Beginning-Principles of Natural Science), where the author of the *Critique of Pure Reason* sought to make good on a promise contained in this epoch-making work and construct the system of nature. Soon after Kant apparently completed the *Doctrine of Law*—it will soon be apparent why I say "apparently"—he announced that he discovered a "gap" or "hole" (*Lücke*) in the "critical system" and that this missing element was intimately connected with his ongoing "transition" project that, so he hoped, would lead from the system of nature constructed in the *Doctrine of Natural Science* to a "pure physics."[4] Comparing his pains to those of Tantalus, Kant tells one of his correspondents that he can see the lacuna but cannot grasp the requisite remedy. As for the *next* doctrinal treatise he published, namely the *Doctrine of Law*, it, too, has appreciable gaps, some of which Kant himself indicates in the published text, whereas others, particularly those that punctuate its early paragraphs, are so glaringly evident that they seem to require no explicit acknowledgment.

Compared to the colossal effort Kant expended in seeking to discover the beginning of law in its conceptual construction—traces of which are visible throughout volume 23 of the *Akademie* edition—it was mere child's play for him to construct the *end* of law. Several years before the *Doctrine of Law* appeared, Kant produced a little treatise in the form of a satirical parody of an international treaty that would inaugurate a state of "eternal peace" among world powers in analogy with the problematic dynamics of a "perpetuum mobile." Such is one of the animating visions of *Zum ewigen Frieden* (Toward Eternal Peace). The capstone of the treaty Kant boldly sketches lies in the "law of world citizenship," which is itself related to the "conditions of universal hospitality."[5] Physical geography thus perfectly accords with its juridical counterpart. By virtue of the spherical character of the earth, its surface is infinite (unbounded) despite its finiteness, and because it also has no "natural" boundaries that would forever impede the movement of sufficiently powerful beings, every rational being capable of self-motivated motion should be allowed to travel through—but not necessarily settle down in—every single spot on the globe. Some lingering legal issues may arise with respect to the temporal boundaries through which travel is distinguished from settlement, but the vision of eternal peace in perpetual motion nevertheless remains unambiguous. The construction of the *beginning* of law is a different matter, however. Kant has only contempt for the fantasies through which much of early modern political thought seeks to secure the beginning of law—the act of unilaterally seizing supposedly unoccupied territory, for instance, or, conversely, the act of "mixing" one's labor with the material world. The reason for the contempt is also the reason Kant finds it so difficult to begin a doctrine of law, despite a vivid vision of its completion: juridical concepts cannot apply directly to phenomena; legal possession, in particular, is radically different from physical detention. In the absence of such application, however, there is no order of right that would promote and secure justice. As Kant explained in various contexts, his inability to close the "gap" in the critical system is a consequence of a confluence of atmospheric and psychophysical conditions that results in an experience he calls "brain cramp" (*Gehirnkrampf*).[6] The thesis of this essay is that a similar "cramp" is responsible for the gaps that mar the beginning of his *Doctrine of Law*—and should be recognized as one of his most far-reaching achievements.[7]

1. From the Metaphysics of Law . . .

The beginning of Kant's conceptual construction of law, as it appears in the published version of the *Doctrine of Law*, is, once again, replete with gaps. This is not simply my own opinion. Recent editors of the *Doctrine of Law* in German and English languages have perceived the lacunae perfectly well but, unfortunately, have chosen to hide them from the reading public. Bernd Ludwig, editor of the Meiner Verlag version, explains the rationale for this reconstructive surgery: "philosophers have only interpreted Kant's *Doctrine of Law* in various ways; the point is to change it."[8] Schopenhauer is more honest, I think, when he says of the *Doctrine of Law* that it "often produces the impression that one is listening to a satirical parody of the

Kantian style, or a bad Kantian."⁹ As with other earlier commentators, including those who had eagerly awaited Kant's contribution to the theory of law during a tumultuous decade of political and juridical uncertainties, only to find themselves disappointed by Kant's meager offering, Schopenhauer fails to ask whether the apparently parodic character of the *Doctrine of Law* is a function not of the philosopher's alleged senility but, rather, of his supererogatory honesty, which, in an operation that perhaps remained hidden even from Kant himself—for honesty cannot be supererogatory—forbade him to send the publisher a "fair copy" of a treatise that would present the beginning of law in its conceptual construction as though it had no gaps, thereby affirming that legal and physical force, hence coercion and violence, can ultimately be distinguished from each other. The focus on forces is one of the two major elements that connect the *Doctrine of Natural Science* with the *Doctrine of Law*: the former treatise cannot quite decide whether the force of attraction should be considered superficial (that is, surface-cohesive) or penetrative (hence, gravitational); the indecision that traverses the latter treatise is perhaps even more serious, for the force under examination must be both superficial and penetrative—penetrative, such that a space can be legally occupied or an object rightfully possessed; superficial, however, insofar as occupation and possession are represented by the boundaries of certain surfaces.

One of the more explicit descriptions of the impasse Kant encountered in trying to begin what would pass itself off as a fully grounded "doctrine of law" can be found in a passage from the *Nachlass* that probably stems from around 1793: "It is difficult to gain insight into how human beings, separated as they are by space, time, and private elective will [*Willkür*], can nevertheless be united with respect to the object of their elective will. . . . Because [however] freedom cannot be subject to sensible laws, [determining] the limitation on a possession with respect to spatial and temporal conditions produces difficulties, indeed the impossibility of an adequate fulfillment."¹⁰ Fully cognizant of the difficulty, Kant experiments in several notes of the same period with the scholastic-Leibnizian concept of virtuality in an attempt to capture the manner in which legal occupation or rightful possession can be distinguished from physical occupation—i.e., detention—which would simply be a function of attractive-repulsive forces. Kant soon abandons this terminology, for it gives away the game, as it were, insofar as the distinction between a "virtual" and a "local presence" (*Gegenwart*) is nothing but a distinction between presence and absence that depends solely on whether a legal or physical limit is under discussion. The terms "virtual" and "local presence" derive from a paragraph in the *Nachlass* whose title is particularly revealing because it is so deeply confusing: "The Limit [*Gränze*] of the Physical Possession of the Ground Is Indeed the Condition But Not the Limit [*Grenze*] of All Legal Possession of This Ground."[11] It is as though the silent difference between *Gränze* and *Grenze* represents the difference between physical detention and legal possession.

All of the confusion could be avoided, the opening impasse overcome, if only Kant were . . . someone other than "honest Kant."[12] Under this counterfactual condition, the philosopher could find himself convinced by Lockean or Grotian arguments and thereby affirm that the beginning of law in its conceptual construction consists in original acquisitions: individuals either "mix" their labor with the material world or "mark" things, including places, that are supposedly *res* or *terra nullius*. These and similar ratiocinations, as Kant explains in both the drafts and printed text of the *Doctrine of Law*, derive from something akin to spirit-seeing, insofar as an object or a space is invested with a "guardian spirit" that facilitates a bilateral agreement between person and non-person.[13] Even as Kant unambiguously disavows these fantasies, he also declines to sketch the path that Fichte develops in a treatise he published in 1796. According to the Fichtean way, the beginning of law in its conceptual construction lies in reciprocal recognition: the "I" produces the full extent of its "I-ness" only by recognizing itself in the form of an alter ego. A proto-socio-legality is thus imputed to "I-ness" in general.[14] Kant seems to have been unaware of Fichte's *Grundlage des Naturrechts* (Foundation of Natural Law), and there is no evidence, as far as I can find, that he develops an argument of this kind, yet the *Doctrine of Law* already indicates why the argument would make no difference to his efforts: it is not reciprocal recognition that generates the founding of law but, rather, reciprocal *coercion*. I return for a moment to the beginning of *Law and Violence*, where Menke quotes the following, decisive passage from paragraph E of the Introduction to the *Doctrine of Law*: "one can posit the concept of law [*Recht*] immediately in the possibility of connecting universal reciprocal coercion with everyone's freedom."[15]

By "everyone's freedom," it is important to emphasize that Kant means precisely *everyone* (*jedermann*), regardless of whether he or she—or perhaps some other sexual variant, about whom Kant speculates in certain passages of the *Opus postumum*, where he worries about the universality and necessity of sexuation—really exists on this, the surface of our current earth or, indeed, on the surface (or in the depths) of another planet elsewhere in the universe.[16] Regardless of when or where he, she, or they happens to find himself, herself, or themselves, everyone's freedom must be connected with "universal reciprocal coercion" in order for there to be the possibility of a legal condition. So conceived, however, the construction of law cannot help but begin in a state of paralysis, for—and this is the sticking point of this essay—the space of law is always already filled before anyone in particular moves anywhere in general. In order to go from place to place, everyone must have secured a right to occupy both the new location and the space in-between, yet every such kinesis potentially conflicts with someone else's freedom of movement—and the "someone else" is altogether general, not a "real person" who physically resists movement, not even a "virtual person" who, once having left a place, could rightfully return, but, rather, anyone in general, for everyone has equal rights, that is, equal permission to occupy his, her, or their own space, beginning with the place of his, her or their body. Conflicts over space can, of course, be settled through sheer physical force, with only slight physical resistance in the case of human beings' relatively slow movement through the earth's relatively thin atmosphere; but no such movement is for this reason "right." And in the absence of law, hence at the beginning of law in its conceptual construction, no motion has a ground to stand on. Kinesis is nothing less than an implementation of physical power—in Kant's term, *potentia* or *Macht* rather than *potestas* or *Gewalt*, as the latter term is used in a phrase that, for Kant, is determinative: "*in meiner Gewalt*," which is to say, "under my control" or "at my disposal."

The notes Kant drew up in preparation for the drafting of the *Doctrine of Law* are right: "Because freedom cannot be subject to sensible laws, [determining] the limitation on a possession with respect to spatial and temporal conditions produces difficulties, indeed the impossibility of an adequate fulfillment."[17] Everyone may be free, but insofar as everyone is free, everyone's movement potentially conflicts with someone else's freedom, with the result that no one can move freely without thereby asserting what, as Menke reminds us, Kant calls "wild lawless freedom."[18] To change for a moment to another idiom, that of the young Hegel, as analyzed in the work of Werner Hamacher: *pleroma* is the basic characteristic of the legal sphere—which is, in a sense, no surprise, for *pleroma* is also, as Kant came to realize late in his life, characteristic of space in general, filled as it is by a certain aether.[19] And to add still another idiom, this one associated with Isaac Luria: by virtue of the original legal fullness, the beginning of law consists in the "breaking of the vessels."[20] If the vessels are shattered in precisely the right way—this is perhaps the underlying thought that prompts Kant to deliver a defective "fair copy" of the *Doctrine of Law* to his publisher—the conclusion of law will be a reconstruction of its original fullness, which Kant construes in terms of an order of international law that secures a right of hospitality, such that everyone can freely move anywhere on the surface of the earth. In less exalted terms, what I am speaking about is, of course, the problem posed by the original division of space, a division that also traverses the surface of the human body, insofar as certain bodily parts—especially those Kant calls "sexual properties"—are not under one's own control, that is, at one's own disposal.[21] In the case of "sexual properties" Kant has a solution, namely marriage, and a method akin to marital law would guide the construction of law if only it could ever begin.

Instead of acknowledging in so many words that any beginning of the law consists in a shattering of the vessels, whereby—unjustly, demonically—physical forces convert something detained into a legal possession whose possession-character is maintained by similar forces, Kant shatters the beginning of his own conceptual construction of the law, that is, the opening paragraphs of his much-delayed and much-anticipated *Doctrine of Law*.[22] Signs of the impasse, however, are evident throughout the resulting shards, including in the following reflection on original acquisition, which runs directly counter to Kant's otherwise consistent demystification of the supposed "guardian spirits" that pretend to secure possession in the absence of a physical possessor: "how far does the authorization to take possession of a parcel of land extend?" Kant asks, and immediately answers, "As far as the capacity to place it under one's control [*in seiner Gewalt*], that is, as far as whoever wants to appropriate it can defend it; as if the land itself were to say, 'if you cannot protect me, you cannot command me.'"[23] To which one may ask the land in return: from what do you need to be protected other than your putative protectors? In any case, the impact of the impasse is concentrated at the beginning of Kant's conceptual construction, especially in the second paragraph, where he proposes what he calls the "postulate of practical reason with regard to law"—a postulate or "demand" that runs as follows: "It is possible for me to have any external object of my elective will as mine; that is, a maxim by which, were it to become law, an object of the elective will would in itself (objectively) have to belong to no one (*res nullius*) is contrary to right."[24] This is to say that everything can be someone's, where "can" means not physically "can" but legally permissible; the postulate, however, not only provides no basis for "me" making anything "my thing," it excludes this transformation in the course of its explication, which depends on two countervailing lines of argumentation, one a juridical argument *e contrario*, the other a logical *reductio ad absurdum*. The first argument is valid under the condition that a new situation may arise that the original legislation could not have envisaged; the second is valid only under the condition that the negation of what is claimed is the only possible alternative, *tertium non datur*—the "tertium" in this case, being (so it seems) the possibility of a donation without a corresponding acquisition. In any case, this postulate represents *e contrario* a stubborn paralysis: everything can become a possession, but the grasping of something in particular is an expression of a particular physical condition, which is to say, contrary to law. If only, in sum, the conceptual construction of law could begin, it ends well—with everyone permitted to travel everywhere on the surface of the earth. But insofar as it can begin only in shards, there is no end to violence.

2. . . . To the Critique of Violence

I now turn to a keen reader of Kant, one who was especially attuned to the late writings, including the *Doctrine of Law*.[25] Sometime during the First World War, Walter Benjamin wrote out a series of *Notizen zu einer Arbeit über die Kategorie der Gerechtigkeit* (Notes toward a Work on the Category of Justice), which he later lent to Gerhard (later, Gershom) Scholem, who then copied them into his diary for the year 1916. For some strange reason, many decades later, Scholem withheld the "Notes" from the editors of Benjamin's writings who were seeking to complete the work that he and Adorno had begun.[26] Regardless of their status in Benjamin's corpus, the "Notes" are of particular interest here because they represent a faithful résumé of the impasse Kant encounters at the beginning of the *Doctrine of Law*: "To every good," Benjamin writes in the first note, "limited as it is by the spatio-temporal order, there accrues a possession-character. But each possession, as something caught in the same finitude, is always unjust. No order of possession, however articulated, can therefore lead to justice."[27] To translate this back into the terminology with which this essay began: the beginning of the conceptual construction of law bars the way to justice. Schelling says something similar in his only explicit contribution to political theory, a 1797 essay that appeared under the ironic title *Neue Deduktion des Naturrechts* (New Deduction of Natural Law). I call the title "ironic" because, far from deducing natural law, where "deduction" is understood in a Kantian manner as the resolution of a *quid juris*, Schelling concludes his sole published contribution to political theory with an outright de-deduction: "Natural law, if consistent (inasmuch as it becomes the right of coercion), necessarily destroys itself, that is, it annuls all law [*zerstört sich nothwendig selbst, d.h. es hebt alles Recht auf*], since the last resort to which it entrusts the preservation of law is physical supremacy [*Uebermacht*]."[28]

The twenty-four-year-old Benjamin is even clearer about the self-destructive character of legal-theoretical construction than the twenty-two-year-old Schelling, whose use of the ambiguous term *aufheben* suggests the possibility that the self-annulment of law amounts to its preservation at a higher level. Nothing of the kind can be found in Benjamin's inquiry into the category of justice. Thus, the second note reads as follows: "Rather, this [the way to justice] lies in the condition of a good that cannot be a possession. This alone is the good through which goods become possession-less."[29] The uncharacteristically awkward phrase, "the good that cannot be a possession," is an abbreviation of the even more awkward expression through which the *Doctrine of Law* develops its supplementary postulate of practical reason: "an object of the elective will (that) . . . in itself (objectively) belong[s] to no one."[30] It would be easy to show that Benjamin's line of argument runs parallel with Kant's exposition of this postulate, for, if anything is objectively unpossessable—if, in other words, something in particular resists acquisition without its resistance being understood as the function of another elective will—then everything in general is unpossessable, for no limit could be drawn that would separate this thing from everything else. Benjamin's "Notes" proceed to describe a misconception common to both bourgeois and socialist political theory, whereby "society" functions as the name of a super-agent that possesses the thing that "objectively" belongs to no one. What remains missing from these "Notes," however, is the name of the good in question—a good, Benjamin suggests, that has a "right" to be what it is, namely a good rather than an evil, which every good becomes as soon as it is used or acquired contrary to law. Again, as recorded in Scholem's *Diaries*, there is no clue as to the name of the outstanding good—perhaps because Benjamin wanted to keep it a secret, or perhaps because Scholem dared not write it down, just as he forgot to provide the editors of Benjamin's *Gesammelten Schriften* with a copy of the "Notes." Nevertheless, a clue can be found in Benjamin's continuation of the line of argument that emerges from his proposed work on the category of justice.

The continuation takes the form of an essay Benjamin sought to publish in a once-renowned literary journal, *Die Weißen Blätter* (*The White Pages*), but ended up in a distinguished journal of social theory under the title *Zur Kritik der Gewalt* (Toward the Critique of Violence). In view of the organizing principle of this volume, I am going to make only three points about this famous essay, after which I quickly conclude.

(1) The prospect of a fourth *Critique*, which guides Benjamin's study of law and justice, emerges directly from the opening paragraphs of the *Doctrine of Law*. It is clear that the word *Gewalt* requires a degree of philological diligence, since Kant clarifies it by means of two diametrically opposed Latin terms. Sometimes, as in the description of the crucial transition from private to public right, it is translated as *violentia*, while in other passages it is translated as *potestas*.[31] Disambiguation of this kind goes only so far, however, for the ambiguity lies in the concept itself, that is, in the concept of a legal force that emerges, as if by magic, from its physical counterpart through an act of reflection: "an object of my elective will," Kant writes in the second paragraph of the *Doctrine of Law*,

> is that which I have the physical capacity [*Vermögen*] to use as I please, that whose use lies in my power [*Macht*] (*potentia*); this must be distinguished from having the same object under my control [*in meiner Gewalt*] (*in potestatem meam redactum*), which presupposes not simply a capacity but also an act of the elective will. But in order to *think* of something simply as an object of my elective will it is sufficient for me to be conscious of having it within my power. It is therefore a representation *a priori* of practical reason to regard and treat any object of my elective as an objectively possible mine or yours.[32]

Here lies, I suggest, the nucleus of a supplementary critique, evident above all in the Latin term Kant declines to translate: "*redactum*," which is perhaps a misprint for *reductum* in the phrase "*in potestatem meam redactum*." This redaction or reduction, as a function of consciousness, cannot escape an amphiboly, insofar as inner and outer determinations are taken for each other, and the amphibolous character of this reflective concept expresses itself in the ambiguity of the word *Gewalt*.

(2) The argument sketched out in "Toward the Critique of Violence" is modeled on the *Critique on the Practical Reason* with a terminological transformation that is transparent from beginning to end. Just as the

Critique of Practical Reason is not a "Critique of Pure Practical Reason," so the critique of *Gewalt* is not a critique of pure *Gewalt*.[33] Like pure practical reason, *reine Gewalt* ("pure violence") is not only uncriticizable; it is precisely what the "critical business" is designed to promote—even if, as both Kant and Benjamin concede, it is impossible to determine in any given instance of practical reason—i.e., *Gewalt*—whether it is pure or not.[34]

(3) Impure *Gewalt* consists, by contrast, in apportionment—that is, in dividing up space and thereafter erecting boundaries, markers for the purpose of demonstrating, justifying, and thus maintaining the resulting division. The mythic character of law follows, too, from the dynamics of division, insofar as myths express the rationale for the apportionment, which is itself reflected in the primordial division between human and divine realms. Much of the analysis of Benjamin's essay, for obvious reasons, has been directed toward its striking deployment of a certain concept of life that comes under discussion on a number of writings he produced during the early 1920s. Nevertheless, it is not the concept of life that generates the critique of violence, not even the concept, drawn from Heinrich Rickert, of "bare life" (*bloßes Leben*).[35] What generates critique is the uncritical manner in which every legal order posits and maintains its divisions. And critique is completed only in a paradoxical mode of practice, whereby action takes the form of non-action; more precisely, in the action of withdrawing from the system of work in its current form; to use Benjamin's words, in the "proletarian general strike"[36] Whereas the beginning of law lies in the division of space, pure *Gewalt*, as problematically exemplified by the "proletarian general strike," is the end of law—not because the strike does away with all divisions and restores something like a lost wholeness, but only insofar as it leaves nothing behind: no boundary markers, no goods *qua* commodities, and above all (this is among the more troubling spots of Benjamin's essay), no bloodshed.[37] In terms taken from Kant's *Doctrine of Natural Science*, *Gewalt* separates itself from the system of physical force and becomes "pure" by departing from the principle of force conservation under which the dynamics of physical bodies can be constructed *a priori*. Physical forces forever reverberate, which is precisely not the case with—to borrow a phrase from Schelling—that force "to the second power" which Benjamin enigmatically names at the very end of his essay "die waltende Gewalt."[38]

In "Notes toward a Work on the Category of Justice" Benjamin identifies a good that cannot be possessed and thus, by making other goods possession-less, leads to justice. He does not name this one good, however. One possible name of this good is *Gewalt*—not as a good-in-itself, akin to the "good will," as Kant describes it, nor as a good-for-something-else, in which case it would be a means to an end, still less as a spontaneous of eruption of "life" that would shake up a system prone to sclerosis. *Gewalt* can be understood as the good around which Benjamin's "Notes" silently revolve only under the condition that it be recognized as a force that vanishes upon its appearance. In other words, it cannot be stored, retained, or preserved in any form. It is inexhaustible because it always only exhausts itself. For this reason, it cannot be assimilated to a natural force insofar as such forces, in whatever form they appear, must be conserved. The difference between the unnaturalness of "pure violence," which Benjamin associates with divinity, and the putative naturalness of legal force, which he associated with the gods of myth, lies in the fact that the law, from its beginning, parasitically relies on physical forces and at the same time seeks to conceal this, its open secret.

Notes

1. Christoph Menke, *Recht und Gewalt* (Berlin: August Verlag, 2011), 33; Christoph Menke, *Law and Violence: Christoph Menke in Dialogue*, trans. Gerrit Jackson (Manchester: Manchester University Press, 2018), 65. An earlier version of this essay appeared as "Il Diritto e la violenzia—da Kant a Benjamin," trans. Paola Morgavi, *aut aut* 384 (December 2019), 127–139.

2. Menke, *Recht und Gewalt*, 34; Menke, *Law and Violence*, 66 (translation modified).

3. Menke, *Recht und Gewalt*, 34; Menke, *Law and Violence*, 66 (translation modified).

4. See Immanuel Kant, *Kants gesammelte Schriften (Akademie Ausgabe)* (cited hereafter as *Ak.*), ed. Royal Prussian (later German) Academy of Sciences (Berlin: George Reimer, later Walter de Gruyter, 1900–), 12:257. See also the letter to Johann Kiesewetter of the same period (Kant, *Ak.* 12:258). The *locus classicus* for the discussion of this "gap" in contemporary scholarship is the work of Eckart Förster, especially the third chapter of his *Kant's Final Synthesis: An Essay on the "Opus postumum"* (Cambridge, MA: Harvard University Press, 2000), 48–74.

5. Kant, *Ak.* 8:357.

6. Kant, *Ak.* 12:296; cf. Kant, *Ak.* 12:321.

7. In the final chapters of two earlier books I sketched aspects of the argument brought together in this essay; see Peter Fenves, *Late Kant: Towards Another Law of the Earth* (New York: Routledge, 2003), 136–161; and Peter Fenves, *The Messianic Reduction: Walter Benjamin and Shape of Time* (Stanford, CA: Stanford University Press, 2011), 187–225.

8. Bernd Ludwig, *Kants Rechtslehre* (Hamburg: Meiner, 1988), 7. The Meiner Verlag edition of the *Rechtslehre*, prepared by Ludwig, naturally accords with his reconstruction of the text, as does Mary Gregor's revised translation of the *Doctrine of Right* published in Immanuel Kant, *Practical Philosophy*, ed. and trans. Mary Gregor (Cambridge: Cambridge University Press, 1996), esp. 401–411. The original translation, also produced by Mary Gregor and published separately by Cambridge University Press in the series *Texts in German Philosophy*, ed. Raymund Geuss, accords with the 1797 text. See Immanuel Kant, *The Metaphysics of Morals*, trans. Mary Gregor (Cambridge: Cambridge University Press, 1991), esp. 68–79.

9. Arthur Schopenhauer, *Werke in fünf Bänden*, ed. Ludger Lütkehaus (Frankfurt am Main: Haffman, 2006), 1:668.

10. Kant, *Ak*. 23:305–306.

11. Kant, *Ak*. 23:287.

12. See Søren Kierkegaard, *Journals and Papers*, ed. and trans. Edna Hong and Howard Hong, with Gregor Malantschuk (Bloomington: Indiana University Press), 2:515, §2236. Kierkegaard calls Kant "honest" because he unambiguously "declares the relationship to God to be a kind of mental weakness, a hallucination."

13. Kant, *Ak*. 6: 260.

14. See Johann Gottlob Fichte, *Grundlage des Naturrechts nach Principien der Wissenschaftslehre* ("Foundation of Natural Law in Accordance with Principles of the *Wissenschaftslehre*," 1796), reprinted in Fichte, *Sämmtliche Werke*, ed. Immanuel Hermann Fichte (Berlin: Walter de Gruyter, 1971), 3:44, 4.

15. Kant, *Ak*. 6:323.

16. See Kant, *Ak*. 21:571.

17. Kant, *Ak*. 23:305–306.

18. See Menke, *Recht und Gewalt*, 7; Menke, *Law and Violence*, 3. See also Kant, *Ak*. 6:361.

19. See Werner Hamacher, "Pleroma: Zu Genesis und Struktur einer dialektischen Hermeneutik bei Hegel," in Georg Wilhelm Friedrich Hegel, *Das Geist des Christentums: Schriften 1796–1800*, ed. W. Hamacher (Berlin: Ullstein, 1978), 7–333.

20. The now-standard starting point for any investigation into Luria's thought and influence can be found in Gershom Scholem, *Major Trends in Jewish Mysticism* (New York: Schocken, 1988), 244–286.

21. Kant, *Ak*. 6:277. For a broader exploration of what is at stake in Kant's conception of "sexual properties," which can be rightfully used only under the condition that they are someone else's, see Peter Fenves, "Marital, Martial, and Maritime Law: Toward Some Controversial Passages in Kant's *Doctrine of Right*," *Diacritics* 35 (2005), 101–120.

22. The clearest, most succinct, and most startling formulation of the paralysis in question can be found in the following note: "All of this"—anything and everything that transcends the limits of one's one body, including the things such as apples that it physically grasps—"I must nevertheless be able to possess, for

otherwise all things [*Sachen*] would be *res nullius*, and my freedom would indeed be independent but would be no capacity [*Vermögen*], and I would do an injustice [*thun unrecht*] either to the things through my appropriation of them or other human beings, regardless of whether I influence them or not" (Kant, *Ak.* 23:280). Both sides of this either/or formulation are strikingly straightforward: I can do an injustice to *things* by taking them, and I can do an injustice to *other human beings* who may nevertheless lie infinitely distant from me in both space and time—if, that is, there is such a thing as a "no one's thing" in the absolute sense.

23. Kant, *Ak.* 6:265.

24. Ibid., 6:246. It is of some interest that one of the earliest formulations of the thesis that will later emerge as this juridical postulate emphasizes its specifically earthly character: "All *iura in re* is ultimately grounded in the right to land. There is no *rem absolute nullius* (which would be an object of the elective will) if human beings are on earth [*wenn Menschen auf Erde sind*]" (Kant, *Ak.* 23:238).

25. See, above all, Benjamin's analysis of Kant's doctrine of matrimonial law in his essay on Goethe's *Die Wahlverwandtschaften* (1923), reprinted in Walter Benjamin, *Gesammelte Schriften*, ed. Rolf Tiedemann and Hermann Schweppenhauser (Frankfurt am Main: Suhrkamp Verlag, 1974–1991), 1:127–129.

26. See Gershom Scholem, *Tagebücher, nebst Aufsätzen und Entwürfen bis 1923*, ed. Karlfried Gründer, Herbert Kopp-Oberstebrink und Friedrich Niewöhner with the cooperation of Karl E. Grözinger (Jüdischer Verlag: Frankurt am Main, 1995–2000), 1:401–402.

27. Scholem, *Tagebücher* 1:401.

28. Friedrich Wilhelm Joseph von Schelling, *Neue Deduktion der Naturrechts* (1797), reprinted in Schelling, *Historisch-Kritische Ausgabe*, ed. Hartmut Buchner, Wilhelm Jacobs, and Annamarie Pieper (Stuttgart: Frommann-Holzboog, 1982), 1.3:174, §162. For Benjamin's interest in Schelling circa 1916, see the remarks recorded in Scholem, *Tagebücher*, 1:134.

29. Scholem, *Tagebücher*, 1:401.

30. Kant, *Ak.* 6:246.

31. Ibid., 6:307.

32. Ibid., 6:246.

33. See Kant, *Ak.* 5:3.

34. Ibid., 5:170.

35. The term "bare life" is an integral element of the "Philosophy of Completed Life" that Rickert presented to a broad spectrum of students—including Benjamin and Heidegger—at the University of Freiburg in the fall semester of 1913. For a description of Benjamin's ambivalently enthusiastic response to these lectures, see Peter Fenves, "Completion Instead of Revelation: Toward the 'Theological-Political Fragment,'" in *Walter Benjamin and Theology*, ed. Colby Dickenson and Stéphane Symons (New York: Fordham University Press, 2016), 56–74.

36. Benjamin, *Gesammelte Schriften*, 2:193.
37. Ibid., 2:199.
38. Ibid., 2:203.

16

Is There Critique in Critical Theory?

The Claim of Happiness on Theory

RICHARD A. LEE JR.

1. Introduction

One would hope that the term "critique" would find its clearest definition in that mode of philosophizing that is called and calls itself "critical theory." Even in the work that should bring precise definition to the term, Horkheimer's "Traditionelle und kritische Theorie," the concept of "critical theory" receives mostly a negative determination in that it is presented in opposition to "traditional theory." Starting already with Kant, "critique" seems to be grasped more in its practice than through a definition. Critique, it seems, is just what philosophers do when they claim to be doing it, rather than a thing in and of itself. Perhaps this is as it should be. It seems that, already from its first use, "critique," i.e., a form of the verb κρίνω, was dependent not only on its object (a critique of X) but also on its content. Something might only call for critique, i.e., a judgment, a decision, an adjudication, in a certain situation, and certain situations might call for the critique of particular "things."[1] From the beginning, it seems, there is no general or abstract definition of critique but only a notion of it in concrete practice.

In book 6 of his *History of the Peloponnesian War*, Thucydides presents a debate among the Athenians about fulfilling a treaty obligation that Athens had with the Egesteans in regard to their battles in Sicily.[2] On one side, Nicias is against further armed conflicts abroad, arguing that Athens should capitalize on what it has accomplished and shore up its current territories. In making his argument, Nicias not only insists that "in going to Sicily you are leaving many enemies behind you, and you apparently want to make new ones there and also have them on your hands,"[3] but also throws in an *ad hominem* attack against Alcibiades: "No doubt there is someone sitting here who is delighted at having been chosen for the command and who, entirely for his own selfish reasons, will urge you to make this expedition—and all the more so because he is still too young for his post."[4]

Alcibiades takes on the *ad hominem* directly: he insists that even with the folly of youth, he has found the "right arguments" in the past to persuade the Athenians to do the right thing. Alcibiades goes on to argue,

> There seems to be, therefore, no reasonable argument to induce us to hold back ourselves or to justify any excuse to our allies in Sicily for not helping them. We have sworn to help them, and it is our duty to help them, without raising the objection that we have had no help from them ourselves. The reason why we made them our allies was not that we wanted them to send us reinforcements here, but in order that they should be a thorn in the flesh for our enemies in Sicily, and so prevent them from coming here to attack us.[5]

In the end, Alcibiades's argument prevails. In an effort to overturn the decision, Nicias then raises the threat level, telling the Athenians they will need to send an overwhelming force. His hope is either to dissuade Athens from sending any troops or to convince them to send a force that could shock and awe their enemies. The Athenians take Nicias at his word and decide to send a force and let the generals decide what is necessary. Nicias decides to take his arguments out of the public assembly and speak privately "in a quieter atmosphere."[6] This last move shows a marked contrast between Nicias and Alcibiades. When Nicias proves to be publicly and politically unsuccessful, he recedes from the public, political space and debate. This seems to presage how the story unfolds—no longer a political debate, the issue turns to the private and the religious.

At this point, Thucydides's narrative breaks from the debate: "While these preparations were going on it was found that in one night nearly all the stone Hermae in the city of Athens had had their faces disfigured by being cut about."[7] Whoever perpetrated this act of extreme impiety, it was attributed to Alcibiades. We can note immediately that this "turn of events" inserts itself into, or is a *supplement to*, the public, political debate about the use of force in Sicily and the obligations of a treaty. The contrast, therefore, is between the arguments presented in the political debate and the event of the impious desecration of the sacred statues. Even if the desecration is a provocation, it is provocative precisely because the profanation is inexcusable, beyond the pale, but also politically relevant. If we take the desecration as a provocation, it is, at the same time, an intervention into the political. We see here something akin to what Vernant and Vidal-Naquet argue about Greek tragedy: the staging of a contest between the religious and the political: "The tragic consciousness of responsibility appears when the human and divine levels are sufficiently distinct for them to be opposed while still appearing to be inseparable. The tragic sense of responsibility emerges when human action becomes the object of reflection and debate while still not being regarded as sufficiently autonomous to be fully self-sufficient."[8] But if there is a contest, then religion and politics must play in the same arena. If the desecration were a provocation, that could only be because religion has political relevance.

Alcibiades's response, however, is entirely political. He asks for what we might today call a "critique," i.e., a judgment, an adjudication, a decision in front of the assembly. Thucydides is explicit on the contest involved: "They therefore exaggerated the whole thing and made all the noise they could about it, saying that the mysteries and the defacement of the Hermae were all part of a plot to overthrow the democracy, and that in all this Alcibiades had had a hand; evidence for which they found in the unconventional and undemocratic character of his life in general."[9] Thucydides's comment here about Alcibiades is telling both about the situation and about the location of "critique." First, it is Alcibiades who asks for a "judgment," a decision, about the situation in which he finds himself. That situation, as Thucydides relates it, is a contest of Alcibiades *against* democracy. However, the crime of which Alcibiades is accused is a religious crime, namely sacrilege. The desecration of the Hermae, therefore, is, for Thucydides, a crime against democracy. That is, the concrete situation in which Alcibiades asks for a critique, a decision, a judgment, is one in which the religious has intervened into the political. Yet Thucydides seems to indicate that the sacrilege is, as such, un- or anti-democratic. Such a situation demands a critique, in the name of justice.[10] Alcibiades, for his part, makes an immediate appeal to democracy in the form of asking for a κριτικός.[11] The trial, its judgment, and the granting of justice would have been in front of the δῆμος and, therefore, would have been democritical as well as democratic. Thucydides own telling of this story, with Alcibiades as the anti-democrat, is, from the beginning, unstable.[12] The appeal of Alcibiades to critique, therefore, is already an appeal to a social context that is, at the same time, a social contest.[13] Religion is inserted into a political context in the sense that religion might *contest* politics. At the crossing, Alcibiades asks for critique, i.e., for judgment, parsing out, and decision. The critique is never not socio-political. However, Alcibiades's appeal for a critique is even more telling; for is it not the case that, in his situation, religion appears as "given"? In the face of that which emerges as given, Alcibiades's appeal for judgment, for critique, is an appeal to look at the social context of that givenness.[14]

2. Traditional and Critical Theory

In the generation before Horkheimer, the method, the mode of operation, the outlook, and the organizing principle of the "Frankfurt School" was not referred to as "critical theory." Even in the generation of Horkheimer and Adorno, the designation "critical theory" was not as common as it is today. The phrase and the designation, therefore, might find its origin in the seminal essay "Traditionelle und kritische Theorie" in which Horkheimer defends a way of theorizing that does not simply confirm what is. Through most of the essay, Horkheimer presents what can only be called a "critique" of "traditional theory" by presenting a different way of theorizing that he most often refers to as "critical." We get a succinct presentation of the difference between these two modes of theorizing when Horkheimer says,

> In this view of theory, therefore, the real social function of science is not made manifest; it speaks not of what theory means in human life, but only of what it means in the isolated sphere in which for historical reasons it comes into existence. Yet as a matter of fact the life of society is the result of all the work done in the various sectors of production. Even if therefore the division of labor in the capitalist system functions but poorly,

its branches, including science, do not become for that reason self-sufficient and independent. They are particular instances of the way in which society comes to grips with nature and maintains its own inherited form. They are moments in the social process of production, even if they be almost or entirely unproductive in the narrower sense.[15]

As his analysis proceeds, Horkheimer comes to call the theory that is in possession of this knowledge "critical." Here, in its negative form, we have a notion of "critique." If we play this out more carefully than Horkheimer does, there are two main moments that are addressed in "critique." The first is the moment in which it is seen that "the real social function" of theory (Horkheimer refers here to "science" but it is clear, as the essay continues, that "science" stands in for a certain way of theorizing) "is not made manifest." The second is the gesture to "human life," which he goes on to speak of in terms of production, "the division of labor," and "all the work done in the various sectors of production."

The first aspect of a theory that engages in critique, therefore, is one that makes manifest the "real social function" of itself. As Marx indicates in the Preface for his *Contributions to the Critique of Political Economy*, "It is not the human consciousness that determines their existence, but their social existence that determines their consciousness."[16] Marx reaches this conclusion by recognizing that the fundamental condition of human existence is something like the reproduction of the conditions of their existence. On the face of it, this seems little more than a simple affirmation of the metaphysical principle, most clearly stated by Spinoza, that each thing, insofar as it exists, strives to maintain itself in its existence. The affirmation that Marx offers, perhaps with a small extension, is that this "striving" necessarily means producing the conditions of existence. That is, since the causes that bring about the existence of any given thing must, perhaps tautologically, bring about the conditions that make that existence possible, the continuing existence of any given thing entails the production again, i.e., the reproduction of the conditions of existence.

When it comes to human existence, we do not need to worry whether humans are by nature social or antisocial because it turns out that we do, as a historical given, have societies in which there are laws and political forms. This is not an empirical point. From Thucydides forward, critique engages not at the level of genesis or even legitimacy but at the level of what appears as "given." Whenever a critique is called for, warranted, or even required, there is a move away from the way in which things are given, particularly as they are given to sensation. It is a point that is developed philosophically and quasi-idealistically already in Kant's "Idea for a Universal History"[17] and further in Hegel's *Philosophy of Right*.[18] The striving to maintain human existence is, therefore, necessarily social and therefore entails relations that are the condition of the production of that existence. Ontology is necessarily, at least for us, social. That means that the principle of "striving to maintain its existence" for us requires entering into relations of the production of the conditions of that existence.

If the metaphysical position is valid, that means it holds as much for stones as it does for angels (and Spinoza's point is that it holds even for *Deus sive natura*). Therefore, for those beings that are material, even if, per hypothesis, only partly, then those conditions of existence must necessarily include material conditions. The production of the conditions of existence for material beings is dependent on the power to produce those conditions, i.e., on the "material forces of production." The result is that the material forces of production condition the social relations of production. Marx concludes that "The totality of these relations of production constitutes the economic structure of society, the real foundation."[19] Here, Marx reappropriates the Hegelian notion of the real from its idealistic snares. As Adorno will point out, what would be other than the forces that are capable of reproducing human existence will always necessarily be parasitic on the material forces of production. Therefore, "real" here must mean not ideal.[20] Just as production is always (even when just thought of in terms of cause or causes) a process, so too the production of the material conditions of existence is a process. As Marx argues, "The mode of production of material life conditions the general process of social, political and intellectual life."[21]

Horkheimer's argument, therefore, calls on this Marxist context, namely that, first, the "real social function" of theory must be related to the social process of production, and, second, this relation is not, in traditional theory, made "manifest." In terms of the first, the fact that theory is not productive of the conditions of human existence does not entail that it plays no role in the social relations of a given mode of production. While Marx's use of the language of "superstructure/base" is often read as presenting a unidirectional—and even causal—relation (the superstructure emerges from out of a given economic base), Horkheimer is here arguing, as Althusser will after him,[22] that the relations between the economic base and the theoretical/cultural/legal superstructure are either circular or have the structure of *causa sui*. As Horkheimer argued, the intellectual, scientific, and religious spheres "are particular instances of the way in which society comes to grips with nature and maintains its own inherited form."[23] If the capitalist form of production is based on the appropriation of labor in the form of value, if the relation between individuals in a capitalist society is actually a relation between things, if, in capitalism, abstractions have gotten out of our heads and become real, then capitalist society faces an almost insurmountable problem of reconciling individuals to an existence that is no longer human.[24] Traditional theory performs this crucial task. In not reflecting its own role in capitalist society, theory works to "naturalize" its present form, making it appear at the very least inevitable, if not a metaphysical necessity. As Horkheimer points out, the current form of society is not natural but is our inheritance that, like Polemarchus in Plato's *Republic*, we take on and further in the hopes of getting a return on our deposit.

This leads directly to the second direction of Horkheimer's argument: the role that theory plays in the ability of society to come to grips with nature and maintain its inherited form is, in traditional theory, "not made manifest." In fact, Horkheimer's point is even more extensive.

> If activity governed by reason is proper to humans, then existent social practice, which forms the individual's life down to its least details, is inhuman, and this inhumanity affects everything that goes on in the society. There will always be something that is extrinsic to humans' intellectual and material activity, namely nature as the totality of as yet unmastered elements with which society must deal. But when situations which really depend on humans alone, the relationships of humans in their work, and the course of one's own history are also accounted as part of "nature," the resultant extrinsicality is not only not a suprahistorical eternal category (even pure nature in the sense described is not that), but it is a sign of contemptible weakness. To surrender to such weakness is nonhuman and irrational.[25]

Traditional theory becomes inhuman the moment in which what is socially and historically conditioned is posited as eternal. Yet the "inhumanity" arises when the tension—if not contradiction—between actual social praxis and rational activity is covered over. In other words, the inhumanity is a confrontation between reason and a social form that is irrational. How are we to understand the irrationality of the current social form and practice?

If reason is characterized by the ability to give an account that is publicly available, i.e., available to all, then irrationality must be characterized as either the failure to give an account—or worse, the positing of that for which no account can be given—or the failure to give an account that is publicly available. From Aristotle through enlightenment thinkers, giving an account is identical to supplying the cause or causes. If there is some existing thing for which no cause can be given, then that means the thing came from nothing. Yet, "from nothing, nothing can come to be." The conditions for "giving an account," i.e., the ground of what counts as reason, must be, at a minimum, the law of excluded middle.[26] In this way, Horkheimer is pointing out that the "existing social practice," as irrational, violates the law of excluded middle and, because rationality is fundamental to human activity, that existing social practice is inhuman. And yet, it continues as if it were "something."

Therefore, the reason why theory needs to be critical, why theory needs critique, is, in a sense, the opposite of the Kantian demand for critique. Once Kant was roused from slumber, he came to two theses that, taken together, make the philosophical response quite complex. On the one hand, Kant recognized that the receptivity of sensation is ineliminable even as it is fundamentally skeptical. On the other, Kant realized that the metaphysical pretensions of reason also, albeit in an importantly different direction, lead to skepticism. For Kant, therefore, critique is required because things are neither as they appear to be nor as they are thought to be.

For Horkheimer, critique emerges at a structurally similar moment: that which—a social process—is, at the same time, a violation of the law of excluded middle and, because of that, cannot be. $A=\sim A$. Therefore, critical theory does engage in critique in a very specific sense. The critique is necessitated by the fact that, as Horkheimer points out, what is given to experience is in violation of the conditions that reason discovers for what can be. Thus, Horkheimer inverts the Kantian notion of critique: we do not need to rein in the pretension of reason; rather, we need to rein in the pretension of what is socially given, and therefore is—socially given to rationality or even reasonableness.

This situation is not structurally dissimilar from the one Kant faced and to which "critique" was his answer: reason makes claims about what is that are unsustainable given what, in fact, is! This is the very situation that pushes Adorno to hold metaphysics to its promise.

3. Critique, Rescue, and the Index of Happiness

In his lecture course *Metaphysics: Concept and Problems*, Adorno makes a curious claim:

> Aristotle . . . critiques the Platonic attempt to oppose essence to the world of the senses, as something separate and absolutely different from it. Above all, he criticizes the Platonic hypostasis of universal concepts as a duplication of the world. In this he makes a very strong and legitimate case, based on the argument that all the attributes of the Ideas are derived from the empirical world, on which they live, rather as the rulers lived on the work of their servants or slaves. At the same time, however, he then seeks in his turn to extract an essential being from the sensible, empirical world, and thereby to save it; and it is precisely this twofold aim of critique and rescue that constitutes the nature of metaphysics.[27]

Metaphysics, Adorno argues, consists of what we might call three "moments." In the first moment, there is a positing of something other than the world of the senses, other than the factical world. In Plato, there is the positing in the Forms or Ideas. Yet, according to Adorno, there is not yet metaphysics in Plato because these Ideas are outside of and opposed to the world of the senses. Because of this, the factical world takes on the character of μὴ ὄν—non-being. Since the factical world is but a diminished similitude of the Ideas, there is no mediation between our world and the Ideas. This lack of mediation is, at the same time, the lack of metaphysics in Plato. This is not because Plato posits a transcendent world of Ideas, and therefore does not think the being of things (which, since Aristotle, would be the characterization of metaphysics). Rather, it is because Plato does not thematize the difference between the factical world and the world of transcendence. He writes:

> While it is true that the tension between the sphere of transcendence and the sphere of that which is merely the case, between τὸ ὄν and τὰ ὄντα, is present in Plato's philosophy, because it is unavoidable, breaking through again and again, his philosophy is not constituted in such a way that this tension is central to his speculation. Now, what I should really like to

> make understandable to you is that the sphere of metaphysics in the precise sense only comes into being where this tension is itself the subject of philosophy, where it comes within the purview of thought.[28]

Let me mark here that Adorno does not claim that, for critique, transcendence is the problem. Rather, he marks the lack of attention to the tension (*Spannung*) between transcendence and the factical. I will return to this after I look at the other two "moments" of metaphysics.

In the second moment, metaphysics is a critique. It is the critique of this lack of tension between the transcendent and the factical. Adorno argues that we can see this critical gesture already in Aristotle: "if I separate the Ideas completely from everything existent and make them absolutely autonomous, I turn them into an existent of a second power, of a second, higher order. In modern terms we would say that I objectify or reify the Ideas."[29]

We should note that Adorno does not argue that the critique that is this second moment of metaphysics is a rejection of transcendence. Rather, the critique that belongs to metaphysics is directed toward the elision of the "tension" that emerges between the factical world and the transcendent world of the Ideas. This is precisely why Adorno points to the lack of "mediation" in Platonic thought. If the Ideas are posited as being—τὸ ὄν—then the factical world is simply opposed as nonbeing—μὴ ὄν. Without mediation, the sphere of the Ideas presents no relation to the factical world at all. On the other hand, without something like transcendence, the factical world is merely the way it ought to be. That is, without something like transcendence, there is no critique because nothing can be said in relation to the factical world as it is.

This, then, leads to the third moment—*Rettung*, rescue. As I have argued, Adorno does not critique Plato for positing Ideas, i.e., transcendence. Rather, he critiques Plato because there is no relation between the factical world and the Ideal. This turned the factical world into non-being, a deficient similitude of the real world that is the Ideas. So there is something that is saved in Plato's philosophy even through the critique. When, according to Adorno, Aristotle turns the Ideas into the essences of things, he brings the transcendent into the factical world. The rescue of the Ideas in the form of essence now allows essence to expose both the failure of the factical world to live up to its ideal and an "otherwise" in relation to the world as it is given. In short, it presents an index by which we can view the factical world or in the light of which the factical world comes to appear in a certain way.

These three moments—transcendence, critique, and rescue—do not belong simply to Aristotle's relation to Plato nor even to metaphysics in general, but, rather, belong to critique as such in Adorno's hands. This is partly because Adorno insists on maintaining the promise of metaphysics, of what he sometimes calls "metaphysical experience." As I already indicated, metaphysics is the exposure of an otherwise in the face of what is factically given. The moment of critique arises when we look at metaphysics in relation to the current state of our world:

> the metaphysical thesis of the inherent meaning of the world, or of a cosmic plan underlying everything that happens, must be called into question at the very moment when a meaningful connection can no longer be established between what has happened and the metaphysical ideas. . . . For I believe we have nothing except our reason; that we have no option but to measure by our concrete experience; and that within the constellations that now define our experience all the traditional affirmative or positive theses of metaphysics—I think I can put it most simply like this—simply become blasphemies.[30]

The blasphemy of metaphysics is that it posits a transcendence and, therefore, a meaning that, viewed from the factical world, is not merely a lie, but an act of evil. The difficulty, however, is that metaphysics, as Adorno understands it, is not merely a philosophical/theoretical gesture but, as we saw in Horkheimer and Marx, a social fact. The metaphysical posit of capitalism is identity in two intricately connected ways. First, in the production of commodities for exchange, 1 quarter of corn = x cwt of iron. This is not merely an equivalence, it is an identity. Corn *is* iron. This is what I meant earlier when I said that, in capitalist societies, the principle of non-contradiction is no longer ontologically binding. Exchange requires that $A=\sim A$. What allows for this contradiction to nonetheless be real? It is a certain kind of abstraction away from use-values and, therefore, from all the sensuous characteristics that make a thing the very thing it is. This abstraction then becomes something real (Marx's famous "ghostlike objectivity"). Yet the identity is borne out because each of the two is identical to some third: $(a=b)=(b=c)$. The third is, famously, labor measured by time.

Yet just as the identity of corn and iron requires an abstraction away from particular, material, sensuous qualities, so too does the labor—otherwise it could not be the ground of identity. For this reason, all labor that grounds the identity of commodities in exchange is equally abstract. Just as all commodities are equivalent to one another, so are all individuals equivalent to one another. The principle and metaphysics of identity that is capitalism brings about the absolute fungibility of individuals.

Yet the response to this fungibility requires that we rescue the promise of metaphysics: "It is, I would say, a metaphysical fallacy into which I should like to prevent you from falling: to believe that because culture has failed; because it has not kept its promise; because it has denied human beings freedom, individuality, true universality; because it has not fulfilled its own concept, it should therefore be thrown on the scrap-heap and cheerfully replaced by the cynical establishment of immediate power relations."[31] The metaphysics that grounds (if this term can be appropriate to a mist or cloud upon which capitalist society rests) capitalism calls out for critique in the sense we have seen in Marx and Horkheimer—an attempt to show that something other than philosophy, other than theory, makes possible the reality of contradiction. Yet in such a reality, simply saying "no" will never be sufficient. "To this end, dialectics, at once the imprint of the universal delusion and its critique, must turn in a last move even against itself. The critique of all particulars, which absolutely posit themselves, is the shadow of absoluteness cast over critique itself, against which also, opposite to its tendency, must remain in the medium of the concept."[32] The delusion, as we have seen, emerges from the context of a society in which what should be false, because a contradiction, nevertheless walks among us. Yet the metaphysical difficulty actually calls for metaphysics or at least the threefold movement that Adorno argues characterizes metaphysics. As he insists at the opening of his lecture course, "Metaphysics . . . always deals with concepts. Metaphysics is the form of philosophy that takes concepts as its objects."[33] The critique that Adorno practices is, therefore, one that does not move outside of the "medium of the concept," i.e., outside of metaphysics. It is because capitalist society, especially after Auschwitz, either reduces all thought to the merely given, to immediacy, or turns the categories of metaphysics into blasphemy. There is, he argues, a demand that both recoils back on metaphysics and requires a rescue of metaphysics. The demand emerges because "traditional" metaphysics, like traditional theory, makes a mockery of our experience. "Dialectics is the self-consciousness of objective delusion, not yet having overcome it."[34]

The delusion is not, however, easily eradicable. If the principle of non-contradiction is no longer binding ontologically, then it is not immediately obvious what is a delusion and what is real. In the end, *Zum Ende*, the critique that belongs to critical theory, at least in the hands of Horkheimer and Adorno—and maybe even Benjamin—is one that sets out from the fact that the social role of theory is not immediately apparent precisely because of the metaphysical posit that stands at the heart of capitalism. Yet that critique is, at the same time, a rescue of the promise of metaphysics. And what is that promise? On the one hand *this*, just *this world*, is not all there is and, therefore, it does not have to be this way. On the other hand, it is the promise of that most traditional of all philosophical concepts: happiness. For Adorno, happiness is intimately related to the task of that form of critique called "negative dialectics."

If negative dialectics strives to prevent the thesis of identity, then it also strives to bring to light the role of non-identity in any positing of identity. It is, in short, an attempt to bring to light "what is" as such and not merely what is thinkable in objects. In this way, negative dialects attempts a restoration. So too, does happiness: "Happiness, the only aspect of metaphysical experience that is more than powerless needing, grants the interior of objects as what is simultaneously removed from them."[35] For Adorno, metaphysics, in positing another world, opens up the possibility of happiness, but only when it is a dialectical critique of the thesis of identity. "The course of the world is not completely closed, and not absolute despair; despair is much more the conclusiveness of the world. As untenable as the traces of the Other are in it; as much as all happiness is distorted by its revocability, the existent is nevertheless shot through, in the gaps which stamp identity as a lie, with the promises, constantly broken again, of that Other. Every happiness is a fragment of the total happiness, which human beings are denied and which they deny themselves."[36] For Adorno, critique is nothing other than a philosophy that works in the light of redemption and reconciliation. "The reconciled condition would not annex the alien by means of a philosophical imperialism, but would find its happiness in the fact that the latter remains what is distant and divergent in the given nearness, as far beyond the heterogenous as what it is its own."[37] The task, therefore, of negative dialectics is the task of critique and it is indexed to happiness. The happiness to which critique is indexed is related, on one side, to reconciliation, the reconciliation of the contradiction that has become flesh and dwells among us, and, on the other side, to the critique of thought turned against itself and what is other than thought.[38]

The second direction, the critique of thought, is the movement toward the fulfillment of the concept of the concept, namely to think that which is. Yet that which is must necessarily be, as Adorno has insisted, *other* (*Fremd*) than thought. It would thus be a critique of the metaphysical posit of thought, viz., that *what* is thought is identical to the thought of it. This identity that seems to belong to thought as such, to theory, and to philosophy, is nothing other than the identity that grounds, in a mystical way, exchange value and the social formation surrounding the production of commodities for exchange. Yet the thought that exposes this, works in the direction of happiness: "In view of what is absolutely, indissolubly individualized it is to be hoped that this is how it already was and would be; only by approaching this would the concept of the concept be fulfilled. It clings, however, to the promise of happiness, while the world which denies it . . . is that of dominating universality."[39] In the end, *zum Ende*, the only form of critique that belongs to critical theory is a Marxist social critique that risks being metaphysical for the sake of a happiness that is the very promise of metaphysics.

This is what Adorno indicates by his claim that now metaphysics has materialism thrust upon it. But I take it this is what he also means at the end of *Minima Moralia* when he insists that "Philosophy, as it is a response to despair, would be the attempt to treat all things as they would be represented from the standpoint of redemption [*Erlösung*]."[40] The despair emerges from the failure of our experience to live up to its own concept. The standpoint of redemption is, therefore, one whose index is happiness, the happiness that would emerge as a possibility in the critical theory that Marx, Horkheimer, and Adorno expose. As Adorno continues, "Perspectives must be fashioned in which the world is shifted, estranged [*verfremden*], its rifts [*Risse*] and fissures [*Schründe*] exposed, as it once will be lying as needy and disfigured in the Messianic light."[41] This messianic light is, according to Adorno, won from out of the inside, as it were, of objects, i.e., from thought thinking what is other without identity. Such a thought, even though indexed to happiness, will also bear the mark of the distortion and neediness of the world from which it emerges and to which it must return, if it is thinking in the light of redemption.

Notes

1. I use the term "thing" here in all its ambiguity. A thing might be a material object, a judgment, a position, or even a social structure.

2. Thucydides, *History of the Peloponnesian War* (London: Penguin Books, 1972), 414 (bk. 6, 8ff).
3. Ibid., 415 (bk. 6, 10).
4. Ibid.
5. Ibid., 421 (bk. 6, 18).
6. Ibid., 425 (bk. 6, 25).
7. Ibid., 426 (bk. 6, 27).
8. Jean-Pierre Vernant and Pierre Vidal-Naquet, *Myth and Tragedy in Ancient Greece*, trans. Janet Lloyd (New York: Zone Books, 1990), 27.
9. Thucydides, *History of the Peloponnesian War*, 426–427 (bk. 6, 28).
10. As the passage cited in the next note shows, Alcibiades asks for "justice" as a result of the "critique."
11. The Greek reads: ὁ δ᾽ ἔν τε τῷ παρόντι πρὸς τὰ μηνύματα ἀπελογεῖτο καὶ ἕτοιμος ἦν πρὶν ἐκπλεῖν κρίνεσθαι, εἴ τι τούτων εἰργασμένος ἦν (ἤδη γὰρ καὶ τὰ τῆς παρασκευῆς ἐπεπόριστο), καὶ εἰ μὲν τούτων τι εἴργαστο, δίκην δοῦναι, εἰ δ᾽ ἀπολυθείη, ἄρχειν. "Alcibiades denied the charges made against him on the spot and was prepared to stand his trial before sailing on the expedition, the preparations for which had now been completed, and to be examined as to whether he had done any of the things with which he was accused; he should suffer the penalty, if found guilty, and, if acquitted, should take up his command."
12. In a text such as this passage from Thucydides's *History*, one might begin to see why the later Derrida began to bring together the instability of a text (the very condition of deconstruction) with the issue of "autoimmunity" that he came to see as ineliminable from democracy. There is not only a shared formal character but also an immanent connection between deconstruction, autoimmunity, and the question of democracy. If Derrida were to use the word, "critique" might mean for him something like "democracy to come."
13. If it is not clear, I am certainly *not* claiming that Alcibiades is a democrat in any sense of the term. Rather, the instability of the term that is present in Thucydides's narration continues in the appeal of Alcibiades.
14. While I do not have the space to pursue it here, the very next use of forms of the word κριτικός in Thucydides comes when Athenagoras picks up the argument in Syracuse and defines democracy against the economic interests of the oligarchy (see Thucydides, *History of the Peloponnesian War*, Bk. 6, 39f).
15. Max Horkheimer, *Traditionelle und Kritische Theorie: fünf Aufsätze* (Frankfurt: Fischer Taschenbuch Verlag, 1992), 214; Max Horkheimer, *Critical Theory: Selected Essays*, trans. Matthew J. O'Connell (New York: Continuum Publishing Corporation, 1975), 197.
16. Karl Marx, *Zur Kritik der politischen Oekonomie*, in Karl Marx and Friedrich Engels, *Karl Marx/Friedrich Engels: Werke*, ed. Instut für Marxismus-Leninismus, et al. (Berlin: Dietz Verlag, 1956–2018), 13.7:9; Karl Marx, *Contribution to the Critique of Political Economy*, ed. Maurice Dobb, trans. S.W. Ryazanskaya (New York: International Publishers, 1970), 21.

17. In the Introduction to "Idea for a Universal History from a Cosmopolitan Point of View," Kant indicates the problem of the merely empirical: "[History], which is concerned with narrating the appearances [of the freedom of the will], permits us to hope that if we attend to the play of freedom of the human will in the large, we may be able to discern a regular movement in it." Immanuel Kant, "Idea for a Universal History from a Cosmpolitan Point of View," in *Immanuel Kant on History*, trans. Lewis White Beck (Indianapolis: Bobbs-Merill, 1963), 11. What is important here is that there is, on the one hand, the appearances of human freedom and, on the other, *history*. It is in the telling/making of a history that Kant indicates that what is merely empirically given as a social reality can also have a rational narration.

18. As with Kant, in *The Philosophy of Right*, Hegel argues that "The absolutely free will, at the stage when its concept is abstract, has the determinate character of immediacy. Accordingly, this stage is its negative actuality, an actuality contrasted with the real world." See Georg Wilhelm Friedrich Hegel, *Elements of the Philosophy of Right*, ed. Allen W. Wood, trans. H.B. Nisbet (Cambridge: Cambridge University Press, 1991), §34. For both Kant and Hegel, the sociality or non-sociality of humans is a question neither of "human nature" nor of the givenness of antagonism. Rather, for both, the actuality of society is a point that can only be taken up rationally, and this means as a step back or aside from what is given. While much of the "social contract" tradition seeks legitimacy of current institutions, Kant and Hegel look for a rational understanding that, when actuality fails to meet it, can be that on which a critique can stand.

19. Marx, *Zur Kritik der Politischen Oekonomie*, in *Werke*, 13.7:8; Marx, *Contribution to the Critique of Political Economy*, 20.

20. When teaching, I frequently tell students that when a philosopher uses a concept that seems unclear, one question they should ask is "As opposed to what?" In this sense, the concept "real" has a complex history. For example, for much of the middle ages, "real" was not a direct opposition but something other than both "rational" and "imaginary." On one hand, there is no "animal" as such, and, therefore, "animal" is merely a rational being. On the other hand, "hippogryph" is not the same as animal in that there are no hippogryphs but there are animals. As I have argued elsewhere, Ibn Sina is perhaps the first to point out that this has ontological consequences because there is nothing existing that is just animal, there are existing things that are animals, and there are no existing things that are hippogryphs. In this sense, in both Hegel and in Marx, we need to distinguish "real" from "actually existing," even if in different ways.

21. Marx, *Zur Kritik der Politischen Oekonomie* in *Werke*, 13.7:8; Marx, *Contribution to the Critique of Political Economy*, 20–21.

22. See, especially, "Contradiction and Overdetermination," in Louis Althusser, *For Marx*, trans. Ben Brewster (New York: Pantheon Books, 1969).

23. Horkheimer, *Traditionelle und Kritische Theorie*, 214; Horkheimer, *Critical Theory*, 197.

24. I allude here to the German Ideology: "Die Ausgeburten ihres Kopfes sind ihnen über den Kopf gewachsen." See Karl Marx, "Die deutsche Ideologie" in *Werke*, 3:13. Even though the editors of this edition of Marx-Engels works are pushing a materialism inspired by Engels, this sentence seems to incite a different materialistic approach. The basic thrust is that what belongs properly to the mind or head has now grown outside of that original home.

25. Horkheimer, *Traditionelle und Kritische Theorie*, 227; Horkheimer, *Critical Theory*, 210.

26. While frequently, as, e.g., in Aristotle, the fundamental basis of rationality is the principle of non-contradiction, the law of excluded middle entails that principle and adds that, in addition to the impossibility of A=~A, there is no third possibility. I will return to this point in relation to Adorno.

27. Theodor Adorno, *Metaphysik: Begriff und Probleme,* ed. Rolf Tiedemann (Frankfurt: Suhrkamp, 1998), 35; Theodor Adorno, *Metaphysics: Concept and Problems*, ed. Rolf Tiedemann, trans. Edmund Jephcott (Stanford, CA: Stanford University Press, 2001), 20. This was a course Adorno gave while he was at work on *Negative Dialectics*. The latter part of the course deals with material found in "Meditations on Metaphysics" section of *Negative Dialectics*. The course begins with general remarks on metaphysics and then proceeds to a reading of Aristotle. While the material dealing with Aristotle does not appear in *Negative Dialectics*, it provides (1) an interesting example of the practice of "immanent critique" and (2) helpful background on the questions and issues that are operative in the closing section of *Negative Dialectics*.

28. Adorno, *Metaphysik*, 1:32–33; Adorno, *Metaphysics*, 18.

29. Adorno, *Metaphysik*, 1:45; Adorno, *Metaphysics*, 26.

30. Adorno, *Metaphysik*, 1:189; Adorno, *Metaphysics*, 121.

31. Adorno, *Metaphysik*, 1:200; Adorno, *Metaphysics*, 127.

32. Theodor Adorno, *Negative Dialektik* (hereafter cited as *ND*), in *Gesammelte Schriften*, ed. Rolf Tiedemann (Frankfurt am Main: Suhrkamp, 1970–1997), 6:397. The published English translation of *Negative Dialectics*—Theodor Adorno, *Negative Dialectics*, trans. E.B. Ashton (New York: Continuum, 1973)—is problematic on many grounds. I almost always prefer the translation of Redmond, which is readily available electronically: Theodor W. Adorno, *Negative Dialectics*, trans. Dennis Redmond, 2001, https://www.academia.edu/39707967/Negative_Dialectics. Since Redmond's translation is unpaginated, it is not readily citable. In what follows, I will cite the text as *ND*, followed by the reference to the Redmond translation and the Ashton translation. For this passage, the reference is Adorno, *ND* 397/ Redmond, part 3, 27/Ashton, 406.

33. Adorno, *Metaphysik*, 1:14; Adorno, *Metaphysics*, 4.

34. Adorno, *ND* 398/Redmond, part 3, 27/Ashton, 406.
35. Adorno, *ND* 367/Redmond, part 3, 9/Ashton, 374.
36. Adorno, *ND* 396/Redmond, part 3, 26/Ashton, 404.
37. Adorno, *ND* 192/Redmond, part 2, 32–33, Ashton, 191.
38. In Richard A. Lee Jr., *The Thought of Matter: Materialism, Conceptuality and the Transcendence of Immanence* (London: Rowman & Littlefield International, 2015), I define matter as that which is other than thought.
39. Adorno, *ND* 366/Redmond, part 3, 8–9/Ashton, 374.
40. Theodor Adorno, *Minima Moralia: Reflexionen aus dem beschädigten Leben*, in *Gesammelte Schriften*, 4:283; Theodor W. Adorno, *Minima Moralia: Reflections on a Damaged Life* (London: Verso, 2005), 274 (translation modified).
41. Adorno, *Minima Moralia: Reflexionen*, 4: 283; Adorno, *Minima Moralia: Reflections*, 274 (translation modified).

17

Critique as Melancholy Science

AMY ALLEN

1. Introduction

The closing aphorism of Adorno's *Minima Moralia*, entitled "Finale," opens with the following memorable passage:

> The only philosophy which can be responsibly practiced in face of despair is the attempt to contemplate all things as they would present themselves from the standpoint of redemption. Knowledge has no light but that shed on the world by redemption: all else is reconstruction, mere technique. Perspectives must be fashioned that displace and estrange the world, reveal it to be, with its rifts and crevices, as indigent and distorted as it will appear one day in the messianic light. To gain such perspectives without velleity or violence, entirely from felt contact with its objects—this alone is the task of thought.[1]

Here we have a striking image of critique as the fashioning of perspectives that reveal the rifts and crevices in the present, cracks through which the weak glimmer of a messianic light cast by the possibility of redemption may break through. This image is not only striking in and of itself, it is also strikingly similar to the image of critique offered by Michel Foucault when he describes his critical project as that of "following lines of fragility in the present" that enable us to see "why and how that which is might no longer be that which is," tracing the "kinds of virtual fracture which open up the space of freedom understood as a space of concrete freedom, that is, of possible transformation."[2] To be sure, Foucault doesn't go quite so far as to invoke the redemptive power of messianic light, however weak, but neither does Adorno commit himself to either the "reality or unreality of redemption itself."[3] What both seem to articulate is a shared vision of critique that is wholly immanent while at the same time, *because social reality itself is marked by cracks and fissures*, capable of attaining a kind of immanent transcendence. Critique, for Adorno as for Foucault, is itself a kind of practice that opens up a space of concrete freedom and glimpses a glimmer of the possibility of redemption by adopting, as Adorno has it, "a standpoint removed, even by a hair's breadth, from the scope of existence."[4]

This is far from the only striking affinity between Adorno's and Foucault's conceptions of critique. One can also find commonalities between their accounts of enlightenment rationality as entangled with domination, their deep and sustained critiques of Hegelian philosophies of history, their deployment of genealogical arguments in the service of problematizing of the present, and their thoroughgoing negativism, that is, their unwillingness to spell out a concrete positive image of utopia. These affinities are so striking and run so deep that they have led some scholars to contend that Adorno and Foucault defend if not exactly the same then at least largely overlapping and mutually reinforcing conceptions of critique.[5] However, some Adorno scholars have expressed reservations about how far and deep these affinities actually go, emphasizing what Karen Ng calls Adorno's critical naturalism and suggesting that this aspect of his thought is incompatible with Foucault's steadfast social constructionism and relentless historicization. As Ng argues, taking seriously Adorno's "critical naturalism" leads in the direction of the conclusion that there is a "divergence between Adorno and Foucault and their respective approaches to historical critique."[6]

These reservations form the backdrop and also the jumping-off point for this paper, which starts with a discussion of Adorno's critical naturalism, organized around his conception of natural history. The aim of that discussion will be to get a handle on what exactly his naturalism amounts to, how it informs his conception of critique, and whether or not it renders his conception of critique incompatible with Foucaultian genealogy. Let me emphasize that the question here is not whether or not Adorno and Foucault have exactly the same philosophical position—as far as I can tell, no one is suggesting that they do, or at least this is certainly not what I am suggesting. Rather, the question is whether or not Adorno's naturalism is incompatible with core Foucaultian commitments, such that his naturalism stands in the way of drawing on their combined insights to forge a conception of critique. The discussion of Adorno's conception of natural history will lead me to a consideration of the concept of transience that stands at its core, and this in turn will prompt some reflections on the distinctively psychoanalytic valence of Adorno's understanding of critique as melancholy science. Although this trajectory might seem to reinforce the argument for the incompatibility of Adornian and Foucaultian critique—especially in light of Foucault's well-documented ambivalence toward psychoanalysis—I will suggest in closing that this is not, in fact, the case.

2. Adorno's Conception of Natural History

In what sense is Adorno a naturalist? What does his naturalism amount to? And what kind of conception of critique does his naturalism imply or generate? In short, what is meant by characterizing Adorno's position, as Ng does, as a *critical* naturalism? As Ng herself acknowledges, the best way to approach these questions is by analyzing Adorno's conception of natural history, not only because this is where Adorno addresses these issues most directly, but also because, as Max Pensky has argued, "the concept of natural history is among the most persistent and influential theoretical structures in Adorno's work, rivalling (of course related intimately to) the concept of the dialectic itself."[7]

The professed aim of Adorno's 1932 lecture, "The Idea of Natural-History," is, as he puts it, "to dialectically overcome the usual antithesis of nature and history."[8] Starting from a provisional definition of nature as the static, fateful, predetermined being that underlies history and a provisional definition of history as the occurrence of the new, Adorno's stated goal is that of "pushing these concepts to a point where they are mediated in their apparent difference."[9] Later, in his *History and Freedom* lecture course, Adorno emphasizes that the mediation between nature and history that he seeks is not an external mediation, according to which history would be grounded in or viewed as an outgrowth of nature, for this understanding of the relationship between nature and history goes hand in hand with unfreedom.[10] Rather, he seeks an *internal* mediation between nature and history, though precisely what this means remains to be spelled out. As he puts it in a famous passage that is repeated in the *History and Freedom* lectures, the goal is "to comprehend historical being in its most extreme historical determinacy, where it is most historical, as natural being, or if it were possible to comprehend nature as a historical being where it seems to rest most deeply in itself as nature."[11] In his "Natural-History" lecture, Adorno first approaches this goal from the side of the "natural," through a critique of Heideggerian ontology; he then switches directions and takes up the discussion from the point of view of the historical, through a sympathetic reconstruction of the concept of second nature in Lukács and Benjamin. On the basis of these immanently critical readings of his philosophical contemporaries, Adorno then articulates his own conception of natural history.

The focus of Adorno's critique of Heidegger is the conception of historicity understood as a basic existential structure of *Dasein*. Reading historicity as the attempt to overcome the opposition between ontology or nature and history, Adorno claims that this attempt fails because it is unable to truly grasp the concreteness, particularity, and contingency of history, and thus it is unable ultimately to do justice to the historical.[12] As Adorno puts this point in his *History and Freedom* lectures, Heidegger offers an "ahistorical conception of history" in which history becomes "mutation as immutability."[13] "Thus," he continues, "to locate the concept of history in existence amounts paradoxically to an ontological inflation that does away with the concept of history by a sort of conjuring trick."[14] In other words, to attempt to think the interrelation of nature and history by transforming history into a natural (read: ontological) structure fails. The implication is that Adorno's conception of natural history, by contrast, will resist the temptation to think the mediation of nature and history by ontologizing or naturalizing history, rendering it as a fixed or immutable structure of reason, consciousness, or human existence. Instead, what is called for is a conception of history that remains deeply and thoroughly historical even as it attempts to understand historical being as natural being. This requires what Adorno calls a "concrete unity of nature and history" where the emphasis is on the concrete—that is, the contingent, particular, and historically specific.[15]

Adorno's reading of Lukács and Benjamin in the second section of the Natural History essay is much more sympathetic. Taking up the question of the relation between nature and history from the starting point of history, Adorno elaborates the concept of second nature found in Lukács's *Theory of the Novel*. Second nature refers to the totality of existing social structures or social reality that have been produced through a process of historical mediation but that have come to take on an appearance of naturalness and givenness.[16] As Adorno explains, "From the perspective of the philosophy of history the problem of how natural-history presents itself in the first place is the question of how it is possible to know and interpret this alienated, reified, dead world,"[17] that is, the world of second nature. Unlike in the case of Heidegger, then, where the point about the transmutation of nature into history is made negatively, through a critique of his hypostasized concept of history as historicity, Adorno credits Lukács with a positive insight into history's congealment into second nature.

At the core of Adorno's understanding of the convergence of history and nature is the Benjaminian notion of transience.[18] Adorno writes, "If Lukács demonstrates the retransformation of the historical, as that-which-has-been into nature, then here is the other side of the phenomenon: nature itself is seen as transitory nature, as history."[19] In other words, what Heidegger misses in his attempt to fix the ontological (natural) structure of human existence through the concept of historicity is precisely the transience of nature, thus of ontology itself: "Nature itself is transitory. Thus it includes the element of history."[20] Of course, Adorno being Adorno, he goes on to say immediately, "likewise the reverse: whenever 'second nature' appears, when the world of convention approaches, it can be deciphered in that its meaning is shown to be precisely its transience."[21] This dialectical reversal is central to Adorno's conception of natural history, which is articulated in the final section of the "Natural-History" essay. There he makes what he calls a "double turn" whereby "ontology is to be concretely and historically radicalized" and, simultaneously, "history itself in a sense presses toward an ontological turn."[22]

I'll come back to this dialectical reversal in a moment, but for now, I want to say a bit more about the notion of transience, since it will play a key role in my discussion later on. Adorno draws inspiration here from Walter Benjamin's discussion of transience in *The Origin of German Tragic Drama*. Benjamin had found in the Baroque German *Trauerspiel* a conception not of sacred history as a story of redemption but rather of natural history as a story of decay and loss. In the *Trauerspiel*, Benjamin wrote, "the word history stands written on the countenance of nature in the characters of transience. The allegorical physiognomy of the nature-history, which is put on stage in the *Trauerspiel*, is present in reality in the form of the ruin."[23] In other words, for Benjamin, history is itself an allegory of transience; it is an interpretation of the ruins of decay and loss that imbues that loss with meaning.[24] Thus, for Benjamin, and for Adorno, natural history has a melancholic structure; as Pensky has argued, it discloses the world as a "world of *loss*."[25] This disclosure of a world of loss is, in turn, related to Adorno's distinctive historical method, which, again following Benjamin, focuses on the fragments, the historical blind spots, and waste products of history. Transience, as Pensky explains, "entails . . . an insight of the historical process itself as generating only concrete, singular, and utterly empirical facts and bodies, each 'transient,' which is to say, incapable of being incorporated into a meaning-giving conception of historical continuity and historical experience."[26]

3. Natural History and Historical Ontology

Adorno claims that "natural history is not a synthesis of natural and historical methods, but a change of perspective."[27] But what sort of change of perspective does it involve? Pensky has argued, convincingly, I think, that Adorno's natural history concept is best understood as instantiating a distinctive critical-historiographical method: a methodology that, as Pensky puts it, "will no longer be beholden to the traditional idealistic versions of timeless nature and historical progress" and will also uncover how historical events "come to appear as the operations of nature."[28] In a similar vein, Tom Whyman argues that natural history essentially serves a "therapeutic function" for Adornian critical theory.[29] Adorno himself implies such a methodological or therapeutic reading when he claims that the program of natural history "is the transmutation of metaphysics into history. It secularizes metaphysics into the ultimate category of secularity, that of decay."[30] Reading nature through the lens of transience, natural history strips the categories of nature and ontology of their theological residue, that is, of their claims to timeless, ahistorical essences.[31] On this view, even nature is not "natural" if by "natural" we mean given, immutable, unchanging. The methodological function of natural history is, as Pensky explains, "to degrade or disrupt the appearance of what is 'given' in experience, insofar as what is given is in itself a reflection of a false totalization of the ensemble of social and material conditions specific to a given socio-economic constellation."[32] For Pensky, the methodological function of natural history is connected to the construction of constellations. Both ways of construing Adornian critical method entail the deployment of fragments, particularities, and concrete contingencies against totalizing narratives of historical progress; natural-historical constellations light up social reality in a new way, disclosing hitherto occluded aspects of experience, and disrupting false totalizations.[33] In this way, Adorno connects "the recovery of the singular, the historically contingent, and the transient" with "the broader aims of unmasking critique."[34]

When read in this methodological or therapeutic way, Adorno's natural history concept ultimately seems to put more weight on the side of history, his professed aim to uncover the internal mediation of nature and history notwithstanding. The concept of transience reveals that nature is (always?) already historical. There is no immutability or timelessness or unchanging essentiality to be found in nature, except—paradoxically—its tendency toward transient decay and loss. The concept of second nature reveals that what appears to us in social reality as natural in the sense of necessary, immutable, or unchangeable is in fact the petrified remains of historical mediations. In other words, the natural is historical and the historical has a tendency to come to seem natural but they are both in fact historical. Adorno seems to admit as much in his lectures on *History and Freedom*: "if we are to speak of priorities here," he says, "then precedence is to be given to society, to the historical sphere."[35] In other words, the weight of Adorno's discussion of natural history, especially if this is interpreted methodologically as a critical-historiographical concept, seems to land on the side of history. This goes some way, I think, toward addressing the worry that Adorno's critical naturalism renders his thought incompatible with that of Foucault, whose commitment to social constructionism would seem to make him wary of any and all invocations of the natural. As Whyman helpfully explains (though without drawing the connection to Foucault), the methodological perspective of natural history does not entitle us to "reach beyond agnosticism about how these things ultimately are, whether the phenomena under investigation really are (in the final analysis) 'natural' or 'historical' or (more broadly than this) precisely how 'nature' and 'history' *as such* are interwoven."[36] Natural history is thus a thoroughly critical concept in the Kantian sense of that term.

Indeed, I would go further than this and argue that there are significant affinities between Adorno's natural history concept and Foucault's notion of historical ontology—a notion that I read as a descendent of his earlier conception of the historical *a priori*.[37] Recall that there are (naturally) two sides of the dialectical reversal at the heart of Adorno's conception of natural history: natural history involves both the radical historicization of ontology ("ontology is to be concretely and historically radicalized") and an ontological turn in history ("history itself in a sense presses toward an ontological turn"). Although Adorno says explicitly that this does not imply a kind of historical ontology, he has in mind here a very different conception of historical ontology than the one deployed by Foucault. Adorno's model for historical ontology is Dilthey, and his critique of this model follows the same outlines as the critique of Heidegger. Dilthey is accused of hypostasizing historical elements ontologically, using them to construct a totalizing intellectual historical picture of the sense of the age, thus failing to take facticity and material reality seriously.[38] Given Foucault's well-known critique of intellectual history, elaborated repeatedly throughout his early work, it is difficult to imagine this criticism applying to him; hence it would be a mistake to read Adorno's critique of historical ontology as neatly extending to Foucault's use of this term. Indeed, in the course of elaborating his conception of the historical *a priori* in *The Archaeology of Knowledge*, Foucault offers a critique of Heidegger that strongly echoes Adorno's critique of Dilthey and Heidegger in the Natural History essay. Foucault describes *Dasein* (obliquely) as "a subjectivity that always lags behind manifest history; and which finds, beneath events, another, more serious, more secret, more fundamental history, closer to the origin, more firmly linked to its ultimate horizon (and consequently more in control of all its determinations)."[39] Here Foucault delineates his understanding of the historical *a priori* in opposition to a totalizing conception of history that hypostasizes historical events. The historical *a priori*, by contrast, like Adorno's natural history concept, is understood positively as "the locus of particular events, regularities, relationships, modifications and systemic transformations,"[40] that is, as the domain of the concrete, the contingent, and the historically specific.

Moreover, although Foucault was surely no fan of dialectical thinking—perhaps because he associated this term solely with Hegelian dialectics rather than with Adornian negative dialectics—it is difficult to deny that the notion of the historical *a priori* has a certain (negative) dialectical ring to it. Even Foucault himself noted that "juxtaposed these two words produce a rather startling effect."[41] Not unlike the natural history concept, the historical *a priori* suggests a complicated double movement whereby the *a priori* conditions of possibility for experience are historicized and concrete historical conditions simultaneously congeal into quasi-transcendental structures. As historical, the historical *a priori* sets contingent conditions of possibility for thought in a particular time and place; as Foucault puts it, "there is nothing more tentative, more empirical (superficially at least) than the process of establishing order among things."[42] But as *a priori*, those conditions of possibility are necessary in the sense that they are binding on us whether we want them to be or not; we can only reject them at the risk of being rendered unintelligible within our socially, culturally, and historically specific context.[43] Thus, Foucault's historical *a priori*, like Adorno's natural history concept, can be understood as both concretely and radically historicizing ontology—by showing how social reality understood as the conditions of possibility for thought, experience, and action is historically constituted—while simultaneously pressing history toward an ontological turn—by tracing the coalescing of concrete, discrete, discontinuous historical elements into a system of thought and practice that carries with it a quasi-transcendental necessity.

When read in this critical-methodological light, Adorno's natural history concept seems not only compatible with but even closely related to Foucault's notion of the historical *a priori*. As I've argued elsewhere, although Foucault largely drops this term from his critical vocabulary after his early, archaeological period, what we might call the historical *a priori* concept remains central to his conception of critique throughout his work.[44] Thus, it would seem that Adorno's critical naturalism as instantiated in his natural history concept, far from being incompatible with Foucaultian historical ontology, can in fact be read as offering a closely related conception of critique.[45]

However, unfortunately for me, I suppose, matters aren't quite so simple. After all, there is another way that Adorno takes up the thought that history is natural, beyond the notion of second nature. For throughout his work he also offers a story about how the drive for self-preservation, construed as "natural" in some sense, shapes the historical unfolding of the dialectic of enlightenment. Indeed, the drive for self-preservation is implicitly invoked in the memorable opening lines of the *Dialectic of Enlightenment*: "Enlightenment . . . has always aimed at liberating human beings from fear and installing them as masters. Yet the wholly enlightened earth is radiant with triumphant calamity."[46] It is our drive for self-preservation that compels us to attempt to ward off fear through ever-increasing mastery and control of inner and outer nature, and it is this drive that propels the development from magic to myth to enlightenment.[47] On Adorno's story, the drive for self-preservation also gives rise to the specific form of conceptuality or rationality that holds sway in identity thinking. As Adorno puts it in *Negative Dialectics*, "Every content of individual consciousness is brought to it by its carrier for the sake of his self-preservation, and is reproduced along with that self-preservation."[48] Moreover, the drive for self-preservation has run amok in late capitalism, perpetuating a society predicated on the absorption of the individual into a totalizing system of cold, calculated exchange relations that are rendered palatable by the machinations of the culture industry. Not only this: for Adorno, the social realization of the drive for self-preservation has, ironically, brought us to the brink of species-wide self-annihilation; it is, as Deborah Cook reminds us, self-preservation that provides the backbone of the negative universal history that connects the slingshot to the megaton bomb.[49]

In a similar vein, we might also consider Adorno's more positive emphasis on the somatic impulse as a resource for morality. One of the crucial points in Adorno's critique of Kant is that the latter associates moral freedom with rational autonomy, and thus with a process of "ruthless rationalization," where Adorno links it to the somatic impulse, examples of which include "naked physical fear" or "solidarity with what Brecht called 'tormentable bodies.'"[50] The contrast between Kant's rationalistic conception of morality and Adorno's bodily, somatic one culminates in the famous line that ends his critique of Kant in *Negative Dialectics*: "the individual is left with no more than the morality for which Kantian ethics . . . can muster only disdain: to try to live so that one may believe himself to have been a good animal."[51] As Christoph Menke explicates this passage, "The action stemming from a feeling of solidarity is the action of a 'good animal'—of a subject that does not separate itself from its 'forces' or 'impulses' for the sake of following the law and in order to make itself freed from them but rather whose freedom, indeed, whose very strength, consists in allowing its forces or impulses to express themselves."[52] I think it is fair to say that Adorno's argument about the role of the drive for self-preservation in the historical emergence of structures of rationality, which is deeply bound up with his appropriation of Freudian psychoanalysis, goes beyond anything that Foucault himself argued (at least as far as I'm aware). But is this account of the "natural" basis of the historical dialectic of enlightenment incompatible with basic Foucaultian-genealogical commitments?[53] At stake here is the broader question of whether or not Foucaultian genealogy is compatible with some version of (psychoanalytic) drive theory. An examination of that question is clearly beyond the scope of this paper, however, here I'd like to note two points that at least suggest that this issue need not be a deal-breaker.[54] First, given what has already been said about Adorno's natural history concept, and in light of Adorno's well-known commitment to deploying Freudian psychoanalytic concepts by historicizing them, the claim to the "naturalness" of the drive for self-preservation has to be understood in a very precise way. However we interpret this drive, it clearly cannot be read as an immutable, timeless, unchangeable force standing outside of history. As we have already seen, that's just not what "nature" or "the natural" means for Adorno. As Jay Bernstein explains, Adorno "always conceives of nature . . . as not an atemporal system of lawful regularities . . . but as in themselves historical," which means that even if, for Adorno, "history is . . . a part of nature and a 'natural outgrowth' from it," it is also the case that "nature . . . is other than the law-governed whole it is depicted to be."[55]

Second, on the flip side, there is a way of reading Foucault according to which the notion of drive—understood in a Nietzschean sense—is central to his conception of subjectivity. As Mark Kelly puts it, "from what is the individual fabricated? The answer is simple and obvious, given Foucault's Nietzschean political ontology: it is made from the animal existence and drives that precede the existence of the individual."[56] This, of course, sounds remarkably close to Menke's gloss on Adorno's point about striving to be a good animal, where this means an animal whose freedom and strength are functions of the organized self-expression of its forces and impulses. Building on this point, Cook suggests that Foucault's conception of resistance would be impossible if he did not presuppose something—some drives, capacities, or instincts—within individuals that escapes total absorption into dispositifs of power-knowledge.[57] Taken together, these two points suggest that even this stronger construal of Adornian naturalism need not be incompatible with Foucault's genealogical project.

4. Critique as Melancholy Science

In his *History and Freedom* lectures, Adorno explains the significance of transience for his conception of philosophy as interpretation. Transience, he claims, points "to the fact that interpretation presupposes the decay of [philosophical] systems."[58] Whatever truth those systems may once have contained has now "retreated into the details, into the individual parts of the system."[59] Philosophy as interpretation is a method of critique that emerges in the wake of this decay, which means that it is a critical method tailored to a philosophical landscape marked by the collapse of grand philosophical systems. As such, it is a conception of critique founded on an experience of loss. Indeed, Adorno argues that most contemporary philosophical concepts have the resonance that they have in virtue of the fact that the "underlying substance" to which they refer has been lost; the metaphysics of time, for example, has emerged as a concern in response to an experience of the loss of time.[60] As Adorno puts it, "The emptier of meaning existing reality appears today, the greater the pressure or the desire to interpret it and to have done with this meaninglessness. The light that is kindled in the phenomena as they fragment, disintegrate and fly apart is the only source of hope that can set philosophy alight."[61] Here Adorno invokes the idea of philosophy as interpretation that he derives from his reading of the Benjaminian notion of constellations in his early programmatic essay "The Actuality of Philosophy."[62] In that essay, Adorno distinguishes his vision of philosophy as interpretation from hermeneutic accounts of interpretation predicated on the attempt to discern the meaning that lies behind perceptible reality. For Adorno, there is no meaning underlying perceptible reality. Indeed, reality appears to us as a riddle precisely because we are looking for a meaning where there is no meaning to be found. The task of philosophy is thus "to interpret unintentional reality."[63] This is accomplished through the construction of constellations that "fall into a figure which can be read as an answer, while at the same time the question disappears."[64] In other words, "the point of interpretive philosophy is to construct keys, before which reality springs open."[65] Since there is no meaning underlying the reality that constellations interpret, the legitimacy of interpretations can only be secured by "the fact that reality crystallizes about them in striking conclusiveness."[66]

Already implicit here is a point that is brought out more clearly in the *History and Freedom* lectures, which is that philosophy as the construction of interpretive constellations is a specific—and, we might venture to add, specifically modern—response to an experience of loss, fragmentation, and meaninglessness. Highlighting this feature of Adorno's conception of critique, a feature that falls out of his understanding of transience, gives us, I think, a new way of understanding what Adorno means when he refers to the work of critique as a melancholy science. This claim, which famously opens the dedication to *Minima Moralia*, is typically interpreted as an inversion of the Nietzschean gay science. Thus, Gillian Rose opens her influential introduction to Adorno's work, which uses this memorable phrase for its title, this way: " 'The melancholy science' which this book expounds is not a pessimistic science. By introducing *Minima Moralia* as an offering from his 'melancholy science'—an inversion of Nietzsche's 'joyful science'—Adorno undermines and inverts the sanguine and total claims of philosophy and sociology, and rejects any dichotomy such as optimistic/pessimistic for it implies an inherently fixed and static view."[67] Rose is one of Adorno's most perceptive readers, and there is certainly ample textual support for this reading of the phrase "melancholy science," insofar as *Minima Moralia* simultaneously mimics Nietzsche's signature aphoristic style while taking critical aim at his affirmation of life.[68] Thus without denying that this is an important component of Adorno's understanding of critique as melancholy science, I want to suggest that our discussion of the crucial role of transience in Adorno's natural history concept reveals an additional, distinctly psychoanalytic valence to this conception of critique, a valence that comes into view when we interrogate in what precise sense the melancholy science is *melancholy*. Rose is correct, I think, to note that melancholy here does not signal pessimistic, nor is it equivalent to sadness or depression (though there is no denying that both of these are typical affective responses to the text). But what the Nietzschean reading of this phrase fails to highlight is the sense in which critique is the melancholy science because it arises in response to an experience of *loss*.

To bring out this connection, I'd like to return to the notion of transience that forms the core of Adorno's natural history concept. While Benjamin is no doubt the direct inspiration for his discussion of transience, Adorno's distinctively and more resolutely secularized version of this concept can also be fruitfully read alongside Freud's essay "On Transience."[69] This short, evocative essay opens with Freud's recollection of a walk in the countryside with a young poet. The poet admired the beauty of the countryside but reported that he could feel no joy in that beauty because he knew that it was doomed to decay. As Freud put is, "All that he would otherwise have loved and admired seemed to him to be shorn of its worth by the transience which was its doom."[70] Freud judged the poet's "aching despondency," though perhaps better than the flat refusal to believe in the transience of all things, still to be an immature response: why, after all, should the transience of the beauty of nature—or of anything—imply any loss in its value?[71] Shouldn't our awareness of transience rather increase the value and worth of the beautiful, by underscoring its scarcity and fragility? Perhaps not surprisingly, Freud's inability to convince the young poet of this point led him to suspect that "some powerful emotional factor was at work which was disturbing [his] judgment" and he surmised that this factor was "a revolt . . . against mourning."[72] The idea of transience gave the poet a "foretaste of mourning over its decease" that he found painful and in the face of which he was recoiling.[73]

At the close of this short essay, Freud notes that his conversation with the poet took place in the summer before the outbreak of World War I. "A year later," he writes, "the war broke out and robbed the world of its beauties. It destroyed not only the beauty of the country-sides through which it passed and the works of art which it met with on its path but it also shattered our pride in the achievements of our civilization."[74] But did it thereby deprive these things of their worth and value to us? Those who think so, Freud argued, were simply stuck in a state of mourning over what they had lost.[75] They had not yet learned how to work through their loss and reinvest their psychic energy in the world, that is, to transform mourning into a productive form of melancholia that Freud later came to understand as central to the formation of all psychic structure.[76] Although the overriding theme of Freud's discussion of transience is resignation—the importance of resigning ourselves to the fact that "what is painful may none the less be true"[77]—Freud nonetheless ends this essay on a hopeful note: "when once the mourning is over, it will be found that our high opinion of the riches of civilization has lost nothing from our discovery of their fragility. We shall build up again all that war has destroyed, and perhaps on firmer ground and more lastingly than before."[78]

As Joel Whitebook argues in his fascinating intellectual biography of Freud, the main claim of this short essay is that "transience and thereby loss" are "essential constituents of human reality."[79] The flip side of this claim is that the desire for transcendence and immortality is an infantile wish, an expression of the pleasure principle that willfully denies the painful inexorability of reality.[80] The mature response to loss—including the loss characterized by the fragmentation, disenchantment, and meaninglessness that accompany the rise of the modern scientific, secular worldview—is to "learn to invest to the fullest in the world despite its lack of objective meaning and the ubiquity of loss."[81] Thus, the ability to mourn successfully—that is, the ability to work through loss and reinvest in the world of objects—is the condition of possibility for living a fulfilled life.[82] This does not mean that we should engage in a manic celebration of transience and loss, which would be another way of denying the pain that it entails;[83] rather, the idea is to transform mourning and loss into occasions for growth and creativity.

Freud thus uses the notion of transience to make a point about the quest for the transcendent or the eternal, a quest that he views as psychologically suspect. As such, his use of the term fits well with Adorno's resolutely secular use of this term. Adorno, after all, famously prefaced his

Metacritique of Epistemology with the fragment from Epicharmus: "Mortals must think mortal thoughts, and not immortal ones."[84] Freud also lays down a challenge here: if transience, loss, death, and decay are essential constituents of human experience, then they are not only core components of the reality principle to which the psyche must yield but also in the face of which the individual must strive to create a meaningful and fulfilling life. The Adornian conception of critique should likewise be understood as a demand to resign ourselves to the painful reality of transience without giving in to a conservative temptation to wallow in despair.[85] As Adorno puts it, critique "represents something like a secularization of melancholy"—not a melancholy that "remains stuck fast in an unhappy consciousness" but rather one that "exteriorizes itself as a critique of existing phenomena."[86] To say that critique is a melancholy science is thus to say that critique resigns itself to the phenomenon of transience while resolving to construct meaning out of the decaying fragments that transience leaves in its wake.

5. Conclusion

Following Whitebook, then, I suggest that we read Adorno's melancholic conception of critique as the attempt to offer a constructive response to an experience of loss, to metabolize that loss by turning it not into psychic structure but rather into interpretive, critical philosophical insight. Critique in Adorno's sense is born of an experience of loss and it is an attempt to make meaning in the face of that loss, and this is crucial to understanding what it means to say that it is a *melancholy* science. Adorno's melancholic interpretation of the transience of nature is indeed a form of critical naturalism, as Ng and others have insisted, but, as I argued above, this critical naturalism is at the same time essentially historical.[87] Thus, not only is his critical naturalism *not* incompatible with a Foucaultian conception of critique, it bears interesting and heretofore underappreciated similarities to Foucault's notions of historical ontology and the historical *a priori*.

For Adorno, insofar as the "philosophical possession of the totality" "has now ceased to be philosophy," what remains is an "unreserved immersion in the individual, specific detail."[88] Precisely this unreserved immersion in the individual, specific detail finds its fullest expression in Adorno's *Minima Moralia*. But even the immersion in the micrological analysis of subjective experience that structures the aphoristic methodology of that book emerges explicitly as a response to the loss of individual subjectivity increasingly accomplished by the totalizing forces of late capitalist modernity. Thus, Adorno writes, "In the period of his decay, the individual's experience of himself and what he encounters contributes once more to knowledge, which he has merely obscured as long as he continued unshaken to construe himself positively as the dominant category."[89] In the face of the hyperbolic declaration of the end of the individual, the immersion in private, individual, subjective experience becomes a response not only to the decay of philosophical systems (which are unable to shed critical light on the present because of the ways in which they are bound up with its logic of totalization) but also to the disappearance of the subject itself. Although this approach may run the risk of devolving into a "sentimental and anachronistic . . . lament over the course of the world," critique lingers in the realm of individual experience "not only with a bad conscience."[90] Instead, it interprets the fragments of subjective experience that remain in the wake of the dissolution of philosophical systems and the absorption of the subjectivity into abstract, totalizing social forms. Resigned to the acceptance of transience and the inherent meaninglessness of reality, critique nonetheless makes meaning by gathering these fragments together into constellations that light up social reality in new, strikingly conclusive, ways.

Although I have endeavored to highlight the similarities between Adorno's natural history concept and Foucault's historical *a priori*, the ensuing discussion of critique as melancholy science might seem to have taken us far afield of Foucault. To be sure, the Adornian invocation of transience as a disclosure of loss and of critique as a melancholy science is strikingly distinct from Foucault's critical method. Although Foucault was certainly interested, at least in his early work, in the experience of the collapse of a historical *a priori* and its giving way to a something else, he tended not to focus on the experience of *loss* produced by such collapse. As Christopher Falzon puts this point, for Foucault, "every human arrangement is historical and finite; it has emerged at a particular time and is also destined to pass away, to be transformed. Nor does this simply amount to a loss, a melancholy realization that everything we value and which defines us is doomed to disappear. Rather it opens up a whole range of possibilities."[91] While this might suggest a point of divergence between Foucault's and Adorno's conceptions of critique—with Foucault adopting a more straightforwardly Nietzschean approach in contrast to Adorno's inverted Nietzscheanism—we might yet wonder who is a better and more consistent practitioner of what Adorno calls philosophy as interpretation than Foucault, especially in his masterworks of genealogy? Digging through the archives, Foucault recovers historical fragments, blind spots, and waste products, the forgotten voices of individuals whose lives have been all but erased by official history, assembling them into constellations that light up social reality in strikingly conclusive ways. Indeed, Foucault may be an even more consistent practitioner of this method than Adorno himself, who, with the notable exception of *Minima Moralia*, tended more to talk about this method in abstract (sometimes incomprehensible) terms rather than simply to practice it.

Notes

1. Theodor Adorno, *Minima Moralia: Reflections on a Damaged Life*, trans. E.F.N. Jephcott (London: Verso, 2005), 247.

2. Michel Foucault, "Structuralism and Post-Structuralism," in *Essential Works of Michel Foucault*, vol. 2, *Aesthetics, Method, and Epistemology*, ed. James D. Faubion (New York: The New Press, 1998), 449–450.

3. Adorno, *Minima Moralia*, 247.

4. Ibid. This is not to say that Foucault and Adorno agree in their assessments of the value of political praxis and its relationship to theory, nor is it to endorse a strong view of the role of theory in generating political transformation. It is just to say that both view "theory"—understood as a philosophical practice of critique—as itself a kind of practice that can have transformative effects. For further discussion of this point, see my response to Guilel Treiber in Amy Allen, "The Ends of Progress: Reply to Critics," *Contemporary Political Theory* (2018).

5. I made an argument to this effect in Amy Allen, *The End of Progress: Decolonizing the Normative Foundations of Critical Theory* (New York: Columbia University Press, 2016), ch. 5. But see also the more detailed and systematic treatment in Deborah Cook, *Adorno, Foucault, and the Critique of the West* (London: Verso, 2018).

6. Karen Ng, "Back to Adorno: Critical Theory's Problem of Normative Grounding," in *The Challenge of Progress: Theory Between Critique and Ideology*, edited by Harry F. Dahms (Bingley, UK: Emerald Publishing, 2019). For distinct but related worries, see Jay Bernstein, "What Do We Owe Other People? On Amy Allen's *The End of Progress*," *Berlin Journal of Critical Theory* 2, no. 2 (2018), 131–148; and Rocío Zambrana, "Dialectics of Progress," *Philosophy Today* 61, no. 4 (2017), 1047–1057.

7. Max Pensky, "Natural History: The Life and Afterlife of a Concept in Adorno," *Critical Horizons* 5, no. 1 (2004), 228.

8. Theodor Adorno, "The Idea of Natural-History," in Robert Hullot-Kentor, *Things Beyond Resemblance: Collected Essays on Theodor W. Adorno* (New York: Columbia University Press, 2006), 252.

9. Adorno, "The Idea of Natural-History," 252–253.

10. Theodor Adorno, *History and Freedom: Lectures 1964–1965*, ed. Rolf Tiedemann, trans. Rodney Livingstone (Cambridge: Polity Press, 2006), 116–117.

11. Adorno, "The Idea of Natural-History," 260.

12. Perhaps confusingly, Adorno equates the question of ontology with that of nature: "For the question of ontology, as it is formulated as present, is none other than what I mean by 'nature'" (Adorno, "The Idea of Natural-History," 253). I address the possibility of reading Adorno's natural history concept as a version of *historical* ontology below.

13. Adorno, *History and Freedom*, 123.

14. Ibid.

15. Adorno, "The Idea of Natural-History," 259.

16. Adorno, *History and Freedom*, 120–121.

17. Adorno, "The Idea of Natural-History," 261.

18. For an illuminating discussion of this point, see Pensky, "Natural History," 233.

19. Adorno, "The Idea of Natural-History," 262.

20. Ibid., 264.

21. Ibid.

22. Ibid., 265.

23. Walter Benjamin, *The Origin of German Tragic Drama*, trans. John Osborne (London: Verso Books, 2003), 177. For helpful discussion, see Beatrice Hanssen, *Walter Benjamin's Other History: Of Stones, Animals, Human Beings, and Angels* (Berkeley: University of California Press, 1998).

24. I'm grateful to Benjamin Randolph for this helpful formulation.

25. Pensky, "Natural History," 234. On the importance of melancholia in Benjamin, see Max Pensky, *Melancholy Dialectics: Walter Benjamin and the Play of Mourning* (Amherst, MA: University of Massachusetts Press, 1993).

26. Pensky, "Natural History," 234.

27. Adorno, "The Idea of Natural-History," 261.

28. Pensky, "Natural History," 231. Yannik Thiem makes a similar argument about Benjamin's development of the notion of transience; see for example Thiem, "Benjamin's Messianic Metaphysics of Transience," in *Walter Benjamin and Theology*, ed. Colby Dickinson and Stéphane Symons (New York: Fordham University Press, 2016), 38–40.

29. Tom Whyman, "Understanding Adorno on 'Natural-History,'" *International Journal of Philosophical Studies* 24, no. 4 (2016), 453.

30. Adorno, *History and Freedom*, 126.

31. For helpful discussion of this point, see Whyman, "Understanding Adorno on 'Natural-History,'" 458.

32. Pensky, "Natural History," 231. For a similar reading, see Whyman, "Understanding Adorno on 'Natural-History,'" 465–469.

33. Pensky, "Natural History," 234.

34. Ibid., 235.

35. Adorno, *History and Freedom*, 122.

36. Whyman, "Understanding Adorno on 'Natural-History,'" 467.

37. Foucault himself noted these affinities in general terms when he aligned his approach to critique understood as "a form of ontology of the present, of present reality, an ontology of modernity, an ontology of ourselves" with a lineage that extends from "Hegel to the Frankfurt School, passing through Nietzsche, Max Weber, and so on." See Michel Foucault, *The Government of Self and Others: Lectures at the Collège de France 1982–83*, ed. Frédéric Gros, trans. Graham Burchell (New York: Picador Press, 2011), 21. Thanks to Daniel Rodriguez-Navas for calling my attention to this passage.

38. Adorno, "The Idea of Natural-History," 265.

39. Michel Foucault, *The Archaeology of Knowledge and the Discourse on Language*, trans. A.M. Sheridan Smith (New York: Pantheon Books, 1972), 121.

40. Ibid., 121.

41. Ibid., 127.

42. Michel Foucault, *The Order of Things: An Archaeology of the Human Sciences*, trans. A. M. Sheridan Smith (New York: Pantheon Books, 1970), 250.

43. On this point, see Amy Allen, *The Politics of Ourselves: Power, Autonomy, and Gender in Contemporary Critical Theory* (New York: Columbia University Press, 2008), 33.

44. Although the term "historical a priori" more or less disappears from Foucault's work after his early archeological period, in his late work, Foucault deploys the closely related notion of historical ontology as a way of characterizing his distinctive historico-philosophical method. For example, in "What is Enlightenment?" Foucault characterizes his overall critical project as a "historical ontology of ourselves" that entails an investigation into conditions of possibility for experience that have been historical constituted so as to appear natural and necessary. Michel Foucault, "What is Enlightenment?" in *Essential Works of Michel Foucault*, vol. 1, *Ethics: Subjectivity and Truth*, ed. Paul Rabinow (New York: The New Press, 1997), 315–316. I discuss the importance of the historical *a priori* for Foucault's overall conception of critique in Amy Allen, "'Psychoanalysis and Ethnology' Reconsidered: Foucault's Historicization of History," *Southern Journal of Philosophy* 55, Spindel Supplement (2017), 31–46.

45. Deborah Cook makes some related observations about the similarities between Adorno's and Foucault's conceptions of critique, though without discussing

either Adorno's natural history concept or Foucault's historical *a priori* specifically. See Cook, "Adorno, Foucault, and Critique," *Philosophy and Social Criticism* 39, no. 10 (2013), 965–981.

46. Max Horkheimer and Theodor Adorno, *Dialectic of Enlightenment: Philosophical Fragments*, trans. Edmund Jephcott (Stanford, CA: Stanford University Press, 2002), 1.

47. For helpful discussion of the role of self-preservation in the dialectic of enlightenment, see Owen Hulatt, "Reason, Mimesis, and Self-Preservation in Adorno," *Journal of the History of Philosophy* 54, no. 1 (2016), 135–151, esp. 141.

48. Theodor Adorno, *Negative Dialectics*, trans. E.B. Ashton (New York: Continuum, 2006), 46. For further discussion of the role of self-preservation in the generation of conceptuality, see Hulatt, "Reason, Mimesis, and Self-Preservation in Adorno," 135–151.

49. Cook, "Adorno, Foucault, and Critique," 967. See Adorno, *Negative Dialectics*, 320.

50. Adorno, *Negative Dialectics*, 286.

51. Ibid., 299.

52. Christoph Menke, "Genealogy and Critique: Two Forms of Ethical Questioning of Morality," in *The Cambridge Companion to Adorno*, ed. Thomas Huhn (Cambridge: Cambridge University Press, 2004), 320.

53. One could go even further and argue that the argument of *Dialectic of Enlightenment* should be read as presenting not a negative teleology but rather a genealogical argument *à la* Foucault. For this reading, see Natalia Baeza, *Contradiction, Critique, and Dialectic in Adorno* (PhD diss., University of Notre Dame, 2012), ch. 6.

54. I discuss Foucault's relationship to psychoanalysis in more detail in Amy Allen, "Foucault and the Problem of Psychoanalysis: Two Aspects of Problematization," *Angelaki* 23, no. 2 (2018), 170–186.

55. J. M. Bernstein, *Adorno: Disenchantment and Ethics* (Cambridge: Cambridge University Press, 2001), 189. On this point, see also Cook, "Adorno, Foucault, and Critique," 970.

56. Mark Kelly, *The Political Philosophy of Michel Foucault* (New York: Routledge, 2009), 96. For related discussion, see Deborah Cook, "Foucault, Freud, and the Repressive Hypothesis," *Journal of the British Society for Phenomenology* 45, no. 2 (2014), 155.

57. See Cook, "Adorno, Foucault, and Critique," 969.

58. Adorno, *History and Freedom*, 127.

59. Ibid.

60. Ibid., 128.

61. Ibid., 129.

62. Theodor Adorno, "The Actuality of Philosophy," *Telos* 31 (1977), 120–133.

63. Ibid., 127.

64. Ibid.

65. Ibid., 130.
66. Ibid., 131.
67. Gillian Rose, *The Melancholy Science: An Introduction to the Thought of Theodor W. Adorno* (London: Verso, 2014), ix. For further discussion of the relationship between Adorno and Nietzsche, see Rose, *The Melancholy Science*, ch. 2, and Menke, "Genealogy and Critique," 304ff. See also Bernstein, *Adorno: Disenchantment and Ethics*, 40–41.
68. On this point, see Rose, *The Melancholy Science*, 32.
69. For discussion of the theological and messianic aspects of Benjamin's notion of transience, see Thiem, "Benjamin's Messianic Metaphysics of Transience," 21–55, and Pensky, *Melancholy Dialectics*, 127ff. Beatrice Hanssen notes the similarities between Benjamin's and Freud's discussions of transience in Hanssen, *Walter Benjamin's Other History*, 177n2. I am not suggesting that Adorno had Freud's discussion of transience in mind when he was working on his "Natural-History" essay—though of course Adorno knew Freud's work thoroughly, having written his first attempted *Habilitationschrift* on Kant and Freud, and implicit references to Freud are scattered throughout his work. What I am suggesting is that Adorno's use of this term could helpfully be read in a Freudian light.
70. Sigmund Freud, "On Transience," in *The Standard Edition of the Complete Psychological Writings of Sigmund Freud*, ed. James Strachey (London: Hogarth Press, 1960), 14:305.
71. See Freud, "On Transience," 14:305.
72. Ibid., 14:306.
73. Ibid.
74. Ibid., 14:307.
75. Ibid.
76. Whereas Freud had earlier understood melancholia as a failure or inability to mourn, he later came to understand it as a process of incorporating lost love objects that is key to the formation of psychic structure. For the former view, see Freud, "Mourning and Melancholia," in *The Standard Edition of the Complete Psychological Writings of Sigmund Freud*, 14:243–258. For the latter view, see Freud, "The Ego and the Id," in *The Standard Edition of the Complete Psychological Writings of Sigmund Freud*, 19:28–30.
77. Freud, "On Transience," 14:305.
78. Ibid., 14:307.
79. Joel Whitebook, *Freud: An Intellectual Biography* (Cambridge: Cambridge University Press, 2017), 332.
80. Freud, "On Transience," 14:306.
81. Whitebook, *Freud*, 333.
82. Note this is very similar to Thiem's interpretation of Benjamin's use of the term "transience"; see Thiem, "Benjamin's Messianic Metaphysics of Transience," 21–55.

83. See Whitebook, *Freud*, 337.

84. See Theodor Adorno, *Lectures on Negative Dialectics: Fragments of a Lecture Course, 1965/1966*, ed. Rolf Tiedemann, trans. Rodney Livingstone (Cambridge: Polity Press, 2008), 80. As Tom Whyman helpfully explains, "when philosophy attempts to do anything more than that—that is, to state something as it exists essentially and ahistorically—this can only amount to thought's 'naïve hypostasis of its own finiteness.'" See Tom Whyman, "Understanding Adorno on 'Natural-History,'" 456.

85. On this point, see Adorno, *History and Freedom*, 158–160. However, for a compelling reading of Adorno that highlights the critical and political potential of despair, see Robyn Marasco, *The Highway of Despair: Critical Theory after Hegel* (New York: Columbia University Press, 2015).

86. Adorno, *History and Freedom*, 134.

87. Thanks again to Benjamin Randolph for this helpful formulation, and to illuminating discussion of these and other issues in Adorno interpretation.

88. Adorno, *History and Freedom*, 129.

89. Adorno, *Minima Moralia*, 17–18.

90. Ibid., 16, 18.

91. Christopher Falzon, "Making History," in *Companion to Michel Foucault*, ed. Christopher Falzon, Timothy O'Leary, and Jana Sawicki (London: Blackwell, 2013), 283.

18

Reality and Resistance

Habermas and Haslanger on Objectivity, Social Critique, and the Possibility of Change

FEDERICA GREGORATTO

1. Introduction

In this chapter, I reconstruct and compare Jürgen Habermas's and Sally Haslanger's contributions to critical social theory.[1] Habermas and Haslanger might seem, at a first glance, like an odd philosophical couple: Habermas's theoretical profile developed, in the '60s and '70s, in close contact with the Frankfurt School. But since the publication of his *Theory of Communicative Action* (1981), he has largely abandoned the Hegelian-Marxist project of an immanent critique of society.[2] Instead, he has committed himself to the Kantian project of reconstructing the normative foundations of the political, social, and cultural orders.[3] Haslanger, for her part, was trained and began her philosophical career as a metaphysician broadly affiliated with the tradition of Quinean naturalism.[4] Lately, however, she has drawn closer to critical theory, taking a special interest in ideology critique.[5] Habermas's main preoccupation, in this context, is the conditions of possibility of social critique, whereas Haslanger's critical work mainly corresponds to a conceptual analysis of concrete social categories, or "social kinds," and especially those of gender and race.[6] Finally, while Habermas has theorized the inevitability of a post-metaphysical thinking, Haslanger has shown how metaphysical considerations are not only unavoidable but can also be beneficial for critical theory.[7]

In what follows, I explore the hypothesis according to which contemporary critical-theoretical endeavors can be enriched by a combination of Habermas's formal pragmatic perspective and Haslanger's socio-ontological framework. More specifically, I contrast and combine Haslanger's idea of critique and her reflections on social construction and reality with Habermas's non-epistemic theory of truth, as he elaborates it after his so-called "realistic turn." Both perspectives, I shall argue, can improve and complement each other. More precisely, I would like to show, on the one hand, how Habermas's formal pragmatic strategy can strengthen Haslanger's commitment to social justice by clarifying where the "urge" to challenge and change unjust social structures comes from. On the other hand, I shall argue that Haslanger's work is more helpful in revealing the socio-structural impediments that block learning processes and emancipatory practices.

The common basis that justifies the comparison between the two authors' different theoretical projects is their quite similar, albeit not identical, views of reality and objectivity. The second section of this chapter is dedicated to this similarity. After that, I shall argue in section 3 that a realistic interpretation of Habermas's so-called formal pragmatism can clarify the critical potential of discursive interactions. While Haslanger's position remains rather vague on this point, Habermas's view allows us to conceive of the drive or need for critique as emerging from a recalcitrant, problematic reality, which pushes toward the challenging and revision of truth claims whose validity has begun to totter. Finally, I want to show, in the last section of this chapter, how Haslanger's reflections on the functioning and effects of social structures offer helpful instruments, which are absent from the Habermasian theory, to reveal the systematic impediments that block critical and transformative practices.

2. Truth, Reality, Objectivity

In this section, I explain the conceptions of objectivity and reality that Habermas, in his later work *Truth and Justification* (1999/2003), and Haslanger, mainly in her famous collection of essays *Resisting Reality* (2012), present and defend. *Truth and Justification* is one of the few texts in which Habermas leaves aside almost entirely issues of practical philosophy and political or legal (or critical) theory, and dedicates himself to issues of theoretical philosophy—and especially to the ontological question of naturalism and the epistemological question of realism.[8] For its part, *Resisting Reality* consists of a collection of assorted papers, almost all written and published between 1993 and 2011. Although Haslanger's book presupposes that philosophy is capable of "unmasking ideology" and also suitable for constructing alternative ontologies that enable us to come "to more adequate and just visions of what is, what might be and what should be," Haslanger does not explicitly identify her work with the tradition of critical theory.[9] Still, even neither text can be considered part of the "canon" of critical theory—if there could even be such a thing—they do provide precious tools for unraveling some issues that its theoretical paradigm can hardly avoid.

The key to grasping Habermas's understanding of objectivity and reality lies in his conception of truth, which since the end of the '90s has undergone a significant process of revision. In earlier works, Habermas defended a discourse theory, or epistemic theory of truth, according to which what "is true is what may be accepted as rational under ideal conditions," that is "if and only if it can be justified in an ideal epistemic situation."[10] A number of discussions with Wellmer, Lafont, Rorty, and Putnam have subsequently prompted him to revise his discursive conception by adopting a pragmatic, nonepistemic concept of truth. According to this new account, there still is a link between truth and rational acceptability, although truth and ideal assertibility cannot be assimilated anymore. As Habermas poignantly puts in another text, "a proposition is agreed to by all rational subjects because it is true; it is not true because it could be the content of a consensus reached under ideal conditions."[11]

Language, as an intersubjective practice of communication and justification, and reality are, on Habermas's view, inextricably intertwined: It would not be possible to isolate "the constraints of reality that make a statement true from the semantic rules that lay down these truth conditions."[12] What is real can be solely explained by relying on the concepts of what is true. Reality is never to be captured as "naked"; it is always permeated by language and the social practices based on linguistic exchanges.[13] For this reason, although truth cannot be reduced to justified assertibility, there must be an internal relation between truth and justification. Argumentation remains the only available medium of ascertaining truth, because there is no immediate, unfiltered access to the truth conditions of empirical beliefs. This is only an *epistemically* unavoidable connection, which cannot be turned into a *conceptually* inseparable connection between reality and discourse.[14]

How can such a nonepistemic, realist conception of truth be conciliated with the idea that the linguistic horizon of our cognitive practices cannot be trespassed? To answer this question, Habermas introduces the concept of an *objective world*, a world which is common to those who relate to each other communicatively. In intersubjective communicative exchanges, linguistic agents refer to an objective world that is presupposed as being the same for everyone involved in the communicative practices of a certain form of life. We cannot reach an understanding—that is, in Habermas's view, we cannot communicate and consequently cooperate with our fellow human beings—unless we "refer to a single objective world, thereby stabilizing the intersubjectively shared public space with which everything that is merely subjective can be contrasted."[15] Only "the realist presupposition of an *intersubjectively accessible objective world* can reconcile the *epistemic priority of the linguistically articulated horizon* of the lifeworld, which we cannot transcend, with the *ontological priority of a language-independent reality*, which imposes constraints on our practices."[16] Objectivity corresponds here to a presupposition undertaken by those who, by engaging in communicative practices and common action, must refer to a world in common. In order to better understand this notion, it might be now useful to situate Habermas's conception of truth within a larger tradition of pragmatist thinkers, from Charles S. Peirce to John Dewey. As Steven Levine points out, the guiding idea of this tradition is that "cognition must be seen as a moment in a larger action-cycle that starts when agents confront problematic situations in the world. In confronting such situations, habitual modes of coping break down giving rise to doubt. To repair this breach and replace doubt with belief . . . agents must undertake high-order cognition and inquiry—i.e., communication, theory and experimentation."[17] In Habermas's theory of communicative reason, "higher-order cognition and inquiry" take place in the passage from communication to *Diskurs*, namely from unproblematic everyday communicative interactions to problematizing and critical practices, in which truth claims, among other claims, undergo a process of discussion and revision. Unproblematic communication belongs to a network of habitual practices, which rely on "more or less implicit beliefs that we take to be true against a broad background of intersubjectively shared or sufficiently overlapping beliefs."[18] Everyday routines, habitual communicative practices, and the resulting actions work by following those certainties we know we can rely on. The background practical context, which Habermas also calls "lifeworld," functions on the basis of "a consciousness of certainty that in the course of action leaves no room for doubts about truth."[19] When no doubts arise, and we act by following stable expectations, convictions, and certainties of action, we can successfully cope with an objective world, which we presuppose to be independent and the same for everyone. The truth of propositions becomes a topic of discussion and inquiry, however, once practices fail and contradictions, doubts, and uncertainties arise.[20]

Such everyday realism, which Habermas contrasts with Rorty's contextualism, is matched by a concept of nonepistemic, unconditional truth that manifests itself, however, only in unproblematic and routine actions. This notion of truth "provides a *justification-transcendent point of reference* for discursively thematized truth claims."[21] The—never fulfilled—aim of discursive practices, namely of practices of justification and problematization, is to grasp a truth that exceeds all such practices. The transcendentalism of this point of reference accounts for the fallibilism of truth claims and their justifications, namely, for the possibility of questioning and changing such claims: "The fallibilist consciousness that we can err even in the case of well-justified beliefs depends on an orientation toward truth whose roots extend into the realism of everyday practices."[22] As Cristina Lafont has rightly noted, the realist sense of the notion of truth—that is, that the only necessary and sufficient condition of the truth of proposition "p" is that "p" is the case—becomes less obvious precisely when such a condition is situated in the context of practices of testing and challenging our beliefs. It is because the unconditional validity of truth is not due to epistemic conditions that this notion can become something like a "fallibilist reserve" vis-à-vis the validity of epistemic conditions and criteria of justification.[23]

Before exploring further the pragmatist way of dealing with (a problematic) reality and its meaning for social critique, I turn now to Haslanger. One of the main goals of the articles collected in *Resisting Reality* is to show that social constructionism does not commit us to reject the idea of a partially independent reality. Haslanger is unwilling to accept the thesis that "because knowledge is socially constructed, there is no objective (and so no independent) reality."[24] Haslanger's strategy relies upon an argument which is shared by Habermas. In Habermasian terms, the epistemic priority of the linguistically articulated (or socially constructed) horizon of the lifeworld can be reconciled with the ontological priority of an independent reality. On the one hand, Haslanger claims that "there is no way we can 'step outside' all conceptualization to determine which, if any, will provide the resources to capture how the world really is."[25] However, on the other hand, she maintains that "even if we grant that the epistemic criteria for applying any term will implicate us in some way, we need not equate such social criteria with the content of our attribution."[26] In other words, although we do not want to deny the existence of an independent reality, our analyses are compelled to critically take into consideration a reality that can be only conceived of as "touched," molded, and shaped by social actors.[27]

As developed in the article "Social Construction: Myth and Reality," the notion of *objectivity*, or better, objectivism about types and kinds, corresponds to some product of human beings' social activity. Objectivity is the result of a process of social construction, which does not, however, make objective social kinds any less real. As Haslanger in many other essays argues, social types or kinds, like "gender" or "race," are objective precisely in this sense. Gender and race are objective social kinds because, as Habermas would put it, we refer to "things" in our world in common that we see and know being "women" or "men," or "white," "black," "brown," etc.—because most of the time we assume, without problematizing such presuppositions, that *there are* women, men, white people, black or brown people, etc. In her debate with Charles Mills following the publication of *Resisting Reality*, Haslanger clarifies that race and gender are social constructions not in the sense that race and gender must be taken as "mere" concepts. In order to understand what things like race or gender *are*, namely the "contents" of their concepts, one should "investigate the world, not the mind." Haslanger's strategy is aimed at capturing what the term "race" (or "gender") "picks out" in the world (e.g., features of persons, sets of individuals).[28]

As I will further explain in the pages that follow, Haslanger is, unlike Habermas, quite successful in showing that certain objective types are the result not just of a social construction or of social communicative practices, but rather of a construction that consists of unjust, exploitative, and oppressive mechanisms. Thus, arguing that certain things in the world are socially constructed calls for a critique of these injustices. But what is social critique? How does it work? Where does the need, or urge, for social critique come from?

3. Resisting Reality and Critique

According to Haslanger, social critique consists of two steps: a *descriptive* step, which depicts social practices in ways that highlight the relevant aspects that will be targeted for criticism, and a *normative* step, which elaborates the concepts necessary for evaluating social practices as more or less just, rational, useful, good, and so on. These two steps are interrelated. On the one hand, in order to describe the world in a way that is appropriate for critical evaluation, one should be able to handle moral and normative concepts (justice, reason, etc.). On the other hand, the normative step should be informed by rich descriptions and theories of the social world.[29] In accounts of her project, Haslanger brings these two steps together in a project of *ideology critique*. In *Resisting Reality*, the method of ideology critique is understood in rather programmatic and provisional terms as encompassing various moments: genealogical reconstruction, exposure of hegemonic discourses hidden in social structures, moral evaluation, etc.[30] In her later Spinoza Lectures, Haslanger specifies the aim of a theory of ideology as the attempt to understand how "we, collectively, enact social structures."[31] Social structures are defined as networks of social relations, namely relationships between people (e.g., being a parent or a lover) but also between people and things (e.g., use, ownership). Social relations are constituted through social practices, which are viewed as collectively organized solutions to problems regarding coordination or access to resources. Solutions to problems of social organization are reduced to interdependences between *schemas* and *resources*, namely between clusters of culturally shared mental states and processes (concepts, attitudes, dispositions, etc.) enabling us to interpret and deal with information and to coordinate action, and all the different things (human, nonhuman, animate, inanimate, etc.) that have positive or negative value for us. Ideology is defined as a "cultural *technē*" or set of interdependent schemas governing a social structure in ways that (a) create relations of domination/subordination (through the production and distribution of goods or in the constitution of selves) and (b) assign values to certain resources and not to others.[32] If we want to successfully criticize ideologies, we should be able to show why certain schemes enable people to subordinate other people and why our modes of valorization are wrong and should be modified.[33]

Haslanger sees her realism as a kind of materialism that is paramount for the critical-theoretical endeavor. She understands herself as a materialist feminist in the sense that she does not intend to enter debates about social justice from a neutral point of view or from the point of view of an abstract rational agent, but she is rather committed to those social movements that entail normative beliefs about the wrongs of sexism and racism.[34] These wrongs imply material deprivations and material harms like those brought about by economic injustice, exploitation, domestic violence, etc.[35] More specifically, her account of ideology "is materialist because the source and structure of a discursive/conceptual frame depends on the complex network of social relations that organizes our relationships to things of (assumed) value."[36] If we want to engage in critical-theoretical work, we also need to examine how "the *physical world*, interpreted and shaped by culture, is arranged to produce and reproduce injustice."[37] According to Haslanger's social ontology, then, there is a physical, natural world that is both human and nonhuman, that is molded by social practices, and the result of such molding is a social, material reality that constrains us in more or less just ways. A fundamental moment in this process of construction (shaping, molding) is the valorization of resources. Social, material reality is thus conceived by Haslanger as the object of critique. But how and why do we arrive at the decision to engage in critical theory? Where does the need, the urge, the drive to challenge certain ideologies come from? What pushes us to see the world through critical lenses and, possibly, to do something to change it? Haslanger's answers to this sort of question remain vague in ways that tend to undermine her realism/materialism. The trigger, or motor, to critical praxis seems in fact to correspond, in her texts, to the conceptual work itself of clarifying descriptive and normative tools, and not so much in those "everyday" experiences that push theorists, and nontheorists as well, to become critical theorists.[38]

Haslanger might object that she does not need to explain how social critique originates, since she has already aligned herself with contemporary social movements. From the perspective of a theorist who is already involved in concrete struggles, the theoretical work that needs to be done would then be aimed at conceptually supporting or orienting ongoing critical practices: e.g., by providing useful and reliable descriptions, by clarifying concepts already circulating within the movements (e.g., "justice") and already employed in problematic ways by other theorists (e.g., "gender," "race"), or else by reflecting on and systematizing the experiences of the oppressed, or even by outlining new values, norms, and forms of practices.[39] For *practicing* critique, moreover, one does not necessarily need a theory of justice or of domination:[40] It is enough to sense, or to know, without relying upon elaborated arguments or justifications, that something is wrong, that certain persons are, for example, treated unfairly because of the color of their skin, their country of origin, or their gender. Critical theorists can (and must!) learn from the experiences and the practical, empirical knowledge of activists and oppressed groups, just as activists can learn from theorists and the oppressed can profit from critical-theoretical work. This approach, however, seems to beg the question. As Haslanger herself is well aware, ideologies function precisely by preventing those who are oppressed from becoming aware of their oppression and even to feel or sense it. Ideology "systematically prevents us from noticing some of what's morally relevant by shaping and filtering experience to provide a practical orientation that reinforces the domination structure."[41] Or, in the words of Theodor W. Adorno, it is "part of the mechanism of domination to forbid recognition of the suffering it produces."[42] So how does the drive for critique, and thus the critical praxis, emerge?

Habermas's pragmatist view of reality might provide some important indications. His (tentative) answer to this question is connected with the thesis, mentioned above, that the formation of an objective world can be explained on the basis of the fallibilism of practices of knowledge and justification. As he writes: "When they [languages and practices] fail, the world stops cooperating as expected. Through failure, we experience in practice that the world revokes its readiness to cooperate, and *this refusal* gives rise to the concept of objectivity. The latter extends, on the one hand, to the *resistance of a world that is not up to us*, that opposes our manipulations on its own terms, and, on the other hand, to the identity of a world shared by everyone."[43] The objectivity of the world is the product of our failures in dealing with the given world and of our attempts to learn from and overcome these failures. It is the fact that some presuppositions become problematic, thus interrupting our habitual communicative practices, that leads to the emergence of a (partially) new world. A renewed objectivity relies on and emerges from the process of critical elaboration of those convictions and truth claims that have become problematic. From a pragmatist point of view, Habermas thinks of reality in terms of resistance, as "the totality of resistances that are processed and are to be anticipated—and it makes itself known to us solely in the constraints to which our problem-solving activities and learning processes are subject."[44] Reality that we experience as resistance—to our habitual practices, to our unquestioned presuppositions, given beliefs, accepted convictions—is what sets the critical and transformative process in motion.[45] This is an "unanticipated" (*überraschende*)[46] reality that makes for a "risk-filled environment" and frustrates us, thus enacting critique, learning and change.[47]

As mentioned before with reference to Lafont's interpretation of Habermas's realism, it is the discrepancy between rational acceptability and truth that allows criticism to take place. If we were to conflate the notion of idealized acceptability with truth, we would anticipate the end of the argumentation process and adopt anti-fallibilist positions. We need nonepistemic references to reality as critical and problematizing instances, which we can rely upon to expose the wrongness of given justifying statements.[48] It is our experience of dealing with a recalcitrant, risky, independent reality that pushes us to elaborate and revise our convictions, habits, and truth claims.

In some passages, Haslanger approaches this kind of pragmatism—for example, when she explains that the point of critical theories is "not to convince someone that there is a problem, or to prove to an unbeliever that a particular belief is the only rational option, *but to answer a question, to address a concern*."[49] When describing the metaphysical "aporematic" method, she also affirms that theorizing starts when we find a "puzzle, tension, contradiction" and want to solve it.[50] In the Spinoza Lectures, moreover, she hints at the fact that schemes evolve by responding to changes on the resource level.[51] Unfortunately, she does not further elaborate on this thought. Still, Haslanger's connotation of "resisting reality" suggests a significant difference, which constitutes the major difference in Habermas's and Haslanger's view of reality and objectivity. In Habermasian terms reality is understood as *what exercises resistance* against habitual communicative and noncommunicative practices and sets the critical process in motion. Haslanger, on the contrary, believes that reality and its thick, unjust, oppressive structures *must be resisted* by an ensemble of activists, critics, and theorists. While for Habermas a resistant reality might come to perform a critical function, a resisting reality is what counts as object of critique in Haslanger's view. On Habermas's account, it is precisely what counts as objective that must be criticized and changed, after having come into conflict with a recalcitrant reality. Haslanger, on the contrary, seems to conflate objectivity with reality.

In this context, it is important to note that Habermas situates his realist-pragmatist conceptualization within the paradigm of intersubjectivity.[52] The relation between subject and object is interconnected by horizontal relationships among members of a commonly shared lifeworld: "The objectivity of the world and the intersubjectivity of communication mutually refer to one another."[53] The experience of a resistant, problematic reality shows in fact the possibility of an intersubjectively shared experience: "We can learn from the performative experience of reality and its resistance to us only to the extent that we thematize the beliefs that are implicitly challenged by such experiences and learn from the objections raised by other participants in discourse."[54] The intersubjective dimension implicit in dealing with reality is relevant for critical theory because it helps to prevent the critical project from being monopolized by a certain group of theorists or even by a certain tradition of thought. The fact that we learn from the experiences and the objections raised by communication partners within the process of dealing with the world has (or should have) the effect of democratizing critical theory. Every critical move, and its results, must remain in principle open to further criticism that might originate from the experiences of other actors. Fallibilism concerns not solely our everyday convictions and habits, but also our critical practices and outcomes. And fallibilism is enabled by the pluralism of perspectives in the intersubjective paradigm Habermas has theorized.[55]

4. Impediments to Critique and the Possibility of Change

How can the intersubjectively shared experience of dealing with a resistant, problematic reality flow into a (collective) critical praxis aimed at emancipatory social transformations? If we seek an answer to this question, Habermas unfortunately does not seem able to help any further. While he sees the reality that frustrates our habits, convictions, and beliefs as the motor of critical and transformative processes, Habermas seems to conceive—at least in *Truth and Justification*—of critique as epistemological or scientific criticism, aimed at revising false beliefs about the natural world, and not as social critique, aimed at revealing and transforming injustices and structures of domination. Habermas is not able, in other words, to conceive of the objectivity of the world in common as natural and social at the same time or to see how this world is the result of discursive practices and processes of inquiry sometimes harboring subordinating, discriminating, harming mechanisms.

This limitation is rooted, I suppose, in his insistence on the distinction between theoretical and practical philosophy, which leads him to distinguish truth claims from justice (or rightness) claims. While truth needs a reference to an objective world of experience, ratified and revised in action, moral validity and justice claims do not. Discussing Neo-Aristotelian and post-Wittgensteinian approaches, Habermas concedes that our form of life relies on "thick ethical descriptions" of things that are "perceived" to be, for example, cruel, loving, or humiliating: such descriptions, which point to the overcoming of the fact–value distinction, are endowed with a "certain objectivity based on the unforced acceptance of routine language games."[56] In Hegelian terms, forms of life constitute an *objective spirit*. Such social objectivity cannot, however, be confused with truth-analogous validity in the sense of the rational acceptability of moral and social norms. While our beliefs about the world can change when confronted by a recalcitrant, problematic reality, our (moral, ethical, but also social) norms have to change internally to communicative practices, namely through exchanges of arguments. The potential or real inclusion of new participants in the discourses, who might raise new, unexpected objections, constitutes an underlying, procedural normativity that can be relied upon for challenging problematic norms regulating social life.[57] The inclusion of other participants is thus only one example of a the ways in which social reality needs to change. What Habermas calls the "resistance of objective spirit"—the fact that certain claims of practical validity become problematic and lose their immediate validity—can be overcome only by "moral learning processes that lead the disputing parties to broaden their respective social worlds and to include one another in a world they jointly construct."[58]

The distinction between these two kinds of objectivity, which is at odds with classic pragmatist thought, relies on the assumption that the social world, regulated by moral and ethical norms and values, is not characterized by the same degree of reality that pertains to the physical, natural dimension, but is "linguistically mediated all the way down."[59] If we follow Haslanger, however, we gain reasons for expanding Habermas's narrow idea of objectivity to include "practical objectivity"[60] as well. The fact that someone is seen and known as a "woman," or, more specifically, as a "black woman," is something that can be challenged both on the level of truth claims and simultaneously on the level of justice or morality. For example, assume that women are (in a certain space and time) subordinated to men because they have less economic power, and they have less economic power because they are more burdened with reproductive work (e.g., care for the children and the elderly, housework, etc.) than men. The justification for such asymmetries that worsen women's economic prospects, as well as their life in general, usually relies on the argument that women, in contrast with men, are "naturally" geared toward the activities of emotionally and physically care for others. Notwithstanding its objectivity—it is true that, in the space and time we are referring to, women do more care work and are thus economically impaired—this conviction might clash with "another" reality. It is not true, after all, that women are better suited for care work, since there are many women who are clearly not "made for it" and have actually actively rebelled against it, just as there are also men who display genuine interest and are very good in rearing children, taking care of the elderly, attending to the everyday tasks of a household, and so forth.

Is this "other" reality easy to accept? Obviously not. To understand why, it is helpful to return to Haslanger's notion of "resisting reality." While the pragmatist-realist approach can give an account of how critique originates, Haslanger's view is able to better explain why critique is so tremendously difficult. Reality is "resisting" as it is congealed, reified, and opaque, and, as such, resists our attempts to conceptually penetrate the structural layers that enable and reproduce injustice and oppression and to practically change even some of them. There are "several specific issues concerning social phenomena that make the task of description and evaluation especially challenging," and a necessary part of the critical work is to understand and possibly dispel them.[61] Haslanger's theory of social structures, social practices, and ideological *technē* is particularly helpful, I believe, in grasping why exactly social critique is challenging.

Recall that Haslanger defines social structures as bundles of interdependent schemas and resources. Schemas are commonly shared patterns of perception, thought, and behavior that are embodied in individuals and bring them to see things in certain ways and to react, act, and interact with others under certain conditions, according to specific habits. As such, schemas are "part of the common ground we rely on to communicate."[62] Resources, on the contrary, consist of various things that schemas put in order, organize, employ, valorize, etc., and grant social structures their materiality. Schemas and resources are interdependent since, on the one hand, material things can become resources for social actors only if there are schemas that make them intelligible, meaningful, and valuable, and, on the other hand, resources allow schemas to function in the context of a social life that also includes material and natural (physical, biological) dimensions. According to such an ontological framework, critique might be difficult because "we respond to the world that has been shaped to trigger those very responses without being conscious of the shaping, so our responses seem to be called for by the way the world is."[63] Consider again the gender binary, namely the belief that human beings can be categorized, concerning their sexual features and identities, only according to two genders—"man" and "woman." The "fact" that human beings can only be (or become) either men or women is mirrored by a series of practices and infrastructures that regulate our world in common: our language (pronouns, etc.), separated sections for men and women in shopping malls, separated public toilets; the necessity to indicate on your identification documents whether you are a man or a woman; surgical techniques that are immediately applied after birth to make intersexed bodies fit into one or the other gender, etc. In short, the habitual disposition to categorize people according to gender binary is supported, confirmed, and reproduced by a bundle of expectations, rules, laws, commodities, marketing strategies, architectural and design choices, etc. At the same time, the material world organized in this way is itself the product of the belief in gender binary. We can speak of an ideology of binary gender, moreover, when we can debunk how and to what extent it brings about the subordination of women and the devaluation—and even disappearance—of all people who do not identify themselves as either man or woman.[64] How can we then experience the world differently? How can experiences that transgress the gender binary cut through this solid system of mutually reinforcing schemes and resources? Social structures, according to Haslanger's account, seem to have the power to prevent reality from becoming recalcitrant, to tighten the entanglements between schemes and resources, to make us feel uncomfortable with our ways of looking at and interpreting reality, and, finally, to convince us to revise some of these ways.

In the previous section, I argued that Habermas's most valuable contribution consists in his explanation of the sources of social critique, namely of the drive that pushes us to challenge and, eventually, revise portions of our (convictions and beliefs about the) world. Critique emerges from our dealing with a reality that does not respond to our usual expectations and contradicts our habitual practices, a reality that has therefore become resistant to our accepted, given strategies to engage with it. Challenging Habermas's distinction between theoretical and practical philosophy, the critical process must be seen as unfolding in this way not only when confronted with the natural, physical world but when confronted with social reality as well—whereby the natural and nonnatural aspects of society are not easy to distinguish.[65] Social reality does, in fact, as Haslanger shows, consist of complex and multilayered entanglements between natural, material, moral, and cognitive factors.

In this last section, I have argued that Haslanger's theory of social structures and practices, which includes an attempt to revitalize the critique of ideology, is central for critical theory—not only because this theory clarifies our conceptual, critical, and normative tools, but also because it makes us aware of the hurdles that social critics do encounter and must confront. Habermas, on the contrary, does not realize the extent to which the reality that provokes critique might inform the terms of that very critique, weakening or even blocking it. An efficacious critical theory is one that includes an account of the sources of both the critical drive and the structural entanglements that block such drive. As a matter of fact, the young Habermas had a sense of this double task, which he articulated in one of his rare references to the method of critical theory (or, as he calls it at that point, critical sociology): "Critical of ideology, it [a critical sociology] asks what it lies behind the consensus, presented as a fact, that supports the dominant tradition of the time, and does so with a view to the *relations of power surreptitiously incorporated in the symbolic structures* of the system of speech and action. The *immunization power of ideology*, which stifle the demands of justification raised by discursive examination, goes back to blockages in communication, independently of the changing semantic contents."[66] "Discursive examination" is what we do when we want to revise the validity claims that have become problematic as result of our encounters with a recalcitrant reality. Reality might come to exercise resistance against our habitual cognitive and practical ways of dealing with the world and, as such, break open those structures that have until now appeared as objective and natural to us, but which are in fact the product of unjust power relations. Critical theory is, however, hindered—not inevitably and not indefinitely—by the same structures it aims at dispelling. Critical theory cannot look away from this conundrum. On the contrary, it must gather every possible conceptual tool it can find to deal with it.

Notes

1. I am grateful to Philip Hogh and Stefan Müller-Doohm for having invited me to the workshop *Der Ort der Vernunft: Habermas im Diskurs* (Oldenburg, June 2015), where I had the chance to present this paper for the first time. For very helpful comments, critiques, and suggestions on the last draft, I warmly thank Steven Levine as well as the two editors of this collection, María and Colin.

2. On the Hegelian and Marxist roots of immanent critical theory, see Seyla Benhabib, *Critique, Norm and Utopia: A Study of the Foundations of Critical Theory* (New York: Columbia University Press, 1986); and Arvi Särkelä, *Immanente Kritik und soziales Leben: Selbsttransformative Praxis nach Hegel und Dewey* (Frankfurt am Main: Vittorio Klostermann, 2018).

3. To be sure, there are scholars who argue that the Kantian tradition of criticism has been an inspiring factor for Frankfurt critical theory from the very beginning; see for example Angelo Cicatello, *Dialettica negativa e logica della parvenza: Saggio su T.W. Adorno* (Genova: Il Nuovo Melangolo, 2001). Furthermore, there are contemporary theorists who rely heavily on a Kantian paradigm for pursuing a critical-theoretical project; see, most notably, Rainer Forst, *The Right to Justification: Elements of a Constructivist Theory of Justice*, trans. Jeffrey Flynn (New York: Columbia University Press, 2012). In this paper, I do not engage with the question of whether Habermas's writings, especially after *The Theory of Communicative Action*, can still be taken as relevant for contemporary critical theoretical undertakings; on this, see Federica Gregoratto, *Il Doppio volto della comunicazione* (Milano/Udine: Mimesis, 2013). It is worth remembering, however, how Habermas himself has expressed strong doubts concerning the Frankfurter project; see for example Axel Honneth, Eberhard Knödler-Bunte, and Arno Widmann, "The Dialectics of Rationalization: An Interview with Jürgen Habermas," *Telos* 21, no. 49 (1981), 5–31; and Jürgen Habermas, "Nach dreißig Jahren: Bemerkungen zu *Erkenntnis und Interesse*," in *Das Interesse der Vernunft: Rückblicke auf das Werk von Jürgen Habermas nach Erkenntnis und Interesse*, ed. Stefan Müller-Doohm (Frankfurt am Main: Suhrkamp, 2000).

4. Sally Haslanger, *Resisting Reality* (Oxford: Oxford University Press, 2012), 13.

5. Haslanger, *Resisting Reality*, ch. 15, 17. See also Sally Haslanger, *Critical Theory and Practice: Spinoza Lectures* (Amsterdam: Koninklijke van Gorcum, 2017).

6. See also Thomas McCarthy, *Ideals and Illusions: On Reconstruction and Deconstruction in Contemporary Critical Theory* (Cambridge, MA: MIT Press, 1991), 130.

7. Unfortunately, I will not be able here to expound on the consequences that post-metaphysical and metaphysical approaches have for critical theory; on the metaphysical commitments of social critique, see Särkelä, *Immanente Kritik und Soziales Leben*, ch. 5.

8. Jürgen Habermas, *Truth and Justification*, trans. Barbara Fultner (Cambridge, MA: MIT Press, 2003), 2. The only exception is constituted by the seventh and last article of the book, in which Habermas comes back once again to the thorny theory/praxis issue.

9. Haslanger, *Resisting Reality*, 112, 379. In her Spinoza Lectures, the affiliation becomes somehow more explicit. In these lectures, as in the introduction of *Resisting Reality*, she identifies as the "starting point" of critical theory its Marxian definition as "the self-clarification of the struggles and wishes of the age." See Haslanger, *Critical Theory and Practice*, 7–8; *Resisting Reality*, 22. Haslanger especially considers anti-sexist and anti-racist struggles to be "struggles of the age." Given the stated lineage, one might wonder why she does not mention the various anti-capitalist struggles that have known a resurgence in the aftermath of the 2008 global economic crisis—but I will not follow up on this oddity here.

10. Jürgen Habermas, "Richard Rorty's Pragmatic Turn," in *Rorty and His Critics*, ed. Robert B. Brandom (Malden, MA: Blackwell, 2000), 45. This article belongs to the original German edition of *Truth and Justification*, i.e., Jürgen Habermas, *Wahrheit und Rechtfertigung* (Frankfurt am Main: Suhrkamp, 1999/2003). See also Habermas, *Truth and Justification*, 36. For a precise overview of Habermas's old and new theories of truth, which I am going to largely follow in the first section, see Steven Levine, "Truth and Moral Validity: On Habermas's Domesticated Pragmatism" *Constellations* 18, no. 2 (2011), 244–247.

11. Jürgen Habermas, *Between Naturalism and Religion: Philosophical Essays* (Cambridge: Polity Press, 2008), 44.

12. Habermas, "Richard Rorty's Pragmatic Turn," 40.

13. Habermas, *Truth and Justification*, 36.

14. Habermas, *Truth and Justification*, 38. See also: "A truth claim raised for 'p' says that the truth conditions for 'p' are satisfied. We have no other way of ascertaining whether or not this is the case except by way of argumentation, for direct access to uninterpreted truth conditions is denied to us. But the fact that the truth conditions are satisfied does not itself become an epistemic fact just because we can only establish whether these conditions are satisfied by way of discursive vindication of truth claim." Habermas, "Richard Rorty's Pragmatic Turn," 46.

15. Habermas, *Truth and Justification*, 41.

16. Ibid., 30 (emphasis added).

17. Levine, "Truth and Moral Validity," 246.

18. Habermas, *Truth and Justification*, 252–253.

19. Ibid., 39.

20. Ibid.

21. Ibid. (emphasis added).

22. Habermas, "Richard Rorty's Pragmatic Turn," 48.

23. Cristina Lafont, *The Linguistic Turn in Hermeneutic Philosophy* (Cambridge, MA: MIT Press, 1999), 312–313.

24. Haslanger, *Resisting Reality*, 85.

25. Ibid., 152.

26. Ibid., 106.

27. Ibid., 95.

28. Sally Haslanger, "Race, Intersectionality, and Method: A Reply to Critics," *Philosophical Studies* 171, no. 1 (2014), 111–112. In his comment, Mills presses Haslanger to give her view on, among other things, those race theories arguing that race is not, or not only, socially constructed, and that there is (also) a biological reality to race; Charles W. Mills, "Notes from the Resistance: Some Comments on Sally Haslanger's *Resisting Reality*," *Philosophical Studies* 171, no. 1 (2014), 85–97.

29. Haslanger, *Resisting Reality*, 16–17.

30. Ibid., 19f.

31. Haslanger, *Critical Theory and Practice*, 12.

32. Ibid., 20–23. See also Haslanger, *Resisting Reality*, ch. 15, 17; Haslanger, "Social Structure, Narrative and Explanation," *Canadian Journal of Philosophy* 45, no. 1 (2015).

33. I will not enter into the details of the normative aspects of ideology critique, and its connection to moral theory, which Haslanger discusses especially in her second Spinoza lecture.

34. "Critical social theory begins with a commitment to a political movement and its questions; its concepts and theories are adequate only if they contribute to the movement. A feminist or racist critical theory does not attempt to be "neutral" on questions of race and gender, but begins with the assumption that current conditions are unacceptable unjust and a commitment to understand and remedy that injustice. . . . Critical theories arise out of social activism." Haslanger, *Resisting Reality*, 22.

35. Haslanger, *Critical Theory and Practice*, 11.

36. Ibid., 25.

37. Ibid. (emphasis added).

38. To be fair, Haslanger seems definitely inclined to think that social critique does emerge from problematic confrontations with reality, but to my knowledge she does not theoretically elaborate on this point in her work.

39. Haslanger herself is more engaged in revising concepts that have been confusingly or improperly used by other theorists, but she advocates for other types of critical work as well. One might add to the list also the conceptual work to coin new terms that could open up new phases in the struggle (consider for example "sexual harassment").

40. Haslanger, *Critical Theory and Practice*, 41.

41. Ibid., 42–43.

42. Theodor Adorno, *Minima Moralia: Reflections on a Damaged Life*, trans. E.F.N. Jephcott (London: Verso, 2005), 63.

43. Habermas, *Truth and Justification*, 255 (emphasis added).

44. Ibid., 27.

45. Ibid., 16. As suggested by the Marcuse quote at the beginning of chapter 6 ("There is an essential connection between freedom and truth, and any misconception of truth is, at the same time, a misconception of freedom"), Habermas seems to think of this process somehow in the emancipatory terms of the first generation of Frankfurt theorists. See Habermas, *Truth and Justification*, 237.

46. Ibid., 256.

47. Ibid., 26.

48. Lafont, *The Linguistic Turn in Hermeneutic Philosophy*, 294, 296.

49. Haslanger, *Resisting Reality*, 23.

50. Ibid., 146.

51. Haslanger, *Critical Theory and Practice*, 23.

52. Haslanger has not explicitly thought about this point, which is not, however, completely foreign to her thinking; see e.g Haslanger, *Critical Theory and Practice*, 425–426; Haslanger, "Social Structure, Narrative and Explanation," 10–11.

53. Habermas, *Truth and Justification*, 16.
54. Ibid. See also ibid., 26.
55. Habermas has most notably presented his idea of communicative intersubjective rationality, discussing its relevance for critical theory, in Jürgen Habermas, *The Theory of Communicative Action*, vol. 1, *Reason and the Rationalization of Society*, trans. Thomas McCarthy (Boston, MA: Beacon Press 1984).
56. Habermas, *Truth and Justification*, 246.
57. Ibid., 248.
58. Ibid., 256.
59. Ibid., 255. For a thorough criticism of the distinction between theoretical and practical validities, see Levine, "In Truth and Moral Validity," 244–259. See also Steven Levine, "Habermas, Kantian Pragmatism, and Truth," *Philosophy and Social Criticism* 36, no. 6 (2010): 677–695.
60. Habermas, *Truth and Justification*, 255.
61. Haslanger, *Resisting Reality*, 20.
62. Ibid., 462–463.
63. Ibid., 468.
64. This example, which is inspired by but not directly taken from Haslanger's pages, reminds of feminists' debates around sex and gender. Haslanger has widely intervened in these debates: most notably, she has criticized Judith Butler for completely dissolving the difference between (natural) sex and (social) gender, thus introducing unsustainable anti-realist commitments (Haslanger, *Resisting Reality*, 152–157).
65. John Dewey, a fervent critic of the distinction between truth and justice claims as well as of the distinction between nature and society, outlines, in his lectures in China (1919–1929), a theory of social struggles that can be relevant here. More precisely, according to this theory, a *resisting social reality* might be interpreted as the moment in which "society is disordered" and "the normal processes of social interaction are disrupted." See John Dewey, *Lectures in China 1919–1920* (Honolulu: Hawaii University Press, 1973), 72. This is the moment when "solid habits" start to "crack." See John Dewey, "Lectures in Social and Political Philosophy (China)," *European Journal of Pragmatism and American Philosophy* 2, no. 7 (2015), 8. Disruptions and confusions of this sort happen because of the emergence of a social conflict between social groups among which there subsist relations of domination. On the place that Dewey's theory of social conflicts can play in critical theory, see Federica Gregoratto, "Agonistic Recognition, Intersections and the Ambivalence of Family Bonds: John Dewey's Critical Theory Manifesto in China," *Transactions of the Charles S. Pierce Society* 53, no. 1 (2017): 127–145.
66. Jürgen Habermas, *Theory and Practice*, trans. John Viertel (Boston, MA: Beacon Press, 1974), 11–12 (emphasis added).

19

The Critique of Law and the Law of Critique

CHRISTOPH MENKE

1. Introduction

Critique and law stand in an indissoluble and at the same time antagonistic relation. On the one side, law is one of the first and most urgent subjects of critique: if all critique, critique as such, is directed against domination (and if law is, in Marx's terms, the "other form" of domination: domination in its other, normative form),[1] then critique always has to become—or at least has to include—the critique of law. On the other side, law is the first instance or the most important and powerful agent of critique; law itself is defined by the operation of critique. Critique is directed against law and performed by law. Critique and law are paradoxically entwined.[2]

    The consequence of this paradoxical entwinement is that, in the critique of law, critique turns against itself. The critique that is directed against law is at the same time directed against the critical operation; the critique of law, consistently performed, becomes the critique of critique (or self-critique). The critique of law becomes a critique of the law of critique, of its own law-like, legal character.[3] And this applies to critique in general: if critique in its essence, i.e. form, is legal, and if the critique of law implies its self-criticism, then all critique, consistently executed, is at the same time critique of critique.

But then how is criticism still possible at all? It is only possible if the paradox of critique—that it must turn against itself—does not annihilate it, but, on the very contrary, makes up for its rule-breaking, liberating force.

I will develop this thesis in three steps: I will first reformulate the sketched paradox of law and critique that leads to a critique of critique. This concerns the possibility of normative judgment, which is at the heart of the critical operation: all critique that judges in the name of a norm proceeds in a legal form and is therefore not a critique of law, but its apology, as I discuss in section 2. This raises the question for a different, a non-legal form of normative judgment and hence of critique. The following sections will answer this question by first outlining a genealogical understanding of critique in section 3 and then showing how this new understanding of critique redefines the normativity of judgment in sections 4 to 6.

2. The Aporia of Critique

What is the ground of the paradoxical entwinement of law and critique that raises the problem? The one side of the paradox consists in critique being directed against law. This holds if we understand critique, following Foucault, as the "art of not being governed quite so much": of "not to be governed like that, by that, in the name of those principles, with such and such an objective in mind and by means of such procedures, not like that, not for that, not by them."[4] Critique *is* the critique of government, of being governed by another, or it is directed against all forms of rule (for rule or domination is the government of the one by the other). Law, in turn, is one of the most powerful forms of rule. This does not only hold, as it is obvious, since law pertains to the power structure by which the state enforces its norms. Rather, law above all is the object of critique because law is a structural feature of normativity as such. Law is not just a special social system that plays historically different roles in the establishment and stabilization of political and social rule; law is a formal characteristic of all normativity. There is no normativity that is not legal, i.e., that has a legal side or shape. Its legality emerges when a norm separates from a practice in order to intervene in it by acts of judgment: to govern the practice from outside—but in the name of its own essence turned against its bad appearance.[5] Because of this constitutive legal externality, every normative order is shaped by an "economy of violence," that is, an economy that binds normative power to factually, i.e., non-normatively operating forces.[6] The legality of normativity consists in its claim to rule or govern a practice (and a norm that does not govern is none). This is the subject of criticism: the art of critique, which is driven by the claim not to be governed "like that, not for that, not by them" (Foucault), has to become the critique of law because (or if) it is directed against the existing normative order and its law-like mode of rule. Because rule is exercised in a normative way and since the rule of the normative defines its legality, critique as such is the critique of law.

On the other side of their paradoxical entwinement, law itself is a practice of critique. Indeed, the origin of the word "critique" can be traced back to law: "Terminologically, the Greeks used the group of words around κριν (κρίσις, κριτής, κριτικός) probably first of all in the legal sphere, whereby both the indictment (the incident) and the judgment (the outcome of the dispute) could be denoted."[7] And when Plato claims the right of everyone to judge another person's claim to truth, he describes this right to critique as the right to be the "judge" of another person's judgment.[8] The critic who distinguishes between true and false is (like) a judge insofar as the judge is already a, if not *the*, critic. Law is critical because law is the systematic unfolding of the operation of normative distinction and decision. Law is the rationalization of the art of normative distinction: it defines (1) its procedure, including the authority position for judging (who is the judge?) and (2) the order of reasons (in the form of rules) that justify the judgment. Law is the formal, systematic, and systemic organization, i.e., the institution or the institutionalization of critique. And this means reciprocally that critique, systematically performed, is law(-like) or legal.

But that is not all. The law can only be critical-judgmental if it also develops an equally critical mode of cognition. Legal cognition is critical because it looks behind the surface. The law does not trust the way things appear. It cannot do that, because the appearance is the opinion and the opinions in the legal case are controversial; each side claims to be right. That is why we need a judge who stands above the parties. And this has been interpreted at least by the law of enlightenment[9] in such a way that the judge is also the one who looks behind the surface of opinions. The judge is an observer who "closes the jalousie, the critic's screen that tests every sound and every word."[10] Law researches the hidden drives, meanings, and perpetrators; it conducts critical hermeneutics. The law is therefore doubly critical: because it is judgmental or deciding and because (or how) it is researching and examining.

The question then is how these two sides of the relation between law and critique relate to each other. The critique of law has a double, an objective and a subjective meaning: the critique (that is directed) *at* law and the critique (that is practiced) *by* law. But can there be any critique of law at all if law itself is already (and nothing but) the institutionalization of critique, if critique is thus constitutive of law?

The claim of a critique of law seems to be caught in an aporia. For either it is a *critique* of law, i.e., an act of normative distinction directed at law—but then it is in truth just an application of law to itself. All critique of law remains immanent to law simply because it is critique. The critique of law just enacts the legality (or the law) of law itself—and is thus precisely not a critique *of law*, i.e., directed against the law and its rule. The attempt at criticizing law will always only repeat its legal logic. Or—the alternative reads—it is indeed a critical questioning of the mode and the extent of the government by law. But then it cannot be an act of critique in the strict sense. For in order to address its logic of domination, the critique of law would have to break with the legal logic, the logic of legality, and thus become not only a questioning of law but of critique itself. The critique *of law* could not be the *critique* of law anymore; it would have to become something other than critique (namely, a creative act that devises a different, non-legal form of government).[11]

According to the first alternative, the critique of law is nothing more than a mere repetition of law and thus its confirmation. According to the second alternative, the critique of law is nothing other than the abolition of critique and law at the same time. On one thing, then, both sides agree: the legal nature of critique. The aporia of the critique of law is that the critique is either immanent to law and hence not directed against law, or it *is* directed against law but then it ceases to be critique. Critique here means on both sides: the normative distinction between right and wrong. And the normative distinction between right and wrong means—this is also part of the tacit agreement between both sides—the procedure of instituting, justifying, and applying a law. Both sides thus agree on the assumption that critique is legal, i.e., legal in its form. Critique has a legal form. The law of critique is law, law is the law of critique.

If this is true, the critique of law is an aporetic endeavor. It cannot be done: there simply is no critique of law. But *is* it true? Is critique, the act of normative distinction, in its nature, i.e. its form, legal? Or can we conceive of an "alegal" form of critique? I will start to explore this question in the following. I will try to show that the statement that brings about the aporia—the law of critique is law—rightly understood also leads the way out of the aporia. The formula of the aporia—the law of critique is law—is at the same time the formula of the solution of the aporia.

3. Critique as Genealogy

At the center of the problem of critique stands the problem of normative judgment, i.e., of the distinction between what is right and what is wrong. Law is the rationalization, the proceduralization and justification of the practice of normative distinction. In this regard, law takes the necessity and possibility of normative distinction for granted. I call this the dogmatism of critique (or critical dogmatism). Legal critique, critique in the form of law, rests on the dogma of normative distinction. The dogma says that right and wrong can be distinguished by certain criteria that allow for their unequivocal identification. Right and wrong can thus be separated as opposite cases: the right way of acting or thinking stands in external opposition to the wrong way.

In his critique of Hegel's philosophy of the state, Marx describes this as the dogmatism of "vulgar" criticism: "Vulgar criticism falls into a . . . *dogmatic* error. Thus, for example, it criticizes the constitution. It draws attention to the opposition of the powers, etc. It finds contradictions everywhere. But this is still dogmatic criticism that *struggles* with its opposite, as for example when in earlier times the dogma of the Blessed Trinity was eliminated by appealing to the contradiction between 1 and 3."[12] This critique is "vulgar" and "dogmatic" because (of the way) it "struggles" with its object. To this, Marx opposes the idea of "true criticism": "True criticism, however, shows the internal genesis of the Blessed Trinity in the human brain. It describes the act of its birth. Thus, true philosophical criticism of the present state constitution not only shows the contradictions as existing, but *explains* them, grasps their genesis and necessity. It comprehends their own *proper* significance."[13] The dogmatism of vulgar criticism consists in struggling with its object in the name of a norm that it presupposes as pre-given: by rejecting the dogma of the Trinity as self-contradictory—the Trinity is meant to be three and one at the same time—it fights it from the outside in the name of a norm, the law of non-contradiction, which it thereby treats itself as a dogma. (Or, by rejecting the dogma of the Trinity as self-contradictory, it turns the idea of non-contradiction itself merely into another dogma.[14]) Vulgar criticism fights against one dogma in the name of another dogma. It thereby means to guarantee the normative distinguishability between the right and the wrong: the dogma provides for a criterion by which the case is rendered either right or wrong.

In contrast, "true philosophical criticism" shows "the act of birth" or the "internal genesis" of its object. For Marx, criticism means genealogy. In the first volume of *Capital*, Marx explains how such genealogy operates, and why, in what sense of the term, it can be called "critical." Marx describes the decisive question that defines his investigation as a *critique* of political economy in the following way: "Political economy has now, albeit imperfectly, analyzed value and the measure of value and discovered the content hidden in these forms. It has never, however, even asked the question, 'Why does this content take on that form, why, then, does labor present [*darstellt*] itself as value?'"[15] To criticize is thus to ask the question of form; more precisely, the question of the form of a presentation (or a representation: *Darstellung*). Criticism takes the existing not as fact or given, but as the presentation of a "hidden" content in a specific form (the presentation of social labor in the form of exchange value). True criticism is thus not interested in what is concealed; for Marx, the critic is not (as Kierkegaard describes it) a "secret agent in a higher service," whose "art" is "to expose what is hidden."[16] Instead, the critic is interested in the genesis, the birth of the form in which this content is presented and thus present. The critic is an analyst of presentations; she is a reader of forms.

In this elucidation of Marx's concept of genealogical critique by way of his later program of a critique of political economy, everything revolves around the concept of presentation (*Darstellung*). On the surface, "presentation" here refers to the depiction of capitalist reality in the ideology of the prevailing bourgeois thinking, that is, in political economy (or economic liberalism). The decisive step, however, is to understand the economic reality itself as a presentation: it is not a mere fact, but a figure in which a content is hidden, i.e., presented. Criticism means the reading of presentations; more precisely, the transformation of what is seemingly simply given *into* a presentation by or through reading.

A presentation is thereby defined by a double distinction: first, the distinction between concealed content and its appearing in a certain figure, and, second and much more importantly, the distinction between the content that appears and the specific way in which it appears, i.e., between the content and the form of its presentation. By reading what exists as a presentation, the critique reveals how—in what form—the content is represented. Only with this second distinction, i.e., with the perspective of form, does the activity of critique begin. To criticize does not mean to unearth some hidden content behind a given piece of social reality; this was already achieved by bourgeois or liberal political economy itself (it already knew that labor was the content of exchange value). Criticism only begins with the question of the form in which this content is presented by that piece of social reality, i.e., by reading reality as a presentation. The act of critique asks not for the content but for why this content, namely social labor, presents itself in the form of value. And to read reality as a presentation means to understand presentation as an act—as the act of formation (*Formierung*). The "genesis" that true criticism explores according to Marx is the genesis of form: the production and functioning of a specific form of presentation.

The critique of political economy is thus not the critique of an ideology as a mis-presentation of capitalist reality. Its critique rather consists in demonstrating that the same act of presentation that liberal bourgeois ideology performs already constitutes reality itself. This presentation is as real as it is ideological. Social reality is produced by an act of presenting that conceals itself. The critique of political economy claims not that the bourgeois way of thinking does not reflect social reality but, on the contrary, that it merely mirrors it: in representing capitalist reality bourgeois thought repeats the presentation that constitutes it and precisely in this way makes its act of formation—of presenting the hidden content in this specific form—invisible. Bourgeois or liberal political economy is "uncritical" precisely because of its "positivism," the mere mirroring of facts (as Marx said, with reference to Hegel's "later writings"[17]).

The definition of genealogical critique is "reading the existing as the text of its becoming."[18] As genealogical, critique is thus the act of transformative reading (a reading that is an act of re-writing): it turns reality into presentation and, more precisely, into the presentation of its form of presenting—into the presentation of presentation or into self-presentation. The activity of critique thus brings about objects, as forms of presentation, that are critical in themselves (or that are self-critical). Friedrich Schlegel calls a philosophy "critical" that offers us "in the system of transcendental thoughts at the same time a characterization of transcendental thinking." To be critical means to present the act of thinking together with the thoughts it produces—to co-present the "producing" (*das Produzierende*) in the "product."[19] Critique is but the self-reflection of presentation which is performed by and in the presentation itself.

Schlegel extends this structure of criticality from philosophy to poetry (as "poetry of poetry") and from there to politics. A politics that is critical in Schlegel's sense is revolutionary politics, that is, politics that co-represents in any act of presentation that which is the politically producing subject or force, *le pouvoir constituant*, the people. Marx goes one step further and relates this idea of critique to social, especially economic forms. To criticize social reality means to transform it, by reading, into a presentation that is critical in itself because it is (read or re-written as) a co-presentation of its own form of presenting. Criticism is the reading of social forms as their self-presentations. Criticism transcendentalizes (or "romanticizes") its object: in its critical reading, the object not only *has* a form, but also represents its form as its act of forming.

4. Beyond Contingency

The critical reading of reality as a self-presentation opens up the field of investigation of the genesis of its currently dominant form. Where, when, and how did the genesis of this form occur? By what act of birth was this form brought about? What step led from the content to this form (in the case of political economy: from social labor to exchange value[20])? According to Marx, to answer these genealogical questions means to "explain" the existence and functioning of a social form. But why, then, is this genealogical explanation an act of critique, or even the only act of "true criticism"? And how is the idea of critique redefined by this program of genealogy? What is critical about genealogy (or about reading)?

A first and quick response to this question is that genealogy is critical in an ontological sense: it is critical because it is anti-positivist, because it dissolves the "myth of the given" and transforms reality into the presentation of the becoming of its form. But if what exists is the effect of a specific way of presentation—of presenting that content in this specific form—it also could be otherwise. Genealogy reveals the contingency of what exists. This is how genealogy defines critique: critique means to dismantle the illusion of necessity and to reveal it as a mere possibility; it also could have taken on another shape.

In the following, I want to sketch a different answer—not because the first one is false but because it is insufficient.[21] The genealogical critique, which shows the genesis of form, does not merely reveal the contingency of the existing social order; it is not merely the de-naturalization of the social and historical. This is only a first step. To stop there misses the decisive point of Marx's genealogical re-definition of critique (and thereby the meaning of critique in Benjamin, Adorno, and Foucault; it misses the point of critical theory). For it misses in what sense and in what way the genealogical program aims at a re-definition of critique in its literal and originary meaning, according to which "critique" is the name of the normative, i.e., the "distinguishing and deciding attitude."[22] The true, genealogical critique rejects the dogmatism of normative distinction but it does not reject (or dissolve) this attitude itself. Genealogical critique is not just about anti-positivism and awareness of contingency. For the genealogical investigation can only be called critical if it performs in a new and different way what vulgar criticism was only able to achieve "dogmatically," namely, to "struggle" against the existing order by way of the normative decision between what is right and what is wrong. The dogmatism of vulgar critique consists in understanding the criteria that define wrong and right as mutually external; it opposes the right case to the wrong one. Genealogical critique—I want to show in the following—reconceptualizes and reconstitutes the act of critical distinction by developing a different concept of the wrong: it understands wrongness and hence the (normative, critical) distinction between the wrong and the right in a nondogmatic way.

5. The Paradox of Law

In order to understand why and in exactly what way genealogical critique leads to the reconstitution of the operation of decision (to the reformulation of the normative concept of the wrong and hence to the reconstitution of normativity as such), we first have to reach a more precise understanding of the "act of birth," the "genesis" of form that the "true philosophical criticism" according to Marx shows. How and by whom is a form born? What is the ground—in Schlegel's terminology, the "producing"—of form? The ground of form is not the content that it presents. The "producing" is also not *a* producer, it is not the act of a subject. Rather, the ground of a form is a contradiction or paradox. The critical-genealogical reading of what exists as presentation shows that the formation of forms consists in the execution of a paradox. The critical-genealogical concept of form reads: a form is the expression, the execution, or the processing of the inner contradiction of a certain thing or object.

With law, this general claim can be outlined in the following way.[23] Law is defined by an inner contradiction. In its fundamental meaning this does not refer to the contradiction between the true idea of law and its only insufficient realization in the existing systems of law (as the concept of immanent critique has it). Rather, the contradiction that defines law and that the genealogy of its forms exhibits is immanent to the very idea of law. For there is no law that is not at the same time the procedure and order of normative distinction, on the one hand, and, on the other, the instance or power of non-normative effectivity. Law is normative and non-normative power at the same time.

Law is, on the one side, *normative* because it distinguishes between the lawful and the unlawful. Or because it practices critique; the law, as we have seen, is the paradigmatic instance of critique. It criticizes in the name of equality; the nomos of law is *isonomia*. The law is, on the other side, *nonnormative* because, by distinguishing between the lawful and the unlawful, it also distinguishes between law and non-law. Law is not only opposed to the unlawful, the violation of the status of equality, but also to any practice, attitude, or mode of subjectivity that is external or alien to law. Law *means* externality; wherever there is law, there are practices, attitudes, and subjectivities that are external to it—and to which law itself thus in turn stands in a merely external relation. This external relation of the normative to the nonnormative can itself only be nonnormative: in contrast to the normative (or critical) relation between the lawful and the unlawful that is internal to law, hence processed by and in law itself, the nonnormative relation between law and non-law is a relation of nonnormative effectivity or power. I suggest to call this potential of nonnormative effectivity of law its "violence": law battles or suppresses the non-law. The relation between law and non-law as categorically external is—can only be—a relation of violence.

Law is the relation between these two relations, between the normative relation between the lawful and the unlawful and the nonnormative relation between law and non-law; it is the relation between normative critique and the nonnormative effectivity of violence. Law is the unity of two distinct relations that cannot be unified. Law thus is, at its basis, defined by a relation that leads to incompatible qualifications and can thus only be represented as a paradox. There is no form of law that is not an effect and hence an expression of its paradoxical unity of normative and nonnormative relations; no form of law that, if the paradoxical unity of the normative and the nonnormative, of critique and violence were dissolved, would still be a form of *law* (it would rather dissolve into either pure normativity or pure violence and become either immaculate, absolute justice or brute domination or suppression).

More exactly, to speak of a "paradox" of law refers to the fact that the relation between the two relations that constitute law can itself only be described in a twofold, indeed, contradictory way. On the one hand, law can only be both at the same time: law is both normative *and* nonnormative at once, critique and violence. This is missed both by the idealistic and the realistic conceptions of law. While the former sees in law nothing other than a normative order of recognition that ensures each person the status of equality, the latter reduces law to a factual arrangement of force that secures the conditions of subordination. Law, however, is neither merely the one nor the other because it is both at the same time.

On the other hand, law cannot be both normative and nonnormative at the same time. The normative and the nonnormative relations that constitute law do not stand side by side; the normative opposition of the lawful to the unlawful operates in the name of equal recognition, and is thus directed against law's own nonnormative relation of violence—law combats the violence that it itself commits. Law is thus not only defined by two incompatible distinctions, the normative distinction between what is lawful and what is unlawful and the nonnormative distinction between law and non-law. Rather, law is defined by two incompatible relations between these two categorically different distinctions: law is normative *and* nonnormative, yet both elements of law also turn *against* each other. The relation between the normative and the nonnormative is a double, even contradictory relation: a relation both of coexistence and of hostility.

This is what the term "paradox" is meant to say: law *has to be* normative and nonnormative at the same time, but it *cannot* be normative and nonnormative at the same time (and both for the same conceptual reason). To express the duality that constitutes law thus means to strive to overcome this duality. (The only true expression of a paradox is the attempt not to express it, but rather to dissolve it.) Law thus turns against itself. Law is not an entity that pertains to two different orders of relations. Because these two orders contradict each other, law is an objection against its own existence. Law thus struggles against itself, against the existence of law; law itself wants to abolish law.

6. Undogmatic Normativity

We have reached the following definition of genealogical (or "true philosophical") critique: critique means to show the genesis of a specific form from the paradox or contradiction in its ground. Or, inversely: critique means to read a given form as the presentation—the execution or enactment—of the paradox that grounds it. Such a critical reading defies the dogmatism of vulgar criticism. This dogmatism consists in its normative presupposition, which is nothing but the presupposition of the normative: the dogmatic claim of normative decidability, i.e., the claim that we can decide between right and wrong in the name of a given criterion and that the right and the wrong therefore exist as separate, independently given cases. The genealogical critique reads the existing forms of law as grounded in a paradox and thereby shows that this dogmatic presupposition does not hold. Law rests on the dogmatic presupposition of normative decidability, and law undermines this presupposition. Without the dogmatic presupposition of normative decidability there is no law. But at the same time, it shows in law that its practice of normative decision produces, on its backside, a distinction that is normatively undecidable.

The pivotal point of this reversal is the duality of the normative distinction between the lawful and the unlawful and the nonnormative distinction between law and non-law. Both go hand in hand. Both distinctions thus overlap and become indistinguishable in the reality of law so that no final decision can be made between what is condemned and punished as unlawful and what is treated and combated as nonlaw.[24] Above all, however, the paradoxical relationship between normative and nonnormative distinction at the center of law calls into question the possibility of critique, just as this relationship makes critique necessary at the same time.

For on the one hand, this relationship requires a critical decision: the nonnormative distinction between the law and nonlaw is a relation of external effectivity. Such a relationship is called violence when it takes place in the space of normativity. As violence, however, the relationship of external effectivity is not normatively neutral; in the space of normativity, the nonnormative relationship is normatively wrong. The law, as practice of critique, must therefore turn against the violence it exercises in relation to the non-law: It must distinguish critically between critique and violence as right and as wrong—for critique and against violence.

But at the same time and on the other hand, it is not possible to decide normatively between the normative and the nonnormative distinction of the law. They cannot be separated from each other and opposed as the right and the wrong—such that one keeps the right side and rejects the wrong one. If the nonnormative relation of violence is but the other side, the hidden presupposition, of law's normativity (as the thesis of the paradoxical nature of law claims), then no normative critique of law is possible that seeks to arrive at a decision that would dissolve their coexistence; the strife between law as critique and the violence of law is not a possible object of critique.

One can summarize these considerations by saying that the genealogical critique—which reads the forms of law as the execution of its paradox—thus stands in an irreducibly double relation to normative critique. Genealogical critique as much dissolves the dogmatism of normative critique as it explains its necessity. As genealogical *critique* it is undermining—for it turns against the dogmatism of vulgar critique. As *genealogical* critique it at the same time explains what it undermines for it shows its genesis.[25] The genealogical critique is thus not the mere other of normative critique. The genealogical critique of normative critique is at the same the insight into its origins. It therefore reconstitutes the normative critique as the effect of the very paradox which normative critique at the same time ignores and suppresses. The genealogical critique thus does not dissolve or even abolish normative critique but brings it about in a new way and shape. Genealogical critique practices a normative critique of second or higher order.

This new understanding of normative critique by genealogical critique can be described as follows: the genealogical critique of the dogmatism of normative critique consists in showing that the possibility of normative distinction cannot be taken for granted; this is the position of legalism, of the normatively inflected self-understanding of law. The normative critic is (like) a judge who dogmatically presupposes the possibility and feasibility of normative judgment. Genealogical critique shows what is wrong with this presupposition: the dogmatism of normative critique cancels the paradoxical coexistence of the normative and the nonnormative that defines the law; it ignores that in each case the unlawful and the non-law overlap and become inseparable. The dogmatism of normative critique consists in repressing the paradox of law. What it thereby represses is, however, its own ground, for normative critique is but one side of law and thus itself emerges from the paradox of law. The genealogical critique of normative critique thus shows that it is dogmatic insofar as it is grounded in the paradox of law but does not acknowledge it. Normative critique denies what it in truth is: it is but one side in the paradox of law.[26]

With this, it becomes clear that the genealogical critique of the dogmatism of normative critique is itself an act of normative critique: for the dogmatism of normative critique, so the genealogical critique claims, *is wrong*. But, contrary to appearance, this does not mean that, in criticizing the dogmatism of normative critique, genealogical criticism simply falls back on or repeats the same dogmatism that it criticizes. For the normative judgment on the dogmatism of normative critique—the judgment that its dogmatism is wrong—works with a different, a non- or undogmatic conception of wrongness. The wrongness of normative critique, as legalism understands and practices it, consists in its inability to acknowledge and represent the paradox of law that is its ground. This, then, is the norm, or rule, of undogmatic critique: its norm is not a pre-given law that it presupposes as given, guaranteeing the possibility of normative distinction (between the lawful and the unlawful); its norm is, on the contrary, the paradoxical unity of the normative distinction (between the lawful and the unlawful) and the nonnormative distinction (between law and non-law) in law itself. Thus genealogical critique also judges and decides between right and wrong; it performs an act of normative decision, a critical act of taking sides. But it does so in the name of the paradoxical structure at the ground of normativity. The norm of genealogical criticism is the paradox of any norm.

7. Conclusion

The procedure of genealogical critique can be reconstructed in three steps. It means:

1. the *reading* of reality as the (self-)presentation of its own form of representing;

2. the *explanation* of form by the paradox that lies at, or serves as, its ground;

3. the *decision* between the right form as the acknowledgment of paradox and the wrong form as the repression of paradox.

The concept of genealogical critique begins by turning against the dogmatism of legal, i.e., law-like, normative critique. And it leads to a reconceptualization of normative decision, of the normative opposition between the right and the wrong form. Does this offer a solution to the aporia of the critique of law that stood at the beginning?

The aporia of the critique of law states that no critique of law is possible because critique itself is (like) law, it is subject to (a) law. This might be a different order of law than the existing one (presumably a "higher" law or court: the law of conscience or, as Schiller believed, the court of theater); but it is still law. Any radical opposition to law could thus not be an act of criticism, of critical decision between right and wrong, anymore. It would have to be something other than critique (maybe an act of creation, of Yes-saying). Critique, it seems, is too immanent *to* law to be a criticism *of* law. So the aporia of the critique of law says: law is the law of critique, the law of critique is law.

This is the formula of the aporia of the critique of law (and of normative critique in general). But, as it turns out, it is also the formula of the solution to, the way out of the aporia (the way into the aporia is, rightly understood, at the same time the way out of the aporia). For law, which is the law of critique, is split within itself; it contains its own other—the other of law. This is the paradox of the legal form. Law is the encounter, the strife, between the law of normative decision (between lawful and unlawful) and the nonnormative distinction (between law as a practice of normative decision and the non-law as the zone of normative indifference). If then *firstly* law is the law of critique, and if *secondly* law is defined by the paradoxical unity of the normative and the nonnormative, it follows that the law of critique is the paradoxical unity of the normative and the nonnormative. Critique—rightly understood—decides in the name of undecidability. And this is not, I want to insist, a mere play on words, a paradoxical pun. It is the definition of a normative critique of a higher order. For it defines a new criterion for what is wrong and what is right: it defines a standard for right, i.e. for true, law. The paradoxical unity of law is the criterion that both allows and calls for the critical rejection of all existing forms of law.

Notes

1. See Christoph Menke, "Law and Domination," in *Critical Theory in Critical Times: Transforming the Global Political and Economic Order*, ed. Penelope Deutscher and Cristina Lafont (New York: Columbia University Press, 2017), 117–138.

2. This article is a revised English translation of Christoph Menke, "Die Kritik des Rechts und das Recht der Kritik," *Deutsche Zeitschrift für Philosophie*, 66, no. 2 (2018), 143–161.

3. But this is also true for law; law and critique share the same fate. If law is critique, and if critique is the critique of (its own) law, then law itself—which is or practices critique—must also become the critique of law. See the discussion in Christoph Menke, *Law and Violence: Christoph Menke in Dialogue*, trans. Gerrit Jackson (Manchester: Manchester University Press, 2018).

4. Michel Foucault, "What is Critique?" in Michel Foucault, *The Politics of Truth*, ed. Sylvère Lotringer (Los Angeles, CA: Semiotext(e), 2007), 44–45.

5. "Once again, the analogy with language is illumination. . . . It can generally be said that not only language and law but all social institutions have been formed through a process of desemanticization and suspension of concrete practice in its immediate reference to the real. Just as grammar, producing a speech without denotation, has isolated something like a language from discourse, and law, in suspending the concrete custom and usage of individuals, has been able to isolate something like a norm, so the patient work of civilization proceeds in every domain by separating human practice from its concrete exercise and thereby creating that excess of signification over denotation that Lévi-Strauss was the first to recognize." Giorgio Agamben, *State of Exception*, trans. Kevin Attell (Chicago, IL: University of Chicago Press, 2005), 36–37.

6. Jacques Derrida, "Violence and Metaphysics: An Essay on the Thought of Emmanuel Levinas," in *Writing and Difference*, trans. Alan Bass (Chicago, IL: University of Chicago Press, 1978), 117.

7. See Kurt Röttgers, "Kritik," in *Geschichtliche Grundbegriffe*, ed. Otto Brunner, Werner Conze, and Reinhart Koselleck (Stuttgart: Klett-Cotta 1972–1992), 3:652 (translation modified). For a more reserved view, see Claus von Bormann, Giorgio Tonelli, and Helmut Holzhey, "Kritik" in *Historisches Wörterbuch der Philosophie*, ed. Joachim Ritter et al. (Basel: Schwabe Verlag, 1976), 4:1249.

8. See Plato, *Theaetetus*, in *Theaetetus and Sophist*, ed. Christopher Rowe (Cambridge: Cambridge University Press, 2015), 170d.

9. See Michel Foucault, "Truth and Juridical Forms," in *The Essential Works of Michel Foucault*, vol. 3, *Power*, ed. James D. Faubion (New York: New Press, 2000), 31–45.

10. Søren Kierkegaard, *Fear and Trembling/Repetition*, ed. and trans. Howard V. Hong and Edna H. Hong (Princeton, NJ: Princeton University Press, 1983), 134.

11. This is the consequence Deleuze draws, following Nietzsche, from the insight into the legal form of critique; see Gilles Deleuze, "To Have Done with Judgment," in *Essays Critical and Clinical*, trans. D.W. Smith and M.A. Greco (London: Verso, 1998).

12. Karl Marx, "Zur Kritik der Hegelschen Rechtsphilosophie: Kritik des Hegelschen Staatsrechts," in *Karl Marx/Friedrich Engels: Werke*, ed. Institut für

Marxismus-Leninismus, et al. (Berlin: Dietz Verlag, 1956–2018), 1:296 (§§ 261–313); my translation.

13. Ibid.

14. As Jan Łukasiewicz objected against the tradition of logic since Aristotle: "[It] appears that even Aristotle at least sensed the practical-ethical worth of the principle of contradiction. At a time of the political decline of Greece, Aristotle became the founder and investigator of systematic, scientific, cultural work. Perhaps he saw in that consolation for the future and the future greatness of his nation. Denial of the principle of contradiction would have opened door and gate to every falsity and nipped the young, blossoming science in the bud. Hence the Stagirite therefore turns against the opponents of the principle with forceful language in which one can trace an internal fervor, against the eristic thinkers of Megara, the cynics of the school of Antisthenes, the disciples of Heraclitus, the partisans of Protagoras; and he battles with all of them for a theoretical principle as if for personal goods. He might well have himself felt the weaknesses of his argument; and so he announced his principle a final *axiom*, an unassailable *dogma*." See Jan Łukasiewicz, "On the Principle of Contradiction in Aristotle," *Review of Metaphysics* 24, no. 3 (1971): 509.

15. Karl Marx, *Das Kapital*, vol. 1, in *Karl Marx/Friedrich Engels: Werke*, 23:94–95.

16. Kierkegaard, *Repetition*, 135.

17. Karl Marx, "Ökonomisch-philosophische Manuskripte," in *Karl Marx/ Friedrich Engels: Werke*, 1, Supplement:573.

18. "Lesen des Seienden als Text seines Werdens." Theodor W. Adorno, *Negative Dialektik*, in Theodor Adorno, *Gesammelte Schriften*, ed. Rolf Tiedemann (Frankfurt am Main: Suhrkamp, 1970–1997), 6:62.

19. Friedrich Schlegel, "Athenaeum Fragments," in *Friedrich Schlegel's Lucinde and the Fragments*, ed. and trans. Peter Firchow (Minneapolis: University of Minnesota Press, 1971), 195 (no. 238).

20. I have tried to answer this genealogical question for the liberal or bourgeois form of (individual, subjective) rights in Christoph Menke, *Kritik der Rechte* (Frankfurt am Main: Suhrkamp, 2015).

21. See Raymond Geuss, "Genealogy as Critique," in *Outside Ethics* (Princeton, NJ: Princeton University Press 2005), 153–160. See also Martin Saar, *Genealogie als Kritik: Geschichte und Theorie des Subjekts nach Nietzsche und Foucault* (Frankfurt am Main: Campus 2007), ch. 7.

22. Walter Benjamin, "Zur Kritik der Gewalt," in *Gesammelte Schriften*, ed. Rolf Tiedemann and Hermann Schweppenhauser (Frankfurt am Main: Suhrkamp Verlag, 1974–1991), 2.1:202 ("scheidende und entscheidende Einstellung").

23. For details see Menke, *Kritik der Rechte*, 103–176, and Menke, *Law and Violence*, 3–76.

24. De-differentiation occurs in both directions. In the first, the unlawful is treated like non-law: the criminal becomes an enemy, the law gives way to a

state of exception. In the second direction, non-law is treated as the unlawful: the lawless becomes a criminal, the law becomes an educational system.

25. All genealogical critique, simply by virtue of being genealogical, thus has an "affirmative" moment, which Hans Joas claims against forms of merely critical genealogy. See Hans Joas, *The Sacredness of the Person: A New Genealogy of Human Rights* (Washington, DC: Georgetown University Press, 2013).

26. Understood in this way, Marx's use of the term "dogmatic" (the "dogmatism" of "vulgar criticism") corresponds to Hegel's definition of the term. For Hegel, dogmatism is the position that does not recognize that the principle that it claims is only one side in an "antinomy." See Georg Wilhelm Friedrich Hegel, "Differenz des Fichteschen und Schellingschen Systems der Philosophie," in *Werke in zwanzig Bände*, ed. Eva Moldenhauer and Karl Markus Michel (Frankfurt am Main: Suhrkamp, 1970), 2:49. Insofar as this also applies to the position of "criticism," it is itself a dogmatic figure; see Friedrich Wilhelm Joseph Schelling, "Philosophische Briefe über Dogmatismus und Kriticismus," in *Schriften von 1794–1798* (Darmstadt: Wissenschaftliche Buchgesellschaft 1975), 161–222.

Works Cited

Acosta López, María del Rosario. "Making Other People's Feelings our Own: From the Aesthetic to the Political in Schiller's *Aesthetic Letters*." In *Who Is This Schiller Now?*, edited by Jeffery High, Nicholas Martin, and N. Oellers. London: Camden House, 2011.

———. "On the Poetical Nature of Philosophical Writing: A Controversy about Style between Schiller and Fichte." In *Philosophers and their Poets: The Poetic Turn in German Philosophy Since Kant*, edited by Charles Bambach and Theodore George. Albany: State University of New York Press, 2019.

———. "The Resistance of Beauty: On Schiller's *Kallias Briefe* in Response to Kant's Aesthetics." *Epoche* 21, no. 1 (2016).

———. "¿Una superación estética del deber? La crítica de Schiller a Kant." *Episteme N.S.* 28, no. 2 (2008).

———. *La tragedia como conjuro: el problema de lo sublime en Friedrich Schiller*. Bogotá: Universidad Nacional de Colombia, 2008.

———. "The Violence of Reason: Schiller and Hegel on the French Revolution." In *Aesthetic Reason and Imaginative Freedom: Friedrich Schiller and Philosophy*, edited by María del Rosario Acosta López and Jeffrey Powell. Albany: State University of New York Press, 2018.

Adelung, Johann Christoph. *Grammatisch-kritisch Wörterbuch der hochdeutschen Mundart*. Leipzig: Breitkopf, 1793.

Adorno, Theodor. "The Actuality of Philosophy." *Telos* 31 (1977).

———. *Aesthetic Theory*. Translated by Robert Hullot-Kentor. Minneapolis: University of Minnesota Press, 1997.

———. *Gesammelte Schriften*. Edited by Rolf Tiedemann. Frankfurt am Main: Suhrkamp, 1970–1997.

———. *History and Freedom: Lectures 1964–1965*. Edited by Rolf Tiedemann, translated by Rodney Livingstone. Cambridge: Polity, 2006.

———. "The Idea of Natural-History." In Robert Hullot-Kentor, *Things Beyond Resemblance: Collected Essays on Theodor W. Adorno*. New York: Columbia University Press, 2006.

———. *Lectures on Negative Dialectics: Fragments of a Lecture Course, 1965/1966*. Edited by Rolf Tiedemann, translated by Rodney Livingstone. Cambridge: Polity, 2008.

———. *Metaphysics: Concept and Problems*. Edited by Rolf Tiedemann, translated by Edmund Jephcott. Stanford, CA: Stanford University Press, 2001.

———. *Metaphysik: Begriff und Probleme*. Edited by Rolf Tiedemann. Frankfurt am Main: Suhrkamp, 1998.

———. *Minima Moralia: Reflections on a Damaged Life*. Translated by E.F.N. Jephcott. London: Verso, 2005.

———. *Negative Dialectics*. Translated by E.B. Ashton. New York: Continuum, 1973.

———. *Negative Dialectics*. Translated by Dennis Redmond. https://www.academia.edu/39707967/Negative_Dialectics, 2001.

Agamben, Giorgio. *State of Exception*. Translated by Kevin Attell. Chicago: University of Chicago Press, 2005.

Aldea, Andreea Smaranda. "Making Sense of Husserl's Notion of Teleology—Normativity, Reason, Progress and Phenomenology as 'Critique from Within.'" *Hegel Bulletin* 38, no. 1 (2017).

———. "Phenomenology as Critique: Teleological-Historical Reflection and Husserl's Transcendental Eidetics." *Husserl Studies* 32 (2016).

Aldea, Andreea Smaranda, and Amy Allen. "The Historical A Priori in Husserl and Foucault." *Continental Philosophy Review* 49, no. 1 (2016).

Aldea, Andreea Smaranda, and Julia Jansen. "Imagination in Phenomenology: Variations and Modalities." *Husserl Studies*. Forthcoming.

Allen, Amy. *The End of Progress: Decolonizing the Normative Foundations of Critical Theory*. New York: Columbia University Press, 2016.

———. "The Ends of Progress: Reply to Critics." *Contemporary Political Theory* (2018).

———. "Foucault and the Problem of Psychoanalysis: Two Aspects of Problematization." *Angelaki* 23, no. 2 (2018).

———. *The Politics of Ourselves: Power, Autonomy, and Gender in Contemporary Critical Theory*. New York: Columbia University Press, 2008.

———. "'Psychoanalysis and Ethnology' Reconsidered: Foucault's Historicization of History." *Southern Journal of Philosophy* 55, Spindel Supplement (2017).

Al-Saji, Alia. "Bodies and Sensings: On the Uses of Husserlian Phenomenology for Feminist Theory." *Continental Philosophy Review* 43, no. 1 (2010).

———. "Creating Possibility: The Time of the Quebec Student Movement." *Theory & Event* 15, no. 3, Supplement (2012).

———. "A Phenomenology of Hesitation: Interrupting Racializing Habits of Seeing." In *Living Alterities*, edited by Emily S. Lee. Albany: State University of New York Press, 2014.

Althusser, Louis. *For Marx*. Translated by Ben Brewster. London: Verso, 2005.

Ameriks, Karl. *Kant and the Historical Turn: Philosophy as Critical Interpretation*. New York: Oxford University Press, 2006.

———. "Reality, Reason, and Religion in the Development of Kant's Ethics." In *Kant's Moral Metaphysics: God, Freedom, and Immortality*. Edited by James Krueger and Benjamin J. Bruxvoort Lipscomb. Berlin: Walter de Gruyter, 2010.
Aristotle. *The Complete Works of Aristotle: The Revised Oxford Translation*. Edited by Jonathan Barnes. Princeton, NJ: Princeton University Press, 1984.
———. *Sophistical Refutations*. Translated by E. S. Forster and D. J. Furley. Cambridge, MA: Harvard University Press, 1978.
Baeza, Natalia. *Contradiction, Critique, and Dialectic in Adorno*. PhD diss., University of Notre Dame, 2012.
Basterra, Gabriel. *The Subject of Freedom: Kant, Levinas*. New York: Fordham University Press, 2015.
Baum, Manfred. "Herder über Kants 'vefehlte Kritik der reinen Vernunft.'" In *Herders 'Metakritik': Analysen und Interpretationen*, edited by Marion Heinz. Stuttgart: Fromann-Holzboog, 2013.
Beck, Lewis White. *A Commentary on Kant's Critique of Practical Reason*. Chicago: University of Chicago Press, 1960.
Behler, Ernst. *Irony and the Discourse of Modernity*. Seattle: University of Washington Press, 1990.
Beiser, Frederick. *Enlightenment, Revolution, and Romanticism: The Genesis of Modern German Political Thought 1790–1800*. Cambridge, MA: Harvard University Press, 1992.
———. *The Fate of Reason: German Philosophy from Kant to Fichte*. Cambridge, MA: Harvard University Press, 1987.
———. *The Genesis of Neo-Kantianism, 1796–1880*. Oxford: Oxford University Press, 2014.
———. "Kant's Intellectual Development: 1746–1781." In *The Cambridge Companion to Kant*, edited by Paul Guyer. Cambridge: Cambridge University Press, 1992.
———. "Un lamento." In *Friedrich Schiller: Estética y Libertad*. Edited by María del Rosario Acosta López. Bogotá: Universidad Nacional, 2008.
———. *Schiller as Philosopher: A Re-Examination*. New York: Oxford University Press, 2005.
Benhabib, Seyla. *Critique, Norm and Utopia: A Study of the Foundations of Critical Theory*. New York: Columbia University Press, 1986.
Benjamin, Walter. *The Arcades Project*. Edited by Rolf Tiedemann, translated by Howard Eiland and Kevin Mclaughlin. Cambridge, MA: Harvard University Press, 1999.
———. *Gesammelte Schriften*. Edited by Rolf Tiedemann and Hermann Schweppenhauser. Frankfurt am Main: Suhrkamp Verlag, 1974–1991.
———. *The Origin of German Tragic Drama*. Translated by John Osborne. London: Verso, 2003.
Berlin, Isaiah. *Three Critics of the Enlightenment: Vico, Hamann, Herder*. Princeton, NJ: Princeton University Press, 2000.

Bernstein, J.M. *Adorno: Disenchantment and Ethics*. Cambridge: Cambridge University Press, 2001.
———, ed. *Classic and Romantic German Aesthetics*. Cambridge: Cambridge University Press, 2003.
———. "What Do We Owe Other People? On Amy Allen's *The End of Progress*." *Berlin Journal of Critical Theory* 2, no. 2 (2018).
Bondeli, Martin. *Das Anfangsproblem bei Karl Leonhard Reinhold*. Frankfurt am Main: Vittorio Klostermann, 1995.
Bormann, Claus von, Giorgio Tonelli, and Helmut Holzhey. "Kritik." In *Historisches Wörterbuch der Philosophie*, edited by Joachim Ritter et al. Basel: Schwabe Verlag, 1976.
Breazeale, Daniel. *Thinking Through the Wissenschaftslehre: Themes from Fichte's Early Philosophy*. New York: Oxford University Press, 2014.
Brude-Firnau, Gisela. "Alexander von Humboldt's Sociopolitical Intentions: Science and Poetics." In *Traditions of Experiment from the Enlightenment to the Present: Essays in Honor of Peter Demetz*, edited by Nancy Kaiser and David Wellbery. Ann Arbor: University of Michigan Press, 1992.
Bruno, G. Anthony. "'As From a State of Death': Schelling's Idealism as Mortalism." *Comparative and Continental Philosophy* 8, no. 3 (2016).
———. "Freedom and Pluralism in Schelling's Critique of Fichte's Jena *Wissenschaftslehre*." *Idealistic Studies* 43, no. 1/2 (2014).
Budd, Malcolm. *The Aesthetic Appreciation of Nature*. Oxford: Oxford University Press, 2002.
Burnyeat, Myles. "Can the Sceptic Live his Scepticism?" In *The Original Sceptics: A Controversy*, edited by Myles Burnyeat and Michael Frede. Indianapolis: Hackett Publishing Company, 1997.
Cain, Patrick. "Practical Cognition, Intuition, and the Fact of Reason." In *Kant's Moral Metaphysics: God, Freedom, and Immortality*. Edited by James Krueger and Benjamin J. Bruxvoort Lipscomb. Berlin: Walter de Gruyter, 2010.
Carr, David. *Experience and History*. New York: Oxford University Press, 2014.
Cassin, Barbara. *Dictionary of Untranslatables: A Philosophical Lexicon*. Princeton, NJ: Princeton University Press, 2014.
Cassirer, Ernst. *The Logic of the Cultural Sciences*. Translated by S. G. Lofts. New Haven: Yale University Press, 2000.
Cavell, Stanley. *The Claim of Reason: Wittgenstein, Skepticism, Morality and Tragedy*. Oxford: Oxford University Press, 1999.
———. "An Emerson Mood." In *Emerson's Transcendental Etudes*. Stanford, CA: Stanford University Press, 2003.
———. *Must We Mean What We Say?* Cambridge: Cambridge University Press, 1976.
Chakravartty, Paula, and Denise Ferreira da Silva. "Accumulation, Dispossession, and Debt: The Racial Logic of Global Capitalism—An Introduction." *American Quarterly* 64, no. 3 (2012).

Cicatello, Angelo. *Dialettica negativa e logica della parvenza: Saggio su T.W. Adorno*. Genova: Il Nuovo Melangolo, 2001.
Cicero. *On Academic Skepticism*. Translated by C. Brittain. Indianapolis: Hackett, 2006.
Coen, Ethan, and Joel Coen. *The Big Lebowski*. Universal City: Universal Studios Home Entertainment, 1998. DVD.
Cohen, Hermann. *Ethik des reinen Willens*. Berlin: Bruno Cassirer, 1907.
———. *Kants Theorie der Erfahrung*. Berlin: Dümmler, 1871/1885.
———. *Kants Begründung der Ethik: Nebst ihren Anwendungen auf Recht, Religion und Geschichte*. 2nd ed. Berlin: Bruno Cassirer, 1910.
———. *System der Philosophie, erster Teil: Logik der reinen Erkenntnis*. Berlin: Bruno Cassirer, 1920.
Cook, Deborah. "Adorno, Foucault, and Critique." *Philosophy and Social Criticism* 39, no. 10 (2013).
———. *Adorno, Foucault, and the Critique of the West*. London: Verso, 2018.
———. "Foucault, Freud, and the Repressive Hypothesis." *Journal of the British Society for Phenomenology* 45, no. 2 (2014).
Correa Motta, Alfonso. "¿Es posible vivir el escepticismo?" In *Convertir la vida en arte: una introducción a la filosofía como forma de vida*, edited by A. Lozano and G. Meléndez. Bogotá: Universidad Nacional de Colombia, 2016.
Crousaz, Jean-Pierre de. *Examen du pyrrhonisme ancien et moderne*. Den Haag: Pierre de Hondt, 1733.
Crusius, Christian August. *Entwurf der nothwendigen Vernunft-Wahrheiten, wiefern sie den Zufälligen entgegen gesetzet werden*. Leipzig: Gleditsch, 1745.
Dahlstrom, Daniel O. *Kant and his German Contemporaries*, vol. 2, *Aesthetics, History, Politics, and Religion*. Cambridge: Cambridge University Press, 2018.
Dastur, François. "Phenomenology of the Event: Waiting and Surprise." *Hypatia*, 15, no. 4 (2000).
de Boer, Karin. "Categories versus Schemata: Kant's Two-Aspect Theory of Pure Concepts and his Critique of Wolffian Metaphysics." *Journal of the History of Philosophy* 54, no. 3 (2016).
———. "Kant's Account of Sensible Concepts in the *Inaugural Dissertation* and the *Critique of Pure Reason*." In *Akten des XII. Internationalen Kant-Kongresses*, edited by Violetta Waibel and Margit Ruffing. Berlin: Walter de Gruyter, 2018.
———. *Kant's Reform of Metaphysics: The Critique of Pure Reason Reconsidered*. Cambridge: Cambridge University Press, 2020.
———. "Kant's Response to Hume's Critique of Pure Reason." *Archiv für Geschichte der Philosophie* (2019).
de Boer, Karin, and Ruth Sonderegger. *Conceptions of Critique in Modern und Contemporary Philosophy*. Basingstoke: Palgrave Macmillan, 2012.
de la Harpe, Jacqueline E. *Jean-Pierre de Crousaz et le conflit des idées au siècle des lumières*. Berkeley: University of California Press, 1955.

Deleuze, Gilles. *Essays Critical and Clinical*. Translated by D.W. Smith and M.A. Greco. London: Verso, 1998.
de Man, Paul. *Aesthetic Ideology*. Edited by Andrzej Warminski. Minneapolis: University of Minnesota Press, 1996.
Derrida, Jacques. *Writing and Difference*. Translated by Alan Bass. Chicago: University of Chicago Press, 1978.
DeSouza, Nigel. "The Metaphysical and Epistemological Foundations of Herder's Philosophical Anthropology." In *Herder: Philosophy and Anthropology*, edited by Anik Waldow and Nigel DeSouza. Oxford: Oxford University Press, 2017.
de Vleeschauer, Hermann-Jean. *The Development of Kantian Thought*. Translated by A.R.C. Duncan. Edinburgh: Thomas Nelson and Sons, 1962.
Dewey, John. *Lectures in China 1919–1920*. Honolulu: Hawaii University Press, 1973.
———. "Lectures in Social and Political Philosophy (China)." *European Journal of Pragmatism and American Philosophy* 2, no. 7 (2015).
Dienst, Richard. *The Bonds of Debt*. London: Verso, 2011.
di Giovanni, George, and H.S. Harris. *Between Kant and Hegel: Texts in the Development of Post-Kantian Idealism*. Revised edition. Indianapolis: Hackett, 2000.
Dilthey, Wilhelm. *Gesammelte Schriften*. Göttingen: Vandenhoeck & Ruprecht, 1913–2005.
———. *Selected Works*. Edited by Rudolf Makkreel and Frithjof Rodi. Princeton, NJ: Princeton University Press, 1989–.
Diogenes Laërtius. *Lives of Eminent Philosophers*. Translated by R. D. Hicks. Cambridge, MA: Harvard University Press, 1925.
Dorion, Louis-André. "Aristote et l'elenchos Socratique." *Les Études philosophiques* 4 (2011).
Dyck, Corey, and Falk Wunderlich. *Kant and his German Contemporaries*, vol. 1, *Logic, Mind, Epistemology, Science, and Ethics*. Cambridge: Cambridge University Press, 2018.
Ertl, Wolfgang. "Hume's Antinomy and Kant's Critical Turn." *British Journal for the History of Philosophy* 10, no. 4 (2002).
Falzon, Christopher. "Making History." In *Companion to Michel Foucault*, edited by Christopher Falzon, Timothy O'Leary, and Jana Sawicki. London: Blackwell, 2013.
Fausto-Sterling, Anne. *Sex/Gender: Biology in a Social World*. New York: Routledge, 2012.
Fenves, Peter. "Completion Instead of Revelation: Toward the 'Theological-Political Fragment.'" In *Walter Benjamin and Theology*, edited by Colby Dickenson and Stéphane Symons. New York: Fordham University Press, 2016.
———. "Il Diritto e la violenza—da Kant a Benjamin." Translated by Paola Morgavi. *aut aut* 384 (December 2019).
———. *Late Kant: Towards Another Law of the Earth*. New York: Routledge, 2003.
———. "Marital, Martial, and Maritime Law: Toward Some Controversial Passages in Kant's *Doctrine of Right*." *Diacritics* 35 (2005).

———. *The Messianic Reduction: Walter Benjamin and Shape of Time*. Stanford, CA: Stanford University Press, 2011.
Fichte, Johann Gottlieb. *Attempt at a Critique of All Revelation*. Translated by Garrett Green, edited by Allen Wood. Cambridge: Cambridge University Press, 2010.
———. *Early Philosophical Writings*. Edited and translated by Daniel Breazeale. Ithaca, NY: Cornell University Press, 1988.
———. *Foundations of Transcendental Philosophy (Wissenschaftslehre Nova Methodo)*. Translated by Daniel Breazeale. Ithaca, NY: Cornell University Press, 1998.
———. *Gesamtausgabe der Bayerischen Akademie der Wissenschaften*. Edited by Erich Fuchs, Hans Gliwitzky, Reinhard Lauth, and Peter K. Schneider. Stuttgart: Frommann-Holzboog, 1962–2012.
———. *Introductions to the Wissenschaftslehre and Other Writings*. Translated by Daniel Breazeale. Indianapolis: Hackett, 1994.
———. *Sämmtliche Werke*. Edited by Immanuel Hermann Fichte. Berlin: Walter de Gruyter, 1971.
———. *The Science of Knowledge*. Edited and translated by Peter Heath and John Lachs. New York: Cambridge University Press, 1982.
Fisher, Linda. "Feminist Phenomenology." In *Feminist Phenomenology*, edited by Linda Fisher and Lester Embree. Dordrecht: Kluwer, 2000.
———. "Phenomenology and Feminism: Perspectives on their Relation." In *Feminist Phenomenology*, edited by Linda Fisher and Lester Embree. Dordrecht: Kluwer, 2000.
Forst, Rainer. *The Right to Justification: Elements of a Constructivist Theory of Justice*. Translated by Jeffrey Flynn. New York: Columbia University Press, 2012.
Förster, Eckart. *Kant's Final Synthesis: An Essay on the "Opus postumum."* Cambridge, MA: Harvard University Press, 2000.
Forster, Michael N. *Kant and Skepticism*. Princeton, NJ: Princeton University Press, 2008.
Foster, John Bellamy, and Fred Magdoff. "Disposable Workers: Today's Reserve Army of Labor." *Monthly Review* 55, no. 11 (2004).
Foucault, Michel. *The Archaeology of Knowledge and the Discourse on Language*. Translated by A.M. Sheridan Smith. New York: Pantheon Books, 1972.
———. *The Essential Works of Michel Foucault, 1954–1984*. 3 vols. Edited by Paul Rabinow and James D. Faubion. New York: The New Press, 1997–2000.
———. *The Government of Self and Others: Lectures at the Collège de France 1982–83*. Edited by Frédéric Gros, translated by Graham Burchell. New York: Picador Press, 2011.
———. *The Order of Things: An Archaeology of the Human Sciences*. Translated by A.M. Sheridan Smith. New York: Pantheon Books, 1970.
———. *The Politics of Truth*. Edited by Sylvère Lotringer. Los Angeles: Semiotext(e), 2007.

Franks, Paul. *All or Nothing: Systematicity, Transcendental Arguments, and Skepticism in German Idealism*. Cambridge, MA: Harvard University Press, 2005.
Fraser, Nancy. "Behind Marx's Hidden Abode." *New Left Review* 86 (2014).
———. "Expropriation and Exploitation in Racialized Capitalism." *Critical Historical Studies* 3, no. 1 (2016).
———. "Legitimation Crisis: On the Political Contradictions of Financialized Capitalism." *Critical Historical Studies* 2, no. 2 (2015).
Fraser, Nancy, and Axel Honneth. *Redistribution or Recognition? A Political-Philosophical Exchange*. Translated by Joel Golb, James Ingram, and Christiane Wilke. London: Verso, 2003.
Freud, Sigmund. *The Standard Edition of the Complete Psychological Writings of Sigmund Freud*. Edited by James Strachey. London: Hogarth Press, 1956–1974.
Frketich, Elise. "Reinhold's Elementarphilosophie: A Scholastic of Critical Philosophical System?" *Kant Yearbook* 8 (2016).
———. "The Starting Point of Reinhold's *Elementarphilosophie*." Forthcoming.
Gasché, Rodolphe. *The Idea of Form: Rethinking Kant's Aesthetics*. Stanford, CA: Stanford University Press, 2003.
Geuss, Raymond. *Morality, Culture and History: Essays on German Philosophy*. Cambridge: Cambridge University Press, 1999.
———. *Outside Ethics*. Princeton, NJ: Princeton University Press, 2005.
Gjesdal, Kristin. *Herder's Hermeneutics: History, Poetry, Enlightenment*. Cambridge: Cambridge University Press, 2017.
Goldman, Avery. "Critique and the Mind: Towards a Defense of Kant's Transcendental Method." *Kant-Studien* 98, no. 4 (2007).
———. *Kant and the Subject of Critique*. Bloomington: Indiana University Press, 2012.
———. "What is Orientation in Critique?" In *Recht und Frieden in der Philosophie Kants: Akten des X. Internationalen Kant-Kongresses*. Edited by Valerio Rohden et al. Berlin: Walter de Gruyter, 2008.
Gonzalez, Catalina. "Pyrrhonism vs. Academic Skepticism in Kant's *Critique of Pure Reason*." *Philosophy Today* 55, Supplement (2011).
Gottsched, Johann Christoph. *Versuch einer critischen Dichtkunst vor die Deutschen*. Leipzig: Bernhard Christoph Breitkopf, 1730.
Gregoratto, Federica. "Agonistic Recognition, Intersections and the Ambivalence of Family Bonds: John Dewey's Critical Theory Manifesto in China." *Transactions of the Charles S. Pierce Society* 53, no. 1 (2017).
———. *Il Doppio volto della comunicazione*. Milano/Udine: Mimesis, 2013.
Grier, Michelle. *Kant's Doctrine of Transcendental Illusion*. Cambridge: Cambridge University Press, 2001.
Grimm, Jacob, and Wilhelm Grimm. *Deutsches Wörterbuch von Jacob und Wilhelm Grimm*. Leipzig: Hirzel Verlag, 1873.
———. *Deutsches Wörterbuch von Jacob und Wilhelm Grimm*. http://dwb.uni-trier.de/de/die-digitale-version/online-version/.

Guyer, Paul. "Kant on Common Sense and Scepticism." *Kantian Review* 7, no. 1 (2003).
———. *Kant on Freedom, Law, and Happiness*. Cambridge: Cambridge University Press, 2000.
———. *Kant's System of Nature and Freedom*. Oxford: Oxford University Press, 2005.
Habermas, Jürgen. *Between Naturalism and Religion: Philosophical Essays*. Cambridge: Polity Press, 2008.
———. "Nach dreißig Jahren: Bemerkungen zu *Erkenntnis und Interesse*." In *Das Interesse der Vernunft: Rückblicke auf das Werk von Jürgen Habermas nach Erkenntnis und Interesse*, edited by Stefan Müller-Doohm. Frankfurt am Main: Suhrkamp, 2000.
———. "Richard Rorty's Pragmatic Turn." In *Rorty and His Critics*, edited by Robert B. Brandom. Malden: Blackwell, 2000.
———. *Theory and Practice*. Translated by John Viertel. Boston: Beacon, 1974.
———. *The Theory of Communicative Action*, vol. 1, *Reason and the Rationalization of Society*. Translated by Thomas McCarthy. Boston: Beacon, 1984.
———. *Truth and Justification*. Translated by Barbara Fultner. Cambridge, MA: MIT Press, 2003.
———. *Wahrheit und Rechtfertigung*. Frankfurt am Main: Suhrkamp, 2004.
Hahmann, Andree. "Die Reaktion der spekulativen Weltweisheit: Kant und die Kritik an den einfachen Substanzen." *Kant-Studien* 100, no. 4 (2009).
Haiven, Max. *Cultures of Financialization: Fictitious Capital in Popular Culture and Everyday Life*. New York: Palgrave, 2014.
Hamacher, Werner. "Pleroma: Zu Genesis und Struktur einer dialektischen Hermeneutik bei Hegel." In Georg Wilhelm Friedrich Hegel, *Das Geist des Christentums: Schriften 1796–1800*, edited by W. Hamacher. Berlin: Ullstein, 1978.
Hamann, Johann Georg. "Metacritique." In *What is Enlightenment? Eighteenth-Century Answers and Twentieth-Century Questions*, edited by James Schmidt. Berkeley: University of California Press, 1996.
Hanssen, Beatrice. *Walter Benjamin's Other History: Of Stones, Animals, Human Beings, and Angels*. Berkeley: University of California Press, 1998.
Harvey, David. *Marx, Capital, and the Madness of Economic Reason*. Oxford: Oxford University Press, 2018.
Haslanger, Sally. *Critical Theory and Practice: Spinoza Lectures*. Amsterdam: Koninklijke van Gorcum, 2017.
———. "Race, Intersectionality, and Method: A Reply to Critics." *Philosophical Studies* 171, no. 1 (2014).
———. *Resisting Reality*. Oxford: Oxford University Press, 2012.
———. "Social Structure, Narrative and Explanation." *Canadian Journal of Philosophy* 45, no. 1 (2015).
Haym, Rudolf. *Herder*. Berlin: Aufbau, 1954.

Hegel, Georg Wilhelm Friedrich. *The Difference Between Fichte's and Schelling's System of Philosophy*. Edited and translated by H. S. Harris and Walter Cerf. Albany: State University of New York Press, 1977.

———. *Elements of the Philosophy of Right*. Edited by Allen W. Wood, translated by H.B. Nisbet. Cambridge: Cambridge University Press, 1991.

———. *Werke in zwanzig Bände*. Edited by Eva Moldenhauer and Karl Markus Michel. Frankfurt am Main: Suhrkamp, 1970.

Heidegger, Martin. *Being and Time*. Translated by John Macquarrie and Edward Robinson. Oxford: Blackwell, 1962.

———. *Kant and the Problem of Metaphysics*. 5th ed., enlarged. Translated by Richard Taft. Bloomington: Indiana University Press, 1997.

———. *Toward the Definition of Philosophy*. Translated by Ted Sadler. London: Continuum, 2002.

Heinämaa, Sara. *Toward a Phenomenology of Sexual Difference*. London: Rowman & Littlefield, 2003.

Henrich, Dieter. "Beauty and Freedom: Schiller's Struggle with Kant's Aesthetics." In *Essays in Kant's Aesthetics*, edited by Ted Cohen and Paul Guyer. Chicago: University of Chicago Press, 1982.

———. "Fichte's Original Insight." Translated by David Lachterman. *Contemporary German Philosophy* 1 (1982).

Hepburn, Ronald. "Contemporary Aesthetics and the Neglect of Natural Beauty." In *British Analytical Philosophy*, edited by Bernard Williams and Alan Montefiore. New York: The Humanities Press, 1966.

———. "Trivial and Serious in Aesthetic Appreciation of Nature." In *Landscape, Natural beauty, and the Arts*, edited by Salim Kemal and Ivan Gaskell. Cambridge: Cambridge University Press, 1993.

Herder, Johann Gottfried. *Philosophical Writings*. Edited and translated by Michael Forster. Cambridge: Cambridge University Press, 2002.

———. *Selected Writings on Aesthetics*. Translated by Gregory Moore. Princeton, NJ: Princeton University Press, 2006.

———. *Werke in zehn Bänden*. Edited by Ulrich Gaier et al. Frankfurt am Main: Deutscher Klassiker Verlag, 1985–2000.

Heßbrüggen-Walter, Stefan. "Putting Our Soul in Place." *Kant Yearbook* 6 (2014).

Honneth, Axel, Eberhard Knödler-Bunte, and Arno Widmann. "The Dialectics of Rationalization: An Interview with Jürgen Habermas." *Telos* 21, no. 49 (1981).

Horkheimer, Max. *Critical Theory: Selected Essays*. Translated by Matthew J. O'Connell. New York: Continuum, 1975.

———. *Traditionelle und kritische Theorie: fünf Aufsätze*. Frankfurt am Main: Fischer Taschenbuch Verlag, 1992.

Horkheimer, Max, and Theodor Adorno. *Dialectic of Enlightenment: Philosophical Fragments*. Translated by Edmund Jephcott. Stanford, CA: Stanford University Press, 2002.

Hulatt, Owen. "Reason, Mimesis, and Self-Preservation in Adorno." *Journal of the History of Philosophy* 54, no. 1 (2016).
Hullot-Kentor, Robert. *Things Beyond Resemblance: Collected Essays on Theodor W. Adorno.* New York: Columbia University Press, 2006.
Humboldt, Alexander von. *Ansichten der Natur.* Edited by Hanno Beck. Darmstadt: Wissenschaftliche Buchgesellschaft, 1987.
———. *Cosmos: A Sketch of the Physical Description of the Universe.* Translated by E.C. Otté. Baltimore: Johns Hopkins University Press, 1997.
———. *Kosmos: Entwurf einer physischen Weltbeschreibung.* 5 vols. Stuttgart/Tübingen: J.G. Cotta, 1845–1862.
———. *Views of Nature.* Edited by Stephen T. Jackson and Laura Dassow Walls, translated by Mark W. Person. Chicago: University of Chicago Press, 2014.
———. *Views of Nature or Contemplations on the Sublime Phenomena of Creation.* Translated by E.C. Otté and Henry G. Bohn. London: Henry G. Bohn, 1850.
Husserl, Edmund. *Analysen zur Passiven Synthesis. Aus Vorlesungs- und Forschungsmanuskripten 1918–1926.* Edited by Margot Fleischer. Den Haag: Martinus Nijhoff, 1966.
———. *Analyses Concerning Passive and Active Synthesis: Lectures on Transcendental Logic.* Translated by Anthony J. Steinbock. Dordrecht: Kluwer, 2001.
———. *Cartesianische Meditationen und Pariser Vorträge.* Edited by Stephan Strasser. Den Haag: Martinus Nijhoff, 1950.
———. *Cartesian Meditations: An Introduction to Phenomenology.* Translated by Dorion Cairns. Den Haag: Matinus Nijhoff, 1960.
———. *The Crisis of European Sciences and Transcendental Phenomenology.* Translated by David Carr. Evanston: Northwestern University Press, 1970.
———. *Experience and Judgment.* Translated by James S. Churchill and Karl Ameriks. Evanston: Northwestern University Press, 1973.
———. *Husserliana.* Edited by Rudolph Bernet and Ullrich Melle. Dodrecht: Springer, 1950–.
———. *Ideen zu einer reinen Phänomenologie und phänomenologischen Philosophie I: Allgemeine Einführung in die reine Phänomenologie.* Edited by Karl Schuhmann. Den Haag: Martinus Nijhoff, 1976.
———. *Ideen zur einer reinen Phänomenologie und phänomenologischen Philosophie II: Phänomenologische Untersuchungen zur Konstitution.* Edited by Marly Biemel. Den Haag: Martinus Nijhoff, 1952.
———. *Ideas Pertaining to a Pure Phenomenology and to a Phenomenological Philosophy (Second Book).* Translated by Richard Rojcewicz and André Schuwer. Dordrecht: Kluwer, 1989.
———. *Die Krisis de Europäischen Wissenschaften und die Transzendentale Phänomenologie.* Edited by Walter Biemel. Den Haag: Martinus Nijhoff, 1954.

---. *Die Krisis der Europäischen Wissenschaften und die Transzendentale Phänomenologie, Ergänzungsband, Texte aus dem Nachlass 1934–1937*. Edited by Reinhold N. Smid. Dordrecht: Kluwer, 1993.

---. *Phantasie, Bildbewusstsein, Erinnerung 1898–1925*. Edited by Eduard Marbach. Den Haag: Martinus Nijhoff, 1980.

---. *Phantasy, Image Consciousness, and Memory (1898–1925)*. Translated by John B. Brough. Dordrecht: Springer, 2005.

Irwin, Terence. "Say What You Believe." *Apeiron: A Journal for Ancient Philosophy and Science* 26, no. 3/4 (1993).

Janaway, Christopher. *Beyond Selflessness*. Oxford: Oxford University Press, 2007.

Joas, Hans. *The Sacredness of the Person: A New Genealogy of Human Rights*. Washington, DC: Georgetown University Press, 2013.

Kant, Immanuel. *Anthropology, History, and Education*. Edited by Robert B. Louden and Günther Zöller. Cambridge: Cambridge University Press, 2007.

---. *The Cambridge Edition of the Works of Immanuel Kant in Translation*. Edited by Paul Guyer and Allen W. Wood. Cambridge: Cambridge University Press, 1992–2016.

---. *Correspondence*. Edited and translated by Arnulf Zweig. Cambridge: Cambridge University Press, 1999.

---. *Critique of Pure Reason*. Edited and translated by Paul Guyer and Allen W. Wood. New York: Cambridge University Press, 1998.

---. *Critique of the Power of Judgment*. Translated by Paul Guyer and Eric Matthews. Cambridge: Cambridge University Press, 2000.

---. *Immanuel Kant on History*. Translated by Lewis White Beck. Indianapolis: Bobbs-Merill Co., 1963.

---. *Kants gesammelte Schriften (Akademie Ausgabe)*. Edited by the Royal Prussian (later German) Academy of Sciences. Berlin: Georg Reimer, later Walter de Gruyter, 1900–.

---. *Lectures on Anthropology*. Edited by Allen W. Wood and Robert B. Louden, translated by Robert R. Clewis, Robert B. Louden, G. Felicitas Munzel, and Allen W. Wood. Cambridge: Cambridge University Press, 2012.

---. *Lectures on Ethics*. Translated by Peter Heath and J.B. Schneewind. Cambridge: Cambridge University Press, 1997.

---. *Lectures on Logic*. Edited and translated by J. Michael Young. Cambridge: Cambridge University Press, 1992.

---. *The Metaphysics of Morals*. Translated by Mary Gregor. Cambridge: Cambridge University Press, 1991.

---. *Philosophical Correspondence 1759–99*. Edited and translated by Arnulf Zweig. Chicago: University of Chicago Press, 1967.

---. *Practical Philosophy*. Edited and Translated by Mary Gregor. Cambridge: Cambridge University Press, 1996.

———. *Theoretical Philosophy, 1755–1770*. Edited and translated by David Walford and Ralf Meerbote. Cambridge: Cambridge University Press, 1992.

———. *Theoretical Philosophy after 1781*. Edited by Henry Allison and Peter Heath. Cambridge: Cambridge University Press, 2002.

Katsafanas, Paul. "Nietzsche's Philosophical Psychology." In *The Oxford Handbook on Nietzsche*, edited by John Richardson and Ken Gemes. Oxford: Oxford University Press, 2013.

Kelly, Mark. *The Political Philosophy of Michel Foucault*. New York: Routledge, 2009.

Kemp Smith, Norman. *A Commentary to Kant's Critique of Pure Reason*. 1918; repr., New York: Palgrave, 2003.

Kerimov, Khafiz. "The Time of the Beautiful in Kant's *Critique of Judgment*." *Epoche* 24, no. 1 (2019).

Kierkegaard, Søren. *Fear and Trembling/Repetition*. Edited and translated by Howard V. Hong and Edna H. Hong. Princeton, NJ: Princeton University Press, 1983.

———. *Journals and Papers*. Edited and translated by Edna Hong and Howard Hong, with Gregor Malantschuk. Bloomington: Indiana University Press, 1967.

Kisiel, Theodore. *The Genesis of Heidegger's Being and Time*. Berkeley: University of California Press, 1993.

Knobloch, Eberhard. "Naturgenuss und Weltgemälde—Gedanken zu Humboldt Kosmos," *Internationale Zeitschrift für Humboldt-Studien* 5, no. 9 (2004).

Kohlenbach, Margarete. "Transformations of German Romanticism 1830–2000." In *The Cambridge Companion to German Romanticism*, edited by Nicholas Saul. Cambridge: Cambridge University Press, 2009.

Kohnke, Klaus Christian. *The Rise of NeoKantianism: German Philosophy Between Idealism and Positivism*. Translated by R.J. Hollingdale. Cambridge: Cambridge University Press, 1991.

Kuehn, Manfred. "The Reception of Hume in Germany." In *The Reception of David Hume in Europe*, edited by Peter Jones. London: Bloomsbury, 2005.

Kulenkampff, Jens. *Materialen zu Kants 'Kritik der Urteilskraft.'* Frankfurt am Main: Suhrkamp, 1974.

Lafont, Cristina. *The Linguistic Turn in Hermeneutic Philosophy*. Cambridge, MA: MIT Press, 1999.

Lange, Victor. "Friedrich Schlegel's Literary Criticism." *Comparative Literature* 7, no. 4 (1955).

Laursen, John Christian. "Cicero in the Prussian Academy: Castillon's translation of the *Academica*." *History of European Ideas* 23, nos. 2–4 (1997).

———. "Swiss Anti-skeptics in Berlin." In *Schweizer im Berlin des 18. Jahrhunderts*, edited by M. Fontius and H. Holzhey. Berlin: Akademie Verlag, 1996.

Laursen, John Christian, Richard H. Popkin, and Peter Briscoe. "Hume in the Prussian Academy: Jean Bernard Mérian's 'On the Phenomenalism of David Hume.'" *Hume Studies* 23, no. 1 (1997).

Lee, Richard A., Jr. *The Thought of Matter: Materialism, Conceptuality and the Transcendence of Immanence*. London: Rowman & Littlefield International, 2015.

Leibniz, Gottfried Wilhelm. *Opuscules et fragments inédits de Leibniz*. Edited by Louis Couturat. Paris: Presses Universitaires de France, 1903; repr., Hildesheim: Georg Olms, 1961.

———. *Philosophical Essays*. Translated by Roger Ariew and Daniel Garber. Indianapolis: Hackett Publishing, 1989.

———. *Die Philosophischen Schriften von Gottfried Wilhelm Leibniz*. Edited by C.I. Gerhardt. Hildesheim: Georg Olms, 1965.

———. *Theodicy: Essays on the Goodness of God, the Freedom of Man, and the Origin of Evil*. Edited by Austin Farrer, translated by E.M. Huggard. La Salle, IL: Open Court, 1985.

Leiter, Brian. *Nietzsche on Morality*. New York: Routledge, 2002.

Levine, Steven. "Habermas, Kantian Pragmatism, and Truth." *Philosophy and Social Criticism* 36, no. 6 (2010).

———. "Truth and Moral Validity: On Habermas' Domesticated Pragmatism" *Constellations* 18, no. 2 (2011).

Ludwig, Bernd. *Kants Rechtslehre*. Hamburg: Meiner, 1988.

Lukács, György. *History and Class Consciousness: Studies in Marxist Dialectics*. Translated by Rodney Livingston. London: Merlin Press, 1971.

Łukasiewicz, Jan. "On the Principle of Contradiction in Aristotle." *Review of Metaphysics* 24, no. 3 (1971).

Macor, Laura Anna. *Der morastige Zirkel der menschlichen Bestimmung: Friedrich Schillers Weg von der Aufklärung zu Kant*. Würzburg: Königshausen & Neumann, 2010.

Makkreel, Rudolf. *Imagination and Interpretation in Kant: The Hermeneutic Import of the Critique of Judgment*. Chicago: University of Chicago Press, 1990.

———. "Kant's Responses to Skepticism." In *The Skeptical Tradition around 1800: Skepticism in Philosophy, Science, and Society*, edited by Johan van der Zande and Richard H. Popkin. Dordrecht: Kluwer, 1998.

———. *Orientation and Judgment in Hermeneutics*. Chicago: University of Chicago Press, 2015.

———. "Relating aesthetic and sociable feelings to moral and participatory feelings: reassessing Kant on sympathy and honor." In *Kant's Observations and Remarks; A Critical Guide*, edited by Susan Meld and Richard Velkley. Cambridge: Cambridge University Press, 2012.

———. "Wilhelm Dilthey and the Neo-Kantians: On the Conceptual Distinctions between *Geistes-wissenchaften* and *Kulturwissenschaften*." In *Neo-Kantianism in Contemporary Philosophy*, edited by Rudolf Makkreel and Sebastian Luft. Bloomington: Indiana University Press, 2010.

Marasco, Robyn. *The Highway of Despair: Critical Theory after Hegel*. New York: Columbia University Press, 2015.
Martin, Randy. "A Precarious Dance: A Derivative Sociality." *TDR: The Drama Review* 56, no. 4 (2012).
———. "What Difference do Derivatives Make? From the Technical to the Political Conjuncture." *Culture Unbound* 6 (2014).
Marx, Karl. *Capital: A Critique of Political Economy*. Translated by Ben Fowkes. London: Penguin, 1976.
———. *Capital*, vol. 3, *A Critique of Political Economy*. Translated by David Fernbach. London: Penguin, 1981.
———. *Contribution to the Critique of Political Economy*. Edited by Maurice Dobb, translated by S.W. Ryazanskaya. New York: International Publishers, 1970.
———. *Grundrisse*. Translated by Martin Nicolaus. London: Penguin, 1993.
Marx, Karl, and Friedrich Engels. *Collected Works*. Chadwell Heath: Lawrence & Wishart, 1975–2004.
———. *Karl Marx/Friedrich Engels: Werke*. Edited by Instut für Marxismus-Leninismus, et al. Berlin: Dietz Verlag, 1956–2018.
———. *The Marx-Engels Reader*. Edited by Robert C. Tucker. New York: W.W. Norton & Co., 1978.
Matystsin, Anton. "The Protestant Critics of Bayle at the Dawn of the Enlightenment." In *Scepticism in the Eighteenth Century: Enlightenment, Lumières, Aufkärung*, edited by Sébastian Charles and Plínio J. Smith. Dordrecht: Springer, 2013.
Mbembe, Achille. *Critique of Black Reason*. Translated by Laurent Dubois. Durham, NC: Duke University Press, 2017.
McCarthy, Thomas. *Ideals and Illusions: On Reconstruction and Deconstruction in Contemporary Critical Theory*. Cambridge, MA: MIT Press, 1991.
McCort, Dennis. "Jena Romanticism and Zen." *Discourse* 27, no. 1 (2005).
McQuillan, J. Colin. *Immanuel Kant: The Very Idea of a Critique of Pure Reason*. Evanston: Northwestern University Press, 2016.
Menke, Christoph. *Force: A Fundamental Concept of Aesthetic Anthropology*. Translated by Gerrit Jackson. New York: Fordham University Press, 2013.
———. "Genealogy and Critique: Two Forms of Ethical Questioning of Morality." In *The Cambridge Companion to Adorno*, edited by Thomas Huhn. Cambridge: Cambridge University Press, 2004.
———. *Kritik der Rechte*. Frankfurt am Main: Suhrkamp, 2015.
———. "Die Kritik des Rechts und das Recht der Kritik." *Deutsche Zeitschrift für Philosophie*, 66, no. 2 (2018).
———. "Law and Domination." In *Critical Theory in Critical Times: Transforming the Global Political and Economic Order*, edited by Penelope Deutscher and Cristina Lafont. New York: Columbia University Press, 2017.

---. *Law and Violence: Christoph Menke in Dialogue*. Translated by Gerrit Jackson. Manchester: Manchester University Press, 2018.

---. *Recht und Gewalt*. Berlin: August Verlag, 2011.

Mensch, Jennifer. "Kant and the Skull Collectors: German Anthropology from Blumenbach to Kant." In *Kant and his German Contemporaries*, vol. 1, *Logic, Mind, Epistemology, Science, and Ethics*, edited by Corey W. Dyck and Falk Wunderlich. Cambridge: Cambridge University Press, 2018.

Merleau-Ponty, Maurice. *Phenomenology of Perception*. Translated by Donald E Landes. New York: Routledge, 2012.

Merrick, Alison. "On Genealogy and Transcendent Critique." *Journal of Nietzsche Studies* 47, no. 2 (2016).

Millán Brusslan, Elizabeth. "Protecting Natural Beauty from Humanism's Violence: The Healing Effects of Alexander von Humboldt's *Naturgemälde*." In *Posthumanism in the Age of Humanism. Late 18th- and Early 19th-Century Cognitive, Materialist, and Idealist Contentions*, edited by Edgar Landgraf, Gabriel Trop, and Leif Weatherby. Bloomsbury, 2019.

Miller, Elaine. "Romanticism and Continental Thought." In *The Palgrave Handbook of German Romantic Philosophy*, edited by Elizabeth Millán Brusslan. New York: Palgrave, forthcoming.

Mills, Charles W. "Notes from the Resistance: Some Comments on Sally Haslanger's *Resisting Reality*." *Philosophical Studies* 171, no. 1 (2014).

Moledo, Fernando. "Die neue Auffassung der Metaphysik als reine Philosophie in der Inauguraldissertation und ihre propädeutische Bedeutung im Rahmen der Entwicklungsgeschichte der Kritik der reinen Vernunft." *Kant-Studien* 107, no. 3 (2016).

Montaigne, Michel de. *Les Essais*. Paris: Librarie Générale Française, 2001.

Moore, Marianne. "His Shield." In *New Collected Poems*, ed. Heather Cass White. New York: Farrar, Straus and Giroux, 2017.

Nagel, Thomas. "The Absurd." *The Journal of Philosophy* 68, no. 20 (1971).

Natorp, Paul. *Logik: Grundlegung und logischer Aufbau der Mathematik und mathematischen Naturwissenschaften in Leitsätzen zu akademischen Vorlesungen*. Marburg: Elwert, 1910.

Nehamas, Alexander. *Nietzsche: Life as Literature*. Cambridge, MA: Harvard University Press, 1985.

Ng, Karen. "Back to Adorno: Critical Theory's Problem of Normative Grounding." In *The Challenge of Progress: Theory Between Critique and Ideology*, edited by Harry F. Dahms. Bingley, UK: Emerald Publishing, 2019.

Nietzsche, Friedrich. *Basic Writings*. Edited and translated by Walter Kaufmann. New York: Random House, 1992.

---. *Beyond Good and Evil*. Translated by Walter Kaufmann. New York: Vintage, 1989.

———. *The Genealogy of Morals*. Translated by Carol Diethe, edited by Keith Ansel Pearson. Cambridge: Cambridge University Press, 1997.
———. *The Will to Power*. Translated by Walter Kaufman and R.J. Hollingdale. New York: Vintage Books, 1968.
Novalis. "Monologue." In *Classic and Romantic German Aesthetics*, edited by J. M Bernstein. Cambridge: Cambridge University Press, 2003.
Nuzzo, Angelica. "'. . . As if Truth Were a Coin!' Lessing and Hegel's Developmental Theory of Truth." *Hegel-Studien* 44 (2009).
———. "General Logic, Transcendental Logic, Dialectic-Speculative Logic." In *System und Logik bei Hegel—200 Jahren nach der Wissenschaft der Logik*, edited by L. Fonnesu and L. Ziglioli. Hildesheim: Olms, 2016.
———. "Sensibility in Kant and Herder's *Metakritik*." In *Herders 'Metakritik': Analysen und Interpretationen*, edited by Marion Heinz. Stuttgart: Fromann-Holzboog, 2013.
Obdrzalek, Suzanne. "From Skepticism to Paralysis: The Apraxia Argument in Cicero's Academica." *Ancient Philosophy* 32, no. 2 (2012).
Oksala, Johanna. *Feminist Experiences: Foucauldian and Phenomenological Investigations*. Evanston, Illinois: Northwestern University Press, 2016.
Owen, David. *Nietzsche's Genealogy of Morality*. Stocksfield, UK: Acumen Publishing, 2007.
———. "Nietzsche's Genealogy Revisited." *Journal of Nietzsche Studies*, no. 35–36 (2008).
Pensky, Max. *Melancholy Dialectics: Walter Benjamin and the Play of Mourning*. Amherst: University of Massachusetts Press, 1993.
———. "Natural History: The Life and Afterlife of a Concept in Adorno." *Critical Horizons* 5, no. 1 (2004).
Pieper, Annemarie. "Editorischer Bericht zu Schellings Briefe über Dogmatismus und Kritizismus." In Friedrich Wilhelm Joseph von Schelling, *Schelling: Historisch-Kritische Ausgabe*. Stuttgart: Frommann Holzboog, 1982.
Pippin, Robert. *Nietzsche, Psychology, and First Philosophy*. Chicago: University of Chicago Press, 2010.
Plato. *Complete Works*. Edited by John M. Cooper and D.S. Hutchinson. Indianapolis: Hackett Publishing, 1997.
———. *Theaetetus and Sophist*. Edited by Christopher Rowe. Cambridge: Cambridge University Press, 2015.
Pomona, Andrea. *The Critical Philosophy of Hermann Cohen*. Translated by John Denton. Albany: State University of New York Press, 1997.
Rawls, John. *A Theory of Justice*. Cambridge, MA: Harvard University Press, 1971.
Reinhold, Karl Leonhard. *Beiträge zur Berichtigung bisheriger Mißverständnisse der Philosophen*. Edited by Faustino Fabbianelli. Hamburg: Felix Meiner Verlag, 2004.

———. *Essay on a New Theory of the Human Capacity for Representation.* Translated by Tim Mehigan and Barry Empson. Berlin: Walter de Gruyter, 2011.
Richardson, John. "Nietzsche's Psychology." In *Nietzsches Wissenschaftsphilosophie*, edited by H. Heit, G. Abel, and M. Brusotti. Berlin: Walter de Gruyter, 2011.
Ridley, Aaron. "Nietzsche and the Re-evaluation of Values." In *Nietzsche's* On the Genealogy of Morals: *Critical Essays*, edited by Christa Davis Acampora. Lanham, MD: Rowman & Littlefield, 2006.
———. *Nietzsche's Conscience: Six Character Studies from the Genealogy.* Ithaca, NY: Cornell University Press, 1998.
Rose, Gillian. *The Melancholy Science: An Introduction to the Thought of Theodor W. Adorno.* London: Verso, 2014.
Röttgers, Kurt. "Kritik." In *Geschichtliche Grundbegriffe*, edited by Otto Brunner, Werner Conze, and Reinhart Koselleck. Stuttgart: Klett-Cotta 1972–1992.
Rush, Fred. *Irony and Idealism: Rereading Schlegel, Hegel, and Kierkegaard.* Oxford: Oxford University Press, 2017.
———. "Irony and Romantic Subjectivity." In *Philosophical Romanticism*, edited by Nikolas Kompridis. New York: Routledge, 2006.
Saar, Martin. *Genealogie als Kritik: Geschichte und Theorie des Subjekts nach Nietzsche und Foucault.* Frankfurt am Main: Campus, 2007.
Särkelä, Arvi. *Immanente Kritik und soziales Leben: Selbsttransformative Praxis nach Hegel und Dewey.* Frankfurt am Main: Vittorio Klostermann, 2018.
Schelling, Friedrich Wilhelm Joseph von. *Ages of the World.* Translated by Jason M. Wirth. Albany: State University of New York Press, 2000.
———. *Friedrich Wilhelm Joseph Schellings sämmtliche Werke.* Edited by K.F.A. Schelling. Stuttgart: Cotta, 1856–1861.
———. *The Grounding of Positive Philosophy.* Translated by Bruce Matthews. Albany: State University of New York Press, 2007.
———. *Historisch-Kritische Ausgabe.* Edited by Hartmut Buchner, Wilhelm Jacobs, and Annamarie Pieper. Stuttgart: Frommann-Holzboog, 1982.
———. *Schriften von 1794–1798.* Darmstadt: Wissenschaftliche Buchgesellschaft, 1975.
———. "Stuttgart Private Lectures." In *Idealism and the Endgame of Theory*, edited and translated by Thomas Pfau. Albany: State University of New York Press, 1994.
———. *The Unconditioned in Human Knowledge: Four Early Essays 1794–1796.* Translated by Fritz Marti. Lewisburg, PA: Bucknell University Press, 1980.
Schiller, Friedrich. *Essays.* Edited by Walter Hindereder and Daniel Dahlstrom. New York: Continuum, 2001.
———. "*Kallias* or Concerning Beauty: Letters to Gottfried Körner." Translated by Stefan Bird-Pollan. In *Classic and Romantic German Aesthetics*, edited by J.M. Bernstein. Cambridge: Cambridge University Press, 2003.
———. *Schillers Werke—Nationalausgabe.* Edited by Julius Petersen und Gerhard Fricke. Weimar: Hermann Böhlaus Nachfolger, 1943–.

———. *Werke in Drei Bänden*. Edited by Gerhard Fricke and Herbert Göpfert. Munich: Hanser Verlag, 1966.
Schlegel, Friedrich. *Friedrich Schlegel's Lucinde and the Fragments*. Edited and translated by Peter Firchow. Minneapolis: University of Minnesota Press, 1971.
———. *Kritische Friedrich-Schlegel-Ausgabe*. Edited by Ernst Behler, Jean Jacques Anstett, and Hans Eichner. Munich: F. Schöningh, 1958.
———. "On Goethe's Meister." In *Classic and Romantic German Aesthetics*, edited by J.M. Bernstein. Cambridge: Cambridge University Press, 2003.
———. "On Incomprehensibility." In *Classic and Romantic German Aesthetics*, edited by J.M. Bernstein. Cambridge: Cambridge University Press, 2003.
Scholem, Gershom. *Major Trends in Jewish Mysticism*. New York: Schocken, 1988.
———. *Tagebücher, nebst Aufsätzen und Entwürfen bis 1923*. Edited by Karlfried Gründer, Herbert Kopp-Oberstebrink and Friedrich Niewöhner with the cooperation of Karl E. Grözinger. Jüdischer Verlag: Frankurt am Main, 1995–2000.
Schopenhauer, Arthur. *Werke in fünf Bänden*. Edited by Ludger Lütkehaus. Frankfurt am Main: Haffman, 2006.
Scott, Joan W. "The Evidence of Experience." *Critical Inquiry* 17, no. 4 (1991).
Seel, Martin. *Aesthetics of Appearing*. Translated by John Farrell. Stanford, CA: Stanford University Press, 2005.
———. *Eine Ästhetik der Natur*. Frankfurt am Main: Suhrkamp, 1996.
Sextus Empiricus. *Outlines of Scepticism*. Edited by Julia Annas, and Jonathan Barnes. Cambridge: Cambridge University Press, 2000.
Silber, John. "The Importance of the Highest Good in Kant's Ethics." *Ethics* 73, no. 3 (1963).
Sloterdijk, Peter. *Critique of Cynical Reason*. Translated by Michael Eldred. Minneapolis: University of Minnesota Press, 1988.
Smith, Norman Kemp. *A Commentary to Kant's Critique of Pure Reason*. 1918; repr., New York: Palgrave, 2003.
Spinoza, Baruch. *Ethics*. Translated by S. Shirley. Indianapolis: Hackett Publishing, 1992.
Spivak, Gayatri Chakravorty. *Critique of Postcolonial Reason: Toward a History of the Vanishing Present*. Cambridge, MA: Harvard University Press, 1999.
Steinby, Liisa. "Zur 'Wissenschaftlichkeit' von Herders Methode." *Herder Jahrbuch/Yearbook* 13 (2016).
Stolnitz, Jerome. *Aesthetics and Art Criticism. A Critical Introduction*. Boston: Houghton Mifflin, 1960.
Taylor, Charles. *Hegel*. Cambridge: Cambridge University Press, 1975.
———. *Sources of the Self*. Cambridge, MA: Harvard University Press, 1989.
Thiem, Yannick. "Benjamin's Messianic Metaphysics of Transience." In *Walter Benjamin and Theology*, edited by Colby Dickinson and Stéphane Symons. New York: Fordham University Press, 2016.
Thordike, Oliver. *Kant's Transition Project and Late Philosophy: Connecting the Opus postumum and the Metaphysics of Morals*. London: Bloomsbury, 2018.

Thorsrud, Harald. "Sextus Empiricus on Skeptical Piety." In *New Essays on Ancient Pyrrhonism*, edited by Diego E. Machuca. Leiden: Brill, 2011.

Thucydides, *History of the Peloponnesian War*. London: Penguin Books, 1972.

Tonelli, Giorgio. "Critique and Related Terms Prior to Kant: A Historical Survey." *Kant-Studien* 69 (1978).

———. "Kant and the Ancient Sceptics." In *Scepticism in the Enlightenment*, edited by Richard H. Popkin, Ezequiel de Olaso, and Giorgio Tonelli. Dordrecht: Kluwer, 1997.

Vaihinger, Hans. *Commentar zu Kants Kritik der reinen Vernunft*. Stuttgart: Spemann Verlag, 1881.

Vernant, Jean-Pierre, and Pierre Vidal-Naquet. *Myth and Tragedy in Ancient Greece*. Translated by Janet Lloyd. New York: Zone Books, 1990.

Vogt, K.M. "Scepticism and Action." In *The Cambridge Companion to Ancient Scepticism*, edited by Richard Bett. Cambridge: Cambridge University Press, 2010.

Waismann, Friedrich. "Notes on Talks with Wittgenstein." *The Philosophical Review* 74, no. 1 (1965).

Weber, Samuel. "Criticism Underway: Walter Benjamin's Romantic Concept of Criticism." In *Romantic Revolutions: Criticism and Theory*, edited by Kenneth R. Johnston et al. Bloomington: Indiana University Press, 1990.

Whitebook, Joel. *Freud: An Intellectual Biography*. Cambridge: Cambridge University Press, 2017.

Whyman, Tom. "Understanding Adorno on 'Natural-History.'" *International Journal of Philosophical Studies* 24, no. 4 (2016).

Willaschek, Marcus. "Freedom as a Postulate." In *Kant on Persons and Agency*, edited by Eric Watkins. Cambridge: Cambridge University Press, 2018.

Wittgenstein, Ludwig. "A Lecture on Ethics." *The Philosophical Review* 74, no. 1 (1965).

Wood, Allen W. *Kantian Ethics*. Cambridge: Cambridge University Press, 2008.

Zambrana, Rocío. "Critique in Hegel and Marx." In *From Marx to Hegel and Back to the Future*, edited by Victoria Fareld and Hannes Kuch. New York: Bloomsbury Press, 2020.

———. "Dialectics of Progress." *Philosophy Today* 61, no. 4 (2017).

———. "Paradoxes of Neoliberalism and the Tasks of Critical Theory." *Critical Horizons* 14, no. 1 (2013).

Zammito, John H. *Kant, Herder, and the Birth of Anthropology*. Chicago: University of Chicago Press, 2002.

Zöller, Günter. "From Critique to Metacritique: Fichte's Transformation of Kant's Transcendental Idealism." In *The Reception of Kant's Critical Philosophy*, edited by Sally Sedgwich. New York: Cambridge University Press, 2000.

Zupancic, Alenka. *Ethics of the Real, Kant, Lacan*. New York: Verso, 2000.

Contributors

María del Rosario Acosta López is professor of hispanic studies at the University of California, Riverside.

Andreea Smaranda Aldea is assistant professor of philosophy at Kent State University in Ohio.

Amy Allen is department head and liberal arts professor of philosophy and women's, gender, and sexuality studies at Penn State University in State College, Pennsylvania.

Karin de Boer is a professor in the Institute of Philosophy at the University of Leuven in Belgium.

G. Anthony Bruno is Assistant Professor in philosophy at Royal Holloway, University of London.

Peter Fenves is Professor of German at Northwestern University in Evanston, Illinois.

Avery Goldman is associate professor of philosophy at DePaul University in Chicago.

Catalina González is associate professor of philosophy at Universidad de los Andes in Colombia.

Federica Gregoratto is wissenschaftliche Mitarbeiterin (research associate) at the University of St. Gallen in Switzerland.

Richard A. Lee Jr. is professor of philosophy at DePaul University in Chicago.

Rudolf Makkreel is Charles Howard Candler professor of philosophy emeritus at Emory University in Atlanta, Georgia.

J. Colin McQuillan is associate professor of philosophy at St. Mary's University in San Antonio, Texas.

Christoph Menke is professor of practical philosophy at the Goethe-Universität Frankfurt am Main.

Elizabeth Millán Brusslan is professor of philosophy at DePaul University in Chicago.

Karolin Mirzakhan is lecturer of philosophy at Kennesaw State University in Kennesaw, Georgia.

Angelica Nuzzo is professor of philosophy at Brooklyn College and the CUNY Graduate Center in New York City.

Daniel R. Rodríguez-Navas is assistant professor of Philosophy at The New School in New York City.

Rocío Zambrana is associate professor of philosophy at Emory University in Atlanta, Georgia.

Rachel Zuckert is professor of philosophy at Northwestern University in Evanston, Illinois.

Index

Adelung, Johann Christoph, 169n9
Adorno, Theodor, 12–14, 187, 194, 308, 320, 322, 324–30, 333n26, 335–51, 352n4, 356n85, 356n87
  "Actuality of Philosophy, The," 346
  Aesthetic Theory, 187
  aesthetics, 187, 197n7, 199n29
  conception of critique, 12, 13, 328, 335–36, 346, 349, 353n45, 385
  critical naturalism, 13, 336–37, 341, 343, 345, 349
  Dialectic of Enlightenment, 343, 354n53
  dialectics, 328–29, 337, 342
  Habilitationsschrift on Kant and Freud, 355n69
  Heideggerian ontology, critique of, 338–39, 342
  History and Freedom, 337–38, 341, 345, 346
  "Idea of Natural-History, The," 337–39, 342, 355n69
  Kant, critique of, 344
  Metacritique of Epistemology, 349
  metaphysical experience, 327, 329
  metaphysics and critique, 325–30
  Metaphysics: Concepts and Problems, 325–28, 333n27
  Minima Moralia, 330, 335, 346–47, 349, 351
  natural history, 336–45, 347, 350, 352n12, 354n45
  Negative Dialectics, 333n27, 333n32, 343, 344
  Nietzsche, relationship to, 355n67
  philosophy as interpretation, 345–46, 350
  psychoanalysis, appropriation of, 344–45, 347
  redemption, 12, 13, 329–30, 335–36, 339
Aenesidemus (Schulze), 121–22, 138
aesthetic state, 98, 103, 110n60
aesthetics, 1, 3, 6–7, 30, 89–104, 185–88, 191–97, 277n1
Africa, 226
Alcibiades, 318–20, 331n10, 331n11, 331n13
Allgemeine Literatur Zeitung, 121, 130n54, 150n41
Althusser, Louis, 322
America, 225
Antisthenes (cynicism), 393n14
Areopagus, Council of, 301
Aristotle, 81n9, 84n74, 202, 324, 325–27, 333n27
  dialectic, 204, 212
  logic, 201, 333n26, 393n14
art, 5, 6, 94, 101, 185, 188, 191–93
  autonomous, 107n19, 176

arts, 156, 163, 168n9
artwork, 5–6, 157, 159, 166, 169n9, 173, 175–76, 194, 197, 348
atheism, 23
Athenaeum (journal), 174, 177, 178
Athenagoras, 331n14
Athens, 318–19
Attempt at a Critical Poetics for the Germans (Gottsched), 2
Aufheben (Schelling's use), 309. *See also* Hegel

Bacon, Francis, 24
Bardili, Christoph Gottfried, 121
base/superstructure, 322
Bayle, Pierre, 24
beauty, 3, 265, 276, 347. *See also under* Kant, Schiller
  of nature, 186, 187, 188, 191, 194, 347–48
Beck, Jacob Sigismund, 131n69, 131n71
Behler, Ernst, 178
Beiser, Frederick, 172n52
Benjamin, Walter, 11–12, 13, 89, 187, 308–12, 314n35, 329, 338–40, 346, 347, 385
  Arcades Project, The, 89
  Concept of Art Criticism in German Romanticism, The, 176
  critique of violence, 12, 105n6, 308–12
  Gesammelten Schriften, 309
  Notes toward a Work on the Category of Justice, 308–9, 311–12
  Origin of German Tragic Drama, The, 339
  "Toward a Critique of Violence," 11–12, 310–11
Berlin, 34n10, 174
Berlin, Isaiah, 168n7
Bernstein, Jay, 345

Big Lebowski, The, 238
Boufflers, Stanislas de, 178
Boullier, David Renaud, 34n6
Brecht, Bertolt, 344
British moralists, 272
Budd, Malcolm, 192–93, 195–96
Butler, Judith, 287, 375n64

capitalism, 8, 221–33, 234n9, 320, 323, 382–83
  and metaphysics, 327–29
  circulation, 229–30
  critique of, 221, 224, 228, 229
  ethical response to, 268–69
  finance, 221–23, 227, 232
  late, 344, 350
  racialized, 227–28, 236n60
Carr, David, 297n3, 299n42
Cassirer, Ernst, 9, 267
Castillon, J. de, 23, 34n5
Cavell, Stanley, 151n44, 154n93, 154n95
Chimborazo, 195
Christianity, 23–24, 26–27, 31, 35n28. *See also* religion
Cicero:
  Academica, 23, 34n5, 35n34, 36n36
  De Natura Deorum, 35n34
Cohen, Hermann, 9, 10, 263, 265, 267–71, 278n15, 279n37
  Ethik des Reinen Willens, 267, 269
  Kants Begründung der Ethik, 267, 268
  philosophy of right, 267–69, 279n45
Collins, Anthony, 35n29
comedy, Aristophanic, 178
commodity, 222, 224–25, 229, 230, 234n9, 328
commodity fetishism, 224, 229–30
Comte, Auguste, 277n1
constellation, 89, 327, 340–41, 346, 350–51

Cook, Deborah, 344, 345, 353n45
cosmology, 42, 48, 49, 50, 51, 64, 69
  general, 55n3, 56n17
  rational, 52, 53
Critcal Age, 174, 181, 188
critical theory, 1, 9, 12–14, 105n6, 187, 197n7, 233, 317, 320, 324–30, 340, 357–59, 367, 370, 371n2, 372n9, 374n34, 385
Critique of Black Reason (Mbembe), 158
Critique of Cynical Reason (Sloterdijk), 158
Critique of Postcolonial Reason (Spivak), 158
critique:
  decision before the assembly, 319–20, 331n10
  doctrine, relation to, 134–37, 137–41, 145, 147, 148
  entwinement with law, 14–15, 377, 380, 391, 392n3, 392n11
  history of term, 1, 15, 30, 39, 81n10, 105n6
  κριν (and variants), 317, 320, 331n14, 379
  materialist, 8, 13, 91, 333n24, 363–64
  See also under individual figures and movements
Crousaz, Jean-Pierre de, 21–29, 34n10, 35n29, 37n52
  education, 26, 35n26
  Examen du pyrrhonisme ancien et moderne, 21, 22, 23–29, 31, 33
  Nouvelle maximes sur l'éducation des enfants, 35n26
  precursor to Kantian critique, 22, 31–33
  skepticism, 22, 25, 31, 34n6, 35n20
  Traité de l'éducation des enfants, 35n26

Crusius, Christian August, 41, 46, 50–51, 55n10, 56n13
culture industry, 344
Dasein, 338, 342
Dawson, Michael, 227
de la Harpe, Jacqueline E., 23, 34n10, 37n52
de Man, Paul, 179
debate, political, 318–19
debt, 8, 221, 223, 226–28, 231, 233–34
deism, 23, 26, 29, 35n29
Deleuze, Gilles, 392n11
democracy, 319–20, 331n12
demos (δῆμος), 320
Derrida, Jacques, 331n12
Descartes, René, 24, 118
Dewey, John, 360, 375n65
dialectic:
  Adorno's conception of, 328–29, 337, 342
  of enlightenment, 336, 343, 344, 354n47
  Plato's elenctic, 204, 213
  See also under Hegel
Dienst, Richard, 226, 232
Dilthey, Wilhelm, 10, 263–65, 271–76, 277n1, 278n15, 279n37, 342
  Critique of Historical Reason, 264
  ethics, formative, 271–72
  philosophy of history, 264, 275
  System of Ethics, 265, 271–75
Discourse on Free-Thinking (Collins), 35n29
dispossession, 224, 227, 230–31
divine, the, 237, 311–12, 319
dogmatism, 2, 4–6, 15, 117–18, 123, 131n67
  and criticism, 134–38, 142–45, 147–48, 151n61, 153n74, 154n90
  and Kant, 29–30, 31–33, 40, 53, 54, 83n60, 134, 136, 145, 149n15

dogmatism *(continued)*
  and skepticism, 2, 21, 22, 28–31, 33
  apraxia objection to skepticism, 25, 34n19
  dogmaticism. *See under* Schelling
  of the Kantians, 158
  of "vulgar" criticism, 381, 385, 388–90, 394n26
  Spinozist, 118, 124, 134, 138, 141
domestic violence, 364

East Indies, 226
ecological degradation, 223, 224, 227, 228, 232
economic crisis (2008), 372n9
Egesteans, 318
elenchos, of Socrates, 204, 212–13
Empedocles, 178
empiricism, 46, 128n24, 169n16, 170n27
  classical, 158–59
  vicious (*rohe*) (Humboldt), 188, 194
Engels, Frederick, 333n24
Enlightenment, the, 27, 31–33, 103, 324
  and Kant, 39
  anti-Enlightenment voices, 61
  conservative form of, 33, 37n54
  dogmatism and skepticism, 31
Epicharmus, 349
Epicurus, 81n9
  See also under happiness
Erhard, J. B., 150n41
eudaimonia, 84n74
exchange, 223–26, 229–32, 268, 327–28, 334
exchange value, 224, 230, 330, 382–84

fact-value distinction, 367
Falzon, Christopher, 350
feminism, 15, 281, 282, 294, 297n2, 363, 374n34
  debates over sex/gender, 375n64
  poststructural, 292

Fichte, Johann Gottlieb, 4, 107n19, 111–13, 117, 120–27, 130n54, 131n69, 133–34, 144, 152n68, 154n95, 164, 173, 177
  absolute subject, 122, 127
  Attempt at a Critique of All Revelation, 121, 124, 130n54
  Attempt at a New Presentation of the Wissenschaftslehre (1797), 124, 138, 150n39
  conception of critique, 113, 122–23, 126
  Concerning the Concept of the Wissenschaftslehre, 111, 122, 126, 131n65, 137
  first principle, 4, 112–13, 121–24, 126, 127, 131n65, 137, 139, 141, 145
  Foundations of the Entire Wissenschaftslehre, 123–24, 126, 137, 138, 139
  Grundlage des Naturrechts [Foundation of Natural Law], 305
  I and not-I, 4, 121, 123, 124, 127, 138–41, 305
  intellectual intuition, 122–24, 131n67, 134–35, 137–41, 143–47, 150n39, 150n41
  law grounded in reciprocal recognition, 305
  Personal Meditations on Elementary Philosophy/Practical Philosophy, 121
  Review of *Aenesidemus*, 121–22, 123, 138–39, 140
  Wissenschaftslehre, 4, 113, 121–24, 126, 131n65, 137–38, 141, 142, 150n41
  Wissenschaftslehre Nova Methodo, 138, 139
fideism, 23, 28, 29
first principle, 4–5, 41, 112, 119–25, 137–39, 141, 145, 147–48, 177, 188
  See also under Fichte, Reinhold

Formey, Samuel, 21, 23, 34n5, 34nn10–11
Foucault, Michel, 13, 335–37, 341–45, 349–51, 352n4
  Archaeology of Knowledge, 342
  conception of critique, 335–36, 343, 349, 350, 353n44, 353n45, 385
  freedom, space of, 336
  government, 378–79
  historical *a priori*, 341–43, 349, 350, 353n44, 354n45
  historical ontology, 340, 341–43, 349, 352n12, 353n44
  power-knowledge, 345
  psychoanalysis, relation to, 354n54
  social constructionism, 336, 341
Frankfurt School, 1, 12, 222, 320, 353n37, 357
  first generation, 374n45
  relation to Kantian critique, 372n3
Franks, Paul, 138
Fraser, Nancy, 8, 221–29, 231–33
Frederick III of Brandenburg, Elector, 22
Frederick the Great, 22
free-thinker, 29, 35n29
freedom, 3, 11, 123, 144–47, 247, 187, 328, 345
  formal freedom of the worker, 225–28
  of subjectivity, 134, 137–39, 141–47
  See also under individual figures
Freiburg, University of, 314n35
French Revolution, 94, 177
Freud, Sigmund:
  melancholia, 348, 355n76
  "On Transience," 347–48, 355n69

Gasché, Rodolphe, 101
gender, 14, 287, 290, 357, 364
gender binary, 369–70, 375n64
gender studies, 15

genealogy, 9, 14–15, 171n41, 239, 363, 378, 381–86, 388–90
  affirmative moment of, 394n25
  British, 262n37
  Foucaultian, 336, 344–45, 351, 354n53
  See also under Nietzsche
general will, 266
genius, 172n47
geography, 117, 190, 302–3
German Idealism, 1, 4, 125, 148, 170n29
  See also individual figures
Germany, 134
given, the, 12, 15, 160–64, 207–8, 320–24, 326–29, 339–42, 381–84, 388, 390
  myth of, 384
God, 154n95, 161
  existence of, 3, 32, 37n52
  See also under Kant
gods, the, 237–38, 257
Goethe, Johann Wolfgang von, 190, 199n16
  Meister, 177
  Wahlverwandtschaften, Die, 314n25
Goldman, Avery, 152n69
Göttingen, 34n11
Gottsched, Johann Christoph, 2
Grammatisch-kritisch Wörterbuch der hochdeutschen Mundart (Adelung), 169n9
Greece, political decline of, 393n14
Grimm, Jacob and Wilhelm, 1–2, 168n9
Grotius, Hugo, 305

Habermas, Jürgen, 13–14, 357–62, 365–68, 370–71
  communicative reason, theory of, 360, 374n55
  epistemic/discourse theory of truth (early), 359, 373n10

Habermas, Jürgen *(continued)*
  ideology, 371
  non-epistemic theory of truth, 358, 359–61, 373n10
  objective world, 360–61, 365, 366, 367–68
  pragmatism, 358, 365–66, 369
  social critique, sources of, 370, 374n45
  Theory of Communicative Action, 357, 372n3, 375n55
  Truth and Justification, 13, 358–59, 367
Hague, The, 34n10
Haiven, Max, 232
Haller, Albrecht von, 21, 23, 34n11
Hamacher, Werner, 306
Hamann, Johann Georg, 160, 169n20
happiness, 12, 72–73, 317, 325, 329–30
  Epicurean, 3, 63, 73–74
Hartung, G. L., 130n54
Harvey, David, 222–23, 228, 230–33
Haslanger, Sally, 13–14, 19n42, 357–59, 361–66, 368–71, 372n39
  Critical Theory and Practice (Spinoza Lectures), 363, 366, 372n9, 374n33
  metaphysics, usefulness for critical theory, 358, 366
  Resisting Reality, 13, 358–59, 361–63, 372n9
  social constructionism, 358, 361, 362, 373n28
  social critique, two steps, 362–63
  social kinds, 13–14, 357, 362
  socio-ontological framework, 358, 364, 369
  technē, 363, 369
Hegel, G. W. F., 1, 7–8, 111, 201–17, 230, 353n37, 383
  beauty, 194
  concrete universality, 214
  constructive ethics, 271
  dialectic, 7, 342
  Difference between Fichte's and Schelling's System of Philosophy, The, 129n34
  dogmatism, 392n26
  "Essence of Philosophical Criticism, The," 111
  freedom, 210, 213, 214–17
  history, philosophy of, 277n1, 336
  letting go *(frei Entlassen)*, 205, 207, 214–17
  logic, science of, 202–3, 206, 217
  objective spirit, 368
  Phenomenology of Spirit, 203, 205–9, 211, 212
  Philosophy of Right, 322, 332n18
  pleroma, 306
  real/actual distinction, 322, 332n20
  refutation *(Widerlegung)*, 204–5, 208, 210–14, 215, 217, 219n44
  Reinhold, critique of, 129n34
  Science of Logic, 202–5, 207, 209, 211–12, 214, 216
  state, philosophy of, 381
  transformative appropriation, 204–10, 214, 215, 217
  Verstandeslogik, 201, 203, 206–8, 211
Heidegger, Martin, 10, 314n35, 338–39, 342
  Being and Time, 10
  Destruktion, 18n31
Henrich, Dieter, 90
Hepburn, Ronald, 185, 192, 197n5
Heraclitus, 393n14
Herder, Johann Gottfried, 5, 155–67
  as counter-Enlightenment, 168n7
  Calligone, 155, 157, 168n2
  co-dependence of thought and language, 165, 171n40
  conception of critique, 156, 162–67, 170n33

critique, material context of, 164, 167
Einfühlung, 166
empiricism, 158, 169n16
expressivism, 166
historicism, 172n52
Ideas for the Philosophy of History of Humanity, 5
impossibility of external critique, 161–62, 166
Kant, crititque of, 156–60, 168n8, 171n40
Letters for the Advancement of Humanity, 168n2
"Metacritique of the Critique of Pure Reason," 5, 155–56, 157, 160, 166, 167, 169n20, 171n41, 172n47
Treatise on the Origin of Language, 171n40
hermeneutics, 270, 277, 346
and law, 379
of nature, 193
historical *a priori*, 291, 341–43, 349, 350, 353n44, 354n45
Historical and Critical Dictionary (Bayle), 24
historical materialism, 8, 105n6
Hondt, Pierre de, 34n10
Hören, Die, 108n30
Horkheimer, Max, 12, 320, 327, 328, 330
"Traditional and Critical Theory," 12, 317, 320–24
hospitality, 302, 307
Huch, Ricarda, 182
Huguenots, 23
Humboldt, Alexander von, 6–7, 185–97
Cosmos, 6, 189–91, 194–95, 200n30
Gesamteindruck of nature, 185–86
Naturgemälde, 6, 185–86, 188–89, 191, 194, 196–97, 199n18
Views of Nature, 188–90, 198n10

Hume, David, 59n62, 118
Dialogues Concerning Natural Religion, 35n34
Enquiry Concerning Human Understanding, 23, 34n5
Husserl, Edmund, 9–11, 282, 284–85, 287, 288, 290, 296–97
Cartesian Meditations, 9
Crisis of the European Sciences, The, 289, 294
On the Origin of Geometry, 9
transcendental approach, 296, 297n2
See also phenomenology

Ibn Sina (Avicenna), 332n20
ideology, 7–8, 14, 17n22, 365, 382, 383
ideology critique, 357, 359, 363–65, 369–71, 374n33
imagination, 162, 170n30, 172n50, 190
See also under individual figures and movements
immanent critique, 11, 13, 333n27, 336, 357, 386
phenomenology as, 281–82, 284, 292, 294, 296
imperialism, 222
intersubjectivity, 5, 14, 156, 157, 265, 283, 359–60, 366–67
irony, 6, 14, 173–82, 193, 199n23
irony of irony, 179
Socratic, 178, 182

Janaway, Christopher, 261n26
Jena, 174
Jena, University of, 117, 121
Joas, Hans, 394n25
justice, 11, 12, 267–69, 274, 279n45, 303, 308–11, 320, 331n10, 358, 363–64, 367–68, 387
distinct from truth, 375n65

424 | Index

Kant, Immanuel, 1–7, 9–12, 21, 29–33, 39–54, 61–79, 263–77, 302–12
anthropology, 85n78, 116–17
Anthropology from a Pragmatic Point of View, 116–17
appearance, 43, 45–49, 51–52, 62–67, 69, 74, 78, 82n27, 161
autonomy, 67, 71, 73, 74, 344
beautiful, 90, 95, 99–101, 108n34, 109n45, 265, 276
canon, 3, 62–63, 67, 68, 71–72, 75, 79, 80n9, 81n11, 85n77, 114, 136, 142, 147
categorical imperative, 67–69, 70, 72, 264, 274
categories, 2, 9, 46–48, 50–52, 57n35, 57n38, 58n54, 63–65, 68, 82n27, 82n28, 114, 127, 135
constitutive critique, 10, 47, 263–64, 265, 275
cosmopolitanism, 79
critical theory, 317, 324, 341
critique, 2, 7, 39–40, 44–48, 80n5, 317
critique and doctrine, distinction, 134–37, 148
critique of metaphysics, 2, 39–54, 61–62, 69, 70, 75, 113, 114, 117, 120, 136
Critique of Practical Reason, 3, 5, 11, 61–63, 69–79, 80n1, 84n74, 86n86, 112, 116, 128n24, 264, 302, 310–11
Critique of Pure Reason, 2–3, 5, 29–32, 39–40, 43–54, 55n3, 55n4, 57n37, 58n45, 58n48, 61–77, 80n1, 80n9, 82n33, 82n39, 84n66, 11123, 125–26, 127n9, 128n19, 131n71, 134–37, 140–42, 144, 149n19, 155–58, 160–61, 163–64, 170n23, 170n29, 187, 201–2, 263–64, 270, 276, 302

Critique of the Power of Judgment, 3, 5, 75, 77–79, 83n65, 89–91, 95, 101, 116, 168n2, 194, 264, 270, 275
"Declaration Concerning Fichte's *Wissenschaftslehre*," 124–26
Dreams of a Spirit-Seer, 36n40, 39, 40–44, 45, 55n3
elective will [*Willkür*], 304, 307, 309, 310, 314n24
faculties, 114, 116, 135, 152n69
free play of the faculties, 90, 95–97, 98, 107n19
freedom, 3, 45, 46, 49, 62–71, 73–77, 79, 82n39, 114, 127n9, 264, 344
freedom of the will, 63, 71, 332n17
German Idealism, early, influence on, 111–27
God, 32, 41, 43, 45–50, 64, 75–79, 82n33, 114, 117, 264, 313n12
good, 3, 63, 68–79, 85n86, 264
good will, 3, 67, 68, 83n41, 312
Groundwork for the Metaphysics of Morals, 3, 67–69, 72, 73, 75, 80n1, 85n85, 87n112, 112, 128n24, 264
happiness, 83n41, 84n74
Hegel's departure from, 201–7
Herder's critique of, 17n13, 155–65
Herz, question to, 54, 57n31
"Idea for a Universal History from a Cosmopolitan Point of View," 322, 332n17
immortality of the soul, 45, 64, 76, 77, 79, 114, 264
Inaugural Dissertation, 39–44, 45, 46, 48–54, 55nn3–4, 56n12, 56n21, 57n31
inclinations, 73, 115
intuition, forms of, 2, 42, 43, 46–49, 51–52, 63, 114, 127, 161
judgment, 29–30, 135

judgment of taste, 90, 92, 93, 95, 97, 98, 99, 101, 265
law, 266–67, 304–6, 314n22
law, philosophy of, 265–68, 271, 301–8
Lectures on Logic, 21, 31, 85n78
legal rights, 267–68
mechanism, 62–69, 74, 75, 77–79, 82n33, 82n39
Metaphysical Foundations of Natural Science [*Metaphysiche Anfangsgründe der Naturwissenschaft*], 4, 112, 117, 302, 304, 311
Metaphysical Foundations of the Doctrine of Right [*Metaphysiche Anfangsgründe der Rechtslehre*], 11, 302–10, 313n8
Metaphysical Foundations of the Doctrine of Virtue [*Metaphysiche Anfangsgründe der Tugendlehre*], 302
Metaphysics of Morals, 2, 10, 11, 12, 112, 117, 125, 265, 272
moral law, 3, 63, 67–68, 70–73, 75–76, 77, 79, 84n66, 84n69, 85n86, 264, 265, 268
moral virtue, 63, 72–79, 85n80, 85n86, 86n89
Nachlass, 304–5
negative critique, 3, 43, 45, 61–62, 72, 77, 113, 114, 136, 149n19
noumena, 49, 51–52, 53, 55n3, 58n54
noumenal sphere, 62, 64, 66, 69, 70, 74–75, 264
On Pedagogy, 117
"On the Author of *Attempt at a Critique of All Revelation*," 130n54
On the Form and Principles of the Sensible and Intelligible World, 2

"Open Letter on Fichte's *Wissenschaftslehre*," 140
Opus Postumum, 4, 112, 305
positive critique, 3, 45, 62–64, 71–72, 73, 75, 113, 114, 115, 149n19
possession, legal, 303, 304–5, 313n22
possession, noumenal, 266–67
possible experience, 44–48, 50, 53, 54, 57n35, 63, 65, 69, 77, 82n27, 90, 114, 120
practical reason, 81n11, 128n24, 276, 307, 309–10
precritical philosophy, 36n40, 40, 155
Prolegomena to Any Future Metaphysics, 59n62, 62
propaedeutic, 2–4, 41–45, 59n57, 81n11, 85n77, 111, 113–15, 120–21, 125, 136, 172n49
pure practical reason, 3, 11–12, 45, 61, 63, 69, 71–77, 79, 80n1, 84n74, 264, 267, 311
purposiveness, 78, 100, 108n32, 276
reason, ideas of, 51, 56n12, 57n35, 62, 66, 67, 69, 70, 76–77, 114
reflective critique, 10, 263, 264–65, 267, 275, 277
reflective judgment, 77–78, 90, 264, 270, 276, 277n5
regulative critique, 10, 263, 264, 265, 269, 275
respect, 71, 273, 274
"Review of J. G. Herder's *Ideas for the philosophy of the history of humanity*," 168n3
Romanticism, influence on, 173, 177, 181–82, 187–88
schematism, 2, 47, 50, 52, 57n38
Schiller's engagement with, 89–93, 95–102, 104n2, 105n7, 106n11, 107n17, 107n19

Kant, Immanuel *(continued)*
  subreption, 2, 41–42, 52, 58n54
  thing in itself, 40, 47–51, 69, 118, 266
  Toward Perpetual Peace [*Zum ewigen Frieden*], 302–3
  transcendental deduction, 47, 135, 207, 214
  transcendental illusion, 52, 54, 58n45, 71, 140–41
  transcendental logic, 201–4, 214
  universal legislative will, 266
  will, 67, 68, 71, 76, 77, 78–79
Kelly, Mark, 345
Kiel, 121
Kierkegaard, Søren, 313n12, 382
Kiesewetter, Johann, 312n4
Klopstock, Friedrich Gottlieb, 217n8
Kohlenbach, Margarete, 187
Königsberg, 130n54, 155
Königsberg, University of, 167n1
Krockow, 130n54

labor, 221, 227, 230, 303, 328, 323, 382–84
labor time, 224, 327
labor, division of, 320–21
labor, reserve army of, 226
Lafont, Cristina, 359, 361, 365
Lambert, Johann Heinrich, 43
Lange, Victor, 176
Latin America, 185, 188
Laursen, John Christian, 22, 23, 27, 31, 32
law, 3, 11–12, 14–15, 98, 108n32, 110n60, 301–12, 321, 344, 370
  and critique, paradox of, 378, 385–88
  critique of, 377–91, 392n3
  inner contradiction of, 386, 388–91
  metaphysics of, 301, 303–8
  mythic character, 311

structural feature of normativity, 378–79
Leibniz, Gottfried Wilhelm, 22, 81n21, 118, 167, 172n51
  freedom as contingent futurities, 64, 65
Leiter, Brian, 244
Lessing, Gotthold Ephraim, 274
  Nathan the Wise, 208, 218n23
Lévi-Strauss, Claude, 392n5
Levine, Steven, 360, 371n1
lifeworld:
  Habermas, 360, 361, 366
  phenomenological, 11, 283, 285, 287, 294
Locke, John, 24, 305
logic, 30, 117
  law of excluded middle, 324
  law of non-contradiction, 121–22, 126, 381, 393n14
Ludwig, Bernd, 303, 313n8
Lukács, György, 338, 222, 224
  Theory of the Novel, 338
Łukasiewicz, Jan, 393n14
Luria, Isaac (breaking of the vessels), 306–7

Makkreel, Rudolf, 30
Malebranche, Nicolas, 24
Marbach, 89
Marcuse, Herbert, 374n45
Martin, Randy, 1, 7, 12, 14, 221–34, 268, 279n37, 327–28, 330
Marx, Karl, 1–8, 7, 12, 14, 221–34, 268, 279n37, 327–28, 330
  abstraction, 222, 224–25, 233
  Capital, 221–24, 226, 229–33, 234n9, 382
  Comments on James Mill, 225, 230
  critique, 8, 12, 15, 221–24, 228–29, 232–34, 234n1, 271, 327–28, 330, 357, 378, 381–85, 394n26

German Ideology, The, 17, 333n24
Grundrisse, 225, 226, 230
  Hegel, critique of, 381, 383
  Hegelianism of, 230
  law as normative form of domination, 377
  Preface to *Contribution to the Critique of Political Economy*, 321–22
  real/actual distinction, 322, 332n20
  superstructure/base, 322
  "true criticism," 381–85, 388
material conditions, 7, 8, 12, 233, 322, 340
Matytsin, Anton, 33
Maupertius, Pierre Louis, 23
McQuillan, Colin, 30
means of production, 227, 234n9
Megara, 393n14
melancholy, 13, 345–50
Menke, Christoph, 13, 14–15, 171n41, 344, 345
  Kritik der Rechte, 14
  Recht und Gewalt, 14, 301–2, 305
Mérian, 23, 34n5
Merleau-Ponty, Maurice, 285, 288, 297n2
  Phenomenology of Perception, 290
Merrick, Allison, 241, 242, 244, 245, 260n10, 260n11
"Metacritique of the Purism of Reason" (Hamann), 160, 169n20
Miller, Elaine, 178
Mills, Charles, 362, 373n28
monadology, 167
Montaigne, Michel de, 35n28, 35n35
moral authority, 238, 257–59
moral parochialism, 252–53, 255
moral rationality, 238, 239, 253, 255–57, 262n34
moral virtue, Stoic, 3, 63, 73
morality, traditional, 252–53, 257

morality, typology of, 9, 251–56, 262n32
multiculturalism, 269–71

Nagel, Thomas, 153n87
National Schiller Museum, 89
Natorp, Paul, 9
natural law, 308–9
naturalism, Quinean, 357
nature, 6–7, 13, 46, 100, 185, 321, 323
  aesthetic appreciation of, 6–7, 185–86, 191–97, 200n30
  as realm of freedom, 186–87, 189, 193–94
  critic of, 185, 189–94, 196–97
  Hegel's philosophy of, 210, 216–17
  See also Humboldt
Neo-Kantianism, 1, 9–10, 11, 278n15
  Marburg School, 267
  See also Cohen
Ng, Karen, 336, 337, 349
Nicias, 318
Niethammer, Friedrich Immanuel, 133
Nietzsche, Friedrich, 7–9, 237–59
  and law-like critique, 392n11
  appropriations by Adorno and Foucault, 350, 353n37
  Beyond Good and Evil, 252, 254, 257
  critique of morality, 8–9, 238, 257
  Ecce Homo, 240, 246–47, 249–50, 257
  external critique, 241–51, 260n10, 260n11, 260n12, 260n13
  gay science, 346–47
  Genealogy of Morality, 8, 240, 244–45, 249–50, 261n25, 262n37
  Human, All Too Human, 246–48, 261n25
  internal critique, 241–51, 260n10, 260n11, 260n12, 260n13
  method and genealogy, 9, 239–41, 251

Nietzsche, Friedrich *(continued)*
  reevaluation (*Umwertung*), 237–59, 259n4
  reevaluation, not grounded on a standpoint, 245–50, 255, 258, 261n24, 262n35
  reevaluation, novelty and scope, 243, 249–51, 262n29
  reevaluation of all values, 9, 238–40, 249–51, 255–56
  rhetorical strategy, 245, 247–48, 255, 261n26
  target audience of, 243–49
  typology of morality, 9, 251–56, 262n32
  will to power, 239
  Will to Power, 249–50, 253
nihilism, 137, 138, 142, 238, 253
Novalis, 174
  "Monologue," 184n33

oligarchy, 331n14
oppression, gender and racial, 8, 222, 223, 224, 227, 228, 232–33
  See also racism, sexism
Oresteia, 301
Owen, David, 241, 242, 244, 245, 260n10, 261n26

Pantheism Controversy, 4, 17n11, 117, 129n32, 134
Pascal, Blaise, 118
Peirce, Charles S., 360
Pensky, Max, 337, 340
phenomenology, 1, 9–11, 281–97
  attitude, everyday, 286, 288, 293, 299n23
  attitude, experiential, 288–89
  attitude, natural-scientific, 289, 299n23
  back to the things themselves, 284
  body schema, 291, 294
  conceivability/inconceivability, 284–88, 291–95, 296
  discomfort, epistemic and normative, 289
  eidetic interest, 281, 286, 291, 293, 294
  eidetic variation, 282, 292–93, 294, 295
  genealogical treatment, 295
  hermeneutical, 282
  historical interest, 281, 286, 291, 294
  imagination, 282, 288–89, 299n32
  imagining-critical stance of, 288–91, 294, 296
  impossibility, 290, 291–95, 296
  intentionality, 285
  kinaesthetic experience, 291, 294
  lifeworld, 11, 283, 285, 287, 294
  lived posibilities, 11, 284–86, 294
  meaning-constitution, 282–84, 286, 290–94, 296
  normalizing stance, 286–88, 289, 290, 292
  possibilities, 286–87, 289–92
  possibility-constitution, 293
  reduction, 282, 284, 295
  teleological-historical reflection, 281–97
Philosophical Journal of a Society of German Scholars, 133
Phyrrhonism. *See* skepticism
piety, 237–38, 319
Pilate, Pontius, 202–3, 205, 214
Plato, 35n34, 327
  Euthyphro, 237–38, 251, 257
  Ideas/Forms, 35n34, 327
  Republic, 323
  right to critique, 379
Platonic Academy, 36n36

pleasure principle, 348
poet-critic, 173, 176, 177, 182
political economy, 8, 222–23, 234, 382–84
political thought, early modern, 303
Popkin, Richard H., 22
positivism, 383, 385
pouvoir constituent, 384
pragmatism, 358, 360, 361, 365, 366, 368, 369
praxis, 323, 351n4, 364–65, 367, 372n8
presentation (*Darstellung*), 94, 97, 382–83
primitive accumulation, 224, 225–26
principle of sufficient reason, 56n13, 64, 82n27
production:
  hidden abode of, 223–24
  mode of, 322
  sectors of, 320–21
property rights, 10, 265–69, 271, 275
Protagoras, 393n14
Protestant Reformation, 118
Prussia, 130n54
Prussian Royal Academy of Sciences, 2, 21–33
  anti-skepticism of, 22, 31, 34n6
  Enlightenment attitude of, 27
psychoanalysis:
  Adorno's appropriation of, 13, 337, 344–45, 347
  Foucault's relation to, 354n54
Putnam, Hilary, 359

race, 14, 87n112, 290, 357, 364, 373n28
racism, 363, 372n9, 374n34
Rawls, John, 275
reality principle, 349
Redmond, Dennis, 333n32
reflective equilibrium, 275

reification, 14, 222, 339, 369
Reinhold, Karl Leonhard, 4, 111–13, 117–22, 124–26, 138, 177
  conception of critique, 113
  consciousness, 118–20
  Contribution to the Correction of Previous Misunderstandings of the Philosophers, 118, 119, 120, 125, 129n34
  Elementarphilosophie, 4, 112, 117–21, 125, 126, 129n39, 131n69
  Essay on a New Theory of the Human Faculty of Representation, 118–19, 129n39
  first principle, 112, 119, 120, 121, 125
  Letters on the Kantian Philosophy, 117, 129n32, 131n69
  On the Foundation of Philosophical Knowledge, 118, 120, 129n39
  "On What Has Been Happening with the Kantian Philosophy," 117–18
  principle of consciousness, 4, 119–22, 126, 139
  representation, 118–20, 121, 126
  systematic spirit, 111, 112, 120–21, 122
religion, 2, 22, 33, 116–18, 120–21, 133
  relation with the political, 318–20
  revelation, 26, 27, 121
  See also Christianity
religious belief, grounding in reason, 26–28
religious education, 26–27
Rickert, Heinrich, 311, 314n35
Ridley, Aaron, 241–45, 255, 260n10, 260n12, 261n15, 261n26, 262n35
Riedel, Friedrich Just, 172n45
Romanticism, 1, 5–7, 173–82, 193
  aesthetics, 186–87
  progressive universal poetry, 187, 193

Rorty, Richard, 359, 360
Rose, Gillian, 346–47
Rush, Fred, 175, 193

Schelling, Friedrich, 4–5, 133–48, 154n95, 203, 209, 217, 311
   critique as method of striving, 5, 134, 148, 168n69
   dogmaticism, 134, 135, 145, 147–48
   feeling of freedom (practical datum), 138, 141, 142, 151n56
   metaphilosophical pluralism, 5, 135, 152n68
   New Deduction of Natural Law [*Neue Deduktion des Naturrechts*], 308–9
   On the I as a Principle of Philosophy, 4, 137, 150n41
   On the Possibility of a Form of Philosophy in General, 137
   Philosophical Investigations into the Essence of Human Freedom, 148, 154n96
   Philosophical Letters on Dogmatism and Criticism, 4, 134–35, 137, 138, 141, 148, 153n83, 154n95
   resistance as condition for consciousness, 145–46
   System of the Whole of Philosophy and the Philosophy of Nature in Particular, 153n76
   unprethinkability, 148
Schiller, Friedrich, 3, 89–104, 391
   aesthetic state, 98, 103, 110n60
   aesthetics, connection with ethics and politics, 3, 89–91, 94, 108n38
   anthropological view, 105n5, 107n17
   beauty and resistance, 3, 90, 92, 94, 96, 106n11, 109n42
   free play of the faculties, 90, 95–97, 99, 107n19, 107n30
   freedom, 96, 97, 100, 108n32, 100, 109n38
   imagination, 92, 95–96, 100
   Kallias Letters, or On Beauty, 91–92, 93, 97, 99–100, 104n5, 106n10, 108n32, 109n42
   Kant's third *Critique*, engagement with, 91–95, 97, 99–101, 104n2, 105n7, 106n11, 107n19, 107n30, 108n32, 109n45
   "misunderstanding" of Kant, 105n7, 107n17
   modern mode of experience, 90–91, 92, 94–98
   natural drive, 90–91, 92, 94–98
   On the Aesthetic Education of Man in a Series of Letters, 92, 93–95, 98, 101, 103, 106n11, 107n30, 110n60
   play drive, 98, 102–3
   temporality of beauty, 3, 89, 92–93, 99–104, 109n45, 110n60
   violence, 91–94, 96–101, 103–4, 106n10, 106n13, 109n38
Schlegel, August Wilhelm, 174
Schlegel, Friedrich, 5–6, 14, 173–82, 187–88, 193, 383–85
   Athenaeum Fragments, 6, 174–76, 182, 187, 193
   Critical Fragments, 174, 176, 178, 193
   critique, 6, 173, 174, 176–82
   Ideas Fragments, 181, 193
   Kant, critique of, 187–88
   Letter on the Novel, 187
   "On Goethe's Meister," 176
   "On Incomprehensibility," 6, 174, 176–77, 182
   revolutionary politics, 382
   unity of philosophy and *Poesie*, 187, 193, 199n27

Schleiermacher, Friedrich, 174
Scholem, Gershom, 308, 309
Schopenhauer, Arthur, 272, 165, 303–4
Schulz, Johann, 131n71
Schulze, Gottlob Ernst, 138–40
  See also Aenesidemus
science:
  empirical, 123, 292
  human sciences
    (*Geisteswissenschaften*), 264, 267,
    275, 277n1, 278n15
  natural sciences, 9, 116–17, 191–92,
    267, 275, 302, 304
  Newtonian, 118
  physics, 9, 39, 117, 118
  relation to art, 191–93, 199n27
  romantic science of nature, 6, 186–94
  Wissenschaft, 122, 193–94
second nature, 33, 338–39, 341, 343
secularism, 33, 340, 347–49
Seel, Martin, 197n7
sex, 287, 296, 305, 307, 375n64
  intersex, 370
  Kant, 305, 307, 313n21
  sexual identity, 369
  sexuality, 290
sexism, 363, 372n9
Sextus Empiricus, 24
Sicily, 318
skepticism, 2, 21–33, 34n6, 35n20, 136
  and dogmatism, 22, 117–18, 136–37
  and Kant, 29–33, 118, 324
  and religion, 23–24, 117
  genre of dialogue, 27–28, 35n34
  invalidity of internal criterion of
    truth, 28, 31, 36n36
  isostenia, 35n34
  mysticism, 26, 28
  Prussian Academy, 22–27, 31, 34n6
  use of skeptical arguments against,
    27–29, 31

slavery, 225–27, 325
social construction, 13–14, 287
  See also under Foucault, Haslanger
social contract theory, 332n18
social critique, urge or drive for, 362,
  364–65, 370–71
Socrates, 204, 212–13, 237–38, 257
Spinoza, Baruch, 4, 7, 124, 142–43,
  145, 151n56, 151n60, 321–22
  Hegel's engagement with, 203–6,
    209–14, 215, 217
state, 107n19, 221, 267–69, 378
state of exception, 394n24
Stevens, Wallce, 175
Stoicism:
  moral virtue, 3, 63, 73–74, 77
  truth criterion, 36n36
Stolnitz, Jerome, 196
Strasbourg, 43n10
sublime, 90, 105n5, 106n11
Sulzer, Johann Georg, 23, 34n5
surplus value, 224, 229
Swedenborg, Emanuel, 40
Syracuse (Greek), 331n14

Tantalus, 302
Taylor, Charles, 166
Teutsche Merkur, Der, 117
theology, 27, 64, 56n17, 58n54,
  130n54
Thiem, Yannick, 352n28, 355n82
Thucydides, 321
  History of the Peloponnesian War,
    318–20, 331n12, 331n13, 331n14
tragedy, Greek, 301, 319
transience, 337, 339–41, 345–50,
  352n28, 355n69, 355n82

use-value, 224, 229, 230, 327

valorization, 229, 231

value, 221
  and anti-value, 222–23, 228–33
  form of, 323, 382, 383
Vernant, Jean-Pierre, 319
Vidal-Naquet, Pierre, 319
violence, 3–4, 11–12, 106n10, 179–80, 194
  critique of, 3–4, 11–12, 106n10, 179–80, 194
  economy of, 378
  of law and critique, 386–89
  See also under Benjamin, Schiller
virtuality, Leibnizian-Scholastic, 304–5

Weber, Max, 353n37
Weber, Samuel, 176
Weißen Blätter, Die, 310
Wellmer, Albrecht, 359
Whitebook, Joel, 348, 349
Whyman, Tom, 340, 341
Wissenschaftslehre
  Schelling's use, 142
  See also under Fichte
Wolffian metaphysics, 40
world. *See* cosmology
World War I, 308, 348

Zurich, 121